Thimayya
An Amazing Life

Brig. Chandra B. Khanduri,
FICHR, FABI

Thimayya
An Amazing Life

Brig. Chandra B. Khanduri
FICHR, FABI

Centre for Armed Historical Research
United Service Institution of India
New Delhi

KW Publishers Pvt Ltd
New Delhi

First Published   March 2006
Second Reprint   January 2009
Third Reprint   November 2009

Copyright © 2006, United Service Institution of India, New Delhi

All rights reserved. No part of this book may be reproduced or transmitted in any form or by any means, electronic or mechanical, including photocopying, recording or by any information storage and retrieval system, without permission in writing from the United Service Institution of India.

ISBN: 81-37966-36-X

Published in India by
Kalpana Shukla
KW Publishers Pvt Ltd
NEW DELHI: 4676/21, First Floor, Ansari Road, Daryaganj, New Delhi 110002
T: +91.11.23263498 / 43528107 E: mail@kwpub.in / knowledgeworld@vsnl.net
MUMBAI: 15 Jay Kay Industrial Estate, Linking Road Extn., Santacruz (W), Mumbai 400054
T: +91.22.26614110 / 26613505 E: mumbai@kwpub.in

Printed and bound in India.

Cover photo presented by Mrs Mireille Chengappa.
Photo shows General K S Thimayya, DSO, as COAS, 1958.

Contents

Foreword	ix
Acknowledgements	xi
Preface	xiii
Introduction	xix
Prologue	1
1. The Coming Events Cast Their Shadows	11
2. Grooming in the Shadow of the Raj	31
3. A Breakthrough	57
4. Stars on the Ascendant Command in World War II	75
5. Towards Tactical Excellence	83
6. An Army in Transit – Member Nationalisation Committee	102
7. The Indian Army on Trial	117
8. Interlude	147
9. For the Honour of India: Chairman of Neutral Nations' Repatriation Commission	161
10. The Trouble Shooter: Commanding all the Army Commands	189
11. The Years of Enthusiasm	201
12. The Honourable Course	243
13. A Distant Trumpet	268
14. The Fateful Years (1959-1961)	282
15. Refusing to Fade Away	311
16. At the Altar of Peace – Commander UN Forces in Cyprus	324
17. The Incomparable Thimayya: The Man of Magic – His Leadership Beyond National Boundaries	341
18. Thimayya at a Glance	365
Glossary	368
Bibliography	369
Index	375

List of Maps

1. Coorg — 10
2. Operation Dash – Capture of 'Poland' — 84
3. The Battle of Kangaw January and February 1945 — 84
4. Western Jammu and Kashmir — 121
5. Area of Operation of Sri Div – 1948 — 123
6. Skardu and its Environs — 133
7. Operation of the Battle of Zoji La — 135
8. The DMZ area, Panmunjom where NNRC Repatriated the POWs — 162
9. Chinese Claims and Intrusions — 244
10. The Western and Middle Sectors as Claimed by the Chinese — 245
11. The Chinese Checker — 310
12. A divided Cyprus as Thimayya Saw it — 326

List of Photographs and Cartoons

1. Captain Thimayya Seen as a Matinee Idol
2. Neena and the Infant Mireille in Fort St George's, Chennai
3. Married in the Kodav Style. Capt. Thimayya with Neena, his Bride
4. A Devastating Scene of the Quetta Earthquake, 1935
5. Prime Minister Nehru During a Visit to Tangdhar, June 1948
6. The Famous 'First Day Cover' Issued by Cyprus Government in 1966
7. Brig. Thimayya in Wax, Representing the Indian Army During the Japanese Surrender Ceremony at Singapore, August 1945.
8. With the Forward Troops at Nastachhun, May 1948
9. Thimayya Visits Troops in Leh, September 1948.
10. Timmy in His Tent at the Hindnagar, DMZ.
11. At the Zenith of the Thimayya Resignation Episode, the Unconvincing Defence of VK Krishna Menon (vis-a-vis Thimayya) by Nehru was Depicted by the *Shankar's Weekly*.
12. RK Laxman Imagined Timmy's Role in NNRC, Korea.
13. Thimayya with the Communist POWs in Korea
14. Mrs and General Thimayya with their MA, Colonel and Mrs Munshi, 1957
15. The Thimayya Family in 1954.
16. Thimayya and V K Krishna Menon at New York During his Visit to the USA.

17. Thimayya 'signing off' a 35-Year Service in Uniform from Kumaon Regimental Centre, Ranikhet, April 1961.
18. Mrs Thimayya Flanked by the Duke of Edinburgh and Nehru During the 1959 Republic Day 'Beating the Retreat.'
19. The Grave of General Thimayya
20. In Cyprus, in the Company of Pauline, George and Bernades
21. Thimayya as Commander UNFICYP, 1964-65
22. Author Holding Medhavi with Lalita and Mireille
23. A Tearful Last Prayer from Friend, Archbishop Makarios, President of Cyprus.

Illustration
1. Thimayya Gate at RIMC, Dehra Dun   359

Dr. Karan Singh
Member of Parliament
(Rajya Sabha)
Chairman
Ethics Committee

Office:
127, Parliament House Annexe,
New Delhi - 110001
Ph.: 2303-4254, 2379-4326
Fax: 2301-2009
E-mail: karansi@sansad.nic.in

Foreword

I first met General Thimayya on 20th June 1949 when, at the age of 18, I was appointed Regent of Jammu and Kashmir by my father Maharaja Hari Singh. Thimayya was at that time commanding the Division based in the Kashmir Valley, and I was immediately struck by his swashbuckling personality, his immense erudition and charm. During my first year up in Kashmir, he personally drove me over the Zojila Pass which he had so dramatically recaptured from the raiders only a few months earlier. Taking tanks over the Zojila was a remarkable feat of military strategy, comparable to Hannibal's taking elephants over the Alps. It was fascinating to sit with him as he drove across the Zojila Pass into Dras explaining on the way the details of the historic Army Operation. We also drove over the Nastachhur Pass to Tithwal and the Razdani Pass to Gurez. Ever since then, until shortly before he passed away in Cyprus, we kept in close touch.

His tenure as Chief of Army Staff would have been even more memorable had not the Defence Minister, Krishna Menon developed a deep suspicion and dislike for him. This unfortunately resulted in his resignation which was later withdrawn, but the episode left an extremely negative impact on the Indian Army. This was proved almost immediately after Gen. Thimayya had been succeeded by Gen. P.N. Thapar, with our ignominious collapse in the face of the Chinese invasion. I have mentioned this in my Autobiography (Oxford University Press), but here I wish to say that had Krishna Menon not pushed Jawaharlal Nehru to adopt the "forward policy" on China, history would have been quite different.

Apart from being a great soldier, Gen. Thimayya was a very impressive personality as was his wife Neena and their only child Mireille Chengappa. His appointment as Commander in the UN Forces in Cyprus, towards the end of his life, in 1964-65, was a tribute to the high esteem in which he was held by the world community. It was in Cyprus that he suffered a heart attack and passed away, but his memory will stay with all those with whom he came into contact.

I am glad that Brig. Chandra B. Khanduri an eminent biographer, has written a full length biography of this remarkable General, who was also a warm and large-hearted human being. He has given his own interpretation of the political developments that led up to the Chinese War, and, coming as it does from an Army man, this will be read with particular interest. I would like to close by paying my homage to Gen. Thimayya who served his country and his Army with great devotion and dedication till the very end of his remarkable life.

Vijaya Dashami
12 October 2005

Karan Singh

Acknowledgements

There are a thousand of people to whom I owe my profound gratitude in writing this book. I have also felt grateful and humbled by the magnanimity of the spirit and the wealth of support from all my friends and well-wishers. The gratitude, of course, is to every one but especially the following without whose personal and intimate help this book could not have been written.

I am most grateful to Mrs Mireille Chengappa and her husband, Major General KM Chengappa for the help they provided. Mireille helped in a hundred ways. I am also indebted to Mrs Pauline Phedonos, her husband Mr George Phedonos and Ms Stella Souliotou for their immeasurable help. So great was the commitment of Pauline that she collected a bag of information from the UN (and persuaded her friends all over the island to share their experiences); she sent precious photos and CD ROMs. "My writing is in jeopardy," so the great lady wrote, "because two of my fingers have developed arthritis and are causing the problem." Yet she was so wonderfully helpful. Then, for Timmy's sake, she dusted hundreds of files "relating to activities and achievements" of the UNFICYP in the UN Public Information Office, Nicosia.

In India, besides Mireille, Dr K K Kuttappa has been a constant source of inspiration.

My effort would have remained only partial but for help provided by General S Padmanavan, the then COAS, in allowing me access to some important official and personal documents relating to General Thimayya's tenure as COAS.

The others whose help has been equally appreciable are:
- Director Nehru Memorial Museum & Library.
- Director National Archives.
- Principal RIMC.

- Kumaon Regimental Centre.
- The great people of Kodagu, each one of who came forward with information on General Thimayya.

My gratitude goes further to:
- My brother, Brigadier PN Khanduri, a veteran of World War II.
- Lieutenant Generals PN Kathpalia, Harbakhsh Singh and Dewan Prem Chand, Late Major General YM Munshi, Lieutenant Colonel NK Sinha, Major DRL Nanda.
- Colonel Fateh Singh, his ADC in Nicosia, who donated some of the rare artifacts.
- Colonel Ravindra Nath, whose help in Bangalore was very appreciable.
- Colonel CN Cariappa, KC Ponnappa and Mr MC Muthanna of the Kodav fraternity.
- Mr. K Dave, IP, formerly of the Intelligence Bureau.
- General KV Krishna Rao, PVSM, for useful advice on Thimayya's tenure as COAS.
- All the authors and publishing houses whose works I have referred to, especially Natraj Publishers, Dehra Dun, and Vision, New Delhi.
- All the newspapers, including foreign ones, quotes from which have been used.
- My daughters, Gitanjali and Meena who helped me with their editorial support.
-The staff at the United Service Institution (USI) of India who provided the library and typing help, especially Pushpa.

And finally, my profound indebtedness goes to the USI, the premier institute of knowledge and learning under a distinguished soldier scholar, Lieutenant General Satish Nambiar as its director. The USI honoured me with its first fellowship of the newly established Centre for Armed Forces Historical Research (CAFHR). The centre, working under Lieutenant General Mathew Thomas, another soldier scholar, and Sqn Ldr RTS Chhina, as its secretary, has helped me immensly. My utmost gratitude to them.

My special thanks also go to Kalpana Shukla, publisher, Knowledge World, who very kindly consented to publish this work, and to Rehana Mishra, the editor-extraordinaire.

CB Khanduri

Preface
In Quest of Thimayya

On 30 March 1906, a prosperous coffee planter couple in hilly, undulating Madikeri, Kodagu, (Karnataka) was blessed with a second son! They named him Kodendera Subbayya Thimayya – later to be known and referred to as "Timmy of India" by the highest and the humblest in the world – all who had the good fortune of personally knowing him, meeting him, nay, even having a fleeting glimpse of this illustrious son of India.

Thimayya later became an epoch-making celebrity, a leader of mankind, an architect of history and one of the dispensers of human destiny the world over. In his span of life of little less than three score years, he brought glory to his country and the world.

All his life, he was the first in war, the first in peace, the first in the hearts of the people, and one of the first whose life was written about even while he served. No general except perhaps Napoleon Bonaparte has had the great privilege of having his biography written even while he served. For only a few men had history woven around their lives; and it is often said that had he been born elsewhere, he could easily have had a place as great as that of Generals Robert E. Lee and Erwin Rommel.

The military career of Thimayya in many ways certainly – and perhaps coincidentally – resembles that of General Douglas McArthur (1880-1964). Both were outstanding military leaders before they shot onto the national and international scenes, and both, it would appear, suffered at the hands of their politicians, whose behaviour appeared to flow from their ignorance as well as personal jealousy.

I had met General Thimayya as a junior officer when he was Chief of the Army Staff (COAS) and I, a subaltern. The difference was one of the euphemistic 'sky and land', but his humanity and humility were so great that he would bend down to hold one's hand or talk to any one. Earlier, at the IMA (Indian Military Academy), I had the privilege of being 'pipped' by him at my commissioning. Then I heard a great many stories of his valour and courage from my brother, who too was an officer from Thimayya's regiment.

There were thousands of others who would say what Brigadier Dalvi had the courage to record:

> I had the great pleasure and invaluable experience of serving closely with this great man, in operational and organisational matters, during my tenure in Military Operations Directorate. I knew with what energy and enthusiasm he started trying to repair the damage done to the army and I saw this confidence being gradually eroded because his advice regarding China was ignored... In one of the farewell speeches before relinquishing command, he told the audience, "I hope that I am not leaving you as cannon-fodder for the Chinese, God Bless You."

Thimayya was a national hero, a statesman of international status; above all, he was intensely loyal to Nehru, the government and the country. He would have given, according to Harbakhsh, his "right hand" to Nehru in deference. No wonder then, Nehru's unkind remarks when he submitted his resignation, made Thimayya feel terribly let down. But his sense of propriety and balance never waned and neither did his moral obligation and patriotism. Under the circumstances, no one else in his place would have continued to serve with such great devotion, as indeed, he did.

For it was in his psyche to rise to every challenge, small or large, disregarding the cost involved. He was indefatigable in effort and inexhaustible in endeavour. His greatness could never be measured then and even now with the hindsight benefit of history, it is unfathomable.

It is Andre Maurois who had observed, "Writing of biography will always be a difficult form of art," as it demands the "scrupulosity of science" and "enchantment of art" the "perceptible truth of the novel," and the "learned falsehood of history." But more than these assertions, the biographer has to probe the emotions of the subject, introspect into the 'time and space', and the small and large cross-currents of situations that influence a life. The opinions one forms of a narrative of situations, and the reactions of the characters involved have to combine scholarship, authority and lucidity with a language that is not only balanced but ornate. It has to essentially generate out of love and reverence for the subject.

Then there are moral and religious aspects and the influence of environments. All packed into one life. So "writing a great man's life," as Carlyle observed, "is like living his full life." I tried to live and imagine his life as I wrote the book and perhaps succeeded to a large extent. For, as my chief pre-reviewer of the book has said, "Thimayya's national and international stature as a great soldier and statesman has been well established in the biography."

General Thimayya, it is often said, never wanted to write an autobiography or have his biography written. This is far from true. He had an almost innate desire to write a book on his 'life and time' as he returned to "Sunny Side" in Mercara, Kodagu. He made no secret of it. In a letter to Nina, his wife, he wrote just before his death: "I now see more straight than earlier when Evans (the man who unauthorisedly wrote *Thimayya of India*) stole ideas from my loud thinking... the book that I will write, will highlight the important, the enduring aspects in the overall perspective of life and the nation."

He had perhaps discussed some aspects of his life with Evans; and he did write a whole book on his experiences in Korea as chairman Neutral Nations' Repatriation Commission (NNRC); above all, he had made an attempt to keep as many papers, letters, media reports and documents, as possible. Some of these were handed over to the Nehru Memorial Museum and Library, New Delhi, the others have remained scattered all over; several reports were hurriedly destroyed by the family. But the valuable ones remain tucked in the vaults of the Ministry of Defence (MoD), Army Headquarters (AHQ), the Historical Division, the UN archives, the archives of the Ministry of External Affairs (MEA) and, of course, in the memories of those fortunate people who had the honour to know him, serve and observe him from close quarters, and who are still alive.

A great effort has been made by Dr KK Kuttappa, Secretary General Thimayya Memorial, Bangalore, to collect a large number of personal letters. Documents are available everywhere, from Singapore to Cyprus, to England, and with the family. Every book of the period of his life has references to him. Some narratives of events are available in Henry Evan's *Thimayya of India*... References are available in General Taylor's correspondence in the USA and Korea. So are they in Nicosia, Cyprus, which his loyal friends such as Mr George and Mrs Pauline Phedonos, and Mrs Stella Souliotou, besides the new President of Cyprus, Mr. Tassos Papadopoulos, have preserved.

What struck me was the way he was withering on the vine till his sixteenth year of service, but a breakthrough came thereafter. Incredibly, in three years he rose from a major to a major general. But with each rank, his shoulders became broader and his heart simpler and nobler as he rose from one height to another and from one glory to several others. How did it happen?

The quest began as soon as I understood the man two decades ago and has continued. So, at the trail of the Thimayya legend, I had earlier met Mrs Nina Thimayya when I wrote a piece on him in my anthology, *Generals and Strategists*. She was kind enough to show me some valuable albums, his letters, citations, war mementos given by a Korean non-repatriated prisoner of war (POW), Lien Tuei. A visit to the Kumaon Regimental Centre, Ranikhet, and 4th

Kumaon, which have Thimayya museums, revealed more. The early books on him stoked the desire to learn more.

I found that Thimayya was a very complex personality – the man, the soldier, the tactician, the strategist, the peace-maker, one who would stand up to any one for a cause that was right. A lion-hearted man but one who was as simple as a child, generous to a fault, a man who would pass onto others all credit for success and not hesitate to share the blame. A man of great foresight and vision whose genius allowed him to anticipate the worst of situations and be prepared for them. A man on whose broad shoulders great responsibilities rested lightly.

He could be – and, in fact, he was – controversial, although having no contradictions of character and conduct. And though a great soldier, who enjoiyed soldiering as romantically as Rommel or Napoleon, his supreme success, I reckon was peace-keeping, which he personally enjoyed. So had he been contributing to the cause of the fight for Indians' rights vis-à-vis the British.

Writing the biography of such a man is evidently difficult. And it has been so. My endeavour has, nonetheless, been to produce a well-written biography of General Thimayya's life, as he himself lived it, the difficulties he faced and the fame he achieved. It has, therefore, been the larger effort to capture on paper, a picture of Thimayya to show how he met challenges in life and how his career enabled him to develop as a soldier, a peace-maker and a legend and to also depict it without concealing the blemishes or frailty behind the placid exterior. Thus, emerges the portrait of Thimayya, the man, and his place in history.

And yet, admittedly, it is only a concise biography. In due course, to do fuller justice to his great life, a more detailed and comprehensive book would need to be written, that I hope to complete before it is too late.

The book runs through 16 major chapters. The first four see his early academic and professional life, his stagnation, and the breakthrough that paved the way for ascendance. The battles he fought as commanding officer of a new battalion showed his tactical skills and innovativeness and gave him the aura of a gallant and outstanding commander. Then came more challenges: Partition, and the J&K War. The next landmark moved him to Korea as chairman NNRC, bringing out the best in him as a soldier-statesman. He would now contend with very complex external and internal security situations that the country began to face – Pakistan, the insurrection in Nagaland, and so on. The four years of his assignment as COAS were most challenging – not so much because of the twin threats posed by Pakistan and China but due to the intransigence of Krishna Menon, the defence minister. Analysis of the facts shows that the ignominy of 1962 could have been averted if the plans Thimayya had made had been followed and his professional advice heeded. He refused to fade away even after his retirement, the final act of which was his supreme sacrifice for the cause of peace in Cyprus. The book also highlights his virtues and traits.

A point needs to be mentioned regarding the oft-repeated allusion to "official documents" and "personal documents" that appear in the book. The former refer to still classified and confidential documents at various headquarters and departments that the author was allowed to peruse, and often browse through, with an oath of confidentiality. The same applies to "personal documents." Because they serve the vital need of seeing the picture in totality and in clearing, what we in the services call "the Fog of War," they have been included and referred to as such. But in keeping with the commitment, no specific references have been made. Readers are entreated to accommodate this.

April 2005   **CB Khanduri**

Maj. Gen. **BC Khanduri** AVSM (Retd.)
Member of Parliament
(Lok Sabha)
Chairman
Parliamentary Standing
Committee on Finance

Office:
114, Parliament House Annexe,
New Delhi - 110001
Ph.: 2303-4140, 2301-7709
Fax: 2301-7709
E-mail: comfin@sansad.nic.in

Introduction

Way back in 1954 when I joined the Bombay Sappers as a young officer, General KS Thimayya DSO was already a "Hero", a 'Charming' General whom everyone – All Ranks – loved. Everyone dreamt of his becoming 'The Chief' soon and bring glory to the Army. When he took over as fourth Chief of Staff of the Indian Army, 1957-61, there was thrill in the air. His appointment was being hailed as the 'beginning of a great era' for the Indian Army.

Thimayya, we all saw, was a 'towering personality' who carried history on his broad shoulders and who, by now, had already created a place for himself in the history of India. Every appointment he held, from being the first Indian battalion and brigade commander in war, commander 268 Indian Brigade in Japan, first Indian General Officer Commanding (GOC) of 4 Indian Division and Punjab Boundary Force and leading the famous Sri Division as a combat ready formation for the J&K War of 1948, bore an imprint of his bold and intuitive personality besides his outstanding leadership.

So did he tackle internal issue of Naga insurgency with brilliance, as indeed, he successfully handled the unenviable task of repatriating the unwilling POWs of the Korean War as Chairman of the Neutral Nations' Repatriation Commission in Korea during the worst period of the Cold War. All these had turned him into an icon, a living legend. The charisma of Thimayya's personality was all pervading and there was not a week when the media, foreign included, did not quote him.

I remember he was 'Timmy' to Nehru and 'Thimayya Sahib' to Vajpayee.

My generation of officers, however, knew the problems Thimayya had inherited: the twin threats India faced from an expansionist Communist China and an ever distrustful Pakistan which was seeking military alliance with SEATO and CENTO, being "armed to teeth" by the Americans, besides creating an incredulous military collusion with China. So was he inheriting an incredibly small army of about seven divisions with antiquated arms and equipment with very poor chance of modernizing – or expanding – to eventually defend the long and tenuous international border. Ironically, it was also an army with high traditions of discipline, loyalty and sacrifice whose officers and men lived through euphemistic 'honourable state of poverty'.

And still worse, in Krishna Menon as the Defence Minister, the Armed Forces would find a man obsessed with his own concept of research and development, indigenisation which believed in producing, 'second class equipment for a first class army' rather than providing it with 'first class equipment' to be able to fight its future wars. On the strategic plane another cause of angst for Thimayya arose as the government of the day continued to call China a 'friend', notwithstanding its blatant physical intrusions and cartographic aggressions from mid 1950s.

He endeavoured for full two years to set the strategic concepts right, but when every stratagem seemed to fail, he took the honourable course of offering to resign. I remember hearing the news one evening, while I was at Poonch (J&K), with utter disbelief. All Ranks – men, officers – were totally demoralized and "shell-shocked". It was great relief to Army when the bad news did not materialize. All the same that action of Thimayya reinvigorated the Defence mechanism, but not with the speed the situation demanded or of the quantum necessitated by the threats perceived by him. Once again disappointments and dejections stared hard into his face, albeit he had retrieved the situation considerably and although he left the service in early 1961 with several misgivings, he was still advising the Government of the day to speedily build up defence forces before seeking confrontation against China. It is a sad part of our History that the then Prime Minister casually told the media that he had ordered the Army "to kick out" the Chinese, during the first week of October 1962. With the hindsight of history it is surmised that the ignominy of the 1962 war could well have been avoided, had his advice and pleadings been heeded. As I look back, I feel sad that Army had to undergo a totally avoidable humiliation.

Thimayya: An Amazing Life is a definitive biography of one of the world's most famous generals of the 20th Century. Thimayya was an international hero and India was fortunate to have him. His strategic vision travelled beyond the historical barriers or geographical boundary. The book focuses, in ample measure, how he imbibed a principled life and his honour-boundedness as forte of his indomitable character. He proved a brilliant tactician and a bold strategist, with a human heart and magnanimity, seldom seen elsewhere. He was a visionary, a dreamer but a doer, who wanted to see the world happy and peaceful. Thimayya lived a virtual whirlwind of a life until his last day on the 'Green Line' of the historic Island of Cyprus. There too, destiny chose it to be his last act of duty to the humanity – a duty to UN peace keeping, which he enjoyed more than fighting wars. Thimayya died in the cause of peace in a foreign land and sealed his place in history. He thus ceased to be merely an Indian and became an international celebrity.

To write the life story of such a great soldier, the author needs not only knowledge of the person, imagination and vision but also an unbiased devotion to his object. I would not hesitate to say that Chandra Khanduri, a distinguished soldier-scholar, who has authored several books successfully, has ornately portrayed the total and true picture of man, soldier and peace-keeper THIMAYYA. He has delved deep into his personality and performance that stand out superbly.

Chandra has been researching on the life and times of General Thimayya for several years and has painstakingly looked for, read, analysed and interpreted events with their cause and consequences on an historical mosaic, giving the best of the biography of a man whose purposeful life created and left history behind and whose life would continue to draw adoration and administration through the centuries. Chandra has filled a long-standing void about the life and time of 'TIMMY'. India, particularly, the Army, would be grateful to Chandra for this brilliant biography of General Thimayya – an all time 'Hero' for the Armed Forces.

I enjoyed previewing this extremely well written book.

November 18, 2005   Maj. Gen. BC Khanduri, AVSM

Prologue

A Wish Fulfilled

What kind of death would I want to die?" General Thimayya (affectionately known as "Timmy" among his friends and "Dubbu" at home) thought aloud before his daughter, Mireille (pronounced Meereh). They had sat down on their garden chairs after a fine morning walk over the dales and turfs of Nicosia. He was jocularly telling Mereille that he was "nearing" his time and he would want it to be without pain or prolonged suffering.

That surprised the girl, who had seen her father all joy and mirth despite the strain of a difficult job. She had been spending her holidays with him, now commander of the UN Emergency Force in Cyprus, known through the acronym, UNFICYP. And earlier he had been known to the world as chairman Neutral Nations Repatriation Commission to Korea and as chief of the famous Indian Army.

She looked into his large dancing eyes with marked displeasure. "Come on, Daddy," she said admonishing him, "must you always pull such fast ones?"

He avoided arguing with her on that account except to say that he would, as a matter of his last wish, like to die in a battlefield. And that perhaps Cyprus was that battlefield, and though it wouldn't be a real battlefield, he would be happy to invite an old Turkish or Greek *gola-goli* or shell-bullet to "complete the work." Mireille knew that her father used to take a sort of pleasure in teasing her mother, who would explode at such pranks. And then looking at her, he would theatrically say, "How I wish I could die in the arms of a beautiful woman."

But he appeared serious this time. "What's the problem?" Mireille wondered. Was it a premonition of the impending events, she wondered.

"Jokes apart," he told Mireille, "I believe in dying on my feet rather than living on my knees." And he began to tell her how he had looked at death too often in the face to be afraid of it any more. "Have you forgotten the Coorg proverb," he chuckled, "Men should die on the battlefield and women on the child bed." "The Kodavs," he seemed to prophesise, "have a *rendezvous* with such a destiny." Then he also recited Shakespeare's famous line, "Cowards die many times " and feigned as if he had forgotten the rest. She completed the line, "The valiant never taste of death but once." Both then laughed and walked holding hands in the garden so beautifully landscaped and maintained by a fleet of Turkish Cypriot gardeners.

She was aware that her father welcomed death preferably in the battlefield, or in its absence, in a brief struggle and a quick *partez* as he called the final act of departure. As they walked in the garden, they were soon on a different 'frequency' and topic – the topic of her marriage. He asked her if she was happy to be marrying Kittu (Major Chengappa) and when should he plan to take a 'break' for the wedding. She replied that Mummy was planning it and she would get back to him when everything get settled.

"Righto," he said.

Soon Mireille left Nicosia, leaving behind her father to look after the UNFICYP and maintain peace in the embattled zone of the divided island of Cyprus.

Death did not have to feel proud with General Thimayya since things seemed to work as he had wished. That morning of 15 December 1965 he was up at 5 a.m. and was soon in the park with his dog, his cane in his hand. He had got used to walking in the cold of the early morning and the fading light of the evening.

No longer fond of writing his diaries, he would pour out his heart in his letters to Nina, his wife and Mireille – the latter especially. And the number of letters to Mireille increased on her return from Nicosia.

After his stroll, Timmy had begun to complain of a cold and a feeling of fatigue. His doctors advised him bed rest for at least seven days. Impatient of inertia, he, however, began to run his office from his residence. Though his staff cancelled his official and social engagements, his friends and well-wishers came in an unending stream.

On the morning of 16 December, he strode into the portico of the house, whistling like a 'Rimcollian Timmy' and was feeling ecstatic. Captain Fateh Singh, his aide de camp (ADC), cum personal staff officer, was close at hand. He had settled down to a cup of tea brought by a servant when he felt a tingling pain in his chest and Fateh saw him perspiring. He told Fateh that he felt nauseous and his heart throbbed loudly and 'stars danced' in front of his eyes.

"It's like a knock-out blow – of the boxing ring – my boy," he whispered, retaining his lifelong sense of humour. His hands and feet were getting limp and he thought it was time to go. He remembered his mother and father, the grandfather who was once his best friend and, indeed, Nina and Mireille.

"God", he prayed, with quivering lips, "Forgive me, if I have sinned." He thought he was gone.

He struggled to his bed. Soon the Norwegian doctor, a nurse, Anne his personal secretary, and Pauline, the great friend of the family with her husband George, were there. Also came his chief of staff and Carlos Bernades, the special representative of the UN secretary general. He smiled at them and said he felt better. "I think the worst is over," he told the doctor. The doctor, however, saw that his blood pressure was unduly high and the cardiogram showed an undecipherable graph. But the flame of life continued to flicker in him.

Fateh suggested that he ring up Mrs Thimayya at Bangalore, but he wanted no panic.

"Listen, I have a cat's nine lives to live," he said, smiling mischievously, adding, "There's still one in the credit." Then he heaved a happy sigh and mumbled, "Ah, I have been lucky all these years and perhaps it may continue..."

Timmy was concealing the pain he suffered and the large sign of interjection that hung between his life and the death that threatened it.

But neither optimism nor his uncanny sense of humour seemed to abandon him.

Messages of Timmy being hospitalised and confined to bed went all over the world; so did the messages come wishing his fast recovery.

"Get well, Timmy" said UN Secretary General, U Thant's message, "The UN needs you...the world needs you."

The President of Cyprus, Archbishop Makarios drove into his house to "look up Timmy." "For Christ sake," entreated His Beatitude, "Recover fast. I need you."

Miraculously, Timmy seemed to recover.

On the following morning, he asked Anne to go through the unanswered mail and put up their replies. The chief of staff asked to brief him on the operational aspects of the UNFICYP. He then dictated a Christmas message to his command and asked Anne to put up the draft. As Anne gave the typed draft back, he read it aloud:

> Whatever the future may have in store, you have every right to be proud of your contribution to the service of peace as members of the force. At Christmas, most of us would rather be at home with our families and friends. Despite the distances to your homeland, I wish you a Merry Christmas and Happy New Year. May God bless, and may good fortune follow you all.

But it did not seem to appeal to him. He modified it to read:

> During the past two years, the UN force in Cyprus has continued to work hard to keep peace and do its best towards restoration of normal conditions on the island. Thanks in no small measure to these efforts, the situation has improved considerably and the general atmosphere is undoubtedly better and more hopeful than a year ago. The secretary general, in successive reports to the Security Council, has warmly praised the work of the UNFICYP and these tributes have been echoed by the president and

the Government of Cyprus, the leaders of the Turkish community and representatives of many nations.

All this fairly reflects the courage, tact, and impartiality shown by the members of the force and the members of the civilian staff and I should like to take this opportunity of thanking you all for your loyalty, devotion to duty, and cooperation during the past year.

Then he added the previously dictated text of the message to it. He read it, re-read it, and sent it across to Brigadier AJ Wilson, his chief of staff, telling him to disseminate it to the UNFICYP "well in time."

Timmy was no stranger to 'future shocks' and he saw how "adversity invades an individual life in full force." "It pours," he used to say "and does not drizzle." It was to be his turn, it seemed. To add to the health problem came the devastating news of a death in the family.

The message he received in the evening from Nina said that Krishna, his "darling sister," had lost her husband near Dehra Dun when the family was on its way to Chakrata. A wall of flash floods caused by rain in the upper tracts of the Mussoorie Hills had swept him down the otherwise small stream. Even the body could not be found. It all happened in a split second as he reconnoitred a passage through the stream – all in front of his wife and children – who helplessly watched him from the bank.

"My God," cried Timmy over the telephone and he asked Nina to ensure that Krishna was looked after. "I will be there soon," he assured Nina.

Fateh recalls that he had never seen General Thimayya more melancholy and distraught than at that moment. He heard him say, "Can it happen... why has it happened?..." He kept the news in his bosom, perhaps, calming himself too. But it was traumatic and became the last blow, perhaps the 'knock-out' one.

The official work, nonetheless, continued. At lunch the following afternoon, his civilian counterparts, Carlos Bernades and Remmy George had joined him. They assured him that the ceasefire of November was holding well and the "Green Line," he had created, was effective.

"Hope I live to see the fruits of our labour," he had quipped.

That evening, Nina was on the line again, telling him all about Krishna and the others. The phone was then passed on to Mireille.

"You know, my darling," he began, "I've always thought, life has been a dream and believe me, I have had an incredibly fine one... Look after yourself, my dear," he continued soothingly and affectionately, as if in a message of parting.

She said nothing but he could hear her sobs on the phone.

"I am feeling tired now. I want to sleep," he said, blessing her again, and put the handset down. A few spoons of soup and he closed his eyes and was fast asleep. Timmy's life, even to his ever optimistic daughter, seemed to be ebbing away.

General Thimayya died at 4 a.m., on Saturday, 18 December 1965, when it was a 'holy hour' in India. He had spent, as he had wished, only 96 hours in the bed. His last word was "Mireille," the only person he never wanted to be separated from his living days. He could see a "shadow in front," as YW Yeats said of "the Horseman," "Cast(ing) a cold Eye, on Life and Death..." The agents of the death god had begun to escort him to his place – assuredly, in heaven.

Death came as he went into the bathroom. He did not realise how weak he had become in just 48-60 hours of illness. As he opened the toilet door, he stumbled and fell on the over-polished floor, his head hitting the side wall. He slumped down. The haemorrhage was severe, and the already weak heart gave up – it failed.

The alert Swedish guard who heard the thud rushed inside. He pulled his body out. Fateh also ran out of his bed into the general's bedroom. The doctor arrived in ten minutes and tried to revive the heart; it was losing its warmth. That great and compassionate heart had finally given up to the vagaries of life.

Friends and ministers of the Cyprus government were there in their dressing gowns, hoping to hear him. Also came Archbishop Makarios, Mrs Stella Souliotou, the health and justice minister, Glafcos Clerides besides Bernades.

But he was gone, leaving everyone in tears. "When I came, I cried/When I went, the world cried," an annonymous poet had written. So 'Thimayya of India' was dead. A great soldier, a patriot, a harbinger of peace in a strife-torn world had ended an era but left behind a history. A man who, to paraphrase, George Bernard Shaw, "put into one common pool of life more than he took out of it," was gone.

"Timmy is dead," the words were echoing throughout Cyprus and all over the UNO, the Commonwealth, more so in India where tributes like, "Ah the last good soldier of India is dead," "A good soldier who was loved and respected, has gone" poured in, for, everyone had seen Thimayya as a man who could rise to any height, and emerge a clean winner. His genius and luck, on the one hand, and his humanity, character and instinct, on the other, had produced a Timmy who, despite all the obstacles, had been "A TOTAL MAN – A SUM TOTAL OF ALL QUALITIES THAT MAKES A LEADER." He had towered over all others during his lifetime and he now appeared taller than the tallest. During his life, he had been a source of inspiration and provided a whiff of freshness when everything else looked dry and dead. In the battlefield, he had been like Erwin Rommel – intuitive, tactically innovative with dash.

His battles for peace had been fought with equal *élan* and relentless pursuit. Such a man, Thimayya was dead.

A Great Soldier at Journey's End
Nicosia – 19 December (Sunday)

At 9.30 a.m., the body of the force commander was moved to the Wellesley Barracks, escorted by four armoured cars of the Royal Canadian Dragoons, where his own battalion, the Royal Highland Fusiliers, the former Highland Light Infantry (with which he began his service in 1926), provided the Guard of Honour and band and pipes.

Was it not then that his last wish, however small, was being providentially fulfilled by the Fusiliers being located in Nicosia?

The body of the late commander remained lying in state at the Wellesley Barracks until close to 1300 hours. At 1020 hours, Bernades placed a floral wreath on behalf of the secretary general of the United Nations on the general's coffin, draped with the Indian and United Nations flags. A few minute later, the Indian High Commissioner, S Sen, who had flown in from Beirut on the Saturday afternoon, placed a wreath on behalf of the Government of India. Then Captain Fateh Singh, his ADC, placed on the coffin, the general's medals and his blue beret and cane.

At 1030 hours, the president of the republic arrived at the Wellesley Barracks to pay his respects to the late commander. He had moist eyes. The ceremony was attended by a number of ministers, the Cyprus Armed Forces Generals SG Grevas and Pokos and other officials, members of the diplomatic corps, who placed wreaths on behalf of their governments. Then came the grieving friends and well-wishers from all over Nicosia.

Two minutes later, the deputation representing Vice President Fazil Kuchuk, and the Turkish community consisting of Dr Niazi Manyera, Fazil Plumer, Bejmal Muftizade and AM Berberoglu also paid their respects.

At 1250 hours, a cortege was formed to escort the body from the Wellesley Barracks to the airport. The skies of Cyprus seemed to have joined the grieving Cypriots, as heavy rain was pouring at this time and it persisted until just before the arrival of the cortege at the airport later in the day.

At the approach to the airport, the route leading to the aircraft was lined by representative detachments of all national contingents serving with the UNFICYP. And, finally, the cortege was carried by the ten members of the Canadian contingent between the two ranks of the two Guards of Honour provided by 2nd Battalion, the Canadian Guards and the National Guard of Cyprus.

The Indian buglers and members of the Indian contingent from the UNEF Gaza, who were flown to Nicosia post haste, sounded the "Last Post" as Brigadier Wilson, the Acting Foreign Minister of Cyprus, Andreas Aracuzos and Ambassador Sen paid their last respects to General Thimayya. A few minutes later, the pallbearers carried the coffin up the steps of the aircraft, an AN-12 of the Indian Air Force, which left for Beirut at 1345 hours, on its first leg of the final journey to Bombay and then Bangalore, his home town.

At Beirut, it was transferred into a chartered Boeing.

At the Nicosia airport, many people wept as they watched the coffin containing the body of their "dear Timmy" disappear into the aircraft. A BBC announcer representing the "collective grieving sentiments" of the people and the UNFICYP, aptly reported to his office in London for broadcast the world over, "Farewell, Apostle of peace. Cyprus is grateful for what you have offered her. May your memory be eternal, General Thimayya."

The coffin arrived at Bombay and thence at Bangalore escorted by Colonel MV Zatar, MVC, and the commander of the Indian contingent of the UNEF.

Bangalore, 20 December
Amid scenes tinged with sadness and solemnity, Mrs Nina Thimayya and Mireille received the body. Both burst out crying inconsolably. A flower bedecked gun carriage brought the body from the 20 km distant aerodrome to the residence of Thimayyas, for the eventual burial of the physical remains of the general at the Wilson Garden Cemetery.

The governor of Karnataka, on behalf of the president of India, and the chief minister, on behalf of the prime minister of India, laid wreaths here. Lieutenant General Moti Sagar, GOC-in-C Southern Command and the three service chiefs were present. So was Dr Thomas of his *alma mater*, the Bishop Cotton School. Major KM Chengappa, the fiancé of Mireille and the would-be son-in-law of the general, was acting as the son who would sprinkle a handful of earth onto the casket before it was lowered into the pit. "Earth into the Earth," he would silently say before saluting the general.

A 17-gun salute boomed as the coffin containing the mortal remains of General Thimayya was lowered into the grave. As troops (which included a small detachment of the Kumaonis) sounded the "Last Post," an estimated 5,000 people from all walks of life stood in silent homage, and several hundred ex-servicemen, including General Cariappa, saluted their friend and colleague, Timmy.

That day, the nation decided to hold prayers in its temples, churches, gurudwaras and mosques as it had done at the time of the death of the Father of Nation. Millions prayed and sang in churches that evening:

"*Treasure Lord in your Garden of Rest,*
While down here he was the Best."

Giving Dignity and Reverence: Shifting the Grave
31 March 1998
Time passed. And the memory of the great contribution of Timmy kept his life in focus. But many people began to see with considerable pain the pitiable condition of Thimayya's grave in the Wilson Garden Cemetery. In fact, letters to the editors of newspapers appeared for shifting it to the Raj Ghat at the capital. While governmental apathy prevailed, the Thimayya Memorial Committee under Dr KK Kuttappa started a crusade to shift it, if not to the capital, then to an honourable place in the cantonment in Bangalore.

The army identified – but not easily – a 60 by 80 feet plot in the Army Supply Corps Centre. Timmy's own Kumaon Regiment then undertook to draw up the plans and design of the site of the grave. In keeping with the aesthetics, an architect of repute was employed, who worked on the final plan.

31 March 1998 was chosen as the great day of honour.

If the scene of the whole of Cyprus mourning on his death on 18 December 1965 was already a historic moment, the next scene was befitting of the man Thimayya. Almost 33 years later, on this date, when in order to perpetuate his honour and to perpetrate his reputation, the mortal remains were shifted to an "honourable place" in the Bangalore Cantonment and a tomb erected for him. This then climaxed the Thimayya Legend, like the climax of Napoleon's legend in *Le retour des cendres* (the return of the ashes) and erection of a tomb for the emperor in Les Invalides, Paris. Such an honour, it may be remembered, was bestowed only only on one other historically known person, Oliver Cromwell (1599-1658) whose grave was shifted by the British in 1700.

The exhuming and shifting of the grave was done in a quiet and dignified manner with full military honours. Dr Kuttappa remembers that the shroud, the casket and the remains of Thimayya inside the casket, looked as "clean as one buried only a week back." It made the soldiers engaged in moving the body spontaneously salute their chief!

The dedication ceremony, Mireille observed, was well organised and was quite touching. The bust of General Thimayya made by TS Baoni was installed and unveiled majestically. It towered over the grave and the tombstone, made of black marble, in the beautifully landscaped surroundings. And that is the final resting place of this man with celestial fire, with a mind like that of Vivekanand, which made a poet see it as "the ecstasy of a living sire;" and for whom, Vinayak Krishna Gokak, the vice chancellor of the Mysore University, composed a ballad:

> *A scion of the Sehyadri range, he rose*
> *To be hero of the Nation new born.*
> *He served mankind as a true Indian*
> *Upholding the peace and helping the forlorn.*
> *Blest by the soil that gave him birth*
> *The men who followed him as Chief and friend,*
> *Timmy the name that's loved and honoured ever*
> *Timmy the name God himself defends.*

Here, in India, it was a phenomenon, the first of its kind. It had to be. For, one wondered at the esteem and reverence people continued to show him. An embodiment of all the qualities of leadership, values and adventure that a country needs in every age, his gallantry, his indomitable courage, his humility, his love for fellow beings, concern for the men he loved shine forth as a bright beacon of what selfless service means. That is his just and enduring reward.

It is amazing how Thimayya, despite being a man in uniform, became an important actor in four of the six major legacies of conflicts of World War II and the Cold War: Kashmir; Korea; the Communist Chinese expansion; and, Cyprus (the other being Vietnam and Palestine). And earlier he had been a part of the occupational forces in Japan, as equally protecting and settling millions of refugees in the newly divided India and Pakistan. His leadership, as Nehru said on his return from Korea in 1954, had, indeed, "extended well beyond the national boundary."

To this it must be added that Timmy is the only general and military leader after whom a boulevard has been named in Nicosia; and, after whom a "Special Stamp" had been issued by the Government of Cyprus. It is his name that is inscribed on a memorial to the Neutral Nations Repatriation Commission (NNRC) in the Demilitarised Zone (DMZ) in the divided Koreas.

Eulogising General Thimayya's role in saving millions of people during the partition of the subcontinent, Faiz Ahmad Faiz, the most eminent Pakistani poet, wrote:

Na Hindu, Na Musalman; Sirf Insaniyat tha Thimayya ka iman.

(Neither Hindu nor Muslim, humanity alone was Thimayya's faith.)

As the scene concludes, I confess, there may be something more in the Thimayya legend, something like Goethe attributed to Napoleon, "which we all know but perhaps we do not know, what."

So the Thimayya Legacy remains immortal. The rest of the effort is to immortalise his greatness. ∎

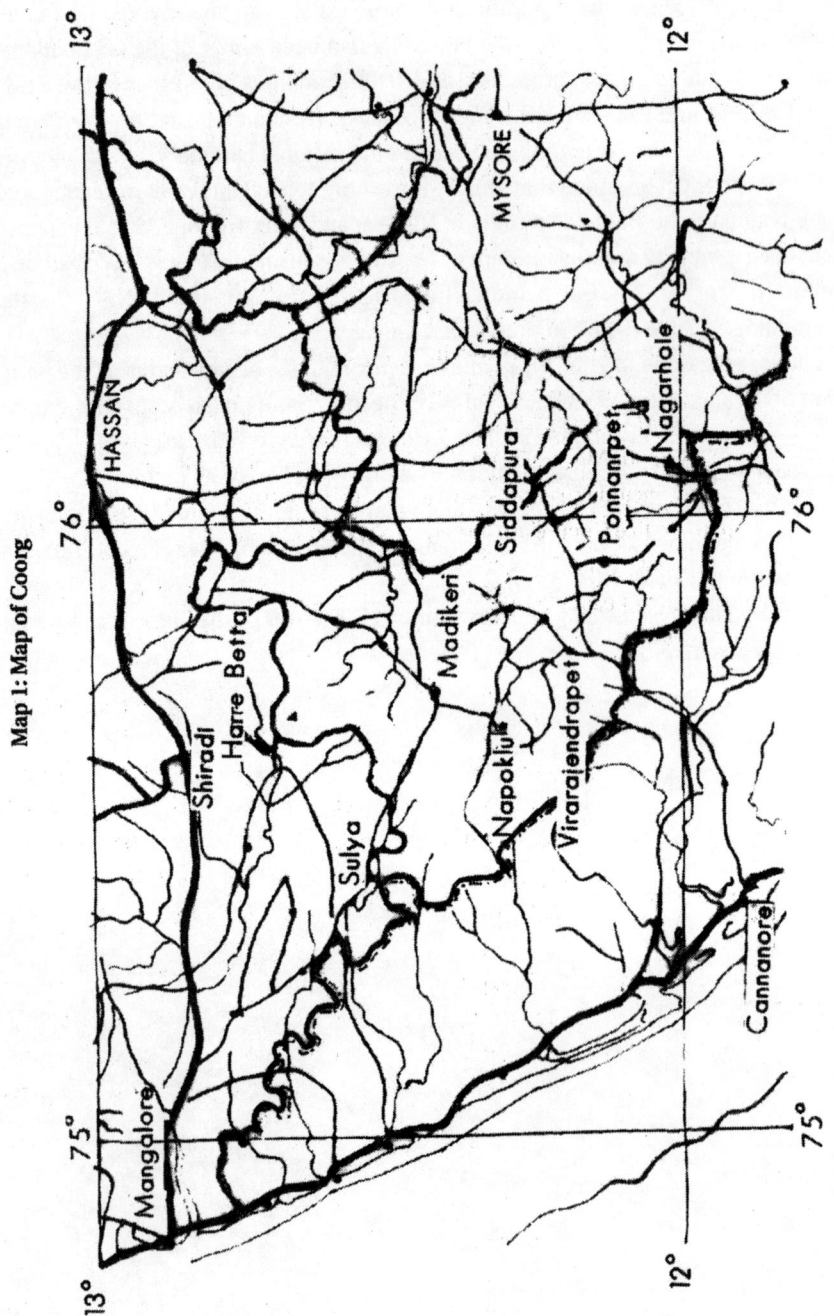

Map 1: Map of Coorg

1
The Coming Events Cast Their Shadows

Vignettes of History

Coorg or Kodagu is a land both old and new, where the legends of a fascinating and often splendid past mingle comfortably with a most lively and energetic present. The Thimayyas belong to this land.

Although limited historical records are available, the Kodavs are considered to be descendants of the Aryans who swarmed across the Indo-Gangetic plains and then fanned out through the Vindhyachal to the Western Ghats, which are washed by the Cauveri or (Kaveri) river, one of the seven holy rivers of India and not only a giver of life but a bone of contention between the states of Karnataka and Tamil Nadu, both vying for the lion's share of this great river's water.

The second theory traces their origin to the Arabs who came over the sea to the Kodagu Hills. Yet others claim that the physical features of the Kodavs suggest their lineage is from a set of people who once formed the invading force of Alexander of Macedonia in 326 BC; and who, rather than make a tortuous journey back to Macedonia, strayed off to the solitude of south India. There is also a school of thought that ascribes the Kodav ancestry to those great but cursed people of Mohenjodaro, who, finding the northern pastures drying up, moved to the verdant hills of the south. Adding to these speculations is the one that this tribe may well have travelled from the Caucasus in the pre-Christian era of migration that brought the Huns to India. But where exactly these non-Dravidian people really come from remains the anthropologist's dilemma and a billion dollar question for the inquisitive.[1]

The *Cauvery Purana*, the oldest Indian treatise that could well be called the recorded history of the Indian races, has a corroborative story. King Siddhartha of Matayadesha had four sons. The youngest, Chandravarma, was the most talented. He came with an army to Jagannath, Thirupati, Kanchi, Chidambara, Ranganatha, Rameshwara and proceeded through to the Western Ghats. He was devoutly religious, so after dismissing his army, he came up and worshipped Goddess Parvati fervently. The Goddess, pleased by his devotion, appeared before him. The king asked for three boons – a wife from his own caste and a faithful mother for his children; victory over his enemies; and entrance into Shiva's heaven after death.

Parvati granted all his wishes except the first one, saying, "O King, you cannot obtain children born of a wife of your caste. But you shall have a Sudra wife who will beget children for you." Thereupon, Parvati created a Sudra wife for Chandravarma who bemoaned his fate bitterly. Finally, Parvati relented and arranged his marriage with the hundred daughters of the King of Vidarbha. The first son had 20 wives, the second 16, the third 12, the fourth 10, the fifth and sixth eight each, the seventh and eighth seven each, and the three youngest had four each. Chandravarma's family multiplied prodigiously. Each of them had more than a hundred sons. Ere long, there was not enough room for them. Thereupon they tore up the hills with their bare hands, dug the slopes and created a place that came to be known as Kroda Desha. Thus, according to legend, Kodagu or the anglicised "Coorg" came into existence. Nonetheless, all these are mere historical conjectures.

Kodagu has had its independence secured over the centuries. During the Vijaynagar Empire, Coorg was firmly established as a small unit under the Hindu Empire. But gradually came the British, nibbling at every state in India. In the south, Hyder Ali and Tipu Sultan were the threats they had to eliminate. The British sought the support of King Virajrajendra of Coorg to help defeat Tipu, who by then had sovereignty over Coorg. This coalition of convenience formed by the British and the Kodavs resulted in Tipu's defeat and death. The process was applied later to Virajrajendra himself and his kingdom was annexed in 1835 to British India.

The mutiny of 1857 that rocked India remained confined largely to the north of the Vindhyachals. In the south, the East India Company continued to consolidate its gains. Coorg, an administrative unit, 95 km by 64 km, tiny in comparison to other states, was made into a commissariat. Nonetheless, it remained the land of the Kodavs. Its importance was augmented as the British made inroads into the Kodavs lives and partook of their produce of coffee and cardamom.

There are few places in India where nature has been so lovingly bounteous as Coorg or Kodagu. Sometimes compared with Scotland, it is more akin to Meghalaya in northeast India. This tiny 6,180 sq km district, with a population of just about 300,000, nestles amidst imposing mountainous undulating terrain, the highest point of which is the 5,729 ft (1,746 m) Thadiyanda Mol.

Tucked away in a corner of southwest India in the lap of the Western Ghats, Coorg is a haven of charm and natural beauty, inhabited by a cheerful people with refreshing and unique individuality.

An old time poet, quoted in the author's earlier book on Field Marshal Cariappa, epitomises the beauty and spirit of Coorg:

And among the flowering trees,
Is the Samige the finest;
Thus is Coorg, a string of pearls,
Loveliest among the kingdoms;
Live in it, my friend and prosper.

Out of this emanates the Coorgs' pride in strength of both body and character, stature and beauty. This concept of beauty entwines with goodness and truth as natural instincts which combine hero-worship of the brave and the noble. The love of ballads, of the heroes, a fiercely independent spirit, a sense of keen competitiveness, an instinctive hatred for servility and sycophancy have turned the Coorgs into a martial race. A sprinkling of social goodness when admixed with respect for elders and ancestry, equal rights to women and social adaptability give the Coorgs an added advantage.

Although the Kodavs do not seem to acknowledge any particular religion, most profess to be Hindus which is evident from their fundamental set of beliefs and practices. They venerate their ancestors, Goddess Cauveri – the river deity – and Lord Iguthappa – a variant of Lord Shiv. The traditional brass oil lamp is lit every morning and evening. All decisions and agreements, including financial and matrimonial are made before this lamp.

The dead are cremated or buried, according to individual will. Gunshots are fired to warn the neighbours of significant occurrences.

They are basically tribals, proud to be Hindus although the evils of caste and creed have been left out, including the ritualistic Brahmins.

Bounded by the Dakhin Kanada district, Kerala, Mysore district and Hasan district, with its green vegetation, endless stretches of coffee and orange plantations and fragrant paddy fields, Kodagu provides an idyllic and enchanting setting, a delightful grandstand panoramic view of which is available from the top of the Brahmagiri Hills.

Madikeri (Mercara), the district headquarters, sprawling across several enchanting hills is a picturesque city. The Veer Shiva Raja's fort housing the administrative officer, Raja's Goddege (graveyard), Raja's seat and the Onkareshwara temple serve as some of its landmarks. So are the two pillars of Coorg's modern history: Field Marshal KM Cariappa, the first Indian C-in-C (1949-53) and General KS Thimayya COAS (1957-61). Rightly too, Coorg or Kodagu is known as the country of coffee, oranges and generals. So much so, every fourth house has a military officer – serving or retired.

Colourful in their attire, the Kodav women who are well built, vivacious and pretty, wear their *saris* in a unique style, covering their heads with silk handkerchiefs. Ornaments of gold and silver complete their ensemble. The men's long coats with gold thread and silk sash, holding the Coorg knives, gives them their identity. Even now, in constant recognition of Kodav gallantry, they are exempt from the Indian Arms and Ammunition Act.

Their weddings, without priests, are a spectacle of their culture; so is the annual harvesting festival of Huttari. Tula Sankramana Kalan to Tala Kaveri, where the Cauveri springs from the hill is an annual pilgrimage in October.

The Kodavs have, thus, been proud to be Hindus although the Hinduism they practise is a refined, ritual-free religion. There is no caste system; there are no priests; they worship deities but, above all, respect and worship their ancestors, with whom they seek refuge in adversity and as a ritual at all major events of life – birth, marriage and death. "In a way," as General Thimayya would say, "the Kodavs are as tribal, as say, the most diehard tribals of northeast India." The Kodavs, however, remain one of the most enigmatic people.

The British influence had its effect on education, and in the Western way of life, but Christianity failed to make any inroads in the Kodav's life or culture.

Brave and proud, the martial outlook of the Kodav held service in the armed forces with great fascination. Colonel CM Ganapathy, for example, is greatly revered as he had earned a Military Cross in the Great War. Then Sir Henry Cobb, the chief commissioner had the best of the Kodav boys picked up for commissions in the army.

Thimayya was born with the proverbial silver spoon in his mouth. His grandfather had a booming business in coffee, cardamom, pepper, ginger and cinnamon. His ancestors had virtually picked up trade in the 17th century when a Muslim pilgrim introduced coffee in Coorg. The British were keen to exploit its temperate climate and ideal soil to grow these crops on a commercial scale. A number of British traders found Kodagu a lucrative coffee growing area and settled down as planters. But the Thimayyas did better.

General Thimayya's father, Kodendera Kuthayya Thimaiah, married his first cousin Cheppudira Sitamma, the daughter of Cheppudira Somaiah. Thimaiah and Sitamma had six children – three sons and three daughters. The first boy, Ponnappa, became a planter and joined the army in the India Reserve of Officers (AIRO), today's Territorial Army. At a later stage he was taken prisoner by the Japanese at Singapore where he served as a colonel in the Indian National Army (INA) in Malaya under Netaji Subhas Chandra Bose. The second boy was Subbayya, who was known after his father as Thimayya (anglicised spelling), and the youngest was Somayya, who joined the Bihar Regiment in the Indian Army.

The Kodav children had peculiar and well sounding pet names; Ponnu, Dubbu (Thimayya), Freddie (Somayya).[2]

General Thimayya's father Kuthayya Thimaiah owned a large estate and a bungalow at Modhur, about 10 km from Madikeri; he also owned a beautiful bungalow at Madikeri, called "Sunny Side"; it had a promenade into the city. Although the family suffered large financial losses during the Depression, its reserves ensured the family's prosperity.

Sitamma Thimaiah, General Thimayya's mother, was an ardent social worker, noted for her hospitality and work for the social upliftment of women and the poor. She helped in the education of women and children and built a water tank at Madikeri. Rightfully, she was the first *Kaisar-i-Hind* of Kodagu; in fact, one of the very few in India.

Of the three daughters, Gangoo married Barrister Kaubiranda Ganapathi, the second married Codanda Jappu Machaia, a senior planter at Pollibetta, and the third girl, Krishna, married an IAS officer, who also worked as private secretary to Mrs Indira Gandhi until his unfortunate death in an accident. Unfortunately, there were many premature deaths in the family. Mrs Sitamma died while Thimayya was in Burma; Freddie would die in 1948; Ponnappa lost his life in a car accident while driving a beautiful lady in Madikeri in 1954; Mr Thimaiah, his father, also died in late 1960.[3]

Born on 31 March 1906, in the Kodendera clan, Timmy was born a year after Ponnu and they grew up together as friends and rivals. Their grandfather, fond of hunting and outdoor life, often took the boys to Nagarhole, then the exclusive hunting ground of the Maharajas of Mysore – just to see the wildlife that abounded there. Antelopes, sloth bears, civets, spotted deer, elephants, panthers, bisons, pangolins and boars, besides many species of birds added to the amazement and education of the boys. During these excursions Timmy would climb *machans* to witness the animals at their water holes. Over the years, these excursions turned Timmy into a lover of nature and a keen *shikari*. His humour was kindled as well. In one of his school essays, he wrote: "Oh dear, not all the Fauna is deer."

Trekking became his obsession, as well as sports at school.

Courage, his grandfather had told him, had both physical and moral dimensions, "Stand up to a bully even if he towers over you. Fight him so that he accepts you as one to reckon with," was the grand old man's advice. "He was my Bhisma, the grandsire of the Mahabharat," he would tell some people later, adding that he would tell them to refrain from bullying others. "But the moral is more important than the physical," said the sire. He would keep emphasising that it involved "standing on the side of the righteous with disregard to consequences to yourself. Understand righteousness, the weight of right over wrong. It is your culture and conscience, besides education and training that will define righteousness to you. Face setbacks, bereavements and uncertainties of life with a stout heart. Stand on your own feet squarely and do your own thinking. And be a good sport in everything, whether in happiness or unhappiness." These became Thimayya's principles of conduct.

At the Royal Military Academy, Sandhurst, it was the 'code of conduct' that set the seal to these learnings. If the grandfather's influence on young Thimayya was overpowering, his mother's was no less. A lady of outstanding beauty and intellect, she was not only a driving force for social upliftment and a leading light but a philanthropist, highly religious – greatly devoted to Lord Onkareshwara of Madikeri. She had a subtle sense of humour as well. When someone said that Dubbu was more Dravidian than Lord Venkateshwara, she replied: "Your knowledge of our history is poor. Don't you know Lord Krishna was swarthy?" Thimayya would, in fact, observe her and imbibe her wit and humour, besides her intuitive outpourings.

Religious tolerance and secularism seemed to blend into the Thimayya family. Most of their coffee labour and servants were Muslims; so were many family friends. The British who practised Christianity were visibly secular. In fact, Hindus and Muslims, since Hyder Ali's days had lived in amity. Even the Onkareswara temple was a blend of Hindu-Muslim architecture.

Thimayya held the British initially in awe, but as his knowledge of history further enlarged, he began to treat them as equals, with a feeling of moral ascendancy that he was as an Indian, a Kodav. He had seen the British as traders who begged his grandfather for succour. Nonetheless, he found them charming, although he never got awed by the colour of their skin or their demonstrated sense of superiority. It was also their history of the conquest of India, their relationship with Nepal and Afghanistan that presented him with a stunning discovery: the British in India were vainglorious; during their campaigns they purchased and hoodwinked the other side but rarely won victories through excellence of military prowess. Most did not display military courage, as history had made out. His association with them until Independence further vindicated his belief.

Schooling and Growth

Timmy, thus, grew up under the umbrella of the inspiring influence of his grandfather, the man regarded as the local *Raja Sahib*, who controlled the coffee and cardamom business not only of his own family but of most of Kodagu.

In his praise, the local Khan Sahib and Qazi Patel would sing "O God, let this Raja be happy throughout his life. Where is the power in a pen to write/O, God, if there is a mistake, forgive us."[4]

Meanwhile, the missionaries had begun to impart Western education seriously and the nearest school was St George's College, Coonoor, in the Niligiri Hills.

The British, had begun their crusade of spreading Christianity with their fabled stratagem of "Bayonet and Bible" and since the missionaries spread English education all over India, south India was no exception. So the nearest school, St George's College, Coonoor, in the Niligiris Hills became the first step towards orientating the Kodendara boys and the girls to modern education. The 240-km tonga journey to this school in 1910 became an experiment, which Timmy's grandfather called "turning men out of the boys"; Timmy, just four years old, was all excited. His sisters were also admitted to a convent school in Coonoor.

The ecclesiastical and academic discipline at St George's College was rigid and medieval at best; and it could be rebelling and frightful to Timmy and his brother

Ponnappa. But what pained the liberal and sensitive young mind of Timmy was the economic stratification of students by the Irish Brothers, who were equally stern and inhuman in their punishment. The economic stratification bordered on open discrimination, from food to the award of grading.

Both Ponnappa and Thimayya would never forget the sadistic treatment the Brothers inflicted on the youngsters. It was here that he heard one day a Brother quote from the Bible:

> He will not cry or lift up his voice, or make it heard in the street; a bruised reed he will not break, and a dimly burning wick he will not quench; he will faithfully bring forth justice.

Timmy decided to ask the Brother why he was not being 'just' to the 'poor' students. He was protesting against the treatment being meted out to some 'sinners' who were made to kneel on broken glass and pray. It was the human conscience that rebelled in Timmy.

Enraged, the Brother made him crawl over the ice-cold dormitory. More punishment followed, in which Ponnu too suffered. They continued to suffer for weeks together. They thought that it was all a part of education and turning "men out of the boys." These happenings could not be concealed from the parents when the boys returned home for the holidays, as they observed their bandaged and injured knees. The tale, reluctantly told, traumatised the parents and the grandfather, who until now had been all praise for their schooling and discipline, besides the refining of the naughty kids.

It was the Spartan discipline, cruel to the hilt, instilled with an iron hand, that made the family come to some conclusion as to why the Brothers behaved as they did. Celibacy and an ascetic life had turned the priests into tyrants and psychopaths. Some of them were behaving like executioners rather than teachers and 'Brothers with compassion.' Eating with the hungry children in the same room became unbearable. Timmy would shudder on looking back at those four years of suffering, comparable perhaps only to the fate of those taken prisoner by the Japanese or the treatment meted out to the Jews in the Holocaust. It was, at best, a reformatory.

Personally, Ponnu and Timmy were not too unhappy as they learnt English rapidly; played games and even 'dated' girls but they found the discrimination of 'parlour boarders, 'first class boarders', and, so on, too difficult to accept. Although resigned to their fate, both wanted to return to Coonoor.

Before this grounding – if it could be called so – could inflict permanent psychological damage on the young children, the parents arranged for them to move to Bishop Cotton School, Bangalore, albeit against the advice of the grandfather. "Where is the need?" he would argue in favour of their staying at Coonoor rather than being shifted to Bangalore.

Many years later, both he and Ponnu recalled that, had they lived in the wilderness of Coonoor, they would have been better off academically. "There were no distractions there," Thimayya would recall. Bangalore had many distractions.

The four years' toughening, in a way, turned Timmy robust, stout hearted and thick skinned, whereas Ponnu, surprisingly, became more sensitive. With a growing frame at eight, Timmy could run faster than the ten-year-olds; he could play all the games, and ride a horse in the slippery Coonoor-Ootacamond trails. He could run up and down the ravines of the Nilgiri Hills and write and speak flawless English. They had turned into good boys, if not 'men'.

So, when the parents got them admitted (against the advice of their grandfather) into Bishop Cotton, they, in fact, went to Bangalore rather grudgingly. To add to it, their welcome in an 'all white' school was with 'fanfare'. On the first day itself, they had a taste of the prevalent discrimination due to fair and not so fair complexions.

As the brothers were entering the school, they became involved in fisticuffs, with two of the students who, when they happened to meet them, said something that demanded immediate retribution.

"God, man," whispered one pointing at the brothers, "what is this school coming to as they have started taking 'niggers' into it."

That was a bit too much for the brothers.

Ponnu leaped ahead and knocked out one of the offenders with a 'left hook,' and Timmy floored the other. That turned them both into heroes. Very soon, they were respected; the bullies adapted themselves to the two Thimayya brothers; and the school itself began to exploit their talents in sports and other extracurricular activities.

The Latin motto of the school was – and remains – *Nec Dextrosum – Nec Sinistrosum* (*Neither To The Right Nor To The Left*). A week into the college, no one however, could explain to Timmy the meaning of the lofty words in the *sanctum sanctorum*. So he walked up to the principal, and asked him if its meaning could be explained to them at one of the morning 'assemblies'.

"There is only one boy," said the principal the following morning, "who asked me what our motto says." He then explained the meaning and the spirit behind it and emphasised its significance. "In difficult situations, when you'll be required to take very difficult decisions, follow the straight course and your conscience. I hope, Timmy you have understood what it means." Thimayya would follow it all his life.

Academically, Thimayya was a high average, although he excelled in outdoor activity. He was especially good in languages. But overall, he would be just in the middle rung. Too much liberty that the new environment offered led to a sudden release of energy in him. He began to turn mischievous with both his co-students and teachers. And when 'gateing' kept him indoors on weekends, he would lower himself out of the school building with ropes or bed sheets. Caught and punished, he would admit his mistake and apologise.

"The masters," so he would tell Evans, "fortunately, never quite gave me up. And they pleaded and reasoned with me. They caned me and they wrote scathingly to my parents..."[5]

In fact, a spate of letters were written by the headmaster to his father, complaining about his activities. One of them was rather distressing, "I write to you," so began the letter, "to tell you about your two sons who are studying here for the past two years. We find Ponnappa is okay, but Thimayya seems to be just muddling along. He is excellent in outdoor activities but his results in studies border on the medium. The reason, we feel, is lack of concentration.

"There are yet other traits of his. Very honest, truthful, forceful, so much so he has begun to regard himself as Alexander of Macedonia or Winston Churchill. He may become a day-dreamer..."[6]

The parents rushed to Bangalore to both admonish and buck him up. When they showed him the letter, he burst out laughing. "Oh Mama," he said, "if this is what the school thinks of me, I'll prove to be one." This event, carrying the concerns of the teachers and parents, nonetheless, spurred him to take his studies seriously.

He was still disciplined and playing most games while admiring the glamour of the British in the cantonment. He was not like Winston Churchill, who would push his teacher into the Thames. Thimayya was actually bored in the ambience of Bishop Cotton. He was looking at a school or college that would make him like General Sir Hore Ruthven, the district commander of Bangalore, an epitome, in his view, of military brass and grandeur. He wanted to live as the British did and not be burning the midnight oil for admission into a first class university.

It was here that his sports master seemed to further influence him. Sergeant John Burgess would constantly remind him that the best profession for him was the army. "Like the princes of the states, you can earn your commission and be an officer. You'll then see the world and be a hero." The young mind of Thimayya began to dream.

PWRIMC, Dehra Dun: A Stepping Stone

Timmy proved to be good in sports but just about a high average in studies. He had joined the 'Auxilliary Force' – a mix of Boy Scouts and National Cadet Corps (NCC). Even his principal opined that he was more cut out for the military service than the civil. There was talk also of joining the family business, which was lucrative. In young Timmy's mind, however, something new was germinating. The environment was helping him to make a choice. And when the overall results of academics suggested a military career for Timmy, and with it an offer of joining the Prince of Wales Royal Indian Military College (PWRIMC), Dehra Dun, he jumped at it.

The PWRIMC had, in fact, been built as the college for the princes and formally established since March 1912. Its object was to prepare selected Indian boys for admission into the Royal Military College (or Academy), Sandhurst. There they would be trained to become King's Commissioned Indian Officers (KCIOs) after a period of 18 to 24 months, to be posted to one of the eight Indianised units.

Catering for 32 cadets, the PWRIMC could not have been located in a better place than Dehra Dun. The lush green valley, ensconced in the lap of the Tons basin, majestically overlooked by the Mussoorie Hills, the PWRIMC was in idyllic surroundings and looked like a modern *ashram*, a hermitage. It was simply exquisite and ideal for training the young. The local military stations of Ghanghora and Garhi added to its charm.

Then under its famous Principal, JGC Scott, its Commandant, Lieutenant Colonel JL Haughton of the Royal Sikhs, it had three sections, named after famous British Generals: 'Rawlinson', 'Roberts,' and 'Kitchener'.

When Timmy joined the PWRIMC in June 1921 at the age of 15, he was almost 5 ft 8 inches tall, 120 lbs in weight and growing rapidly. He looked big for his age and was well built and strong. His rich class fellows were, however, mostly overage, overfed and under-exercised, and little interested in serious studies and other chores. But still worse was the naivete of his guardian – Mr Kittermaster. He would embarrass him by asking questions such as how many wives he had; and, if he believed in *Sati*, and such stuff and nonsense. That obviously, was seen by Timmy and others not only as ignorance but colonial arrogance.

The British had agreed to the establishment of the PWRMC and later to the Indian Military Academy in 1932 under intense political pressure. As they had acceded to sending selected Indians to Sandhurst from 1918, and under this pressure only, they would accept the 8-Unit Indianisation Plan. At the PWRIMC, the staff trained the cadets with enthusiasm and zeal. There was a good dose of indoor academics mixed with outdoor activities – drill, physical training (PT) and games with excursions, mountaineering and trekking. In academics, English, Mathematics, History, Geography and Science were compulsory subjects, while Urdu and Intermediate Mathematics became optional subjects. Drill and PT, besides games, carried no marks.

Drill Sergeant Major Gorman of the Durham Light Infantry would drill them with a voice that "caused landslides on the Mussoorie Hills"! And his caustic remarks in Cockney on the drill standards of some of the awkward cadets were hilarious. He tore Timmy to smithereens when, while standing at attention on a ceremonial parade, he had ventured a look at the visiting Prince of Wales. He recalled: "The sergeant major caught the misdemeanour. After the parade, he approached me; his face livid."

"I saw you Thimayya," he shouted. "Disgraceful! Shame on yer! Why did you lower your eyes?"

"I wanted to see the Prince of Wales."

He ground his teeth with fury and said, "Don't let it happen again."

"When would that Prince of 'Wails' come again?" thought Timmy, but the drill major had let his steam out. Gorman, the 'Maulvi', 'Pandit', and his schoolmates made life enjoyable. And he would regale all his friends in Kodagu with anecdotes of the Doon days.

The training and education was good; and, for once Timmy was enjoying himself. He was seen as a boy of "great hopes." By 30 June 1922, when he was 16 years and four months old, Thimayya had completed one year at the PWRIMC and had to his credit excellent academic results. Scott found that Timmy had "worked very well throughout the term and he was putting the advantage of an excellent early education to good use." Colonel Haughton saw Timmy as "an attractive boy with a good deal of character." He regarded him as being "among the most promising material." He congratulated him on a "very satisfactory term's work."

By December 1923, he was "on top of the college" with "excellent term work." As a 'cadet captain', he was acknowledged as "very promising material," by both Scott and Haughton.[7]

At 10 stone (140 lb, 62 kg) 5 ft 9 3/4 inches (172 cm) tall, the 18-year-old Timmy was heading for the coveted interview with the viceroy for entry into the Royal Military Academy (RMA) Sandhurst, one of the most illustrious military institutions. The final PWRIMC report of the commandant on Timmy was both sanguine and optimistic:

> Probably the best all round cadet we have at the college. He is now sitting for the Sandhurst examination at Simla and I expect him to pass.

Personally, Timmy was confident, without any worries. He had enjoyed his stay at the PWRIMC and was eagerly looking forward to the interview by the viceroy. Mr Scott and Colonel Haughton were coaching him, so that he did not stumble through this very last step for which they had prepared him for the past three years. The college was vindicating its motto: *Ich Diem* (I serve).

"You have intelligence, you have knowledge and you are courageous. You have luck too," observed Haughton before wishing him good luck. Timmy was fluent in English, with a workable knowledge of Urdu. He had also developed a keen sense of humour and was known for his wit and mature opinions. His values and convictions were firming in. There was another subtle observation that was impressing his young mind – that the British, though, colonialists, were not parochial at the teaching and training levels. They disseminated knowledge as freely to Indians as they would do to their own kind; and they valued merit. Nonetheless, that sense of values and tolerance was not extended to those who failed in study and drill. And several cadets were expelled without a second chance.

By July 1924, Timmy had been interviewed and cleared by General Sir Claude Jacob, chief of General Staff, General Headquarters, Delhi. he was then sent to Simla for the interview by the governor general and the viceroy. He was accompanied by his cousin Bopayya. "Ten minutes is the time," he was told by the British military advisor to the viceroy, "You make it, or you don't. Keep your wits about you, what?"

He had, in fact, been briefed by others and had prepared himself for the interview thoroughly, particularly on Coorg (Kodagu). In Thimayya's words, "The great door swung open and I found myself in an awesomely hushed and majestic room. In the centre in a great chair sat the viceroy..." Thimayya thought that if the Christian explanation of creation were the correct one, then the Almighty with his archangels must look like this.

The viceroy glanced at a paper. "You are Thimayya," he asked. "Where are you from?" was the next question, and Thimayya began his monologue on 'Coorg, its Past, Present and Future,' the topic he had prepared, and he burst through. The viceroy smiled. And after a question or two on games that he played, an aide stepped up to his side and escorted him out. Then he heard the viceroy say, "Hope you enjoy your stay at Sandhurst."

It was too good to be believed; the first success of his life.

He recalled that the military adviser to the viceroy congratulated him on his success. He offered him a glass of port before he left and flattered him by saying that he had shown *sangfroid* and that he was a connoisseur of great drinks!.

RMA Sandhurst

The success at the interview was heady wine! But he would begin to see that the viceroy, after all, lived miles above every one. Perhaps that was the reason for the pomp and deference that were heaped on him. He was the king of kings. Later in life he would realise that the British in India were regulating their lives by a "warrant of precedence" whose seventy-seven ranks established, for example, where people should be placed at dinner, or where they socially stood. That also seemed in tandem with the traditional caste and class ridden Indian society. It was so with the native princes and their feudal anachronism whose territories formed about one half of the empire.

The entry of the Indian aspirants for the Indian armed forces into the Royal Military Academy (RMA), Sandhurst, had a long history of political struggle. Like it was for establishing an Indian Military Academy (or College) at Dehra Dun. But in 1923-24 it looked a distant dream. Sandhurst was to be the *alma mater* of all the KCIOs – some 100 or so after him, who would be commissioned from there.

Timmy joined RMA Sandhurst on 29 August 1924, and his training was completed on 23 December 1925. At Sandhurst, Timmy was a part of the No 14th Platoon of No 4th Company.

Sandhurst, then the 'Mecca' of all military leadership training, proved to be an institution of repute. It turned raw material into a fine product. The result was a 'chiselled out' Timmy. The regimental sergeant majors (RSMs), legendary in their own rights, could cause landslides, as they voiced words of command and even invectives.

"O, you bloody Timmy," one would say, "You're walking like a pregnant duck." Calling one a "dog" or "swine" together with "Sir," was common. The RSMs have their reputation intact even today and Timmy having had some taste of this tribe at the PWRIMC, enjoyed performing on the Drill Square. Then there would be the 'Putti Parade', and 'gateing' for minor breaches of discipline, sometimes ludicrously funny ones, such as "tunic button dirty due to perspiration!"

Lectures and sports, socials and dinner nights were an essential part of the training. Debating and boxing were carried out as demonstrations of confidence acquired and as essential part of development of officer-like qualities. For the British, gentleman cadets (GCs,) the appointments rising up from lance corporal to senior under officer were common, although to the Indians and other cadets from the colonies, they were denied. But then it mattered little as one learnt, passed tests and examinations, and played better than the British and other whites from the British dominions, and enjoyed the training.

Lieutenant Colonel Sturgess, Tummy's official guardian, apparently did not impress him; neither did he seem to make those under his guardianship, comfortable. But both Camberley and Sandhurst charmed Timmy, nonetheless.

The Royal Military Academy trained GCs not only from the British dominions but from all over the world. As usual, Timmy found the juniors or newcomers being shunned by the seniors, besides being ragged. One had to pass the "Drill Square" before one was allowed "liberty" or outpasses. He found the staff "strict but fair" in their dealings with GCs, although the drill and physical training staff could find one "bone idle" "dirty," "inattentive" on parade.

The instructional staff at Sandhurst represented a good cross-section of the British Army. Among the staff who impressed him were Captain Sir Robert (Boy) Browning, the adjutant; his own company commander, Major Jackson of the Royal Scottish Borderers and the Commandant, Sir Charles Cochrane. Then there were memories of his 'batman', an ex-serviceman who had seen war all over the world, including the Great War, who, typical of all those who went through Sandhurst (or the Indian Military Academy), he found "simply marvellous." Speaking in Cockney, Welsh or Scottish, these simple souls were content getting their weekly "rum allowance" from the GCs, or an extra pound sterling before Christmas. He learnt several ballads from these wonderful people, who did not mind referring to the awful years of the so-called Great War as an internal "balls up" or "cocks up."

What he enjoyed most was the learning of tactics based primarily on the trench warfare of the Great War, the fiasco at Gallipoli, and the slogging matches in Mesopotamia. Lessons of military history which *ipso facto*, turned out to be the British history of disproportionate gains in their colonial wars and successes, would be learnt and unlearnt.

At the personal level, another aspect made him believe that luck was the most important quality in a successful soldier. If Timmy awed the RSMs for his "thundering self" on the hard metalled Drill Square, it was again this epitome of peace-time military hero that drilled into his young mind the unfaltering place of luck. RSM McNeil would narrate the story that Captain Winston Churchill had written of how an incompetent commanding officer, on the verge of what appeared a 'sure sack' was awarded a Victoria Cross, in the Boer War! Timmy became a fatalist. And he seemed to believe that so long as luck held, all obstacles and obstructions could be skirted. In later life, he would humbly accept that although he was a little lower than those much more gifted and brave, he had been lucky to have been recognised. It was, in fact, his inborn modesty, but his infatuation with luck survived, turning it into a Napoleonic obsession.

The whole curriculum at the RMA was designed to enable a young officer with leadership qualities to command a platoon of 30 to 36 men on joining his regiment. It gave a good idea of the basic infantry and tank tactics, with a fair idea of how other arms and supporting services worked. It taught military history, military geography besides science and humanities. Equal attention was given to the customs of the services, etiquette, and above all, development of character and leadership qualities. A 'code of conduct', naturally formed part of the training.[8]

The 18 months training at the RMA, Sandhurst, had a tough and rough exterior. The military side of the training was, indeed, tough but Timmy enjoyed it – and fared better than most. In academics and general awareness, he was comfortably placed. What he imbibed also was a world vision of the European races with, unfortunately, the discrimination the British harboured against the Indians. It was then that the concept of an Indian Sandhurst in India, for the Indians, was gaining momentum and there was subdued whispering in England too. "The Indians should first learn to walk," said a civilian teacher at Sandhurst to the Indian cadets, and later, as if spewing venom, he added, "Before, they jump." It was true but difficult to accept. Slavery under a foreign yoke could at best be cursed. But the young Timmy and other Indians were bitter. There was more to add to that bitterness.

Cadet Sant Singh (commissioned on 29 January 1925), an outstanding hockey player, for instance, was never included in the RMA, Sandhurst's Hockey Eleven, when it played against outside teams, when it was all whites, although Sant Singh, like Apji Randhir Singh, a much later entry, was a Hockey Blue. Discrimination in such matters would later become the cause of institutionalised prejudice and prevarication.

The advantage of birth and nobility vis-à-vis merit was also quite blatant. These 'toffs' were always over and above the commoners and as time passed, Timmy's young mind became sanguine that the British, whenever required, should be squarely faced, on equal terms. He pointed out the obvious discrimination to his battalion commander and even the commandant at the time of his passing out interviews. In doing so, he took considerable risk. For he was told that his views bordered on the unjust, undemocratic and unprincipled paradigms, and if he persisted, he might have to opt out. It was a kind of subtle British intimidation, a shut up call to Timmy. So he decided that discretion was the better part of valour. He was advised by his sponsor, Lieutenant Colonel Sturgess, to remember that "a sense of indispensability was dangerous and it could be fatal, if he took matters as granted." The lesson was registered well by young Timmy.

JN (Muchu) Chaudhuri, who joined the RMA when Thimayya was passing out, also found traces of discrimination. "At work, without exception," he wrote, "there was no differentiation between the British and the non-British. The exception was that no foreign GC either got an executive rank or was ever put in command over the Britishers." It was a short-sighted policy as it built up resentment and complexes during the training period. There was, nonetheless, no social taboo on intermixing at Sandhurst, while in later life in India, the British were not 'wholly comfortable' in mixing with the Indians. Habibullah saw the British as generally friendly in the UK, but changing colours as they crossed the Suez Canal.

By the time Thimayya was passing out to the strains of *Auld Lang Syne* from the Sandhurst parade ground, the "8-Indianised Units" were already a reality. He, like all other Indian young officers, would be commissioned into one of them. He had asked for infantry, for which he was also recommended; the unit to which he would be commissioned would, nonetheless be revealed after he had completed his attachment with a British unit in India. Until then, he would be designated as ULIA – the Unattached List Indian Army!

In 18 months of training, Thimayya had been very much an extrovert. He played hard, trained hard, even danced with English girls, despite his guardian's displeasure. He took time out to meet the English gentry and found them amiable enough to have a young Indian in their midst for a glass of ale or a cup of tea. The men in uniform, however, remained officious.

There was an intermission between his sailing to India and the closing down of the RMC Sandhurst. And he joined a French Army family who exposed him to the French social life of Paris, its Moulin Rouge, the Maurice Chevalier shows, to French sensitivity and even obscenities, rather shocking and quite capable of corrupting a young mind – and body.

With the Scots

Commissioned into the Indian Army, Timmy joined the 2nd Highland Light Infantry (HLI), a Scottish Unit, for one year's attachment, at Bangalore. At 20, he was tall, debonair, with the grace of a young tiger.

The HLI had won laurels in the Great War where large numbers of officers and men had laid down their lives. The unit, determined to lead a comfortable life, appeared like a 'club' to Timmy. It was an experiment in extravagance. There were brawls over the opposite sex and there appeared sufficient cause to believe that the traditional Scottish-British rivalry was rife even in the colonial army.

The Scots and the English suffered virtually congenitally from the mutual suspicion that their temperamental differences and intellectual abilities made them poles apart. A sort of prejudice seemed to have so gripped both that they would often collide. Dr Samuel Johnson, the first Briton to have compiled the English language dictionary, is said to have made no bones that his Scottish biographer, James Boswell carried a "chip on his shoulder." The playwright and Fabian, Bernard Shaw, as an Irishman, took potshots at the English and the Scots and said famously: "We live in an atmosphere of Shame. We are ashamed of everything that is real about us; ashamed of ourselves; of our relatives; of our income; of our experiences just as we are ashamed of our naked skins."

The hatred – and even distaste – between the English and the Scots was historical too. In the 18th century, the Highland Scots had been feared and hated by the English, and by the lowland Scots. But in the Victorian era, they had been domesticated and metamorphosed into 'Noble Savages', after which the English swooned to the swirl of their bagpipes, kilts, and Kilmarnock caps.

Thimayya was to hear and learn from the first day that the Scots literally "carried chips on their shoulders" with regard to almost everything. He would see its various manifestation, especially in the attitude of the Scotsmen to the English officers.

Established in 1800, the 900 metre above mean sea level cantonment of Bangalore was ideally suited for the British troops and traders. With the advantage of location and climate, it soon became a small European cosmos that also provided them adequate facilities for training and recreation. As part of the cantonment, the Parade Road, stretching 1.5 km from east to west, surrounded by a mall called Rotten Row, became the hub of the area.

Famous people like Sir Winston Churchill had lived in, and eulogised, Bangalore for its polo, picnics and parades, besides several 'gossip columns' on flirtations, adultery, wife swapping and sweet romances. Serving with the 4th Hussars, Churchill, with an imperious zest for experience and adventure, would get bored here and join the Malakand Field Force, besides the Boer War.

Bangalore's United Services Club offered shelter and solace to the British who treated it as a 'home away from home'. It provided entertainment and social contacts. For the Indians, it became a symbol of social status if not snobbery to be a member. But like normal British snobbery, it was 'off limits' to the Indian officers. Undeterred, some Indians like Sir M Visveswaraya had established a purely Indian club called the "Century Club", which, ironically, was opened by the commissioner of Bangalore and Karnataka, Sir Marc Cubbon, in whose name a park and road stands even now.

On his arrival at Bangalore, Thimayya was received by a colour contrast of subalterns – Lieutenants Gray and Black. The HLI had been instructed by the Station Headquarters to "handle Thimayya – a ULIA – tactfully." The reason was the growing political agitation that had caught up the mood of the Indian people after the 1919 Jallianwala Bagh massacre, the renunciation of knighthood by Rabindra Nath

Tagore, and the movement begun by Gandhiji. The government had already been compelled to accept the "8-Indianised Units" and General Sir Andrew Skeen had been put on the job of raising an Indian Military Academy, after the eyewash of running a course for the Indian cadets at the Daly College, Indore, 1917-18.

So Mr "Ulia," as Thimayya began to be addressed until this acronym was dropped at his behest, was interviewed by his commanding officer, Lieutenant Colonel Sir Robert Seagraves, Bart (Baronet). "Learn the most, be sincere and genuine," were the words of the 'old man', the commanding officer, who himself looked pleasant and sincere.

He was placed under Major Sir Telfer Smolett, for training and administration. Smolett was a fine officer who began to train him, whatever little he could; for it looked as if training as a whole had been relegated to a lower priority in preference to socialising. The result, Timmy noticed, was that officers squabbled over Anglo-Indian girls, men resorted to sodomy and prostitution. Sexually transmitted diseases and indiscipline naturally infected the men. He was not impressed with the way the battalion was being trained or administered. But he decided to learn and be sincere in everything he did. Smolett had a word of counsel for him too, "Your men will respect you if you influence them with sincerity of purpose. You are here to learn good things. Do so."

If some of the officers were villains who thought morale could be raised by affluent and good living, there were good officers who spent time with the men, and trained and boosted their morale. But both good and bad types of officers were by and large opposed to socialising with the Indian officers or easily letting them join the club. The more liberal ones led by the commanding officer, ensured that Thimayya, the only Indian officer, was not stopped at the gate. Friends and relatives were also permitted entry – both, however, remained non-members.

Living, to quote Thimayya, was "darn cheap." A full Indian lunch in the best restaurants did not cost more than one tenth of a rupee, and petrol at a rupee a gallon could make Timmy look like a Maharaja. Thimayya bought a Ford car and made a good use of it, as Lieutenant Colonel Cariappa would reminisce: "Timmy, known to the family as Dubbu, was stationed at Bangalore in 1926. He visited our family there quite often. I remember as a five-year-old, how he would drive his Ford, carrying sometimes piglings, strapped to its carrier, as gifts for the family. At home, he would amuse us by trying to sleep on our baby cots, thus arousing mirth and curiosity amongst me, my brother Bunny, two years my junior and our sister Bollu, then about 17. In the evenings he would drive the three of us, my young sister Bollu, Bunny and self, to the scene of the waterfall at great speed and go round and round the huge tree (still there) located at the waterfall View Point." In later years, when the time to settle down came, Timmy would find a life companion in his house, marrying Bollu's sister, Nina.

He was taking his profession seriously and he began to train his company and coach them in sports. Timmy was the champion athlete of his regiment. At an athletic meet of the British units (held exclusively for the British units) of Southern Command, Thimayya was the champion athlete of the HLI, and the command. The British objected to his having participated in an "All British Championship." But the commanding officer of the HLI threatened a walkout, if Thimayya's championship was rejected. That settled the issue, on the one hand, but it showed Thimayya's immense popularity in the HLI, on the other.

Club, mess and sports were, indeed, the major attractions for the officers of the HLI and Thimayya blended with them. But he volunteered and took his men out trekking through the nearby sandlewood jungles. They became tougher. A sojourn to the nearby Nilgiri Hills was refreshing; besides, he learnt to admire the beauty of nature. Coonoor was another place he often visited.

Here he would be treated as 'hero' by the once "abominable" and "despicable" Irish Brothers. Though stiff, they were keen to exchange notes. He was invited to address the boys and girls. He was blunt in recalling his and his brother's 'penance' in the dormitory. But he summed up the 'VIP Speech' by saying, "Without these Fathers and Brothers, I would not have been a soldier today... For a soldier must have discipline built into his bones and be able to endure privations." The growing and training, he told them, was not only "ascetic," but "harrowing," yet the right type for every youth who dreamt of joining the armed forces of the country.

Christmas always brought great happiness to the men, most of whom were without their families and had made local friends who invited them over to their homes on this and other occasions. Thimayya too was determined to enjoy the day.

"On Christmas day," so Colonel Cariappa recalled, "there was a big party at the local club, and we all left for the party, including Dubbu (Timmy). At the party, when everybody was enjoying himself, someone sufficiently sozzled, got up to sing. His voice sounded no better than a 'fog horn'. In his enthusiasm to silence the singer, Dubbu threw a potato at him which landed straight in his open mouth. There were roars of laughter amongst the revellers." He could be naughty!

Thimayya was surprised to learn that his commanding officer was maintaining an unobtrusive watch on his finances. He was told in clear terms that he was drawing too much loan from the contractor and would do better to "clear his debts" and "have no more in future." And then the first lady, as the commanding officer's wife was addressed, advised him "not to marry before he was mature enough." Sound advice, indeed.

During his one year's attachment, the battalion saw a new commanding officer; Lieutenant Colonel Hikitt who assumed command a few months before he left.

Evaluating Thimayya's performance and growth, Sir Robert Graves had found him "energetic, good tempered, tactful, reliable with plenty of brains." Hikitt, who recommended Thimayya's retention in the army as "desirable and likely to be advantageous to the service," had found him "promising, who would improve with experience."[9]

His effort to learn Scottish from Sir Smolett made little headway. "Timmy," he said affectionately "It's hell of a job to get their accent correct. You have been taught English in the clipped, cut-glass way, more Oxonian than the colloquial Cockney. Don't be alarmed when I tell you, I also have to strain my ears to make some sense out of it. Like many of the Indian languages, you'll be surprised, Scottish, Welsh and Cockney are poles apart."

The Scots were tough and like Highlanders the world over, tended to be simple, straight and blunt. Thimayya had a problem understanding their language, and even manners, still more their violent ways, especially after drinks. But he played hard with them, led them on long route marches and exercises. They had grown fond of him.

His one solid lesson with the HLI was that *to be a good officer, whom he led was less important than how he led.* A very fine lesson that he never unlearnt, right from his days as a subaltern to a four-star general.

He too had begun to treat the HLI as his own regiment as he would in later years do to the 4th/19th Hyderabad, to which he was finally commissioned. With the HLI, he would maintain life-long contact; he would meet them whenever he visited England; he would present leopard skins for their Pipe Band and tiger heads for their officers mess, all being shot by himself.

Little did he know that fate had destined him to also end his career – and life – with the Highlanders. It was perhaps his last wish. ■

NOTES

1. In *The Study Of Origins of Coorgs*, Lieutenant Colonel KC Ponnappa, in an erudite study, has examined several ethnographical linkages of the Kodavs and he concludes: "The Coorgs seems to have come from the Punjab area via Rajasthan and west coast of India migrating gradually into Coorg... Their origins are connected most probably with Brachycephalic and Alpine people of North Iran and the Caucacus," p 50.
2. Why this confusion in name? According to the Kodav tradition, his name should have been "Kodendera Subayya Thimaiah" and "Subayya" and not "Thimayya". There is a small story to it. When his grandfather took him to admit him into the school at Coonoor, the Irish Brother suggested that he be called KS Thimayya. "Thimayya," said the Brother, "is more emphatic, and romantic. It'll be received well." So this anglicisation.
3. The above information is based on private correspondence with Mrs MM Belliappa, a relative of Mireille Chengappa.
4. From private correspondence. It also serves as a good example of the growing importance of the English language.
5. *Thimayya of India* by Evans, p39.
6. From private correspondence.
7. Courtesy RIMC, Dehra Dun.
8. During his research at Sandhurst, the author found that the syllabi of that period included

Human Psychology and Metaphysics. The study of Metaphysics being abstract and least popular, was dropped later.

9. The guidelines for evaluation were objective. The pen-picture was to highlight both strong and weak points. As commander, the superior was to evaluate "energy", "determination", "independence of thoughts", "the extent he would be able to carry heavy responsibilities". Whether "impulsive" or "deliberate"; gets results by "leadership or by "driving"; "resourcefulness" and "initiative," whether "elastic"; his "expression"; and "overall personality". "Outstanding" grading was reserved only for those who had the characteristics for the highest rank.

ADDITIONAL NOTES

1. Some of the Indians at Sandhurst with Thimayya were: Kalwant Singh, NS Gill; Sant Singh; LS Soin; NJ Khan; KM Idris; BS Chaudhuri; TS Batra; SK Ghose; DS Brar, TS Bal; SPP Thorat; PN Thapar. Interestingly, General JN Chaudhuri, OBE, and Field Marshal Mohammad Ayub Khan were his compatriots.
2. British Government Order placed them on Unattached List 2nd Lieutenants (for appointment to the Indian Army).
3. Thimayya's elder brother became a planter and served as an officer in the Army in India Reserve of Officers (AIRO), in the 14th Mercara Battalion from 1924. During World War II, he was mobilised to serve as an ECO with the Frontier Force. He was taken as a POW in Singapore and later joined the INA.

2
Grooming in the Shadow of the Raj

I - Iraq: The Grooming and Brooming (1928-1929)

4th/19th Hyderabad[1] (Hybd) was a standard infantry battalion with the versatile role of fighting in any type of terrain within and outside the British Empire. Consisting of about 800 officers and men, it was composed of four fighting companies, two of which were double companies of about 120 all ranks; it had one company of Kumaonis of the Uttaranchal region; another company of Muslim Ahirs of Delhi; the third company was of Rajputs of western Uttar Pradesh and Rajasthan; and the fourth company was of Jats from Haryana. To support the assaulting companies, there was a company with mortars, machine guns, signal communication equipment and pioneers. To be able to administer the battalion logistically, yet another company with a quarter master, transport officer and doctor, and a platoon of nursing orderlies and stretcher bearers, had been added.

Although 4th/19th Hybd had not joined any theatre of the Great War, its men were excellent, its drills and operating procedures practical and its overall morale was very high.

Thimayya was transferred to 4th/19th Hybd, one of the eight Indianised Units in March 1927. The Indianisation, to recall, had been the most ungracious and grudging concession that the British government had agreed upon.

The "Eight Unit Scheme of Indianisation" envisaged commissioning of Indian officers into the eight selected units from 1918-19: 7th and 16th Light Cavalry; 2nd/1st Madras Pioneers; 4th/19th Hybd, 5th Royal Marathas, 1st/7th Rajputs, 1st/14th and 2nd/1st Punjab Regiments. A trickle again, as the British accepted just five infantry battalions out of 104, two cavalry regiments out of 21, and one pioneer battalion out of seven. The percentage varied between 5 and 10 per cent. Ten years later, there would follow another eight units. This slow governed pace saw the commissioning of 69 officers between 1918 and 1930 at an average of about five KCIOs, for both the Indianised units and the State Forces.

Nonetheless, a small beginning had been made in the 1920s to let the Indians join as second lieutenants. An Indianised Unit did not mean that it had to be totally officered by Indians; most senior officers were British, including the commanding officer and the second-in-command. In 4th/19th, of the 16 officers, there were just three Indians before Thimayya joined the unit in end 1927. Captain Harbishan Singh Brar was the first KCIO who joined the unit in 1924; he was followed by Daulat Singh and Mohammad Istifaq Majid.

The British brigade had two battalions in Iraq: 3rd/5th Marathas and 4th/19th Hybd. Both the battalions had been in Iraq for some time and were employed principally in guarding the oil dump in the Shatt-al-Arab and Tikrit areas, with headquarters at Basra and Baghdad. But for that, the companies rotated while the bulk of the strengths remained at Basra, with an additional role of maintaining internal security against the Iraqi rebellious elements.

The problem was a continuation of the fallout of the Great War too. Turkey, the seat of a once great Ottoman Empire (which encompassed Iraq too), had been an ally of Germany, and was defeated. Although Turkey was spared the ignominy of the Versailles Treaty, by virtue of it being the seat of the Caliphate, the Iraqis by and large, remained anti-British.

Historically, the ancient land of Mesopotamia had been colonised by Britain at the end of the Great War. The collapse of the Turkish Ottoman Empire that followed the Turkish defeat resulted in its division between France and Britain, secretly achieved by the intamous "Shyes-Picot" that placed Syria and Lebanon under France and Trans-Jordan and Iraq under the British, the latter already under the occupation of Libya and Egypt.

Not that the Iraqis accepted the British rule; as they rebelled, forcing Britain to employing its newly found 'secret weapon,' the RAF, to put down the rebellion. Thousands were killed.

King Faisal, a Heshemite, became the monarch and a system of supremacy of the feudal chiefs was encouraged by the colonialists. Soon the 'black gold,' as the oil wealth of the Middle East came to be known, had the Anglo-French-American triumvirate take charge of three-fourths of the Iraqi oil.

By the time 4th/19th Hybd joined the British garrison in Iraq, in 1926, the Anglo-American Treaty of 1922 and the 1925 Oil Agreement had not only shackled the country to the 'coloniser's vice' but aimed clearly to keep Iraq in the dark ages. The Iraqis were extremely unhappy.

The common Iraqis, like the Indians at home, were resentful of the British – and the Indian troops in their country. For the British, it mattered little as long as their strategic oil reserves and the Persian Gulf and area east of Aden remained in their firm control; as also their naval bases and submarine cables that were stretched all over the world.

The dislike by the Iraqis of the Indian Army and their British officers, the torrid heat and dust storms for most part of the year, the Muslim faith that normally kept the local population aloof, all added to create self-imposed isolation for officers and men. It was then that the clubs, hunts and cruises in the Persian Gulf became the sought after pleasures for this occupational force. The "women of Iraq," as Majid would say, "offered cheap sexual entertainment to most of the British officers and men."

To Thimayya's good luck, Colonel Hamilton-Britton, his commanding officer, became instantaneously fond of him. While serving with the Karnatic Regiment as a subaltern, he seems to have liked the Kodavs. Generally sympathetic to all Indian officers, he fought for their membership to the otherwise purely white Basra Club. He was always trying to achieve some sort of Indo-British amity in the battalion. "We are an experimental Indianised Unit," he would reiterate, and forthrightly tell the British officers, "We are here because of the Indian officers." Not that every other British officer agreed with him.

Personally, he began to guide Thimayya, in whom he found all the likeable traits a good officer is expected to possess: good manners, boundless energy and a keen desire to learn.

But while Hamilton-Britton was a good CO, just and candid, the other British officers were distant and indifferent, and some were downright hostile to the Indians. This group was led by the Irish second-in-command. He served the essential cause of tension and bad blood between the British majority and the struggling young Indian officers. And there were historic reasons for such hostility.

Overall, the story of Britain's pursuit of the spread of the empire from 1650-1947 was one of its civilians' and soldiers' dreams of global supremacy, on the one hand, and fears, on the other. The fears were of seeing an 1857 again; of their countrymen "going native" by converting to Islam and getting circumcised, or marrying Hindu wives; or otherwise blending more culturally by adopting the local customs.

These fears gave rise to complexes, discrimination and even brutality. Denying social interaction in clubs was in pursuit of this ideology.

But the more clever and opportunist among the British saw the indispensability of keeping the Indians along with them to further enlist or ally with the favoured groups of Indians such as the heads of state forces and other influential people. Equally, the imperial needs made them accept the Indians in the administrative and police services, councils of the governors and governor generals, besides officers of the Indian Army. The KCIOs and ICOs were accepted, albeit, grudgingly. But what the British sought, and obtained most willingly, was the cooperation from the over 500 princely states, comprising almost half of the Indian territory.

Thimayya had realised that British prejudice and discrimination arose mostly due to their overwhelming power combined with a sense of superiority. Most of the British demanded of the KCIOs that they turn into the fabled "Brown Sahibs" and shun their Indianness. Most did adapt, but a small minority rebelled.

The prejudices and the inflated sense of superiority, besides the inflated egos of the British in India were also generated due to patchy background knowledge of Imperial India that they were imparted at Sandhurst. Nor was their academic base as large as that of their counterparts in the Indian Civil Service or the Indian Police and in other spheres of British service in India. While the latter category were prepared deliberately in England and encouraged to learn more about the Indians, their culture, civilisation, religion and psyche, the same was unfortunately denied to the British officers of the army. Ensconced in their cantonments, living in colonial bungalows, training in military institutions and socialising in their exclusive clubs, they generally developed a paranoiac view of the Indians including Indian officers.

While some like Philip Mason had words of praise for the Indian officers; or some like Wavell, Auchinleck, and Slim saw the true worth in 'native' officers, most refused to accept them as equal and worthy of merit, notwithstanding their upbringing, education, selection and training. It is only during, and in the aftermath of, World War II that the British were made conscious of their fallacious impressions and evaluations, and how the 'little Englanders' among them did the damage.

In the 4th/19th Hybd, Thimayya found that the British efforts to turn the Indians into "Brown Sahibs" led to extremes of Indian outbursts. Daulat Singh, for example, would don a *dhoti* for his *puja* and he always ate and served Indian food at his house. He would refuse to attend any club function too. He became an icon of the anti-British rebels.

The discrimination was, thus, rife among the officers and it often led to acrimonious situations and simmering conflicts. Captain Bull, a British officer, even aired his frustrations at the Indianisation so dramatically that he told Thimayya that his coming into the army would probably "deprive his son of a commission." Although he himself had no son, the issue he raised obviously had Daulat retort with equal vigour and anger that "Bull's forefathers had deprived Indians of their rightful place in the army to command their own troops in their own country, besides causing millions of death in famine caused by the British policy of globalisation of Indian goods and causing deficiencies in India."

Further trouble began when unwritten orders stipulated that an Indian captain should take orders from a British subaltern. (It was so even with other colonial troops e.g. an African sergeant was to take orders from a white private.)

This discrimination was widespread and even endemic. VR Khanolkar, (later major general, commissioned into the Sikh Regiment) would be deprived of war experience since he fought for his rights. Ranjit Rai (later lieutenant colonel), another Sikh officer, was forced to travel by train in a class lower than that given to his British junior. E Habibullah (later major general) found the British very nice as long they were in Great Britain, but they changed like a chameleon as they neared the shores of India. There were others, including Cariappa, who were barred entry into the "British only bars" and clubs. The manifestation of this discrimination was eventually to become one of the major causes of the rise of the Indian National Army (INA) during World War II.

If the British were mostly inimical to the KCIOs, they, incredibly, exuded affection and love for the men. Thimayya was told that he was "privileged" to command and lead the best men in war. For they had vowed to be "true to the salt," (be *namak halal*) as the euphemism for fidelity went. He, therefore, had to be worthy of their command.[2]

Being worthy became the sole purpose of his life. The first step for Thimayya, therefore, was to understand his Kumaonis, Jats, Rajputs and Ahirs, the men who composed the battalion. He observed that the British officer not only understood but loved his men which became the basic reason for the men's loyalty and devotion. In the first month of service, someone recited to him two badly written lines of poetry by one Lieutenant Hodgson, but which quintessentially conveyed, the enduring relationship between a jawan and his officer, "You were only their fathers, I was his officer," Hodgson had said.

More than parents, the officer was a jawan's *mai baap*. To be so, he himself had to be *namak halal*, a man who would truly replace the divine role of a father. That's what the British officers created. A role model and the image that was, thus, built up was formidable. Timmy had to create that image of a good officer and gentleman for himself. The men reciprocated his endeavour in enormous measure. "They humbled me, respectfully and with wit, humour and gentle tact and they taught me to be a soldier," he said.[3]

The quality of life in the battalion, as everywhere else, besides its social component, was good. For, above everything else, the British sense of justice prevailed and was admired. And there was a larger reason for it: the man and officer relationship rested on mutual respect and trust, besides the understanding of human nature. He was told by his company commander, for example, that a "Kumaoni truth was not the whole truth, nor their lies entirely false," and the Jats were simply obdurate, while the Ahirs needed to prove their worth everywhere before being taken for granted.[4]

But he would soon find them fully trustworthy, responsive, caring and prepared to sacrifice themselves for the cause of the *izzat* of the battalion; above all, however, they needed to be well led.

It is in this kind of ambience that Thimayya began to go through his regimental service. Character building and professional competence took priority in the battalion, then deployed in Iraq on Internal Security (IS) duties, part of which he did in the Iraqi royal palace of King Faisal. In trying to save a 'damsel in distress,' he virtually invited his own demise. His company provided the guard and protected the palace by constant perimeter patrolling. While riding along the perimeter one day, he was attracted by the shrieks of a woman who was being molested. He dashed across in his cavalier fashion.

"Two swordsmen attacked me, one almost got me but for my horse which was skittish and danced aside," he would recall later. Thereafter, he acquired the reputation of getting "close to the harem and remaining alive!" But it clearly showed in him the exemplary traits of courage and even chivalry.

With this reputation behind him, Thimayya was to replace an air force provost marshal, court-martialled for keeping a Russian sex worker in his quarter besides causing a riot in a 'red district'. So Thimayya was assigned by the CO to take over the duty of keeping the garrison out of the "many fleshpots and trouble spots of the town's frenzied night life."

In assigning young Thimayya to this cesspool of vice, Colonel Hamliton-Britton gave him to clearly understand that if he erred in maintaining the iron hand of a provost marshal, he would not only destroy his own career and life but would help vindicate the narrow and bigoted views of the British, "I told you so types,"[5] who were openly resisting the policy of Indianisation and saying that "Indians cannot make good officers; they just don't have it in them."

He would not let that happen and got on to the job with energy and enthusiasm. It was tiring and taxing as he would run into nefarious gangs.

Having worked assiduously and successfully, his reward came from the CO. "I am proud of you, my boy," he said, as the ship sailed back to India. That was more than enough.

In his first annual report, Colonel Hamilton described him as a "zealous, energetic professional King's Indian Commissioned Officer who had the regiment and profession at heart." He saw him as popular among officers because of his "temperate and nice manners."[6]

In this one year, Thimayya, now 21, had grown in maturity and stature and had done better than most of his contemporaries. He was confident that he could handle responsibilities as they appeared. The Viceroy Commissioned Officers (VCOs), the men and all the British, including the Irish short tempered prejudicial second-in-command too, were friendly with him now.

The mission in life he set for himself was to learn from others, seek counsel from every one to do a job better.' "Be a good officer," became his motto.

II - Lessons in ID and Vignettes of Political Thinking (1930-31)

The 4th/19th Hybd now moved to the Hindu holy city of Allahabad. Venerated as the confluence of three holy rivers, the Ganges, Jamuna and the underground Saraswati rivers, Thimayya would see how Hinduism as such had taken shape, how the flames of the agitation for freedom was being fanned, and would even meet some of the political stalwarts of the time. In his fourth year of service, he was becoming more mature.

At Allahabad, one of the IS (also called Internal Defence – ID) Stations, to which the battalion had been posted on its return from Iraq, he was often out in the field maintaining law and enforcing order. His principle was not to behave like the police in an IS situation but like a soldier. He implemented the principle of use of minimum force, harboured no malice towards civilians, and worked towards minimising the chances of malice or sadism from the crowd as well.

Allahabad was then the seat of political activities. All the political leaders like Mohammad Ali Jinnah, Madan Mohan Malviya, Moti Lal Nehru, Sarojini Naidu would often congregate there. So did Jawahar Lal Nehru who was interned at the Naini prison. Thimayya would meet with them and discuss the political situation. His sensitive mind even led him to suggest to Moti Lal Nehru that he would leave the service and join the political battle if that was what he wanted. "Do not do that," said Moti Lal, but added, "For thirty years we have fought for Indianisation (and) if you give up, no one but the British would be greatly pleased."

"We are winning the battle," said he, "(and) if you give up we shall have lost it."

He told Thimayya and the other three Indian officers who had met him over dinner, that on the retreat of the British, which was inevitable, the country would need officers like him. "Our survival would (then) depend upon men like you."[7]

Although future events took their own shape, Moti Lal generally proved right.

Then followed Thimayya's meeting with Sarojini Naidu and Mohammad Ali Jinnah. Over lunch with Mrs. Naidu, he found her (unlike Gandhiji) overtly anti-soldier. She was for non-violence, the Gandhian philosophy of *Ahimsa* although *Ahimsa* in its more practical sense did not mean or imply surrender to a bully or aggressor. It meant application of full force against them, without, of course, inflicting violence on those who followed the right and just path. Mrs Naidu's non-violence was not too convincing for the young Thimayya. He told her that he was a soldier and he wanted to be a good soldier. Then he asked her: "What would you do if you were in my place?"

"I really don't have any answer," she said and turned him over to Jinnah, who invited him to dinner, a few days later.

Jinnah dominated the entire conversation that evening, ignoring even his young wife who would have otherwise enjoyed exchanging notes with a young subaltern with an open and enquiring mind. By the time the proceedings were over, his conclusion was interesting. "I felt Jinnah did not regard me as a person but rather a type. His lawyer mind probed me with questions and wanted to absorb all that I had learnt since I entered Sandhurst." Jinnah the man did not impress Thimayya but his mission did.

The effect of this meeting was lasting. Thimayya concluded that the "intelligence" of these people and the "singleness" of their purpose made the winning of independence a surer possibility, the conditions and circumstances, indeed, generally remaining favourable.

Within the battalion, he found the Indians ignored and kept out of the Allahabad Club. It was happening for the first time in his service. In the all-white clubs in the heart of the Indo-Gangetic Valley, the KCIOs were to be left out of an institution of social status. The Indian officers were bitter. They were being ill-treated, relegated to a lower social order and boycotted. The Indianisation was really proving a *façade*.

The enduring image of an Englishman as racist hurt Thimayya immensely. The British officers, on their part, were driven by what Lord Milner, the champion of "racist patriotism" was urging the Empire's inhabitants to do – think "imperially." The result was that while some British officers were known to be good and liberal minded, most were proving to be arrogant, brick-faced, tight-lipped and even downright stupid in their racist attitudes.

"I told you so," was the reaction of the anti-British Captain Dalip Singh. "They will use you and then chuck you out," was his opinion. But Thimayya, wanting to assuage Dalip's and the others' pent up feelings, replied, "Dalip, it may not be so. The British, after all, are superior officers with a bigger status than you and I." He suggested the KCIOs use that period of club life to intermingle and socialise with the Indian intelligentsia and even freedom fighters, several of whom had already opened their doors to them.

Socialising was not to be the be all and end all, nor was acquiring a social status equal to the British. What was clear to him was the need to prove to the British that Indian officers could match and even beat them in every aspect of the profession. He had tested the required traits of a good officer in the 2nd HLI, and in Iraq. He would endeavour to be accepted as an equal. Professional competence and acquiring sterling qualities of character were to be the *sine qua non*.

Opportunities would open the door for improvement, more learning and excellence.

Soon Thimayya would be fully committed to the Kumbh Mela, receiving the King's Colours, the reorganisation of the battalion and the perpetual headache of the army – IS duties.

For a young officer, there could be nothing more exciting than the ceremonial presentation of the King's Colours to the 4th/19th Hybd. Colours, the proudest possession of a battalion or regiment, the rallying point of a battle, has been romanticised in history. Imagine Napoleon admiring the Colours of an enemy regiment held firmly in the frozen hands of a dead soldier in the battlefield outside Moscow, so magnificently portrayed by Count Leo Tolstoy in *War and Peace*. The fleeting image caught one's fancy. And Thimayya looked forward to the occasion. He would be the proud bearer of the flag in the Colour Party. And, finally, the Colours were being presented by the viceroy. Great moments to live by.[8]

Then came the Kumbh, held once in twelve years at the Triveni. It took the 4th/19th Hybd great effort to make the massive arrangements to help India's Hindu population, then estimated at 10 crores, take the holy dip at the confluence of the holy rivers. While he was overwhelmed by the righteousness of most devotees, he was pained to see kidnappings, prostitution, and much else all done in the name of religion. He feared that Hinduism had become a religion in decay and one without intellectual discipline. How long would it last? he kept wondering. Those fleeting moments would also pass by. Later in life he would realise that a few miscreants could not destroy an ancient religion.

The battalion was reorganised; in fact, it lost the Rajput company and gained an additional Kumaoni company. It was part of the second phase of the Indianisation process. Among the new weapons introduced were the .30 inch air-cooled medium machine guns (MGs). Thimayya was trained in this new weapon and he organised a new sub-unit. It was then regarded as a big technology leap, although the MGs had been used in the American Civil War and the Great War. Its introduction was welcomed by the battalion.

Captain Daulat, the vehemently anti-British officer, asked for release and was eased out. But three more young officers joined from Sandhurst: Niranjan Singh Gill, Yadunath Singh and Ganpat Ram Nagar.[9]

A tenure at Allahabad could not have been peacefully completed if a battalion did not operate an IS column in Allahabad and the areas around. The reason for this deployment on IS duties was the visit by Gandhiji to Allahabad. Thimayya saw the whole world go crazy to see this messiah not only of Indian politics but of the conscience of the masses. A Gandhian mesmerism prevailed in the holy city.

At Gandhi's meeting, the British had disrupted power supply and, hence, no microphones worked, but the contents of Gandhi's speech were relayed by word of mouth from the front to the rear, from the centre to the flanks. It was simply incredible to both Thimayya and his CO who had quietly joined the function.

The biggest fear his new CO, Colonel Nicolls, had at this moment was, "if the troops were to mutiny." "No, Sir," he would reassure the colonel, "it will never happen. The oath of allegiance we have taken will never be snapped."

But then the story that his beret, which he tossed over to Betty Nehru, the pretty daughter of Moti Lal, had been consigned to the fire, had shaken Nicoll's heart. He asked Thimayya if it were true, which he confirmed.

"Timmy, could you be so silly to do a thing like that?" rebuked his CO.

"A lady was wanting a small thing; surely Sir, I couldn't ignore her," was his reply that bordered on naiveté.

"Oh, you damn Timmy, this is too much of chivalry," barked a visibly amazed CO. He remained standing at attention.

"Get married," was the advice of his CO now. So all was well that ended well.

That evening he would call on the CO and tell Mrs Nicolls that the thought of tossing over his beret had an English background. "Ma'am, do you remember Sir Walter Raleigh spreading his cloak on the path of the British Queen?"

"Yes, I do," said the lady.

"And all for a lady, Ma'am." Then looking at Colonel Nicolls, he said: "Chivalry was part of my training at Sandhurst, Sir."

Timmy was proving to be quick-witted and good-humoured.

There was no mutiny; no more bonfires of British textiles. But news of trouble from neighbouring villages agitated the district commander. And although Philip Measure, the district police superintendent, had calmed down a group of agitating ladies, the 4th/19th Hybd was off to the villages. They carried the band, their wrestlers, and volley balls with nets, along with a bandolier of ammunition which the officers personally controlled. Thimayya's company formed the vanguard of the battalion.

Thimayya's company moved from one village to another with the customary "welcome banner" being displayed prominently by the *tehsildars*. There was loud music, singing and games in every large village; and people followed the battalion. And when the beat was over, they were garlanded. At Kannauj, the perfume factory presented them with their special perfume products. By the time the battalion returned, the officers and men smelt, in his words, "like the world's most heavily armed, perambulating whorehouse."[10]

At Kannauj too, he was confronted by a historian who romanticised the spot at which a battle was fought between Humayun and Sher Shah Suri in AD 1540 and which resulted in the former being defeated and fleeing to Persia. "Of course," said the man, "Humayun returned after 14 years and restored the Mughal monarchy." Here also in this town, were two legendary brothers – Allaha and Udal. "Some exposure to our history," Thimayya would say, "teaches us to reflect on how small bands of marauders could exploit the deep schism that existed primarily among the Hindu rulers before the invasion of the Muslims and how the destiny of this great nation was changed owing to their suspicion of neighbours and lack of unity. We have to be a strong nation, united and powerful after these *goras* are evicted." A thought had begun to germinate.

One of the lessons he learnt while on IS duties was to be considerate and humane in dealing with political agitators; they had, of course to be to be boldly confronted yet handled deftly. Bloodshed, as far as possible, had to be avoided. He ensured that fire was not opened on the public and better sense was made to prevail among the agitators. It created suspicion in the British mind that the treatment the agitators were getting was soft and one of appeasement. But Thimayya would prevail and advise his CO that by aggressively employing troops in IS against the unarmed civilians, the government would further alienate the people to a degree of hostility, and no army could successfully fight a war against its external enemies without the people's support. However, the British would continue to commit such blunders like the Jallianwala Bagh massacre, follow their "Butcher and Bolt" policy in the North-West Frontier Province (NWFP), both of which drove the proverbial nail harder and deeper into the British coffin in India.

The British were observing the Indianised Units closely for symptoms of inefficiency and disloyalty. Their prime concern was focussed upon the Indian officers who, they claimed arrogantly, were "flooding the units." Both the KCIOS and the

ICOs came under this scrutiny. Their attitudes to the political influences generated out of the freedom movement, especially in sensitive places like Allahabad, were closely watched. As a result, several officers and men in uniform were singled out. The easing out of Dalip Singh was most likely caused by his more pronounced anti-British outbursts. Thimayya, on his part realised that restraint and perseverance were the prime needs of the hour; he remained a good, apolitical soldier and his British superiors acknowledged it.

His professional knowledge and competence continuously improved in a steady manner and he became the Machine Gun Company commander and adjutant. In both these appointments, Thimayya was adjudged as "above the average." He was seen to be imbued with "keenness," "energy" and "zealous soldier's attitudes." His other attributes of "strictly temperate habits," "correct attitude," possessing "sound judgement" made him in every way an "ideal Indian officer." Timmy was a very popular officer with his British seniors.

Brigadier SB Norton, commanding the Allahabad Brigade and sub-area, predicted that he would "make a useful officer in all aspects." He recommended him for Staff College. He especially remarked: "Has charm, sense of humour and personality, and is clearly above the average." He predicted that Thimayya "would go far, if he maintained his present standard,"[11] a remark that his CO had not omitted to include. He was now the adjutant.

The 4th/19th Hybd was now due to be moved to the NWFP for an operational role. It was a part of the fixed cycle of relief programme of the units – a sort of alternating of tenure between a foreign country, a peace station with IS responsibility and the NWFP. Unless war broke out or disturbances enlarged, this cycle was adhered to.

III – In the North-West Frontier Province

Before looking into the NWFP tenure, one is tempted to peep into the overall British colonial policy. It may be remembered that India was the "jewel in the crown" and was the permanent symbol of British power and Imperial Britain. For it was here that the wealth lay. So the sea routes to India were protected through the intermediate territories. And threats to it from the north i.e. Russia and China over Afghanistan and Tibet had to be countered. Acquisition of Gibraltar, Malta, Cyprus, Aden, the Cape, the Suez Canal and control over the Malacca Strait were all part of this grand strategy.

The introduction of the English language, the adoption of Urdu – a blend of Persian and Arabic called *Zabaan-e-Hindwi* – saw the British firm and deeper in the Indian society. The proselytisation by the Christian missionaries saw the bridgehead deepened. English education popularised the British cause. Their philosophy of altruism and philanthropy, social upliftment, resulting in abolition of their own slave trade, equal status for women and abolition of the evil of *Sati* – the heinous custom of burning the Hindu widow on her husband's funeral pyre – seemed to provide a lofty motive to what Rudyard Kipling called "the white man's burden." So even in the 1920s, the British were fully entrenched in virtually all spheres of the Indian society. Timmy saw several vignettes of this transformation in Allahabad and rightly concluded that it would be many decades, if not more, before any political change would occur in the existing state in India.

The battalion arrived at Fort Sandeman in April 1933. The train journey from Allahabad to Lahore took a week; then a two-day drive in trucks to Peshawar. The last part of the trek by foot saw the battalion settle down to a small period of rest, relief and refit.

Ironically, this fort on the river Zhob had been established in 1860, named after Sir Robert Sandeman, ICS, the deputy commissioner of Ghazi Khan. Sandeman had offered an alternative to the "Butcher and Bolt" or "Forward Policy" with his "Backward Policy" of preventing direct contact with the tribals. While the British officially disclaimed the "Butcher and Bolt" policy, they, nonetheless followed the "Forward Policy" of selective forays into NWFP and Afghanistan – and maintained surveillance through British officered militias. The fort continued to serve as a military station and a logistical base for operations into the NWFP.

Fort Sandeman had two units, while two more units were located at Lorali. The headquarters of the Zhob Independent Brigade was also at Fort Sandeman while the command headquarters was at Quetta along with a unit of the Zhob Militia, officered by the British. They were *elites* in their own right. A battalion of the 8th Gurkhas, (the 1st/8th) was the second unit. The third battalion was the famous 47th Sikh, the Duke of Connaught's Own 5th/11th Sikhs. The cavalry, artillery, sappers and miners and others formed the garrison.

The situation in the NWFP had remained very unstable and difficult. With violence, slaughter, brigandage, rape and arson, these tribal fanatics looted anyone who showed a slight slackness, took pot-shots at key personnel, before melting into the mountains. Thimayya would recall: "An imaginary grievance, a fancied insult, delay in payment even of keeping peace or changing of a dishonest contractor would create problem for months on." In the circumstances the British were only maintaining a tenuous peace through retribution and bribing the local war-lords and chieftains. At Sandeman, a system was adopted which served as a base for logistics, of granting allowances to the tribesmen for various military duties such as collection of revenues.

The British retribution ingrained in the "Butcher and Bolt" policy would be to destroy the standing crops of grains or opium, besides levelling the huts. And the tribesmen would look for a *Saragarhi* kind of situation by immobilising all British succour to it before annihilating its inmates. Tit for tat was the principle.

The operations involved the move of the battalion columns into the country, linkup with posts already established, interaction with known friendly tribes and punishing of the hostile ones before returning to the fort. Thimayya called them "flag marches," with a view to show presence and convey the message that a flag march could always become a deadly affair, if opposed or encountered.

The move, to be safe, had to be through a series of pickets (or piquets) based on *sangars* established over the high peaks along the axis of advance and had to be recoiled only after the troops of the advanced guard had crossed the danger zone, and build into the rear guard that followed at some distance.

Then there was a code of conduct and a code of honour. Troops were not to return unless the mission was complete; they were not to be harsh to women, the elderly and children; they were not to lose any weapon nor leave behind a dead or wounded comrade.

Life, for Thimayya, thus moved on from the grandeur of Colour presentations and social events, to the rough and tumble of the NWFP terrain, made more hostile by the tribesman and their *Faqirs* of Ippi. It was a busy and tough life requiring extreme physical fitness and a positive attitude to the warlike situations.

Thimayya had been on leave when the battalion moved to the fort. Colonel Lewis had taken over command. Upon his return, he was expected to take over the adjutant's appointment. But because he returned late to the unit, he was asked to command a company, instead. He felt aggrieved but soon got on with his duty. Colonel Lewis was a fair and efficient commanding officer, who would spare no erring British officer, nor would he stint on praise for the well performing Indian officer. Thimayya was subsequently appointed as the adjutant.

It was then that another flag march was ordered and he saw how the tribals kept the Indian Army on its toes. One night, while they rested, the tribals fired at a picket and stray shots around their camp. That was the closest he came to being fired at in anger or being shot at. He was not impressed with the tribal marksmanship but their hospitality certainly made a mark. What pleased him was the attitude of the tribals to the Indian officers. They expressed great happiness in welcoming them. They were happy, they said, in seeing a smart and handsome Indian (Timmy) among the *goras* (the whites) and predicted, the day was not far, when they would bring in peace and *aman* (tranquillity) to the area. They were disseminating the message of the *Faqir* of Ippi.

Back at the fort, he found the Indianised 4th/19th Hybd being seen as an inferior unit, since unlike 5th/11th Sikh (also Indianised but more cohesive), they were 'mixed'; besides the Sikhs were outstanding sportsmen. The Gurkhas were 'pure' and living in their own 'home ingrown group', refusing to interact with the Indian units. They too looked down upon the Hybds. They dominated the brigade in football and boxing.

It was another thing that the British officers were keeping the Gurkhas not only isolated from the rest of the troops but at a low level of education. The knowledgeable could see that their lack of education would turn into a marked disability in fighting future modern warfare that would require technical knowledge and a high degree of individual initiative. It was evidently a case of perception. The British viewed the Gurkhas as simple and uncomplicated people, who could be misunderstood or carried away. To them, the Gurkha was, as Major General W. Ross Stewart said, "the simple-minded hill man with the manners of a king." Divide and rule, after all, had been the instrument of British policy since 1857, when the role of the Gurkhas in quelling the Mutiny became prominent alongside that of the Sikhs.

In this ambience of oneupmanship, one of the tasks Lewis assigned to Thimayya was to 'show by results' that the 4th/19th Hybd was in no way inferior to others. The key result areas, he told him, were operational security, competitiveness, and consequently high morale, for which Timmy as adjutant had to work hard.

Security was the topmost concern and warranted that foolproof arrangements were made for safe custody and carriage of weapons, while another requirement was to do well in all competitions organised by the brigade and the command. "The miracle," said Lewis casually to Timmy one day "is to beat the Sikhs in hockey and the Gurkhas in football. The Sikhs in particular were cocky and had humbled us (the 4th/19th Hybd) in hockey by heaping on us two dozen goals in the last competition." The CO was contrite and asked his adjutant, who played hockey so well, to do something about it. "I leave it to you as to how you do it but I don't want to see those two dozen again," were the CO's parting words.

Could he do it, he wondered. Between the games of football and hockey, he thought he would concentrate on the latter. It was the Sikhs who had after all gone trumpeting about their success and if he could spring a surprise against them, it would redeem the Hybd's prestige.

He spoke with a few of his trusted VCOs about training the hockey team so as to put up a good show in the next competition and to challenge the Sikh supremacy. Then he selected potential players and formed them into four teams. He took on himself the responsibility of training all four teams and finally selected two strings, a month before the match. Extra diet, early morning and late evening practice, coordination and team spirit saw the emergence of a spirited 4th/19th Hybd Eleven praying to their deities for success against the mighty Sikh Eleven. In his own words:

> For ten months I trained the team secretly and then reluctantly accepted a challenge from the Sikhs. During the match my team played superbly. The Sikhs, however scored two goals and we equalised, finally winning the match in extra time. The Sikhs were stunned.

It was all as a result of Thimayya's efforts. While the yelling was carrying on, Colonel Lewis called Thimayya aside and asked him: "In heaven's name what did you do to these men of ours?"

"Why nothing, Sir, I only gave them a few pointers."

"Pointers be damned," said Lewis and added, "And a spirit like that is more important than winning a match."

This then became his *mantra* for leadership in both war and peace. He built up an indomitable spirit in himself, enthusing all those whose command he would be privileged to assume. Personally, he began to see the possibility of creating an "indomitable spirit," in every endeavour. He would stretch every ounce of his energy to achieve the best results everywhere.

The rewards he received for a job well done had been well recognised.

The Indianisation process had continued to augment the number of Indian officers – MS Wadalia and SM Shrinagesh joined the battalion, the former from Sandhurst and the latter after disbandment of the Madras Pioneers.[12] That gave the unit six Indians among 14 officers. A ratio of four British to three Indians was not too bad. But what was distinctly discernible was the snail's space at which the Indianisation process was moving. Six officers in 12 years was ridiculous and the Indian political leaders, who were keeping tabs on the developments, would hit the governor general in the Council hard, but to no avail. The British evaded, very cleverly, the issues that appeared to threaten their existence in India.

Discrimination against Indian officers continued. Thimayya's brother Ponappa (an AIRO), attached with the 5th Baluch, Capt AA Rudra, posted to the Royal Mahrattas and Capt Bhonsale would all feel this unjustified discrimination.[13]

Although proud and sensitive, Thimayya got into the groove of regimental life enthusiastically. It was a clean life and equally thrilling, where not a moment was dull. And he enjoyed it, above the din of low-keyed, much (British) hyped tribal warfare of the NWFP. Thimayya, above all, found the Fort Sandeman tenure one of learning and enjoyment.

Thimayya had developed his own concept or image of a CO. To be a good CO, he learnt, one had to be wise, mature, sincere and courageous besides being humane. The CO was no good if he failed to command himself, which implied self-control. In addition, he had to have broad shoulders. In short, he needed sterling qualities of head and heart to be able to lead the battalion in war.

Thimayya saw in Colonel Lewis, an example of a good commanding officer who expected nothing but perfection as a yardstick for normal performance. Because Lewis expected the best, "men responded to his belief by giving their best." Thimayya himself would accept nothing that was sub-standard. Later in life, overtly he never demanded extra spit or polish, but his command always did that as a matter of habit and in reverence to the unwritten standards set by him.

Thimayya had been Lewis' adjutant and a successful one. Two occasions that influenced his young mind about Lewis were distinctly imprinted in his memory which he would recall in later years with affection and even awe. The first was when he as adjutant, was bone tired after being out on a column and was evidently slack in his duties. The CO asked him to hand over the charge of the adjutant's appointment to Major

Bull, a Staff College qualified officer. Timmy thought it was his weakness which had compelled the CO to relieve him. When he requested the CO to reconsider his decision, Lewis replied, "I know you are a good officer, I shall expect a great deal from you but until you are used to this climate and altitude, I want you to go slow."

In later years when responsible for the grooming and training of hundreds of gentlemen cadets at the National Defence Academy, Dehra Dun, and in various important appointments of the army, from CO to Chief of Army Staff, he would observe the effects of long hours of duty, fatigue and slackness in his subordinates and advise them to take a break, while a fresh incumbent with fresh energy and ideas was moved in to do the job better.

The second was after the 4th/19th Hybd defeated the 5th/11th Sikh at Fort Sandeman. Lewis openly praised Thimayya for being one of the few Indian officers who could inspire the jawans to great heights. In fact, Lewis had inspired Thimayya to set high goals for himself. A good CO made an officer; the bad destroyed him with equal intensity. "A superior in the armed forces," Thimayya would repeatedly tell everyone with whom he came in contact, or whom he addressed, "reflects the way his subordinates prosper or die." On another occasion he would equate a superior with a "gardener who tended new saplings."

And in his years of responsibility, Thimayya would become one – the proverbial 'friend, philosopher and guide' to the KCIOs – and later the Indian Commissioned Officers, ICOs – who were gradually increasing in number in this Indianised battalion. With his help, they began to grow in confidence and stature. He felt greatly elated in doing his bit. He was strict but always lent a helping hand, when needed.

Colonel Lewis was a just and fair CO. He saw in Thimayya a "very considerable force of character and power of command." He admired his "initiative" and "sportsmanship with ability to be highly competitive." He has been a "good adjutant," wrote the brigade commander. Lieutenant General JS Matterson GOC-in-C Command found in him, "a very promising officer, whom he considered "suitable for Staff College."[14]

IV – Marriage and the Challenge of the Quetta Earthquake

In the meanwhile, 4th/19th Hybd had a new commanding officer, Lieutenant Colonel P Penn, who told him: "Frankly, dear boy, I shall expect you to take over all of what might otherwise be considered my duties. And if I have to spend more than an hour in the office, you are inefficient." He was the real *koi-hai* type, who would prove a negative pole to the former CO, Colonel Lewis.

The 4th/19th Hybd had arrived in Quetta on 7 November 1933. Under Colonel Penn were eight British and 11 Indian officers. They included: Majors Rickets, Hall, Bull, Leech, Worllidge and Colsey; Captains Agnew, Thimayya, Sen, BS Lamba, MI Majid, NS Gill, Shrinagesh, Nagar, Yadunath, MA Khan, Bahadur Singh and Balwant Singh.

Fortunately for 4th/19th Hybd, they moved from the operational duty of Fort Sandeman to the peace environs of the 5,000 ft high Quetta cantonment which the British referred to as the "Aldershot of India" (In fact, it was a wrong comparison as Quetta was – and remains – far superior to the British station.) There, the planning for training, manoeuvres, major events, including ceremonials, was centralised in the brigade and command headquarters.

Timmy had experience of the post-War British Army of India in the 2nd HLI, at Bangalore that was run like a club. At Quetta, he would see the 4th/19th Hybd form part of a larger British club where shedding the puritanism of the Victorian era, the British in India – and perhaps in the UK – were more liberated in their views. Quetta being a peace station had its share of vices where the British often indulged in promiscuity and a gay abandoned life. He witnessed adultery, wife-swapping, dishonesty and embezzlement rock the Quetta station, with some of the Indian officers also joining the bandwagon.

The unfortunate part was that his new CO, as a captain, had deserted his first wife to elope with the wife of one of the subalterns. In sheer fury, and perhaps seeking revenge, this subaltern had asked for the hand of his CO's first wife. In an ironic twist of fate, both the ladies were in the station and would snarl at each other!

Meanwhile Gandhiji was challenging the British from a moral high ground. Calling the British *mlechhas*, or unclean, he exhorted the Indians to gain ascendancy over the British morality. In his considered opinion, while British historians were adulating their highly moral Queen Victoria, they ignored the fact that during her reign from 1876-1902, an estimated 12.2 million Indians had died in famine. Ironicaly, more than $ 100 million had been spent on the Queen's Diamond Jubilee of 1897 while any substantial aid to India to alleviate poverty and hunger was not forthcoming. Gandhi had essentially embarked on his political campaign against the British rule and his utterances did not seem to penetrate into the tight security cordon of the cantonment life at Quetta. But it did move the more sensitive ones like the Garhwali platoon at Peshawar that refused to fire at the agitating Pathans. So political turbulence had its peripheral effects on the uniformed men.

Moving back to Thimayya's life. By this time, Thimayya was big and what the Americans call "husky." He was no doubt the best Indian officer in his unit and he had developed a *savoir-faire* that left an instantaneous impression on people. And perhaps, he was the best "guy east of Suez" in the marriage market.

His mother was seeking a good match for him among the Kodavs. She asked him about his choice and his reply pleased her, "Your choice is mine."

Soon, Thimayya went on leave, and his mother was determined to see him married to a good Kodav girl. Tales of the British ex-marital goings-on in the cantonment, and their loose morals had shaken her up. "Dubbu, I hope you've no *memsahib* in mind," she would quiz him and warn him from blundering into an alien woman's arms. She would not hesitate to tell him: "You will marry and if it works, you'll lead a good life but if it doesn't – and the chances are that it may not – you'll turn into a Buddhist monk."

She had, in the meanwhile, made up her mind regarding a beautiful young girl called Nina Cariappa, who had just returned from Paris. Nina was the daughter of Codanda Madiah Cariappa, a hydro-electric engineer at Sivasundarum, and her mother was a social worker. Nina had been educated in Paris where Cariappa had been on deputation.[15] Nina's paternal grandfather was the first Coorg to be inducted into the Maharaja of Mysore's Executive Council. Besides, Nina's father was the first Coorg chief electrical engineer of the princely Mysore State. Her antecedents were, therefore, impeccable. Soon, Nina's family settled down in Bangalore. Nina herself did her schooling between the ages 13 and 18 years in Paris. The Cariappa family was extremely popular and Field Marshal Lord Birdwood was a frequent guest.

Thimayya was romantic to the hilt, very free with the fair sex, which often made him the envy of both men and women and, on occasions, the subject of gossip. His falling head over heels in love with Nina was narrated by himself: "I paid a courtesy call on people called Cariappa... At the door, I was met by an attractive girl who said, '*bon jour, comment allez vous, monsieur.*' I had one look at her and that fixed me. '*Entrez monsieur*' followed; a short call became a long story... courting and so on. Marriage was fixed."

He had his leave extended and Nina and he were married in the traditional Coorg style on 27 January, 1935. He was nearing 29 years and some described him to be as handsome as the matinee idol, Clark Gable. At 20, Nina was described in the local papers as an Ava Gardner. In fact, Nina was an admirable mix of Indian and Western culture and would add great happiness to this meandering celibate.

A happy married life began amidst the *bonhomie* of regimental life. Thimayya, already a role model to the Indian officers and much admired and envied by the rest of the officers in the station, was also a favourite of Sir Norman Carter, the commissioner, and Major General Karslake, the military commander. Both of them had served in Coorg and had a soft corner for the Kodav couple. Life was moving along beautifully. The Thimayyas had hired a colonial bungalow in the cantonment. Although he was still the adjutant, and, therefore, very busy, he and Nina would often go for short holidays to the cool climes of Murree or the scenic vale of Kashmir. Living was cheap and one could drive to far away places without feeling the pinch. At Quetta itself, besides the training and peace-time routine, they mixed with many friends and official functions kept the couple happily engaged.

Then came the infamous 1935 earthquake.

On the night of 31 May, a massive earthquake rocked Quetta. The disaster that occurred on that hot and sultry evening of 31 May was sensed by the animals and the birds. Thimayya's horse had become most restive. The *sais* (syce) reported this to him in the midst of a party in his house. He asked the syce to tie the horse in the open. The birds in the meanwhile had begun to fly about distractedly. It was only human beings who ignored nature's warning; perhaps no one understood the warning.

By about 1 a.m., when the guests had departed and the Thimayyas were asleep, the earth shook violently, tossing their beds like nine pins. In minutes, Quetta was buried under its own rubble.

Measured at 7.4 on the Richter Scale, it was what the *Morning Post* of Saturday, 1 June 1935 would describe as: "Mother Earth shrugged her shoulders." Among the thousands killed were, prominently, the meteorologist's family, over 200 Europeans, including 50 men of the RAF. While the military station including the Staff College escaped damage, bungalows crashed like a pack of cards. The earthquake set off fires that swept over Quetta. The entire police force was wiped out, along with most of the civilians.

The damage occurred mostly in Quetta city. The civil and railway areas were razed to the ground. The tremors travelled some 200 km all round, more so to the west. The Kandahar, Herat, Kalat areas saw houses destroyed and inmates killed; roads and telegraph lines were destroyed. The mountain villages were all in ruins.

The devastation continued into the following days, and large areas of Quetta trembled, as earthquakes sent residual tremors. The rumblings panicked people and many began to flee the area. When Thimayya drove around the city, he found that his friend Muqbool Khan had disappeared with a family of eight; people were sitting speechless with shock; Sir Norman Carter's son had died; many living were buried under debris and their heart-rending shrieks could be heard for miles. Scenes of an apocalypse appeared everywhere.

But soon Nina and Timmy joined the surviving gentry who pressed themselves into rescue and relief work. In the din of nature's wrath, the Pathans from the NWFP joined the looters, jackals and vultures. They had to be driven off. It was here that one found the caste Hindu and the Sikh religious and social prejudices still haunting the jawans when they initially refused to lift the dead bodies. But eventually they worked as assiduously as the officers and other civil gentry, and saved thousands trapped inside rubble and fallen structures.

The ferocity of the widespread devastation was broadcast by the *Morning Post* of 2 June 1935. "Quetta in ruins. 44 RAF men killed. Police Force wiped out. Mountain villages destroyed. (But) Military Station escapes, although bungalows crashed like a pack of cards. But Staff College not seriously affected. City on fire. Kandahar (in Afghanistan) in ruins. Chaman, 80 km northwest, destroyed. Devastation for 160 km southward to Kalap with four-fifth of population killed."

The rumbling shocks continued for months. The final toll was estimated at some 60,000 dead with more than 100,000 injured and rendered homeless. Rescue operations were further geared up.

A message of sympathy from the King Emperor to the viceroy was received. It read: "The Queen and I are greatly shocked to hear of the tragic disaster in Quetta involving the loss of many valuable lives among the European and Indian population. Our hearts go out in sympathy to the bereaved, the injured, and those whose homes and property have been destroyed. Please keep me informed of any further news."

To the Thimayyas this earthquake presented a veritable hell on earth; a desolate landscape, dark even by day, a common undug cemetery of thousands, some of whom clung to life but were being nibbled away by jackals and vultures. There were human vultures from the hills – the rampant tribesmen who found the human misery no less attractive than the booty. It was sickening and rebelling to see what so-called humans could do to their fellow beings. The Thimayyas had lost six of their best friends – something that Timmy and Nina could never get over.

On their part, while Nina ran a clinic for some 10 families at her home, Thimayya was everywhere, organising relief, driving away the looters and vultures. It was a true example of selfless and devoted service. After the situation eased and the tremors reduced, Thimayya was one of the many who would reflect on life with a philosophic equanimity and write to his father: "Nature can be kind as well as cruel. One cannot take life for granted. Natural calamities could be worse than war, for, there is method even in the madness of war, while Nature's fury has none."

Nina's services were well recognised as she was awarded a *Kaiser-i-Hind* by the government for her "yeoman service."

Nina, with her usual aplomb, told her husband: "I told you, these British have run out of their vocabulary. How can a woman do 'yeoman' service? They need another Dr Samuel Johnson!"

There was another interesting incident. Out of the city in ruins survived a *Maulvi*, members of whose large family had been rescued by the 4th/19th Hybd. After a month or so, when the tremors had died down, the *Maulvi* called on the Thimayyas with a copy of the *Koran*. He had come to thank the *Sahib* and the *M'em Sahib*. He wanted to read a *Sura* (99) of the *Koran* to them. Please listen to it, he pleaded, as he read:

> When the earth is shaken in her last convulsion and when earth brings forth its burdens... on that day, mankind will come in broken bonds to be shown their labours. Whoever does an atom's weight of good, shall see it and whoever does an atom's weight of evil shall also see it.

He told them, "You both are righteous in Allah's eyes," and departed.

The Quetta earthquake made Thimayya's role a recurring topic of conversation. In fact, both husband and wife had risen high in the esteem of the whole station. They were respected and sought after. It showed them at their best in meeting a challenge posed by Nature. Both Thimayya as a soldier and Nina as a human being were being regarded as exceptionally gifted.

Personally, the gains were much bigger and almost life-long. He had won the confidence of all his seniors, equals and subordinates. Colonel Penn saw him "in every way a good officer – as good as a good British officer." He was sanguine that given a chance, "Indians could spontaneously rise to any height."

He wrote further, "A first class adjutant, with high soldierly bearing and an excellent example to the KCIOs. He has been a great, great help to me in dealing with difficult situations that came in the Indianised Unit; totally trustworthy, who can keep the worst secrets." Colonel Penn had evaluated him "above the average" for his rank in "military knowledge and ability."

Brigadier Charles Brook, commander 4th (Quetta) Brigade who, liked him immensely, found in Thimayya "strength of character and loyalty" and considered him "one of the best adjutants of the Indian Army." He especially praised his services during the earthquake period and recommended him for the Staff College course.

The Commander Baluchistan Area, Major General HJ Huddleston, DSO, MC, rated him as an "excellent officer." The GOC-in-C found him "fit for Staff College."[16]

The qualities of Thimayya's character were blossoming and his conduct and acumen as a soldier was being fully recognised.

It was ironic that the military bureaucrats who were to select and detail him for the Staff College just ignored all the flowing praise that he, as a KCIO, was earning. "A first class regimental officer," Colonel Penn observed, "who by education and temperament was ideally suited to be trained as a staff officer," – even such adulation made no dent in the British policy of keeping the Indians lower than the British.

The battalion also received a special certificate of thanks from J. Freeman, secretary to the Earl of Willingdon, the governor general and viceroy of India. It contained fulsome praise for the unit:

> Deeply impressed by gallant and devoted conduct of the officers and men of His Majesty's forces during and after the earthquake of 31st May 1935. 4th Battalion, 19th Hyderabad Regiment for their share in acts of rescue and succour which saved many lives and mitigated so much suffering on the occasion.

V – University Training Corps, Madras (Chennai) (1937 – 1939)

It was customary for all military officers to visit the recruiting areas of their men at least once every five years, if possible. Called the "British Officers' Winter Tour," it found some of them, along with half a dozen mules loaded with rum and rations and with adequate logistical support, trudging through their areas. The aim was two-fold: to orient these officers to the background of their men; and to meet ex-servicemen, besides getting a feel of the pulse of the people whose sons were their soldiers.

Nina was keen to join Timmy on such a tour. So both, accompanied by some VCOs and men proceeding on leave and a few mules loaded with their essential kit, trekked through the Kumaon Hills, western UP and Haryana, for almost a month.

They met as many of the families of the men serving in the 4th/19th Hybd, as they could. It was a matter of great satisfaction for them not only to understand the socio-economic conditions of the men but their culture and the environment that helped produce these fine soldiers.

The good times spent with the Jats, Ahirs and the Kumaonis became a tonic besides a pleasant memory for the Thimayyas.

Eleven years comprised a long period for continuous service in a battalion. Enjoyable no doubt, challenging and satisfying too, but it had its problems. It turns one into a good soldier but not a good commander, for which, no doubt, an enlarged vision, a broader spectrum of duties and responsibilities must be shared and learnt. It was so then and it remains so now.

There was also the service need for selecting and training officers for higher staff and command assignments.

For a regimental soldier it was necessary to learn not only the art of warfare but also the aspects of staff duties, planning and coordination of operations of larger formations in various operations of war, and to understand the doctrinal issues of modern war. To rise higher in his career, Thimayya would need to understand the philosophy of warfare in the larger perspective, understand strategy and the implications and impact of science and technology on modern warfare.

To be considered for selection to the Staff College, every officer needed to do a stint of lower staff and extra-regimental employment (ERE) such as instructional appointments. It was with his 'chit' of good work in Quetta that Thimayya approached General Huddleston, the army commander, requesting him to recommend him for a staff or an ERE assignment. He explained how he was turning into a 'regimented' type and how he needed a break. "If nothing else, Sir," he pleaded, "could I replace my cousin Captain Boppanna, at the 5th (Madras) Battalion UTC Madras, as he is now overdue for relief?"

General Huddleston acceded to Thimayya's request and soon Timmy replaced his cousin Bopanna, as adjutant of 5th (Madras) Battalion UTC.

Fort St George, which housed the UTC, was a complex of offices, training establishment, living quarters together with an Anglican church. Both the fort and the church had plaques that said that Robert Clive (1725-74) of the East India Company had lived, and had been married, there. It was historic.

At Fort St George, as adjutant, Thimayya was to work under a senior British captain, as his officer commanding. The overall control of this establishment, with 12 to 13 officers, rested under the commander, Madras District, Bangalore, and general commanding Madras District, Madras. The governor of Madras was the unit's officio-colonel.

Thimayya observed that the five colleges that were under the UTC Battalion did some training, including Sunday parades and a 15-day camp. But no potential officer candidate joined; none, therefore, was selected. The UTC was set up to train selected Indian post-graduates for a commission. The UTC was, in fact, an eyewash, a facade, to assuage the pent up national feelings of the politicians. Thimayya was disgusted at this colonial camouflage, feelings which he openly expressed to General Norton and the governor. His superiors did not take these observations too kindly, and Thimayya was conveyed their displeasure and explained that policy matters were best left to those empowered to formulate policy and that he should stick to his own charter of duties.

Thimayya would rebel at every type of discrimination the British practised to exclude Indians professionally and socially. He found this discrimination applied locally. For even as the adjutant, he was not allowed to live within the fort, although there was adequate accommodation. He convinced his superiors that it was necessary for him to move in. They reluctantly agreed but maintained a social distance from the Thimayyas.

By virtue of being the adjutant, he was the master-gunner too, and it was on his personal orders that the gun located on the ramparts of the fort could be fired on special occasions or for rehearsals. So when one day a girl told him how thrilled she was at the governor getting a "31-gun salute," he had the gun fired. The British considered it a sacrilege, but for him and other Indians, it was a small act of defiance. It was perhaps equally a demonstration of frustration. For, frustration was dawning on Thimayya. While most other Indians survived through subservience to the colonial masters, he would stand up for his rights and privileges. He suffered, like all good Indian officers, from pangs of conscience in such situations.

It is here that he began to see the very bleak future for Indians in the armed forces. Among the seniors, for example, KM Cariappa of the Rajputs, with over 17 years of service was still struggling as a major; he was himself languishing in an ERE appointment. "To be a slave, in your own country, is a bigger curse," he would tell the boys who came for training and exhorted them to be more patriotic, often repeating Moti Lal Nehru's words.

It was a period of pessimism, when his future appeared bleak and non-purposeful. And this helplessness would even turn him rebellious. However, some good also came out of this period of almost four years for the Thimayyas. It proved to be one of relaxation, enabling them to lay a foundation for their family life. Their only daughter, Mireille (Asha Lata Mireille) was born here on 27 January, 1937. And this lovely child would grow up amidst great care and love. Thimayya's concern for Mireille was constant. Nothing mattered to him in life except the happiness of his only child.[17]

Nina, now began to learn Bharata Natyam, and Thimayya, in addition to sports, took up meditation and lessons in Yoga. "If Nina can enthral the audience with her Natyam, like Rukmani Devi, then I certainly can train my mind to work under the worst tensions of a battlefield and even of peace," he would tell his friends.

He also used his time to attend classes in Indian philosophy and did a short course at the Madras University. It was here that he improved his knowledge of military history and technology. It helped to widen his knowledge and contacts. He would be called to address the faculty of military science to give a *tour de horizon* on military operations in the NWFP and other facets of his experiences in Iraq and elsewhere, besides the Quetta earthquake.

In the midst of his personal developments, an interesting phase of life seemed to dawn on him – and India – with the appointment in mid-1939 of CR Rajagopalachari, as the Indian chief minister of the Madras Presidency.[18] This ushered in the beginning of Indian self-rule in a selective way. While this event chilled the British bone marrow, Thimayya was excited and happy, and he called on Rajaji. Thimayya told him how proud all Indian officers felt about his achievement; the old man smiled and said: "We are making some progress but we still have far to go."

"The march has begun, Sir," Thimayya spontaneously said, as he saluted him and took his leave.

About the same time, war had broken out in Europe. By March, Hitler's stormtroopers were in Czechoslovakia. By August, Hitler would reinforce his eastern front by signing a German-Russian Peace Treaty and Europe was mobilising for the inevitable war. On 30 September, the Nazis invaded Poland and divided the country between themselves and Russia. And with that, despite Chamberlain's "peace of our time treaty," Britain and France declared war on Germany. The Indian Army was also mobilised. Thimayya was posted back to his unit, now in Secunderabad.

Although relieved of his duties from the UTC, Thimayya was ordered to rejoin the 4th/19th Hybd; and be ready on orders for general mobilisation for war. "Strike the drum," as Christopher Marlowe wrote in 1587, "and the march had begun."

The four years' tenure at Madras was "a jolly good paid holiday," to quote his own words. Although a sedentary job, he had kept himself updated with the changes that were taking place in the army. "Keep your powder dry," the words engraved on the walls of Fort St George, always reminded him that he was a soldier and was there, for, at best, a side-show. The real show would begin any time.

The reports, as the annual evaluations were called, generally reiterated his character and professional qualities. "An excellent type, who left a mark"; "one who gets the best out of subordinates"; "with perfect command of English"; "socially, a man of the world"; and so on were the accolades he received. It was the normal way for the British to write about a subordinate when they wanted to let the reportee go happily unprotesting and seeking no redressal.

But the others found him, as Tara Ali Baig says, "a man of singular joyness, adored by his men." He was also a ladies' man, and his humour was such that "his wife Nina, a fiery Coorg like himself, used to walk out on him with monotonous regularity."[19] That apart, Thimayya was not a supporter of the theory Napoleon propounded – "marriage is good for nothing in the military profession" – nor among those who thought marriage turns a good soldier into one "left out of battle." He saw the need for soldiers to be married, for them to be braver and humane – braver because cowardice by a married man, in his opinion, was inconceivable, and human feelings and humanisation were the sure byproduct of a happily married soldier.

By nature, a man of martial spirits, the sounds of the trumpets and the alarms of the war for him were calls to march against the enemy. "We are for this day," he told the staff and officers of the UTC and all the faculty of Madras University who had invited him for an *au revoir*, "How will you feel safe at home, otherwise," he joked. ∎

NOTES

1. The origin of the Hyderabad Regiment dates back to the eighteenth century when its senior units were raised as part of the army of the Nizam of Hyderabad. For many years, including during World War II, it was known as 19th Hyderabad Regiment. Nawab Salabat Khan raised two battalions in 1788, one of these was 4th/19th Hybd, the oldest battalion of the regiment. Sir Henry Russell, the resident of Hyderabad raised two more battalions in 1813: one of which was 3 Para (Kumaon) and the other, the Kumaon Regimental Centre.
2. *Thimayya of India*, p. 105.
3. Almost two decades later, while opening the Armed Forces Academy, a forerunner to the National Defence Academy (NDA), in 1950, Sardar Vallabhbhai Patel, India's deputy prime minister had said, "During our struggle for freedom, the Indian Armed Forces, were the most difficult hurdles to cross... Nevertheless, we found our officers and men safely installed in positions of honour."
4. Similar impressions on the character and the characteristics of the troops are reflected in the Handbooks written by the British on various tribes.
5. n. 2, pp. 107-108.
6. From Official Document.
7. By 1932, the IMA was established due primarily to the efforts of these politicians. Earlier, Indians' entry into the IMA, Sandhurst and even Daly Cadet College, Indore, was due to that. In addition, eight more units were Indianised in 1932-1933, bringing their strength to 16. Readers would see that the Thimayyas became fond of the Nehrus, as were the Nehrus fond of the Thimayyas.
8. He would receive the King's Colours back at the National Defence Academy, Dehra Dun, in 1952. And then 4th Kumaon (the former 4th/19th Hybd) would be the first Indian battalion to receive the President's Colours on the eve of his retirement in 1961.
9. Gill joined the INA during the battalion's captivity in Singapore in 1942 and later became India's ambassador to Thailand. Yadunath Singh would be a hero in Rajauri–Punch link up in 1948.
10. n. 2, p 123.
11. From Official Document.
12. MS Wadalia, a fine sportsman, was later transferred to the Indian Cavalry, retiring eventually as vice chief of the Army Staff. SM Shrinagesh had been the first Indian instructor at

the IMA during World War II. He became the third chief of the Army Staff.
13. In *Major General AA Rudra: His Service in Three Armies & Two World Wars*. Rudra being swarthy of complexion, was really discriminated against more for the colour of his skin than being an Indian officer.
14. From Official Records.
15. Nina's younger brother, Colonel Cariappa, who will often be referred to in the book later, commanded 3rd/9th Gurkhas.
16. From Official Documents.
17. He would remain so all his life. His long time ADC, Major DRL Nanda, confirms it. "My father never slept until I returned, however late. We always ate together. There was not a moment when I saw him get angry with me or he did not want my company," said Mireille to the author.
18. "Rajaji", or "CR" was an astute politician and incisive thinker and was one of the greatest living Indians. An ardent freedom fighter, he served as chief minister of Madras, governor of West Bengal, and first governor general of India.
19. In *Portrait of an Era* (Chapter 4), pp, 82-83.

ADDITIONAL NOTES

1. Readers will find in this book the spellings of the Nepalese citizens who voluntarily seek recruitment in the Indian armed forces as "Gurkhas" and "Gorkhas". They were called "Gurkhas" during the British days, whereas the Indian Army after Independence began to address them as "Gorkhas." The Nepalese in the British Army retain the former designation.
2. The consciousness among animals, as evident prior to the Quetta earthquake, is a well-established natural phenomenon. Birds begin to seek safer shelters as the solar eclipse darkens a bright day. Horses flatten themselves to put their ears to the ground to note seismic turbulence prior to an earthquake. Similar has been the observation regarding the tsunami of 26 December 2004, that killed hundred thousands of people, but preemptive consciousness among animals enabled elephants to break free of their chains, and other animals to run into the safer areas of the hinterland, well in time to save themselves.

3
A Breakthrough

Missing the War by a Hair's Breadth

The few years the Thimayyas spent at UTC, Madras, took them virtually to the beginning of World War II. Here Mireille was born, and here Thimayya could see India gradually, but haltingly, moving to self-rule. His meeting with Rajaji seems to have built optimism in him.

Nina decided to stay on in Madras for a few months before joining her in-laws at Mercara. Upon his return from UTC, Thimayya found a dangerous schism prevalent between the British and Indian officers of the battalion. The Commanding Officer, Lieutenant Colonel D. Stuart, MC, and his second-in-command, (2IC), were apparently responsible for it. There was also a larger reason for it – the Indian officers demanded that they be treated as equal to the British; equally, there was British consternation at their demand. "Learn to walk before you run," was the advice to many Indians.

It could have been worse, as was evident from Colonel Stuart's outburst at Thimayya at his first interview. He lambasted him for failing to write a letter to him or his 2IC, before his arrival. Service courtesy did demand that; Thimayya apologised for the slip-up, although he said he had been ordered to "move forthwith." But the CO would not stop. "If you think, Thimayya," blurted an angry Stuart, "you have the temerity to think that you and other Indians can be good officers, you are sadly mistaken; your behaviour proves it otherwise. You people just don't have it in you."

It was a little too much for Thimayya and he said: "Sir, you are being unjust and pre-conceived. Indians are as good as any British but the British prejudice will not help us."

"March out," yelled the CO to the adjutant.

He saluted him and marched out.

What a welcome back, he thought. He was trembling with rage and despair. But he calmed down and began to devote his time to his company. Shortly thereafter, the battalion was, as expected, mobilised; its destination was kept secret, and was to be divulged only at Madras on the high seas. There was speculation that it could be Europe or the East. A special troop military train was lined up at Bolarum by 20 July 1940.

His absence from the battalion had seen another change in the organisation. The battalion consisted now of five companies: four rifle companies and a headquarters company that catered for both administration and long range weapon support. Subedar Bahadur Singh was his 2IC, while Lieutenants Dilsukh Maan, and SM Hussain were his company officers, commanding platoons.[1]

He had another 'scrap' – this time with the 2IC who seemed to hate the Indians even worse than the CO himself. He abused Thimayya in front of the whole battalion, lined up for inspection on the railway platform before boarding the military special.

"Have you finished," he asked the bully of a 2IC, and added in cool and collected sentences, "You might as well know that I shall never obey orders given in an un-officer-like fashion." He had rightfully ignored the 2IC's order to "double up" to report to him, as "bullshit" and undignified for an officer.

The 2 IC gulped it down without further ado. Later, the same 2 IC would ask him why he had become so defiant. "Well, because you were making me do a thing which has never been part of the tradition of this battalion. Officers do not run in front of the men, especially at someone's angry word of command." The matter seemed to end there.

The battalion transferred the whole of its strength of 26 officers, 699 men including seven warrant officers, and 64 followers into SS *Tilwana* by 30 July. It was to sail for Singapore on 1 August after taking on board 5th/14th Punjab, 15th Field Company and a detachment of RIASC.

The religious priests had attempted some *puja* (prayers) at the pier, but a sudden cloudburst washed out every thing. "Not a good omen, Sir," said the young priest. "It will be all right, Panditji," shouted the angry CO, who apparently did not believe in superstitions. "We are going to war," he said. "Do not bother." The priest grumbled in disagreement.

The CO was, in fact, annoyed at Thimayya's insistence on visiting Nina and Mireille before boarding the ship. He had agreed to Thimayya's out pass of about six hours most grudgingly only after he heard Thimayya tell Shrinagesh, the adjutant, that he might even be AWOL, 'absent without leave'! Thimayya realised that the absence of human sympathy on the part of the British officers could be totally damaging for good cohesive spirits necessary for victory in war, for which they were moving, in any case. Although the CO would ignore small aberrations in discipline by the Indian officers on board the ship, he did nothing to maintain their dignity or willing cooperation. To add to the already bad and uncomfortable ambience, another irritating situation built up in the ship during the voyage. It related to the Indian officers sleeping on the upper deck during the night. This was not only disallowed but these officers were insulted before the men and the British officers who also slept there. It made Thimayya seek an interview with the CO where he submitted to him that "the morale of the Indian officers had succumbed to the lowest" and he, out of desperation, was prepared to resign his commission and leave the service.[2]

The CO prevailed on Thimayya's good sense and calmed him down but it saw the end of what little *bonhomie* the British sometimes feigned to show to the Indians. Indianisation, evidently was anathema to the British. Only the most generous among them were able to reconcile to it.

The 4th/19th Hybd was a fine mix of Muslims and Hindus. This mix was never a cause of *angst* for its officers; on the other hand, this mix could lead to keen competitiveness, and healthy rivalry. The British, however, were restive about it, at least, among themselves. They feared that the Indian officers could 'steal' the loyalty of the troops. The creation of the rift between the Indian and the British officers by the CO seems to have been part of the generally followed British policy of "divide and rule." Such paranoiac policies, especially in a fighting unit, could prove highly counter-productive, and could result in the proverbial 'man trying to ride a tiger ending up inside.'

At Singapore, where the ship docked on 10 August, 4th/19th Hybd was accommodated at the Tyersall Barracks and placed under the command of Major General Fitzsimons, the fortress commander. Soon, new machine guns and two-inch mortars were added to the battalion. So were seven 'recce' (reconnaissance) trucks and 10 'bren gun' carriers. And the Hybd became a part of "Force Emu," the forerunner to the establishment of 3rd Corps, that would eventually comprise the 9th and 11th Divisions in Malaya and fortress Singapore.

Malaya, Singapore and Hong Kong comprised the eastern window of the British Empire. Although the Japanese had not declared war against the British until December 1941, there was sufficient cause to move forces into, and fortify, Malaya, Singapore and Hong Kong.

In Singapore, however, life moved at its normal British imperial pace and style. But it was *naïve* for the British to think that war in the East would not break out, especially when Japan was a member of the German-led "Axis." The US, on its part had renounced the 1919 Trade Treaty with Japan and frozen Japanese assets in the US. And Great Britain was continuously threatening it with dire consequences. As a counter, Japan drummed up propaganda for the march of the "Asian Co-prosperity Sphere." That war would occur was inevitable. The only doubt that remained was when! In any case, in a week-long meeting at Singapore in April 1941, the British, Dutch and Americans had also concluded a contingency plan for war. But the plans were kept secret.

While the War Office in London was still haggling over a strategy as to whether

Malaya formed the essential component of the strategy here or whether fortress Singapore was the pivot, some thinking did take place about the training of troops in jungle warfare. Accordingly, Thimayya's 'D' company was assigned to do the training in Mersing and Kota-Tinggy in Malaya. Thimayya was given "knives perang" and "bill hooks" for training in jungle lane cutting, However, *dah* and *khukri* also came in handy. Thimayya now began to train his company. Along with it came his deployment in Kota-Tinggy and thence Klaung. Living in that jungle with meagre rations and resources made Thimayya see whether the fastidiously vegetarian Jats would eat non-vegetarian tinned food. He would do the same later in Burma as a CO. The Jats, at the end of it all would say how "they almost lost their religion but saved their lives," and laugh over it.

In the meanwhile, the battalion was shifted to Nee Soon and a new CO, Lieutenant Colonel EL Wilson-Effendon, was posted. Along with it, NS Gill and Shrinagesh were posted out.

His company rejoined the unit.

It was now the turn of the whole of 4th/19th Hybd to be sent to Kota-Tinggy and Mersing to be trained in jungle warfare during November–December, the wettest months in Malaya. His company, in fact, had become the training company, providing knowledge of its experience in jungle warfare. Further reconnaissance of Klaung, Mawai, Kuala Lumpur, Johore, and so on, continued. By the beginning of 1941, the battalion was placed under the command of 12th Indian Infantry Brigade, as Force Emu was being wound up and 3rd Corps was made formally responsible for the entire defence. Companies were deployed and carried out their training *in situ*.

Gradually, but mysteriously, there were internal troubles brewing up in the unit. One evening in April 1941, Thimayya and his friends Pratap Narain, Kochar and Kumar were having a memorable evening in Hotel Cathay and were, according to Narain, being entertained by "the prettiest girls of the Island wearing skirts with extra long slits." A sudden spurt of telephone calls for Thimayya was ignored by him. "That clod of a 2 IC, may be there," he said.

Narain only got to know the following morning that the Jat company under Captain Zahir had mutinied and the battalion, as the rumour had it, was under orders of being disbanded.

The whole thing happened as Zahir, who had a German woman friend (said to be a *Mata Hari*) was living with him in his jungle training camp – unauthorisedly. Zahir and his friend seemed to have mesmerised the men too. The news travelled to the CO who ordered the company back to Singapore, and Zahir was relieved of his appointment. This aroused the Jats to protest. They even refused to eat the food. But Wilson-Effendon considered it mutinous conduct and reported so to the Brigade Headquarters which ordered the Scots to surround the unit, disarm the Jats and others and take over the kotes or the armoury. With that, the Ahirs also joined in what was now a real mutiny.

Thimayya got back to the unit late at night and found himself being challenged at the gate by Scottish troops.

"Where are the 4th/19th Hybd and what are you doing here?" he asked the Scottish officer who met him.

The officer explained that his battalion had mutinied and the Scots were now controlling the key areas, guarding the mutineers besides safeguarding the kotes. The men had been disarmed and herded into an enclosure.

Thimayya rushed to the office building where the CO and the other British officers had taken refuge, and bolted the doors from the inside. He asked the CO as to what he should do, in the prevailing situation?

"Please control these mutineers," came the pathetic reply.

Then Thimayya requested all the officers to come out in the open and be seen. Instead, the CO sought protection from the Scots and moved to the Brigade Headquarters.

There was no time to be wasted. He surveyed the so-called mutineers, and put the other Indian officers (who "looked lost,") to organising some food. To his great happiness, he found that the Kumaoni company and his own mixed company had stayed away. They were put to getting the administration going in some form. So food was cooked.

In the meanwhile, the fortress commander spoke to Thimayya and discussed plans to end the rebellion.

"Things are not so bad," he reassured General Fitzsimons. "I have persuaded the CO and others to come out of their self-imposed isolation and see how things can be improved." (The CO had of course, abandoned his own battalion.)

The general asked Thimayya to keep him informed. While he reassured the fortress commander, the Scot CO, however, kept painting a grim picture about the mutineers.

The island of Singapore had been, and continues to be, a city-state where it takes very little time for news to spread. And soon reports of the mutinous conduct of the Indian troops in its exaggerated form, began to trickle down to the civilian areas and the city, setting off waves of fear. The events of 1918 when a Pathan battalion had run amuck on the island were recalled. People began to keep indoors and the police was out in strength.

In Hybd, the CO had *de facto* handed over command to Thimayya! He approached the sullen men cautiously, offering first the *hookah*, the hubble bubble, as the British called it. The men ignored it. He then asked them what had gone so wrong that they mutinied.

The senior VCO, Subedar Sant Ram, volunteered to answer.

"We did not mutiny. We were only protesting against the removal of Zahir Sahib."

"Then why could you not do it peacefully?"

"I did but I was told by the adjutant to shut up."

"You could have gone to the 2 IC, and the CO."

"Before I could do that, some more agitated JCOs and NCOs raised a hue and cry."

"And then?"

"Then we were told we were mutinying and within a short time the *Gora Paltan* (the Scots) arrested us and our arms were removed." He then broke down as he said their well intentioned motives had led them to that situation.

"We are now mutineers and let them do what they want to do," said the VCO in total resignation.

He talked with some more – VCOs, NCOs and a few riflemen. Like typical obdurate men, they all said they were not prepared to return to barracks and obey orders.

"But you cannot refuse to obey my orders. I have been your adjutant, you and I have lived together, drank and smoked together. Even then, you wouldn't obey me, eh?" He looked at their faces sternly, seeking obedience.

The rebels refused to budge an inch. He did not give up either. While he talked, he got some tea served but no one drank it.

'You now rest. I'll see you tomorrow morning," said Thimayya, in slow admonition.

Before leaving, he had the men's blankets and pillows sent to them.

Then he and other Indian officers met the British officers. The CO was resentful; the others looked very worried. He too could not conceal his angst. For, within an hour Thimayya was back with the men, most of whom had gone to sleep by then. He talked with the VCOs again. The Scots had increased the guard, but he asked them not to intimidate the men.

It was morning when Thimayya again met them, this time with the priests who recited verses from the *Gita* and the *Koran* which enjoined on soldiers to refrain from acts of infamy, explaining that mutiny was one such act.

Playing on their psychology, he told them that the ignominy of a bad name, ill-repute, was as bad as defeat and desertion in the face of the enemy. "Tales of your indiscipline and death or dismissal on its account, will spread like wildfire in your villages. Your parents will not forgive you, neither your wives. You'll be a pariah even in your death and punishment. Do you want it that way?"

One man murmured. He sobbed. More murmurs and sobbing followed. The VCOs broke down, apologised and sought forgiveness.

"You have always been our best officer. You are today our *mai baap*. Tell us what to do?' said Sant Ram.

"Rejoin and apologise for your mistake. Forget about Zahir Sahib."

They were back. So were the British officers.

The fortress commander visited the unit and asked the Scots to hand over the guard duties to Thimayya's and the Kumaoni companies. "Captain Thimayya has assured me that his men can look after his security and I have no reason to not trust him," said the general. To rebuild the trust of the men who had strayed, he said, he would see them at PT and then at the firing range.

The Jats and even the Ahirs who had been under the Scottish Guards were back at PT, and also the short range, doing their firing, looking as if nothing had happened.

The CO trembled with remorse but could hardly believe that normality had returned to the unit.

The storm was over, but contrition and shame hung on. Both the mutineers and the British officers could not look straight into the eyes of the Indian officers. Covering up their own defects and act of cowardice in hiding from the protesting men, the CO, and other British officers whispered to their British commanders that it was all as a result of the Indian officers' "starting the fire and then putting it out too." It was rumoured that the Indians had done all that for self-glorification and to show up the British in poor light.

The court of inquiry took a heavy toll of the good name of the 4th/19th Hybd, and it took the unit a long time to rebuild not only the trust but the spirit of the unit. Zahir was court martialled and his German friend deported to Australia, while most of the mutineers were moved out to other battalions.

A superb unit under a bad CO, and a scallywag of an Indian officer, was virtually shaken but saved from being destroyed.

General Fitzsimons and other senior officers were, however, enormously pleased to see Thimayya's leadership under this second challenge – the first being the Quetta earthquake some five years earlier when he and Nina played a sterling role, and now in averting this mutiny.

"You have done wonders, my son," said he to Thimayya.

"If you are really pleased with me, Sir, I'd like to leave," urged Thimayya.

The general asked him to wait, as the Japanese intentions were still not clear. He asked him to remind him after the monsoons. Thimayya waited for a few months and then one day met the general at the golf course, and told him how the CO continued to harbour ill feeling against him.

"Sir, It is the time I leave," Thimayya pleaded.

"If the war was around the corner, I would have never allowed you to leave but I think there will be no war now. You need a change and there is a need to have good officers in the new units being raised in India," said the general benignly. He approved Thimayya's posting to 8th/19th Hybd.

To cover up the fiasco, the war diary of the 4th/19th Hybd recorded interestingly:

> There were rumours that the Indian soldiers were not content with their service conditions in Singapore and Malaya. 'At homes' were arranged and two weeks sojourn was allowed to them, for looking after their personal problems."[3]

Any sensible officer could have seen that this would happen. That night when he was stopped by a Scottish sentry outside his own unit gate and told of the incident, he felt as if lightning had struck him. "Could it be true?" he moaned. Then hanging his head in shame, he had muttered, "My God, these people (the CO, and the 2IC,) have really done what I could never imagine!"

The Hybd, according to Peter Elphic (in *Singapore: The Pregnable – A Study in Deception, Discord and Desertion*, Hodder & Stought, London, 1995) Zahir had been anti-British right from the beginning. In one of his letters he wrote to an Anglo-Indian lady, Mrs Grantzer, in Calcutta, he had said that the "days of British in India were numbered." His staying with a German woman added to his troubles, which the censors were keeping under scanner. When he was being ordered home, the Ahirs – and Jats – mutinied. The Argyll and Sutherland Highlanders had taken over the perimeter.

The court of inquiry attributed the cause of mutiny of the Hybd to the "political education of Ahirs by Zahir and encouragement to mutineers by the junior officers." It was circumspect on giving any credit to Timmy, and added that the Hybd was "unreliable," and recommended to remove it from Malaysia. However, the cause for the overall mutiny was attributed to the "poor leadership of the CO and burrowing into the loyalty of the Indian troops." The CO was removed from command prematurely, and replaced by Major AD Brown.

On the side of history, it is amazing how adroitly the Japanese kept their operational plan secret. Thimayya recalled later in December 1941, General Fitzsimons telling him, "Now the Japanese attack is very unlikely to happen, so you can leave." Back at home, Sir Hugh Elles, director of Military Training, UK, was also saying: "The Japanese are no danger to us and are eager for our friendship."[4]

His posting out of the battalion, as the records show, may well have been done on purpose since the CO, on the quiet, had been asking for a "thinning out" of the Indian officers from the battalion. Shrinagesh and Gill had already moved out. Thimayya would add to the list. This was done very discreetly so as to not arouse any suspicion.

That, however, did not detract the fortress commander from officially recognising his worth as a good officer. In his report, he wrote that Thimayya possessed "considerable tactical sense," and had "the making of a good officer." For his good work, especially in averting the mutiny and getting the troops back to normal, C-in-C, Headquarters Second Echelon, 'Force Emu,' "*commended Thimayya for good work in regimental affairs.*"[5] His role, in fact, had been boldly highlighted by the Court of Inquiry, while it had no good words for the other officers, both Indians and British.

In the circumstance, Colonel Wilson-Effendon was not allowed to report on his officers. Earlier, Colonel Stuart was more than fair to him when he wrote of him: "A most attractive personality with charming manners, cool under all circumstances." He, however, found him extravagant and counselled him to "control his finances," a euphemism for extra socialising.

As Thimayya sailed back with a heavy heart, he wondered why luck was playing truant. Whatever may have happened or what the future held, this was no time to leave the battalion, he thought. But at Agra where he reported on 27 August 1941, Nina would tell him that all that was happening had something good in it. She was right. For, the ticking of the second hand of destiny had begun. By early November, the US ambassador in Tokyo warned Washington of a possible Japanese attack on the US positions in the Pacific. A week later, Sir Winston Churchill was saying that he would join the US, "within hours" in case of war with Japan.

When the Japanese struck in early December 1941, Thimayya felt aghast at the incredulous intelligence failure and the naivete of the British high command.

The Japanese proving absolutely meticulous in concealing their intentions sprang a surprise when they struck Pearl Harbour on 7 December, and a day later sank the *HMS Invincible* and *HMS Repulse* outside Singapore, coordinating it with a ground invasion of Malaya through Thailand. They destroyed 3rd Corps and captured some 70,000 prisoners, including the 4th/19th Hybd. It was a rout worse than Dunkirk and soon more humiliating as the Japanese forces would pursue the retreating British through Burma to eastern India.

***

Thimayya suffered through the period of thirteen years from 1927 through to 1941, where Indians, though equal, were never treated so by the British. Discrimination and prejudice made the lives of the Indian officers unhappy and gave them no job satisfaction. Thimayya thought a miracle had to happen if the situation was to improve. A suffering Indian community prayed for that miracle. And it did happen. Thimayya called it the "Reincarnation of Lord Krishna" when Hitler began to agitate against the injustice of the Versailles Treaty and propagate Aryan supremacy over the lower European races. In the East, it was the Japanese who began their march extolling the virtues of the "Asian Co-prosperity Sphere," which was an agenda for expansion. The war removed several discriminations by its nature and demands but not wholly.

The emergency brought in thousands of ECOs, both British and Indian, and gradually official discrimination reduced.

As British prestige was now at its nadir, there emerged what was termed as the "Loyalty Oath Paper," containing an affirmation of the oath of allegiance to the King Emperor, besides confirming an apolitical attitude and total commitment to the war. Thimayya's brother Ponnappa had been taken as POW at Singapore and rumours were afloat that he had joined the Japanese-organised Indian National Army. It was, therefore, necessary for Timmy to show no personal proclivities for politics, if he were to remain in the army. He signed the loyalty oath paper; so did most. Those who demurred, were eased out of service.

Thimayya was suffering, indeed, but indirectly, he was contributing to the Indian struggle for independence in a unique way. By his continuous revolts against the

British policy of denying Indians opportunities for leadership responsibilities and higher command, he was simply refusing to accept their superiority. But this was done with a *savoir-faire*, and in a disciplined manner for which he even offered to resign.

The years 1940-41 were, by all reckoning, frustrating years. Thimayya had to serve under two COs who were thoroughly anti-Indian. Two bad COs ruined the spirits of an outstanding unit such as the 4th/19th Hybd. They simply played havoc with the cohesiveness and morale of the unit, and handled it so badly that the inevitable revolt took place. The unit, already a dispirited lot, would become POWs, and suffer the most.

He would cry now for his battalion, as he would cry later when the emaciated 'old faithful' would meet him on their emancipation in 1945.

8th/19th Hybd: The Raising

The expansion of the Indian Army had begun with a bang. In 1941 itself, some 50 units were raised and raisings would continue unabated, until the army reached a strength of 2.5 million. It was half the strength of the five million called to arms from British dominions/colonies.[6] The Hybd's share of raising in 1941 would be two battalions along with a machine gun battalion, all at Agra where the training centre was located. His CO, Lieutenant Colonel Charles Attfield, was a pleasant man to work with. Being sufficiently senior, Thimayya became the 2 IC of the unit.

Agra also saw two more developments: the establishment of the war-time Central Command; and, an influx of Americans. Central Command Headquarters was principally to look after raisings, training and fitness of the units for war.

The Americans at this stage were on a logistical air support mission for supplying the Kuomintang (KMT) troops of Chiang Kai-shek in China over the 'Hump,' besides establishing their future air bases. As part of their SOS (Supply of Services) project under Brigadier General Raymond K Wheeler, they had set up depots all over India, Agra being one, Ramgarh in Bihar (where the Chinese troops trained) was another, as also another at Jorhat in Assam, and so on. At their peak, the Americans had over 79,000 troops and civilians located in British India.

With their resources, the Americans could move the earth and change its face, thought Thimayya. Within months, working round-the-clock, they had prepared a large operational airfield at Agra. The Indians found them lively, though a bit loud. They loved children and admired the Indian women in their colourful *saris*. Some of them openly sympathised with the plight of the Indians under the British yoke.[7]

True to the feelings of the famous American writer Mark Twain, they found India a "land of wonders" – one of the wonders being the famous Taj Mahal. The erotica at Khajuraho added further to their interest.

Although Mark Twain would be remembered for his lines, "East is East and West is West and the twain shall never meet," he had observed more specifically of India: "Nothing has been left undone either by man or nature to make India an extraordinary country that the sun visits on his round – India the only foreign land I ever day-dream about or deeply long to see."

The Americans impressed Thimayya. Some of them became family friends and one Colonel d'Isle even married Nina's sister, Bollu. That would, of course, turn into a marriage of convenience. Thimayya had counselled Bollu to consider what Mark Twain had opined – the cultural and ethnographic differences were too large a divide for a durable marriage.

But the free spending and boldness of the Americans as an enterprising people had certainly impressed him as he saw them in the British club, at sports and training. They could be a nuisance too; and had to be handled carefully after a few heady drinks when they would turn rowdy and aggressive.

The training of the new recruits and old soldiers who were forming part of the 8th/19th Hybd was completed fairly soon.

Even as the war efforts continued unabated, the agitation for independence did not die down in sympathy. The Indo-Gangetic Valley was rocked again with Gandhiji's *Satyagraha*, the peaceful protests through the use of non-violent methods. And the 8th/19th Hybd was to have its share of IS duties to perform. As 2 IC, Thimayya was active in planning the IS column, sometimes leading the odd one. He would remember his experiences in Allahabad and apply the lessons he had learnt there – that while the army had no differences with the countrymen, it had to maintain law and order. It could be done by a show of force rather than the use of force, and invariably, with persuasion.

A few columns that the 8th/19th Hybd sent out controlled the mobs and returned without opening fire. While the public praised it, the Press highlighted it and Thimayya had a difficult task convincing Attfield that it could best be done in this manner. Attfield would, of course, soon see the results himself, and reluctantly accept Thimayya's views. "There is one man who is at least taking me seriously," he would tell Attfield, later in a letter from Quetta. "Like this, dear Timmy," replied the colonel, "the Indian Army would turn into a saintly army!" Attfield added, "While you may be influenced by non-violence here, I wonder if you'll be able to apply it in war." "Remember," Attfield quoted McCauley, "moderation in war is imbecility."

The British were, indeed, circumspect about the developments taking place. For, as the news – and the rumours – trickled down from the Singapore front, there were wild stories about the way the units and the Indian officers and men had changed their loyalty in favour of joining the INA. Ponnappa, his elder brother who moved straight from the ship to the Changi POW Camp had also joined, the INA. It was the failure of the British high command, as indeed, the deep-rooted resentment against discrimination among the Indian officers that had become the principal cause of such behaviour amongst the men. Back home, it was feared that mutinies would be sparked off and 1857 repeated. So fresh oaths of loyalty and allegiance were solemnised and a watch kept on those who could breach them and incite the men. With the exception of a few minor cases, the officers and men adhered to their oaths and trust. The politicians agitating for independence wisely decided not to politicise the army. It proved an act of wisdom, as any breakdown of the armed forces would have accelerated the Japanese "March to Delhi" and replaced one colonial power by another, as proved in all other occupied territories.

There were lighter moments too. Nina's younger brother (later Lieutenant Colonel) Cariappa had joined in the ranks and his regiment was located at Mathura, a short distance from Agra. Coincidentally, Thimayya's younger brother, Freddie, now an officer of the Bihar Regiment, was also located at Agra. Family get-togethers were held regularly.

There was another occasion to remember. The emergency saw the flooding of the centre and units with ECOs. Big bungalows were hired for them so that 10 or more could stay there, on a station pool basis. Freddie and Cariappa were in one of the bungalows. But they had to dine in the mess, which normally served English food, of which every Indian officer was sick at heart, if not in stomach. They longed to eat Indian cuisine wherever possible.

On a week-end, these ten decided to have a beat up in their bungalow with dancing girls in attendance and the best Indian cuisine from a local hotel. But because it was not allowed to entertain women and guests or have food in the bungalow, the ten subalterns first joined their colonel at the dinner and later excused themselves. Normally, they would have had to wait till after dinner when liquor and a card session would continue into the wee hours of Sunday.

By 9 p.m., when they cycled back, the servants had the food and snacks laid out, along with a bevy of comely dancing girls accompanied by musicians from Jaiselmer to entertain them. The night was young and the dancing, and music began on joyful note. They lost count of time as the liquor intake made each of the ten see the dancing girls as fairies from the outer cosmos.

In the meanwhile, the colonel asked the duty officer to ascertain if all was well with the "sheepish looking youngsters." "They may be up to some mischief," he remarked, as he tasked the duty officer to surreptitiously observe and report. Upon return from the bungalow, Captain Brown, the duty officer, stated the bare facts to the colonel, "They are enjoying themselves." "Ah, well," burst out the colonel.

Thimayya, as 2IC, responsible for the discipline and training, was then asked over by the CO to the mess for a drink, by about 11 p.m. Realising that there must be something wrong, Thimayya joined the colonel and soon they were at the bungalow.

"Everything came to a standstill," remembers Cariappa. "We were paralysed, the girls froze and the musicians began to pack up. We were all standing to a frozen attention. The effect of liquor was instantly lost." In this mayhem, the colonel suddenly spoke, "Why stop?" and looking at Thimayya, asked if they too should join in the revelry.

Cariappa still cherishes that memory:

> Dubbu, ever ready for fun, agreed wholeheartedly. We were so relieved and all of us had fun, the colonel and Dubbu joining in shaking their legs or dancing with the girls. The party gave over about 2 a.m., with the colonel having to stagger home. We put both of them on their square feet, but before they left, Timmy invited all of us to lunch again. He was absolutely normal.

Staff College Quetta and Staff Appointment (4 February 1943 – 19 August 1943)

Agra provided a good opportunity to Thimayya to start looking at his profession more seriously than he had done thus far. A balanced career, especially to an officer of the combat arms, could only be ensured if he qualified for, and was trained at, the Staff College, Quetta.

The Staff College now ran two short courses a year instead of the year-long normal course. The selection to attend the course was based on an officer being recommended by his CO up the chain till the army commander. And, finally, the Army HQ or GHQ, India, drew up a list of merit.

It was Thimayya's luck that Lieutenant General Polk, GOC-in-C Eastern Command visited the unit. He had known Thimayya and had formed a very high opinion of Major Thimayya from his exemplary service at Quetta. He asked him why he had not attended the Staff College Course as yet, when he was "virtually getting overage" for it – and for which he thought him ideally fit. Thimayya explained that he had been a sort of rolling stone and perhaps gathered no good reports, and added that perhaps he was not fulfilling the criteria for selection.

Hearing this, Polk thought that injustice was being done to the officer for no fault of his. At the same time, he thought it was possible to still earmark him for the war-time courses. He asked the CO to initiate a special report recommending him for the next course, due to begin in a few months. Although his CO, Lieutenant Colonel Attfield, had not yet completed the minimum period to initiate a report on Thimayya, General Polk asked him to recommend him as a special case to attend the Staff College at Quetta. He asked him to leave the rest to him. In recommending him for the course, General Polk stated that "great injustice as it was, had been done to Thimayya; it would exacerbate if he was denied the course now and the Indian Army would lose an outstanding Indian officer of the future." Some of the British officers could really be soothsayers. Polk was one.

General Polk ensured that Thimayya was at Quetta, to attend the 7th War Course from 22 February 1943 to 17 July 1943. Quetta in Baluchistan was not a new place for him. He and Nina had done yeomen service there during the 1935 earthquake, which took some 100,000 lives, if not more. Turbulent, with tribal warfare and icy cold even in March, the fear of an earthquake always loomed large here. While sleeping under canvas had become the rule, war in Europe and the Far East and Middle East had no effect on the social life of the Staff College.

But the course, condensed to six months from its normal one year, demanded hard slogging in which Nina would help him. With 16 years of service as his anchor, Thimayya competed with co-student officers generally junior in service to him but with inflated war ranks of lieutenant colonel and long stories of their war experiences. Yet Thimayya's practical knowledge, clear thinking, service with troops in various theatres of operations, his innate understanding of the jawans, his vision and needs of war, placed him among the best officers. He finally stood second on the course, which had 140 officers, only six of whom were Indians.

By end 1942, the war in Europe, Asia and Africa had advanced sufficiently. The Germans, already in Russia, were being opposed by the Russians through their offensives in the Caucasus but the Germans held on to their advanced position, extending it to the Black Sea. The battle in the Pacific was still in favour of the Japanese. They had forced the withdrawal of the British forces from Malaya and Burma. In North Africa, Rommel's *Afrika Korps* had twice driven the 8th Army to the Egyptian Delta. In India, the Congress was opposing the positioning of American troops in India as well as pressing for an early departure of the British from India. However, by the end of the year, El Alamein had been captured. The Americans had landed in Tunisia and Algiers. The Russians had launched their counter-offensive on Stalingrad. The Japanese had reached the extremity of their advance to Gudalcanal and the Andaman–Nicobar Islands. The politicians in India also seemed to tacitly go slow with their agitations. And the enthusiasm of the Indian youth to join the armed forces did not seem to decline.

The Staff College course was eagerly following these historic events while getting into the nuts and bolts of staff duties. It was enjoyable and educative as well.

Thimayya was repeatedly asked about what went wrong in Malaya and Singapore where he had served.

In his analysis, the mistakes had been both strategic and in the mindset he saw in Singapore, barely two months before the Japanese struck. "General Percival, as Principal Staff Officer to Lieutenant General Sir William Dobbie, the Fortress Commander in 1937," he said was "instrumental in suggesting that the defence of Singapore lay in Malaya." History was still incomplete and several key facts were unknown or skilfully concealed. In fact, the Chiefs of Staff Committee in London had dithered over the plan, eventually allocating 3rd Corps (9th & 11th Divs) for Malaya. But the myth that the defence of Malaya lay finally in "Fortress Singapore," saw the outcome of war. This was forsaking all initiative.[8] Eventually, fate ordained that Percival became the victim of his own design.

The mindset he alluded to and which he explained, was what the Fortress Commander General Fitzsimons told him before his departure and added, "No one was wanting to believe that there could be a war and those who did, like I, were not only 'shunted out' but were not forceful enough to express the urgency."[9]

In his Staff College report, the chief instructor credited Thimayya for his "wide sweeping practical knowledge to handle units and formations up to brigade level."

The commandant was more impressed with his "deliberate thoughts in matters military and his grasp of strategy." "Given adequate opportunity and encouragement," he remarked, "Thimayya will rub shoulders with the best of his rank in the Indian army." His report read:

> A strong personality with plenty of character. Always cheerful with very equable disposition. Has a well developed sense of humour. Possesses charm of manner and is both tactful and tolerant. Level headed.
> A good organiser and leader who gets the best out of everyone. Very popular.
> A good, sound, practical brain. Full of common sense, capable of handling detail and working hard. Thoroughly reliable.
> Produces sound, common sense, practical answers neatly and accurately.
> Recommended for a G (OPS) or Q Appts (Appointments) with troops.[10]

In assessing Thimayya's potential as a staff officer capable of planning not only operations but appreciating the strategic paradigms, the directing staff at Quetta had been fair. So were their grading and recommendations. That is where the problem began.

Paradoxically, the British were against any Indian holding an appointment which would lend him access to operations and all the inputs that help evolve the plan – the intelligence, enemy reactions, own design of battle, the activities of the INA, the influence of political developments, and so on. It was a matter of trust and the British were not prepared to do so. Secondly, Thimayya himself realised that the "British were against the idea of an Indian acquiring experience in this ultimate of military science."[11]

Graded Staff and Window of Opportunity

What Thimayya stood posted to was typical of the British. Though graded as GSO 2 (Operations) of a division, he was being earmarked to fill the vacancy of a GSO 2 (Staff Duties), the latter apparently a low grade appointment. Thimayya protested and wanted a posting back to his battalion rather than serve along with the 'overpaid, overranked office boys' at the GHQ. His representation paid off. He was posted as GSO 2 (Ops) of 25th Indian Division under raising at Madras where he reported by 20 September 1943.

General HL Davies, CBE, DSO, MC, the GOC was not only difficult and prejudiced about Indians but was keen to have a British officer as his GSO 2. He told Thimayya so when the latter's biodata showed him as a 'regimental type'. However, reluctantly he agreed. Davies incidentally, had been Chief of Staff to General William

Slim in 1942, when 15th Corps withdrew in absolute tatters, disintegrated, demoralised and ineffective.

Life was never dull for Thimayya and he seemed to have a knack of initially getting into a scrap with everyone he served with then, or would serve with later. And soon a scenario would be enacted. Davies was practising a divisional advance and withdrawal manoeuvre. As GSO 2 (Ops) he was the author and coordinator of the exercise. During the manoeuvre, Davies got lost, for which Thimayya was held responsible. Although it was the provost who had misguided the GOC, Thimayya apologised for the fiasco.

But when the general equated that episode with his inefficiency, he offered to be posted away. That too did not seem to satisfy the GOC. As a last resort, Thimayya wanted to put in his papers, rather than be humiliated. Sensitive to the core, Thimayya never learnt to cultivate a thick skin. However, an "imperial rocket" by General Davies set him on the right course.

"I wouldn't stop you from going, if you must," argued Davies in the end, "but you must know I would be happy if you stayed." He instantly changed his mind. Perfecting his phlegmatic sense of humour, Thimayya later told his friends and wrote to Nina at Bangalore that "had Davies concurred in his request, he would have to go counting beans in Coorg." His luck had held on.

Thereafter it was smooth sailing. He learnt a lot professionally. He acquired experience in operational planning and coordination unequalled thus far. Well trained and guided, Thimayya was an efficient GSO 2 (Ops) of the division that moved into the Arakans to finally join 15th Corps under Lieutenant General Sir Philip Christison.

This corps already had 26th Indian Division, 81st and 82nd West African Divisions, 50th Indian Tank Brigade, besides 22nd East African Brigade and 3rd Commando Brigade. The Arakan offensive of 15th Corps was opened by the 25th Division by advancing astride the Mayu Peninsula on 12 December 1944 supported by the African Divisions in the Kaladan and Kalapanzin Valleys.

Timmy was to be fully baptised to battle conditions and to the fury of the Japanese artillery and aerial attacks during his GOC's forward visits to the troops. It was here that he found that despite all his military experience of service in the NWFP, and elsewhere, he stood to learn from a poor sweeper how to behave under fire. The incident took place while General Davies and he drove straight to an observation post of a forward company of 4th/1st Gurkha Battalion near "Able Hill." As the company commander began to indicate the Japanese positions, the Japanese fire controller, who had all this time kept the movement under his telescope, brought down a sharp artillery 'crunch' on the post. Both Davies and Thimayya jumped into the nearby trenches, Thimayya landing on a sweeper (*safaiwala*) already inside the trench. He bore Thimayya's 70 kg weight until the shelling ended.

But, finally, when the fire seemed to lift, Thimayya jumped out, apologising to the *safaiwala* for the inconvenience. Ignoring those words from Thimayya, the *safaiwala* shouted to him to jump back into the trench as the Japanese would pause and bring down another salvo that would cause more casualties. When Thimayya did return to the trench and the *safaiwala* was proved right, he thanked him. "You must know your enemy," said the lowly non-combatant unenrolled (NCU), "and if you don't, learn about him from others who know him." Words of wisdom, Thimayya would always say, should even be learnt from the seemingly lowest.

Thimayya found that the operational headquarters area albeit fire-free, was still tense. General Davies, who seemed to be overwhelmed by the weight of operational responsibilities and his inability to bear the burden more cheerfully and confidentaly, seemed to be wearing himself down. On the other hand, he found Colonel Sharma, director, Medical Services of the Division,[12] to be a fearless religious man who kept the morale of the troops and Medical Services high. But General Davies appeared to crack faster than expected, although he would continue to be the GOC when Thimayya showed his tactical ingenuity as a battalion commander under him.

Thimayya had now been found "fit to be promoted to command a battalion." Thimayya's staff appointment was just for eight months and he had done well. He asked for a posting back to his own battalion i.e. 8th / 19th Hybd then in 25th Indian Division itself and deployed in contact with the enemy. He was excited to be back as the second-in-command.

It was 18 May 1944.

Thimayya had done almost 18 years of service, and was 38 years old. That made the difference. He was young, but with fairly sufficient experience in both staff and regimental duties. And, above all, destiny had whisked him away from the ignominy of being a POW. Instead, these were to be his years of action and glory. This also would give him the sobriquet of being the "first Indian to command a battalion in war." ∎

NOTES

1. Major JB McLeod commanded HQ Company. 'A' Company was commanded by Major HL Hill, 'B' (Jat) Company by Captain NS Gill (later Zahir would take over) 'C' (Kumaoni) Company by Captain MI Majid. His own 'D' Company was a mixed company with a platoon each of Kumaonis, Jats and Ahirs. Captain SM Shrinagesh was the adjutant. With the declaration of war and emergency, the unit strength rose to 26 officers, of whom only five were British. The Indian officers were now a numerical majority.
2. This was the first time Thimayya would seriously think of resigning his commission and leaving a service which he dearly loved. But, in order to uphold his dignity and *izzat*, he was prepared to forsake one of his dearest possessions.
3. The War Diary of 4th/19th Hybd.
4. Norman Dixon's *On the Psychology of Military Incompetence*, p.164.
5. From the Thimayya Papers and Official Records.

6. The sacrifices the Indian Army made of approximately 170,000 dead comprised almost 70 per cent of those killed in action. It would earn 31 Victoria Crosses, almost half won by the whole force.
7. Some American writers like Wendell Wilkie, Pearl S Buck, Louis Fishcher and Mrs Gunther eloquently advocated the Indian nationalistic cause, engendering Indian goodwill.
8. From Papers on *War in Singapore*, kept in the archives in Singapore.
9. In *Singapore, the Japanese Version*, p. 99, Colonel Tsuiji talks of the pains the Japanese took to prepare for war. The single, biggest reason for the British rout, he observed was the "lack of anti-tank defences."
10. From Personal Reports. G(Ops) and Q Appointments mean General Staff Officer dealing with operations, whereas Q imply logistics both vitally important.
11. *Thimayya of India*, p. 183
12. Later director general Medical Services, Indian Army. His four sons did him greater honour: the eldest Som Nath earning the first PVC (posthumously) the second rising as engineer-in-chief and a third as COAS Indian Army. The son younger than Som Nath had been killed in World War II in Burma. A very rare military family.

4
Stars on the Ascendant Command in World War II (May 1944-January 1945)

Thimayya's transfer to 8th/19th Hybd was both a matter of luck and opportunity. While serving under 25th Indian Division, where he was GSO 2 (Ops), a situation developed when the commanding officer of the unit, Lieutenant Colonel FW Gibbs, was wounded in Japanese shelling. Thimayya had been approved for promotion and stood posted as 2IC of the battalion, and true to the environs, he stepped into the war-like reception from the enemy. On his way to his battalion headquarters from the divisional headquarters, as his jeep meandered through the dusty track, he was blocked by a caravan of loaded mules that drew the enemy's fire. The 8th /19th Hybd were stunned by the unexpected enemy salvo. He saw the previous CO being evacuated, telling him to "take over" and wishing him "good luck" in command.

It is a great welcome, he thought, and drove onto the battalion headquarters. It was under intense shelling by the enemy. He was received by his adjutant and the 2IC. Soon the subedar major sahib also met him. While briefing him, he found that there was great anxiety among all ranks of the unit. The following day, as he went around the defences and talked with the officers and the VCOs, he observed the anxiety again.

He assured them that he would soon find means to improve the defensive posture and see how best the casualties could be reduced and, indeed, administration improved. He insisted on publishing a "special order of the day" that briefly recorded his policy regarding the conduct of war and points of special emphasis. "*I see you in good hearts and fine spirits. Although under the enemy fire and tactical disadvantage, I admire your courage. I am certain we will soon beat this enemy and show him that the Hyderabad can decisively beat him.*" Deep in his heart, however, he knew it was not only a challenge before him but a test of his command. He prayed to God to give him courage and strength to prove his battalion as the finest fighting unit.

And then he asked the adjutant to disseminate the order to every company. The battalion was getting to know that Lieutenant Colonel KS Thimayya was one of the first Indian COs who had taken over a battalion in war. Everyone, including the men and the British officers, were observing him for his style of command.

During his meeting with the commander and staff at the brigade headquarters, he was told by his commander that the "entire commonwealth would watch him for efficiency" and he assured him help to the extent possible. Thimayya reassured him of his complete loyalty and devotion.

A Self-Styled Attack

Like his previous battalion, the 4th/19th Hybd (now prisoners since February 1942), the 8th/19th was an Indianised Unit. Except for five Indian officers who were mostly junior officers, and Surgeon Captain KC Dasgupta, IAMC, the other eleven officers were British. Major FJO Kelly (2IC), led the other British officers: Major FW Macdequigley (later, Major Buxton), DC Gray (later, Major Bobby Fowler), HD Paed, HN Horsfold, Captains CW Burgess, SC Arnold, and Surgeon Ronald Ross formed the team.[1] There were, of course, four subalterns. He found all of them on the ball except Gray whose 'gray area' was deficiency in man-management of the Jat company, which was on the verge of a rebellion.

8th/19th Hybd was in no better shape than 4th/19th Hybd had been when he left it in Singapore in 1941. The reasons being both the Japanese actions and inflexibility of command. The companies were widely dispersed and were constantly under enemy fire and domination from a 100 metre (approximately 400 ft) high feature which was held by about two Japanese companies. The situation was somewhat akin to the trench warfare of the Great War![2] The Jat Company was a divided lot under their Australian company commander, Major Gray. The worst were the VCOs, the culprits who had divided the men on caste and regional basis, affecting their promotion and overall cohesiveness.

The Ahir Company was in good heart and its morale, despite being badly deployed, was high. So were the two Kumaoni Companies, which though totally dominated by the Japanese from their tunnelled defences, kept their spirits high. Internally, therefore, he took immediate action to get the Jats on the grid, by removing some of the VCOs and changing the company commander. The troops felt at ease.

He then began to analyse the major cause of worry: the pitiable conditions of the men under direct enemy domination and observed fire. He knew there was only one solution to the problem: to somehow capture and hold the feature. But it would require a full-fledged assault for which clearance, if not help, from the higher formations would be necessary. From the depth position he was shown the three enemy localities of 'North Pimple', 'Green Hill' and 'Green Tree Hill'. To his dismay he found that the enemy could even sling stones into the unit to cause casualties and harassment; and there were reverse slope positions to protect them (the Japanese) against artillery and air attacks.

He decided to carry out a preliminary reconnaissance of the Japanese position. On 21 May, along with Buxton and Arnold, he went to a vantage point to see the approaches to 'Green Hill'. Buxton then investigated the 'Bird Nalla,' on the east, that led to the eastern face of the Japanese defences. He then took an officer patrol to the northern side. He came to the conclusion that, if permitted, he would have a crack at it and perhaps secure it. Even if he did not succeed in overthrowing the Japanese, he would, at least, secure a foothold, on which the division could plan further expansion.

He discussed his proposal with Brigadier Angub, his commander, who agreed with it but asked him to obtain General Davies' approval. The general agreed with the plan of action but ironically tasked a British battalion, now in reserve, to do the task. Thimayya felt disappointed but again volunteered his full cooperation with the British CO in terms of fire support, going, deception, and so on. That was turned down by a haughty and peeved CO, who felt that his battalion was unnecessarily being dragged into this unachievable task.

The British assaulted the objective in a manner that any defender would desire his enemy to do. They were noisy; they followed an obvious, gentle western approach; and as the leading platoon attacked and some men got killed, the CO called off the whole operation, which was an easy thing to do. It was equally easy for this CO to tell the GOC that the Indian suggestion had led to an untenable situation, and should not really have been agreed to in the first place. General Davies agreed with the judgement of the British CO and placed the "onus of the British failure and casualties" on Thimayya.

"You made a rash judgement," he told him "and I have lost faith in your tactical advice. I wouldn't trust you any further."

As one of the first Indians to take over operational command and whose orders for the appointment were yet to be formally confirmed, this was shattering to Thimayya as CO. This was also most damaging to his reputation, which he was beginning to build in the formation. If the present impression of his superior percolated to his men, he feared he would lose their trust too and his overall image would suffer. This thought traumatised him. But he could not just twiddle his thumbs and let the heavens fall and overwhelm him.

In a conference with all his officers and VCOs, he asked their opinion on what should be done now that the British had failed. The majority was for action. "Let's do it ourselves," was one voice that helped him restore his own morale, lowered sufficiently by the British failure and GOC's condemnation.

He began to plan the attack in such a way that it would achieve maximum surprise and knock the hell out of the Japanese, who, he thought, regarded the British or Indians as incapable of any offensive action. The best enemy becomes complacent against a non-reacting and passive opponent. They had seen the British battalion being routed from its assault. So were they enjoying the scene of the Indians scurrying for cover whenever their guns opened up. An aura of invincibility reigned supreme among the Japanese. "That's what needs to be exploited," he told Kelly, his number two.

But what if the plan he was making failed? He would not only be court martialled and booked for life, but disgraced. Would his men forgive him for failure and the inevitable fruitless sacrifices? He was in two minds, in a dilemma of command that every good CO often faces.

Thimayya gave out his views to some more of his officers and asked their opinion, once again. His 'planter' adjutant, Captain Burgess, was a civilian in uniform, a man who needed to be goaded to perform. But his one sentence made Thimayya sit up.

"What Sir," said Burgess, "If a *gola* or *goli* takes your life away... wouldn't you regret? Why not take a risk with 50 per cent chance of success?"

Thimayya's face brightened up. "Yes, my man," he mumbled.

So Thimayya was on the job again, determined to go in. He would rebut: "In my judgement, the hill could be taken cheaply. (But) if I was wrong, I had to know now; otherwise, I would never be sure of myself again. If I did lack judgement (as General Davies had concluded), I deserved to be removed from command... I decided to take the risk."

It was then that his 'planter' adjutant and Captain Ross of 8th/19th Hybd contingent serving as medical officer followed the planter's humour. "Sir, I wouldn't let any *goli-gola* touch you."

So more officers' patrols were sent out to reconnoitre all the approaches to the Japanese held position and in its rear. Both Bobby Fowler and Kuldip Singh, carrying 'K' rations, ascertained vital information on the "going," "time and space." These were followed by patrols led by Som Nath Sharma and Subedar Bahadur Singh. Similarly, a company under Buxton went on a "fighting patrol" through the 'Bird Nalla.' Every avenue was explored, including the vertical wall.

His silent and careful reconnaissance of the least expected approaches for assault gave him two vertical climbs from the north and south walls. The attack, to succeed, had to be launched in the dark, well before dawn – the first light hour. The Japanese had to be caught off guard. But the assault had to be made with audacity and *élan*. To disguise the noise created by the men clambering up the vertical walls of loose rocks, he would have to lay an artillery barrage on the Japanese positions, firing intermittently throughout the night until 4.30 a.m., which matched his appreciation of "time and space" for the movement, and then it had to be lifted to the rear areas and flanks. And while other radio communications were to remain normal, there was to be total radio silence about this operation till the success signal lit the sky; the headquarters in the rear also were to be kept in the dark.

The Kumaoni peasantry who formed his forward companies were ideal to negotiate the vertical approach; they were also adept at their *khukri* charge, like the Gurkhas. They were to be led by those who had been on earlier patrols. Special training, however brief, had to be organised for them. It had to be a close quarter battle, and a charge without remorse, pity or fear. The Jats and the Ahirs could support from flanks or act as reserve.

The plan then fructified with two Kumaoni Companies climbing along the two difficult and least expected approaches to the hill top, with the Ahirs climbing up the 'Bird Nalla.' The rock climbing by the Kumaonis was covered by the artillery in direct support. The Kumaonis reached the top by 4.30 a.m., and then waited for morning light to diffuse the objective. By 5.30 a.m., they attacked and caught the Japanese napping in their tunnels. Attacking them with their *khukris*, grenades and bayonets they killed more than 100. About 100 escaped through the tunnels. About this time the Ahirs also charged from the east. Up went the success signal!

Thimayya could not take this success for granted, and wanted to see things for himself. He took the Jat Company along the approach, where a fortnight earlier the British had stumbled, and reached the top in record time. He was met by the jubilant Kumaonis who had totally surprised the Japanese, killing many. The mopping up dug out more Japanese from their tunnelled defences, only to be killed. The two machine guns covering the western approach were captured. Over 100 of the estimated 230 Japanese had been killed, and the others fled into the jungle.

Before the Japanese could react from the rear, half the unit was on the feature and around. With that success, there was jubilation. "I felt sick with relief," Thimayya reflected.

What followed is equally interesting. Thimayya and his battalion, as mentioned, had managed to keep the whole plan secret and not a whisper was passed to higher headquarters. His situation report gave no impression of any extra activities. The gunners too were brought into the planning at the last minute, giving them a feeling of firing an impromptu plan. So the brigade and other headquarters knew nothing of the ongoing preparations, as, indeed, of the successful assault, until Thimayya confirmed the extent of success.

Thimayya was not a very religious man, but piety and righteousness were ingrained in him. Spiritually, he was upright and faithful to "God's ways" that also had turned into his concept of morality. He didn't believe too much in prayer as a ritual but his heart never missed his faith in God's mercies. The night, as his two companies moved to their objective, he stood at the start point, looking into the eyes of each man, bidding him, "Ye man, be brave." He also looked for reassurance from their silent expressions of doing their best for the honour of his battalion. There was also an unexpressed entreaty from him to those now moving in single file with camouflaged faces, weapons slung, grenades filled into their pouches and *khukris* and water bottles knocking on their hips. His silent hope and request was, "If you do your best, which I know will be the best, neither you nor the battalion will be let down."

He wondered anxiously whether he would see these men again. Like a father, worried and anxious for his sons on a perilous adventure, he was pacing up and down the headquarters, looking at his watch, and the objective in front. The artillery was firing as planned on a timed basis, having started at midnight and finally ceasing at 4.30 a.m. When his watch showed 5.00 a.m., he began to panic but then the attack went in, and with it, the war cry, the explosion of grenades, and more war cries as the men fought and ran from bunker to bunker in their *khukri* charges. The result was a silent attack well executed by the unit, which saw the Japanese thrown out of their defences. The Japanese were caught in their tunnels with their rifles standing against the walls. A perfect success – the first thus far in the 25th Divisional sector. The whole corps was agog with Thimayya's success story.

Thimayya's amazing plan and success was received by the British commanders with individual nuances. The brigade commander called it a "jolly good show." The corps commander congratulated him, showering him with words of praise. General Davies, the GOC, was incredulous, flabbergasted and did not rest till he himself drove up to the feature, saw the results and then as if getting out of his soul, forgetting even his residual annoyance, he told Thimayya: "You took a big chance… you had a close shave…" And as he drove away he lauded Timmyya's luck.

He had pulled a *fait accompli* for his commanders – something they themselves had hoped for. Personally, he had used what the Americans of the new world seemed to believe in, defining the term initiative: do something you are not supposed to be doing and which succeeds.

That luck, indeed, had not come out of the high heavens. His boldness paved the way for lady luck to appear on the high feature. He told his officers and men: "We have been lucky this time and done well. But war demands that we be continuously brave and bold. So let's continue." He shared the credit for the success with all the men. And he was also realising that success, as the proverb went, had many fathers, although no one had really fathered his plans.

By June, the season of confidential reports appeared. Brigadier TH Angub, the brigade commander, saw him emerge as a "first class officer, cool, imperturbable with sound judgement," who should command the battalion in more operations. General Davies combining his assessment of a Grade 2 staff officer at his headquarters and CO Hybd said: "He took hold of his battalion most effectively and at a time when it was in close contact with the enemy." He was certain Thimayya would make a good CO. "Aptitude and imperturbability in the worst of the circumstances," he opined, "would see him triumph further." General Slim confirmed him in command; it was a formality.

* * *

The battalion now stretched between the old defences and the newly captured feature and remained dug in for another month. The Japanese were hammered and harried by the entire corps. The defeat in Kohima and Imphal had made the Japanese higher command shaky. It was time for the units to consolidate and recuperate before the advance to Akyab was resumed. Thimayya's first priority now was to improve the morale of the Jat Company, who felt left out after the Kumaonis and Ahirs earned glory in the operation. He assured them that they too would have their chance for glory. Alongside, fire control was improved against Japanese jitter attacks, and the idea of smaller and stealth patrolling was introduced.

A few days in the reinforcement camp in the rear further improved the men's mental and physical health.

For Thimayya, it was Rommel's famous infantry attack, if not Napoleon's Austerlitz. The brigade, division and corps had gained their springboard to victory from this small but significant action.[3]

The story would not be complete without reference to one more man who would move with Thimayya as a shadow, knowing him more intimately perhaps than his kith and kin. This was Ram Singh, his orderly, the "most bone-headed" in the battalion and an example of "monumental ignorance," but who loved him like a mother. He would serve him through thick and thin for seventeen years, like no other man would. He would demand that he be given a decoration as big as Thimayya Sahib got, as he too had been through the hazards of war as much his *sahib*.

The battalion now settled down on the new feature and remained under continuous Japanese attacks. Fire control was necessary, as was more innovative and offensive patrolling. So was the need to improve the men's health and their recreation facilities in a detached and safer rear area. He would once again experiment with non-vegetarian food on the purely vegetarian Jats. Kidney soup became a favourite item with them. He had to take some unorthodox measures to see that no one inadvertently or otherwise spilled the beans. "I was prepared to deceive the men for a good cause," he would say.

Last, but not the least, would be the act for him to bloody his Kodav knife. Every Kodav in battle wants to see it smeared with the enemy's blood. One day he sat on bait, on a forward trench to slice off the head of Japanese crawling towards it. And as his own heartbeat grew faster like a novice's in a boxing ring, he suddenly found his bone-headed but brave orderly Ram Singh do the trick. He placed a primed grenade on the parapet of the trench where Colonel Thimayya stood with the knife in his hand. The grenade did everything for him. But not quite, as along with the Japanese being blown into smithereens, Thimayya and Ram Singh would have joined him, had providence not saved them.

This monumental folly of Sepoy Ram Singh would make his CO laugh until his ears began to pain due to the blast.

It was time for Thimayya to get some rest and recuperation – 28 days war leave at Bangalore and here like a young fawn he would watch, adoringly admire Nina do the Bharata Natyam and the eight-year-old Mireille teach him how to play "steppu", and enjoy her songs and dances.

"If I can't do Bharata Natyam, I certainly can attempt meditation and some yogic exercises," he told Nina.

He did. The result – his tranquillity spread to all.

Often he would walk into the Bishop Cotton School and regale the school with stories of the Japanese, and his friend Ram Singh. ∎

NOTES

1. Captain Ronald Ross was later associated with his research on eradication of malaria, and knighted.
2. The 8th / 19th Hybd had been raised on the new organisation of two Kumaoni Companies and a company each of Jats and Ahirs. Now there were an administrative and a battalion headquarters company.
3. Allusion being made to infantry attacks by Rommel.

5
Towards Tactical Excellence

1944-1945 were the years of intense political activities for "self-rule" and "independence" in India. The INA too added to the British anxiety. A *cause celebre* of the politicians was that although Emergency Commissions had opened the door to the Indians, they were still being marginalised and kept away from higher appointments. Consequently, it was said that the morale of the Indian officers was low. As a sop, and to please the revolting Congressmen in India under Gandhi's Non-Cooperation Movement, the British decided on the formation of an experimental "All Indian Brigade" of three battalions. 51st Brigade that was picked up for this, lost its 8th York and Lancaster (Y & L) Regiment and was replaced not by a Gorkha battalion as per practice but by 2nd/2nd Punjab. Though still under a British brigade commander, Brigadier R A Hutton, it had now all three Indian battalions commanded by three Indians, each known for his principles, loyalty and dash.

Lieutenant Colonels S P P Thorat, L P Sen and K S Thimayya commanded 2nd/2nd Punjab, 16th/10th Baluch and 8th/19th Hyderabad (Hybd), respectively. The three battalions developed not only a healthy rapport but intense competition, the fruits of which were to be seen in the forthcoming operations, where each of the COs was awarded a DSO and the tally of bravery awards by other officers and men rose high. The brigade was to become a springboard for the Indians to either "leap high or drown themselves," as the gossip in the British circles in Delhi went. So all eyes were on 51st Brigade.[1]

At the higher operational level, Lieutenant General ARP Christison, the corps commander, was to prepare for the winter offensive when roads became traversable, and the logistics support for a larger force, feasible. Better operational flexibility would then help gain the initiative from an infrastructure of better command and control. The British had acquired absolute mastery of the skies, and the age-old

Map 2: Operation Dash – Capture of 'Poland'

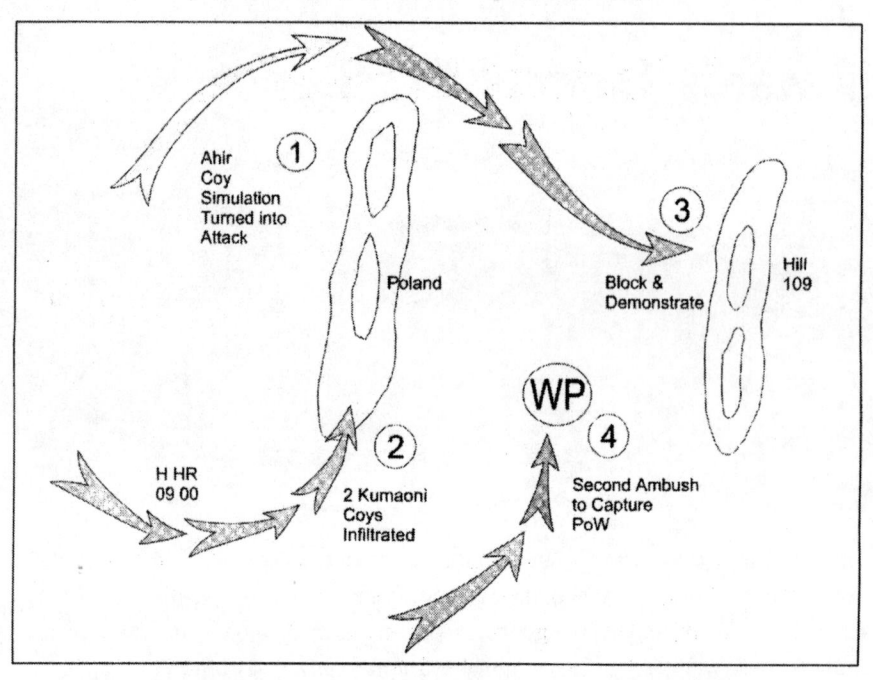

Map 3: The Battle of Kangaw, January and February 1945

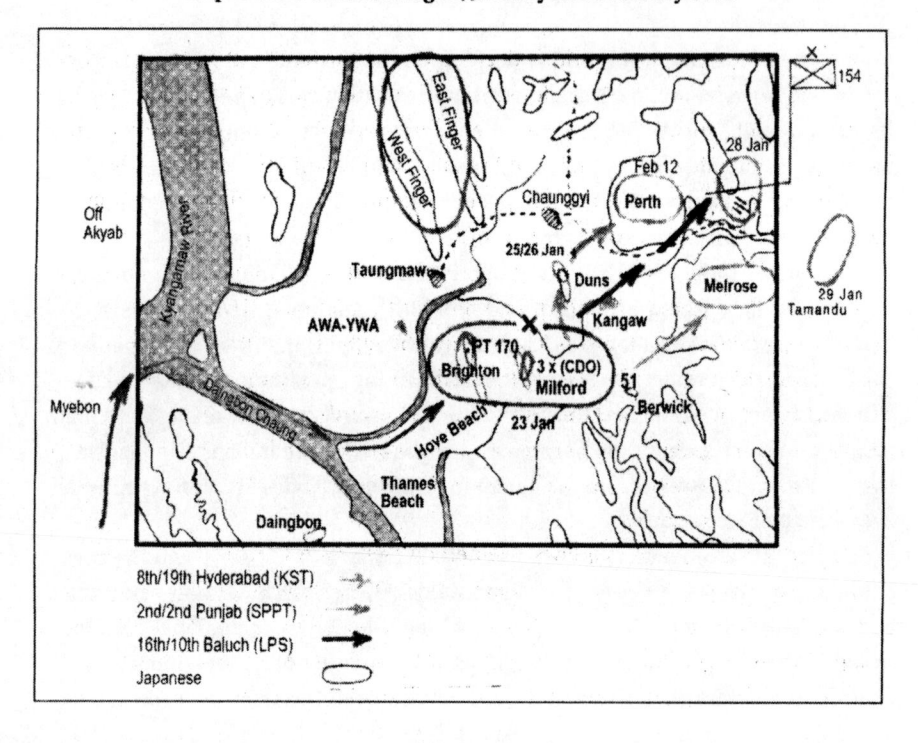

principle of war was being further violated by the Japanese in developing and sustaining their lines of communication (L of C). They were strung out and were at their proverbial tether's end, while the British communications were short, several and maintainable. What, however, remained was the ghost of invincibility of the Japanese. For, as late as October 1944, Headquarters 25th Division had offered to any man of Thimayya's battalion (as also others) a cash award of a thousand rupees for the capture of one Japanese. This happened even after a decisive victory in Kohima and Imphal. The legendary Japanese heroism kept the British guessing; it was eventually the Indians and the Gorkhas who were able to beat them.

***

Operation Dash Capture of 'Poland' (22 November – 24 November 1944)

The capture of the tunnels on the Mayu Range became the objective of the first brigade of 25th Division immediately after the monsoon of 1944. It involved an advance from Maungdaw to Akyab. General 'Sammy' Wood had taken over the division from Davies, evacuated due to the stress and strain of war. Although Thimayya had been on temporary duty as GSO 1, he managed to return to his command from the divisional headquarters just in time to lead his battalion again to a larger victory against more formidable challenges.

51st Indian Brigade under Brigadier Hutton, as averred, was an all Indian brigade. A British battalion Y&L, was now available to the brigade for information gathering and reserve tasks. The objectives involved the capture of a feature called 'Poland' for Hybd, a hill feature called 'Point 109' for the Baluchis and further extension of 'Point 109' for the Punjabis. Occupied by about three to four companies of Japanese, 'Poland' was dominating and its capture was important for the success of the brigade's operations. It had to be captured through unconventional tactics, if success was to be ensured. Several attempts by other battalions of the division had earlier failed to unnerve the Japanese.

Thimayya's study and reconnaissance revealed that the top of the feature was waterless, which, earlier information had revealed, forced the Japanese to move downstream to collect water. Close observation also revealed that here regularly arose a mist on the hill top between 9 a.m. and 9.30 a.m., which obscured it from view for a precious 30 minutes. It offered a fleeting advantage to the attacker. These factors would influence the plan considerably.

If the success of the earlier operation was a result of Thimayya's personal dash and the *elan* of his battalion, this *Operation Dash*, true to its designation, had to be another and larger example of sharper thinking, detailed planning by him and resolute execution by the troops. But for success, intelligence had to be absolutely accurate. This had to be obtained through relentless air and ground reconnaissance, virtually from all directions, utilising all the resources. The strength and density of the Japanese on the feature that dominated the road Buthidaung on the Mayu Range in the Arakan Hills, was, therefore, ascertained to the fullest extent that helped evolve a plan.

Thimayya would take no chances. "An enemy can always prove formidable," he would say, "if preparations are not thorough and contingencies are not planned," quoting Napoleon – who equated genius with thorough preparedness.

The plan of attack envisaged two Kumaoni Companies infiltrating onto the objective from a flank which was considered unassailable. The Ahir Company was to stimulate an attack along the expected southern direction. The Jat Company was to establish a block and demonstrate against 'Hill 109' – the brigade's second phase objective.[2]

In execution, as always, it happened differently. The Ahir ('A') Company actually preempted the attack and captured part of the objective from the south before the Kumaonis could start the assault. The Kumaoni Companies had to fight a close quarter battle thereafter. In the flush of the battle, the Jat ('B') Company decided to attack, rather than be content with demonstrating against 'Hill 109' -- and captured it too. Thimayya's battalion, thus, captured two-thirds of the brigade's objective – a cause of envy to all but not to the Baluchs who were thoroughly peeved.

And as the Hybd had captured feature Hill 109 too, in a real 'dash,' Bogey Sen grumbled in protest, for it was his objective, which he wanted back so that the Baluchis could occupy it. Rightly too, Bogey Sen took it as being deprived of the thunder. The tension eased off as Thimayya asked the Jats to melt away before the Baluchis stormed feature '109'! He then had a crack at him: "If I were you, I would ask the commander to stand you a bottle of Scotch for nicknaming the operation as 'Dash.' Damn it, Bogey, it put wings onto my boys." Bogey was too piqued to retort or appreciate the humour of the moment.

In *Defeat into Victory*, Slim described the Japanese defences here as a fortress. He wrote: "The Japanese defences were tunneled far into the hills with living accommodation, store rooms, dugouts 20 to 30 feet below the surface. There were innumerable mutually supporting machine gun posts. The extent of their preparation and extreme formidableness, of course, was then not fully known to us but it was obvious that they would be hard nuts to crack."[3]

It was Thimayya's gift of the 'Birthday Bowl,' as somebody euphemistically called the feature, to the brigade!

It was here that Thimayya's luck played its part well. As the successes of *Operation Dash* came on the air, he went rushing up in a jeep. His vehicle ran over a landmine that tossed him up. He was hurled through the air and slammed into a ditch. He was intact, though he lost his clerk. His orderly Ram Singh and the gunner too were unscathed. The only damage seemed to be a deafening sensation in his ears. Lieutenant NK Sinha, his quartermaster, who was following him in another jeep, retrieved him. Sinha recalls how he himself had been moved out from the CO's jeep just before they started. Thimayya told him to move into another vehicle, saying, "It is not safe to keep all the eggs in one basket." How true![4]

Thimayya emerged as a hero who would soon become, in his own words an "acting, unpaid, temporary, brigadier" for about a month in place of a Briton evacuated from the area, but soon he reverted to his own command of the battalion. It was during this period that he planned several brigade operations clearing the axis Tunnels – Foul Point.

Thimayya was deservingly due for war leave. A soldier looks forward to it as something of a boon, a gift from above. The jungles of Burma, the leeches, rain, mud and the ever-lurking Japanese ambushes and never ending artillery harassing fire, could turn a soldier stoic, philosophic and homesick, seeking the security of a place with some peace and tranquillity. The strain could become unbearable to some not psychologically attuned. Leave, therefore, acts as a tonic. Every day of leave becomes a chapter of life, specially when one knows it could be the last one.

Timmy's war leave for 29 days, which he spent with Nina and Mireille, became one of the happiest periods of family life at Bangalore and in Coorg. He would roam around the gardens with Mireille on his shoulders; then go for a drive in his old car, or simply sit and watch a movie in the evening. Nina was still learning Bharata Natyam and Timmy was fascinated by the beat and rhythm.

Back in the Arakans, Thimayya was officiating GSO1 for a month or so before reverting to his command. As the rain stopped and the road surface got firmer, 15th Corps advanced astride the spine of the Mayu Range.

Given below is the excerpt from the Operation Order written by Colonel Thimayya on *Operation Dash*. It is the historical value that is of relevance and is reproduced here in original abbreviated form:

Dt: 20-11-44

1. 51st Ind Inf Bde Op Instr No.17 received for *Operation Dash* to be carried out from Nov 22nd. This op is to be a series of tasks to be carried out by each bn with 9 Y & L under command to obtain information as to enemy strength and identification east of Mayu.

2. Op 'A'
   (a) Comd. Lieut Col K S Thimayya.
   (b) Tps. 8 Hybd.
   In Sp: Arty teams (Capt Stramock) 37/47 Btys 27 Fd RA
   34 Med Bty
   RE Recce team
   Det Bde Sig.
   (c) Task:
      (i) Hold "Ticker' (the firm base).
      (ii) Ascertain str on 'Poland and Pt 142.'
      (iii) Later to Punkori.

3. 'C' and 'D' moved to firm base. 'D' delayed H Hr changed to 0940 hrs.
4. Results
   (a) 10 Japs killed; others fled.
   (b) 6 rifles, 1 LMG captured.
   (c) Jap flags; 1 officer sword.
   (d) Own cas: one wounded.

***

The Kangaw: the War in the Chhaungs (18 January – 17 February 1945)

History has a habit of throwing up some non-descriptive names – and even persons – into prominence. One such was the little Burmese village of Kangaw (pronounced Caango) in the Arakans. This village commanded the coastal road and served as a focal point to the An Pass, leading to central Burma. It became the scene of one of the fiercest battles of the Burma Campaign.

The XVth Corps offensive under General Christison with its regular divisions, the 25th Indian Division, the 81st and 82nd African Divisions, 3rd Commando Brigade, 50th Indian Tank Brigade, and some 150 fighter aircraft, alongwith a naval task force was a massive force.[5]

The British had developed an organisation called Combined Operations Pilotage Parties (COPP), which was an organisation of 'Force W,' the sea-arm, under Rear Admiral BCD Martin. Their job involved reconnaissance and piloting of the amphibious force. They charted not only the routes but marked them with buoys as close as possible to the assembly area and forming up places, and then guided the assaulting echelons onto their objectives. The air support was provided by Air Commodore the Earl of Bandon's 224th RAF Group.

But such was the fear of the Japanese ability to spring surprises that Christison was taking no chances. Perhaps rightly too, as each Japanese soldier was prepared to kill and die as valiantly as the highest gallantry award winners of the Allied armies. This was no understatement – for, it was the Japanese tenacity which compelled the Americans to drop their atomic bombs on Japan later in August.

To the Japanese command, Arakans had provided an air base for threatening eastern India, interfering with the shipping in the Bay of Bengal and perhaps capturing Chittagong and Calcutta later in their "March to Delhi." However, by the autumn of 1944, there was a reversal of fate in favour of the British. And the Japanese were out on a limb. Their logistics was failing and reinforcements had become a trickle. No air force or naval guns were available to support the ground forces. Courage and determination had, however, not abandoned them. They would fight determinedly. Against Christison's corps there was a regimental group (154th) of two battalions, with an artillery battalion and an engineer company, that stretched itself around the village of Kangaw occupying small knolls in the paddy fields – 'Fingers,'

'Perth,' 'Melrose' – with a view to dominate and deny the road axis Kangaw-Tamandu. And as the events of January–February would show, the approach by their enemy from the Arakan Sea over the *chhaungs* was regarded as less likely.

In order to keep the 14th Army rolling forward to Rangoon, the final objective, it was necessary to: (a) secure the road at Maungdaw-Kangaw-Akyab and to the east, Yenangyaung; (b) secure airfields at Akyab and Ramree; (c) secure the mouth of River Kaladan and hold the country as far south to the Meybon Peninsula.[6]

With this aim in view, Christison's corps began its offensive on 12 December. Three days later, Buthidaung was captured by the 82nd Division. This naturally upset the Japanese plans of an orderly tactical withdrawal. Japanese General Miyazaki had orders to hold a strong unbypassable position for as long as possible. It was to ensure that the rear troops and heavy stores could be pulled back intact. To ensure a clean breakthrough, Miyazaki chose Kangaw, that denied two lateral coastal roads across the Arakan Yoma, situated 80 km south of Myochaung, the old capital of the Arakan state, and another road leading to the An Pass. It was a position with defence potential and consisted of 'Hill 170' and a conglomerate of features that rose as high as 130 m or 500 ft north and south of it, providing defences in depth. Its tidal swamps were so densely covered with spikes of mangrove roots that even a foot could not be placed between them. The tributaries of Daingbon *chhaung* offered the usual resistance.

While it was possible to develop an amphibious operation against Kangaw from the sea and over the hinterland flow of the *chhaungs*, it was nonetheless essential to capture Meybon before that. Although approachable from the sea through the narrow *chhaungs*, these were, however, a mirage of mangrove swamps, the optical effect of which is sometimes seen at sea and, of course, invariably in deserts.

"At low tide," observed Mankekar, "the mangrove swamps studded the landscape like so many mushrooms and the *chhaungs* diminished to weak, slender streams. At high tide, the *chhaungs* swelled and swallowed the mangrove islands, leaving a vast expanse of water in their place, lending an eerie touch to the scene. The mangrove islands varied in size from tiny uninhabitable dots of wild green vegetation with semi-liquid soil, to large islands with villages and paddy fields. In Ramree Island, at least, a hundred hunted Japanese ran into the mangrove swamps for refuge and got stuck or sank in the treacherous liquid soil, and were gradually buried alive."[7]

These was a labyrinth of mangrove swamps intersected by tidal *chhaungs* and the channels through them were narrow and treacherous. Partially reconnoitred and chartered by COPP, they still provided the needed axis. The pilots of these crafts, Thimayya found, were not only unskilled personnel but unclear about their charter of duty.

8th/19th Hybd was supporting the securing operations of the 3rd Royal Marine Commando Brigade in Meybon. That, however, was not an operation the Japanese contested much. The Hybds would soon move with the commandos. The war diary of the unit of 12 January (1945) has an interesting entry.[8]

The battalion was loaded in a cruiser on January 18th and by 8.15 a.m., landed and embarked on two minesweepers and taken off to LCA, landed at Meybon beach. CO, IO, went to Div HQ and thence recce of concentration area, preparatory to taking over from Commandos at Kauntha. On January 20th, battalion was made to march back to beach transit area and prepared to embark for the Kangaw Beach by 9.30 a.m.

Meybon in hand, the next step was the capture of a beachhead to Kangaw by the Commando Brigade, intimately supported by the 8th/19th Hybd and subsequently by the whole of the 51st Brigade.

The commandos moved to Akyab and the Hybd followed them in the troop ship *HMS Phoebe*. The sea voyage of three to four days proved to be a great tonic and a period of recuperation to the war-weary troops, their officers and the CO who found himself fresh and fit as he reported on the evening of 15 January to Brigadier Campbell Hardy. He found Hardy and his deputy Colonel Young – both as relaxed as Major General Orde Wingate of the Chindits – sitting and gossiping over drinks in a forest where the brigade had concentrated for the impending beach operations.

The Commando Brigade consisted of the "Green Berets," with earlier landing experience in the Mediterranean coast. They were asked to capture beachheads and hold them for about 24 hours when they could be relieved by other regular troops.

On landing, having been taken to Hardy, Thimayya asked for orders. "Orders? There are no orders," Hardy casually replied. "We push off at 6; you tag along after us at about 9." That was to be on 22 January.

Could things be so simple, he wondered. He, in fact, had a premonition that the commandos were launching themselves with little or no preparation. He thought they could at least have air photos, if not the benefit of ground reconnaissance (recce). The following morning he saw the commandos depart with confidence. He still looked forward to some good combined operations and instructed his own command to act only on his instructions.

As a CO, Thimayya ensured that while every officer was treated fairly and with concern, there was no let up in discipline. As it was, cases of malaria beyond 2 per cent of the strength could get a CO sacked. There could, therefore, be no slackness. He was a stickler for drill too. It was the Hybd alone which would be seen doing drills in the breaks between the fighting. Maintenance of weapons, vehicles, issue of new clothing according to the size roll, besides his usual "*josh* talks" were the techniques of his command. He was fortunate in having good officers. Major Kelly as second-in-command was an able help. Majors Quigley, Pead, Horsfold, Fowler were good and there also was the 'great' Assistant Surgeon, Captain (later Sir) Ronald Ross, the man who would revolutionise the treatment of malaria. Amongst the good officers were S N Sharma (later the first PVC of the Indian Army), Kuldip Singh, his intelligence officer, Abu Naser, the QM, besides Sinha, the signals officer. In combined operations of the kind the Hybd were to be engaged, Colonel Thimaya knew that even an odd slip up in understanding the commandos would be fatal and inexcusable. He had, therefore, decided on controlling the operations of his battalion himself.

Reverting to the battle of the *chhaungs*: three hours later, his own flotilla of old boats slowly moved uneventfully and trudged along the 13-km-long *chhaung*, about midway there was an SOS from Hardy. It asked him if he could accelerate his movement, as his commandos on Hill '170' were under fierce attack and needed urgent help.

The commandos had landed on the *chhaung* mud bank and approached the village across a tidal swamp. In their path rose the narrow, wooded Hill '170', which, though part of the Japanese defensive layout, was not held. A shattering bombardment by Thunderbolts and Beaufighters, backed by the guns of the sloops *Narbada* and *Jamuna* from Meybon had made their beachhead entry unopposed in broad daylight. The surprise was effective but not for too long. For, as the Japanese noticed the commandos on '170' and spreading further to 'Fingers,' 'Milford' and 'Pinner' they reacted violently. Their shelling with 175 mm guns and 120 mm howitzers began to inflict heavy casualties on the commandos who were in the open, with no digging tools.

It was then that the SOS came and Hardy realised he had made a mistake in not keeping Hybd available within easy strike. Thimayya tried to speed up the movement but the barges could not respond.

And even the COPP wanted his men to disgorge in the swamps. He had to move them at pistol point. When he disembarked at 4 p.m., the beach and '170' were facing a "solid wall of flying steel," and then as usual, his battalion came under own 'friendly fire' from the naval guns. The hazards of war, after all! Miraculously, the battalion got through these initial setbacks without suffering casualties. Soon the evening shadows of the winter sun were lengthening. Hardy asked the Hybd to capture 'Fingers.' Thimayya told Hardy he would ascertain the situation before committing his troops. Hardy's deputy Young volunteered to join in the recce.

That night's 'recce' in a gun boat by Thimayya and his 'recce group' would have left the battalion 'headless' as not only was the patrolling aborted but they were fired at by every Japanese from 'Fingers' and the neighbouring areas. Luckily, they managed to abandon the boat and swim across to safety. "We jumped overboard and swam across and hid in a jungle while the pilot managed to get the boat to safety," Thimayya recalled his close shave with death. The operation was called off, though Young and Hardy treated the whole thing as a joke. He admired their philosophical equanimity while the muck flew.

In an effort to enlarge the beachhead, the commandos captured 'Pinner' and soon built up to a strength of 130. The Japanese, who had been thrown back, plastered the small feature with all available artillery the whole night and many men in the open were killed. Of the 130 who had moved into the feature, only 30 survived. Over 77 per cent casualties shook Hardy. He asked Hybd to do something.

Thimayya, who had taken 'D' Company and the Pioneer platoon to relieve the commandos, saw dismembered bodies lying everywhere. "My men and I," he said, "had to step over the arms, legs and unrecognisable parts of humans." He instructed Major Quigley, the company commander to "dig, dig and dig." The war diary gratefully notes: "digging saved lives," and the "commandos were grateful for evacuating the wounded, burying the dead, above all for relieving them from that wretched 'death hole.'" He would later refer to this as a "scene from hell," to which he became witness, for the second time, the first, the Quetta earthquake, having remained in the deep recesses of his mind.

Soon he sent another company to reinforce the first on 'Pinner,' and ensured that their defences were fully coordinated. While 'C' and 'D' Companies were now on the objective, the other two were still at '170.'

By 25 January, the rest of the 51st Brigade under Brigadier RA Hutton arrived in the beachhead to take over the defences and clear Kangaw. Along with it came up a troop of Sherman tanks. Liberators, then strategic bombers, were also pressed into bombing the Japanese positions. But it left the Japanese firmly resolved to stay on, irrespective of their losses.

While the brigade plan of attack was under preparation, the Hybd sent two strong patrols to 'Duns' and Kangaw village on the night 25/26 January. 'Duns' dominated the road leading to 'Perth' through Kangaw, and both were strongly held – the former, more so. As a first step, he himself led a recce patrol to 'Duns' and had 'A' and 'B' Companies build up near and around Kangaw, while 2nd Punjab provided the flank protection.

The brigade plan envisaged, the 16th/10th Baluch under Bogey Sen to capture 'Melrose' and Hybd, the feature of 'Perth.' It involved clearing two hills from the east and southeast. The feature 'Duns,' situated on the north, would also interfere with the assault on 'Perth' and was required to be neutralised. Besides, in the village of Kangaw itself, there was a formidable Japanese presence.

As part of his plan of attack, he relieved the two companies from 'Pinner' and moved them to secure a base for the assault on 'Duns.' Concurrently, while the air and artillery kept the enemy engaged, he, along with his recce party and mortars, moved with 'A' Company to the crest line from the west to be in position by early dawn. And commanders of the Sherman tanks and mortars arranged the pre-assault and later supportive fire on and beyond 'Duns.'

The attack went in at 7.30 a.m. The company secured the area with no casualties, but within hours a very large number of Japanese surrounded 'A' Company, and 'B' Company sent to reinforce, was also under siege. Thimayya now ordered 'D' Company (Jats) to go on a "bayonet charge." "This is your chance," he told the Jats, who went wild. They evicted the enemy but in the process lost heavily.

The Liberators came bombing again. The Japanese counter-attacked the 'Duns.' In this close quarter battle, 'A' Company killed 14 Japanese. But more recces showed 'Perth' strongly reinforced as also Kangaw further reinforced. The idea of capturing these objectives was shelved for a while, as a bold *Kamikaze* assault was being built up by the Japanese on the commandos on '170.' The battle was now turning into what Slim would call the "crisis of the Arakan operations."

"The enemy, whom Radio Japan was exhorting to fight as 'Sons of God,' had not taken kindly to the encirclement of Kangaw by the Hybd," records the history of the Kumaon Regiment. "To recover it, he put in repeated attacks, mostly at night... After day long shelling of the village and 'Pinner' where the battalion headquarters was still located, the Japanese attacked 'B' Company's position on Kangaw hill. The Hybd held on. Next morning, thirty-six Japanese bodies lying around the perimeter were buried and one wounded Japanese was taken prisoner – the first one."[9]

'Melrose' was now attempted by the Baluch under Bogey Sen, but was halted half way. It was finally captured by Thorat's Punjabis, as part of the brigade plan.

All this time, 'Perth' remained the Hybd's objective while it continued to retain the foothold around the village of Kangaw.

The Japanese were now suffering but stoically not giving up their battle. True to their reputation, they would have to be cleared of all the areas they held. It was revealed subsequently that a portion of the Japanese 54th Division (Matsue Detachment) had been operating in the Kaladan Valley to delay the Allied advance. Immediately after the landing of the commandos and other troops at Kangaw, Miyazaki ordered them to move there with all possible speed. As a result, the regiment at Kangaw was supported by two artillery brigades. With ammunition already dumped at Kangaw, the Japanese gunners had their proverbial 'field' day. The arrival of this force was signified by the launching of "the most determined counter stroke of the whole Kangaw battle" on 31 January on Hill '170.' The key to the area was the main Japanese target whose loss could cut off 51st Brigade from the beaches. It was a desperate yet bold effort, analogous, though on a smaller scale, to the German battle in the Ardennes!

Reenacting the true *Kamikaze* spirit, some 90 screaming Japanese sappers carrying explosives, charged the northern end of "170" and knocked out two of the six Shermans deployed there. And then their infantry attacked *en masse* the commandos in the shallow trenches. There ensued, the whole day, attacks and counter-attacks. The fight moved into the night. By first light, as the fog hovered low and battle ceased, some 340 Japanese lay dead; so were over 100 commandos, with three times their number seriously wounded.

The history of the Hybd (Kumaon) Regiment observes admiringly of the enemy as it states: "It must be said to their credit that they had captured a part of the Hill. Attack and counter-attack raged for full thirty-six hours before the Japanese were driven off the feature. The Commandos and 7/16 Punjab bore the brunt of the fighting." It was a desperate battle and the superior fire support saw the battle won by the commandos.

The battle now raged all round. 74th Indian Brigade was exerting pressure from the north. The Allied air force was active; so was long-range artillery. But the Japanese with their characteristic *Kamikaze* traditions of suicidal tenacity and fanatical bravery, unless one caught them off balance, were still a formidable foe.

That 'catching them off balance' Thimayya was now prepared to exploit. He began to threaten the defenders of Kangaw; however, the Japanese though stunned, were determined to hold the ground. A sudden smashing attack on the village by the reorganised companies of the battalion under Major AL Fowler on 13 February, nonetheless, saw the seizure of the objective. Exploiting the same speed of success, a platoon under "one of the bravest Naiks" (Naik Jagmal) and selected men of the battalion, carried out a lightning attack on 'Perth' and caught the Japanese by surprise. Most were killed in their defences but some broke off in confusion, to die finally of wounds and hunger.

This Ahir Company made it a demonstration attack. The Hybd history again records: "The rest of the battalion had been watching the Ahir Company's action. They were thrilled to see Subedar Matadin and his platoon chasing the fleeing Japanese with bayonets. Jagmal had reason to be proud of his feat. When (wounded) he was being carried to the regimental aid post, he said to his commanding officer, pointing towards 'Perth', 'I got it and I made the Japs run.' Thimayya smiled and gave him a CO's salute. After the battle, 25 dead Japanese were counted around their bunkers. Our causalties were 3 killed, 6 wounded."

***

The citation of Colonel Thimayya for the award of a DSO highlighted his "outstanding performance" in planning, and execution of battalion operations for Poland, his command of the brigade and conduct of operations opening the road to Buthidaung and to Foul Point. At Kangaw, the citation said, "In spite of considerable casualties, repeated enemy counter-attacks and heavy fire... Thimayya handled every situation with cool judgement and cheerful confidence," showing "leadership of a high order, an indomitable spirit inspiring every officer and man under his command." (See Appendix)

Thus, ended the battle of Kangaw, which had lasted 22 days. On its conclusion, the GOC in a special "Order of the Day" said: "Every man who landed on the Kangaw beaches can recall the fact with pride." Field Marshall William Slim called it "the fiercest battle fought in Burma where bravery and pluck of the highest order paved the way to eventual success."

As the Japanese defences crumbled, the battle zone shifted to south Rangoon. Thimayya had made a niche as deputy commander of 36th Brigade in the Ramree Island operation. And as luck would have it, the brigade commander was removed and he was appointed commander 36th Brigade – the first Indian to command a brigade in war.

The Hybd had also formed a lasting friendship with the commando brigade. The acknowledgement of its gratitude and indebtedness to the unit is inscribed on the silver trophy presented by Brigadier C R Hardy, DSO, commander 3rd Royal Marine

Commando. The inscription on this trophy which is proudly displayed in the officers' mess of 4th Kumaon reads: "*In commemoration of the historic beach landing at Kangaw, January 1945, in which the 8th Battalion the Kumaon Regiment (now 4th Kumaon) distinguished itself under command of Lt Col K S Thimayya, DSO.*" A similar trophy from the Hybd finds a place of honour in the commando officers' mess in the UK.

The exposure to battle fatigue, exacerbated by bad water infected Thimayya with jaundice and it was with considerable difficulty, including a threat to resign his commission, that he was given command of the brigade again, now at Rangoon. The British effort to marginalise him could succeed no longer.

About this time, the war corespondent DR Mankekar was sent to visit the "All Indian Brigade." He wrote:

> The press hungry All Indian Brigade welcomed me with open arms. They were particularly happy that when at last a correspondent did arrive, it was an Indian, who, they were confident, would do justice to them. No wonder, therefore, that the three Indian battalion commanders laid out the red carpet and vied with each other in playing host to me. I had to eat a meal at each one of the three battalion headquarters. Timmy fished out Scotch besides laying on some sherry and wine and rice *Pullav* and tinned mutton *kurma* for dinner. That was the first time I was meeting the three Indian officers; Thimayya struck me as a hail-fellow-well-met, tall, athletic personality. His uninhibited laughter chased out the blues and put cheer into your soul. He was also a good *raconteur*. He was adored by his men as well as officers, who included Britishers...."[10]

The official assessment of Thimayya by his superiors did not materially change from the cumulative write-up for his decoration.

A mention has been made earlier regarding the INA. One of the several developments that shook the British during and after World War II was the rise of the INA to which some 37,000 Indians of the 70,000 POWs in Singapore changed their allegiance. Captain (INA Colonel) Ponnappa, Brigadier Thimayya's brother, had became the chief administrative officer to the INA forces in Rangoon. In an irony of fate, Thimayya's 36th Brigade entered Rangoon first and was to also capture or take the surrender of the INA personnel, including Ponnappa.

The British officer who captured Ponnappa told him that although his brother was not present, even if he were, he would have thrown him into the sea.

"You are wrong," retorted Ponnu, "Timmy would give me cold beer, hot curry and he would have thrown me into the clink."

Thimayya differed with his brother and all the others who joined the INA. To him, it was breach of trust and violation of the oath of allegiance – both totally reprehensible to a soldier – a fact he would even highlight during his tenure as chairman NNRC.

World War II ended in 1945 and a great honour came his way. In representing the Indian officers at the surrender ceremony, Lord Mountbatten invited him to sit at the high table while Japanese generals led by Yamashita surrendered their swords. With his immense historical sense, Mountbatten had collected and displayed a transcript of General Percival's address during the British surrender ceremony of February 1942. It was like Versailles recreated by Hitler at the fall of France in 1939!

Then came a deeply depressing and hurting scene. Thimayya accompanied Field Marshal Slim to the prisoners of war camp – first to the British and subsequently to the Indian, including his own 4th/19th Hybd. The jawans, emaciated and veritably living skeletons, had tears of joy and smiles on their faces! He was overwhelmed with both sorrow and joy.

"To me," he admitted, "those were the saddest moments of the war. I was not ashamed of my own tears." After all, he had loved them through the years from Baghdad to Singapore, like his own. Then again a fleeting, though momentary thought crossed his mind. In the change of the battalion, something good had been in store.

"God's ways," he sighed, wiping his tears. He would also rejoice at meeting them. And he remembered the parting words of the subedar major of 4th/19th Hybd on his posting to the new battalion (8th/19 Hybd) at Singapore, "You were the only hope of ours and you too leave us!" His heart welled up again.

He was off to Manila, representing the Indian Army at the Independence Celebrations of the Philippines on 4 July 1946 where the mayor gave him the "Key to Manila." A singular honour!

Above all these frills of the victor's war, the frailty of the unfortunate prisoners and the vanquished, and the humiliating sorrow that he now was witness to, he had been deeply impressed with the brilliance of warfare. He had seen it turn into a fine art in the hands of commanders adroit in their profession. "If I have to remain a soldier of free India," about which he had no doubt, "then I must be the best." So a new resolve!

The breakthrough that came virtually after seventeen years of a slogging, arduous journey within India, through Iraq to Malaya – Singapore turned out to be a successful odyssey in Burma. It proved, in many ways, the test of his penance or *tapasya* and as a soldier, the climax of his fortitude and boldness. Although things looked uncertain and several times he thought of leaving the job and unceremoniously fading away, in his own terms, to "pick beans" in Kodagu, he would reconcile and be back at his duty. In all those overtures, he would show reason and wisdom.

Luck, indeed, had played its role in providing opportunities to him. The more one scrutinises this period, one is tempted to agree with him that luck, indeed, has a role in the scheme of things and opportunities. But the ability to grab them and translate them into real time action, was his. It was in his personality and psyche that enabled him to rise to any challenge – small and large. That alone had turned him into an outstanding, gallant and distinguished soldier.

***

Commander of a Brigade as Part of the Allied Occupation Force

Following the surrender of Japan on 14 August 1945, the American occupational Commander General Douglas MacArthur soon produced a new Constitution for Japan which *inter alia* had come to be known as the "peace clause," and "renouncing war as a sovereign right." In its wake came the Anglo-Saxon occupational forces of both the Americans and the British Commonwealth.

It brought in among the defeated and traumatised Japanese, a masochistic feeling of servility towards their conquerors. The new Constitution seemed to have shackled a once proud country under the American Military Government (AMG). As a society, as Thimayya observed, the Japanese nation seemed crushed and numbed by its fate.

Under those awful circumstances, Thimayya's 268th Indian Infantry Brigade was selected to be part of the British Indian Division (Brindiv) commanded by Major General DT Cowan CB, CBE, DSO, MC, formerly of 17th Indian Division that formed part of the Allied Occupational Force, Japan. 268th Brigade had the pick of Indian units. 5th/1st Punjab was Field Marshal Auchinleck's own; 1st/5th (Royal Marathas) was a Victoria Cross battalion; the 2nd /5th Gurkhas had two living VC awardees in the battalion; added was the 7th Light Cavalry, another reputed armoured regiment which formed part of Thimayya's brigade.

268th Brigade was, in fact, one of the four brigades under Cowan – the other three being one each from Australia, New Zealand and Britain. The whole force was commanded by the Australian Lieutenant General Sir Brian Robertson and later, General Northcote.

In its occupational deployment in Japan, the force spread from Kure Bay to Hiroshima, Simomasake to Matsue, with Hanada, Okayama and Tottori included. The AMG regulated the life of the occupation force which had asked the local Japanese military commanders to surrender to Thimayya and others.

There was very little to do except remain prepared to handle any case of defiance or disorder. The feeling that grew among the officers and the men was similar to what he had experienced in the second year of his service in Iraq: relax and enjoy the fruits of victory over the vanquished.

Out of this grew more disorder and indiscipline among the Allied troops than defiance from the Japanese who were suffering under the wheel of humiliation, and economic depredation. Both these led the Indian soldiers to depart from their sobriety and even righteousness, the hallmark of the Indian Army.

The first scene that Thimayya was confronted with was the jawans bathing in the nude along with Japanese men and women. So women became a problem. Deprived of the male population who had been killed by the millions, these women were either widows or unmarried. They would offer themselves to the soldiers for even a cigarette.

Thimayya was acutely aware that in any war, disturbance, or social disorder, it is the women who suffer the most. As the brigade commander, he saw that the men had begun to contract sexually transmitted diseases in large numbers. He had to take recourse to harsh measures to control it.

The problem of women remained, although on a diminished scale with the Indian units, who, once warned of the dangers involved, began to tighten their loins. But not the Gurkhas of 2nd/5th who were moved to the Divisional Headquarters of General Cowan at Kure and Okayama. In their over-zealousness to fraternise with the local females, especially those who cheaply sold sex, they clashed with the military police, who they thought, were discriminating between them and the white troops. It sparked further into a fire and a mutiny when the Australian MPs arrested a few Johnnies under dubious circumstances. The result: "600 Gurkhas with drawn *khukris* poured into the street roaring like demons... a terrible sight and all traffic on the street vanished..."[11]

Lieutenant Colonel Virendra Singh, the adjutant and quartermaster general (AQMG) of the division who happened to pass through, stopped them from wreaking vengeance on the British and the Australians, who, they claimed, had been hurling insults at them. The good counsel of Virendra prevailed and the Gurkhas returned to their barracks. The issue was squashed, hushed up and ignored.

Not for long though; as the battalion was moved to Ikado, Tokyo, the women problem again raised its hydra-head, forcing the British officers to repeat in the barracks what the MPs had earlier done. The result was that, one morning, 2nd/5th refused to appear on parade. There was a 'sit-down' protest like that of the 4th/19th Hybd in Singapore. Like Singapore too, Thimayya was told to "somehow resolve the problem." He was, after all, the brigade commander, he was told by Cowan.

"That's true," said Thimayya. "But Colonel Townsend, the Gurkha CO, had not thought it appropriate even to call me over to the unit except once. I hardly know the boys," remonstrated Thimayya.

"Please Timmy, come over. We know you have magical powers," pleaded Cowan.

"Hardly, Sir, but I'll try," replied Thimayya.

Thimayya was in Tokyo the next day and drove straight to the Gurkhas and met Townsend. A puritan and of spartan discipline, he had, no doubt, tightened the noose on his Gurkhas after the earlier incident. Thimayya remembered that "the men simply had been pushed too far. But to Colonel Townsend, it was as if his own sons had repudiated him. He was a broken man, and I pitied him. The Colonel would not – or could not – help me, even by arranging to see the men. I had to work it out on my own."

Employing his charm, he persuaded the Gurkhas to give up the path of confrontation and protest, and return to the barracks. Exploiting every strategem of better sense and reasoning, he enabled a highly decorated battalion with two living VCs to retain not only its honour but also its reputation.

Thimayya had learnt the fine art of assuaging the pent-up feelings of the men, who under duress and poor COs, threw their discipline, good sense and even propriety to the wind. "Control," he would say, "had to be like a concertina coil which had its coefficient of tension. It breaks beyond a point. The art of man management, which, in most cases, remains in the text-books, is to gauge this coefficient."

In later life, he would tell an erring subordinate, and some superiors, that they were failing in understanding their men and the organisations they formed. "The men are an officer's best friend, so long you yourself do not fail them."

Reflecting on the two instances of rioting and mutiny by this illustrious Gurkha unit, he came to the conclusion about the cause of the mutiny in 2nd/5th Gurkha: the wrong policy the British followed with regard to the Gurkhas vis-à-vis the others. He had seen even as a junior officer how the British segregated them from the mainstream and then told them that the Indian troops and officers did not like them; and when the Gurkhas misbehaved, they followed a wrong approach to punish their misdemeanors or violation of good order and military discipline, harshly. Thimayya would tell the officers, whenever he had a chance with regard to these unfortunate events that "crises have a nasty way of exposing pretensions."

The 14 months tenure as part of Brindiv highlighted his "broad mental horizon," his "loyalty" his "charming personality," his "leadership and initiative," "independence of thought" and "well balanced acts." [12]

He would now return to India to become a member of the Nationalisation Committee.

Among his compatriots he had earned the sobriquets of 'pot-shot Timmy" and a "diplomat among the uniformed." With the addition of these two vital characteristics to the already growing list of virtues that he had by now, the list had become weightier.

Thimayya went through a titanic period of struggle to become the epitome of an officer and a gentleman, as required by the British system aimed at turning a raw civilian into one. For 16 years he struggled – like any other Indian officer – to rise from anonymity to distinction. It turned him somewhat rebellious too, but without irretrievably damaging himself. In this march, however, he assimilated fine character qualities, intellectual and professional refinement and lion-hearted courage, which would emerge more prominently whenever challenges arose. A sort of *coup d'oeil* grew in him to see through the fog of war. It was his crucible. ■

NOTES

1. Jumping the gun, so to say, after the success of Operation Dash, Lord Mountbatten came congratulating Thimayya and his battalion and his remarks were: "The Press says the morale of the Indian officers is low. Look at Thimayya. He has been doing so splendidly. Does he look disgruntled?" The success of the brigade was expected to help the British commanders to prove to the world that Indians, whose merit deserved rewards, got it without discrimination.
2. Excerpted from Official Records History Division, MOD.
3. See Chapter XX, *Defeat Into Victory*.
4. Interview of Colonel Sinha. This officer had a long innings with Thimayya. But one lesson that is often forgotten is the saying, "Do not keep all the eggs in one basket." It happened when he was the QMG; it was much worse in 1963, when Lieutenant General Daulat Singh and several of his officers died in Punch in a helicopter crash.

5. Commanding these divisions were: Major Generals G Wood, Loftus Tottenhem and GS Bruce respectively.
6. "Akyab," wrote Frank Owen, "itself is a port of 45,000 people staying on an island about 50 miles (80 km) south of the India-Burma border. It served the Japanese in Arakan, as Chittagong up the coast served the British Indian forces as a reception point for troops and supplies." It was 'captured' by an air OP on 2 January 1945, as the Japanese had vacated it. He boldly landed there.
7. D R Mankekar, *Leaves From A War Reporter's Diary*, p119.
8. From Historical Division, MoD. The commandos by charter were to capture and hold a beachhead, sufficient for assaulting troops for 24 hours, before returning to reserve. The Commando Brigade had the 1st and 5th Army Commandos besides the 44th and 45th Royal Marine Commandos.
9. Extracted in original from the official history of the Kumaon Regiment – the former Hyderabads.
10. References based on *Thimayya of India*; *Leaves From A War Reporter's Diary*, interview of Colonel Sinha who was a subaltern under Thimayya and *History of Hybd* the (Kumaon) Regiment.
11. *Thimayya of India*, in chapter on "Matsue."
12. Based on the official evaluation.

Appendix

Unit	Personal No	Rank and Name (Christian Names must be stated)	Action for which commended (Date &place of action must be stated)
8th Bn 19 Hyderabad Regiment	AI 944 Regular Indian Army Commmission	Sub Major/Ty Lt Col. KODENDERA THIMAYYA COORG HINDU "Sunny Side" Mercara, Coorg	ARAKAN. Lt Col THIMAYYA commands the 8th Bn 19th Hyderabad Regt. This Bn was involved in much fighting SOUTH of MAUNDAW in the spring of 1944 and has been engaged in a series of actions since the end of the 1944 monsoon. In Nov 1944 Lt Col THIMAYYA planned, and executed with skill and determination, the Bn Operation which resulted in the capture of POLAND, a strongly bunkered Japanese position, and in thus securing the concentration area known as the BIRTHDAY BOWL. During Dec 1944 and Jan 1945, he officiated as Bde Comd and conducted the Bde operations which opened the road to BUTHI-DAUNG and cleared the spine of the MAYU RANGE from the TUNNELS to FOUL POINT. On 28 Jan 1945 his Bn launched the

			attack which culminated in the capture of KANGAW and the cutting of the Japanese escape route. In spite of considerable casualties, repeated enemy counter-attacks and constant heavy enemy fire of all natures, Lt Col THIMAYYA handled every situation with cool judgement and cheerful confidence. 2. Throughout he has displayed leadership and devotion to duty of a very high order and his indomitable spirit has inspired every officer and man under his command – Comd 51 Ind Inf Bde 3. Recommended. The performance of Lt Col Thimayya's bn has been outstanding. Recommended DSO Immediate Maj Gen GN Wood, GOC 25 Ind Div 19.2.45 "He is one of the Indian COs in the all Indian Bde which won the decisive battle of KANGAW. Specially recommended." - Lt Gen ARP Christison, Commander XV Corps l 3.3.45 DSO Recommended: C-in-C Allied Land Forces SEA 20.6.45

HONOUR FOR DSO
GEORGE THE SIXTH BY THE GRACE OF GOD
Of Great Britain, Ireland and the British Dominions beyond the Seas, Kind, Defender of the Faith, Emperor of India, Sovereign, of the Distinguished Service Order, to our Trusted and well beloved
KODENDERA SUBBAYYA THIMAYYA
Major (temporary Lieutenant Colonel) in our Indian Army.
Greeting.
Whereas the above thought fit to Nominate and Appoint you to be a Member of Our Distinguished Service Order, we do these presents, Grant unto you the Dignity of a Companion of our said order and we do hereby authorise you to have, Hold and Enjoy the said Dignity as a Member of our said order, together with all and singular the Privileges thereto belong or appertaining.

Given at our Court at St. James's under our Sign Manual this FIFTEENTH day of NOVEMBER 1945 in the NINTH YEAR OF OUR REIGN.

By THE SOVEREIGN'S COMMAND S/d The Principal Secretary of State for the War Major (Temporary Lieutenant Colonel) K.S. Thimayya 19 Hyderabad Regiment Department Indian Army.

6
An Army in Transit – Member Nationalisation Committee

The long cherished dream of Independence was finally coming true. It was Sardar Baldev Singh, the new defence member, who set-up a "Services Nationalisation Committee" to review the problems that India may face after independence.' Sir N. Gopalaswamy Ayyangar, CSI, CIIE, was appointed as chairman, and Pandit H N Kunzru, Mohammad Ismail Khan, Major General DAL Wade CB, OBE, MC, Sardar Sampuran Singh CB, Brigadier K S Thimayya, DSO, Wing Commander Mehar Singh, DSO, Commander H Mohammed Siddiqui Choudri MBE and Lietutenant Colonel L P Sen, DSO were members. Lieutenant Colonel B M Kaul was secretary to the committee with Major Muhammad Musa as his assistant.

During the committee's meetings, Thimayya actively questioned over 45 'experts' who were called in for enquiry. The views of some of them were for longer retention of the British as part of the Indian Army of the future. When, for instance, Vice Admiral Geoffrey Miles, KCB, C-in-C Royal Indian Navy suggested that it would take about seven years to train all the Indian technicians, Thimayya contested the point saying that if one year's training was considered adequate during the war, why not treat the training of the Indian staff as on a 'war footing.'

Having interacted with the Indian naval officers, he would vouchsafe that all Indian naval officers have full confidence that they can "man, maintain and run cruisers efficiently with reduced training." It was evident that the British wanted to retain their hold over the Indian armed forces for as long as possible. (In subsequent years, the British would sell fairly modern aircraft such as the Canberra to the Royal Indian Air Force (RIAF) and the Royal Indian Navy (RIN) would acquire *HMS Achilles* (later *INS Delhi*), and so on. The rationale was to ensure dependence on the UK, for both officers and equipment.)

Discussion ranged on every issue including those under the axe of demobilisation.

Air Observation Post (OP) squadrons had been kept in suspended animation and needed to be reactivated. Thimayya urged the committee to consider speedy Indianisation and thought that civilian technicians could be brought in to replace the British and commissions could be granted to them. But the problem was not confined to the RIN and the RIAF and some of the arms – the Royal Indian Artillery, Engineers, Signals, Electrical and Mechanical Engineers, and so on. So retention of some officers, warrant officers, had to be seriously considered from among the willing British. But to have a senior Indian brigadier as a major general (and equivalent ranks in other services), the committee recommended that the deputy chief of each service be Indianised. The committee also agreed on posting Indian officers to foreign missions as military attaches.

The ten Gurkha regiments, which the British had kept as their preserve, were recommended to be Indianised. In this the British had a large stake as later developments would show. It seems the amalgamation of the princely states numbering over 526, was discussed as one of the peripheral issues. "Princistan" and "Pakistan," as Sir Winston Churchill had called these, then were distant and indistinct possibilities. If the army was recommended to be reduced by almost one-third, the committee also wanted to reduce the RIAF to 10 squadrons with each squadron of eight aircraft as opposed to the normal 16. The RIN was already a tiny force, and, hence, needed to be improved rather than drastically cut like the other two services.

Among the other recommendations the committee made were: India to stay part of the Commonwealth and training of staff to be reorientated to ushering in a "national outlook" among the Indians. "Members of the armed forces of a free India must not only be nationalised but also be national minded," emphasised the civilian members led by Dr Kunzru. The British case for retention of Independent (Undivided) Armed Forces of India, seems to have been vindicated.[2]

The report of the committee had, nonetheless, drawn some heated discussion on the question of the period for Indianisation. The British insisted that the process of Indianisation would take a decade and a half, as against the half a decade estimated by the Indian members. The Indians remained vocal in asking the committee to accept the shorter time-frame.

Two things stood out at the end of the deliberations: General Wade's stress on retaining the maximum number of British after 1948, the likely year of Independence; and an ominous note of dissent by M Ismail Khan, in support of the 'two-nation theory'. In the committee itself, its civilian members, Nawab Mohammad Ismail and Pandit Kunzru, clashed on elementary issues. And while Wing Commander Mehr Singh, Commander Choudri and Brigadier Thimayya developed unanimity of thoughts, Lieutenant Colonel B M Kaul, the secretary, would differ even in recording the minutes.

The enquiry and recommendations of the Nationalisation Committee, willy-nilly became the referral points in the larger designs of partition, the Partition Committee and Reconstitution Committee.

The breakneck speed at which the wheels of Independence moved could be gauged by the fact that the machinery for Partition was agreed to on 3 June 1947 – barely 40 days ahead of Independence, by which time the committee would have completed the study. But why this breakneck speed from the earlier agreed to June 1948 date by the Attlee government in London? History holds Lord Mountbatten responsible for advancing this date and the subsequent chaos and the communal violence of the Partition. He would shift the onus of responsibility on the Muslim League and its leader, Jinnah.[3]

I – The Enigma of Reconstitution

Partition of the country, like the division of parental property after the demise of the head of the family, began with the clauses of the will of the deceased. In this case, the sad process started with a number of committees that Lord Mountbatten set up by establishing a Cabinet Committee for Partition. Helped by a Steering Committee, the Cabinet Partition Committee had ten committees – Organisation and Records (No.1); Assets and Liabilities (No.2); Revenues (No.3); Contracts (No.4); Currency and Coinage (No.5); Economic Relations (No.6 & 7); Matters Relating to Domiciles (No.8); Foreign Relations (No.9); and Armed Forces (No.10). The larger Partition mechanism was called reconstitution – in fact, a misnomer, for the division that would take place.

In the meanwhile, Thimayya was moved to Amritsar to take over 5th Infantry Brigade (4th Infantry Division) on 20 May, relieving Brigadier P R McNamara, DSO. He was, soon thereafter called up as a member of the Armed Forces Reconstitution Committee (AFRC) administered under Major General B Temple. The deliberations and haggling at this committee resulted in the following distribution:

(a) Area India and Pakistan 4:1 (1,219.6 thousand square miles: 336.4 thousand square miles)

(b) Population: 31m: 6.7m.

(c) Armed forces 63 per cent (Including Gurkhas 7 per cent): 37 per cent.

In terms of army formations, the AFRC divided the Indian Army (by then in the process of demobilisation) as:

India	Pakistan
One armoured division plus one armoured brigade	Two armoured brigades (approx.)
One airborne division less a brigade	One airborne brigade.
Two infantry divisions plus one brigade group.	One infantry division plus One infantry brigade group.
Indian Gurkhas (less HMG's Gurkhas).	Seven Frontier brigades.

Upon return from Delhi, Thimayya was moved to 11th Infantry Brigade in about one month when Brigadier Tyrrwhit Wheeler (popularly nicknamed "Tyre & Wheel") decided to leave the Indian Army and virtually left without orders. Thimayya took over command of this brigade on 25 June and continued until 9 September.

The partition of the armed forces on communal and dominion bases along with immediate movement to Pakistan of all Muslim majority units, concurrent with the move of non-Muslim units to India became one of the major and avoidable curses of this period of flawed and bloody history. In the meanwhile, the British barrister, Sir (later, Lord) Cyril Radcliffe (like the fabled Solomon), supported by Justices Mohammad Munir, Mehar Chand and Teja Singh, as members, formed the committee set up to demarcate the frontier between India and Pakistan, and, to create a Pakistan consisting of portions of both the eastern and western regions of India. An equally vital issue was the division and movement of the newly formed Pakistani armed forces, termed by Jinnah and Liaquat Ali as the "vertebrae" of the new nation. Along with it came the movement and resettlement of millions of unfortunate civilians from both sides who would be uprooted by this Partition. And with Jinnah's insistence to annex Jammu and Kashmir (J&K), a fistula would be planted on the body of Indo-Pakistani relations.

II - Punjab Boundary Force and GOC 4th Division

To control the entire juggernaut, transmigration of the civilians and the movement of the army units and sub-units, a Joint Defence Council was established under the Supreme Commander, Field Marshal Claude Auchinleck, until recently the C-in-C Indian Army. And the two new armies were to be placed under General Sir Rob Lockhart (Indian Army) and General Sir Frank Messervy (Pakistan Army). There would, of course, be C-in-Cs for the navy and air force of the two dominions, as well.

Under the Partition Council, a Punjab Boundary Force (PBF) was created based on 4th Infantry division located in the Punjab and commanded by Major General T W (Pete) Rees. It was to build up to a strength of 50,000 from 12,000, with a number of British officers still with the units and headquarters, but there were to be no British units under Pete Rees. In order to control the anticipated communal violence, this force was to be located in the twelve districts of Punjab and control a 60,000 sq km communally troubled area with a 15 million population. And true to its diversity, Punjab's demographic divide was Muslims, Hindus and Sikhs with a ratio of 55:25:20.

There were 15,000 villages to guard/protect by about 300 platoons, all weakened by demobilisation and carrying out migration at the same time. There could not have been a better scenario for climactic, if not wholly disastrous, events.

A further damaging dimension was added to this period by the so-called, "standdown" instructions given to the British officers.[4] These not only restricted the involvement of British officers from areas of conflict, but also discouraged them from actively participating in controlling the communal violence. Although what was conveyed was categorical about the British non-participation, the same would be mellowed down for the Pakistan armed forces. In consequence of this clever diversion of instructions, the British officers who served with the Pakistani armed forces provided frontline leadership and vital advice to them when fighting took a serious turn in J&K from 1948. Overall, these instructions caused more damage to the camaraderie of the British and the Indians at this last stage of the Raj.

When the PBF was created, its military composition consisted of two brigades of 4th Div and three more brigades. These were 14th Para Brigade (3/7 Rajput, 3/10 Baluch, 4/13 F F Rifles); 43rd Lorried Brigade (1/2 Punjab, 2/7 Rajput, 1/10 Baluch, 3/17 Dogra, 2/8 GR) and 114th Infantry Brigade (4/10 Baluch, 5th/13th FF Rifles and 2/17 Dogra). These units had not been divided.

The force commander was given Brigadier D S Brar of India and Brigadier M Ayub Khan of Pakistan as military advisers. Later, Brigadier K S Thimayya of India and Brigadier Nazir Ahmed of Pakistan joined them as alternate advisers and as the situation turned grave, 50th Para Brigade, 77th Para Brigade and 123rd Infantry Brigade were also made part of the PBF and the strength rose to over 50,000 troops.[5]

But it was too late, as by early August, more than 7,000 people had lost their lives, and their properties were completely destroyed. In total insanity, Master Tara Singh was threatening to kill Jinnah, accusing him of being fully responsible for the planned genocide of Sikhs in the newly acquired Pakistan.

The areas of contention both in the east and west were so many that there was no acceptable solution. The Radcliffe Award on 17 August, saw a huge population of over 10 million uprooted. Then began one of history's worst mass migrations in which thousands lost their lives and property, and many atrocities were committed by both sides. It was a monumental folly of all those responsible for it.[6]

Added to this were other contradictory and confusing situations such as the mechanism of division of the army along with the trans-migration taking place. From 3 June, knowing that the Indian Army had been ordered to be divided, the attitudes of the men going to Pakistan changed; similar was the case of the non-Muslims in units located in Pakistan. There was a need to rebuild these sub-units and units and in the absence of experienced senior Indian and Pakistani officers, it had to be left to the British. But the British officers and men had also begun to lose interest, as they themselves, in a reversal of fate, had been told to choose to serve as a mercenaries, either as part of Pakistan or India. For most, it was a "hell of a come down" and they chose to return to the UK with a three months' notice. To top it all, Auchinleck's headquarters, as averred, had issued secret instructions to all British officers to stand-down, implying no serious involvement in the disputes arising out of Partition – not even for alleviating the human suffering thus caused.

The Raj was ending, but there were still available in plenty the ruler's snobbery, false pride and deep-rooted prejudices of the white man's claim to superiority. So when, for example, Ayub was nominated as adviser from the Pakistan Army to Pete Rees, he hated to give even a 'dime' to him.

To Thimayya too, Pete Rees' treatment bordered between being bollocked to summary dismissal and as if of no consequence. Even though Thimayya's brigade had been effectively handling the cases of rioting with a firm hand and he had a well-established reputation as a brigade commander, Rees was dismissive.

On completion of the work on the Reconstitution Committee, Thimayya was told that another important assignment awaited him. In addition to command of the brigade, he would act as an alternate adviser to Rees.

Having been appointed as an alternate military adviser, he reported to Rees at 6 a.m., on 24 June. Rees, attired only in a towel, was shaving. Thimayya wished him.

"How much service do you have?" Rees asked abruptly.

"Twenty years," Thimayya answered.

"I have got thirty years," the general said. "If you think I intend to listen to your advice, you are mistaken."[7]

There could be no further argument. If the general felt he needed no advice, Thimayya, obviously, saw no need to hang on. Prejudices die hard, thought Thimayya. He saluted and walked out. Rees was least courteous and his attitude would lead eventually to all the Indian and Pakistan officers later demanding division of the PBF. Thimayya returned to Jullundur (now Jalandhar). Soon the communal frenzy caught on. The insistence of Jinnah and Liaquat Ali – with the reluctant agreement by Nehru and Patel – to divide the army and police, made the minorities, left in Pakistan, lose all confidence in the new government. They were being systematically wiped out.

On 17 August, though the PBF was deployed in a rag-tag way, Nehru admitted to the Press, "Ghastly tales are being heard." And as rioting and killing and looting were carrying on unabated, there were not only rumours of the "British officers appearing indifferent to the fate of the two new countries," but responsible men like Maulana accusingly saying that the "army looked on while people clashed."[8] There were even calls to break the PBF up. A panic-stricken Nehru, in a letter addressed to Sardar Patel, dated 31 August, stated "....In the military set-up I am insisting that brigadiers should be Indians. Rees is creating difficulties... Major General Thimayya is going to be in charge of our brigade."[9] (On this date, Thimayya was still a brigadier.) In July, Nehru wrote to Mountbatten that it was "incongruous for the army of a free country not to have its own officers in the highest ranks."

There was confusion not only among the refugees but also among those responsible for their safety. What could the army units do while they themselves were broken and dispatched to their new country? The military units moving across had nightmarish experiences too. The regimental histories of both the Indian and Pakistan Armies abound in tales of those ghastly days.

Lieutenant General Eric Vas, then a captain, posted to 2nd Dogra from a Baluch unit, recalls how his unit returned to India, and how the 4th Division was collecting the bits and pieces of units to complete its order of battle.[10] In the case of the Sikh Regiment, it lost one-third of its Muslim strength, its three battalions i.e. 16th Sikh, 17th Sikh and 18th Sikh, built up on some 20 battalions of the Punjab Regiment and the Frontier Force. The organisational problems of the Indian Army were equally bad as along with this reorganisation, a large-scale demobilisation had taken place. "What a way to vivisect a country! What way to destroy its fibre," Thimayya wrote to a friend, and added, "It's only the genius of the British who could credit themselves in such grandiose designs."

That is something the Muslims realised, to the folly of their Muslim League politicians as the juggernaut of displaced people took the shape of a "diaspora in distress." Interestingly, after Pakistan lost its eastern wing, East Pakistan in 1971, the former General Muhammad Musa wrote: "The Punjab Boundary Force had failed to serve the purpose, namely movement and protection of the Muslims and non-Muslim refugees... For, in the whole of the Pre-Partition Army, there was not even one single Muslim infantry battalion and a cavalry regiment as such. Consequently, when the defence forces were divided, the Muslim elements were moved to Pakistan as company, platoon, odd detachment or like me individually..."[11]

It is true that while Hindu regiments, by and large, were pure, the Muslims were never so. The British did not seem to wholly trust them, not that they trusted others, for that matter.

The consequence of all these developments was cumulative. Pete Rees found bitterness among the Muslims and non-Muslims at its peak. He would confront the private armies of the Muslims, Sikhs and Hindu *Jathas*, especially the Sikh *Jathas* influenced by Master Tara Singh, with diffidence. He did not know how to really control the situation, he merely muddled along, hoping that things would sort themselves out.

The migration which began as a trickle in June-July, had become a continuous stream of human exodus from both sides. Nehru and Patel, fully seized of the problem, were on the move, visiting refugees, attending meetings at Lahore, Karachi and Delhi. They issued orders to the PBF to "protect Muslims at all cost" – the cost of which they hardly had any idea. At Amritsar and Jullundur, Thimayya gave firm orders to the Sikh *Jatha* leaders to stop the killing. But in the absence of adequate force, he could only marginally control the situation. Killing and vendetta continued. And as the storm of dissatisfaction with the performance of the PBF grew, the Indian and Pakistani officers met and decided to tell their respective prime ministers to divide the PBF into its Indian and Pakistani components. This, they would do, without informing Rees or their British Cs-in-C, or even Auchinleck.

In the meanwhile the situation continued to drift from bad to worse. Barely a week beyond Independence, on 21 August, Mountbatten called Auchinleck and observed, "In spite of conferences, telephonic messages, the situation was out of hand in the

Punjab and the PBF had proved ineffective." Further, the prime minister and defence minister proposed that General Rees be given additional officers and that the PBF be divided, under an Indian officer for East Punjab and the other half under a Pakistani officer for West Punjab under General Rees' overall command.[12]

On 22 August, while Thimayya and Sardar Baldev Singh toured both India and Pakistan, Nehru wrote a letter to Liaquat Ali saying, that "blood of many million innocent people has flowed, Congress will, however, continue to protect minorities." He was soliciting a reciprocal assurance on the safety of the non-Muslim minority in Pakistan. Musa recalls that "Muslims in India were abandoning their villages and seeking the shelter of refugee camps...people in Pakistan feared that thousands of families were likely to be wiped out." While Thimayya saw the carnage in India and Pakistan, Musa required bulldozers to bury the dead refugees. It happened, he says, because the ad hoc battalions and regiments of the Pakistan Army were "too tired and weary" to continuously patrol and protect the non-Muslim refugees in Pakistan.[13]

By 25 August, Pete Rees himself admitted in a JDC meeting at Delhi that he feared that the PBF was fatigued and their mood explosive. He also defended the British officers' performance and felt that nothing better could be expected. The situation became so frightful that General Rees himself threw in the towel by recommending to the JDC: "Now that the Partition has taken place, the two dominions should individually assume their responsibility of movements and safety of the refugees." The JDC deferred discussion and a decision on it.

In the meanwhile, the civil war and its mayhem spread. The PBF tried to control the mobs in Sialkot, but only after over 200 Sikhs and Hindus were killed; in Montgomery, Muslim mobs flooded the non-Muslim villages by breaking the canals. In retaliation, an unaccounted number of Muslims were killed in Batala and Gurdaspur. The blame on the PBF was increasing – Nehru and Liaquat Ali were both blaming it. The politicians, who were really the cause – and the consequences of this undeclared war – on both sides, had been squarely targeting the PBF under Rees. As is common with this class, they had found a scapegoat.

It was only on 30 August that a decision was taken that from 1 September, the PBF would revert to the control of the respective governments. But discussions and parleys continued; Mountbatten especially wanted Nehru to go slow. Nehru helped, as Major General SBS Chimni headed the Military Evacuation Organisations for both India and Pakistan, and though he tasked Thimayya to take over the PBF (India) on this day, the decision to formally appoint him as GOC 4th Division and commander PBF was accepted only on 14 September.

Thimayya reorganised the PBF (India) into smaller self-contained mobile groups with transport and radios. They carried their own rations and petrol and could move swiftly to trouble spots. Yet the killings continued unabated, as it was difficult to restrain the animal instincts of the evacuees. Meanwhile, trains moved with escorts, as did the transport columns. Ignoring protocol, Thimayya would lead the convoys of the refugees, barge into troubled spots in Pakistan where lawlessness and mayhem were worse than in India. His forays into Sheikpura one night opened his eyes and strengthened his resolve to catch and punish the fundamentalists with a heavy hand. This column was especially unparalleled in individual bravery and courage. He was determined that the communal madness had to be bridled through firm actions and no effort was too great for it.

Sheikpura, however, remained embedded in the deep recesses of his memory. Having woken up from a nightmare at 2 a.m., one night, he intuitively headed for Sheikpura, the Sikh village, along with a small convoy. He could hear the cries of the wounded and dying. Although he was the commander of the PBF, with freedom to move, the Pathan sentries allowed him to proceed only after much loss of time. He caught the perpetrators and abettors of the crime and the guilty policemen. He brought back the living, some of whom had been saved by a *Maulvi*.

That day, even as his heart ached, he did not lose all faith in the impartiality of soldiers – he had, however, become sceptical about the nobility of human beings, especially in times of adversity. For, he was now seeing both hell and a little glimmer of heaven, too, when he saw amidst the ruins, a man like that Muslim *Maulvi*.

These could be exciting days too. General K V Krishna Rao recalls how his commanding officer, Lieutenant Colonel Khalid Jan, had handed over to him his Mahar Machine Gun Battalion and how he drove off to Pakistan.[14] Similar was the case of Brigadier RCB Bristow, commander 11th Brigade. He recalls how Liaquat Ali Khan and Pandit Nehru with their advisers, Brigadiers Ayub Khan and Thimayya, visited Hoshiarpur. Thimayya wanted him to deliver a detailed briefing, which he says he did. A few days later, Krishna Rao saw Thimayya appointed as GOC 4th Division. Krishna Rao's battalion was then sent to Multan and placed under Brigadier Munir Tiwana for the safety of about 100,000 non-Muslim refugees huddled in a refugee camp. He evacuated them efficiently. At the end of this job, Thimayya wrote to Rao: "Will you please tell your officers and men how proud I am of having them under my command. I'll take my first opportunity of thanking them personally."

Many more came in contact with General Thimayya – Serbjeet Singh and his brother, who made photographic history of the J&K War, especially of Zoji La. The two brothers received help from Thimayya.

On 13 September 1947, a day before Master Tara Singh had threatened to wage a crusade, a Sikh *dharamyudha* against the Muslims in India, the cry of *Jihad* came from the Pakistani fundamentalists. It set in a panic reaction from Generals Lockhart and Messervy who were visibly shaken. Mountbatten was alarmed and wanted immediate steps to be taken to avert a tragic carnage and the loss of lives. While Nazir and Ayub were alerted in Pakistan, Thimayya, who still worked under Rees' overall command, was sent off to Amritsar to calm down Master Tara Singh and get an undertaking from him that the Sikh *Jathas* would not attack a train of the Muslim refugees due to go from Jullundur via Amritsar to Lahore. At Amritsar, Thimayya did not hesitate to apprise an infuriated Tara Singh that the army would not hesitate to even move tanks to control the rioting.

An incredulous Tara Singh then asked Thimayya: "You will use tanks against your own people!"

"Yes," said Thimayya, "if Muslims, who are also our people, are threatened."

"In that case," said a pacified Tara Singh reluctantly, "*Jathas* will not attack the Muslim columns."

Master Tara Singh kept his word.[15]

Back from Amritsar, Thimayya joined the JDC meet at Lahore on 14 September. It was here that he suggested to Prime Minister Nehru to implement the considered opinion of both Indian and Pakistani officers "to divide the PBF and replace those British officers who wanted change." After a stormy session, the PBF was split – with the Pakistanis retaining most of the British, and India being selective. Thimayya's promotion as GOC 4th Division was also announced and as the Indian commander for the PBF (India), he had his headquarters at Lahore and Jullundur.

General Sir Rob Lockhart resented this action and was furious with him for "going over Rees' head" and "letting him down." Thimayya was candid enough in telling Lockhart, "Surely, I am obliged to advise my prime minister about the matter on which my knowledge gives me authority to speak." Lockhart admonished Thimayya and told him that even though he may be right, he should, nonetheless, have submitted his views through General Rees. Thimayya realised that under the circumstances, it may be desirable for him to put in his papers. He began to write his resignation.

It was a stand-off that cooled only after Rob Lockhart realised that the whole thing had been inflamed by Pete Rees' kow-towing to the Indian and Pakistani officers. At the same time, Brigadier Thimayya's "writing his resignation" turned the tables.

If the madness of trans-migration, the rioting, arson and cold-blooded massacres were proving Punjab to be the killing fields of millions, there were other problems too. The Jam Sahib of Junagadh and the Nizam of Hyderabad were refusing to join the Dominion of India; Jinnah, at the same time, was trying to wean away or snatch Jammu and Kashmir from India. The cost he had paid for Pakistan, after all, had been nothing. He was like an obdurate child who got what he cried for!

Mahatma Gandhi's soul was the most troubled one during this period. He was constantly goading the Congress leaders to save the Muslims in India and safely bring back the non-Muslims out of Pakistan. He was wanting to visit Pakistan and meet Jinnah. It was then that Nehru met General Thimayya on 25 September in the presence of Mahatma Gandhi and Mountbatten. The note records in *Mountbatten and India*:[16]

> I asked General Thimayya to speak quite frankly and fearlessly on the situation and not to consider my (Mountbatten's) feelings since all I wanted was the truth. I asked him for a categorical answer to the question: "Do you consider that the British

officers of the Punjab Boundary Force discharged their duties faithfully, correctly and impartially?"

General Thimayya replied in a firm tone, "I have no difficulty whatever in answering that question; in my opinion, it is 'yes.' Of course, in any particular group, an exception may be found, but that is not peculiar to the British; but in the main, I have no doubt whatever that they did was their best in the Punjab Boundary Force as, they are doing to this day." He continued: "In Punjab the Boundary Force suffered from the disadvantage that they were not directly responsible to any government; the force large as it was, was inadequate to deal with the magnitude of the outbreak and it is doubtful whether a force, large enough to deal with such a mass rising could have been produced to suppress it. I myself as liaison officer was travelling around East and West Punjab and I have no doubt that no force could have stopped the rising. Furthermore, my two British Brigade commanders and my own staff, which is at least 50 per cent British, are working themselves to death and loyally fulfilling their duties. We all owe them a great debt.... But there is feeling of frustration among them and more are sending their three-month notice."

The Raj was ending and the British officers were still maintaining their traditional fairness in assessing their Indian subordinates. Despite the extensive discrimination that the Indian officers suffered under their colonial bosses, they still maintained their Solomon type of evaluation. Overall they were fair. A vignette.[17]

General Dudley Russel GOC-in-C, Delhi & East Punjab Command, graded him OUTSTANDING and wrote a pen picture that befitted Thimayya's personality:

A forceful character and excellent commander. Possessing a clear brain, he expresses himself well. Not afraid of saying what he thinks. Professional knowledge of a high order, cheerful, good company. He will benefit considerably when he can get his division under command for training instead of being employed on ID (Internal Duties) and evacuee work. Always cooperates well, frequently anticipating what is required of him.

General RMM Lockhart (predecessor to Bucher) as C-in-C Indian Army endorsed Russel's view-point on 19 December 1947 (before he was forced to resign). Awarding an 'Above the Average' Grading, but not ignoring the incident of the PBF, he wrote:

He is undoubtedly one of India's best officers. He has done extremely well in his present difficult appointment. He needs more experience to realise that all commands form part of a vast machine and action taken on any one part may often affect the rest and commanders must, therefore, weigh this aspect. I have no doubt he will soon appreciate this and go far.

It may not be far off the mark to suggest that Thimayya should have been rewarded with a *Nishan-e-Pakistan* and *Bharat Ratna* for all that he did to save the suffering humanity of both nations. Alas, such a noble thought hardly struck the leaders of the two countries. The sympathy wave created by Timmy's humanitarian acts, nonetheless, moved the best of the human concerns from the newly created Pakistan. The great poet Faiz Ahmed Faiz wrote in his praise:

Na Hindu, na Musalman,
Sirf Insaniyat Thi
Thimayya ka Iman

He was turning into a messiah.

PBF operations became unprecedented in world history, without being named as such. "Uprooting ten million people from their hearths and homes in the name of a new nation of the pure – Pakistan," said Thimayya "beat all records of exodus and Diaspora. Even Stalin didn't do it." He would hesitate to name the people who put the clock back. But he always felt sad about it. "There was no method in this madness," he would say.[18]

To Lord Mountbatten, who continued to be criticised all his life and even after death for his actions and inactions, it was a maddening affair. Jinnah is said to have lamented the decision to get the country divided and millions killed.[19] President Iskander Mirza had referred to it as "mayhem." Musa saw it as "saga of courage and conviction against the genocide of Muslims." Such thoughts and perspectives, no doubt, showed it in differing scenes in a sordid *son-et-lumiere*. In the words of Lord Ismay, "Jinnah's creation of Pakistan and exodus of that great mass of humanity caused an upheaval in Delhi." It was, indeed, a simple way of passing the buck to Jinnah, while the British role behind the scene in the division of India was more prominent than Jinnah's or the Muslim League's.

Nehru gave it a national and political nuance as he saw the refugees settle down by January 1948. "In future history," remarked Nehru after Partition, "it will be said that vast and colossal as the problem was, something which might have shaken the foundation of the government and the social order, the people of India stood upto it bravely, tackled it, and I hope ultimately solved it to the advantage of the nation."[20]

Baldev Singh had more sympathy with the PBF as he wrote in the same book: "Rarely in peace-time has a fighting force suffered such great vicissitudes... Army had to be divided and reconstituted which meant breaking of the battalions, regiments, training installations."[21]

Thimayya's response was measured. "*We felt a thrill of pride when we read of ceremonies (of independence) that took place. But real independence would come only when peace had been won and harmony necessary for progress, had been established between the two new countries.*"[22] Personally, it was, by his own admission, the "unhappiest period of his life." Nonetheless, in this din of death and destruction, he found people capable of rising above passions and maintaining their sanity. There were many who physically had forsaken their own safety for the good of others and gave human behaviour a sense of value and decency. But they were only a numbered few. He saw the awful and beastly side of many, who were simply abominable.

If his faith in general human rationality was shaken, he was proud of the Indian (and some Pakistani) young officers performing their duties magnificently, as also civilians and the police, when motivated to work.

Personally, Thimayya could look back with great satisfaction on the fact that he had been able to serve and save a part of humanity doomed to suffer. It was the triumph of his courage and humanity. Eric Vas, who figures elsewhere too, records his impression of an ideal general through the eyes of a very junior officer:[23]

> This, my first contact with Timmy, revealed so many aspects of his character and leadership qualities, the charm with which he dealt with a brash young officer's overconfidence and inexperience; the skill and understanding with which he encouraged a junior officer's self-expression without dampening his enthusiasm; the freedom he allowed his subordinates and the control he could exercise when this was required; the calm and cool manner in which he accepted the news that our armed forces were being dispatched to J&K; the tact he displayed when he told me that my plan to raise a battalion was haywire and was not going to be implemented; his decisiveness and the kind gesture of using me not only to inform the battalion of the radical change in their destination and mode of movement, but to re-unite me with E Company. In this one episode you can find that which goes to make the Thimayya legend.

Thimayya's intelligence, speed of decision, courage of conviction and ability to react to situations had left a deep and indelible imprint on Gandhi, Nehru, Mountbatten and Sardar Baldev Singh. Under these same trying circumstance others looked unsure, confused and indecisive. In the case of Ayub, he confessed to Rees that he came "under severe criticism and a good deal of blame." Ayub attempted to wriggle out of his responsibility by saying that he was an "outsider" and was in an "advisory role," although he claimed to have saved some Muslims from Amritsar. He also saw it as an unhappy period of his life.[24] Overall, he was an example of failure.

What of Pete Rees? Indubitably, Rees' task was unenviable. But he threw in the towel rather fast, especially as the dimension of the problem seemed to overwhelm him from 20 August. The residual colonial British 'pride and prejudice' seemed to have been his undoing.[25]

History was moving fast. Junagadh had acceded to India by 6 November 1947, although Lord Mountbatten, along with General Lockhart, had supported its accession to Pakistan. Plans were also being finalised to end Hyderabad's ambivalence.

J&K was assuming a very complex shape. The Pakistani intransigence had forced Nehru to review the force level. Because Nehru had a hunch that the Indian C-in-C and his British counterparts were in league with each either, he would seek advice from Cariappa and Kalwant, but more so, from Thimayya, because of the confidence he had built up in Nehru by his handling of the PBF.

Nehru's trust in Thimayya grew, as evident from his letter of 25 December 1947, to the Maharaja of Kashmir in which he wrote: "...We asked General Thimayya to come over from Amritsar and he was present at our conferences... It is clear that we (have to) mobilise total effort..."[26] He mentions the raising of regular and irregular forces. It was Nehru who selected him to command the forces in the Valley.

By January 1948, the refugees were under control but the national tragedy of the assassination on 30 January of the Father of Nation, Mahatma Gandhi, had upset Nehru's undivided attention to J & K. To this had been added some 10 million people uprooted from their homes and hearths due to the hurried Partition of the subcontinent by Lord Mountbatten, causing about a million deaths in the ensuing uncontrolled panic and violence.

In the meanwhile, Thimayya continued to command and train 4th Division in Punjab. ■

NOTES

1. From Official Records.
2. Excerpt from the Thimayya Papers.
3. Independence was scheduled to be granted in June 1948. Lord Mountbatten advanced the date.
4. The stand-down Auchinleck signal of 20 August read:
   "Owing to immediate risk of outbreak of open hostility between the armed forces of India and Pakistan, all British officers and other ranks shall cease forthwith to take any part in the command or administration of armed forces of India or Pakistan... nothing to be allowed to impede it."(quote from original documents reproduced by C Dasgupta's *War and Diplomacy in Kashmir*, p. 18.)
5. *The Red Eagle, A History of Fourth Division*, p 152.
6. This sense of mayhem can also be appreciated from the US book, *The Chronicle of the 20th Century* which recorded: "August 15. At the stroke of midnight India won her long awaited independence from Britain. And Muslims won a degree of freedom from Hindus..." In its rhetoric, it called India a "killing ground," quoting some Hindus as saying that they would not be satisfied until every Muslim is driven out of India into Pakistan. The poison of enmity and hatred was difficult to ignore.
7. *Thimayya of India*, p. 250.
8. *India Wins Freedom*, p. 202.
9. Nehru to Mountbatten 11 July 1947. Also see Sardar Patel's correspondence (1945-50),

Durga Das Navjivan Trust, 1972.
10. *Fools and Infantrymen*, p. 98.
11. *The Pakistan Times*, 14 August 1979.
12. Larry Collins and Dominique Lappierre, *Mountbatten and Independent India* (16 August-18 January 1948).
13. *The Pakistan Times*, 4 August 1979.
14. *In the Service of Nation; Reminiscences*.
15. n. 7, p. 252
16. Ibid., pp. 108 and 121.
17. From Official Records.
18. As recalled by Lieutenant Colonel Cariappa, his one time ADC and brother-in-law.
19. In *End of Empire*, Lapping says, "Jinnah realised the creation of Pakistan was a mistake."
20. In *After Partition, Mountbatten and India*, pp. 108 and 121. See also pp. 163 – 64, It is said that when a train accident in Pakistan caused the death of hundreds of non-Muslim refugees, General Messervy ordered an enquiry. A colonel sent as a member to this enquiry by Thimayya is said to have returned thoroughly brainwashed.
21. Ibid.
22. n. 7
23. n. 10, pp.98-101.
24. *Friends And Not Masters*, pp.14-17.
25. *While Memory Serves*, Francis Tucker, doubted the ability of the PBF to enforce law and order due to lack of administrative support. In *Divide and Quit*, Moon saw the PBF's role and expectations as unrealistic and that its disbandment was a foregone conclusion. By 29 August, the pace was set. So have been the deductions of Andrew Roberts in *Eminent Churchillians*.
26. *Selected Works of Nehru*, Second Series, Vol 4, pp. 13, 181 and 393.

7
The Indian Army on Trial

Over the years, it has become absolutely clear that the tribals who attempted to invade J&K in 1947-48 were, in fact, ex-soldiers of the pre-Partition Indian Army and deserters of the J&K State Force. They had a good sprinkling of Pakistani regular forces and ex-INA officers. Their knowledge of the local terrain and ability to live off the land made them good fighters. The tactics that suited them and they used well, were of infiltration and envelopment.

The other arm of this invading force comprised the tribals from the NWFP. Imbued with a war-like spirit, revenge and brutality, loot, mayhem, and rape became their bestial methods of terrorising people even though they were their co-religionists. The third comprised the Chillas and the Gilgit Scouts, armed with modern weapons, including 3 inch mortars and 3.7 inch howitzers. They acted as a good guerilla force that would operate against Skardu, Zoji La and Ladakh. The Pakistani regulars, who moved behind the irregulars, were armed, equipped and organised like the Indian Army. Their tactics and capabilities were similar, but they would not hesitate to maintain a screen of cattle and the local people.

Several developments were taking place that had focussed the Indian government's full attention to J&K, the other troubles being regarded as mere "flashes in the pan." When Pakistan continued to press its offensive into Kashmir, Nehru had begun to toy with the idea of taking the war into Pakistan with a view to attack and destroy the bases in Sialkot, Gujrat and Jhelum, from where the bulk of the invading force was operating. This had happened even after Mountbatten's meeting with Jinnah in a personal capacity on 1 November, at Lahore, where the Indian governor general surmised that the invasion had taken place with the Quaid-e-Azam's explicit connivance.

While discussing an appreciation, which had been prepared by the three Cs-in-C on future operations in J&K, Nehru also faced a stonewalling effort by Mountbatten and his British chiefs against any offensive toward Domel or Mirpur, for reasons of "apparent lack of wherewithal." The prime minister, however, insisted that he viewed the capture of Domel, the holding of Poonch (or Punch) and the advance to Mirpur as an essential part of the Indian strategy in J&K.[1] A via-media was then followed, rather grudgingly. As a result of this interim measure, Major General Kalwant, GOC J&K Force, was directed to relieve Punch town of the raiders; undertake an advance on Bhimbar, and consolidate the position at Uri.[2]

By November, the fall of Jhanghar, held by Brigadier Usman's brigade, added to the government's anxiety. It was then that General Thimayya was hastily summoned from Jullundur for a meeting at Delhi and his views were sought on the likely future course of the war in J&K and the redeployment of the additional force that was under his command. In order to counter the Pakistani raiders, it was also decided to raise an irregular force of 10,000 in the form of the J&K Militia. Thimayya was tasked to raise six Frontier Constabulary battalions for the J&K force under Kalwant Singh.

Sending of the invading force as raiders was an uncalculated gamble by Jinnah. He had hoped Srinagar would fall, and as Pakistanis often chuckled, the Maharaja would either run away or be caught in his sleep! He could then make the Indians twiddle their thumbs as the Pakistani Army could consolidate faster. But the 27 October landing in Srinagar of 1st Sikh saved Srinagar and Kashmir. When the news reached Jinnah, he ordered General DD Gracey to use the Pakistan Army to capture Srinagar. Gracey, realising that the new Pakistan Army would be destroyed, refused to obey the order. Instead, he contacted Auchinleck. The following morning, the supreme commander made Jinnah see sense.

The thaw in the refugee movement by January 1948 gave Thimayya time to get his division into some shape. He began training and had the armoured brigade located in Ambala grouped with his brigades for joint operational training and coordination. The artillery and the sappers began their training camps. But suddenly, as always happened in his case, he was on the move, this time to the battlefield of Kashmir.

He was posted as GOC JAK Force. He arrived at Jammu on 22 April on which date a much harassed Kalwant was relieved. Having taken over as GOC-in-C, DEP, by 20 January, General K M Cariappa already had the plans to bifurcate the operational responsibility on either side of the Pirpanjals. The government had also accepted the creation of these divisions by the beginning of April. Similarly, a sub-area had been raised for administration. As part of this reorganisation, Thimayya was moved to Srinagar to take over the newly formed Sri Div (19th Divison) and Major General Atma Singh to command a similar formation on the Jammu-Punch axis.

Kashmir was, indeed, assuming strategic importance for India, not by virtue of its geo-strategic position alone; it had begun to serve as a new gateway for the Muslim invaders – as in the past. V P Menon linked history to it when he wrote: "...Within ten weeks of establishment of the new state of Pakistan, its very first act was to let loose a tribal invasion through the northwest. Srinagar today. Delhi tomorrow..."[3]

Nehru was also clear about its significance. "The first thing to be understood," he wrote in a note, "Kashmir is of most vital consequence to us and we are deadly earnest about it..."[4] He wanted offensive actions to be planned.

For Mr Jinnah and his newly formed army, Kashmir (and the whole of J&K) was a fabled "Alladin's lamp," in any case. It was Thimayya who heard of the Pakistani officers' dream from the horse's mouth, so to say. At Lahore, he heard the Pakistanis dividing Kashmir between their regiments – Probyn's Horse at Gulmarg, 13th Lancer at Pahelgam.[5]

Thimayya had been essentially picked up to direct operations in the Valley for the capture of Dommel-Muzaffarabad and to free Ladakh of the invaders. But as Akbar Khan also confirms, the Pakistan Army was fully aware of the impending operations – surprise had already been compromised. "By the middle of April 1948," he wrote, "it seemed that a serious Indian offensive was to be expected in Kashmir..."[6] Gracey, being more loyal to the Pakistani Army he was serving than Bucher, warned the Pakistani government on 20 April, that in order to prevent an easy victory to the Indian Army (which would result in breakdown of Pakistan), more troops must be rushed to, and be deployed on, the axis Chakothi-Muzaffarabad and down south. "It is imperative," his note, emphasised "that the Indian Army is not allowed to advance beyond general line Uri-Punch-Naoshera."[7]

As a result, Pakistan began its *Operation Venus*, where Major General Loftus Tottenham's 7th (Pak) Division[8] reinforced the approximately one mixed brigade of regular and militia plus thousands of tribals with a brigade in the general area Pandu-Chakothi-Bib Dori and another stretching from Muzaffarabad-to Tithwal occupying the heights astride the Kishan Ganga.

The stage was now ominously set. As Noel Baker was urging the UN to enforce a ceasefire, Gracey had Tottenham's 7th Division reinforce the defences opposite Uri and Punch, and Lord Mountbatten was using his charm on Nehru by telling the latter about the incalculable harm any wrong military action could do to both India and Pakistan. The British were doing everything possible to ensure that India's *Operation Summer Offensive* was a "non-runner."[9]

The JAK Force was now directly under Cariappa who had the tactical headquarters operating from Jammu. But a proposal to set up headquarters to coordinate the operations of these two divisions, the independent sub-area at Jammu, and other troops, was under active consideration. It would come up as the J&K Corps at Udhampur. Lieutenant General S M Shrinagesh would become its first GOC.[10]

As Thimayya landed in Srinagar on 4 May, he found Skardu and the rest of Ladakh on the verge of collapse. Working directly under the new Pakistan Army Headquarters at Rawalpindi, the deserters of 6th J&K Infantry, a large force of tribals, and the Gilgit Scouts with four wings with 1,200 rifles and supporting weapons, had been trying to besiege the small sub-unit of the non-Muslim Kashmir force since the last August. Concurrently, it had sent the remnants, principally the deserters of 6th J&K Battalion from the Northern Area to the Kargil-Dras-Zoji La area. Additionally, the Pakistanis were attempting to move from Lamayaru to Kargil under one Colonel MS Jilani. Major Sherjung Thapa, the OC there since November, made frantic calls for relief. An aerial reconnaissance done by him in a Dakota on a supply dropping mission, showed him that Skardu was, indeed, indefensible and he would have to seriously plan to withdraw, in case the situation became untenable.

The Summer Offensive

By 4 May, the Sri Div had been formed. Under its order of battle were L P Sen's 161st Brigade at Uri, 163rd Brigade at Handwara with Katoch taking it over and Nair's 77th (Para) Brigade was joining it.

The directive issued to Thimayya on 7 May for *Operation Summer Offensive* generally tasked him to capture Domel and prevent the enemy action from that direction. He was to "particularly" ensure the security of Srinagar, hold the essential outposts at Uri, Baramula, Handwara, Skardu, Leh and Kargil; and secure at all times, the administrative communications of all the garrisons mentioned. It was a prodigious task.

He was happy that 4th Kumaon formed part of 161st Brigade along with other famous battalions: 2nd Dogra, 6th Raj Rif, (the Sawai Man Singh) and 7th Sikh. So were 1st Sikh, 1st Madras and 3rd Garhwal with 163rd Brigade. The 77th (Para) Brigade, in a ground role, had equally good battalions. "It is the battalions which eventually are supreme in war. They deliver the goods or jettison them under stress," he said, during his first meeting with battalion and brigade commanders.

Thimayya was told to recreate his own reserves. He intended to capture the bridges at Domel and Muzaffarabad while containing the enemy on the northern flank; protect the Line of Communications between Sonamarg and Kargil; and in order to drive the raiders from Kanzalwan, operate towards Bandipur and the Gurais Valley. He was equally anxious to ward off a Pakistani major riposte from the south, where reports of a large concentration had begun to trickle in. Thimayya's priority task, therefore, was not only to clear the enemy from these areas but carry the battle to the doorsteps of Pakistani territory and, thus, free the area of their occupation. It would involve an advance up to Muzaffarabad and Domel, and if the situation warranted, a link up with Punch over the Haji Pir hump.

With the resources crunch, the plan he made out as a result of his military appreciation was simple and implementable. It catered for contingencies that could arise out of the military situations on the border. We reproduce it in its entirety as a document to the book.[11]

The plan, simple and executionable, nonetheless showed that actionable intelligence as required for the assault was lacking. He was not aware that Tottenham, now

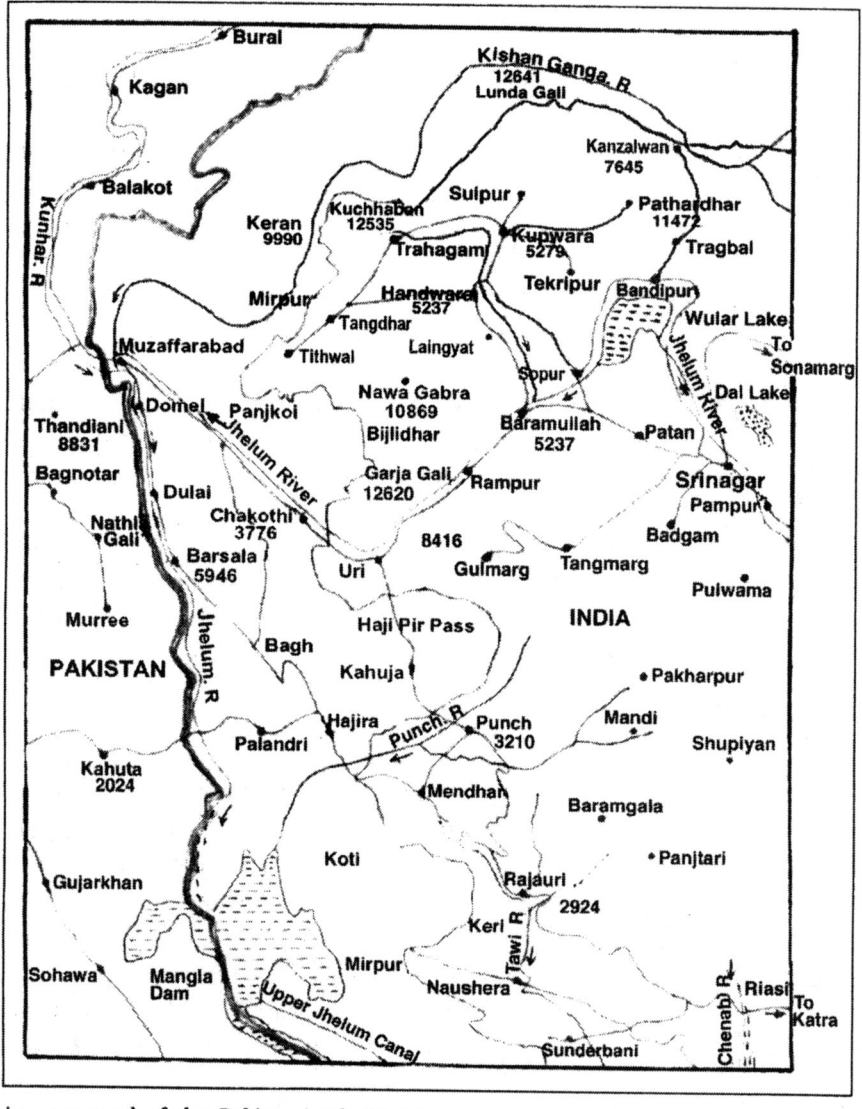

Map 4: Western Jammu and Kashmir

in command of the Pakistani 7th Division, was opposing him on the main Uri-Muzaffarabad axis. Secondly, Leh and Kargil were vital objectives and would involve capturing and holding them. An advance to Leh may, therefore, have to be planned subsequent to completion of the primary task, namely, capture of Muzaffarabad and Domel. Insofar as Skardu was concerned, he could 'draw in his horns.' Until the major task was done, efforts had to be made to keep it going and succour could be provided.

The basic elements of the plan were:

(a) Raiders were to be driven out from the Valley.

(b) His biggest worry remained Skardu but he thought it would get solved as soon as the main objectives were cleared and then he could advance to capture it from Kargil and Gurais.

(c) He wanted to withdraw most of the troops from east of Kargil but kept the option of moving to Leh either through the surface routes or the air routes.

The plan that was worked out hinged on:

(a) Brigadier Katoch's (later Harbakhsh's) 163rd Brigade to climb over the Nastachhun Pass, capture Tithwal and continue the advance to Domel-Muzaffarabad astride the Kishan Ganga axis. That would happen on D-Day. This was expected to draw the enemy reserves.

(b) Brigadier LP Sen's 161st Brigade to advance to Domel-Muzaffarabad astride the main road Uri-Chakothi axis, starting 72 hours after 163rd Brigade.

(c) Brigadier H L Atal's para brigade, already in the process of joining him from Samba, to hold Uri and also support 161st Brigade, besides warding off the enemy attacks across and astride Haji Pir-Ledi Gali features in the south.

(d) As part of this offensive, the Punch Brigade was to advance to Bagh to provide him necessary flank protection.

The staff worked out an alternative and contingency plan for him that would cater for an offensive into the south and east. "Keep it handy," he told them. "No plans even in thin air have gone according to those initially laid. We have to continuously rehash our plans." It would happen without exception.

The operation began on 18 May with 163rd Brigade reaching the Nastachhun Pass by 21 May by which time Katoch, having fallen ill, was replaced by Harbakhsh. Some raiders who had got that far ran helter skelter. Two days later, Tithwal was captured. The expansion continued as 1st Sikh captured features of Points 7895 and 7802 on the west of Nastachhun. 1st Madras crawled up to Point 7229 across the Kishan Ganga and 3rd Garhwal having earlier taken Nastachhun Pass, remained at Tithwal. So on the 163rd Brigade front, the 1st Sikh provided great stability to the defences south of the Kishenganga by capturing Richmar Gali. North of the river line, the Feature 7229 and Ring Contour (near point 9444) had been captured with great sacrifices by the 1st Madras but they were finding it difficult to hold onto it due to lack of logistical support.

As battlefield commander, Thimayya was everywhere, more so at Harbakhsh's brigade now on a "wild goose chase," as he would call it:[12]

"It was in the early morning of the 19th May 1948, in the valley of Kashmir, when I was listening to a report from the Liaison Officer who had been with the forward troops during the night along the axis Handwara-Kupwara," recalled Harbakhsh, "that I noticed General Thimayya come up to the hill feature, Zechal-Dor which was my tactical headquarters for the operation and without disturbing me, he quietly sat on a boulder nearly 10 metres away from me ... He was there but did not wish to interfere with his subordinate commander. This gracious gesture on his part as a senior commander in the battlefield was rare in the Indian Army of the day. I have had experience of senior officers who preferred to conduct operations, and give

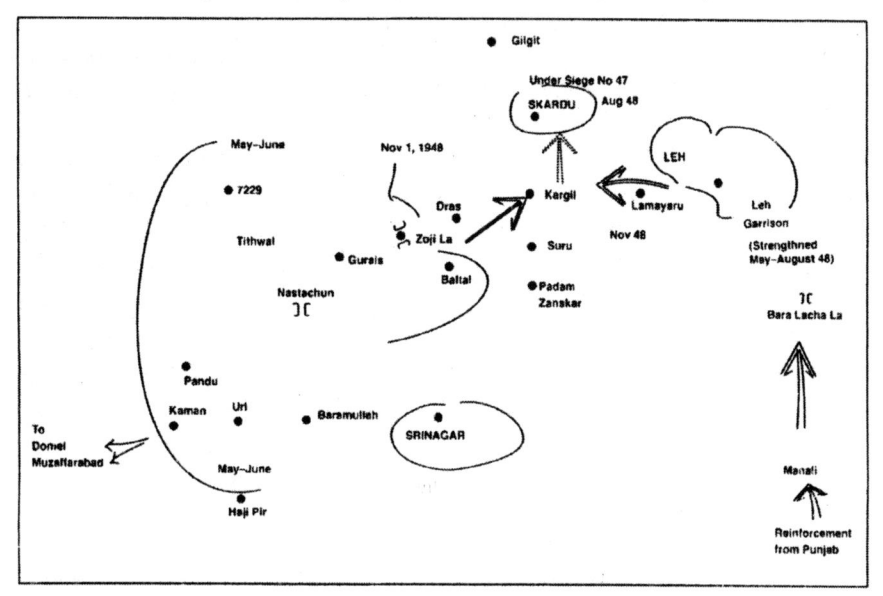

Map 5: Area of Operation of Sri Div – 1948 (Schematic)

tactical orders from the armchair of their centrally heated offices in Srinagar, rather than come up to the battle and see things for themselves."

General Thimayya had travelled nearly 32 km from his tactical headquarters at Baramula over an indifferent road. His goal was to give, by his presence, encouragement and confidence to the commander and his troops and to feel the pulse of the battle. After hearing from Harbakhsh about the progress of the operations and exchanging pleasantries with the men at headquarters, he left to visit the other part of the brigade operating in the area of Pahelgam.

Timmayya, in fact, was extremely worried about sending a brigade on an axis which was akin to a goat trail without any worthwhile logistical and gun support. He really suffered "doubts and anxiety," as Evans recorded, "about the fate of this force."[13] But the units and formations rose up to the challenge and got through the pass onto the Kishan Ganga.

He was again with Harbakhsh on 30 May, when 163rd Brigade was executing *Operation Surya*, the planned dash to Domel over the Richhmar Gali, west of Nastachhun.

The operations of 163rd Brigade made excellent initial strides and Tithwal was captured by 23 May, but then it slowed down, to the great relief of Pakistan. Harbakhsh, rather then make a dash to Domel, began to occupy half-way-house features, besides waiting for the jeep track to come up. No doubt, the airdrops were limited and the operational progress slow. Even Lord Birdwood observed: "Pakistan's situation was now grim, and had India only used air supply more agressively to maintain the impetus of this outflanking success, her forces would so severely have threatened Muzaffarabad as to force Pakistani withdrawal from the whole of the northern sector. Luckily for Pakistan, they paused."[14]

Sen's 161st had almost a whole Pakistani division against it. On the first day, the 2nd Dogras could reach only the ridge line based on the "Kaman post," on the Jhelum. Sen attributed this failure to a "poor calibred commanding officer." However, 4th Kumaon made steady progress by capturing up to line Pandu. When further advance towards Chakothi-Domel was opposed by at least two Pakistani brigades, Thimayya halted the advance and instead diverted his effort towards south. The 6th Rajputana Rifles and 2nd/3rd Gorkha Rifles captured the ridge line Kathi-Pirkanthi-Ledi Gali on the south of the Jhelum. Unfortunately, the operations of 2nd Madras (Para) to Haji Pir remained unsuccessful.

In the midst of operations, a personal tragedy struck Thimayya on 5 July. His younger brother, Major Somayya (Freddie), an officer of 2nd Bihar, then deployed at Pandu-Chhota Kazinag, had come down to Uri for a weekend. Uri then was a death trap as the withdrawing Pakistanis had left several booby traps and mines irregularly sown all over the area.

Freddie had a dog, which, one morning ran into one of these and was severely wounded and lay dying in the minefield. Freddie rushed into the minefield to rescue his dog. He too stepped on a mine and was instantly killed. The dog and his master, true to their fidelity to each other, could be retrieved only after some time. It was one of the saddest days for General Thimayya. He wrote a long letter to his mother, saying how proud he had felt due to Freddie being with him in the battle so far and how misfortune had befallen.

Controlling his grief and sorrow, while on a visit to Uri, Thimayya had said: "I have lost several sons and brothers, Freddie is yet another sacrifice for the defence of Kashmir." He had the body flown to Madikeri for burial. Among several messages of condolence which the family received, one was from Sardar Patel. He wrote to General Thimayya: "Your brother died for a noble cause, and that should be some consolation, if there can be any consolation while mourning the death of a brother while in the prime of life."[15]

Operation Summer Offensive had, limited success as Domel remained out of reach, from both north and west. His right hook landed at Pandu but Haji Pir remained with the enemy. The Tithwal expedition could have done better but for grave logistical problems and in the final analysis neither the 161st nor the 163rd could achieve the divisional objectives. Both made limited gains. The *Summer Offensive*, as Sen described it later, remained a "toothless offensive."[16] There were several reasons for this partially completed task: lack of resources; and, some of the battalion commanders not exerting themselves. Also the brigade commanders were being extra-cautious.

Thimayya's greatness now – as in the past – lay in his measuring up to adversities and challenges. He was not prepared to leave the heights that dominated the Uri bowl in the north and south and preferred at least to consolidate the possession tactically. It was the same on the Kishan Ganga front.

While Bucher had, indeed, a major role in this dubious game, Air Marshal TW Elmhirst would complement it. For, as late as 20 September 1948, he told Colonel SHFJ Manekshaw, MC, the Director of Military Operations that no reconnaissance could be carried out by the RIAF into Pakistan nor could they fly even close to the international border, except in POK. Group Captain Ranjan Dutt, commander No 1 Operational Group had instructions from his air chief that even disallowed attacks on Mangla, Kotli and Gilgit when the Pakistan Army was fighting a war inside J&K.[17]

If all this made the *Summer Offensive* a lost case, there was what Bogey Sen called "frustrating denial of encouragement and support" (p. 295), and the division was stifled by refusal of more formations." He considered Army Headquarters under Bucher to be responsible for it. Neither he nor Thimayya knew of the larger game behind all this.

Then came the UN enforced ceasefire, which Pakistan refused to accept. The Indian government regarded it as sacrosanct and instructed the field formations to take no fresh initiative, whereas Gracey and Tottenham continued their offensive. Pakistan's tail was virtually up after a mishap with 2nd Bihar and 1st Madras resulted in the loss of Pandu and Point 7229 north of the Kishan Ganga positions; certain deployment was also necessitated on the Richhmar Gali. "It has not led to any loss of morale; accept that such things do happen in war, but be prepared to win larger victories," Thimayya told the units whose morale had been somewhat shaken. But 'rockets' went to the commanding officers and brigade commanders whose troops manned Pandu and Kishan Ganga defences. "My report says, not only did the defenders abandon their positions without a fight but the reinforcement took their own time to come to the help of these posts,"[18] he wrote and demanded that such mistakes should not be allowed to recur. But there was no witch-hunting thereafter. With the resources available, Thimayya appeared content with the gains achieved.

Thimayya's priority was now focussed on the northern and eastern sectors for which he had identified four principal tasks: the capture of Gurais to eliminate any threat to the Valley from that direction; the securing of the Zoji La, and as much support to Skardu as possible; the relief of Leh, all of which had been under siege and holding out against great odds for six months; and the subsequent restoration of the Srinagar-Leh L of C.

The enemy, firmly seated over Zoji La, had also intruded into Dras and Kargil, to Lamayaru and the Zanskar Valley, *ipso facto*; he isolated and threatened Leh from the west. So Thimayya and Commodore Mehar Singh did the incredible feat of landing at Leh. The story merits recall.

The situation in Leh had become so precarious that it was a matter of touch and go. The only way Thimayya felt the situation could be resolved was by making the RIAF agree to do the impossible. He called Mehar Singh (Baba) to his headquarters and talked him into what was almost *hara-kiri*. Over strawberries and cream, Thimayya broached the subject of landing at Leh with Mehar. "Baba," he said, "You know I have some Dogra boys at Leh but they cannot hold on for too long. I want to take more boys there. The Leh polo ground is not too bad. It will be cleared if you make a trial landing."

"I am ready to go," said the flying Sikh without flinching, "but what of the Dakota? It has no de-icing facility or pressurisation."

"But I will go with you," said Thimayya. The thought of de-icing had evaporated from the minds of these two dare-devils, who had both been decorated with the DSO.

"Oh well," replied Mehar with a smile, "then we go."

On 24 May, while boarding the aircraft, Thimayya casually informed his staff that he was on a reconnaissance flight. Mehar Singh's radio report relayed the same information. Airborne, trouble soon began brewing over Zoji La and Fotu La. The Dakota, flying at 24,000 ft, suddenly began to lose height. Mehar wanted to turn the machine back, but Thimayya reminded him of his promise. Mehar heroically brought the aircraft under control and landed at Leh.[19] Having flown over an uncharted route and over some of the world's highest mountains, above 23,000 ft, landing on an 11,500 ft improvised landing strip was by itself a world record then.

On 30 and 31 May, six aircraft carried 35 well-equipped troops with their arms and ammunition for the defence of Leh. While Mehar Singh was telling his pilots: "You're lucky pioneers. Keep it up," General Thimayya gave the pilots a first salute and thanked them. To the Gorkhas he added, *Ayo Gorkhali*. It gave a marvellous thrill to both the Gorkha Johnnies and the pilots of the 12th RIAF Squadron which would continue to fly some 696 sorties to build up the garrison.

The 24 May flight to Leh opened the vital possibility of induction of more troops to Leh and their maintenance by air. He asked Cariappa to let him have more hill troops who could be easily acclimatised at the rarefied atmosphere of Ladakh. 2nd/8th Gorkhas, part of the 43rd Lorried Brigade in Punjab were ordered to move early, despatching one company at the earliest.

The battalion moved one company under Major Hari Chand on 28 May pioneering the rest of the battalion's 210 miles (336 km) expedition, humorously called *Chapathi*. Taking the Pathankot-Manali route, it crossed the 17,000 ft Baralacha La, reaching Leh only in early July. But the rest of the battalion would be warned to move in early August. (We will see more details on it subsequently.) Thimayya had, in fact, initially asked for the whole battalion but Bucher is said to have agreed initially to a company. In August too, only one more company was sent when Cariappa had ordered the whole battalion and told the HQ to confirm their arrival. Had the battalion arrived in July, as the rest of the company did, the overall effect would have been much better.

Gurais

By early August, Thimayya reorganised, and recreated two groups of assaulting forces. He tasked 77th Brigade to advance to Leh via Kargil; or if Leh holds, to advance to Skardu after the capture of Kargil. And the second force of a composite group of two battalions that had built up in the Valley, to clear the areas of Gurais. The two battalions were: 2nd/4th Gorkhas and 1st Grenadiers, both working under the Grenadiers commanding officer, being senior.

In the meanwhile, the motorable road up to Bandipur was planned to be extended to the Gurais Valley which was swarming with thousands of raiders. He planned to capture Rajdhan Pass, first, by 1st Grenadiers and then send 2nd/4th Gorkhas from the east over the rugged mountains. The sudden appearance of Gorkhas at Kanzalwan so panicked the Pakistanis that they bolted into the hills, abandoning their arms and ammunition. The battalions had only a few days notice but they did an excellent job and not only captured Gurais but held onto the pass, in the thick of the winter.

The Crisis of Leh

Operating from Gilgit (which had been built during the winter months as a forward base) the raiders advanced along the Indus Valley. Bypassing Skardu which had been invested since December 1947 but was still gallantly holding out, the Pakistani forces advanced into Ladakh and occupied Kargil and Dras early in May 1948, thus, paving the way for their coveted objective, Leh.[20]

This enemy force consisted of approximately four or five battalions of mixed Pakistan Army regulars, the so-called Azad Kashmir forces and tribesmen from the NWFP and Chitral. By the end of July, a brigade strength had arrived in the vicinity of Leh and established its headquarters at Kargil from which it could operate conveniently to the west of Zoji La, east to Leh and south to the Zanskar Valley. Simultaneously, it kept its supply route to Gilgit/Skardu open. The investment of Leh proper began early in July – the advance upon this fortress being along two routes – along the Indus and Shyok Valleys.

The arrival of the company of Gorkhas had improved the morale of the troops and militia under Major Prithi Chand, who had been in Leh since March. The Pakistanis had reached the outskirts of Leh and occupied piquets of varying strength all around the airfield, the strongest among them being around Tharu and Chiling, northwest of Leh. Gradually they built up regulars at Lamayaru, Nimu, the Nubra Valley, moving down to Padam in Zanskar. In Nubra itself, there were same 400 armed men of a Baluch Regiment; in Lamayaru, over 600; and on the outskirts of Leh at Chiling and Tharu, a battalion plus 500 to 600 guerillas under one Major Qureshi of the Pakistan Army.

The enemy attacked Tharu on 13 July but the attack failed. A second attack on 22 July could make no dent, although some invaders were seen in Leh itself. The last attack on Tharu came on 20 August, three days before Colonel Parab landed with his mortar platoon. The RIAF fighters also took on some opportunity targets. By the end of the month things began to look up. 5th/11th Gorkha Rifles was crossed into Suru Padam/Kargil Valleys to comb the area of the invaders. They killed some 400 of them.

2nd/8th Gorkhas, as mentioned, then part of the 43rd Lorried Brigade in Punjab, was first asked to send a company which it did under Major Hari Chand, but later the whole of the battalion was marching up the road-cum-route to Manali-Leh. It would fetch up in Leh only in September – just in the time of crisis. While the Gorkhas marched under the second-in-command, Colonel HS Parab was whisked away from his marching column from Pathankot with his platoon of 3 inch mortars and was at headquarters Sri Div by 20 August, where he was to be briefed by the GOC.

General Thimayya briefly described what was happening in Ladakh and then handed Colonel Parab his charter as *military governor* in Leh, giving him complete military, political and judicial authority over that area. He was to save Leh from the enemy, no matter what the cost; he was to be given absolute power to do his job and against his actions there would be no appeal. His charter was signed by Bakshi Ghulam Mohammed, then deputy prime minister (and subsequently prime minister) of Kashmir.[21]

In Leh, the Pakistani fifth column had succeeded in painting a very confused picture of enemy strengths and intentions – and in war nothing is more demoralising than confusion. Prithi Chand, in the absence of any agencies at his command, had been unable to make a clear appreciation of the situation and was undecided on his course of action – whether to go forward to meet the enemy or concentrate his forces for the immediate defences of Leh.

Leh, therefore, had begun to get more and more panicky, and in the absence of any social or political control, the situation was truly appalling. Upon the advice from Thimayya, Parab began a civic action plan. He made an English missionary, locally named "Driver," the prime minister; his wife, the health minister, and a Buddhist businessman named "Tunissia," the finance minister. The situation improved as this motley crowd of ministers moved with the swagger of Parab. "Short of turning yourself into a Ghenzis Khan," Thimayya told Parab, who seemed to be enjoying the job, "You've freedom of action. All I want is for you to destroy the Paki presence in the land of lamas." Parab assured him of his whole-hearted commitment.

The enemy at the gates of Leh was then planned to be liquidated or driven back to Baltistan.

The garrison strength comprised about 250 regulars and about 250 mixed militia men and armed civilians. This meagre force faced an enemy numbering well over 4,000 – of whom nearly 2,000 were actively engaged in investing Leh. Reports of build-up of a section of two 3.7 inch mountain guns were being received. In the meanwhile, Parab raised a company of guerillas for commando tasks.

When Thimayya met him on one of his flying visits to Leh, he explained the task further to Parab: "You now have some good strength. You should defend Leh as it is but the best form of defence is to be on the offensive. Harrass the enemy line of supply, raid his guns and mortars. Go for his mule columns. Starve him and he will run back, if he can, otherwise he'll die and vultures will feed on him."

Thimayya asked Parab to marshal as many riding ponies as possible and make his guerilla company mobile. And he advised him to call his force the "Leh Brigade."

"I'll ask the staff at HQ to include you in our orbat (the order of battle)."

Encouraged and emboldened, Parab was now a "Lawrence of Ladakh." Riding his charger, he was leading missions of his force against the Pakistanis who were struggling to survive without local support, amidst the vagaries of weather and terrain. Parab let it be known to the enemy, through agents, that all the IAF Dakotas, which were daily flying in with supplies and ammunition, were bringing fresh troops to Leh, and that the intention was to increase the garrison strength to a brigade, if not more.

By the end of September, Major W S Nene, the second-in command of 2nd/8th Gorkhas brought the battalion completing, thus, *Operation Chapathi*. Utilising the "Mongols" against the "Moghuls," as General Thimayya would say, the scene was set for Parab to make a final sweep of the invaders.

Then followed a raid by Parab at Lamayaru in early October, killing Pakistani muleteers along with 40 mules and capturing a prisoner. The Pakistani 3.7 inch howitzer at Bagso became the next target which was destroyed in a bold raid in September. A long story of exploits continued, which were fully supported by Thimayya. The rapidity of all the raids and attacks on the enemy's columns made one of them while vacating the Tharu position, pass a garbled message on the radio to the headquarters at Kargil: "*My brain does not function. The enemy is everywhere and means business every time. Wah Allah! You come and plan the attack yourself.*"

And individual acts of gallantry like that of Jemadar (later Colonel) Rinchin, the two Chands and others added to this chapter. So Leh was saved, but the link-up was yet to come.

Skardu: A Tragedy; A Dien Bien Phu

Skardu was already under siege and would remain so until the Pakistani Independence Day, 14 August 1948. From the first week of December 1947, Major (later Brigadier) Sherjung Thapa of 6th J&K Infantry kept at bay a vastly superior force with a handful of Sikhs, Dogra and Gorkhas of the Kashmir forces and carved a niche for himself in history.

The local Muslim population had already seized and appropriated the property of all 229 non-Muslims, who had sought refuge in the Skardu Fort. Subsequently, however, 41 Muslims including 22 prisoners joined the refugees. They also killed some of the non-Muslim government officials. Thapa, on taking over, readjusted his defences for a long protracted battle, although he always hoped that there would occur a link-up or a timely withdrawal.

Soon the Muslim deserters, along with thousands of others, began their attack on Thapa's position and laid siege, though the supplies continued to be air-dropped and fighter planes appeared whenever weather and other commitments permitted.

During February 1948, two reinforcement columns under Captains Probhat Singh and Ajit Singh added 160 more men to the garrison, improving the strength to 285. Concurrently, Thapa's garrison repelled the enemy attacks on 11 February with mortars and machine guns, and repeated the same in the first week of March. Thapa's men, imbued with a fine fighting spirit captured some weapons of the enemy too, but in the process seven were killed and 16 wounded. Thapa was also compelled to shrink in his garrison by abandoning Point 8853, which the enemy occupied.

Thapa then rightly pleaded for succour in reinforcement and logistics. It was agreed in principle that the State Forces alone would do that rather than regular forces, the same being committed for the coming operations. Upon arrival at Srinagar, Thimayya asked the State Forces, which had almost a brigade in Srinagar, to send relief columns post-haste. Three high powered relief columns were organised: one under Brigadier Faqir Singh of the State Forces, the second under Lieutenant Colonel Sampuran Bachan Singh, the former CO 1st Sikh, now liaison officer with the State Forces and the third under Brigadier Kirpal. Faqir, along with a company reached Thergo defile after one month, but as an enemy party ambushed part of his column, he retreated to Kargil.

By May things were again going from bad to worse and Thapa's message to Thimayya was desperate. "We will defend Skardu to the last round," it said, "provided we are saved from starvation." He asked for air strikes at Point 8853, besides supply airdrops. Thimmayya had supplies dropped and ordered air strikes at the Pakistani concentrations. But because supply drops were attempted from too high, most fell into the enemys' hands. Then small packets were dropped by fighter aircraft.

On 14 May, when deeply involved in the planning of the *Summer Offensive*, but trying to bolster Sherjung's morale, Thimayya's message read: "Your fine stand will be remembered as a landmark in the Kashmir campaign; continue as bravely as you have done so far. Recommending Naik Chatru for an immediate award." (M M Chatru attacked an enemy post near the fort and compelled it to withdraw). Even earlier, on 21 April, Cariappa praised Thapa and added, "Remember, you all are far superior to the enemy in every way. Expect reinforcement shortly."

Thapa continued to fight local actions gallantly although continuously requesting for reinforcements and supplies. It was not unusual to see signals coming, "We have done our task but no air force, no reinforcement for three months, no air strike."

Another effort was made to move a column under Lieutenant Colonel Sampuran

Bachan Singh, with a company of 5th J&K Infantry in May itself. Thimayya personally told him, "to make a supreme effort to save the garrison." This column also ran into the enemy and returned without a link-up. Not given to despondency, another attempt was made. A third column was pushed up in May itself under Brigadier Kirpal Singh of the State Forces. His force reached Mirpigund, a little short of Pirkuta where it was intercepted. It also retreated, in a rather disorganised manner. This time, the enemy became bolder. It pursued it in larger strength.

Skardu was now left on a limb with all its other lines of communications and logistics under Pakistani control. This shattered all hopes of a ground link-up and all that Skardu could hope for now was sustenance from the air or a full-fledged operation by the Sri Div. As the transporters could not fly, the air force used its fighters to drop survival rations. The link-up operation was given more thought and Thimayya was amenable to detaching a two battalion force under a senior colonel to finally rescue the besieged garrison. But as *Operation Summer Offensive's* success was more vital, the plan remained unexecuted.

As a last resort, it was thought that the Skardu garrison should be withdrawn to a base near Kargil. That possibility was, however, ruled out by Thapa himself. He had not only the combatants but civilians, the wounded and sick to be moved back through the enemy now in control of the route to Kargil. He suggested that he be allowed to fight out his battle. But he wanted regular supply of rations and ammunition, though his request for reinforcement never ceased; and like a good soldier, he assured his superiors that he would stick to his post.

Skardu was now virtually a sitting duck. An enemy attack came in on 16 June which Thapa's brave garrison repulsed. By 18 June, the enemy, reinforced with Chitralis, Gilgitis, Pakistan Army personnel, closed the noose. Colonel Shahzada Mate-ul-Mulk, the son of the Mehter of Chitral, asked Thapa over a loudspeaker to "surrender" or face "an all out attack." He had also sent a man with a white flag. Thapa returned a message: "Do not underestimate our resolve to fight it out."

The RIAF increased its attacks with rockets and 20mm guns on two consecutive days i.e. 20 and 21 June. But the enemy continued to shell the position intermittently. To replenish ammunition, Tempests dropped a small amount of .38 ammunition, 3 inch mortar bombs and 800 rounds of .303 ammunition. Two days later, on 30 June, the RIAF strafed the enemy position. Enemy pressure, however, continued. Occasionally, RIAF jets attacked them, and extended activity to Gilgit, destroying a wireless station there on 6 July. But air supplies dropped to only a kilogram where a quintal was required. Lack of supplies had reduced everyone to just one *chapathi* a day.

The enemy kept up the harassing attacks, attacking once more on 3 August. The RIAF was prompt to retaliate but the enemy was nevertheless able to close in during the night, and snipe by day. Personally, it was time to take a hard decision – to either withdraw the garrison or let it fight it out or let the commander decide! The signal

Thimayya addressed to Army Headquarters and Corps on 7 August not only showed his helplessness but self-admitting moral failure.

He said he had advised Thapa to withdraw as the whole force was on the verge of capitulation. Although he and Thapa were doing their best, it was impossible to continue to 'deceive' the garrison any longer. The signal read:

> August 7, 1948: TOPSEC HQ Sri Div (Main)
>
> To: JAK Corps; West Com
>
> Ind Army (MO/MI) (.) decided to ask Thapa to withdraw from Skardu on acct (account) of following reasons. alfa (.) apprehension on part of grn (garrison) cdr (commander) of mass desertion on acct of low morale (.) bravo (.) difficulty of maint (maintenance) of grn half-starved and practically of no amn (ammunition (.)Charlie (.) no prospects of relief (.)
>
> Secondly (.) have asked grn not to surrender without permission this hq (headquarters) pointing out danger of complete annihilation of grn and civilian refugees (.) have assured of reg (regular) maint through specially fitted Dakotas (.) impossible to continue to deceive grn any longer on false hopes of maint and relief (.) in case reg maint not possible in near future request permission be granted (for) withdrawal or surrender of grn.[22]

This made Cariappa consult General Sir Roy Bucher, who asked Air Marshal Elmhirst to employ fighter aircraft to save the garrison. All that happened was the usual delay in the use of the air and further enemy pressure from the ground. By 14 August, the post had been captured.

So ended this tragedy of Indian history, after a struggle of 285 days, by a brave garrison under Sherjung Thapa. Just for solace, compare it with the 143 days of Kut-Al-Amara (World War 1), 64 days of Kohima (World War II) and 890 days of misery of Leningard in World War II that killed over one million civilians.

Thapa is said to have met Thimayya soon after his repatriation to India. Thimayya told him that considering the feat, valour and bravery of his (Thapa's) men, he did not have the heart to give him the orders to surrender. However, Thimayya, in one of his messages to Army Headquarters, had specially mentioned the brave feat and had said that the sacrifice and gallantry of Thapa and his men had saved Ladakh for India. Thimayya reasoned and explained that being heavily overstretched during the J&K operations, the army did not have the strength to attempt to break the siege as had been done in the case of Kargil. "Perhaps that would have been possible if the garrison survived the winter of 1948," he had told not only Sherjung Thapa but also Cariappa, and continued to say so. It remained a deeply etched event in his memory as one more act of barbarity on the part of the invaders.

After the surrender, the Pakistanis started to indiscriminately kill non-Muslims, soldiers and civilians alike. After having killed 40 or so, they began to target the male

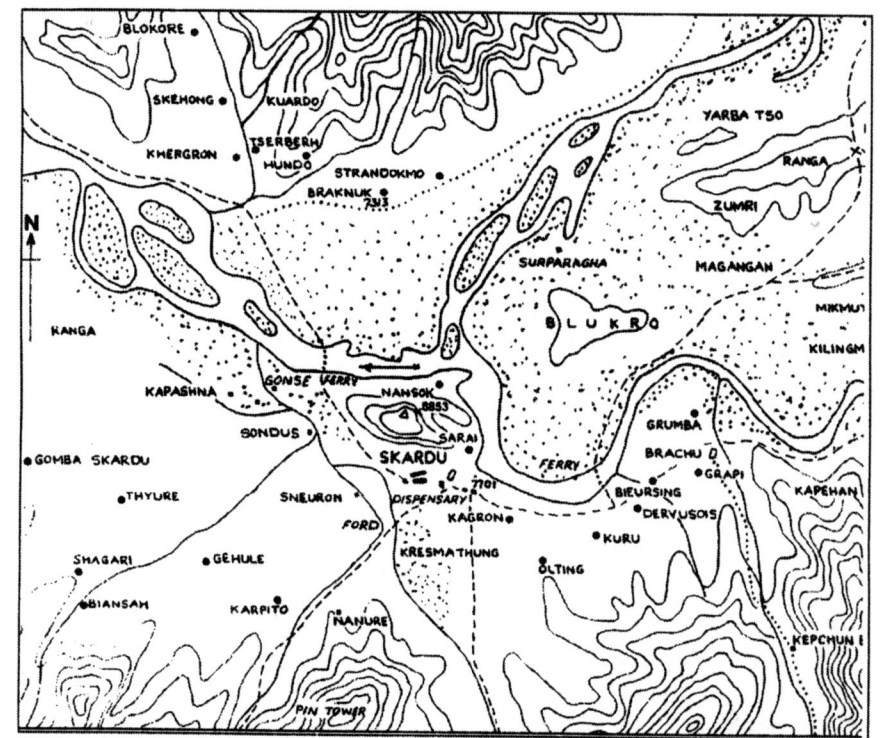

Map 6: Skardu and its Environs (Schematic)

Sikhs only. Among the unfortunates was Captain Ganga Singh, an excellent officer. The women who were spared were kept for other forms of bestiality. These hapless people suffered dishonour and humiliation. At the end of this savagery, the Pakistani megalomaniac commander's intercepted message had read: "All Sikhs killed, all women raped!"

Blitzkrieg at Zoji La Climaxes the Feat

By August, the overall situation in J&K was at a boiling point and Thimayya's angst for the areas east of Zoji La grew. The more he thought, the more anxious he became about Kargil and Leh, the two extremely important communication centres, across which stretched the 640-km-long Tibetan border. In the context of the overall long-term strategic consideration, the Srinagar-Dras-Kargil-Leh route linked the Indian subcontinent with Chinese Turkestan, via the Karakoram Pass. It had dominated the "Roof of the World" from time immemorial and its future importance needed no overemphasis.

The bottleneck of this critical axis was the 11,500 ft, over 3-km-long Zoji La (Pass), with rugged peaks and ridges. Soaring from 14,000 to 17,000 ft, its three dimensional sharp curving trails and many canyons with rocky, slippery gradients of 80 to 85 degrees could send a chill down the very bravest of spines! While ascent to the top of the feature on both sides of the deep gorge through which the jeep trail meandered on the right side was possible from the north, all other sides required the rock climbing ability of the mountain goat.

At Zoji La, the enemy occupied all the features dominating the axis from Matayan to the mouth of the pass, some of which came to be nicknamed as 'Chabutra,' 'Mukand,' 'North Hill' 'MMG Ridge', and so on.

In early August, 77th (Para) Brigade under Brigadier HL Atal was accordingly tasked to clear the pass as early as possible. Reconnaissance showed the enemy was well entrenched with machine guns, mortars and 6 pounder anti-tank guns to cover all approaches. As the battle commenced, own artillery fire, and fighter aircraft which were pressed into attacking the enemy, proved ineffective. The monsoon rains and moss on the rocks made any ascent time consuming. Foot patrols managed to clamber up the slope, but found themselves unsuccessful in closing with the defences. The first attack failed.

Atal attacked once more on 3 September and the attacking echelons comprising two battalions reached the top to discover the enemy had readjusted his position further back and to the flank. Besides, the troops were day-lighted. The second attack also proved the futility of a conventional attack even by the most determined and rugged Indian infantry. On reflection, Thimayya attributed these two failures to the inability of the assaulting troops to capture the objectives in the hours of darkness. It was further exacerbated by the lack of suitable areas for digging defences on the captured rocky outcrops. All the gains that the battalions made during the assault were lost as day broke and they became sitting ducks and had to pull back. Thimayya sent the 1st/5th Gorkhas to cross the Kot Kulan Gali on a wide flanking attack, but had to pull them back for lack of fire and logistic support.

He ordered a sand model to be prepared from the available maps and air photos, and then conducted a brainstorming session to which he called all his commanders, commanding officers, staff, the air force and the squadron commander of the armoured cars. Cariappa and Shrinagesh joined as observers. The results of the three-day-long tactical deliberations were mainly three: to ask for a parachute drop between Gumri and Matayan and combine this operation with a frontal attack from Baltal; or, to move the brigade through Suru-Kargil and then wheel major part of it west to capture Zoji La from the east; or to move a squadron of Stuart light tanks from 7th Cavalry undergoing maintenance, rest and refit after their 445 km of operations south of Pirpanjal.[23]

At the operational discussion itself Thimayya's military genius had found the answer to the Zoji La riddle – the use of armour. "I had only a few weeks before winter," said Thimayya "before the onset of winter and heavy snow. The plan of opening Zoji La had, therefore, favoured a *blitzkrieg*. The Germans did it in Europe, in better terrain. I needed to attempt it here."[24] Surprise became the keyword. Boldness became the motto. The tanks became the decisive factor for winning the war, the

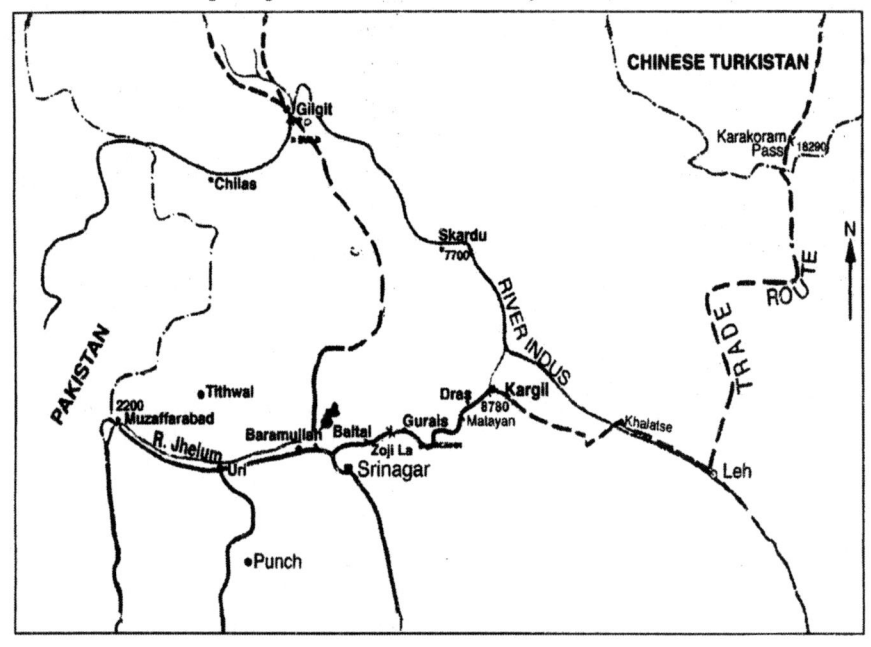

Map 7: Operation of the Battle of Zoji La (Schematic)

failure of which would be more cataclysmic than Skardu.

More discussion the following day saw Lieutenant Colonel Rajinder ("Sparrow") being called in for urgent discussions by Thimayya. On a reconnaissance of the Pass, Sparrow said that he could do it if the road was improved. The same day, the commander Engineers confirmed that his engineers would construct the road and make it fit for tanks. 13th and 433rd Field Companies (Madras Engineers) were on the move to Baltal. So, a foundation for the capture of Zoji La was laid, the most spectacular operation of the J&K campaign.

No battle like Zoji La had ever been fought even during World War II. The altitude, lack of communications, extreme weather conditions, all added to the difficulties of operating in the areas. Thimayya became the architect of the venture, to which Shrinagesh and Cariappa agreed.

The regimental headquarters and a squadron of tanks were moved from Jammu to Srinagar. A distance of 322 km was completed in five days. The tanks were dismantled and loaded as "water tanks" into larger vehicles; they were moved as part of a carefully organised convoy. The deception was an outstanding facet of Thimayya's ingenuity.

Another 80 km from Srinagar to Baltal took a night. No risk was taken with security. Srinagar and adjoining areas were placed under strict curfew. This kept many of the Pakistani spies and informers indoors and they were kept guessing. To keep the move secret, the turrets of the tanks were removed and vehicles had to be winched across light bridges. The turrets were carried in three-ton trucks and finally reassembled at Baltal, which became off limits to the unauthorised.

The *Tambis* of Madras Sappers did as large a wonder as the Sikhs of 7th Cavalry, under the very noses of the enemy observing from atop. They converted a 13.2 km jeep track into a road fit for tanks in about three weeks. Often the enemy opened up, but dauntlessly the men of 433rd and 13th Field Companies continued to work; they would later extend the road from Matayan to Dras, put up a bailey bridge at Pindras, and have the road ready by end October, by which time 682nd Field Company also joined.

Innumerable difficulties cropped up in 'engineering' the road and negotiating tanks on it. Sparrow was not sure if the tank engines could produce enough power in the rarefied atmosphere of Zoji La, or if they could negotiate the sharp gradient. The trial at Baltal showed that wooden chocks or blocks would be required to be placed behind the moving tanks to prevent rollback. The negotiation of hairpin bends was another problem; one skid would take the tank and the crew to their sure deaths thousands of feet below. Another fear was that the enemy may have mined the track with explosives and anti-tank mines or would do that just before the move. So both secrecy and engineering effort to see the plan through were necessary, including continuous, harassing artillery fire and occasional air strikes. Fortunately, the engineers did a marvellous job in widening and reinforcing the shoulders of the narrow trail. It was all done without the use of explosives – just with field kits and often with bare hands.

A trial run by one tank in conditions of blizzard and minus $20°F$ temperature was attempted. It took eight hours for the first 5 km; the rest took as much time, though the last part to Gumri had to be left out due to the secrecy of the plans.

The plan envisaged tanks leaving the start point at 10 a.m., preceded by two infantry companies on mortar carriers to test the ground. The tanks were to clear the enemy line of communications, establish a fire base at Gumri, where the infantry was to 'marry up' for providing close infantry support to the tanks. Then the entire 77th Brigade was to move after dark and mop up the enemy at Gumri and capture the high ground.

After two delays on 21 and 25 October, providentially it snowed on the last acceptable day for the operations – 1 November. It served both strategic and tactical causes well: the enemy commanders and their British bosses had written off any operation now; and the Pakistani troops freezing in their "boots and bottoms," as General Thimayya humorously put it, saw the beginning of "this winter vacation begun."

Serbjeet Singh, the famous painter and documentary film-maker, who stood at the starting point of the operation to capture Zoji La, recalls in his *Zoji La, 1st November 1948*: "A visionary in more ways than one, Thimayya realised the importance of a visual record of the history of those tumultuous times... It was a gray morning on 1st November 1948 as we assembled at the jeep head at Zoji La. A report was received from the air force meteorological officer forecasting a snow storm. Thimayya paused for a while as his commanders looked anxiously at his face. Soon he turned to them and pronounced, 'to hell with a meteorological report! We will join the battle. It is now or next year."

Not that the weathermen were wrong. It began to snow soon and later a blizzard raged. But had he dithered, a ceasefire might have been enforced, with Sri Div wringing its hands at the base of Zoji La, while the Pakistanis controlled every thing east of Baltal. It would have been a sheer disaster.

The tanks (Thimayya in the lead tank) broke through without difficulty, creating a terrifying echo over the rarified air of Zoji La. The brigade which was to move by night, reached Gumri in daylight. These tanks disorganised the enemy position allowing the infantry to follow and mop up. By 2 p.m., they were at the Gumri Basin.

As the tanks churned and moved forward firing their guns, the sound echoing and re-echoing through the pass, the Pakistani commander panicked and reported on the wireless set about the advancing tanks. Confused and deafened, the enemy commander reported the situation as something big and horrendous building up against him.

"The enemy may be using high explosives to improve the road," he was told.

"But I can see the T-16 carriers which look like tanks," he said. He was instructed to check again and hold fast, until the tanks were really on his 'top.' An intercept:

> Headquarters at Skardu/Kargil: We have told you there are no (repeat, no) tanks in the area... They may be jeeps camouflaged as tanks ... it is impossible for tanks to move on this track.. Roger so far, over.
> Local commander: Roger, but believe me they are tanks. I see with my own eyes.
> Headquarters: You are tired, hallucinated... order from commander, hold your position, over.
> Local commander: (keeps silence in disgust but adds) Nothing heard... Sorry all over again.
> Headquarters: Come in again. What's the matter with you.
> Local commander: Over, over, all over (silence as the tanks were firing.)

The plan continued to be changed. Thimayya always asked his commanders and troops to accept this as "part of the ever changing mosaic of war." "No plan survives the first contact with the enemy," he would replicate the words of Napoleon. As the enemy bolted out of 'Mukund' and 'Chabutra,' the Patialas just mopped up. At Gumri, to which the attacking force advanced straight, the 1st/5th Gorkhas swerved to the rear of the enemy and then attacked it, along with the Patiala and the Rajputs assaulting frontally. In fact, that became just an 'exercise' as the enemy fled in panic. Machoi was taken by the Patialas which captured it along with its artillery pieces.

"From now on it was just a case of speed to prevent the enemy from reorganising and holding up our advance," wrote Thimayya in his "lessons," that he compiled at the end of war. And he continued to expand the theme. "The enemy made one attempt to hold us at Batkundi, where he held a strongly entrenched position on a precipitous feature which covered the exit from the Matayan plain. This involved a brigade attack and then there was a through run to Kargil."

Matayan, 18 km from Zoji La, fell to the 4th Rajputs on 4 November. The Patialas secured Dras by 16 November to celebrate victory on the holy birthday of Shri Guru Nanak. The brigade captured Kargil on 23 November, when Parab's guerillas and marauders also linked up from Leh. It was a great show, under a great commander.

Thimayya would pass on the lessons of the campaign learnt. They were almost universal: occupy heights in defence, do not let the enemy dominate or surprise you, rely on intercepts and cultivate sources; capture the enemy's base; keep force available to pursue the enemy; have a deception plan; give 'Q' (administrative branch) early planning time. His suggestions for improvement consisted of better clothing, equipment, footwear, headwear and puff tents. And his best point was more specific: "Never commit troops to uncharted ground."[25] Lead by example was what he was proving.

After the operations, Thimayya whole-heartedly praised the "fine operational role" of each major unit as well as the lesser units. About Major Thagaraju and his Sappers, he said they had tackled a "clearly impossible task and established a record." Any one could be proud of this feat by the *Tambis*, but the inspiration came from the enthusiasm and infectious optimism of their GOC. Each unit was so motivated that it took the task as a competition.

"Working at temperatures below 20° F," said Major (later Major General) Niranjan Khullar, the brigade major to Atal, "was by itself a test of physical fitness; it was equally a resolve to survive and succeed."[26]

His praise for Lieutenant Colonel Narain Singh, RIASC Battalion, was as lavish as his praise for the commanding officers of the arms. He wrote, "Your last feat will go down in the history of your Regiment and the Indian Army. You supported and maintained 77th Parachute Brigade in their push from Zoji La to Kargil. Both men and animals were tested with extreme hardships, and you carried out your tasks successfully."

To the commanding officers of 17th Para Field Regiment, the J & K Mountain Battery 11th Field Regiment, who occupied the highest gun positions at 11,533 ft, his praise was unbounded. "Even Napoleon Bonaparte, a good gunner himself, would have envied you all," he wrote.

Thimayya was from the school which taught him what Field Marshal Lord Wavell had observed, "*A bold general can be lucky but no general can be lucky unless he is bold.*" He believed in doing things. Luck would help, as it had so far, and would in the future.

The Divisional Ski School
Thimayya was a thinking general. The snow of Kashmir that covered the hilltops and vales – 40 ft of snow in a continuous fall of seven to 10 days – made Thimayya

wonder why it could only be utilised for sporting events. Surely, it could be used in training for high altitude warfare for officers and men operating in the north.

In a letter to the director of Military Training, he contended: "India may or may not join any Power Bloc but we cannot afford to lag behind in training and equipping our army on modern lines. Besides this, we have to defend an undefined and undemarcated sprawling border in the north stretching from Assam to Gilgit, passing over one of the highest mountain ranges in the world. India is in dire need of at least one 'Alpine' Division equipped with modern weapons and equipment and trained in snow warfare. The fact cannot be over-emphasised."

He also forwarded an outline plan to open an Army Ski School to train army personnel in snow warfare with the help of experts from Switzerland, Norway and France. For lack of funds and certain other technical difficulties, the Army Headquarters were not able to implement the scheme, though it was accepted in principle.

Thimayya, however, started the Division Ski School in Gulmarg that winter on a small scale. Skis and other equipment were loaned from the Ski Club of India (which had not been functioning since the winter of 1946-47). Since there were many limitations like paucity of skills, funds, etc, each course had to be limited to a small number of students. This then laid the foundation of the Army's High Altitude Warfare School (HAWS) Gulmarg.

The Image

Thimayya's *joie de vivre* has been aptly recorded by Dr Karan Singh.[27] "Dashing and witty Divisional Commander General K S Thimayya... Timmy was in great form and exuded charm and charisma. He was adored by his troops and also very popular with the civilian administration..." He goes on: "Timmy was in high spirits, driving our jeep himself, regaling us with graphic details of the battles fought to free the areas from invaders only a year ago...The cordiality between the army and civilians was also impressive..." And, "Later we did a similar trip across Zoji La where in *a historic manoeuvre easily compared with Hannibal's crossing his elephants over the Alps, Timmy had taken tanks for the first time in human history to such heights and routed the startled invaders.*"

He was prepared to take calculated risks, his limitations in resources, notwithstanding. Flexibility, both of plan and manoeuvre, were his undiminishing assets and an indispensable part of his generalship.

Timmy was fortunate in having some of the finest brigade commanders – Sen, Harbakhsh, Atal, Parab – all on the ball. Then there was Candeth, the artillery brigade commander, and Shergill, the CO of 7th Cavalry. The list is endless. He was equally lucky in having reputed battalions with World War II reputations. However, he was well aware that the junior officers needed more command experience, boldness and mental flexibility.

There was official recognition by his admiring superiors – Lieutenant Generals SM Shrinagesh, GOC J&K Corps and KM Cariappa GOC-in-C Western Command.

Shrinagesh evaluated Thimayya thus:, "A first class divisional commander who has genuine interest and knowledge of humanity. Has fighting will to win. A good judge of character with real affection for troops under his command, with knowledge of tactics and topography... I have great confidence in his ability. Popular with all, including civil administration."

Cariappa, as GOC-in-C Western Command fully endorsed the corps commander's assessment. He advised Thimayya to "guard against over-optimism over practical reasonableness." He saw him take "considerable interest in the welfare of his command and commanding a happy division." He wrote further: "He had a difficult task in Kashmir Valley which he successfully carried out through his energy, common sense, and determination. A very popular officer. Of sound military knowledge.. Very good all round officer."[28]

The war over, with the demarcation of the CFL and the presence of the UN observer (for India and Pakistan), and Kashmir began to acquire a semblance of its pristine beauty. "The Vale of Cashmere," its placid lakes, flowering gardens, the valley of emerald green, with towering snow-clad mountains, evoked a boyish excitement in Thimayya. He was often on the ski slopes of Gulmarg, trekking and rock climbing. He would visit troops as often as possible, sometimes with Nina, who had joined him.

Then a sudden illness!

He would land up in a hospital, recover and then be back on his job. He was posted to the Armed Forces Academy cum-National Defence Academy, the ideal place to recoup his energies after a gruelling 30 months of active service. And though he was evacuated to the hospital, he dictated long letters to his PA (who moved with him) to the brigade headquarters and commanding officers for all major units, the gist of which was: "You have proved yourself brave, offensive and done everything – every task with success. I have come to love and admire you. Shall remain grateful to you, for you all did to make Sri Div a fighting division." ∎

NOTES

1. See Ch. VIII, *War & Diplomacy in Kashmir 1947-48*, quoting the minutes of conference.
2. *Government of India Operations*, pp. 83-85, Also see Ch. 7, *Carippa...* Nehru note of 19 December in *Selected Works* Vol 4, pp. 375-78.
3. *Integration of Indian States*.
4. *Selected Works*, Vol 4, pp. 375-78.
5. *Thimayya of India*, p. 264.
6. *Raiders in Kashmir*, p. 99.
7. Top secret telegrams of 26 March 1947 from Shone to CRO. Quoted by Dasgupta, p.147, f.n. 10. Even Akbar says, at pp.102-104 that about a brigade worth troops were already located

there. So does Sen highlight it in *Slender was the Thread*.
8. Tottenham had commanded 81st African Division in Burma and was rated as a good battlefield commander of World War II. Also see *Operations in Jammu & Kashmir 1947-48*, GOI, *Cariappa* (Chapter 7).
9. Earlier, as mentioned, Auchinleck had issued 'stand-down' instructions to all the British officers of both the dominions, restraining them from joining either Indian or Pakistani forces in their conflicts that were ensuing. Lockhart, in dissuading Nehru from taking action in Junagadh, J & K and Hyderabad, had represented to Nehru that the British on the roll of both these armies were on a 'single list.' This policy was surreptitiously changed by the British for Pakistan, where Gracey used it to its full advantage. (NMML, New Delhi.)
10. To begin with, it was called J&K Corps; later V, and subsequently XV. Located at Udhampur; later Srinagar.
11. Courtesy Major General Surendra Shah, VrC, GOC 19th Infantry Division. See Appendix at the end of the chapter.
12. From letters of General Harbakhsh to author, dated 15 January 1999.
13. n. 5, p. 268.
14. *A Continent Decides* (quoted from Amrinder Singh's *Lest We Forget*, p.70).
15. From personal records.
16. Sen, n. 7, ch.19 ("An Offensive Without Teeth").
17. From official records. Even Lieutenant General Wilson hints at it when he says Roy Bucher made considerable efforts to contain the "fire from spreading in the J&K." "Problems: The Truth," *USI Magazine* April-July 1997.
18. It was established that in the case of Pandu, the enemy had been trying to capture it over three nights, and the post was not reinforced. Instead, reserves were allowed to remain at Uri who could not reach the area when the enemy finally assaulted. In the case of Pt 7229, the basic tactical error was allowed to go unchecked. This feature was dominated by a higher feature in the immediate vicinity which was left unoccupied and one night the enemy made it a firm base for attack on Pt 7229.
19. See *Cariappa: His Life & Times...* chapter 7 (Indian Army on Trial).
20. Major (later Major General) O S Kalkat was the brigade major of the Gilgit Brigade before the Partition. In his memoirs – and repeated in a letter to the author in 1982 – he said: "A confidential letter from General Messervy C-in-C Pakistan Army to my commander, Brigadier C P Murray had been erroneously (or out of curiosity) opened by me. It had said unambiguously that Pakistani Armed Forces abetted by tribal raiders would attack Kashmir from north and west and he should be prepared to plan and organise it on as large a scale as possible. I was in Gilgit and reached Delhi, where I told S Baldev Singh and later Nehru about the impending Pakistani plans. But apparently it was not taken seriously in 1947."
21. From Thimayya Papers, containing the report of Colonel Parab. Thus, Parab became the first military governor from the Indian Army. Others who followed in his footsteps were: Major General J N Chaudhuri (Hyderabad) Major General Candeth (Goa).

22. From records in Historical Division of MOD.
23. From *We Lead – 7th Light Cavalry 1784 -1990*.
24. n. 5, chapter XVII.
25. Ibid., pp 52 and 53, and records of Sri Div.
26. War Diaries of the Brigade.
27. *Heir Apparent* (Oxford Press, 1982) p105.
28. The assessments purported to the period May 1948-December 1948. The quality of evaluation shows the inability of the officers of that time to gauge operational successes, then demonstrated qualities and potential for higher command and leadership. And then Cariappa and Bucher were niggardly in recognition of Timmy's generalship, leadership and the larger influence of his dynamic personality. While he deserved a very high award, both military and civil, they awarded him a Mentioned-in-Despatch for the J&K Operations.

Appendix

Appreciation of the Situation by Major General K S Thimayya – Commander Srinagar Division made at Srinagar on May 13, 1948.
(As Originally Written)

Object

1. To drive the raiders out of my area of responsibility and then to prevent them from reentering Kashmir territory.

Factors

2. *Enemy Tactics.* He has concentrated a strong force on my main line of advance which is the Uri-Domel Road and is operating in small bodies of troops along all the approaches to the Kashmir Valley from the West and North.

Deduction

3. He is obviously trying to make me dissipate my strength so that I should not be able to put in a major thrust whereas he will concentrate a strong force to penetrate the Kashmir Valley.

4. *Topography.* The country adjoining the Kashmir Valley is very mountainous with very definite lines of approach into it, either along rivers or mountain passes. He is using these definite lines of approach and on approaching the edge of the Valley, he fans out into small parties and operates on a wide front making it difficult for me to destroy him.

    (a) *In the North.* He is based on Gilgit from where he comes down to Skardu and from there he advances down to Kargil and Leh. He is also using the Burzil Pass from where he has moved to Kargil and Gurais.
    Deduction. I must hold Kargil and Gurais and if possible operate towards the Burjil Pass.

    (b) *In the West.* He is based in Muzaffarabad and Domel from where he enters Kashmir territory along the Kishan Ganga River to Tithwal and Keren and along the Jhelum River to Garhi and then to Uri and Bagh respectively.
    Deduction. I must secure the bridges over Kishan Ganga and Jhelum Rivers at Muzaffarabad and Domel.

    (c) *In the South.* There are lines of approach from vicinity of Poonch (Punch) towards Gulmarg and Pir Panjal Pass.
    Deduction. I must watch these approaches and if the enemy uses them for an advance I must be able to destroy him.

5. *Maintenance*

    (a) It is impossible for me to maintain the garrison at Skardu due to the difficult terrain, lack of mules and porters, lack of purchase, impossibility of air supply and my inability to protect the L of C against enemy action.

    (b) Similar difficulties will arise if I try to garrison Gurais, so I must limit my operations to Tragbal, until a jeep track is constructed and I can avoid having to use more troops in protecting a long and hazardous administrative tail.

(c) Operations towards Tithwal will have to be maintained by mules and porters until a jeep track is made. Air supplies will have to be arranged in case there is delay in this advance. Beyond Tithwal I understand the enemy are in the process of making a road.

(d) Operations towards Domel along the main road may be delayed in case bridges on the road are blown and, therefore, air supply will have to be arranged.

Deductions.

(i) I must withdraw all troops beyond Kargil where I will form a base.

(ii) I will control my operation towards Gurais from Tragbal in accordance with the construction of the jeep track.

(iii) I can risk operations towards Domel and Muzaffarabad owing to the availability of air supply, if road supply becomes impossible.

6. *Morale.* From all accounts received from our agents and the enemy's reluctance to face an encounter and due to the heavy casualties incurred by them in Jhangar and the previous fights at Uri, I consider that the enemy's morale is low. On the other hand our troops are in very high spirits and have found the measure of the enemy.

Deduction. I must use this state of affairs to launch an offensive quickly and boldly.

7. Relative Strength

Area	Enemy	Own Troops Plus Two J&K State Battalions
Leh, Skardu, Kargil, and Gurais area	500 tribesmen from Gilgit with an equal number of deserters from J&K State forces. Expecting further reinforcements from Gilgit. All well armed with rifles and automatics and some mortars	Spread out between Skardu, Kargil, and Sonamarg. One infantry battalion to boost up the above Operations from Sonamarg. one infantry battalion in the Bandipur area operating towards Gurais.
Keren, Tithwal and Handwara area	1,200 Mahsuds, Swatis and Pakistan Ex-Army personnel well armed with rifles, automatics and some mortars.	One infantry brigade of three battalions and two companies J&K Militia. Two batteries of artillery one squadron armoured cars.
Domel, Uri, Mahura, Baramula area	Two brigades, one based on Chinari operating forward to Uri and the other on Domel operating towards Chinari. Two gun areas reported in Chinari.	Two infantry brigades based on the Uri-Baramula area. Two squadrons armoured cars. Three batteries artillery.

Area	Enemy	Own Troops Plus Two J&K State Battalions
Bagh and Poonch (Punch) area	Two brigades, one around Poonch (Punch) and one in Bagh.	One infantry brigade containing the enemy around Punch

Deduction. I can only contain him on my northern flank as I have no effective striking force. I can hit out in the direction of Tithwal and Domel, but must be prepared for an offensive by the enemy on my southern flank from Bagh.

8. *Time and Space*
   (a) In the Northern Sector, as the snow melts, more tracks will become available to the enemy and he will be able to "build up" in the Kargil and Gurais area. I must, therefore, try and establish my bases there as soon as possible I can achieve this soonest in the Kargil area by pulling in my horns from the Skardu area, any attempt on my part to depend on the one battalion now advancing towards Sonmarg will cause great delay due to the long difficult L of C and the "turn round."
   (b) In the west, the further I advance, my L of C becomes extended and thereby more vulnerable whereas that of the enemy shortens and enables him to reinforce his forward troops. Any offensive I put in must be done with speed and I must have sufficient forces in reserve to keep up the momentum of the attack.

Courses Open

9. To The Enemy
   (i) To carry on guerilla tactics on all fronts. To make me dissipate my troops and thus force me to remain on the defensive.
   (ii) In addition to (i) above, he may concentrate a strong force in the Chinari and Bagh area and put in a strong encircling movement on my Southern flank and thus force me to withdraw to the edge of the Kashmir Valley.
10. *To Me.* There is only one course open to me and that is to contain him in the north where his L of C is long and difficult, and attack his main concentrations on the Uri-Domel Road and capture his main L of C over the Jhelum and Kishan Ganga Rivers at Domel and Muzaffarabad. To maintain a reserve in hand of at least one brigade for any enemy offensive towards my southern flank. After completing the above operation to attack and destroy the enemy on my southern flank if he has not withdrawn as a result of my offensive. Finally, to push the enemy from my northern flank in the direction of Gilgit and Skardu operating from bases at Kargil and Gurais.
11. *Intention.* To contain the enemy on my Northern flank and to advance and capture the bridges at Domel and Muzaffarabad

Right	163 Brigade Group (Katoch)
	TASK: Capture Tithwal and continue advance on completion of Jeep track from Solur to Tithwal.
	D. Day 17/18 May.
Left	161 Brigade Group (Sen)
	Task: Capture Chinari, Garhi and Domel.
	D.Day. 20/21 May.
Res	77 Para Brigade
	Tasks: (i) Hold a firm base at Uri and he prepared to operate behind 161 Brigade to maintain the momentum of the attack.
	(ii) Be prepared to operate against any enemy advance from the southern flank.
Poonch (Punch) Brigade	To carry out a battalion operation in the direction of Bagh with the object of preventing the enemy withdrawing from there and reinforcing the defence along the Uri-Domel road.

12. *Plan.* Withdraw all troops beyond Kargil and establish a firm base there using Patiala based on Sonamarg to protect and maintain the L of C from Srinagar to Kargil.

1 Grenadiers based on Bandipur to operate towards Gurais and establish a base there when the jeep tracks are completed from Bandipur to Gurais.

Advance on Muzaffarabad and Domel with two brigades.

8
Interlude
(1950-1952)

Adding to His Image

An interlude of two years between May 1950 and May 1952 served for Thimayya as a period of alternating between miracles and the moral high ground. He had been through World War II under the British and had risen from being a virtual non-entity to a hero whose brilliance had continued to shine through the holocaust of the Partition and Pakistani invasion of Jammu & Kashmir. He was a miracle man, a leonid that appears, so astronomy says, rarely.

In the interlude, he was appointed initially as commandant of the National Defence Academy (NDA) and subsequently as the quarter master general (QMG) at the Army Headquarters.

In his third year in Jammu & Kashmir, Thimayya was in his forty-fourth year. It was March 1950. Young and adventurous, he was climbing mountains beyond 16,000 ft (4,877 m), pioneering skiing in the Killenmarg heights, trekking up the steep gradients of Khardung La, flying over the Karakoram Pass, Khurnak Fort and across the Aksai Chin, then still a distant dream to the People's Liberation Army. The region was tranquil but the terrain vast, uncompromising and exasperating.

During the conduct of the operations from Pandu to Tangdhar, Zoji La to Leh, he was everywhere. Officers and men, much younger than him, were finding it difficult to stick around against the vagaries of terrain and climate of northern Kashmir and Ladakh; and some of them had been evacuated to lower heights and hospitals. But he was in the forefront, advising commanders, bucking up the weaklings and the underdogs. He would hold the hands of those faltering and pull them through along with those stout hearts and bodies. While already a hero to his officers and men, he would spur their fighting spirit and sustain their sense of what he would surprisingly call, "spiritualism," by appearing at places least expected and hazardous – especially where a situation could be turning nasty, where commanders needed direction and troops, resoluteness. When, for example, a Pakistani brigadier threatened the 1st Sikh guarding Richhmar Gali and had the temerity to say he would present it to Pakistan as an Id present, he visited them during the battle. And as the Sikhs knocked the hell out of the enemy, he told the subedar major: "*Sahib*, now you can send the Pakistanis some *kara prasad.*"

And, as if to control his breath, and share the discomforts of the troops, he would sit down on a rock to see how the battle was developing, ignoring the *gola-goli* (shells and bullets) that would keep the lesser souls behind cover.

Leading from the front was his motto and life-long principle. He expected others to devise their own concepts and styles; every nuance was acceptable to him, as long as the mission did not fail. "Use any initiative," he would repeatedly tell everyone "to make a success of it." He was himself setting a pioneering pace. He was generally satisfied with the way the operations progressed, albeit, failure at Skardu continued to trouble him. He realised something more could have been done to save the garrison.

Throughout 1949, there were violations of the CFL and several 'communications' came to his office from Lieutenant General M Delovie, the commander of the UN Observer Group for India and Pakistan, He would often call Pakistani Major General Nazir Ahmed, GOC, Pakistan Army in POK to 'flag meetings' and ask him to refrain from violating a mutually accepted CFL. "You and I look after what has fallen as our share," he would appeal to the better military sense of Nazir. "Let our leaders decide upon a course best suited now. And we on our part keep peace here."

In the UN, the battle for vacating the Pakistani aggression as an essential precondition for plebiscite and subsequent withdrawal of Indian troops assumed the form of a ding-dong battle, the ding-dong being replicated astride the CFL. While Pakistan was further fortifying POK by raising the so-called Azad Kashmir forces, some consolidation was also evident on the Indian side. For, within a year of the ceasefire, the Udhampur based JAK Corps had become 5th Corps, being finally a forerunner to the current 15th Corps.

Earlier, in the preceding week, he had been busy in delineating the Line of Actual Control with his Pakistani counterpart. A UN-enforced ceasefire had been prevailing since January when the UN Observer Group for India and Pakistan consisting of members from Argentina, Belgium, Columbia, Czechoslovakia and the US, were in location, supervising the uneasy truce.

It was then that a 'flag meeting' was arranged by the UN Observer Group at Chakothi, 80 km from Muzaffarabad, where the Indian and Pakistani officers met in an atmosphere of what Germans call – *Kreig ohne hass*, an ambience of no malice. While the officers hugged, embraced and warmly shook hands with each other, with much laughter, the men who accompanied them exchanged notes about old times. Ram Singh, his old faithful, who had carried his cooked meal, shared it with a Pakistani soldier from his home town, Sonepat. So while Ram Singh exchanged views with his one time neighbour of Sonepat about the quality of buffalo milk, the officers indulged in light-hearted banter regarding a lady news announcer of All India Radio! This *bonhomie* between the two enemies whose guns on the heights across the Jhelum river were fully deployed against each other, greatly surprised the UN observers.

The shedding by India and Pakistan of dominion status saw a new secular republic in Delhi; while the one in Rawalpindi, a Muslim republic, was strengthened, especially after the demise of Jinnah. This appeared to reinforce the Pakistani will to call Kashmir a case of "historical grievances," the "core issue" between the two countries, and so on, and keep the guns booming in one form or the other.

The transformation of India as a 'republic' had large ramifications, both political and military. For the latter, it was the eventual "burial of the stuff royal," Thimayya would jocularly say. For those who were nostalgic about the prefix "Royal" such as in Royal Indian Navy, Royal Indian Air Force, Royal Artillery, Royal Sikhs, Garhwal and Gorkhas, etc, it was a sentimental day. To Thimayya, it all meant the final and ultimate stage of becoming fully Indianised in just three years as against the fifteen that the Nationalisation Committee, of which he had been a member, vouchsafed. And his own Hyderbad Regiment was now the Kumaon Regiment.

The reputation of General Thimayya as an officer and gentleman, a fine general and a rising star spread throughout the Indian Army. While his own regiment appointed him as its Colonel of the Regiment, there were others who 'pitched in' their request. Colonel AD Iliff, commandant, Indian Grenadiers Regimental Centre, Nasirabad, asked if he would accept the colonelcy of the Grenadiers. He offered his regret saying, "Once a Grinder, always a Grinder. Wouldn't the Kumaonis and the Grinders clash?"[1]

The 4th Prince of Wales Gorkhas Lieutenant Colonel NK Lal requested Thimayya to take over from Major General Sir AM Mills, CB, DSO. He politely refused.[2]

In one of the grateful acts to honour soldiers, the Indian government instituted the award of Param Vir Chakra (PVC), as a worthy successor to the Victoria Cross (VC), and its first awardee became Major Som Nath Sharma of 4th Kumaon, (the former 8th/19th Hybd) on 26 January 1950. Thimayya wrote to Major General AN Sharma, the father of Som Nath, (and now director general, Medical Services): "As Colonel of the Regiment I would like to convey my congratulations on the highest award being granted to your son. This has raised the morale of the whole regiment. Major Sharma's act will go down in the history of the Indian Army as one of the regiment's greatest achievements."[3]

There was another personal event for him and all officers, borne on the strength of the Indian armed forces: the signing of the new Form of Affirmation, a new paradigm of fidelity to the Constitution of India. He signed it on 7 February 1950:

No A I 944. (Rank) Maj Gen (Name) KS Thimayya. I do solemnly affirm that I will bear true faith and allegiance to the Constitution of India as by law established and that I will, as in duty bound, honestly and faithfully serve in the Regular Army of the Union of India and go wherever ordered by air, land or sea, and that I will observe and obey all commands of the President of the Union of India and the commands of any officer set over me even to the peril of my life.

A living legend, God ordains, must live longer, is an age-old Coorg saying. Perhaps as an indication, when after a dinner with Sheikh Abdullah on May 14, he felt uneasy and was hospitalised. Diagnosed as a case of jaundice (infective hepatitis), it was eventually attributed to have been caused by his continuous exposure to the high altitudes without being acclimatised. He was signing off his Kashmir assignment.

The infective hepatitis that he suffered from was expected to require about a year or so of resuscitation. The doctors advised a softer appointment for him and General Cariappa, now C-in-C, thought the newly reorganised National Defence Academy (NDA) – from the Armed Forces Academy – needed him to train the cadets of the three services until he could pick up another useful appointment for him.

"Timmy, would you be happy," the military secretary had asked, "if you were posted to the NDA?"

"Who, on God's earth, least of all a Rimcollian, would not want to go to the Duns?" Thimayya had replied over the hospital telephone. His boyish enthusiasm was back again.

While still in hospital, one day Colonel Carriappa (his one time ADC) found him dancing in the club while the doctors were searching for him. The hospital duty officer had to bring him back in a staff car; the following morning, he was discharged, given a posting order and was heading for the Duns to take over the academy.

He was in the NDA by mid-May. But ere long, he would be sent out to the UK for the Commonwealth Conference to act as military adviser to Sir Girija Shankar Bajpayee for the Paris and Geneva meetings on the "J & K Negotiations."

In Sri Div, he had proved to be a "first class divisional commander" who had "fighting will to win." He had inspired "great confidence" among his superiors with his "ability" and his troops had developed a "titanic faith" in their commander. He was, overall assessed as a "brilliant commander both in war and peace," who managed his relations with the civilians with "charm and dexterity." A man who had shown not only professional brilliance but also magnanimity and humility. He could, as General Cariappa thought, sometimes be "over-confident."[4] But then, that was what he could be loved for. The opinion of him by two superiors – Major General Tara Singh Bal and Lieutenant General Shrinagesh, the deputy and the corps commander of 5th Corps – putting his leadership in a larger perspective, was that they saw in him "a winning, attractive personality with independence of thoughts," a man with *savoir-faire*, clearly above the ordinary generals.

Commandant NDA

At Dehra Dun, Nina joined him and she would soon get immersed in the unique responsibility of being the commandant's wife – the 'Madam Commandant,' as the cadets got to know her. Perhaps her youthful looks, her natural charm and grace, her interest in Bharata Natyam and above all, her Ava Gardner style of holding a cigarette appealed to the young minds. With Timmy's charisma and Nina's talents, the Thimayyas were to be loved and remembered forever.

To Timmy, there could be no better job than to be the head of India's Sandhurst – in fact, an institute better than Sandhurst. It was as good, if not better, than the American West Point and the French *Ecole de Guerre*.

The establishment of the NDA had been an interesting historical experiment.

As Brigadier Barltrop, the last British IMA commandant left and Brigadier Mahadeo Singh, DSO, took over as the first Indian commandant, the visionary idea of Field Marshal Auchinleck in creating a Tri-Service Academy, at a cost of £100,000 sterling, donated by the Government of Sudan, primarily for a war memorial in India, had also taken shape. The genesis of the gift of £100,000 sterling from the Government of Sudan lay in the recognition of the courage of the Indian troops of 4th Indian Division (later reinforced by 5th Indian Division) in Sudan in 1941.

Auchinleck felt that there was a great need to doctrinally integrate the services by having an academy where cadets from the army, navy and air force could train and live together for the initial common military training. When the money was finally available, he conceived the idea of a "War Memorial Academy," which could fulfill the concept.

Auchinleck envisioned the building of this institution alongside the IMA. No better place could have been located than the infrastructure left at Clement Town, where adequate assets existed from World War II, to immediately begin the new wing of the institution with its subsequent Key Location Plan (KLP) being built up. It was, however, only on 2 May 1945, that a committee was appointed by the governmnent to prepare a scheme for what was then accepted by Mountbatten and Auchinleck for a National War Academy (NWA) to be built at Dehra Dun, with the IMA retaining its old accommodation at Prem Nagar but adopting a new name, "Military Wing" and the Tri-Service assuming the name of the Inter-Service Wing (ISW) (later Joint Service Wing, JSW). The actual initial combined training would take place at the JSW. In principle, then, the cadets of the JSW would move to the Military Wing and the Naval and Air Force Academies, for their final pre-commission training until such time – and if possible – the NWA could assume the sole responsibility of producing all officers for the armed forces. At the JSW, the army and naval cadets would do two years and the air force cadets three years before moving into their own academies.

The NDA was then a long story of experiments, and it had two wings: the Military

Wing at Prem Nagar, having been redesigned from the Indian Military Academy; and, the Joint Services Wing at Clement Town.[6]

Thimayya soon settled down, often looking back on his Sandhurst days. He found the IMA better organised, better attuned to the needs of the Indian Army leadership than any other academy in the world. While at Sandhurst, he had seen that the mission of the Indian cadets was to aim at getting a commission and to also take full advantage of an army career of adventure, travel and glamour, but they were oversupervised rather than helped to develop their personalities and broaden their outlook. The Indian cadets, therefore, turned more regimented than their British counterparts – an obvious inherent aim of the British.

The cadets at the IMA, General Thimayya thought, could neither be treated as school boys nor as soldiers. There had to be a balance between control and freedom. On this premise, he began a liberalisation programme. Gentleman cadets could discuss any subject with the staff and himself. And he expanded the theme of 'liberalisation' to their participation in *shikar*, polo and cricket, besides social events. He knew they could be naughty too.

For, in one of the 'pipping ceremonies,' Gentleman Cadet Sandhu went to the extent of asking Mrs. Thimayya, why she "looked like the general's daughter." Even though, Nina fitted into the "age group difference," such a remark was least expected of a 'gentlemen cadet,' passing out in a few moments to become an "officer and gentleman" of the famous Indian Army. Sandhu was hauled up by the adjutant who even recommended that his commission be stopped.

"Ignore it," said Thimayya. "He will enlarge his vision. In any case, his remarks to my wife are flattering," he laughingly said.

"Success isn't about being intelligent," he would tell the teaching faculty and cadets. "It is about what you do with the intelligence you have. Because, even if you were highly educated but you didn't know how to apply your knowledge, it would remain a paper degree. We are not looking for professors but practical soldiers with sufficient common sense. If you don't have that, you'll never beat your enemy tactically and technically."

He wanted them to take advantage of a career in the armed forces, which could provide adventure, travel, gallantry and glamour. "Without taking pride in one's uniform," he emphasised, "you'll not be recognised as a soldier and 'an officer,' your conduct and character alone would give you gentlemanly qualities, through which the world will recognise you and your subordinates will respect you."

He ordered a thorough reevaluation of the syllabi and evaluation system. The two wings, the Military Wing and the JSW, located 20 km apart, *per se* remained separate wings. For, while the JSW was a military university, according to a remark made by Jack Gibson (its principal), the Military Wing was running four types of courses of different duration for the JSW, Direct Entry, Technical Graduates and cadets of the NCC.

The amalgamation of the JSW and the Military Wing began when Thimayya's tenure was almost eight months old, as the First ex-JSW Course joined the 10th Regular Course on 15 January 1951. (The naval and air force cadets joined their academies). Thus, far more objective information was available to the ex-JSWs (the junior wing of the NDA) when they joined the Military Wing, where they did wonders in the field of sports two years hence.

Two years of hard work, coaching and training produced a miracle team of young soccer players of the NDA, that shook the greats of Indian football in the Durand Finals, and won praise from everyone. It was really a gate-crashing of the "Blue Riband" of Indian football, the credit for which went to GC Puran Bahadur Thapa and GC MK (Mike) Lahiri. Thapa was, however, credited for "taking the team from one seemingly impossible victory to another." Similarly, the IMA produced fine boxers, cricketers, and tennis and polo players.

In the winter of 1950, two more events took place at the NDA that brought it into focus in the Commonwealth, if not the international arena: the laying down of the King's Colours of which the NDA became the repository; and the visit of the UK's MCC team playing against the Indian XI. The second event, first. The MCC team played its first test against the India XI at the Military Wing (IMA) grounds for which Pandit Nehru was present. It required superb management, which Thimayya ensured. Lieutenant General Pettengell, then a battalion commander at the IMA, remembered how skillfully the whole thing was arranged by the Academy.

The practice of carrying the King's Colours on parade had to be discontinued. They had to be either returned to England or be laid up in the Chetwode Hall, the repository of the old Colours since 1934.

India had now turned a new and glorious page in history as an independent nation and it was fitting that the last vestiges of the Raj – the Colours – should be laid up. In the new era ushered in on 26 January 1950, the symbolism of the old regime, must, in the nature of things, give way to the new and there could be no better place for these old Colours than the NDA, the home of the future officers of their armed forces, where they would inspire the future generations of young men with all that was best and noblest in the profession of arms.

On 23 November, the 36 oldest and most famous King's Colours, many of them battle-scarred with their gold crown pinions were handed over for safe custody to General Thimayya in the Chetwode Hall, after a majestic and picturesque parade by the NDA. The ceremony heightened the emotional flow as one by one officers of the respective regiments surrendered to the general the proud Colours. The ceremony was attended by Sardar Baldev Singh, minister for defence and Sir Archibald Nye, who represented the king. This then marked the end of a chapter.

The High Commissioner of Australia Mr HR Gollan, and the High Commissioner of Canada, Mr Warwick F. Chipman, the Defence Secretary, Mr HM Patel, and the Commanders-in-Chief of the Indian Army, Navy and Air Force,

General Cariappa, Vice-Admiral Parry, and Air Marshal Ivelaw Chapman, were among those present.

While there was great understanding and depth of feeling among the members of India's armed forces in showing respect to these Colours, which, on many an occasion served as an insignia in war and peace, there was also deep appreciation of this spirit by Sir Archibald Nye.

After a picturesque parade, the King's Colours, many of them looking bright in the sun, were marched off into the Chetwode Hall of the Academy amid the playing of *Auld Lang Syne* and "God Save the King."

At the ceremony, the defence minister asked Sir Archibald Nye to convey to the king the grateful thanks of the regiments and the high esteem in which their Colours would be held.

Sir Nye, responding to the defence minister's words, said: "Nobody could have been present today without having a very deep feeling of the solemnity of the occasion. But today's act is symbolic and something deeper. It happened not only because India is now a sovereign republic but also because she has decided, of her own will, to remain a member of the Commonwealth and to recognise the King as the symbolic head of the Union." Later, Sir Archibald in a talk with the special reporter of *Hindustan Times* confessed that despite the fact that "we Englishmen are supposed to be so unemotional, during the ceremony it became difficult at moments to suppress a throb in our throats."[7] India after all, had been the jewel in the British Crown and this was the removal of a permanent symbol of British power and imperialism.

Thimayya was the sort of man to whom exciting things would continue to happen. Taking a quiet after-dinner stroll in his bungalow at the IMA one night he sighted a panther in the bushes. He seized his rifle and shot it on the spot. Indeed, his whole life was exciting. A similar feat was accomplished when he shot a man-eater in Bangalore. Later he would say, it was not eating a man but a cow but then there had to be an "excuse for everything in life and for death."

On another occasion, while returning from an outdoor exercise of the gentlemen cadets (GCs) he again saw a panther staring hard at him. Timmy asked the driver to keep the lights focussed on the beast while he himself ran inside the house, loaded his gun, and returned and shot it. "Shotgun Timmy," would say his friends, "can never miss a *shikar*."

The NDA accepted no laxity. While those who failed to secure the satisfactory gradings were relegated to lower terms, others, weak, with vulnerable character qualities or corruptible traits, were removed. GC (later Lieutenant General) YS Tomar remembers a defaulting gentleman cadet being marched upto the commandant in 1950. "GC KD Ram Pal," said General Thimayya in a stern voice, moving his eyes from the offence report, to his face, "I withdraw you." He was marched out, moved into a vehicle waiting outside which conveyed him to the railway station where he was put on a train to his home. He was gone before anyone knew about it.

He was forthright with his assessment and evaluation of cadets. Any cadet who could not make the grade despite serious efforts was counselled by him to look for another avenue where he might make a better name. "If you are not cut out for the army, you waste your time in training and later, in pursuing the wrong profession," he would tell the boy while wishing him all the best. But GCs whom he had thought could make it and yet would turn into "misfit monsters" in later years, he would withdraw without remorse or pity.

Thimayya would recall how boys, apparently unsuited to the profession of arms were also trained at RMC, Sandhurst. He saw a course mate commissioned into the Gorkha Brigade in India, merely on his father's reputation. However, he had to resign his commission a few years later. As commandant NDA, parents would plead with him to reinstate a failed cadet but he learned the greater kindness of preventing a boy not cut out for a military career from wasting valuable years. The same boys did exceedingly well elsewhere. NN Vohra, for example, had to leave the NDA. He became the defence secretary. There were others, too, who succeeded in business, politics, and so on.

If the NDA observed no laxity in the training and upbringing of the GCs, it could be achieved only through the training staff. In one way it was helped by General Cariappa, the C-in-C. He had posted some of the best lieutenant colonels of the Indian Army in the appointment usually held by majors and captains. "Until we have suitable junior officers," Cariappa would say, "seniors will have to be there."

But some juniors still made their way in: Lieutenant Mathew Thomas as physical training officer (PTO) and Captain Kundan Singh as platoon commander. Mathew looked as young as the cadets of the JSW and was moved to the Military Wing to under study the PTO, from whom he finally took over. In Thomas' words: "One day when I was seen by General Cariappa, the C-in-C, I was quizzed on my service. I said two years. Next day, I was packed off to my battalion." But Kundan (later lieutenant general) stuck on. The story was told by him, "One day General Thimayya saw me take a class in tactics. He wasn't impressed with my English. He said nothing to me but later asked Lieutenant Colonel PS Bhagat VC, GSO1, to pack me up. I represented that if English was the only reason for my marching orders, then could I perhaps be given a three months probation period to improve. It was agreed. Being from the ranks, this was definitely my weak point. But determinedly, I learnt English from the English wife of an officer. Three months later, I was seen by Timmy and he said I had improved. And I was retained." There were many others who were given a chance to prove themselves.

Thimayya remained committed to other activities too. As the Kashmir question came up before the Security Council in early 1951, six more weeks were given to Dr Graham, the mediator. Meanwhile Major General Thimayya and Colonel

Manekshaw (then DMO) were sent to New York to advise BN Rau, India's permanent representative to the UNO. Thimayya would also join in, helping Sir Girija Shankar Bajpayee in Paris and Geneva; in Thimayya's absence, Colonel MM Khanna, MVC, his deputy would officiate and if the cadets feared anyone, it was Khanna!

The working period of Thimayya as commandant NDA, was barely one year i.e. two terms – too little to do anything serious. At the time of his departure in August 1951, he was contrite and said, "I have been here for a very short period and was not, therefore, able to do all that I wanted." However, he was happy and observed that the NDA could compare with the best institutions of the world, especially, now that Major General MS Wadalia, a friend, was taking over.

General Thimayya left an indelible imprint at the NDA. The *IMA Journal* of September 1951 paid tribute to him, addressing him as a "gentleman, a keen sportsman, an amusing and generous host and a great soldier." About Mrs Thimayya, the words were equally poignant. "We remain grateful to Mrs Thimayya for her inestimable contribution to the life and atmosphere of the Academy."

By this time, Thimayya was being recognised as a "forceful yet pleasant personality." An outstanding officer, he was regarded by his superiors as an "asset to the Indian Army." His balanced judgement and practical approach, loyalty and integrity as adjudged by Generals JH Wilkinson, director Military Training and SPP Thorat, chief of General Staff, was shaping his image as the man who would lead the Indian Army one day to great heights.

Thimayya would return to both the NDA and IMA at every opportunity. For, it was here he could tell the future officers what he valued the most in the profession of arms.

"At all times, you will have men placed under your command. These men are some of the finest men in the world and man-management and leadership of a very high order will be required." He asked them to add "glamour to service by wearing your uniform, maintaining your exemplary bearing and your conduct all the time. *The greatest glamour is when you return from battle. The one and only reason why you have chosen this career is to enable you to lead your men into battle. If you are killed in battle, yours will be a hero's death, if you come back alive, it will be a hero's return.*"

But he would always win their young hearts and inquisitive minds with his humour. He would recount his own 'home made,' personal humour. In one of the parades he told the passing out GCs:

> Don't be in perpetual debt like I have been all my life. Among my several creditors was the famous Jenkins & Co who stitched my clothes on credit. They would remind me, as a matter of drill, every month that I owed them money. I got cheesed off and wrote them a reply cyclostyled by my PA: "You are among the many creditors I have and I clear the bill of one of the many each month out of my meagre pay,

by drawing lots. This month, regrettably, your name didn't figure. But I promise to pay you as soon as the lottery works. In the meanwhile, please stop harassing an officer and gentleman."

The newspapers carried the anecdote and whole of India was amused by Timmy's jokes.

Quarter Master General (QMG)

From the NDA, Dehra Dun to New Delhi was not too great of a distance but the job was altogether different – the feeding, billeting, movement of troops beside operational logistics of the whole Indian Army was his responsibility. As QMG, he was also to improve the material welfare of the officers and men and raise their quality of life.

Living in a large bungalow at 6, Tughlak Road, the Thimayyas were happy to be in Delhi.

There was already a large staff to assist Major General SBS Chimni, his one time senior in Kashmir from whom he took over the charge. And things moved with some efficiency, although there were areas that needed change. Accommodation was one segment which suffered. There was a colossal 60 to 70 per cent deficiency in accommodation for married officers and men! Then came the question of improving conditions in field areas, improving field rations, enhancing travelling allowances and upgradation of the authorised travel class by railways, and so on.

By his own admission, he succeeded only partially in improving the state of accommodation in peace stations. The Partition of the country had seen the bulk of the cantonments remain in Pakistan. The demobilisation of the Indian Army and reluctance of the government to be financially more liberal to the army made Thimayya say in one of his addresses to officers in Amritsar: "I regret to tell you that both the C-in-C and I have failed to make up the deficiency. But you have my authority to raise this issue with anyone, including ministers. And you can always quote me." There was both sincerity and truth in what he said.

What he could achieve substantial results in was the creation of canteen services and change in the contractor system; these again were done in 'Timmy style' – unconventionally. He wanted radical changes and deplored his predecessor's *status quo*.

In the contractor system, a legacy of the British Raj, the contractors supplied units, centres, schools of instructions and even the forward posts from the bases. They also hired and controlled the ancillary services such as tailors, barbers, washermen, confectioners and money-lenders and those operating large cinema halls and transport systems. In a way, their utility was established, and some of them were honoured with British awards and rewards like Rai Sahibs and Rai Bahadurs.

Even after Independence, the contractors were deeply entrenched in the administration and welfare system. As a result, some of them were among the richest people of the country, with property worth millions. Thimayya had always seen them not only as parasites on the welfare system but also as a direct consequence of the failure of the military system to assure that the lowly paid and suffering soldiery of the Indian Army were afforded some semblance of a just system. For, he (the jawan) would be fleeced even in the merchandise supplied, and would be compelled to use material of inferior quality; he would run into debt, and once again, be exploited by these contractors and their men. Calling it "legalised robbery," he convinced General Cariappa, the C-in-C and Sardar Baldev Singh, the defence minister – and his successor – that the system needed change, even abolition altogether. He even convinced Prime Minister Nehru, whose government itself was busy in abolishing the landlord (*zamindari*) system. "Another abolition, Sir," said Thimayya, "would add to your programme of nation building."

Having got the required support, without a notice or warning, he published the orders, terminating the contractor system.[8]

"What a storm broke about my ears," he would recall, "what screams of anguish!" He was inundated with calls for interviews by individuals and unions of these contractors.

"My grandfather supplied Kitchener," said one, "We have been most loyal servants of the army and the Indian armed forces."

"Who are you to turn us pariahs?" lamented others.

"We'll not leave you in peace," threatened the group when Thimayya refused to budge.

Some tried to bribe him with artifacts ranging from foreign liquor (of Thimayya's choice) to sheafs of currency notes. But Thimayya was too honest to be bribed, or intimidated into rescinding his orders. So they took recourse to taking a delegation to the minister for defence, who patiently heard them and then courteously turned the protest down.

There would follow a malicious canard against Thimayya by these people but soon everyone was reconciled to the changed system, although some of them would join the bandwagon of the Thimayya detractors in 1960.

When Thimayya obtained official approval for the abolition of the contractor system, he was asked how he would – for Heaven's sake – substitute an army-managed system efficiently. He suggested the creation of a Canteen Services Department on the lines of the American PX system where stores, including liquor, were bought on a wholesale basis, and stocked and supplied to individual units and headquarters. Cheaper bulk purchases and use of military transport would result in handsome profits and would, thus, help in generating canteen profits for the users, which would contribute to the welfare of the men and their families.

Another idea came to him from what every defence minister was talking about: grow more food through self-help. He allowed training centres to have their farms and livestock. Soon the contractors were sent off, although some influential ones would make their way back in other forms.

A landmark, which proves Thimayya's proverbial "nine lives," occurred when he was on an exercise being conducted by UP Area under Major General Chimni at Lucknow. He had with him in the twin engine Devon aircraft, Lieutenant General SM Shrinagesh, Major Generals SPP Thorat, DSO, Sardanand Singh, MS Chopra and Brigadier Ajaib Singh. It was a day-long operational discussion at Lucknow. The plane, while returning late in the evening that day, caught fire and one of its engines burnt and dropped out but the pilot saved the top brass he was flying, by belly-landing in a field.

When news of this accident reached the nearby hospitals, a fleet of ambulances reached the spot within hours of the accident. There had, fortunately, been no fatality but anxiety was writ large on most of the faces, except Timmy's who had taken the whole episode as a professional hazard. Instead, he cheered up everyone by telling the officer-in-charge of the rescue fleet, "Sorry chaps, no luck today, Sorry to disappoint you." That made the strained faces lighten up in amusement.

Within days of this incident, Pandit Nehru invited this lucky ensemble of army-air force fraternity along with their wives to an informal dinner, but in *de rigeur*. Dressed in his dinner jacket, Nehru was in a pleasant mood. As dinner got over and sherry was being served, he asked the survivors of the mishap what exactly was their last thought, as they helplessly saw the burning aircraft which might explode and go down in flames, causing sure deaths.

Shrinagesh, the seniormost, took the lead and said he remembered his mother. Thorat, more religious, prayed to his deity "Jotiba." The thoughts of the others had wandered between their gods and the grieving families they would leave behind. It turned the ambience sombre as everyone narrated the parting scene of a gathering of soldiers heading for their death. Even Nehru appeared to grow serious.

Then came Timmy's turn. His remark rocked the Teen Murthi House. He said in as simple words as possible: "My thoughts, Mr Prime Minister, were altogether different." He paused and then added. "I always wanted to die on a battlefield. But God, what a way to die! Now I wished I could die in the arms of a beautiful woman... that would have made dying so easy."[4]

Such was the man Thimayya. Always truthful, always loving life but never attached to it. He was a *Yogi*, who faced life as realistically as possible. And, above all, his humour always brightened even the dullest ambience. ■

NOTES

1. From Official Documents.
2. From Official Documents of the Kumaon Regimental Centre.
3. Ibid.
4. Ibid.

5. From Official Documents.
6. Subsequently, under political pressure, the JSW would be dissociated and moved to Khadakvasla and established as the NDA The NDA remained at Dehra Dun all through Thimayya's tenure.
7. *Hindustan Times*, 25 November 1950, and the records of the Indian Military Academy, Dehra Dun.
8. From Official Documents.
9. The IAF was generous in presenting the seats of this aircraft duly silver-polished as a souvenir to all its lucky passengers. Timmy presented his to the Kumaon Regimental Centre, where it remains a piece of undoubted attraction.

9
For the Honour of India: Chairman of Neutral Nations' Repatriation Commission (NNRC)

(1 September 1953-23 March 1954)

You have become a veritable Mahatma in the Army...The bloodless victories you have won in Korea entitle you a permanent place in the annals of the Army of India and the UN. It is simply unrivalled.

– **Armstrong Hamilton, editor, *Foreign Affairs*, USA.**

...NNRC is carrying out one of the most difficult missions ever entrusted to any nation any time.

– **John Foster Dulles.**

In end May, Thimayya had come to Madikeri, his home town, on a six-month-long leave, while major decisions were being taken in the UN Security Council on how to end the impasse over the Korean War. Meanwhile Nina and Thimayya began to renovate their ancestral home "Sunny Side." Instead of painting at her easel, Nina joined him, and others, in painting doors and woodwork, the goal being to refurbish the place as his mother might have done.

Then came a "Top-Secret" letter from General Rajindra Sinhji telling him that the "prime minister had appointed him as chairman of the Neutral Nations' Repatriation Commission (NNRC) Korea." The commander-in-chief, however, assured him that "preliminary arrangements" would be made before he returned to Delhi. Having confirmed the receipt of the letter, Thimayya was off on a week-long trek to rediscover the "inherent decency of jungle life," and return recharged.

Thimayya had a fortnight in Delhi to understand the genesis of the Korean War, the current situation, and analyse the task he had been assigned and evolve an approach to the problem he would have to handle.

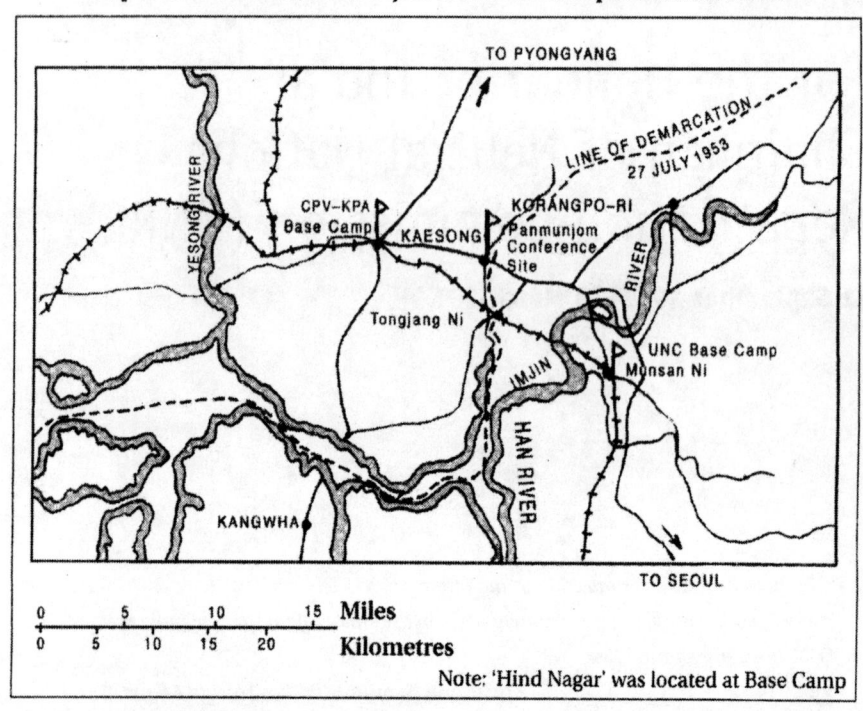

Map 8: The DMZ Area, Panmunjom Where NNRC Repatriated the POWs

Note: 'Hind Nagar' was located at Base Camp

In 1945, Korea was divided into two halves astride the 38th Parallel and it then became the playground of the two superpowers who began to experiment with the theory of proxy war here, with the North under Kim Il-Sung being supported by Communist China and the South under the fiery Dr Syngman Rhee helped by the USA and others.

Korea had, in fact, been the playfield of the Chinese, Japanese and Western colonialists since the 1870s; it could not have remained peaceful – even after it was divided. Continuous tension and urge for reunification eventually led to the invasion of South Korea by the North Korean People's Army (NKPA) in June 1950, which, in a *juggernaut* pushed the South Korean Army to the Pusan perimeter. It led further to the formation of the UN Command, arrayed to fight against the North Koreans.

In the North, the Chinese joined the North Koreans in combat, with the full diplomatic, moral and material support of the former USSR. Calling its People's Liberation Army Expeditionary Force the Chinese Peoples' Volunteer Force (CPVF or CPV), their military contribution became substantial in restoring the situation in North Korea. Between the two of them, they formed the Northern Command. The conflict dragged on for a full three years as a see-saw war, with both adversaries finally settling down on a six-km-deep "no-man's land," called the Military Demarcation Line. It was, at best, "a no war, no peace" affair where there was "no victor, no vanquished."

The Armistice Agreement of 1953, coming after year-long wrangling, envisaged: complete cessation of hostilities in Korea; establishment of a Demilitarised Zone (DMZ) from which all military forces would be withdrawn; repatriation of all POWs; and those who refused to be repatriated to be settled through the NNRC which would act in accordance with the laid down Terms of Reference. The problem hinged on the repatriation of those prisoners held by both the commands who refused to be repatriated (non-repats) to their own countries in contravention of the 1949 Geneva Convention.[1]

At the UN, India's representative Mr VK Krishna Menon, suggested that a commission under the chairmanship of a neutral country may have four to five members, two each from the Communist Bloc and two from the Western Block, each carrying a vote, including the chairman. On formulation of procedures, legality and final decision, they could be given a mandated time-frame, of say, 90 days, and terms of reference to facilitate interviews and explanations of the "observers" of the side that the individual non-repat belonged to, with the ultimate aim of persuading a non-repat to decide as to which country he (or she) would want to go to or to change his (or her) mind to return to the parent country. The commission, by nomenclature and designation, was to ensure absolute neutrality and fairness without any coercion, fear or animosity.[2]

India, then a truly non-aligned country, was asked if it would provide a chairman and a custodian force. The Indian government accepted both commitments of making available a chairman with his team and staff and a custodian force of appropriate size. That is how Lieutenant General KS Thimayya, DSO, already appointed as army commander Western Command, was selected as chairman and Major General SPP Thorat, DSO, then chief of the General Staff, Army Headquarters, as the general officer commanding, Custodian Force India (CFI). These appointments were made public on 25 July 1953. The government decided to send to Korea a team comprising RK Nehru, the foreign secretary and Thorat for an on-the-spot study, from which they returned by end-August.

Comprising initially a brigade group, the CFI was moved by ship and air commencing from 18 August and concentrated in the DMZ, which came to be known as Hindnagar from 6 September. Those who were transported in ships had a really rough time in the monsoon-turbulent high seas from Madras to Inchon. Added to it was the inexplicable hostility of South Korean President Dr Rhee who regarded the Indians as pro-Communist. He would continue to threaten them while in the DMZ too.

Hindnagar, the CFI Camp, had 26 General Hospital, 60 Para Field Ambulance and 7 Field Hygiene Section from India. 64 Field Hospital was providing initial medical back-up to the 28th British Commonwealth Brigade. There were also Joint Red Cross teams besides the Indian Red Cross under Dr Balwant Singh Suri.

The induction of the CFI led to one of the largest heli-lift operations of the

Korean War, when on being transferred from ships, the troops were shifted onto a US aircraft carrier at Inchon. They were then flown by helicopter to the DMZ. Some 1,800 sorties found mention in the Guinness Book of Records.

In the hour-long discussion, Prime Minister Nehru had apprised Thimayya about India's position in the Cold War and the situation he was likely to face. But as chairman NNRC, what his task would involve remained obscure. He had to understand the whole gamut on his arrival in Korea and decide on the best course to be adopted. All Nehru told him was "to charter his own way."

The initial orbat of the CFI consisted of 190 Infantry Brigade under Brigadier RS Paintal. The major units were: 5th Raj Rif under Lieutenant Colonel Sarup Kalan; 3rd Dogra under Lieutenant Colonel P Hazare; 6th Jat under Lieutenant Colonel M R Badhwar, MC; 3rd Garhwal Rifles under Lieutenant Colonel Ujjal Singh. Subsequently airlifted in five Globe Masters was 2nd Para (Maratha) under Lieutenant Colonel TR Jetley. The CFI also included one company Para Mahar Machine Guns, 74th Field Company Engineers, Field Workshop, Field Ambulance, Postal and Provost.

The staff at HQ 190th Infantry Brigade consisted of Major PN Khanduri as BM, Major KV Janardan as DAA&QMG. Brigadier BM Kaul was Thimayya's Chief of Staff (COS), while Major YM Munshi was his PSO, and Captains Jasbir Singh and SK Bahri were his ADCs.

Thimayya also found himself being given a conglomeration of civilians, the high-powered ICS, IFS and IP, with some experience in administration and foreign affairs. The team comprised: BN Chakravarty, ICS, as alternate chairman, PN Haksar IFS, IJ Bahadur Singh, NV Rao, AK Dave Indian Police, Brigadier BM Kaul as COS along with another 40 officers at the Headquarters.[3] Also included were Lieutenant Colonel Streenivasan as the chief PRO with a team of seven others.

The CFI, as mentioned, was under General Thorat; the others being his Deputies – Brigadiers Gurbakhash Singh, RS Paintal, commander 190th Infantry Brigade and SP Bhatia (director of Medical Services). There was a Red Cross team too.

The two delegations representing the Communists comprised the Czechoslovak and Polish delegates under Colonel Ladislav Simovic and Stanislaw Gajewski with more than 50 officers each. The non-Communist world was represented by the generally neutral countries of Sweden and Switzerland. Major General Jan Strenstrom and Dr Daenikkar, each with a four dozen strong staff, joined them. Added to these was a fleet of liaison officers, besides the scribes.

In Thimayya as chairman of the NNRC, Nehru had picked up his best commander for this task. He had known him as commander PBF and Sri Div besides commandant NDA. For, in him he had found a general of potential. He wanted him to be firm, friendly and fair to all individuals and states. Thimayya was to be the custodian of India's reputation.

So, Timmy became Nehru's emissary in Korea. Nehru told him, time and again, over tea, at cocktails and in the office before he left, that the job he had been assigned was totally new to him and, hence, difficult and he would have to be both a soldier and a statesman to do a "neat job" of it. Mahavir Tyagi, the minister for defence also told him to do well, "for the honour of India." The motto then became "For the Honour of India."

In Delhi, he was handed over a sealed confidential envelope containing five copies of the sacrosanct Terms of Reference – one each for the four members and one for the chairman. He found them interesting – very interesting – as he would reveal in a lecture at the USI, Delhi, in later years.

The Terms of Reference, *ipso-facto* were the directive to the NNRC from the UN secretary general. They required of the Commission to function in accordance with the provision of "Article 132 of the Geneva Convention." The Terms of Reference stipulated that after having taken custody of prisoners for the next 90 days, the NNRC was to give freedom and facilities to the representative of the nations to which the prisoners belonged so that they could explain to them their rights and their freedom to return to their homelands (or be repatriated to a country of their choice). The unwilling non-repatriates were then to be referred to the Political Conference for another 30 days. On termination of 120 days, the non-repats were to be given civilian status and repatriated to a neutral country. By the 150th day, the NNRC would cease functioning.[4]

With these broad Terms of Reference that spread over 25 clauses, the chairman NNRC assigned the CFI under Thorat to hold and administer the non-repats; not to use force or coercion, threat of force or violence against POWs; and, be absolutely impartial without any political responsibility.

Getting Down to Brass Tacks

While the CFI and its Headquarters concentrated in *Hindnagar*, the tented camp in the DMZ, Thimayya and his personal staff arrived in Tokyo on 8 September. Having flown through Rangoon and Bangkok, Dr MA Rauf, India's ambassador to Japan, received him at Tokyo. He was taken through the city and 'deposited' in the Imperial Hotel. A battery of cameramen and journalists gave him his first idea of the news value of the mission and of the publicity that henceforth was to attend his every move. The *Asahi*, a leading newspaper of Japan, in its 9 September edition was predicting that "though it is a heavy responsibility for India to take custody of the prisoners refusing repatriation, it will be a good chance for a neutral country to gain experience and education." The cautious opinion of the paper, however, acknowledged that neutral India held the "key to war or peace in Korea."

The next morning, Thimayya, along with the Swiss and Swedish delegates, met General Mark Clark in a "God-Almighty-lives-here" atmosphere (just like the viceroy of India whom he saw during his interview for Sandhurst) but found Clark to be an amiable and friendly soldier, who, he observed, looked detached from the ostentation of his office. General Clark also expressed a personal apology for Syngman Rhee's anti-Indian overtures and expressed full faith in the Indian troops.

Thimayya would, nonetheless, soon find that the officers of the UN Command would treat him according to the decision he took, either in favour or against, and that automatically turned him a hero or a villain – nothing in between.

On the Northern Command side, Lieutenant General Lee Sang Cho represented the NKPA while General Ting Kuo-Yu was the general officer-in-charge CPVF. Both displayed a stoic similarity in thoughts and expressions. Enigmatic though they were, this served as a good lesson for Thimayya to understand the Chinese character. Unpredictability and ruthless pursuit of ambition were the Communist Chinese traits, he discovered. He would see them so from 1957 onwards.

His NNRC delegates, those representing the West and the Communists, were equally interesting individuals. Of the Swede and the Swiss members, General Strenstrom and Dr Armin Daenikkar respectively, Strenstrom was, social, easy-going, generally neutral, correct and punctilious about protocol. Daenikkar, was more emotional than rational, which he displayed in his anti-Communist utterances and decisions Of the Communist delegates, Colonel Ladislaw Simovic of Czechoslovakia and Stanislaw Gajewski of Poland made a good team. Gajewski, a lawyer by profession, sarcastic, though witty and amusing, was the cleverest. Often he led the assault against Daenikkar and keeping the peace between these two men was one of the major tasks of Thimayya – in order to keep the Commission going.

So the two sets of people, the contenders, had begun to be understood by Thimayya as he was introduced to them. And he was careful to modulate his relationship with them in accordance with his astute observations. "They held the Damocles sword over me and played their own orchestras," he would say laughingly.

Thorat would keep a strict watch on the pulse of the prisoners. The CFI under him was motivated to undertake any job, for the "*honour of the country*," as he would repeatedly tell everyone. Chief of Staff, Kaul was to coordinate all the activities.

Amongst the brigadiers was Gurbakhsh Singh of the former Patiala State Forces who, as a Japanese POW in Singapore, unlike many others, had managed to keep himself out of the temptation of joining the INA and had retained his image as a steadfast soldier. He would be remembered by the North Korean prisoners, one of whom, then under the Japanese control, had slapped him.[5] Gurbakhsh proved a good deputy to Thorat. Then there was RS Paintal who commanded the troops.

The troops of the CFI had a daunting task. They suffered the inherent privations uncomplainingly. The men would have a rough eight months in the DMZ, not because of the highly volatile and militant prisoners, but because of the cold, fatigue and nerve-wracking demands of custody, security, and keeping their cool despite being jeered (rather than cheered) at by the POWs.

The prisoners' camp built by the UN Command to house the prisoners had been constructed in 17 separate compounds, each to accommodate 500 prisoners. Basic tented amenities, including electric lights and coal heaters, had been provided. Seven to ten compounds were grouped into an enclosure. Enclosure 'A' contained the questionable prisoners and those already segregated for return. 'B,' 'C,' and 'D' held the Chinese; 'E' and 'G.' the Koreans, and 'F,' the hospital. While the North Korean and Chinese prisoners numbering 22,604 were in a separate area, the 359 KPA-CPV (Northern Command) prisoners, including five South Korean women, were at a distant place called Song Gong-ni.

The inner area of each rectangular compound – the size of a couple of football fields – was surrounded by barbed wire fences 15 feet apart. Outside was a second pair of fences, about 50 yards away. The prisoners occupied the inner rectangle. The CFI guard had a couple of tents in the outer strip. Sentries patrolled the perimeter. The meetings of the NNRC and others were generally held in the Peace Pagoda, a sort of large conference tent.

Both KPA-CPV and UN Command prisoners were organised with a leader and had their own community life and military police. They cooked their own food. The UN Command maintained its secret contacts with the prisoners through radio sets smuggled through supplies, heliographs, and through the hospital staff.

Thimayya arrived in the DMZ on 9 September and was greeted by a Guard of Honour provided by the CFI. He was accompanied by the Swiss and Swedish delegates. That afternoon, the other two members i.e. Czech and Pole had arrived by train through China and were living at Kaesong. He held a meeting that afternoon itself to consider the methodology for taking over the prisoners. At that meeting, the first thing that happened was a meeting with two Northern Commanders, General Lee Sang Cho and General Ting Kuo Yu.

"We were to be introduced to the two generals of the Northern Command," he recalled. "They were particularly keen on protocol. They and the NNRC were supposed to enter the Peace Pagoda at the same time since one party going before the other would mean that the party entering later is in some way superior to the other." He told them that he did not mind going earlier. "They wouldn't even do that too," he would say. Eventually, the timings went wrong and he entered the conference room about 10 minutes before them. As they came in they shook hands with General Lee Sang Cho. He then made a long speech to introduce Thimayya to General Ting Kuo Yu. This speech was translated into Chinese and then into English.

Thimayya was rather amused thinking how melodramatic the situation would turn if he spoke in *Hindustani*!

"Then I got up," General Thimayya recalled "and began by saying *apki nani ke do sar hain*." Kaul transliterated it by saying that the chairman wore two hats (rather than the literal, your grandma has two heads). The effect was immediate and he found, the Poles and Czechs shaking hands with him. One of them asked, "How do you do, Mr Chairman?"

"I asked them if they knew English."

"They said, 'Yes'."

"Thank God," I said. I was just wondering, how long this Commission would last at this rate.[6] So, they were to become his 'Knights of the Round Table.' General Thimayya was also introduced to the Swedish and Swiss members of the Commission and they settled down happily.

At the meeting that afternoon, three points came up: the presence of observers; the presence of 'agents'; and, the right to the list of POWs. According to the Terms of Reference, every operation carried out by the NNRC was to be attended by observers from both sides. These terms also mentioned that POWs would be handed over to the custody of the NNRC through their agent to the CFI and, therefore, the observers would be present at the taking over of the prisoners. The UN Command strongly protested that this was a unilateral action between the UN Command and the CFI and, therefore, no Communist observer should be present. The Northern Command was insistent and drew the Commission's attention to this paragraph. So the Commission took a unanimous decision to allow observers to be present.

The Northern Command had told the "Advance Party" of the CFI, that there were agents planted in the compounds by the UN Command and that they had organised these people to resist repatriation.

But the facts showed that the UN Command had picked on these prisoners for their leadership and intercommunicability – and perhaps slow brainwashing was part of the process. They also selected them for their knowledge of English and Korean, as well as Chinese. They were all prisoners and, not inducted from outside as Rhee or the Chinese government made out. Although the UN Command had claimed that the so-called 'agents' had been segregated and excluded from the non-repats after the Koje and De-Choje incidents,[7] they were recognised by the prisoners later in the Explanation Tents. Thimayya was, thus, cautioned and told to remove the 'agents,' before non-repats were explained.

A point was then raised by the Northern Command about the list of POWs held in the camp. They pointed out that the list of POWs handed over to the NNRC by the UN Command should be given to them to enable them to check for the presence of agents amongst them. Refusing to accept this, the UN Command quoted a paragraph of the Terms of Reference, according to which the Commission could only send them a statement every week showing the number of prisoners who chose repatriation and not the whole list. But because the issue had been raised, General Thimayya asked the UN Command regarding its objection to handing over of the list of the POWs to the Northern Command. Pat came the argument that the Communists would kill the relations of POWs in China and North Korea, if they handed over the list to them. When he mentioned this to the Northern Command, they were furious and questioned the chairman: "Do we look the sort of people who would instruct innocent people to be exterminated?" Thimayya obviously nodded, "No."

The Communist member on the Commission then argued: "Well, Chairman, we are all members of this Commission. We presume all documents in your possession are our property, as well."

General Thimayya delayed the handing over of the list to the members for a month or so by saying that he did not have enough staff or the carbon paper to make out the copies but eventually conceded and asked Thorat to observe the 500 men carefully.

Out of the list of so-called 500 agents, they identified 40 to 50 but could not find them doing anything wrong. A few of them were compound leaders. The names given by the Northern Command were chiefly of the battalion commanders, company commanders, platoon and section commanders. There was, thus, no reason to arrest them.

To his disgust, Thimayya found both the Commands, his members and even the prisoners refusing to accept any decision he gave – or would give – as an umpire. *And the first lesson he learnt was that he was being challenged, and he would continue to be challenged, unless he stuck to his own iron rules and his own conscience.*

The next day, during the taking over process, he saw two men being beaten up because they wanted to go back home. So here was evidence available to the NNRC that some prisoners were, indeed, keen to go back home but were being prevented by others.

Interestingly, when the Americans had those people in their camps, they were faced with exactly the same problems as the CFI in the DMZ. In trying to convert Communists, they created organisations with leaders. They would just not let anybody interfere with their discipline or organisations within the camps. It was an estate within an estate. So the American role had been well-founded. Persuading such well-indoctrinated people to return to Communism, Thimayya was becoming aware, was a difficult job and would require sustained, humane effort. Was that possible within a short span and in an ambience of one-up-manship from both Commands?

He found the attitude of the Northern Command more reprehensible when they suggested to him that the prisoners and so-called agents be shot, in case of misbehaviour or violence. If he had agreed, it would have served the cause of the Cold War well. But for the NNRC, it would have implied bloodshed and greater trouble. Weighing the pros and cons, Thimayya decided to take disciplinary action against the defaulters rather than take recourse to what was being suggested.

Dichotomy of the Terms of Reference

How did the Terms of Reference make a desperate situation, worse?

Whenever the Commission interpreted a paragraph in a certain manner, the UN would show the NNRC their draft, made during the negotiations and the negotiatior's verbatim reports to indicate what they meant. Then the Northern Command would show the Korean and Chinese drafts and verbatim reports. They were always different. In fact, Thimayya found them the most amazing of documents published by the two sides – the interpretation of every paragraph was disputed by the other side despite the fact that both sides had signed them. In certain cases, he would jocularly say it was not agreed to even by one side! So they were both dichotomous and controversial, and if not firmly handled, would return the proceedings to *status quo ante*. But he was sanguine that the sole purpose of setting up of the NNRC was to enable transfer of custody of prisoners; to enable parent nations to offer "explanations" to them to return to their countries within the period stipulated and with reasonable extensions.

The first paragraph of the Terms of Reference, for example, said that representatives of both sides should be permitted to observe the operations of the Repatriation Commission and its subordinate bodies, to include explanations and interviews. The Northern Command wanted representatives of both sides to be permitted to observe all the operations of the NNRC and its subordinate bodies, including "explanations and interviews." The UN Command, on the other hand, maintained that only explanations could be observed by both sides. The words "observers, interviews" in this paragraph could be twisted to mean what suited either side. The NNRCs interpretation was that observers from both sides could observe all operations, including the interviews and explanations.

Similarly, Paragraph 2 of the Terms of Reference stipulated that on the expiry of 90 days after the transfer of the custody of the prisoners to the NNRC, access of representatives to captured personnel shall terminate, and Paragraph 3 envisaged "no force or threat of force shall be used against the prisoners of war specified in Paragraph 1 above to prevent or effect their repatriation, and no violence to their persons or affront to their dignity or self-respect shall be permitted in any manner for any purpose whatsoever (but see Paragraph 7 below)." It also required the NNRC to ensure that prisoners of war, shall, at all times, be treated humanely in accordance with the specific provisions of the Geneva Convention, and in the general spirit of that Convention. Then Paragraph 7 added another twist, as it said, "notwithstanding the provisions of Paragraph 3 above, nothing in this agreement shall be construed as derogating from the authority of the NNRC to exercise its legitimate functions and responsibilities for the control of the prisoners of war under its temporary jurisdiction."

So here the NNRC was confronted with Paras 3 and 7. It was its job to give an opportunity to the explaining side to explain to the POWs and then leave it to them to do what they liked. The prisoners, however, had their own understanding about this. They maintained that they need not attend the explanations under threat. (Paragraph 3 prohibited use of force.) The question then arose as to what action the NNRC could take if the prisoners refused explanation. It was perforce agreed that "minimum force" should be used in the circumstances. The members too agreed, with certain reservations. These then became the most quoted and fought over paragraphs of the controversial document.[8]

Para 8, nonetheless, was quite clear. It stipulated that the nations to which the prisoners of war belonged shall have freedom and facilities to send representatives to the locations where such prisoners of war were in custody to explain to all the prisoners their rights and to inform them of any matters relating to their return to their homelands.

However, the UN Command argued that the NNRC had no right to ask these people to attend explanations and that it was only required to give facilities and transport arrangements for the representatives of the explaining side to go and explain to the prisoners there. Their interpretation was that explainers should go there and explain to the prisoners over a loudspeaker. But, because of the existence of subversive organisations and the high-strung mental state of the prisoners, the NNRC knew that if the explainers went on air and explained to the prisoners over loudspeakers, those people would have cut the wires and would have played the brass-bands and their own music systems to drown out the explanations. The explainers would never get the chance of being heard at all.

Hence, Thimayya decided that every prisoner would be explained to individually. The prisoner in the explanation tent would be by himself for about 20 minutes. Also present would be a subordinate body of the NNRC, an observer from his original side, an observer and a representative from the detaining side and interpreters from both sides. That, Thimayya thought, would ensure that the prisoner could freely elect repatriation without any fear or coercion even within the constraints of time.

Yet, these Terms of Reference, rather than simplify the procedures, had introduced an inherent dichotomy, which he could see later building "a mountain of recrimination, vituperation, charges and counter-charges" – a repeat of the days of the long war that caused some 300,000 casualties.

The Troubling Times

The trouble began from the early days. An altercation with US General Lawton while the Communist POWs were being taken for reconciliation fouled the atmosphere. Lawton blamed the NNRC for "leaning right over to Commies." using the deogatory word for Communist. He advised restraint to Lawton. He also had to refuse a Communist demand to reshuffle the POWs in different groups than had been originally formed. For, according to them, agents and gangsters had been infiltrated into the compounds. Radio Beijing castigated Thimayya in harsh words for this so-called "bungling." But he remained firm on his principles within the Terms of Reference as interpreted by the Commission. While he could handle all those who posed problems from outside, a secret organisation among the POWs that prevented repatriation became his stumbling block. Incrimination, doubts and suspicions were being hurled at him by both sides, if it did not suit their demand and concern. Coercion was proving successful in neutralising the natural instincts among the prisoners to return to their countries.

It took time as the process of validation progressed and repatriation began for China and North Korea. But this was negligible compared to what followed. Trouble began when on the first day, nine prisoners escaped and sought repatriation. Out of these, one unfortunate man was caught by the other prisoners and meted out the most heinous treatment. They hanged him upside down and while living they ripped open his heart and distributed it to the others to eat, warning them that their fate would be no better if they sought repatriation. Dave recalls such ghastly sights.[8A]

On the second day, when the prisoners were being transferred, as they were marched in, finger-printed and their kits searched, the Northern Command officer was attacked. The troops of the CFI controlled the ensuing mayhem with difficulty. General Lawton again blamed Thimayya. The same day, the prisoners of the Northern Command tried to bully him, demanded a reshuffle and use of force against those who resisted orders. But Thimayya refused to either reshuffle the prisoners, or use force.

The barrage of fire that came both from the UN Command and Northern Command made him sit up. While the UN Command sent a long letter of complaints under General Clark's signature, the Northern Command continued to castigate him in broadcasts over Radio Beijing.

More trouble followed on 15 September, as two officers of 6th Jat were detained by the POWs. Luckily, they managed to get out of a tricky situation.

Although explanations were to commence on 26 September, they were delayed to mid-October owing to objections to the explanation sites, that led to the selection of new sites and subsequent construction. It was the two concerned parties, namely, the UN Command and Northern Command rather than the prisoners of war that had begun a "Cold War" which from then onwards became a *battle royale*.

Then came the trouble of 24-25 September – a case of rioting – and which, but for the intelligent handling and wisdom shown by General Thorat, would have totally undermined the NNRC and the image of India. It followed the repatriation of a Chinese prisoner, Sergeant Won Chu, who had been the leader of Compound 31/D. In the mass demonstration that took riotous shape the following morning, the prisoners nabbed Major Grewal and Captain Sukhjit Singh, besides a driver, Thakur Singh (who, in the tradition of the army, decided not to abandon his officers). Thorat rushed in and through persuasion, calmed the situation. "What sort of Chinese are you?" said Thorat to assuage the POWs anger and added, "I and my men have been your guests but you have not seen it fit to offer us a cup of tea or even a cigarette...." said Thorat in a masterpiece psychological stroke that had magical effect.

In recommending General Thorat for an award, Thimayya explained the situation and concluded: "This action on the part of General SPP Thorat was far beyond his normal duty and at the risk of his own life, and by his daring and coolness, he took a calculated risk which not only rescued Major Grewal but also prevented an outburst of violence which might have caused many deaths both to the prisoners and to our officers and men." And, further, "This act on General Thorat's part was in the highest traditions of the Indian Army and not only raised his prestige among his own troops but also brought him admiration from the POWs who gave him a Guard of Honour as he left their compound."[9]

Thimayya was unsure of the type of recommendation he could make for Thorat and others who showed conspicuous courage at this moment. In response to a letter from Major General JN Chaudhuri, CGS, he wrote: "I am pleased that the chief has asked me about Thorat: I hesitated to make a recommendation as I was not quite sure as to the reaction, especially as the past policy has laid so much emphasis on decorations in battle. I am convinced that Thorat did a very fine job in that particular situation and did not realise even the risk that he ran (into). In fact, I had given him a 'friendly rocket' and asked him not to repeat his performance, which might cause us real embarrassment in rescuing him. He fully deserves this award...." He had left the column for "award" blank requesting the chief to fill it suitably. Thorat was awarded an Ashoka Chakra Class II (now Kirti Chakra).

Mayhem of Explanations

In drawing up the Rules of Procedure for explanations, the NNRC had struck a judicious balance. In twelve of these the NNRC sided with the Swiss and the Swedes and in the other twelve with the Czechs and Poles. But it had trouble over the construction of the Explanation Area. The Northern Command insisted that it should be done in the manner in which the explaining side wanted it. The UN Command had already constructed explanation structures in consultation with the CFI. But the Northern Command completely turned it down saying that it was most unsuitable and at a wrong place, being on the tip of the ground on the UN side, so that the prisoners coming to the area would be 'guided psychologically' to go back to the UN Command side. They wanted it on the tip of land on their side and the whole thing spread out.

Eventually, when a new site was selected and buildings constructed at Thimayya's personal request to General Clark, the NNRC had lost three precious weeks – a delay caused on purpose by the Northern Command.

How were the explanations conducted?

In the explanation hut, the explainer sat on one side. Opposite him, sat the prisoner. Facing the door through which the prisoner came in, sat the subordinate body of the NNRC, backed by interpreters from both sides. Then there were representatives and observers from both sides. The troops of the CFI had to perforce protect the explainer, and had to place barbed wire between the prisoner and explainer. Both Commands, but more so the Northern, did not want to have a wire obstacle between the prisoner and the explainer, as they alleged, it would have a "psychological effect" on the prisoner to go back, and demanded that the NNRC should ensure that they were not attacked.

The Commission was in for more trouble. The first day when a prisoner entered the explanation tent, he made a rush towards the explainer and a wrestling match ensued. So the CFI soldiers had to restrain the prisoner and put him back in his seat. The first thing the explainer did was to read out a message from Marshal Kim II Sung. The explainer then asked the chairman of the subordinate body if he could present the document to him. He walked across over to the prisoner slowly. As he got near the prisoner, the latter got up and attempted to attack him and spit at him. Another prisoner blew his nose at the explainer! But the people who wanted to go back to the Communists, came in, shook hands with the explainers, tore off their American supplied clothing and went back straight. Very few went back to the Communists due to these explanations.

The Communist side had 359 prisoners, all thoroughly brainwashed. They too had their share of outrageous behaviour. They would listen to the speech and ask for permission to reply and then lambast the explainer in the most unparliamentary language. The explainer would then say, "We don't want such talk." But the prisoner would insist on having his say and insult him.

The 22,000 prisoners of the UN Command had also been tutored on how to resist explanations. As soon as the explainers came, they would start shouting "Tai-Wan" "Tai-Wan," and would not listen to the explainers at all. The explanations, thus, turned into demonstration of intensified sentiments, exaggerated emotions and melodrama. On the first day, the Northern Command were able to explain to about one thousand prisoners giving 15 to 20 minutes of explanation to each. When they found that by this method only 5 per cent or so people had asked for repatriation, they resorted to prolonged explanations; at times, explaining to one prisoner for two to three hours. The prisoner would say that he didn't want the explanation, but the explainer would insist that he had not finished his explanation. The Communists maintained that it was for the explaining side to decide how much explanation would suffice. Thimayya maintained that it was, in fact, for the NNRC to decide on a rough time schedule. But that was contested not only by the Commands but the delegates of the NNRC, and the delegates would walk out if it did not suit their side. So in this unsatisfactory manner the explanations carried on.

The UN Command too continued to influence every prisoner before he came up for explanation. They would send in radio sets and instructions in ration bags and the South Korean division near Hindnagar would relay messages to prisoners through heliographs. But the UN Command quickly assured the NNRC that they would rectify these errors – which they did. It was a game of wits, after all.

As the explanation process picked up, it became evident that both Commands and even the Czech and Pole delegates had little interest in the repatriation of the non-repats. The UN Command was in the meanwhile cleverly turning the 64th Field

Hospital into a spy centre through the staff and prisoners under treatment. The explainers too suffered indignities and threats to their lives.

Media's Role

As chairman NNRC, Thimayya had to deal with the two rival Commands, the uncooperative non-repats, occasionally with the governments of Seoul, Delhi, Beijing and Washington, and there appeared another agency claiming full attention: the reporters, some 200 of them. This category was worrisome, wearisome, unaccountable and unmanageable. They were not only breathing down his neck but breathing fire. Whether one liked them or not, they were there, and could not be ignored.

Thimayya's public relations officer (PRO), Lieutenant Colonel Streenivasan had a hard time explaining to the media, who continuously played on the theme of the "battered and beleaguered" plight of the Indian troops, on the one hand, and the forcible repatriation by them of the prisoners, on the other. *The Star & Stripes*, an unofficial US Forces newspaper was directly implicating the troops of CFI, often carrying stories in which facts were mixed with fiction and fantasy. It called for a continuous 'battle' to lift the 'fog' to prevent such reporting from spreading disinformation and panic.

The explanations had also drawn criticism, even from the Indian papers. For example, he had to explain to K. Rangaswamy, editor, *The Hindu*, the correct position.[10]

A bad Press, Thimayya knew, would have the worst effect at home. All sorts of personal opinions had begun to appear. The effect was visible even at Delhi. BB Ghosh, an official from the Ministry of External Affairs, India, for example, counseled him on India's "impartial role," and advised him to have exposure only to "guarded publicity," even in an incident when KPVA Lieutenant Kim Yon Mo was saved by Lieutenant Colonel Ujjal Singh. Thimayya obviously felt hurt about it, as he wrote back: "Every newsable news gets out of here in any case as there are some 200 Press correspondents." He added: "This is a very tough assignment you have managed to push us on and I think there are worse things ahead. Anyway, I am keeping my fingers crossed and hoping for the best. Jai Hind."[11]

Thimayya knew that the media would "paint white whiter and black blacker" and would often make scandalous observations. But careful preparation and unanimity of all members of the Commission would help. *The Stars & Stripes* was a paper that had to be silenced; but the Press all over, including in India, was making mountains out of molehills; their perspective too had to be corrected.

He decided to call a meeting of the Press with the entire NNRC on 6 October. He anticipated most of the questions he would be asked. His deliberate and convincing replies to all queries changed the attitude of the Press, the basis of which focussed on the fact that the *Commission was there to protect the interests of the prisoners and (to that effect) to guarantee them real freedom of choice*.

The *Time* magazine of 19 October (1953) gave a glimpse of the effect: "One day last week, Thimayya summoned UN and Communist correspondents to Panmunjom for his first Press conference. For two hours, coolly, he sought to allay UN fears that the POWs would not be coerced by Communist 'explainers' into going back to their Communist homelands. 'The POWs would have to go to the explanation huts,' he said, but wondered 'how to make a man listen?'"

Time added, "One by one, UN newsmen voiced specific UN worries. How long would each explanation session last? I think we can ask the POWs to listen for five or ten minutes. Would POWs have to take more than one explanation? He did not think it possible. Would the 90-day explanation period be lengthened, as the Communists demanded? Not unless both sides agreed. (The UN does not.) Could his men stop a breakout? Yes, but 'with terrible slaughter.' Would he stop one? 'Yes,' he said."[12]

The New York Herald Tribune of 8 October, 1953, observed on this: "Lieut Gen KS Thimayya, the Indian Chairman of the Neutral Nations Repatriation Commission in Korea...in the midst of a highly explosive situation, invited newspaper and radio men to a Press conference in Panmunjom Tuesday; about fifty Allied correspondents sat side by side with twenty-five Communist writers and fired questions at him regarding the handling of the 22,500 Chinese and North Korean war prisoners who refused repatriation... smoking cigarettes, he answered coolly ; asked whether he would attempt to stop a mass outbreak of POWs, he said he didn't think so ; the slaughter would be too terrible."

The sensational heading that appeared frequently, especially in South Korea and America would say: "Indians wouldn't attempt to stop breakout." That would further enrage Dr Syngman Rhee. Gradually, however, the ambience brightened up and reduced the "burdensome, worrisome pretty bloody situation," as he wrote to Chaudhuri. "Diplomacy," he remarked to another friend "is at its rawest stage and I am no diplomat." Even seasoned diplomats would have thrown in the towel at this 'unmitigated muddle.'

After the October briefing of the Press, the media had become a friend of Thimayya. "A turning point," he called it. His sense of humour never left him, as he wrote: "We achieved a semblance of popularity. At best, however, popularity was an uneasy virtue. *Only when each side was accusing me of collusion with the other, could I feel sure that I was being neutral.*"[13] Although critics could never be eulogisers, most were making his job easier by objective reporting. *Handling of the media was one big lesson he learnt, and he excelled in it all his life.*

Indian Commitment

The NNRC was primarily a commitment on part of the Indian government. Nehru made it clear to the Parliament repeatedly that it was so and that "Thimayya as Chairman, represented India." So, it was India's reputation that was at stake. Thimayya, indeed, stood up to the challenge, as did his officers and men. He was determined to see that the NNRC stayed on course, despite all the wrangling. The government too, ensured that political advice was available to Thimayya in critical situations.

Syngman Rhee's anti-India canard had by now reached a crescendo, and he did everything in his power to provoke both the UN Command and the anti-Communist non-repat prisoners to prove to the world how inept the Indians were in handling the problem. Syngman Rhee, it must be understood, had succeeded in keeping America involved in Korea, more or less on his terms. For, Rhee was unhappy at the signing of the Armistice itself. The release of 27,000 Communist prisoners of war from South Korea and non-cooperation with the CFI and the NNRC were the outcome of this.

Dr Rhee made several insinuations against the CFI which included the "arming of the Indian troops to the teeth," that they would shoot helpless prisoners; that explanations were forced and of long duration; that trials of prisoners were being held for no reason; that the Communists were being allowed to broadcast and they rigged their explanations; and so on. Most of them were refuted not only by the NNRC but supported by Arthur H. Dean, secretary to John Foster Dulles, and by the Indian government, including Krishna Menon, the Indian delegate to the General Assembly in November 1953.

Prime Minister Nehru would support the cause of the NNRC, finally on 24 December 1953, when the question of return of the POWs hung in jeopardy. He explained India's stand as he spoke in the Parliament:

> India went to Korea to solve the problem and the Government under me would accept the challenge not once but a 'hundred times.' We are not a great military nation, nor a rich nation but we have certain standards by which we act as a nation ... because President Rhee says something that we do not like, can we call back our troops and upset the whole apple-cart? War or no war, massacre or no massacre, we are going to discharge the work to the best of our ability...[14]

Thimayya realised his job involved reconciling the irreconcilable; untying virtually an irrational knot and turning centripetal forces into centrifugal ones. The battle astride the 38th Parallel had moved to the tables where each side tried to outmanoeuvre and outwit the other. The prisoners, tired of the brain-washing, had been taken to a point where they became disloyal to their own army and country by seeking non-repatriation. They had suffered more humiliation in the prisoners' camps than in the hazards and privations of the battlefield. They were pawns in the captors' hands. Two small warring groups had been introduced into the Commission to carry on this sinister ideological battle, and the attitude of the two Commands was trying to place India as chairman and custodian force, between the proverbial "devil and the deep blue sea." The responsibility of completing an impossible task naturally fell on the shoulders of Thimayya. Even Thorat, as the Custodian Force commander under Thimayya, observed the ambience, as of the Cold War.[15]

If the Northern Command and Radio Beijing were lambasting Thimayya along with Dr Rhee, the American UN Command under General Mark Clark was insinuating that he was "failing to uphold the principle of freedom of choice." It was evidently part of the UN Command's pressure tactics to go slow on "observers," "explanation" and "repatriation." The Northern Command too resorted to innumerable tactics to retard the process, though its *modus operandi* was deliberate and persistent.[16]

By the end of October and Nehru's Deepawali greetings to the Indian soldiers on the All India Radio (AIR) on 8 November, people became aware of the thankless task Thimayya was entrusted with. Nehru's address recorded by the AIR stated: "Our soldiers have a difficult task. From all accounts, they have borne themselves worthily and our country feels proud of the way they have discharged their duties with quiet efficiency, peaceful and disciplined behaviour."

But the Cold War effect would not cease. The United Nations Command and the United States protested that the prisoners were being "unduly influenced." The Commission rejected these protestations and said that "it could not be guided by any interpretation other than its own." A letter was addressed by the chairman to General Clark in reply to the commander-in-chief's letter of 15 October. The UN Command was assured that "the Commission was fully conscious of the responsibility it has taken and it would continue to discharge its obligation with complete integrity and strict impartiality and with full understanding of what is involved, bearing in mind the history of the POWs issue."

Testing Times

On 15 October, when explanations had already begun, the prisoners were in no mood to listen to the explainers. However, after much persuasion, out of 490 Communist prisoners, a mere ten opted for repatriation. This saw the explainers depressed at the loss of face. The UN representative, however, showed great jubilation. The result was that no one would appear the following morning and, hence, a "show of force" had to be staged by the CFI. On 16 October, the stratagem of a "show of force" to "force" the prisoners to attend explanations, led to a situation – which if adopted – would have a Koje, De-Choje repeated, the NNRC discredited, and with it everything else that the UN and India had at stake.

If luck played truant, Thimayya's wisdom, courage, better sense and firm control restrained the massacre. As a result, while the process of explanation suffered and was delayed by a fortnight, the situation was pulled back from the very precipice of defeat.

On this day, the North Korean prisoners of two compounds were to undergo explanations. They refused. A show of force by the Dogras had no effect. Then it appeared as if the prisoners would attempt a break-out and as the Dogras readjusted their positions to meet this contingency, the prisoners got infuriated.

Virtually insane, the prisoners rushed to the barbed wire fencing and attempted to climb over the wire obstacles. But as the Dogra troops advanced, the prisoners melted into the camp; however, they refused to come out for explanations. Thorat had the Commission's authority to use force but instead – and fortunately – once again wanted a confirmatory order to open fire, if necessary. He told Thimayya that opening fire could, of course, result in some 300-400 casualties.[17] Upon this, the Communist delegate speaking on behalf of the Northern Command, took offence to Thorat's intended inaction and walked out, but the Swede and Swiss supported him. Thimayya, as chairman, was "not prepared to use force without unanimous consent of the whole Commission." So orders for resorting to fire were rescinded.

It was a loss of face for the Dogras, who were jeered at by the prisoners and being highly sensitive about their *izzat*, were demoralised. It led to a stormy session within the Commission too but the tempest blew over only after the sustained effort by Thimayya. While the world around was enraged and virtually set on fire, and the two warring Commands watched expectantly, and the Communists fumed and fretted, General Thimayya withdrew to a quiet corner, smoked his cigarettes and reflected on the episode phlegmatically:

"As chairman of the NNRC, as the Indian delegate and as a military man, I was not prepared to condone a mass slaughter of unarmed men. I felt such slaughter would mean the failure of the NNRC."[18]

He was quite prepared to forgo his own and his subordinates' ego but was sanguine that "if lack of strong action" could end the NNRC, he would accept the full blame. It infuriated the Czech and Polish delegates who walked out, bringing a crisis within the Commission to a head and towards disaster. The subsequent meeting was turning into the fabled Tower of Babel. But using his charm and wit, cool headedness as always, Thimayya had everyone back to the Peace Pagoda and working. The troops too recovered and got on with their job.

Refining the Instrument

Following the unprecedented event of 16 October, the prisoners became his key result area. He realised, albeit rather late, that so much persuasion of the prisoners to attend the explanations was not necessary. It was barely necessary to convey to them that unless they individually cooperated, their fate and future hung in the balance. They, therefore, had to cooperate. Gradually, he began to reach out to them in an informal manner and found that the leaders of the compounds reacted favourably to his conversations, often asking for more time to go back.

It became increasingly clear to him that the issue of use of force should have never arisen. In his own words: *"After the surprise of my first real contact with the prisoners, I began to wonder about them as people. How did they get there? What are the differences between them? What are their motivations? I realise now that both sides had forgotten to think of these men as human beings, and were treating them as pawns in a bitter game of politics."*

Thimayya also became conscious that anxiety and fear were clouding the already traumatised souls and minds of the prisoners. Winning their confidence and assuring them that, irrespective of ideological differences, their human freedom, dignity and above all, their individual interests alone would solicit willing cooperation for them.[19]

Propaganda from both sides had made out that the Indians (including Thimayya and the CFI) were pro-Communist. That prejudice also had to be also removed. It involved his personal interaction with every prisoner.

Neutrality was the cornerstone of the NNRC. *Nonetheless, the true meaning and application of neutrality, as Thimayya observed, was to ascertain the true desire of the non-repat POWs.*

The American parents and friends of prisoners were persistent in their request to Thimayya to do 'something' to convey their messages to their wayward sons. He would advise them to wait for the change of heart by the American explainers. Although he adopted a proforma-response to the anxious Americans about their non-repats, these prisoners continued to be both an enigma and a source of study to him. He observed, "American non-repats interested me the most, probably because there had been much publicity about them.... This group's conviction was based on rationality.... Most of them came from the poorest and under-privileged groups in the US. Three of them were African-Americans who seemed to feel that they were escaping from racial prejudice in their country."[20]

The UN side, Thimayya observed, had its own 'brand of troubles' in its 359 pro-Communist non-repats, who included 23 Americans and one Briton. Their explanation was delayed till as late as 3 December, and ended without disturbance. None of the prisoners opted to be repatriated, as each said "no use inducing me," "I would rather marry a Korean girl," and refused to receive explanations. On 23 December, the final day, the UN Command made a general broadcast but to no effect.

The prisoners assured him that they trusted India but wanted him to ask the Indian troops to be friendly. (The problem was of language and not of behaviour or attitudes.) He told them, "If you are prepared to give me a guarantee of good behaviour and military discipline, I shall have no guard."

Even after the beginning of explanations which only commenced from 31 October (and ended on 23 December), he was meeting the prisoners, the last time being his visit to the Song Gong-ni Camp of South Korean prisoners on 11 December. Persuasion was the keyword, while confidence building was the purpose of his visits. "I persuaded them to trust me that they would be treated fairly," he told the Press reporters on 15 December. "For the NNRC was not only responsible for repatriation, but the CFI under it was to look after their discipline, welfare and morale as well."

There were murders in the camps and an international tribunal was appointed to conduct an inquiry into these cases. Brigadier KN Dubey was the president of this tribunal. When one of the accused was asked, "Did you kill them?" he replied, "We killed them, the whole of the compound killed them."

Ironically, the trial that commenced on 6 January 1954, dragged on till 23 January, to be finally called off, as on this day, the witnesses refused to attend. Another case where four people had been strangulated was also dropped.

Thimayya was often discreetly told that nobody loves an ump (umpire). But he remembered Nehru's words, "Though neutral India maybe unpopular but that's what you will have to do and prove in every aspect in Korea." He really had to do some tight-rope walking.

Appreciation

Thousands of people wrote appreciating Thimayya's role. E Ronald Walker, Australia's ambassador to Japan, made a broadcast on 19 November, highlighting the "tedious task" that the NNRC was assigned – and was doing. Thimayya assured Walker that the NNRC was not there to find fault with either side. "All I would like, to do," he wrote "is to settle the future of these poor miserable prisoners who have been behind barbed wire for over two years and for me it is a real human problem."

Mr HD Black, the American ambassador to Thailand, for example, said that use of force could not possibly compel non-repats to change their minds. Recognising the brave role the NNRC and the CFI were playing, he emphasised: "*It is to the everlasting credit of India that she has refused to use force, and has been backed by the Swedish and Swiss representatives.*" (Emphasis added.)

The Economist, of London, wrote of Thimayya in the 23-29 November issue: "The behaviour of the hard pressed custodian force under the direction of General Thimayya, the Chairman of NNRC, has won much praise for its tact and impartiality as well as for its determination to carry out its most invidious task in spite of every kind of external pressures. As a result, there is a considerably better feeling between the Indians on the spot and the American officers of the UN Command."

Armstrong Hamilton, the editor of *Foreign Affairs*, called him a veritable Mahatma in the army, who even in the face of the gravest provocations, would not allow a single round to be fired at the prisoners. He wrote, "The bloodless victories you have won in Korea entitle you a permanent place in the annals of the Army of India and the UN. It is simply unrivalled." [21]

While doing the job, he was communicating with the highest and rubbing shoulders with the commoners – a typical Thimayya trait. To thousands who wrote letters to him, some of whom were the anxious parents of the POWs, he would promptly reply. In the din of activities, he would have time for his officers and men too. The troops of the CFI, he observed, were perpetually on guard, and tense as they feared an assault by the POWs while they like Jesus Christ offered their "other cheek." They were exhausted due to their interminable duties and the bitter cold of Korea but the Indian soldiery could rise to any challenge when the *izzat* of the country and their regiments was at stake. Thimayya was beside them as often as possible. The officers and men of the CFI adored him.

The promptness of the concern he showed for the problems and queries of everyone was legendary. When Air Vice Marshal M M Engineer, deputy air commander, Air Headquarters wanted to find out if Wing Commander Baldwin was a prisoner, or had died in the Korean War, Thimayya replied within a fortnight, confirming the latter. He was in communication with editors of newspapers, explaining the correct position; as well as with various ambassadors.

He replied to letters from "Jail Baba" of Bandipur (of his J&K days), his own Kodagu *Samaj* in Mercara, a IXth class boy from the Aurobindo Ashram who sent ten rupees from his meagre pocket money for the "welfare of troops." "Noble sentiments, boy," he wrote back, "you qualify to be a soldier of India." He thanked BN Chakravarty, his alternate chairman and political adviser, who was evacuated due to acute bronchitis, for all the good work he had done.

"I sometimes wonder," wrote Chakravarty after being evacuated, "what brand of cigarettes you smoke; for, it has something to do with your tact and patience while presiding over the NNRC or watching the operations of the prisoners. I salute you."[22]

Then came an incredibly astonishing letter from US Secretary of State John Foster Dulles. Dulles, known for his anti-India feelings and utterances, was appreciative of the NNRC. His message read out by the US representative at the pre-political conference at Panmunjom on 19 November expressed this appreciation. "*India as Chairman of the NNRC and through the presence of her Custodial Forces in Panmunjom is now directly contributing to the stabilisation of the Armistice in an important and able way and humanely and nobly carrying out one of the most difficult missions ever entrusted to any nation any time.*" (Emphasis added.) Appreciation for a job well done was also received by the Government of India from the Chinese Prime Minister, Zhou En-lai, and head of North Korea, Kim Il-Sung. More pointed and appreciative was the letter of President Eisenhower, as evident from his letter to Nehru:[23]

> *Dear Mr Prime Minister,*
>
> *Now that this mission of Indian Troops is drawing to a close in Korea, I want to express to you my appreciation and that of my countrymen for the performance of the Indian Custodial Forces.*
>
> *No military unit in recent years has undertaken a more delicate and demanding peacetime mission than that faced by the Indian Forces in Korea. The vast majority of the prisoners placed in their charge had, from months of imprisonment and uncertainty, became highly nervous and volatile. The confidence inspired by the exemplary tact, fairness and firmness shown by the Indian officers and men led by their two able commanders, Lieutenant General Thimayya and Major General Thorat did much to alleviate the fears and doubts of these prisoners. The performance of these officers and*

their troops was fully in keeping with the high reputation of the Indian Army. They deserve the highest commendation.

With best wishes,

Sincerely
Dwight D Eisenhower

His Excellency Jawaharlal Nehru
Prime Minister of India

Korea revealed him in many a splendoured form.

Grand Finale to an Experiment

The final dispersal of POWs was governed by Paragraph 11 of the Terms of Reference which said, "At the expiration of 90 days after the transfer of custody of the prisoners of war to the NNRC, access of representatives to captured personnel as provided for in Paragraph 8 (above), shall terminate, and the question of disposition of the prisoners of war who have not exercised their right to be repatriated, shall be submitted to the Political Conference recommended to be convened in Paragraph 60, Draft Armistice Agreement, which shall endeavour to settle this question within thirty days, during which period the NNRC shall continue to retain custody of those prisoners of war. The NNRC shall declare the relief from the prisoner of war status to civilian status of any prisoners of war who have not exercised their right to be repatriated and for whom no other disposition has been agreed to by the Political Conference within one hundred and twenty days after the NNRC has assumed their custody. Thereafter, according to the application of each individual, those who choose to go to neutral nations shall be assisted by the NNRC and the Red Cross Society of India. This operation shall be completed within 30 days, and upon its completion, the NNRC shall immediately cease its function."

Later, the Northern Command wanted the NNRC to hold the prisoners indefinitely. But Thimayya told them that at the end of 120 days, it would be going home. Finally, on the 121st day, the prisoners were handed back to the two commands – the UN Command willingly accepting them, with the Northern Command doing so sulkingly, as it wanted the NNRC to do so only after the Political Conference was over. However, the best thing the Indian Government did, was to tell them to take the prisoners back at the end of 120 days as per the Terms of Reference.[24]

Of the 3,222 prisoners who were put through the explanations, only 4 per cent chose repatriation to their homelands. The fear in the minds of the prisoners and the indifference of the two Commands was responsible for the low figure. It was a clear battle of the Cold War for propaganda victory, with the unfortunate prisoners becoming the victims – for the second time; the first was to have become prisoners and now repats. And at the end, the results of repatriation made it evident that almost 96 per cent of the Chinese and North Korean and 90 per cent of the UN Command repats refused to return to their own countries. But left to General Thimayya, the outcome would certainly have been far more assuring, besides satisfying.

In all, 21,805 prisoners were handed back to the UN Command and 347 to Red Cross representatives of North Korea and China. During the period of CFI custody, 629 prisoners of the UN command and 359 of KPA-CPV sought repatriation and returned to their respective Commands. CFI brought back 88 non-repats who wished to settle in India.[25]

According to the UN sources, the operations of the NNRC had cost $ 30.5 million, a dollar being valued at Rs 4 at that time. It was a small cost for a large useful *coup d'essai*. Truly, it would seem the whole thing remained an "experiment in neutrality" but, fortunately, the prisoner non-repats were not made into guinea pigs, as the concerned parties had seemed to want to do.

There were errors made by him as chairman and by others of his commission and command. There was a mix-up in accounting and, worst of all, the thought of use of force was reprehensible. It was Thimayya's trait not to brood over things and he believed in letting the storm pass over. He would take responsibility for the mistakes of his subordinates and even of those only indirectly concerned, and attempt to rectify them. He understood the difficulties and the possibilities of errors. He believed, and practised it too, *that praise, and not censure, should be passed on to his subordinates. That was his magic wand of command and in this situation, a stroke of statesmanship. His rewards would be immediate and pleasant. Sometimes they looked miraculous too.*

The best miracle, he realised had happened in Hindnagar before his departure. Dr Rhee, acknowledging the sincerity of his purpose and the enviable task done by the CFI, agreed to let the troops return to Inchon by the South Korean Railways. Short of meeting them, he did everything possible to make their return journey enjoyable – although the US forces heavily guarded the track all over the South Korean stretch. The change of heart – and perspective – had been slow, but finally it did happen.

"There is an Indian General," he is reported to have said, "who, as Chairman of the Commission, didn't sway from his mission." Such words coming from an anti-Indian Dr Rhee transcended all other praise received by General Thimayya.

The CFI had a precious load of 88 non-repats, including 86 from South Korea! While the CFI moved back after a brief holiday in Singapore, Thimayya with his ADC, Captain KS Bahri, flew back to Calcutta after a brief intermission in Tokyo.

Delhi was agog with the news of the return of Thimayya and his contingent. At a reception hosted by Sham Nath, president Delhi Municipal Committee, Thimayya, speaking in Hindi, said he could not say whether they had been successful or not but he could say "without any fear of contradiction that all officers and the jawans of the Indian Army had, by their exemplary behaviour, raised India in world esteem." He assured the countrymen that the army was ever willing to make any sacrifice in the interest of the nation.

Above all else, he did not fail to emphasise, his life-long, inalienable love and affection for the soldiers of the Indian Army and admiration for the virtues of a noble profession. Calling them our "honourable jawans," he saw them as "uncomplaining and cheerful men with strong sense of *izzat* and devotion to duty." "Emerging from an atmosphere (of Korea) of mayhem and chaos, privations and challenges, belaboured and beleaguered, we would see their triumph now and later," he said.

Then came a personal and magnanimous gesture from Prime Minister Nehru. He called General Thimayya to his office, and presented him with his own autographed photograph. Thimayya kept the photograph in his house, on a table where people could see it as they signed his Visitors' Book. It meant more to him than the government's award of the Padma Vibhushan, the citation for which read: "In recognition of his most outstanding role as Chairman of the Neutral Nations' Repatriation Commission, Korea 1953-54 and in enhancing India's prestige in the cause of world peace."[26]

Korea marked General Thimayya's meteoric rise to fame. He became India's international celebrity from "an otherwise Indian Army general" – like several others, but he was head and shoulders above them. He was now a soldier-statesman, and some politicians, fearing his unprecedented popularity, quietly began to treat him as a *bete noire*; others, however, loved him. And although he repeatedly disclaimed to have any talent for diplomacy or politics he, indeed, had it in abundance. Korea enabled the great showing of political genius, that could make this military commander supreme.

Personally, it had been an "eight month long harassment," for him. But the reward he received was what the official *janm-patri*, or the horoscope had proclaimed. General Maharaj Rajindra Sinhji, the C-in-C Indian Army, in his annual assessment of General Thimayya referred to him as the "Pied Piper of Panmunjom." "The army would benefit," wrote the C-in-C, "by being placed under his leadership at an early date."[27] ∎

And a Memento

What General Thimayya valued the most, however, was a letter and a few gifts from a lowly suffering but a self-assured non-repat. A monument, he told all, when he received Lien Tuei's letter. He would often quote from Somerset Maugham: "The great man is too often all of a piece: it is the little man that is bundle of contradictory elements. He is inexhaustible. You never come to the end of surprises he has in store for you." Tuei was offering that pleasant surprise through his letter.

"To

General Thimayya

Since the time we entered the neutral territory, you have given us every facility for our living and carrying out our work. We sincerely thank you all for your spirit to serve for freedom and liberty.

We know that the task for which you have taken the responsibility is an extremely difficult one but you have taken a righteous stand based on human freedom to fully protect our right to freedom and struggle. This has given perfect satisfaction and earned high respect of our group of anti-Communist patriots.

The aggressive Chinese and Korean Communist followers are using every ingenious device to scatter and break our anti-Communist resolve and make the smooth working of the Korean Armistice Agreement impossible. You had to deal with each problem one by one and this has received praise of the whole world. The way of your dealing with problems is deep and your attitude is righteous and bright.

Now we venture to express our friendly feelings and sincere thanks for the friendly help given by you during this short period. We have the honour to present to you 6 Chinese paintings, 4 tea cups, one battleship made of wood, one medium type tank, 2 cigarette case sets, one pair cotton shoes. We hope that his kind of friendship will be maintained till the end and we will advance together in friendship for the sake of just and righteous freedom.

The Chinese Anti-Communist Prisoners of War Camp – 13 group (Lien Tuei)"

NOTES

1. The Armistice was signed on 27 July 1953, at Panmunjom. And while the prisoners' numbers varied, there were reports of a large number of them not having been declared by the Communists; some 27,000 POWs were made to escape from South Korea, presumably under Dr Rhee's orders.
2. Terms of Reference. Some explanation follows as the text progresses.
3. Although, initially Thimayya had thought that the civilian officials were not really required, he would realise their usefulness very soon. Chakravarty, as alternate chairman, would help in settling the diplomatic issues; the others would also play very useful roles in sub-committees of the explanation mechanism. "I was impressed," said Dave, "by General Thimayya's frankness in telling us to our faces that we had been thrust on him against his wishes by the PM, and he would not be utilising our services. He (however) remained cordial and distant...His was a commanding personality. He had the great qualities of courage, fair-mindedness and sportsmanship."
4. The prisoners, whose numbers continued to change until after being handed over, stood at 22,959:
   - UN Command: Chinese – 14,700; North Korean – 7,904.
   - KPA–CPA or Northern Command: 330 men, 5 women – South Korean, 23 Americans and one British (Total 359)
5. See author's *Generals and Strategists : From Kautilya to Manekshaw*, ch 16.
6. All quoted conversations are of General Thimayya, excerpted from a lecture he gave at the

USI, New Delhi, in June 1954. Most of the quotes are from his address.
7. At Koje and De-Choje, the prisoners rioted which forced the Americans to open fire. They killed or wounded some 3,000 of them. The Americans failed to control them thereafter, compelling them to agree to some other agency, taking over the prisoners. The NNRC was, in many ways, that agency.
8. *Experiments in Neutrality*, p.144. The Commission had circulated the Terms of Reference to all the POWs' compounds, to ensure that their rights and obligations were safeguarded. Based on these Terms of Reference, the Commission had prepared its own standard operating procedures, which were called "Rules of Procedure." These were circulated to the *Commands, etc but not among the POWs.*
8A. Interview of K Dave, IP, who formed part of the NNRC.
9. From Official Records.
Sepoy Driver Thakur Singh was also awarded a decoration for "conspicuous display of loyalty to his officers."
10. Letter to the editor, *The Hindu*, dated 20 November 1953.
11. Semi-official letter of BB Ghosh on behalf of Sir Raghvan Pillai, secretary general, External Affairs.
12. He admitted frankly that this first Press conference made him "nervous" and the whole Commission sat behind him for "moral support." *Experiments in Neutrality*, p.162.
13. Ibid., p.164
14. Jawahar Lal Nehru's Speeches Vol. III (March 1953 to August 1957, pp. 244-45)
15. In *Reveille to Retreat*, at p.156, Thorat says: "...acrimonious discussions and gradually prisoners faded into the background. Then the only thing that mattered was the political prestige of the country involved...both sides aimed at wrecking the 'Explanation' and pass the blame on the other side. It was a Cold War ideological conflict at its worst."
16. The US government finally adopted a more positive attitude to the final settlement of the Korean problem after General Eisenhower promised the Americans to "bring the war in Korea to an early end." Soon, General Clark, who represented the McArthur school of thought, was replaced by General Hull, a more moderate officer, who had instructions not to collude with Dr Syngman Rhee in his misadventures of 'reuniting Koreas through war' and even regarding India as its enemy. General Taylor was shifted to command the US 8th Army and General Hull was appointed as commander Far East Command and UN Command. Taylor became Thimayya's life-long friend.
17. n. 15, p.199, mentions General Thorat's personal experience.
18. n. 12, p.173.
19. Ibid., p108. Why some of the Communist prisoners did not want to be repatriated also became clear to Thimayya. He observed the case of a Chinese lieutenant. "My CO was prejudiced against me," he said. To Thimayya, his was a case of "emotional stultification."
20. Private correspondence.
21. In a private letter, dated 30 November 1953.
22. Ibid.

23. Ibid.
24. The quotes here and earlier are from a lecture General Thimayya gave to the members of the USI, in mid-1954.
25. n. 15, p.155.
26. His citation, quoted from the *Gazette*.
27. From Official Records.

Additional Notes

1. The scars of this awful conflict, as predicted by General Thimayya, have continued to remain septic, cancerous, if not fatal. Though these were the officially declared figures of UN POWs handed over to the CFI, according to other sources, more than 1,000 American prisoners had been siphoned off to Russia. Colonel Philip Corso, an intelligence officer to General Lawton, the head of the UN Truce Team in Korea, claimed so in an article in 1993 when the end of the Cold War Treaty was being signed. According to the *International Herald Tribune* of 30 October 2002, "North Korea is following through with promises to cooperate with the United States on recovering the bodies of more than 8,000 Americans still listed as missing from the Korean War. US military officials said the North had agreed on the return of 11 sets of remains, to be flown from Pyongyang to the US Air Force base in Yokota, Japan, en route to a laboratory in Hawaii where specialists will examine the bones to determine their authenticity."

    One does not know what happened to those non-repats who got spread all over the globe, including India. However, there exists in India what is known as a "Korean War Veterans Society." Its members frequently visit the DMZ.

    Fortunately, the traumatic developments of the Korean War are receding into the background as some positive developments have taken place towards the unification of the Koreas. However, assuming all things remain generally unaltered, it may take a decade or more for this process to be completed. The "Sun-Shine" policy adopted by South Korea, the extension of surface communications, visits of families, and so on, justify optimism. But the foundation stone for it had been laid in 2000 when South Korean President Kim Dae Jung and North Korean Chairman Kim Jong-Il held their first ever North-South Summit in June. It is said that the Pentagon in its Quadrennial Defence Review of 2002 also assumes that reunification of the two countries may be more probable than ever before.

2. General Thimayya wrote the drafts of the book *Experiments in Neutrality* as "Neutrals in Korea" in 1954. The drafts were read by Pandit Nehru, who advised him to delay publication until after his retirement. Thimayya was told that an American publisher was prepared to buy the script for $80,000. Apart from the financial aspects, the book, if published then would have served as a guide to the UNO and the world community which has provided – and employed – troops for upkeep of peace and reconciliation.

10
The Trouble-Shooter: Commanding all the Army Commands

The Chhad Bet

Thimayya was approved for promotion to the rank of lieutenant general by January 1953. In the normal course of events he should have commanded a corps before being considered for the appointment of army commander. His outstanding performance, however, made the government override this requirement and Thimayya was appointed army commander Western Command, with headquarters at Shimla and for the defence of the homeland responsible from the Rajasthan desert to northwards to the CFL in J&K and Ladakh.

Thimayya had two brief stints as Western Army commander. The initial one from May 1952 till August 1953 was disturbed by his eight-month assignment in Korea as chairman NNRC. He returned to Shimla by mid-May 1954 and remained there for exactly one year before being moved as GOC-in-C Southern Command, Pune. No one knew the reason for this change. Rumour had it that it was to accommodate Lieutenant General Kalwant Singh (a home posting).

At Shimla, two events left an imprint of Thimayya's personality: meeting the challenge of Liaquat Ali's 'mailed-fist', which mobilised the army and dispatched it to the border; and planning offensive actions. During this period, the Ladakh border remained quiet for the most part. The Tibetan exodus, which had begun, was mostly left to the IB to handle.

It was his second tenure that made him conscious of the Chinese threat, despite clear evidence of the Indian government's friendly relationship with the Communists. He had discussed with the director of Military Intelligence the problem of maintaining surveillance over eastern Ladakh that had been virtually left devoid of habitation, and the presence of police, IB, or even regular patrols. The IB, that operated occasionally and on need-based intelligence requirements, was generally ignored in this sector.

A man of vision and with intimate knowledge of the Chinese history and now the part they had played in the Korean War and the confused news of their oppressive self-imposed reign over the peaceful Tibetans, made Thimayya view the likely Chinese threat seriously. Maj Gen WD Lentaigne, commandant of India's Staff College and even Lord Mountbatten had warned him not to trust the Chinese.

Even here, in these 15 months, Thimayya surreptitiously used own informers in the form of pilgrims, porters, grazers and traders to collect information of the Chinese activities in Tibet. It had to be done with utmost care, as of more concern than the Chinese, was the sensitivity of Prime Minister Nehru. Nehru did not want anything done that could, as he openly told General Cariappa, "sabotage" his policy of befriending China through *Panch Sheel*, border trade, support for UN membership, and so on.

Thimayya moved to Southern Command, Pune, once again for fifteen months from May 1955 to September 1956.

As GOC-in-C Southern Command, Thimayya had to deal with the Pakistani intrusion into Chhad Bet in the Rann of Kutch in February 1956. It had a deeper history.

The Kutch-Sindh boundary dispute originated in 1843 when the British annexed Sindh. The dispute remained after the Partition of 1947. For eight years, the dispute simmered between Pakistan and India until in early February (1956) the Pakistanis attacked the post of 7th Grenadiers and captured it and then occupied the whole of Chhad Bet by 18 February.

Owing to logistical problems, this former State Force battalion, equipped with camels as their main source of conveyance, had been split into three positions along the axis Bhuj, Khavda, Chhad Bet. It was thin on the ground, especially at Chhad Bet, opposite which the Pakistanis, supported by better communications could build up more than a brigade on its one battalion deployed on the border. And when small incidents of cattle straying into each other's areas enraged the Pakistani Punjabi battalions and they attacked the Grenadiers on the Indian side, a large skirmish could be anticipated.

The protests and pleas to the Pakistanis had little effect. Thimayya, therefore, moved 112nd Infantry Brigade from Dharangdhara to Chhad Bet and evicted the Pakistani marauders.[1]

Thimayya, himself had reconnoitred the area with the commander of the brigade (Brigadier Ajit Singh Guraya) and trapped the Pakistanis in a pincer movement and temporarily occupied their posts at Waghi, Pareli, Jat Talai and Baliari. These were vacated only after obtaining a firm assurance from the Pakistanis that in future they would refrain from such incursions.

The loss of camels and some weapons by the 7th Grenadiers was making the authorities think of disbanding the battalion. Thimayya, however, acknowledged the courage of some of the men, one of whom was awarded a VrC. Considering the treachery of the enemy, Thimayya stopped the disbandment. Soon the area of Chhad Bet was connected by border roads, and the border outposts were manned by the Central Reserve Police. To keep the track open to Chhad Bet, a three-km-long *bund* was made by the brigade. Before moving out of the Command, Thimayya visited the battalion in July and assured them of their retention in the army as a regular unit.[2]

The IAF, on his recommendations, established an all-weather airfield at Bhuj and landing strips at Khavda and Chhad Bet.

After Chhad Bet was restored, Dr KN Katju, the defence minister, met Thimayya. Congratulating him for driving the aggressor out of the territory, he asked him: "General *Sahib*, tell me why you allowed the Pakistanis to intrude, in the first instance and why you could not capture Karachi?"

Thimayya briefed Katju on the Pakistani belligerence and unwarranted provocation and added that he would carry the battle into Pakistan through the plains of Sindh, if the Pakistani misadventure was repeated. Suffering from extremely impaired hearing, Katju had to rely on his hearing aid, to comprehend even normal conversation. As a result, he figured that Thimayya was wanting to invade Pakistan and start a larger war. The minister did not care to read the official report either; so, the erroneous impression lingered on and it set Nehru thinking when the same was conveyed to him by Katju informally.

Nehru sought Thimayya's explanation through General SM Shrinagesh, the then COAS. What finally turned out was a piece of humour. It had been a strategic thought process which Thimayya had shared with the defence minister and had nothing to do with invasion plans. Dr Katju was known for such "strategic hilarities," and the MoD was accustomed to such distortions due perhaps to the minister's habit of often switching off his hearing aid!

At the end of this brief operation, General SM Shrinagesh congratulated Thimayya, and 112nd Infantry Brigade. "I have no doubt," said his message to Thimayya "that your personal influence and direction avoided an operation which might have been a long-drawn one."[3] General Thimayya's decisiveness even in minor skirmishes, prevented the situation from escalating. The Pakistanis licked their wounds, seeking another opportunity for revenge, but had to wait till 1965 when a whole division under Major General Tikka Khan would invade the area once again. It then served as a prelude to Pakistani grandiose designs of *Operation Gibraltar*.

Winning Over the Nagas: A Psychological Approach

Thimayya, the trouble-shooter was now to move to Headquarters Eastern Command at Lucknow and handle the Naga problem that had begun to escalate in all its violent manifestations by January 1955 when AZ Phizo organised his Naga National Council and built up an armed cadre of some 2,500 to 5,000 Naga rebels, calling the outfit the Naga Federal Government. Armed with a large number of weapons and led by fairly well trained deserters from the Assam Rifles and Assam Regiment, they had declared the independence of Naga Hills-Tuensang Frontier Agency (NHTFA or NHTA) from the country.

Indications of secessionist activities had been continuously building up when the tribals boycotted the 1952 and 1956 General Elections, and the visit of Pandit Nehru accompanied by U Nu of Burma on 30 March 1953. Concurrently, the NHTA saw a spate of murders, violence and looting. The NHTA was declared a "Disturbed Area," and the army was moved in at the recommendation of General Shrinagesh, COAS, from January 1956. Major General RK Kochar became the first GOC Assam under Lieutenant General Sant Singh, GOC-in-C, Eastern Command. GOC Assam had his main headquarters at Shillong with the tactical headquarters at Kohima.

From the civil side, NHTA was placed directly under the governor of Assam, with Colonel PN Luthra IFAS, being the commissioner. The army moved in gradually and by July 1956, NHTA saw 45 platoons of Assam Rifles with a sprinkling of Armed Police from Bihar, Assam, Madhya Pradesh and four army brigades, comprising:

- 181 Infantry Brigade
- 201 Infantry Brigade
- 301 Infantry Brigade
- 192 Infantry Brigade

All under GOC Assam which would, in due course, form into GOC Nagaland and 23 Infantry Division.

Nicknamed *Operation Raji*[4] (Reconciliation), the army units and sub-units swung into action, systematically clearing the area from Dimapur to Kohima and further east. It resulted in the killing of some 400 rebels in pitched battles, encirclement and combing of villages and search operations. A large number of armed Nagas surrendered with their weapons. Among them were Phizo's three daughters aged 19, 17 and 13 along with two of his sons. That forced the underground Nagas to resort to guerilla warfare. They would inflict casualties on the security forces, then melt into the jungles and eventually to the safe sanctuary of Burma (Myanmar).

General Kochar coordinated the movement and deployment of his troops, systematically clearing the area, deploying Police and Assam Rifles posts. Learning from the 'Malayan insurgency', even "grouping of villages" known as "stockades," was begun; these groupings were aimed at providing security to the villagers and isolating the hostiles from their families and sources of sustenance.

The hostiles then resorted to a reign of terror and retribution, sometimes burning down villages and livestock. The atmosphere that existed was one of suspicion and distrust, which the hostiles exploited well to launch a well-planned canard against the army. One such opportunity, regrettably, came about with the shooting on 3 July, under suspicious circumstances, of Dr Haralu, a politically connected resident of Kohima.

Brigadier Sukh Dev Singh, commander 181st Infantry Brigade, after a court of inquiry, had exonerated the two sepoys of 2nd Sikh who were involved in the incident, as he opined:

"Troops have been working under constant stress and exposed to hostile fire everywhere and at all times. Under the circumstances, the death of late Dr Haralu is purely accidental because of the extraordinary situation prevailing in this area." He firmly ruled: "No one is to be blamed."

General RK Kochar, GOC Assam, concurred with his findings and opinion. The Special Services Bureau, however, sent a conflicting report emphasising the 'trigger-happiness' of the men involved.

The prime minister called for the proceedings of the Court of Inquiry and doubted the army's version. On 24 July 1956, he wrote a long note to the defence minister, which he instructed, was to be shown to the COAS too:[5]

> ... I am much troubled by this occurrence. Apart from this, it brings some very unpleasant aspects about the behaviour of some of our men, including some officers. Our Army has a proud record not only of courage but of good behaviour. It maintained that record in Kashmir. An incident like this one resulting in the death of Dr Haralu and subsequent attempt to cover this up, leaves a bad mark on this record.
>
> Ever since the beginning of operations I have been laying stress on our Army making friends with the Nagas and trying to win them over. Nagas are our fellow citizens... We have had trouble in Telangana area of Hyderabad... I recognise fully the inherent difficulties of the situation in the Naga Hills. Nevertheless, we have not acted effectively and have yet to come to grips with the situation... Whenever necessary, we should change this set-up and our plan of approach. I should like the Defence Minister to consider this aspect in consultation with COAS...

Earlier, on 13 July, Pandit Gobind Ballabh Pant, the home minister, too had "praised the army's efforts to gain control in NHTA and appreciated their difficulties" but expressed "great distress at Dr Haralu's death on account of mistaken identity." He had feared that incident would act as a "setback to peace efforts."[6]

Generals Kochhar and Sant Singh came under a lot of pressure after the Haralu incident. Added to this was the fact that the civilian population was under pressure from the hostiles to rise against the security forces and false cases of rape, stealing, etc. were maliciously being attributed to them. The senior officers of 3rd Sikh LI, for example, were under consideration to be removed for "inefficiency." And as often happens in such circumstances, there was also a crisis of confidence between Sant Singh and Kochar, the brigade and battalion commanders.

Simultaneously, 2nd Sikh and 3rd Sikh LI were relieved by other units, ignoring their sacrifices and devotion to duty. The security forces had themselves suffered 68 killed and 240 injured. Their good reputations were, however, vindicated, as later records show how contrite Nehru was over his initial outburst. Added to this, the police had been abandoning their pickets at the slightest threat, one such being Aochagalini. The police was neither trained nor well-led for counter-insurgency (CI) operations.

Taking advantage of the deteriorating situation, the reported mistrust between the army and the politicians and emboldened by their successes, the Phizo Nagas were threatening to hoist the rebel flag at Kohima on 15 August to declare their independence. The instructions that Nehru issued to the administration show his ever-increasing anxiety about the NHTA.

"Make sure," he said, "these rebels are allowed nowhere near Kohima."

Intelligence reports indicated that Naga hostiles had begun to acquire arms from Pakistan, the Revolutionary Communist Party of India (RCPI), the Communists of Burma and possibly China. That the Naga rebellion could get out of hand, now became clear. It was some time in the mid-1950s, recalls Brigadier GL Sachdeva, that General Thimayya was at Ambala to felicitate Tenzing Norgay who had climbed Mount Everest with Edmund Hillary in June 1953. When the official function was over, Thimayya requested the media and the civilians to depart, as he had something purely military to discuss with the army officers.

It was then that he discussed *inter alia* the situation in the Naga Hills (NHTA). He said: "The insurgency in NHTA is really alarming. And unless the government does something urgently about it, the insurgency may spread to the Lushai Hills (Mizoram-Tripura) and the entire Indian Army wouldn't be able to quell it."

He added that while the army and security forces could douse the fire started by Phizo, "the reconstruction and rehabilitation of the people, renovation of their battered economy, and winning their confidence could only be done by the government."

In this situation, some changes had become inevitable. In his letter of 24 July, Nehru had suggested to "change the set-up" and "plan of approach." Thimayya became the choice as a replacement for General Sant Singh, who had himself wanted a less strenuous appointment. It would mean his moving to Lucknow. A one-to-one change with Sant Singh was agreed. He was called to Delhi to interact with all concerned, as also act as officiating COAS, in the absence of General Shrinagesh, then on tour. In his appreciation of the situation in NHTA, he saw the force level as somewhat inadequate. He convinced the IAF to raise and establish No. 3 Tactical (Air Support) Group in support of GOC Assam. Then he asked the government to raise HQ 23rd Infantry Division to assimilate all the loose brigades into a cohesive formation. In this appreciation, he apprised the MoD that "India's security needs will continue to augment, placing higher demands on force level both of the army and the para-military forces." He requested that an immediate study be undertaken on it.[7]

"Gentlemen, I am not in the news," said Timmy to the media persons before he left Pune for Lucknow to take up his new assignment as GOC-in-C Eastern Command. He was visibly moved when thousands gathered at Command HQ and the Victoria Terminus to see him off to the city of *nawabs*. He moved to Lucknow on 16 September.

He was soon on the move to Shillong, Kohima and all over NHTA. But major discussions were held and decisions taken, at Shillong with the Governor, Fazal Ali, and

Chief Minister BR Mehdi. Here, he persuaded all to agree on the following: BC Kapur, the senior secretary to the governor to be the liaison officer (LO) to GOC Assam; since the operation was in aid to civil authority, police officers to accompany army columns as LOs[8]; tribal officers to be placed as political assistants to DC Kohima; the need to arm loyal Nagas selectively be considered; PROs to be placed at various places and media to be regularly briefed; loyalist villagers to be fully supported, including grouping them in camps; and, the military operations to be relentlessly pursued by a psychological approach to the insurgency. The battle in this, he emphasised, had to be more for the 'hearts and minds', than only physical control.

He knew that the missionaries were helping the rebels in their propaganda of "Naga Hills for Nagas" and "for Christ." But they too had to be used as an instrument to the larger strategy of defeating the rebellion. Years of neglect of these tribal people had, unfortunately, aroused the feelings and impulse for secession. This was manifesting now. And though the larger majority were not for the idea of independence from India, they were bent on having their own home state. As a sequel, an All-Tribal Meeting was held in Kohima on 22 August, where they demanded the amalgamation of Naga Hills and Tuensang, but no solution could be found due to their insistence on this unit being separated from Assam. This had to be handled with care.

Thimayya began to study both the ethnohistory and the causes of the Naga problem. It meant studying all the tribes and their recent history. An interesting mosaic presented itself. Comprising 13 main tribes, the Nagas were spread over not only today's Nagaland, but Assam and Manipur as well, and were claiming an ethnic similarity in neighbouring Myanmar. The tribes of these areas included the Angami, Ao, Chaksang, Chang, Khienmugan, Konyak, Lotha, Phom, Sangtam, Sema, Yichungar, besides the Zeliang and Rengma, the last two being a minority.

The cause of most of the problem, in fact, was the Nine-Point Agreement with Sir Akbar Hydari, governor of Assam, which was signed by the Government of India with the Nagas during the British period in June 1947 – just about the time when the Atlee government announced freedom to India and its Partition. It virtually transferred all legal, executive and administrative control to the Naga National Council. The worst part related to the boundary which *inter alia* recommended to "bring under one unified administrative unit, as far as possible, all Nagas."[9]

The problem was compounded by the ethnic divide as well. The British had, through their missionaries, firmly and deeply rooted in the Naga psyche the feeling that "Nagas were not Indians, just as Indians were not Nagas." They would harp on "Nagaland for Christ," when they gave independence to India. Out of this psyche-cum-myth arose a few anti-Indian Nagas, Phizo pioneering their cause, ever quoting Gandhiji's words, "If Nagas want a separate homeland, let them have it." Gandhiji's views had, after all, emnated from a moral, rather than *realpolitik* view-point.

With a view to making a fuller assessment of the Naga situation, prior to launching an intensified multifaceted operation, Thimayya, accompanied by KL Mehta, adviser to the Assam governor on NEFA, and Kapur, was in Mokukchung by 3 October. The peaceful Nagas congregated in the thousands and presented him a shawl and a *dah*[10] at a civic function. Here he announced: "Hostiles will be finished but I hope Semas and Aos will see reason and surrender unlicensed weapons to the authorities, as the Angamis are doing." He said the army was on the offensive and would provide security to the farmers in different areas. But he wanted every peace-loving citizen to support the administration and the security forces with every means available to him. "He (the soldier) is here to help you and protect you," he emphasised.

He was then in Tuensang where the locals honoured him with a Naga warrior's outfit. It is here that he asked one of the *gaonburhos*,[11] "Where is the bead of heads? Like you, I am a head hunter." And recounted his experiences of war, the Pathan warfare and, of course, his tiger shoots.

At Zunheboto, while accepting the war dress, he was at his best. He addressed them: "I am not only honoured but would like to tell you, I am like you, a tribal. I assure you that the government, under the benign leadership of PM Nehru, will bring a peaceful atmosphere." The appeal was again the same: bring peace for prosperity; we are all one.

Here he donated Rs 10,000 for a General Shrinagesh Dispensary. For the widows, who had lost their husbands to the Naga rebels, he donated Rs. 500 each. These were considerable sums in those days.

The journey through the Naga Hills, Tuensang and Manipur continued. The villagers everywhere accorded him a civic reception and pledged that they would give an ultimatum to the rebels, assuring him that they would bring the rebels back to the mainstream. On his part, Thimayya assured them that their villages would be protected.

The Thimayya spell had begun to show its effect. The troops were on the job; the civil administration had begun to feel confident; Kochar and his brigade commanders were no longer under the threat of unceremonious removal.[12] Based on the assurance of the government, he asked General Kochar to offer amnesty to the rebels. In a Press conference at Imphal on 16 October, he said that there were some 2,500 to 3,000 guerillas with about 300 modern rifles. Having visited the Tuensang Frontier Division in NEFA, Kohima, Mokukchung, Lhota, Rengma and Southern Sema areas, he found that the progress of military operations was "beyond his expectations."[13] He was hopeful that once the administration was established with the support of the army, the situation would further improve.

As a result, a group of eleven Nagas met Nehru, who asked them to be courageous and urged them to be associated in a bright future for India. He also announced formation of a new Frontier Division Administrative Service, an addition to Assam Rifles and more socio-economic improvements in the hills. Nehru also advised the officials to treat the tribals as "friends and equals." "Let them grow naturally," he told them.

In March 1953, 14,000 Nagas had gathered at the district headquarters of Kohima to convey their grievances to Prime Minister Jawaharlal Nehru and U Nu, the then premier of Burma, who were touring the frontier regions on a mission of pacification. According to an eye-witness of the *Christian Science Monitor*, this is what happened: "A long line of Naga chiefs in their best feathers and cane dresses awaited the two leaders with gifts in their hands. They were, said the Nagas, 'our honoured guests.' But a few moments before the prime ministers' arrival, a deputy commissioner of the Naga Hill districts, took it upon himself to announce that the prime ministers would accept no gifts and no addresses were to be presented. For the audience, this was a violation of the age-old tribal custom of hospitality which was claimed to be among the best in the world. When Nehru and U Nu finally arrived, the offended Nagas were streaming homewards, leaving the Indian prime minister to demonstrate his annoyance in unmistakable terms to the embarrassed Indian officials."[14] The PM was naturally reminded of what happened three years earlier.

Operations progressed satisfactorily. In mid-October, Thimayya briefed the media about the achievements of the security forces. He said:[15]

> Jawans have acquitted themselves remarkably well in an extremely difficult operation. The back of the revolt has been broken and it is hoped that the mopping-up operations, now in progress, will be completed before the end of the year. The army's job is normally to fight an outside enemy. It is distasteful to the Indian Army to fight the Naga tribesmen, who are part and parcel of India. Force, therefore, has to be judiciously used. And along with force, has to be blended political acumen aimed at conciliating the tribesmen... The present revolt has erupted, so it is claimed by competent critics, out of the bunglings and arrogance of the civil administration. In dealing with a tribal people, particular care has also to be taken to respect their custom and tradition. We all have to learn from the past experiences.[16]

He also said the liberal Naga leaders were now making appeals to all Nagas to surrender arms and ammunition and to settle the political matters peacefully; more and more Nagas, he said, were joining the liberals. He further said that he came to Imphal to check the infiltration of hostile Nagas into the territory of Manipur state. He expressed satisfaction at the response to the offer of amnesty made by Kochar.

By October, people were keen that life should return to normal. Eventually, and in full consultation with the Nagas, the Assam and NHTA administration, and the local commanders, Thimayya decided to review the process of grouping of villages. The hostiles were, nonetheless, still undecided: some favoured surrender without arms, others were for complete independence. They continued to raid villages and engage the security forces. In that ambience of uncertainty Thimayya told the village leaders that he would let them return to their villages if they "pledged abstinence from violence and support to hostiles."[17]

They agreed. He made the villagers sign a pledge for *degrouping*. In the meanwhile, a select committee was appointed by the government to examine various aspects of the adminstration. As a consequence of the political parleys, the select committee made a resolution on 26 October 1957 that the peaceful and loyal Nagas would accept a new administration within the framework of the Indian Constitution.

Overall, that was a breakthrough and the results were there for all to see. For, although the Naga rebels' propaganda continued and they called themselves the "92nd Government," children were returning to the schools, the farmers were tilling their fields and the underground rebels were agitating to come over ground. The beginning was made on 2 March 1957, when 146 Naga Hostile guerillas and families surrendered with serviceable weapons at Henina. They included some self-styled brigadiers and other officers.

As a result, a delegation of Ao, Phom, Konyak Naga tribal leaders pledged peace in their areas and promised to widen the peace horizon before the state Governor, Fazal Ali, at Shillong, on 21 April. Thimayya, along with others were present. It was then that General Thorat took over the responsibility of settling the Naga Hill problem under General Thimayya as COAS

The performance of Thimayya in NHTA was under close scrutiny not only by the government, but also by the media. *The Statesman* of 15 January 1957 would review his role:

> But the time to rest was not his. The Naga troubles on India's vital eastern frontier, almost requisitioned his services, so to say. After appointment as GOC- in-C Eastern Command in September 1956, the direction of operations in the Naga Hills Area has been occupying his full attention. By firm and friendly handling of the Naga rebels and by personal visits to every part of the disturbed region, he was able to restore a measure of faith among the inhabitants of this region, who had hitherto been subjected to the worst depredations from the Phizo group.
>
> This was a proper rehearsal, indeed, for General Thimayya, before his assumption of the high office of Chief of Staff of the Indian Army.

The Indian Army had fought conventional wars all these years – with elan – but lacked knowledge of guerila and unconventional warfare. He saw the units' performance suffering due to long and tedious jungle bashing and avoidable casualties. The counter-guerilla warfare techniques involving small unit operations, quick responses to situations, mobile operations in pursuit of guerillas together with the battle for the 'hearts and minds' of the locals (psychological warfare), needed special training. He started a jungle warfare school at Ghaspani (near Dimapur), to train units in the basics of guerilla warfare, knowledge of the Naga characteristics and customs besides introducing Dos and Don'ts for them. This orientation, however, brief, began to help the units.[18]

The fight against the hostiles now became a multi-dimensional battle. Though violence continued, intimidation of the locals by hostiles ebbed and flowed. By July 1960, NHTA was officially one entity and placed under the Ministry of External Affairs. It was Thimayya's effort that two Naga Regiments were formed out of surrendered hostiles; later, two more would form battalions of the Border Security Force. Yet opposition to these measures continued to erupt from the secessionist group called Naga National Conference, which called for a "war of resistance" against the Indian and Burmese governments, actively supported by the Chinese. The NNC even had a "government in exile." Concurrently, the peace process also showed some success.

With Thimayya's bold leadership, and his adopting a psychological approach, more signs were visible now of restoration of confidence among the Nagas. The security forces, especially the army, had also regained their image. The depredations and ravages caused by hostile Naga bands were being fast cleared and repaired by the government. Normal life, which had been disrupted, was gradually returning. Basically this was the army's triumph. But a great share of this credit must go to the Assam Rifles, the civil administration and the Naga people at large who contributed to the common mission. As a result, the weekly *bazaars* in Mokokuchung and elsewhere were being held again and normal business had begun to take place in poultry, vegetables, tobacco and other essential commodities. *Bazaar* gossip was afloat that smuggling from across the Burma border had stopped! Hopes of a reconciliation built up. In the meanwhile, the Border Roads had begun to improve the 86-km Mokokuchung–Tuensang jeep track into a class 18 road.

Times were changing and the government had introduced several welfare measures with a view to bettering the lot of the men and women in NEFA and NHTA. At women's welfare centre at Tuensang, for example, Naga women were taught various types of handicrafts. Thimayya laid the foundation stones of several welfare centres, schools, dispensaries and, above all, football grounds for Naga children; besides, an atmosphere of well-being was being ushered in. Wherever he went, Thimayya was received with thunderous ovation, with dance and music true to the Naga tradition of welcoming an honoured guest. He had brought about an ambience of hope for the future.

Unfortunately, what he initiated and Prime Minister Nehru approved, was overtaken by the developments of India's deteriorating relationships with China and Pakistan. The secessionists found succour and encouragement from both these adversaries. And although by 1962, 8th Mountain Division with 36 battalions was looking after both the Naga Hills and Manipur (to which insurgency spread in 1961) and the NHTA had became a full-fledged state, its security environment remained volatile. The peace process traversed through the 1964 Peace Mission, the 1975 Peace Accord and an unending series of ceasefires and parleys. ■

NOTES

1. The Pakistanis have, on their part, played down this operation. In *Khaki Shadows*, (Pakistan 1947-1997) General KM Arif merely says (at p. 41), "In 1956, India's border forces impounded the intruding cattle and drove out the Pakistani villagers from their ancestral homes. A small contingent from Pakistan returned the Indian compliment and evicted the Indian forces from the area. An uneasy calm returned to the Unit... In 1965, the Indian patrols adopted a provocative aggressive posture."
2. The War Diary of 7th Grenadiers records the event with great adulation: "This act of kindness of the Army Commander greatly improved the unit morale."
3. Official Documents History Division, MoD.
4. Ibid.
5. Ibid.
6. Ibid.
7. Official Records.
8. Until the Armed Forces (Special Powers) Regulations 1958 conferring special powers on officers of the armed forces came about, this arrangement remained in vogue.
9. The NSCN demand to include all areas of the northeast into Nagaland emnates from it, and remained a ploy for negotiations even in 2002-03.
10. A sharp-edged Naga knife used for multi-purpose jobs.
11. The village elder whose leadership is unquestioned.
12. *The Bombay Chronicles* of 23 April 1957 called it "Thimayya on secret talks with Nagas." Thimayya was, indeed, soliciting the help of all *gaonburhos* and the Naga intelligentsia to hold talks with the political leaders as also with military commanders.
13. Carried by the *Indian Nation*, 17 October 1956.
14. As quoted by the *Indian Nation*, 20 October 1956.
15. *The Pioneer* (Lucknow), 13 October 1956 carried excerpts from it.
16. *Amrita Bazar Patrika*, 20 October 1956.
17. This then became the foundation of today's CIJWS (Counter-Insurgency and Jungle Warfare School), Virangte.
18. What began as a rag-tag Naga Army of Phizo had reorganised under a so-called C-in-C with four commands and several battalions. This proliferation would take place from May 1961, as Thimayya demitted office.

11
The Years of Enthusiasm (1957-58 – Leading to 1959)

The Thimayya legend had already spread far and wide when he took over as India's fourth COAS. Indeed, he deserved to be recognised by the highest honour that the country could offer this illustrious son. He was internationally known and his countrymen literally doted on him as their military leader. His deft handling of the NNRC had turned this battle-scarred soldier into a statesman-diplomat. Quick-witted and good-humoured, he was given the sobriquet "Pot-Shot Timmy," although to the members of his large family in Kodagu, he continued to be known as "Dubbu." Socially, the dashing soldier Timmy and his French educated wife, Nina, were in great demand in the social circles of New Delhi. If Thimayya was tactically unconventional, so was Nina with her slacks and long cigarette holder.

Every inch a soldier, he stood erect at 5 ft 11 3/4 inch (180 cm); he was a magnificent specimen of a soldier – tall and healthy; sturdy and athletic. Thimayya took over the Indian Army when peace was uncertain and dangers to India's security had increased. His appointment was naturally welcomed by 400 million Indians who could rely on his leadership.

Thimayya really qualified for what was said of him by Surjit Singh Majithia, the deputy defence minister. "There is a Chinese saying," Majithia had remarked, "a thousand soldiers are easily got. But a single general is hard to find." Thimayya, the minister said, "knows the art of war and he loves his soldiers and they love him too."[1]

By March, when the government confirmed the news of Thimayya as COAS-designate, he was in his 50th year, with three decades of illustrious service behind him. He had great stature and he inspired enormous hopes for the future. A source of envy to India's enemies, he was truly an example of leadership to the military and the country as a whole.

As he was stepping into the office, most of his officers and men who served or had known him, were also seeing a principled man assuming the appointment. He would have no cronies, nor favourites, but would expect every soldier to do his duty. Personally too, he would ensure that he did nothing that would impair his honour and conscience. Thimayya had moral ascendancy over all others due to his quality of life and principles – loyalty to those above him, service to those under him, and comradeship to those alongside him. To the government, which had reposed special trust and confidence in his fidelity, his whole life was available.

The message to the armed forces, which was broadcast on All India Radio on the eve of his assuming appointment, read:

> I am proud to take over from General Shrinagesh today as Chief of the Army Staff-designate. I shall strive to fulfill the trust placed in me by the government in the full realisation of the great responsibility that I shall bear. I have served in both peace and war with you and I admire your gallantry, steadfastness and high sense of honour and integrity. I will try to give you that leadership and support to maintain those high standards of discipline and behaviour which are the hallmark of this army of ours. Finally, I wish to remind you that our principal duty is the defence of our country, and everything that we do must lead us to maintain the highest state of efficiency in carrying out this role.

To the officers, he said he was "looking forward to mutual loyalty and cooperation in the future in building up the army and in providing it as a real instrument of support for the progress and greatness of India."

On 8 May, the feeling he had was one of great elation with some nuances. He reflectingly recalled: "As CO of 8th/19th Hyderabad (Hybd) in Burma in the thick of an uncertain war, I prided in this similar moment. I had thought of the battalion as a unit; it was as an instrument assigned to me to use as effectively as possible. I could not think of the army as a unit. I saw it, instead, made up of separate individuals held together less by military regulation than by shared experience, common duties and similar problems."[2] It had to be a persuasive leadership to weld this army into a cohesive and efficient organisation.

Thimayya knew that the army faced a serious threat, the strongest since the ceasefire of 1949 and deep down, he knew that it was not well-prepared to meet it. The efficiency of the army, all these years of soldiering had taught him, was based on the fighting quality of its troops, the leadership and the state of its equipment. Although motivated, the soldiers' morale in the army remained generally high, however, all these deficiencies needed his special attention.

The establishment of the MoD that then existed was that the Defence Minister, KN Katju, had moved to become the chief minister of Madhya Pradesh and V K Krishna Menon had been designated as the defence minister; he took over by 18 April. The two deputy defence ministers i.e. Surjit Singh Majithia and Kotha Raghu

Ramiah, were already in position. M K Vellodi, the defence secretary was stepping aside for O Pulla Reddy, ICS, to take over. The ICS era, like the KCIOs in the army, was still doing well.

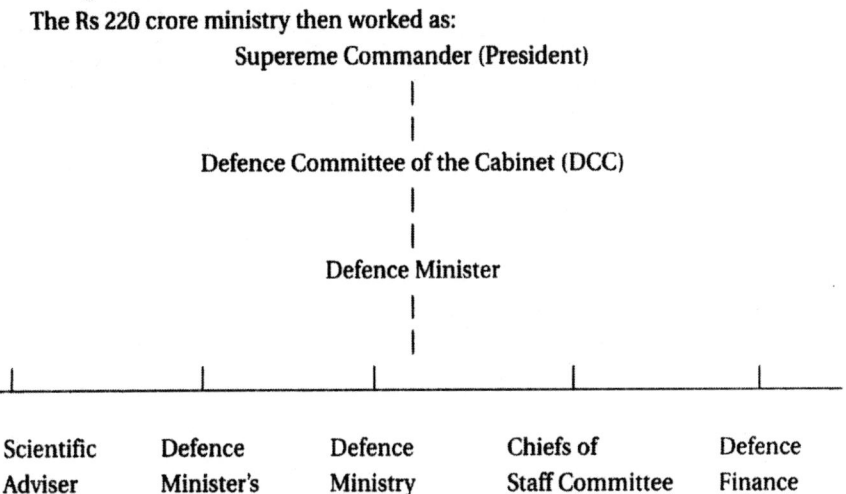

The Rs 220 crore ministry then worked as:

```
                    Supereme Commander (President)
                                 |
                                 |
                  Defence Committee of the Cabinet (DCC)
                                 |
                                 |
                          Defence Minister
                                 |
                                 |
_____
   |           |            |              |              |
Scientific  Defence      Defence       Chiefs of       Defence
Adviser     Minister's   Ministry      Staff Committee Finance
            Committee       |
            (DMC)        Defence
                         Secretary
_____
   |                        |                            |
Army HQ                  Naval HQ                      Air HQ
(COAS)                   (CNS)                         (CAS)
```

What were the lacunae?[3]

First, the chiefs' command over their service was hurriedly circumscribed with their new designation of Chief of Staff, from the earlier C-in-C. Second, they could have access to the Defence Ministry or the minister either through the defence secretary or through the Chiefs of Staff Committee. Third, no effort was being made by the government to integrate the services like it had been during the British period, or like what progressive nations such as the UK and US had done by accepting the Chief of Defence Staff and chairman of Joint Chiefs of Staff. These lacunae would exacerbate as the crisis grew over a strategy to be adopted to meet the twin threats of Pakistan and China, and need to prioritise the real-time needs of the services. Then there existed the well-known dichotomy of centralised control, by the MoD acting as a superior headquarters without being accountable for operational efficiency, success or failure in operations. The MoD required urgent reform.

To add to the misfortune, as a sole example among all the major nations of the world, India alone had no men of military experience among its statesmen, legislators and administrators. Cariappa, who by right should have remained the "grandsire" of the services and an adviser to the government on defence matters, was, in his own words, "shunted out" by Nehru to Australia and New Zealand as a high commissioner, and the others had little to offer, voluntarily or otherwise. So, the services continued to suffer.

The Chiefs of Staff Committee was headed by the Army Chief General Thimayya. At AHQ, Lieutenant General MS Wadalia had become the deputy chief of Army Staff. Among his ADCs were Captains CG Alvares and DRL Nanda. Major YM Munshi was the military assistant.

Of the other sister services, Air Vice Marshal Subroto Mukerjee, OBE was already the chief of the IAF and Vice Admiral Stephen Carlill, KBE, CB, DSO, was the last British naval chief who would hand over to Rear Admiral R D Katari in April 1958.[4]

The three commands namely, Southern, Eastern and Western, were under Lieutenant Generals PN Thapar, SPP Thorat, DSO and Kalwant Singh. In the staff under him at AHQ were Major General PC Banerji as MS, Major General SD Verma as CGS, besides Brigadiers Amrik Singh, MC and D Prem Chand were DMO and DMI respectively. Among other principal staff officers (PSOs) were Lieutenant General K Bahadur Singh, Major Generals Daulat Singh and KP Dhargalkar as the AG, QMG and MGO respectively. Major Generals RE Asarappa, PS Gyani and AC Iyappa were the E-in-C, director artillery and director signals respectively. Normal changes would see Major Generals SD Verma and LP (Bogey) Sen, DSO becoming the CGS, and so on.

The relationship between the service chiefs, despite Carlill still heading the small but growing navy, and Subroto Mukerjee now in his third year of command of the IAF, was most cordial. In due course, Indianisation of the service would be complete as soon as Rear Admiral RD Katari replaced Carlill in 1958.

"While the services maintained a most cordial and cooperative relationship," to quote Lieutenant General SPP Thorat, DSO who was the CGS before his command of the CFI in Korea, the same with MoD "was, to say the least, only lukewarm." He adds: "From our side, we blamed the defence secretary and the financial adviser, who in our opinion lacked a proper understanding of the army's problems and needs and had an unsympathetic attitude towards them... We had come to believe that they and most of the senior officers of the Defence and Financial Ministries had an exaggerated opinion of their own ability and status and rather looked down upon the senior army officers. Some of them even believed that they knew more about army affairs than we professional officers did. They were in a position to rough-ride us because of the tremendous influence which they wielded with the Defence Minister, Sardar Baldev Singh, who was a perfect gentleman, but did not have courage to control officers of his ministry, even when he was satisfied that they were being unreasonable with the sole object of establishing the superiority of the civil services over the army."[5]

With Thimayya's reputation and standing, it was hoped the MoD would change its attitude to "warm" from being "lukewarm." But much, no doubt, would depend on Krishna Menon, the new minister for defence.

The hopes of the services pinned on Menon were, in a way, reflected in the welcome that the magazine of USI published in its 1957 issue, with great fanfare: "The appointment of Shri VK Krishna Menon as defence minister has been welcomed by all ranks of the services. Shri Menon is held in high esteem as one of the foremost Indian political figures, championing not only India's cause abroad for years, but also that of world peace, particularly in the UN. That a statesman of his eminence should guide India's defence forces is a matter of great satisfaction. They feel that their future is secure and bright in his hands."[6] Very high hopes, indeed.

Strategic Developments in Neighbourhood Vis-à-Vis Own Response

After its occupation of Tibet in 1950, China quickly consolidated its position. It assured India of its friendship. Diplomatically too, China was playing its cards well. It had joined the Bandung Conference and become the exponent of the Nehru-pioneered *Panch Sheel* or five principles of international conduct and even signed an agreement with India on 14 October 1954, for "Trade and Cultural Intercourse." It envisaged establishment of trading agencies at New Delhi, Calcutta and Kalimpong in India, and at Yatung, Gyantse, Gartok, Lhasa, Phari and Shigatse in Tibet. Trade was to be transacted over the passes on the border of India and Tibet at Shipki La, Mana, Niti, Kungri-Bingri, Daruna and Lipu Lekh.[7]

In a rare, yet unreciprocated, gesture, the Indian government withdrew the old Indian counsel generals along with the flag flying posts, located there since the 1905 Younghusband expedition, from Lhasa, Gyantse, Shigatse and Yatung. Thus, all vestiges of Indian claim or liaison with Tibet were fully removed in 1954 after the symbolic posts of the Indian Army were pulled back without equivalent treaty rights. This newly acquired friendship was accelerated as Menon would be asked to support wholeheartedly Communist China's entry into the UNO. In this euphoria, even KM Panikkar, India's ambassador to Beijing would devote much of his time and effort in acting as special plenipotentiary to the Chinese government during the Korean War (1950-53) rather than apprising Delhi of the changing Chinese colours.

In 1954 itself, Zhou En-lai had confirmed to Prime Minister Nehru that his country accepted the McMahon Line as the *de facto* India-Tibet(China) boundary. As the Sino-Indian tension heated up on the bleak and high altitude of Ladakh, NEFA, UP-Tibet border, Zhou would rescind his stand. Ironically the border trouble had begun to simmer at Bara Hoti, a few months before even the Treaty of Trade could be implemented.

In 1954, at the height of the Sino-Indian *détente* and the *Panch Sheel*, the People's Republic of China published "China Pictorial" (or *Le Pai-Hua*) a map that depicted its dream of the fabled "Middle Kingdom." It showed twelve neighbouring countries and regions as a part of China. Listed in it were the then Soviet Republics of Kazakh (Kazakhstan), Kirghiz (Kirghiztan), Tadzik (Tajikistan), the Pamir-Sinkiang region, Nepal, Bhutan, Sikkim, the whole of NEFA, Burma, Taiwan, Vietnam and Outer Mongolia. Some called this a Chinese "neo-colonialism."

However, China attributed it to its earlier loss of these territories, except for Tibet, and to its "weak period of history."

That year some more developments were taking place. Korea remained divided in spite of the 15-month-long war. While Zhou En-Lai was saying that China had no intention of invading Taiwan, the People's Liberation Army (PLA) had fought in Korea and despite the Armistice, and the NNRC tension on its account continued to ebb and flow. In Vietnam, the French had been routed from Dien Bien Phu and the two halves of Vietnam were at war. The situation had been steadily deteriorating since 1950, thanks to the Cold War between the two superpowers. Geo-strategically, in early 1957, Asia had steadily become a zone of conflict owing to the Cold War and in part due to the rise of the China's power, since its occupation of Tibet, and its unbounded territorial ambitions.

In the immediate neighbourhood, Pakistan, orchestrating fears of its neighbour, India, of which it made no secret in all international fora and organisations including the UNO, was aligning with the US dominated Southeast Asia Treaty Organisation (SEATO) and Central Treaty Organisation (CENTO).[8]

In dealing with Sino-Pak collusion, the strategy that China had followed since 1957 needs to be recalled. While trying to neutralise the Indian position in Asia and the world, China had attempted to isolate – and highlight – India as an arrogant nation and the odd man out in the comity of neighbours. As part of this strategy, it was attempting to cut into the traditionally friendly relationship of India with Nepal, Bhutan, Sikkim, Afghanistan, Sri Lanka and Burma, and further escalate the already tense relations in the case of Pakistan. To that effect, borders were realigned with some adjustments in respect of Nepal, Burma and Afghanistan and a hostile Pakistan was made to secede a 5,200 sq km area of the Shaksgam Valley from the Northern Areas of POK. In return, Pakistan was allotted the Karakoram Highway (KKH) and a military collusion ensued.

The Chinese plans began to unfold with the construction of the Xinjiang-Tibet road passing over 180 km of the Aksai Chin plateau, reports on which had begun to emerge from 1955.[9] Deploying more than 30,000 armed and unarmed labour, this road was ready in 1956 and was formally opened in October 1957 with ceremonies held in Lhasa, Beijing, Urumqui and Gartok. It entered Indian territory at Jarig-Jilgng and then ran southeast towards Amtogar-Lake, Yangpa-Khati, Haji Langar. Although Thimayya as GOC-in-C Western Command had sent an officer patrol under Second Lieutenant Tilak Raj of 8th Gorkha Regiment, along with a few others, including a volunteer US Central Intelligence Agency (CIA) agent Sydney Wignall[10] into Taklakot, to ascertain its rough alignment near Haji Langar in June, officially the two patrols were sent only the following year[11].

And while the "letter warfare" continued between the two governments, there were events that showed Sino-Indian relations as being "normal." In 1956, for instance, while the Chinese established a base in Bara Hoti, Zhou En-lai and

Marshal Chien Ye (regarded as the founder of the PLA along with Chu Teh) visited India. In January 1958, a firepower demonstration and defence installations were shown to the visiting military delegation. From the Indian side, Major General JN Chaudhuri took a delegation to China along with Commodore Chaturvedi and Air Commodore PC Lal. They spent a fortnight in conducted tours at the invitation of the Chinese, in what they called "an exchange between two peaceful neighbours." On its return, the delegation mused: "*It is good to have the Chinese as friends, but they will make formidable foes.*"[12] Zhou would visit India twice again, in 1958-59 and finally in 1960.

Reports also had begun to trickle down through intelligence, media and rumours that the Chinese were behind inciting the Nepalese government to close down the Indian wireless stations in Nepal and even to wind up the military training teams. Reports of Naga rebels under Phizo attempting to obtain modern arms and training in guerilla warfare from China also became available. And still worse seemed to be happening. The Pakistanis had begun to play with both the Americans and the Chinese. While General Ayub Khan, now C-in-C Pakistan Army was actively collaborating with the US and its defence secretary, Major General Iskander Mirza was on a fact-finding mission to China.

So, there was Kashmir, a victim of the Cold War; there were China and Pakistan – China building a road inside Indian territory and justifying the encroachment, and Pakistan sparring to somehow see India down, if not out.

The Indian government, rather than face the challenge, was following a policy of ambivalence admixed with self-deception, in the belief that the Chinese would not blatantly violate the Indian border; and if inside, would reel back their position to their side of the traditional border i.e. the McMahon Line.

It was further backed up by assurances. For example, while replying to a question during a debate on the Defence Estimates, in April 1956, Nehru had said: "... the members fear an attack on India from neighbours. It wouldn't; I assure you and if it did, the Indian armed forces are strong..." To this when further pressed about the "state of the Indian Armed Forces vis-à-vis the adversaries," he told the Parliament, "A people that has vitality, strength and unity can never be defeated (and) in the final analysis what counts is not your soldiers or their military weapons, but the spirit of the unity of the people to survive in spite of difficulties..." He added, "The right approach is to avoid having unfriendly relations with your neighbours."[13]

And as the Chinese notes and utterances became menacing, denouncing the McMahon Line as the boundary, and claiming that Tibet was an "inalienable" part of China and they would accept no interference, Nehru, in a doctrinal *volte face*, told the same Parliament, "We are living in a world full of menace.... The Armed Forces are, indeed, the spearhead of defence... they are to bear the brunt."

There was rhetoric again, but this time from the defence minister. Writing a foreword to "The Indian Armed Forces," 1957, Menon remarked: "The Indian armed forces are not meant for aggression but solely for defence. (But) I have seen troops all over the world and nowhere have I seen such magnificent men as in India." The emphasis did not appear to tilt even when danger was so obvious. In 1958, when the Chinese already had their Aksai Chin Road, Nehru was saying, "I should like Indian defence forces to be known not only for their efficiency and daring but also for works of peace and friendship." Then, in 1959, Nehru would talk like a philosopher as he said, "No weapon had been devised that can conquer the spirit of man." True, but the ground realities warranted a more phlegmatic approach.

On yet another occasion, the details of which follow subsequently, Nehru would advocate India's preference for what he called indigenising "second class equipment" rather than importing expensive equipment from foreign countries. As a prime minister, no doubt, he avoided leaning on either power bloc, so as to uphold the nation's independent policies. He could not be faulted, at least morally. However, he erred in his estimation of India's adversaries. A neighbour like China which was evidently expansionist and making no secret of its intentions, both overtly and covertly, could be only contained by meeting it on equal terms. That meant strong and modern armed forces, capable of becoming an instrument of India's non-aligned policy.[15]

Bundle of Problems

On the eve of Thimayya's entry to the office of COAS, the newspapers were welcoming in "A Soldier-Statesman Thimayya" (*Tribune*, 17 February), "Thimayya Promises to Sustain the High Traditions of the Indian Army During his Command," (*Hindustan Times*, 10 March). More specifically *The Times of India* warned him through discreet, but frank remarks in the 11 March issue, "A malaise saps the officer cadre today. During the last few years the Army's morale has been steadily on the decline, for reasons which are best left to its new chief to investigate. The demoralisation of officers is most often expressed in terms of the admittedly low pay scales and, worse still, their lack of promotion prospects – neither of which has so far been sympathetically considered. *But pay and promotions are not the only guides to morale. The malaise is more deep-rooted than that; it is only with patience and understanding that the evil can be rooted out.*" It went on to the next three points, namely, the state of our obsolescent arms and equipment that had remained static since Cariappa's time, the problem of higher direction and bureaucratic control in which the Defence Ministry worked as a superior inter-Service Directorate; and it asked Thimayya to seek "immediate reforms."

The Indian Express (13 March) pointed out the pathetic state of accommodation in peace stations, the low pay scales of the services vis-à-vis their civilian counterparts, withdrawal of concessions of schooling of the children of service personnel, etc. It warned Thimayya not to let "such things drag on if the morale was to be raised." There were reasons for all these public disclosures about the issues of the army! And General Thimayya acutely became aware of the problem areas.

The army had inherited several problems, both operational and of welfare. They required to be attended to urgently. The development of the northern border had remained neglected. The force level had stagnated at seven divisions. And it was primarily responsible for the Pakistan border. The northern border had remained with the police and paramilitary despite the Chinese presence in Ladakh.

The committee under Himmat Sinhji, deputy defence minister, to recall, had conducted, in 1951, a survey of defence requirements for the Chinese border. It recommended coordination of intelligence under the IB, construction of border roads and border deployment of the police. Lacking expert knowledge of terrain and strategic perception, the report was essentially patchwork, and that too was accepted only in part for implementation. Its recommendations, whatever their worth, were termed by Prime Minister Nehru as "provocative militarisation of the border." It especially left out Aksai Chin, including the areas of Lingzi Tang, Aksai Chin, Soda Plains and Deepang Plains from being manned; later, the same became the greatest cause of embarrassment. Even summer patrolling, that the committee had recommended, seems to have been ignored; when India woke up to the existence of the Aksai Chin Road and other incursions, China could lay its historic claim and vehemently refute the existence of the McMahon line. *What China implied was: territory is claimable only if it is legitimised by physical occupation.*

The committee, as mentioned, had also made recommendations to extend roads to 9 Mile-85/0-Shipki La; Manali-Leh; Shimla-Chini; Siliguri-Gangtok-Natu La; Mokukchung-Tuensang; Margherita-Khonsa; Kimin-Ziro; Sadiya-Denning; Lakra-Kimin; and, Passighat-Sagong. But so tardy was the progress, that in 1957, most of them were nowhere near being completed.

The roads needed to be extended expeditiously to the borders. But the state and Central Public Works Departments had no priority for them. Thimayya, therefore, asked his engineer-in-chief to reconnoitre the areas, evaluate the work force that could be assembled to complete those roads and plan building them by a special task force.[16] Similarly, the responsibility for wireless communication was given to the signals-in-chief. Since the collection, collation and dissemination of intelligence of strategic value had been passed on to the IB under Mullik, the traditional military intelligence collecting agency, the MI, had been marginalised not only for funds and resources but also analyses and evaluation. This arrangement was defeating the very purpose of strategic intelligence and depriving the prime user, the armed forces, of its benefits. Thimayya was determined to bring this lacuna to the notice of the government. He was also keen to apprise the prime minister about the need for the border to be strengthened without delay, and to let the army control the border, as it was required to, by its charter.

There were several other problems too: the services were not integrated; the defence mechanism was *ad hoc*; the research and development however nascent, was detached from the main users – the armed forces. There was a need to modernise but the government mindset on development, prioritised over defence, had a stonewalling effect over funds for procurement, *et al.*

When on 10 May, Thimayya formally went to call on Nehru at an appointed time, the prime minister had also called Krishna Menon. He had told Menon that they could have an informal chat with Timmy (as he often addressed him) while he came to pay his regards and seek his blessings.

"The Chinese would play their Checkers," Thimayya told Menon and Nehru, when they asked him as to what the Chinese were capable of doing. "They have a wide choice over the 3,500 km of the border. Better roads and air routes, larger force and improved logistics afford them flexibility." But he recalled his own impressions of the Chinese from the NNRC days. In his report to the government he had plainly stated that the Communist Chinese delegation from the Northern Command, despite their smooth external countenances and silky ways, could not be trusted. They would be ruthless in following their own interests, ignoring the other party's well established and founded ground realities and covenants.

He, therefore, urged that while diplomatic efforts to make the Chinese vacate their aggression could continue, defensive measures would need to be activated without further loss of time. He said he would examine the problem of deployment, the requirement of troops, fire support, build-up of logistics, communications and forward his recommendations to the government soon.[17]

By 3 June, the aerial reconnaissance confirmed the alignment of the Aksai Chin Road and the Chinese military build-up. On 6 June, Nehru wanted to know about the strategic implication of the road for India. Thimayya apprised the prime minister that it had both immediate and long-term consequences and then went on to explain how the Chinese had stationed three armies (equivalent to three Indian corps) consisting of nine to ten divisions in Xinjiang and Tibet; and how the quickly expanding roads within Tibet and Xinjiang to the borders in the north, west and south provided the ability to move two to three additional divisions into Tibet at a notice of 45 to 60 days. The PLA AF (PLA Air Force) was busy carrying out trials for the MiG 17s and 19s in and around Lhasa and Shigatse. The plateau provided innumerable landing grounds and airfields. The airborne troops were undergoing training in both the Gobi Desert and on the southern banks of Tsangpo. "All these could be concentrated against Ladakh or elsewhere," he remarked.

Ironically, Mullik, director IB, in his book, seems to make a case, saying "...he (Thimayya) tried to play down the importance of the (Aksai Chin) road and 'throw doubts' on intelligence reports about its existence."

There was no doubt in anybody's mind, including the foreign secretary's, about the road; what was doubtful was the Indian capability to undo the damage in any lucrative way. While the possibility of military offensive was clearly negated, the defensive capability that Thimayya would recommend, remained. Even the MEA, in Mullik's words, thought it "pointless to pick quarrels over issues in which India had no means of enforcing claims." (*The Chinese Betrayal*, pp.205-06, published in 1971, six years after Thimayya's death.)

With the Aksai Chin Road in the news and confirmed through the reports and reconnaissance, Thimayya sent a note to Menon in July 1957. In it he summarised the information that had been gathered and suggested that (a) the army take over the defence of entire Ladakh; (b) the police, IB and militia be placed under it; (c) he be allowed to move a brigade into the area of the Pangong–Spangur Lakes from the Punjab border which would be made up by new raisings.[18]

He also recommended that to contain the Chinese from further spilling into Indian territory, the army had to move into proper defensible areas, denying major axes of western ingress, but logistics had to be ensured. He explained the requirements of roads, landing strips, and so on.

Menon read through the note and told Thimayya: "The enemy is on the other side. Ignore China."[19]

Notwithstanding the defence minister's cold-shouldering of Thimayya's note, a quick evaluation of the threat became further necessary. He tasked the CGS to do so with immediate priority. So the intelligence and military operations staff set to evaluating the threat and the options available to the Chinese and Pakistanis. A full intelligence appreciation would be available by July when the Army Commanders Conference was to be held.

Because Nehru was playing down the Chinese threat, Krishna Menon too played the piper's tune for political reasons. But Thimayya could not play politics with the country's borders, nor with the lives of his men and the *izzat* of the army. He undertook extensive tours of Punjab, Kashmir, including Ladakh. At Headquarters XI Corps, he reviewed the offensive/defensive roles of the formations and approved the plan for an offensive to Lahore across the Ichogil Canal "in principle," as Joginder recalls.[20] He asked 26th Infantry Division at Jammu to be responsible for defence rather than defence-offence. At XV Corps Headquarters at Srinagar, he directed them "to pay more attention to the Ladakh Sector." The joint efforts of Thimayya and Subroto saw the C-119 begin to land at Srinagar and Leh, and Western Command could, thus, improve its logistical ability to eventually build up the defence of Ladakh.[21]

Within days of his appointment, Thimayya was in Calcutta (Kolkata) to visit all the army units, especially the Cossipore and Ishapore factories, to assess for himself the progress of their production. Earlier, he would spend a few days with his Kumaonis at Ranikhet for their reunion. "It has been a pleasure," he said in a handwritten "Special Order of the Day" to the commandant, "to meet so many of my old friends, men and officers who served with me and I have been fortunate to meet all the commanding officers.... I particularly congratulate you for the Kumola Model Farm, which I hope will be the model for all..."[22]

Thimayya and Mukerjee joined Menon on his first visit to Kashmir, then under Bakshi Ghulam Mohamed. Sheikh Abdullah had been placed under house arrest and the state had adopted the Indian Constitution as its new Constitution[23]. Menon's oratory was again at a sharp edge. " We will not allow violation of Indian sovereignty or by proxy... not allow to be plucked or pillaged."[24]

During the first Army Commanders Conference that was held in end July 1957, Thimayya reviewed the defence preparedness, discussed the broad assessment the intelligence appreciation had given, then decided on holding two operationally-oriented exercises that would evaluate the Chinese-Pakistani threats, along with the Naga insurgency. It was also here that he would accept the regularisation of what came to be humorously known as "The Thimayya Commission"[25] to all the non-regular emergency commissioned officers, temporary commissioned officers who had fought gallantly in World War II and in J&K in 1947-48, but could not fulfill some conditions to become permanent regular commissioned officers. He remarked on how unfair and bureaucratic some senior army officers had been in failing to recognise the "worth" of these officers. It did good to the army and the 3,000-strong deficiency in the officer's cadre could be partially made up by this.

The service conditions of the men were as bad. They served for seven years and were then discharged with an eight years reserve liability. Assuming that a man enrolled at 18 years, he would be in civvies at 25 and then nobody's responsibility. "Who would join an army on those terms and conditions?" he asked. "It is criminal to have men serving for seven years and officers living in animated suspension," he said while informing the government that his positive recommendations in these regards should be approved. During his tenure, he saw to it that both these issues were set right.

The conference, which was attended by the prime minister, defence minister and finance minister (Morarji Desai) served as a good forum to give his views on the need for modernisation. He said: "If men get antiquated equipment, they will lose faith in themselves. It is essential, therefore, that old and obsolescent equipment and weapons are replaced. The army should be sound, well-trained and with a high morale. Its morale would reflect on the people, and nation as a whole, giving a sense of security and confidence in facing the future."[26]

Then came the question of boosting the army and he was frank in adding it to his "agenda for the government." He said: "We need to expand our strength to be able to match the threats. No longer is Napoleon's saying, 'An army marches on its stomach' wholly relevant. All armies now move with their heads. We need technicians to man our improved and improving equipment. Our combat arms need more trained men. The time, therefore, is suitable to make the services attractive by increasing not only the intake but increasing the 'colour service' of a jawan from seven years to 15 years; increasing pay, perks and pension. A retired soldier must be made to maintain his dignity among the civilians and thus serve the cause of patriotism and the army better." He then would narrate the pathetic condition of some of the ex-servicemen whom he met all over the country.

The deficiency in accommodation for married officers, JCOs and men had alarmed him too. The earlier defence ministers (Gopalaswamy Ayyangar and Dr KN Katju) had been trying to persuade the chiefs to raise this accommodation through "self-help," voluntary works and had even proposed that the army does what the PLA was already doing in China: grow own food, undertake public works on roads, bridges and airfields, *et al*. But this had to be seen in the light of the overall operational preparedness. Would it not hamper the training and affect morale?

He explained here – and later he would explain at every forum – including public addresses to ex-servicemen, to students and the NCC cadets that "an Indian soldier was neither a farmer nor an artisan nor a pioneer to undertake unsoldierly tasks." He needs time to train and adopt new techniques of fighting and administration in war and during peace time. He has to mobilise as a fully trained man at the shortest notice. He cannot, therefore, do ancillary jobs." Rebutting those who compared the jawans to the Chinese troops, he would explain to them that even in the PLA, it was the militia and not frontline soldiers who did the *kheti-bari* – the farming.

***

A chief is always busy and so was Thimayya. In June, he had been to the National Defence Academy, Khadakvasla, where Major General E Habibullah, an old friend, was the commandant. At the passing out parade on 1 June, he reiterated the advantage of "friendship to be of value for integration."

"We pride ourselves," he also told the passing out cadets, "in obliterating any parochial or provincial feelings, and, we are first and last Indians."

The Cold War scenario had its advantage for a non-aligned country like India, like an eligible bachelor still in the marriage market. Both Russia and the USA were wooing India. And Thimayya would soon find himself first in Russia and later in America. It turned out to be Russia first at the invitation of its defence minister, the famous Marshal GK Zhukov. The American visit would take place after another year.

Marshal Zhukov had visited India in May. Included in his itinerary were all the defence establishments, including the NDA and IMA. Zhukov's visit was preceded by the much publicised visits in 1955 of Khrushev and Marshal Bulganin. The Russians had shown steadfast support to India on its position on the Kashmir dispute in the UN, besides helping in setting up the Bhillai Steel plant.

During his visit to the prime minister's office, Nehru introduced Thimayya as "our most gallant general and strategist."

Zhukov had then asked Thimayya the number of divisions he commanded during World War II. On being told that he had commanded only his battalion and a brigade, the marshal had highlighted how he himself could be credited with having set an unbeatable record of commanding over 200 divisions. Zhukov though ostentatious, meant no offence to Thimayya. For, it was only in India that he got to know that the

Indian Army officers, despite their capabilities, had to struggle to take the command of a brigade in war and peace, "I am certain," he told Nehru, "your general would have commanded more divisions than I led in war if he were born in Russia."[27]

The Russian Visit

The visit to Russia took place in July 1957. The two service delegations, one led by General Thimayya, and the other by Commodore A Chakravarti, deputy chief of the Naval Staff, had a fleeting glimpse of the Soviet armed forces at the Navy Day celebrations at Leningrad and at the various service training institutions they visited. A series of field exercies carried out by Soviet ground and air-borne troops provided a *grand finale*.

The delegation's two-week itinerary included a four-day visit to Leningrad, where on 14 July they, along with several other European and Asian delegations, watched the Navy Day review, which is regarded as a national festival in the Soviet Union. Here they also visited the Krilov Naval Academy and some Soviet naval ships and submarines.

The next five days at Moscow were employed in visiting some of the premier officer-training centres, named after eminent Soviet scientists and military leaders, including the Frunze Military Academy, the Dzerzinski Artillery Academy, the Voroshilvo Higher Military Academy for officers of all the three services and an institution devoted to higher studies in armour. At the Kubinka Air Force Station, frontline supersonic military aircraft and the newly-developed civil airliners were on display. In token of their visit to some of the academies, General Thimayya and some senior members of the delegations were made honorary graduates and presented with the emblems of the respective academies they visited. The Zhukovski Air Academy also presented its graduation badge and an army air landing unit, its paratrooper's badge to the distinguished Indian soldier.

Replying to a toast proposed by the host, Marshal Zhukov, at a reception held on the eve of the delegation's departure for India, General Thimayya said, "We have seen how the Soviet armed forces are trained and what weapons they use. We have also seen Soviet forces exercising in the field. And while I cannot claim to have sufficient experience or complete knowledge, it has not been difficult for me to appreciate and admire the height of fitness and efficiency at which the Soviet serviceman stands. Apart from the educational value of our tour, we have been overwhelmed by the warmth and affection shown to us by officers and men and everyone else throughout our visit."

The general continued, "I will not find it difficult to explain to our jawans that the Soviet soldier is like him, who I am told, is addressed as 'Ivan.' *All I have to tell our jawan is that he is like your Ivan.*"[28]

Following his visit, the Russian delegation that came to New Delhi under General Macek offered T-34 and T-54 tanks, IIiyushin-14s and MiG-15s, besides 7.62 mm rifles along with 130 mm guns – all on 30-year soft loans. The government, however, refused to accept the generous offer.

Thereat Perceptions and Projections

Upon his return from Russia, Thimayya sat with Major General LP (Bogey) Sen, the Master General of Ordnance (MGO) and asked to be briefed on the earlier projections that had already been made to the government for modernisation of the army. He found that in an ongoing process, the earlier Cs-in-C and COAS had wanted the old .303 rifles to be replaced by 7.62 mm semi-automatic rifles. Similarly, the 3 inch mortars needed replacement as also the main artillery guns, 125 pounders and 5.5 inch medium guns. The list was long and included anti-aircraft guns and missiles, lighter and mobile tanks, clothing for high altitude, composite rations, and so on.

Although the US Colt AR-15, and Belgian 7.62 mm F N rifles were offered for sale, the government had begun to try to manufacture 7.62 mm semi-automatic rifles at Ishapore, which were expected to take a much longer period than proposed. Rejections of more modern replacement in other equipment had been also been continuously done by the government due to the extra cost in foreign exhange, or purely as a matter of policy.

Thimayya was aware that although the foreign exchange required for essential minimum 'inescapable' quantities was not wanting, nevertheless, there were three impediments: one, Defence Minister Krishna Menon's obsession with his indigenous capability to manufacture modern weapons, thus, saving foreign exchange; two, the prime minister's policy to prioritise development over defence and security; three, Mr Nehru's firm belief that despite blatant Chinese intrusions into the Aksai Chin and other areas, it was merely "bluff" and the police and militia would offer adequate deterrence to their further ingress.

There were other issues of perceptions, but these three, offering a "stonewall" to border security and better border management, could only be removed if he could make the government see the seriousness of a larger threat or threats from two modern armies – that of China (the PLA) and the American-equipped Pakistani armed forces.

He asked the MGO to project the requirement to the army afresh, highlighting the urgency of:
    (a) Phased procurement through foreign sources and seeking their collaboration in helping indigenous production.
    (b) The need to arm, at least, one-third the present strength of infantry for operations in high altitude areas as soon as possible.
    (c) To approve extra forces for which a separate projection would follow[29].

Based on the "Intelligence Appreciation," IB inputs and studies by Commands, an operational discussion was held on the assessment of the Chinese threat and requirement of additional troops for deployment on the Chinese border. It was sent to the MoD in early July barely a week after the urgent note on modernisation of the army.

The deployment pattern of the forces recommended was modest. It recommended a brigade group along with the militia and Ladakh Scouts for the defence of Ladakh, on suitable defensible and well maintained features west of the line held by the Chinese. It considered necessary the raising of a division for the defence of NEFA which was being claimed by the Chinese on their maps. True to his thinking, Thimayya recommended a strike division to be located suitably for offensive tasks. A battalion each of frontier corps or militia was also required for Sikkim and Bhutan for internal security. In addition, he asked for deployment of more intelligence and communication resources all over the border, besides developing the essential artery of surface communications enabling not only the logistics but also movement of artillery and reinforcements.[30]

A brief note that mentioned that most of the projections contained in the note would, in due course, be met from indigenous production, was received from the MoD in January 1958. Thimayya would now seek another opportunity to apprise the minister about the state of obsolescence of the army's equipment.

No Change in Recruitment Policy

In the meanwhile, the MoD under Krishna Menon, under pressure from the politicians, especially the Communists, began to ask the Army Headquarters to reserve vacancies for the Scheduled Castes and Tribes in the army. In his well-considered note, Thimayya apprised the government about the validity of the existing recruitment policy.

He apprised that prior to independence, certain classes were referred to as the "Martial Races." Beginning from the time of General Cariappa, the concept of class composition was discarded for arms and services other than the armoured corps, artillery and infantry. Consequently, recruitment to all arms and services except those three arms, was thrown open to all Indian nationals, irrespective of any consideration of caste, religion or region.[31] Even within the three arms, new classes were gradually being inducted. As a result, by the late 1950s, the armoured corps and artillery had about 10 per cent mixed classes – and this trend continued to be encouraged.

While Thimayya regarded the army as not the preserve of specified tribes or castes, he explained to the ministry the basics of soldiery. "It is laudable," he wrote "that a break has been called to be made to the present class composition; however, care should be taken to see that the new proposed arrangement should under no circumstance impair the fighting qualities, and cohesiveness of units based on intimate sense of kinsmanship and traditions."

"It is easier" he wrote further, "to take an academic view of this matter but it would not give the quality to the army that we must have. Equally, we need to see that the Indian soldier is deeply imbued with regional, linguistic and social ties. Any radical departure from the present concept of class composition in the fighting arms is, therefore, fraught with grave danger and I do not recommend it."[32]

The government accepted his recommendation.

To the UK, Egypt and Back

By August (1957), he was in Camberley (UK) attending *Exercise Forecast* as part of the meeting of Commonwealth Army Chiefs of Staff, conducted by Field Marshal Sir Gerald Templer, CIGS. Having been to Russia and sufficiently clear on the shape and design of the USSR, he was interested in the "Armageddon" being fought by the two nuclear power blocs. The exercise, true to its nickname was forecasting mutually assured destruction as the acronym "MAD" suggested. It was, in fact, chiefly, concentrated on whether the brigade group system or the standard divisional system was to be adopted or not in a nuclear environment. "Apart from this," the general quipped, "the average men and women in the UK, as always, centre their attention on the latest football scores, the latest shows in town and the growing housing shortage."

During the summing up, Thimayya spoke only one sentence that dawned sobriety among the Cold War warriors. "After my recent visit to Russia," he remarked, "I am convinced that they genuinely desire peace." He suggested cooperation be preferred to confrontation by the North Atlantic Treaty Organisation (NATO) in dealing with the Warsaw Pact.

He met the Indian Journalists Association in London at a luncheon hosted by them. Here he declared that the Indian Army was "an Army of Peace," and "its functions were linked with India's foreign policy." He said: "We do not want to get involved in either bloc but we are prepared to be used to resolve tensions that divide Russia and the West."

Another point, he made was about the attitude of the services: "We have been very clearly directed not to be trained for an offensive but purely for the defence of India." As usual, he spoke warmly of the Indian soldier who never lost even once, his equilibrium in the most difficult situations, in Korea or Kashmir. No soldier in his place could genuinely be happy with a passive policy of defence but Thimayya knew that the art of generalship, to a large degree, coalesced diplomacy with strategy.

On his way back, Thimayya had two more programmes on his itinerary: a visit to Egypt; and, to the Indian battalion deployed at *Deir Al Balah* on the Armistice Line of the UN Emergency Force in Gaza.

Received at the Cairo airport by India's Ambassador, Nawab Ali Yavar Jung, and General Mohamed Rashad Hasan, he met the Egyptian Army Chief of Staff General Mohamed Ibrahim. The afternoon of the first day he visited the Sun Boats and the Sphinx. Then he flew off to Gaza where he was received by General Mohamed H A Latif, Egyptian administrator, and General Burns, commander UNEF, both of whom praised the Indian troops. "I found the troops engaged in a delicate and difficult task which was being tackled with tact, tolerance and efficiency," he said to the Press while praising the dedication and discipline of 1st Paras committed to an "international obligation." A cocktail with Burns and then he drove to the battalion headquarters to spend the night with the Paras under Lieutenant Colonel Inder Gill, MC. He visited all the troops the following day.

By 27 August, Thimayya was in Cairo where he visited the Egyptian ammunition factories, and armoured units, and lunched with President Gamel Abdel Nasser, an old friend in whom Prime Minister Nehru had great trust[33].

By the evening, he wound up his visit by seeing the Military Museum at the Citadel and the Mohamed Ali Mosque at Al Jawhara Palace, before attending a reception in the Indian Embassy. On 28 August, he was flying back.

Upon his return to Bombay, Thimayya was met by Lieutenant General P N Thapar, Army Commander Southern Command. Kalwant Singh, who officiated in Thimayya's absence, had sent a long brief summarising the events on the Pakistani border and how the Chinese had kept 'Bara Hoti' post under tension, how the Khampas in Tibet were active and that despite the brave speeches by the prime minister, the bombshell of the Aksai Chin Road may publicly explode "any time." He said Thorat was handling the Naga problem although most of them had found sanctuary in Burma and were perhaps on their way to China. In Pakistan, Ayub and Iskander Mirza were getting restive and it could not be said how developments would shape there. He would also mention some of the highlights of President Eisenhower's 21-day 11-nation visit, including to India.

Among the important issues he suggested to the chief was to hold two exercises or operational discussions on NEFA and Ladakh and apprise the government of the army's views once again as there had been no response to the earlier notes.

It took Thimayya another year of work and he was in a position to give an indication again in the following Army Commanders Conference, about measures being taken up to step up recruitment to the Territorial Army, liberalisation of the pensionary and other benefits, besides his proposal to introduce a contributory children's education scheme in the army. He wanted the army commanders to expedite the 'works' on buildings and communications.

One of the most resented episodes of 1957 in so far as the services were concerned, was the visit to India of a high-powered Chinese military delegation under marshals and generals. The delegation was sent to all military stations with orders to "show them everything!" A continuing fallacy of the *Hindi-Chini Bhai-Bhai*.

Impetus to Sports

Himself an outstanding sportsman, he motivated the Services Sports Control Board to exert itself. Sports and sportsmen really got a fillip now. The army athletes had done the country proud and put India on the international sports map. The army dominated every field: athletics, aquatics, boxing, cricket, football, hockey and golf.

Then began the Army Headquarters Mountaineering Association and an army team climbing Annapurna. The establishment of the Himalayan Mountaineering Institue (HMI), Darjeeling, followed. At his behest, the country reconstituted a 15-member All India Council of Sports under Dr P Sobbarayam. Thimayya shared its membership with Raj Kumari Amrit Kaur and the Maharaja of Patiala. As president of the Delhi Golf Club, he was most active. On relinquishing its presidency to Dharma Vira, the *Week End Golf-Notes*, recorded:

> Thimayya held office for two years and during that period, an important chapter in the club history was written. It included planning and contribution of a new wing and holding of Delhi's first ever Amateur Championship, both events with extremely satisfactory results.

Not only golf, Thimayya also encouraged sailing, and polo, not only in Delhi, but also in the metropolitan cities and Bangalore. The great sportsman in him was now reinvigorating the sporting spirit of the Indian Army. On another important occasion, the Army Commanders Conference of December 1958, he remarked: "A sportsman makes a good soldier and I am happy that the army has dominated most sports events this year; some of them are bringing laurels in international sports. I hope to provide facilities to promote sportsmanship and assist in its standards generally in the country." He continued to strive for it.

He was delighted to hear that Captain Narinder Kumar, Lieutenant Y K Yadav and Lieutenant (I N) Mehta of the HMI had ascended Trisul[34]. Jemadar Milkha Singh, the "Flying Sikh" had won his 200 and 400 metre races at the Commonwealth Games, Cardiff. Five gold medals had been won by the services boys at the Asian Games in Tokyo. Havildar Lila Ram had won in wrestling.

Naturally, Thimayya, in his great enthusiasm and appreciation, promoted all of them one rank up, not knowing two facts over which he would later laugh heartily. Timmy Sahib did not know that Lila Ram consumed a mythical "Kumbhkaran's" diet of three to four kilos of milk, 600 grams of ghee, 500 grams of almonds, besides one kg of meat, plus eggs – all contributed by his friends in the Regimental Centre – a true White Horse. And secondly, Milkha, the Flying Sikh was looking for a commission as an officer and not as a mere subedar which his sporting prowess had already helped him rise to from a cook. Above all, being an amateur sportsman, someone reminded him that it was not in order to formally recognise their performance. Thimayya's reaction was characteristic: "Yes, this is interesting and there is a great deal of truth in it. But I do what my boys deserve."

The army continued to do well. On 24 June, the 20,596-ft high Bundur Puchh (Monkey's Tail) was climbed by Captain Jagjit Singh and his team. While Thimayya congratulated the mountaineers in South Block, Krishna Menon walked in and asked Jagjit: "Was your ascent in tune with the infinite?."

Jagjit was non-plussed. Then Thimayya, adding his humour, told Jagjit, "The minister would like to know if you found a Hanuman up there?"

***

By August, the water supply of Delhi had been badly disrupted due to the change in course of the Jamuna and overall recession of its water level. Water could not be pumped for three days. Thimayya proved to be the saviour. He suggested that water should be brought to the intake mains at Wazirabad. The Sappers then took charge and restored the supply. The army also ensured that all hospitals were supplied water through its own bowsers. The capital was grateful to him – and the army.

The hostile Nagas, despite all his efforts of 1956, were now reorganising into so-called four commands under Phizo as C-in-C. The inconsistent policy followed by the government was responsible for it. After Dr Haralu's incident, the security forces were working under several constraints. Besides, following the enquiries against the units and their relief which hurt their pride, the enthusiasm to pursue the hostiles had weakened. The rebels were emboldened and had organised themselves into battalions, volunteer parties, courier parties and women's volunteer force. They began to loot *bazaars* and kill peace loving villagers, who refused to part with their grain or sons and daughters. The establishment of village guards organised by Thimayya and fully implemented by Thorat, was doing well. But overall, the situation was hardly satisfactory as the political solution to the Naga problem was far off.

At Delhi, the winter sports saw the services cricket team led by Thimayya beat the team of the members of Parliament led by Nehru. A great deal of *bonhomie* brought in the end of 1957.

1958

The year 1958 augured well. On 15 January, the Army Day Parade attended by Prime Minister Nehru and a large number of guests, showed the regard the prime minister had for General Thimayya. Briefly speaking at this grand but austere display of arms in this ceremonial parade, Thimayya said:

> The object of the celebration of this day is to draw the attention of the people of India to the work, the loyalty and steadfastness of the army to its country. I do not think I need enlarge on this. The work you have done and, will continue to do, is sufficient proof of this. We are the largest nation-building organisation in the country today. Apart from our purely military responsibilities, we instill discipline and we teach hygiene and sanitation and make the men take pride in themselves. All these are necessary in making you into useful citizens of the country and thereby add to the strength and development of our country.

The IX Republic Day Parade had also gone off well.

Three days later, he was on All India Radio[35] addressing the "Youth in the Defence of Nation." It is here that he spoke of the border aspects of the problems of defence, the problems the country faced and the manner in which the youth could cooperate and play a major part. He found the educational system was still far behind in producing youth who were good leaders but he hoped things would improve. "Toughness," "spirit of enthusiasm" and taking part in what the prime minister called the "great experiment," were the needs of the day.

Returning to technological sufficiency, he said, "To fight effectively, it is necessary for the armed forces to be equipped with modern and efficient weapons. Hitherto, owing to lack of industrialisation and lack of encouragement that we have had in producing our own weapons in defence equipment and stores, we lagged far behind in our own production and in order to be self-sufficient, we must create an army of technical workers. We must develop scientists, production men without whom we can never be self-sufficient. Our colleges, technical institutes and factories, both in the private and public sectors, must play their full part in producing these men. There is an extreme shortage of all types of technical and scientific personnel. A large number of these will have to be in uniform, others will be civilians, but whatever clothing they wear, they are important in achieving our success."

The Battle Within

The peril from the north now called for full attention. The Chiefs of Staff Committee under Thimayya's chairmanship, seized of the impending danger, decided to reiterate to the government the urgent need for arms, equipment, ammunition, ships and aircraft. Although the defence minister himself began to devote full time to indigenisation, at what he called "full-throttled" speed, the chiefs admired his "foresight and vision" for long-term defence self-reliance. However, they were forthright in pointing out to him the "immediate needs" of acquiring new equipment for the services, specially of the army and IAF.

Menon would chuckle and say, "Where are the threats; if it is Pakistan then, you tell me you can handle it, and I say, China will not attack India."

However, they managed to make him project an increased defence budget for 1957-58 slated at Rs 278.14 crore (a dollar then being approximately Rs. 4 and a pound sterling Rs 16). Although inadequate to meet even normal requirements, nonetheless, it generated some heated discussion in the Parliament. Acharya JB Kripalani, the leader of the Opposition would hackle Menon, so much so that Nehru would have to explain the requirement for additional funds under the "mounting list of equipment and its maintenance." Yet under political pressure, the defence budget for 1959-60 would be brought down to Rs 242.68 crore, reducing the previous one by Rs 35.46 crore.[36]

The Opposition could not be convinced by the government on the need for a higher defence budget despite the Chinese designs of aggression being amply clear. It was also not being appreciated that a higher defence budget than the one projected was inescapable for raisings and equipping the forces that would soon become responsible for guarding the 14,880-km-long land frontier and 5,656-km-long coastline. Even population wise, it came to just Rs 8 ($2) per head, a negligible amount for the defence of a long border.

By the end of 1957, Tibet, 'dragooned' under China's heavy heels, had become a cause of further anxiety for India. It had also become a topic of the UN General Assembly debates. Rebellions seemed to have picked up momentum on the "Roof of the World" and some dissent was discernible in Xinjiang, in the far west.

Although the Aksai Chin Road alignment was generally clear, to test the Chinese reaction to own ground reconnaissance and movement of troops in close proximity to the road, General Thimayya suggested that confirmatory reconnaissance be done at the earliest, and he asked the government to decide on this policy soon. He also urged the defence minister to approve both the new raisings and equipping of the forces he had earlier recommended, at least, in principle, so that further action could be taken by him to meet the Chinese threat.

While the government took some time to dig out the files gathering dust in the MoD and reexamine these requests, he asked HQ Western Command, Shimla, to move as many patrols forward as possible. These were necessary to confirm the road alignment made available through air reconnaissance. Concurrently, the government also approved the movement of two patrols – one led by Lieutenant Iyenger, a Sapper; and another by the IB's Inspector Karam Singh, simultaneously during July-August – to assess the northern and southern extremities of the said road.[37]

Karam Singh moved cross-country in the south to Amtogar and having ascertained the alignment, returned safely. Iyenger's patrol moved from Hot Spring via Shamul Lungpa, Dehra Compass, Shinglung to Haji Langer where Iyenger confronted and informed the Chinese that he had been assigned to a mission of survey and was well within the Indian territory, which the Chinese objected to. He asked them to take him to their officer-in-charge, to whom his line of explanation was the same that he was on a fact-finding mission and, therefore, was in no way, there to pick a fight with them. He asked them to let him return as Chinese and Indians were *Hindi-Chini Bhai-Bhai*. The Chinese regarded Iyengar's patrol as an enemy reconnaisance against their forward defence. They apprehended his party and began extensive interrogations. This carried on for almost two months, after which the party was released only on the night of Diwali of 1958.[38]

About this time, on entreaties by Mullik, the MoD asked Thimayya if the army could take over deployment in Ladakh. In accepting the requirement, the Army Headquarters drew the MoD's attention to their earlier projections and urged the government to approve the raisings, prioritise the building up of communications, and logistics to enable forward deployment. Simultaneously, it also asked all other agencies now manning the border to be placed under its command. Until that happens, the army contended, it could reconnoitre the area and remain in contact with the Chinese through patrols.[39]

Unfortunately, the army's request to hand over the border to it so that necessary strategic developments matching the Chinese could take place, had been continuously ignored. Thimayya had anticipated that some day the government would realise its folly and order the army to step in. Having been ignored all this time, the Army Headquarters, on approval by Thimayya, agreed only to occasional patrols as it was not in a position to establish posts since both logistics and communication were lacking. "We will mobilise as many troops and fire support means as required, as soon as the bare minimum requirements are made available," the note added.[40]

As a professional soldier and strategist, Thimayya would not have rushed headlong against the vastly superior Chinese Army. He wanted a deliberate build-up of defences before taking on the Chinese. In fact, right from 1957, he had been urging the government to hand over the defence responsibility of the border to the army, which Menon refused and Nehru did not encourage until after August 1959, when the enemy action would compel the government to act, or be succumbed.

The next battle line soon emerged: indigenisation versus modernisation. Thimayya would continuously recall that within the first month of his appointment, he had reminded the government that the army had many obsolescent weapons and equipment and it needed a wide-range of modern weapons and equipment to replace them as an operational priority.

He had the MGO assess the requirements, and then send a note. The whole project, he reminded the minister, worked out at about Rs. 500 crore with a 30 to 40 per cent of foreign exchange component. The priority he accorded was for replacement of old .303 rifles with 7.62 mm, 4.2 inch mortars with 120 mm, 5.5 inch gun with 155 mm, of existing tanks with universal lighter and medium tanks, with amphibious capabilities and better bridging equipment, helicopters for artillery, communications and logistics, long range and more secure radio communications, and so on. But Menon would emphasise that his indigenisation programme was there to cater for it.

The Baldev Singh Committee report on the "Reorganisations of Ordnance Factories" had already recommended the formation of an autonomous Defence Production Board and had also suggested establishment of the post of Chief Controller of Research and Development. Out of these, Menon prioritised some projects which would cater for both defence and civil requirements, in addition to capitalising on their political fallouts. Nehru would support this policy when he declared open the first *Defence Production Exhibition* in New Delhi on 6 September, 1958.

"Defence production, in common with the rest of industrial development," Mr. Nehru declared, "has to be thought of in terms of its ability for peaceful purposes." The exhibition succeeded in its attempt to familiarise the public with the efforts so far made by the ordnance factories and several defence installations in the country for meeting the requirements of the armed forces, as well as in aid of civil industry, in both the public and private sectors.[41] It also gave an idea of what indigenous production was aiming at in the defence industries during the next three years. This was followed by explaining the government policy, as the prime minister added, "*A reorientation is necessary from the old 'Maginot Line' thinking, and revitalisation of existing resources to the best advantage. By far, it is better to have second rate weapons made in the country than to depend on the first rate ones from outside....*" (emphasis added).[42]

Earlier, Nehru had inaugurated the manufacture of the Shaktimaan vehicle in the Gun Carriage Factory, Jabalpur. Ordnance factories had begun to undertake production of tractors and bulldozers, in collaboration with a Japanese firm. AVM MM Engineer was shifted as general manager to Hindustan Aircraft (Private) (later Aeronautical), Kanpur, replacing J M Shrinagesh, ICS. The list would add fuel gas plant, pressure cookers, coffee percolators, project for a 7.62 mm rifles and Brandt mortars, besides the more prestigious HF 24 (Marut) and Vijyant tanks at Avadi Heavy Vehicles Factory. While negotiations for the *HMS Hercules* (later *INS Vikrant*) were afoot, Mazgaon Dockyard was to produce ships. Similarly, AVM Harjinder Singh, a 'blue-eyed boy' of Krishna Menon, was working on assembling the AVRO-748 transport aircraft.

While reviewing the position of equipment and weapons in the army, during the December 1958 Army Commanders Conference, Thimayya had said that the introduction of trucks and tractors would greatly help solve the transport problem and he thanked the minister for it. "Alertness and fitness to fight," was the theme of the conference. He, however, observed that these systems and equipment, being selective and barely touching the tip of a large requirement, would also need a gestation period of, at least, seven to ten years – if not more. "The question, hence," he said, without dramatics, "what happens if a war is suddenly thrust upon us in the not-too-distant a future?"

"Time, tide and the enemy," he remarked "do not wait for anyone. It is my experience, they strike when they want or when you least expect."[43]

This began to irritate Menon. In rejecting the projections, he had asked the army chief to have patience with the indigenisation and trust that brand new weapons would be available soon, even the production of a universal tank; the HAL Kanpur would have the transport and fighter aircraft and helicopters, Ishapore would have the 7.62 mm semi-automatic rifles; so would mortars and guns and vehicles be available aplenty. He would quote the prime minister's policy of second class indigenous weapons being preferred to first class foreign ones.[44]

Another meeting was held some time in April 1958 to discuss the issues. At this meeting, the service chiefs were frank and forthright and explained that they fully supported his indigenisation policy and programmes but that could be a futuristic thing, say 10 years or so, if all went well with production and quality. They, however, suggested to him not to reject or defer the projections being made by them as their immediate requirements which had become operationally inescapable to meet the threats. Some more vital recommendations were made by the service chiefs with regards to immediate purchases, raisings of formations for the Chinese border and speeding up construction of border roads for which a separate Border Road Organisation was suggested.

The service chief, now all Indians, Admiral Carlill having been replaced by RD Katari, were clamouring for better integration of the services to evolve joint strategies and plans for the armed forces. They were also wanting their voices to be heard by the government and their professional advice to be heeded. An overhaul of the system was being suggested where the bureaucracy at the MoD and the Service Headquarters would be acting as one organisation rather than the former being treated as bosses on matters over which they had neither experience, nor knowledge, nor expertise. A legitimate appeal. While O Pulla Reddy, the defence secretary, himself in discord with Krishna Menon, was for every kind of adjustment with the chiefs, he would, nonetheless, want an approval of the minister, even to discuss this proposal.[45]

While the MoD and the services agreed only tangentially on vital issues of strategic conceptions, the aggression continued. By June 1958, the Chinese visited Khurnak Fort, well inside Ladakh and turned it into a firm base and established posts at Spangur and Digra. The dragnet expanded into other areas too. In September, they carried out deep reconnaissance in Di Chu Valley of Lohit Frontier Division and then retreated. The next month, they established posts on Sangcha Nalla and Lapthal in the Central or Middle Sector. The air space of Spiti Valley was also violated by the Chinese Air Force in October. The Khampa rebellion in Tibet had brought in thousands of refugees into India all over the frontier. Thus, there were no doubts of the Chinese intentions and yet the MoD continued to play it down; so did Menon himself.

Thimayya, however, did not give up. The proposal for force-multipliers of all arms and services to meet the twin threat was being tossed up and down between the Army Headquarters and the MoD. With the defence budget being sliced, it was not unusual. However, his recommendations to improve the officers situation by accepting additional intake from the NCC, technical entries, ACC and even accept temporary, emergency and short service commissions in an emergency, was under progress. Instructions also went to all institutions imparting training to officers and men to make arrangements for the extra intake.

To meet the manpower requirements in an emergency, he proposed to maintain a regular army reserve of officers. As a result, released short service regular emergency and temporary commissioned officers as well as former state forces' officers, cadets of the senior division of the NCC with Certificate 'C' and other civilians within the prescribed age limits on 1 January 1959, all became eligible for being commissioned in the "reserve."

The need for specialised training was felt as the northern border became active.

General Thimayya realised the need of training every infantryman and some selected from other arms in skiing, rock climbing and special missions, besides general survival in extreme cold and high altitudes. As GOC Sri Div, he had set the ball rolling for the Ski and Winter Warfare School in Gulmarg. This was formalised further as the High Altitude Warfare School. Along with this had come the mountaineering institutes – in Darjeeling and subsequently in Uttarkashi. The idea of a joint land-air warfare school had been floated to the ministry, as were the institutes of material and defence management.

Thimayya was also persuading the government to accept the proposal for a National Defence College (NDC) at Delhi on the lines of the Imperial Defence College of the UK.

Successful 'live' drop trials with Indian-made parachutes produced with indigenous materials were held at the Parachute Training School, Agra, during the month of June. A jeep with an indigenously made platform was dropped for the first time from a C-119 Fairchild aircraft, undamaged parachutes made from indigenous silk materials and subjected to dropping trials at various altitudes, wind velocities and loads with 'dummies,' proved a complete success. Encouraged by these results, 40 more such parachutes were made and successful 'live' drop trials held at Agra.

About this time, the Chinese too were impressing Nepalese Prime Minister B P Koirala and his Foreign Minister S P Upadhayaya with a massive parachute drop in Tibet, with the object, as Mullik observed, "that China could at any time capture Kathmandu and India could do nothing to prevent it."[46]

Humour and wit enhanced Thimayya's personality. "We are the only ones who defy common sense in a calculated manner," he told the parachutists amidst a roar of laughter. "We leap before we look. But there is a logic in it – we see no evil."[47] On another occasion, he would tell the "Red Berets," "The human mind acts like a parachute, it only works when it is open."

Need for Further Analysis

By mid-1958, China offered a red herring to India on the 20-km simultaneous pull back by both sides from the prevailing positions in Ladakh; Nehru, recognising this stratagem as a Chinese effort at legitimisation of their aggression into Indian territory, especially in Ladakh, deprecated it. China, now unashamedly insinuated that India was "aiding the rebellion" in Tibet. To disprove it, Nehru offered to visit Lhasa, which the Chinese disallowed for "reasons of security." They had already unleashed a reign of terror and destruction in Tibet. But Nehru still hoped that better sense would prevail and the Chinese would prevent the situation from turning irretrievable.

Thimayya's sixth sense could see the yellow peril firmly spilling over across the McMahon Line, not only in Ladakh or the UP-Tibet border, but into NEFA; worse still, into Sikkim and Bhutan, if it became an all-out war. The more he reflected on the possibilities, the more convinced he became of the possibility of a war. But the government appeared in no haste to hand over the border to the army, or develop logistics and surface or air communications. He realised that having lost precious time since 1950, creating a capability equal or superior to the PLA in the immediate future would be next to impossible, but shrewd diplomatic handling by the government might still give him time to build a deterrent by suitably deploying even small, self-contained forces on major axes of ingress. The doctrine he enunciated was: "*We will not rush forward to the border but fight from the ground of own chosing, easily defensible and sustainable... In the bargain, every piece of ground or every square on the map south of the McMahon Line cannot – and need not – be expected to be defended.*"[48]

It was a sound principle to work on. He was certain that the government would concur in the proposal. It was necessary then to further carry out detailed terrain analysis of the entire Chinese border which geographically fell within the Western and Eastern Commands. He asked General Kalwant (GOC-in-C Western Command) and General Thorat (GOC-in-C Eastern Command) to reconnoitre the areas of their responsibilities, and, evaluating the threat, ascertain the defensive pattern they felt was essential to adopt against the Chinese along various areas.

Thus, originated *Exercise Lal Quila* for General Thorat and *Exercise Sheel* for General Kalwant and his successor. He tasked the DMI and DMO to also work on their plans independent of the Commands but with Mullik's intelligence inputs. The DMO was to also liaise with the Survey of India to provide maps of the areas already surveyed and speed up work on the unsurveyed tracts.

He asked the scientific adviser and director general Medical Services along with the defence psychologists to examine the problems arising out of high altitude deployment and fighting by carrying out trials in both Ladakh and NEFA realistically. They were to educate the troops. It was to become a mass movement in the army. He was also pursuing the case for a Border Road Orgnisation. Both perseverance and enthusiasm were required to get anything moving amidst the inertia of the ministry.

Before Thimayya left for his overdue visit to the USA, he embarked on a whirlwind visit to major stations in all the three Commands. The highlights of his addresses to the officers, and where possible, the men, were the "threats as they had arisen and the shape they could assume." He made it clear that now that China had breached India's frontier in such large strength and it was conniving with the hostile Nagas and with Pakistan, war had become inevitable. And although the border had not been formally handed over, the Indian Army should be under no false impression that it would not be deployed and, hence, it needed to be built up, learn to live and fight on those difficult heights.

"In case tomorrow, I am asked to take over the border, I'll do it. My battle at present is to get it now so that infrastructures are developed, more formations are raised, trained and deployed before it is too late. I hope I can prevail on the government to acknowledge the urgency," he would emphasise.

September-October saw Thimayya visit Canada and the USA. He was accompanied by Major General Daulat Singh, QMG and Brigadier B D Kapur, chief controller of research and development. Daulat, besides being the QMG was an expert in armoured warfare and tanks. Kapur would see the R&D in the USA and Canada. The mission was to get acquainted with the most modern Western systems that could be adapted for the Indian Army, still organised primarily on the British lines.

To Western Continent

On 5 September, he inspected a guard of honour at Palam and was seen off by Ellsworth Bunker, and Chester A Roning, the ambassador and high commissioner of the USA and Canada respectively, besides Dr D S Kothari, scientific adviser MoD and Lieutenant General Kalwant Singh, the seniormost army commander.

At Ottawa, he conferred with the Canadian Defence Minister, G R Peakes and the chairman of the Canadian Chiefs of Staff Committee, before undertaking a week-long visit to the Canadian defence establishments. While in Canada, he did not forget to greet the Madras Regiment on its bicentenary celebrations. "I hope your glorious past will continue to be equalled by your glorious future," his message said.

His visit to the USA was interrupted by his sudden illness. He met General Layman L Lemnitzer, the vice chief of the US Army Staff in Washington. The following day, he was admitted into the Walter Reed Army Hospital for respiratory infection and a bleeding gastric ulcer. He would recover only by 1 October. Laughingly, he would tell everyone, that he had been forced by his overworked system to 'switch off.' With Walter Reed's motto, "Here any GI gets the same medical care as a Prince of Arabia or the President of the US," he recovered well and fast.

One Lil Doc who had looked after him here, wrote him an affectionate letter with "feelings in the innermost depths of my heart." He sent her a painting of Kashmir later.

On 3 October, he was honouring the American dead by laying a wreath at the "Tomb of the Unknown Soldier." The following day, he was at Fort Meyer, Virginia, where George V Allen, former US ambassador to India, received him. A guard of honour by 1st Battle Group, 3rd Infantry Regiment followed. At Fairfax, he conferred with the US Army Secretary, Welbur Brucker, and met his old friend, General Maxwell Taylor. A meeting at the Pentagon with the defence secretary proved interesting as it was here that an assessment of the Chinese capability in Tibet was presented to him by a representative of the CIA and an offer of essential arms and equipment, tanks and aircraft was made by the US government.

Thimayya had been sufficiently impressed with the US service helicopters and showed interest in the S-62 Sikorsky. Suitably modified, he thought, they would prove a ready solution to meeting the logistical requirement of troops and police on the Chinese border. The US secretary for defence arranged a flight for him and others on 12 October to the Sikorsky Helicopter Factory at Connecticut. It proved a boon, as he could also fly to a place called Derian, which had continued to have a

Derian-Mercara Committee (a proposal begun by General Cariappa). He was able to see "Shakuntala," the baby elephant donated by Mercara to Derien and renew his offer to the mayor to visit Kodagu.

Earlier, on 10 October, the UN Secretary General, Dag Hammrskjold, had invited him to the UN Headquarters at New York. Krishna Menon who had attended the General Assembly meeting, was also there.

In Canada and the USA, getting down to the nitty-gritty of defence, he studied particularly their systems of commissioning officers, which he had observed was the Indian Army's chief defect. He said, "I found both of them, apart from their military academies at Kingston and West Point, maintain a very large reserve of officers through their militias and reserve of officers training course. In fact, every graduate who passes out of a university is also a potential officer and unless we adopt some such system in this country of concentrating in a greater measure on the training of the NCC, we will never be able to maintain or build up a large reserve of officers to deal with an emergency." He, therefore was going to concentrate on the extra training of the NCC in the coming years.[49]

Despite having fallen ill, he enjoyed a visit to the Infantry School at Fort Benning, where over 2,000 officers (both reserve and regular) were undergoing training and some of the items that he saw were most impressive. At West Point, he was particularly impressed by the great emphasis placed on academic training and the necessity of obtaining a B.Sc degree before an officer was commissioned. This, he thought was a real necessity for increasing the study of science as a part of modern warfare. It also enabled an officer to obtain civilian employment at any stage in his life, being in possession of a recognised university degree. He wished India could send more officers there for training, but unfortunately the foreign exchange situation was drastically low.

It was time to return. Both Daulat and Kapur had moved around according to the planned itinerary while Thimayya recuperated in Walter Reed. The team sailed back in the luxury liner *Queen Mary* from New York to London. By 30 October, they touched down at Santa Cruz. But General Thimayya had another hop to West Germany.

While he personally briefed Nehru and Menon on the outcome of the visit, a long shopping list accompanied the report that also had the American assessment of the Chinese in Tibet. Nehru read it, but Menon, on his return from the UN, asked Pulla Reddy to "mouthball it in a pigeon-hole." The minister hated to see anything reported against the Chinese; least of all by the CIA.

While in the USA, Thimayya had heard of the coup in Thailand, where General Sarit Thanarat seized power on 20 October. Seven days later, there was a coup in Pakistan, bringing to power General Ayub Khan. With Burma and Pakistan under military rule, the politicians in India, no doubt, felt uncomfortable. There was an undercurrent, a whispering campaign that General Thimayya too could spring a surprise. Such feelings, however unfounded and facetious, had their effect on the growth of a cordial relationship between Menon and his service chiefs – already on a slender thread.

While it was hard to form an opinion on the cause and consequence of coups elsewhere, Thimayya was led to reflect on Ayub's act. He had known Ayub from their Sandhurst days and had heard of his poor battlefield performance in Burma; and, he was least impressed by his handling of the refugee problem in Pakistan. How would such a mediocre officer with a lot of brawn but less brain, rule the country? "Rule or misrule, it's his funeral," he told India's ambassador to America in response to his query. "We have to guard Kashmir against his adventures, which people like him are capable of springing. [50]

Project Amar: A Surprise

The army had lost nearly 75 per cent of its permanent living accommodation to Pakistan, and the officers and troops had been living under canvas since the availability of family accommodation was negligible. This was beginning to have an adverse effect on the morale of the rank and file, as many of them had been separated from their families since the time World War II began. A scheme for permanent construction of barracks and family lines was put forward to the ministry by AHQ. Krishna Menon backed the idea more for self-aggrandisement than the welfare of the troops, since the credit for providing accommodation to the army would be his. In Kaul, he had found someone to give it shape, as it involved troop labour. Thimayya had earlier convinced Menon that such "an adventure," should not be undertaken. This happened before his sojourn to the US.

In his absence, after manipulating his way through Menon and Kalwant, Kaul commanding 4th Infantry Division had volunteered to construct accommodation at Ambala. It became a *fait accompli* now. The ceremony that took place at Ambala on 20 August 1958 was marked by the presence of the prime minister. "We are proud to have with us today," said Thimayya, "our prime minister who has consented to declare completed this fine project and the defence minister whose idea it was." And he paid a personal tribute to General Kaul for the "leadership and the motivation he provided for completing the project in seven months." His praise went to each officer and jawan too, who, despite numerous difficulties, succeeded in the mission, howsoever "unsoldierly" and "undignified" some of them might have regarded it. In order to maintain the dignity of his minister and Kaul, he took upon himself the onus of approving the project.

Personally, Kaul was building up his image as a go-getter, and creating avenues for special consideration for his vertical elevation. While politically, perhaps without his superiors' knowledge, he had already established links with Menon, he continued to impress the army chief by discreetly sponsoring the scheme to the defence minister and then volunteering to execute it. And as merit alone mattered to Thimayya, he naturally expressed high praise for what he called "an experimental housing project," providing living accommodation to 1,400 personnel.

At the conclusion of this ceremony, General Thimayya seemed to realise that both Menon and Kaul were closer than the desirable level of friendship-cum-acquaintance required. He knew Kaul was the nephew of the prime minister and even earlier placing him under his command, in various appointments, Nehru, evidently wanted Kaul to "grow." He became aware of Kaul's stratagem to get Project Amar going primarily for self-promotion. Although he ignored this as a skewed up affair, and true to his nature, was most generous in acknowledging Kaul's contribution and capability, Kaul's method had not pleased him a bit. Kaul, he thought, would need to be discreetly controlled.

What was, however, a cause of worry for him was the methodology the defence minister had begun to adopt to get his plan executed without getting the cheerful assent of the heads of the services. Thimayya was finding a new kind of vortex – a vortex destiny seemed to create for him now onwards.

Through the Opaque and the Transparent

It was customary for the service chiefs to address the students and the teaching faculty of the Defence Services Staff College, Wellington, Niligiri Hills, at least once during their tenure. The subject usually would be the strategic scenario. General Thimayya, however, decided to dwell on his impressions of his visits to Russia, the UK, Canada and the USA. (In addition, on his return journey, he had spent five days in Bonn, during which time he took the opportunity of meeting Mr Strauss, the defence minister of West Germany and the senior officers of their new army.) His aim was to provide a vista vision of the other nations, he said:

> On the whole, after a visit to these countries, I can happily say that our own training, in its small way, and within our financial means, is sound, that our officer corps is being well trained, that our men are of the quality, well disciplined and able to carry out their task with utmost confidence, but we will try to adopt some of the methods in the other advanced countries I have visited, to improve our training. Our equipment state is not satisfactory, but owing to our shortage of foreign exchange, rather than throw our money out in making purchases from outsiders, who want large profits from us, we are putting the same money into our production, the reorganisation of our scientific development and production in our own ordnance factories has been expanded enormously even in the last few months, and I am more than satisfied at the strides they have made, though the effects will not be felt immediately.

He hoped that within the next three or four years, the services would be self-reliant in most of the weapons with which they are armed. But he was candid in expressing his fears: *"Tanks, aircraft and missiles will be a longer programme and I do hope that with the foreign policy that we have adopted, this programme of ours will not let us down."* (Emphasis added.)

Speaking on Pakistan, he had a few words of sincere advice for Field Marshal Ayub Khan, then hobnobbing (he would call it *kowtowing*) with the American and the Chinese. "I would just like to say a word about our Pakistani friends across the border. Though General Ayub Khan has said that he would even go to war to solve some of his problems vis-à-vis India, I think that one sentence of his which follows in his statement, has not been emphasised and that is that 'if we go to war, both countries are doomed.' Therefore, I think that if he retains his balance of mind and is prepared to appreciate a military situation as taught to you in the Staff College, it will be foolish of him to attack India. We are quite clear in our own minds of our plans that we intend only defending India and he would require an army 4 to 5 times the size that he has today to enable him to attack us successfully. Even though he may be equipped in some cases, with a little more modern equipment than we have, *I have no doubt in my mind that if he attacks us, he will come off second best and that though it may not lead to the doom of this country itself, it may lead to the doom of Pakistan. For us, therefore, it is necessary that we keep our minds cool and collected and those of us who have the good fortune of serving on the frontiers, will always deal with every situation in a cool and calculated manner and will do nothing that can be mistaken for aggression on our part.*" (Emphasis added.)

He also wanted a change of attitude; for, he was now addressing the professionals and not the Press, say in London. "Let us not put too much emphasis on defence; that is always a bad thing and no army has succeeded in the history of the world, which is able to fight and defend their country merely on defensive methods. If Pakistan attacks us, we would have to hold this attack and subsequently launch a counter offensive, if necessary."

He was asked a question on the Chinese threat to India. He replied that as a military man he recognised the threat but the government was busy in handling it diplomatically.

He said that in all his travels abroad, he had found India's stock was high in the world, whether it was in Egypt, in Lebanon, in Syria, in the UK, in Canada and America, or in the USSR. He had been, he said, proud to be an Indian and he had always shown respect and consideration for the stand the country had taken on most of the world's problems.[51]

Integration

By the end of 1958, Thimayya, as head of the Chiefs of Staff Committee also had to face the question of improving the integration of the services in the fields of "common activities and concerns towards a better defence response to national security."[52] Some thought had been given to it earlier but he saw the need to review it. He had known how the gradual stripping away of the power and authority of the chiefs had been systematically done earlier. Then the role and charter of the chiefs (army, navy and air force) had been turned anomalous by the bureaucratic maze of the MoD. In

1957, he was neither a C-in-C, nor a genuine chief as was the case with the other service chiefs. Shrinagesh and his counterparts did not want to rock the boat during their tenures. Then there was the Chiefs of Staff (COS) Committee constituted under a charter, assigned to joint planning on a joint-service-basis. It was, on paper, responsible for strategic planning, joint logistics, and strategic plans, besides coordinating its activities with the planning committee. On the ground, however, policies were implemented on the whims and priorities thought to be appropriate by the minister of defence and junior officials in the ministry.

Added to it, the COS Committee was not part of the Defence Committee of the Cabinet. Further, the chiefs had no say in the defence production and R&D even when the minister was in the process of planning the production and acquisition of defence related aircraft, ships, weapons and equipment, he did as he thought right. Strategic intelligence was another area that had been conveniently passed off to the IB from the MI, the latter being left with just the acquisition and analysis of tactical intelligence. Since most of the border security responsibility had rested with the state police, the feedback of intelligence input that the services received was filtered and partial.

The "analysis"[53] which Thimayya forwarded to the MoD on integrating the services with the ministry, contained recommendations on a "phased" integration: the first phase combining joint subjects such as training, electronics and communications, engineering and medical services, intelligence and psychological warfare. Among the other recommendations he made was to coalesce the MoD with the COS Committee (or vice versa) which he thought, needed a permanent chairman rather than one who was ad hoc and 'moving.'

"If it was to be responsible for strategic planning," he argued, "it must be part of the Defence Committee of the Cabinet. It will then fulfill its role adequately."

Finance for defence was another issue the analysis considered. It highlighted its present role that bordered on "preventing irregularities in defence spending, financial administration and scrutiny of defence budget." He suggested that the Defence-Finance Ministries be "integrated colleagues of the services." They need to be assisting the services rather than acting as impediments and hamstringing. He was emphatic in his suggestion that they should be coopted into "working out the war economy and national defence planning," rather than be "auditors."

A joint cell for perspective planning that evaluated threats not only from hostile neighbours but also internal security, the biosphere, and communalism was the last item of the first phase, which he considered needed to be tackled immediately.

The requirement to make command headquarters and other subordinate headquarters exercise effective operational control over their formations and units in geographical areas and to co-locate similar IAF headquarters, was considered essential by this study. It suggested that Shimla and Lucknow hardly served this purpose for the Western and Eastern Commands respectively and could, instead suitably be located in the Punjab and Bengal or Assam. Similarly, the navy needed to build up on the eastern and western coasts beside the Andaman-Nicobar Islands and Lakshdweep, for which amphibious capability was necessary.

In the second phase, which could telescope with the first phase, he recommended the restructuring of the armed forces to meet the new threat from China along with that from Pakistan.

The list increased with the recommendation for a Defence University, a repeated appeal for a National Defence College and an Institute of Strategic Studies as a think-tank for national issues.

The file travelled up to Krishna Menon.

All this remained, what Thimayya and the other chiefs began to call, a "labour of love." Defence, despite the twin threats, insurgency in the Naga Hills, an uncertain situation in Kashmir, became a secondary issue.

Krishna Menon, by this time, was fully aware of the great professional competence, force of character and courage of General Thimayya. His popularity the world over, the confidence he inspired and his established role model as a hero to the country, seemed to overpower Menon, especially, with a latent sense of jealousy. He found the army chief too overpowering and convincing to be ignored. By this time, an uneasy feeling also grew in Thimayya – and even the other chiefs – that Menon's grasp of security matters, despite his jugglery with statistics, was a sham. And that he was counting the proverbial trees rather than seeing the forest, as was evident from his unintegrated approach even to the indigenisation of the defence industry.

Personally too, Menon's idiosyncrasies were being seen by all the service chiefs as bordering on eccentricity, worsened by his protracted celibacy and 'weddedness' to his ministry, as it would humorously be known. It was irksome too to be called to a meeting without an agenda, or be sitting at discussions with little or no relevance to strategy and defence security. These, Thimayya would remark, were "the pitfalls and lawlessness of a genius." He was decidedly "a square peg in a round hole" or vice versa insofar as the defence portfolio was concerned.

1959

January 1959 began on a note of confidence. Nehru took the salute at a colourful Army Day Parade on a misty and cold 15 January, at New Delhi's garrison parade grounds. Marshal Tito, on a visit to India and the chief guest for the Republic Day, had been accompanied by Nehru himself.[54] Later he would be joined by Prince Philip, General Maxwell Taylor, the US Chief of Staff (Army), and other guests.

Nehru made a passing reference to the new and mightier weapons that were being made and tested in the West and said that in the ultimate analysis, it was the men behind the weapons who counted. "With strong, brave and determined people, there is no danger to the country," Nehru said and paid a warm tribute to the spirit of patriotism and efficiency of the forces and said they had helped in fostering unity.

There were men in the forces, he remarked, belonging to different castes, states and communities. They had merged into one family to serve as a model to the country. He was very gratified to know that much was being done to educate the jawans. It was the aim of the government, he said, to banish illiteracy from the country.

After complimenting the men of the armed forces for their good showing in sports, Nehru said he had no doubt that the armed forces would have a notable part to play in the development of the country. He referred to the manufacture of defence needs in India and said the country could no longer afford to depend on supplies from abroad.

While it was depressing to note the damp squib that Nehru had put on the modernisation of the forces, his address acted as a tonic to morale. These brave words of the prime minister were badly needed, as the situation on the northern border were growing precarious.

And soon the 24-year-old, 14th reincarnation of Chen-re-zi, Tibetan God-King, the Dalai Lama would be compelled to flee to India, to seek asylum. That would happen barely two months hence.[55]

General Thimayya saw it as one more stage to the final hostility with China. The Chinese left no doubt that India was behind the Tibetan revolt. On the ground, they had extended their occupation of Aksai Chin by moving to the heights overlooking Chushul and Rezang La. Cartographically, Zhou had totally renounced the McMahon Line as the international boundary – coincidentally, through his letter of 23 January to Pandit Nehru. Declaring Tibet an "inalienable part of China," Kalimpong, in the Chinese eyes had become a "base of Tibetan reactionaries," and any discussion on Tibet in the Indian Parliament was tantamount to "interference in Chinese internal affairs."

Even at this stage, when the Chinese menace had no possibility of abating, the state of the armed forces, especially of the army, remained deplorable. Even a Rs 305 crore defence budget was being asked to be reduced, when the actual need stood at double this amount. In supporting this little increase from the previous budget, Menon was telling the Parliament on 10 April that with it, "the defence forces would meet the attack to the best of their ability and capacity."

The two exercises-cum-war games that Thimayya had assigned to the Eastern and Western Commands the previous year were ready. He held both of them in February 1959 – the first half being devoted to Thorat's Eastern Command at Lucknow and then Kalwant's Western Command at Shimla. For both, a team of officers under Major General PP Kumaramanglam was assigned to act as the enemy – mainly the Chinese, in this case. Thimayya himself directed the exercises while the army commanders did most of the conduct.

In *Exercise Lal Qila*, Thorat appreciated that of the eight to nine Chinese divisions in Tibet, he could expect about half the numbers against NEFA and Assam although owing to lack of communication from the border into India, the Chinese initial offensive would be limited to troops that could be supplied by animal transport or air drops. It was deduced that the ingress would form a number of simultaneous threats, i.e.

    (a) Towang (Tawang) – Bomdi La in coordination with or without thrusts through North Bhutan.
    (b) Longju – Daporijo – Ziro.
    (c) Rima – Kibithoo – Teju.

But all these, it was argued, would suffer from lengthening of communications which should be exploited by occupying easily defensible vital grounds. The defence line stretching laterally envisaged was Tawang/Bomdi La-Ziro-Daporijo-Along-Roing-Tezu-Hayuliang. But the area between the McMahon Line and this line was to be filled by some 90 platoons of the Assam Rifles in an early warning role, who, on contact with the enemy, would harass his line of communications, provide information on the enemy's concentration and axes of advance, to enable suitable counter-actions by the regulars, commandos, guerillas etc.

Futher ground reconnaissance would have modified the plan.[56]

While Thorat saw the Chinese main threat as against NEFA, Thimayya was of the view that the Chumbi Valley salient of southern Tibet could pose the largest threat. In his opinion, the PLA could invade it from both north and east, combining incursions into Bhutan and threatening the Siliguri corridor with or without support from East Pakistan. But with the opening of the Gangtok-Nathu La road, the defenders could be reinforced and given offensive capability. He wanted an operational priority to be given to it by the Eastern Command.

The main conclusion of the exercise, in Thorat's words, was pessimistic but an eye-opener in that "with the troops, weapons, equipment and communications available at that time, it was difficult to contain or even delay any aggression by China." And logically, therefore, immediate action to raise and build up adequate forces was to be undertaken to make up deficiencies.

At Shimla, where Kalwant was conducting *Exercise Sheel*, it transpired that the terrain and other indications suggested that the Chinese would strengthen their defences on the line they then held and attempt to capture as much area on the west, as possible. The offensive capability to the PLA was given at about a division, with Leh as its prestigious objective. Thimayya wanted to make full use of Kalwant as he had also been connected with the deliberations of the 'Himmat Sinhji Committee Report' and implementation of those recommendations as CGS.[57]

In both the cases, the PLA AF was expected to support the invasion and, hence, own IAF was envisaged to be offensively employed against the invaders from day one of the war. This capability was to be enhanced by improving airfields, radar stations and meteorological facilities in North Bengal and Assam.

Time was at a premium and the Chinese intentions were emerging clearly. Combining both the exercises and further discussions that were necessitated owing

to Chinese belligerence, an initial deployment pattern was recommended by the Army Headquarters to the MoD; its main components were:
   (a) A division for NEFA with a brigade in the Tawang-Bomdi La sector; a brigade in the Daporijo-Limeking Sector; and a third in reserve for the remainder of NEFA, to be deployed as reserve, or, according to the situation.
   (b) A division to be located in Gangtok-Kalimpong for both defensive–offensive tasks (in the Chumbi Valley and Shigatse plateau, if required). Some light armour to be grouped with it. Communications were to be further extended to the border to enhance the division's offensive capability and close offensive and transport air support was to be integrated.
   (c) A brigade (to be further increased to a division) in Ladakh which would have two or more local militia battalions under its command for containing the Chinese further expansion. (He had in mind the availability of a larger force that could be employed in offensive/counter-offensive role in Ladakh, perhaps towards the Soda Plains.)
   (d) Assam Rifles type of battalions for UP-Tibet and Himachal-Tibet borders.
   (e) An increase of ITBP battalions.
   (f) An additional force of 10 to 15 AR battalions.

The force level required for raising, thus, was about three divisions along with increases in Assam Rifles and Militia. These then laid the foundations of 17th ('Black Cat') Division, 2nd Division and the 3rd Division – all infantry to begin with, but with the ability to transform into what Thimayya called the "Alpine" or "Himalayan" Divisions and eventually "mountain" divisions.[58]

In order to wage guerilla warfare against the Chinese marauders, the idea of irregular, locally raised forces was also considered. These were to be raised by recruiting and training the manpower of the border areas.

This force level had, in fact, already been projected in diminished form in 1957 and almost two years had been lost. He urged the government to approve it now. This force level, he pleaded, would need to be doubled as soon as funds were made available in the next two to three years. And, in order to maintain parity with the Chinese on the border, with some reserves, besides augmenting the force level against Pakistan, he recommended a larger force level on a long-term basis.[59]

The appreciation, with an outline plan for force level, raisings, training and deployment was projected to the defence minister with a request to provide an additional monetary outlay for the new defence budget.

The outcome of this exercise reached Menon by May. He took no cognisance of the same, nor was any effort made to study and evaluate the ground dispositions. What Menon did was to dump it in a diagonally crossed almirah, marked "Remove Me First in Case of Fire!" But on being reminded, he pulled it out, rather reclu ctantly.

A discussion took place in the MoD some time in June 1959 on the new accretions that Army Headquarters had projected. Menon presided. Present were all the service chiefs, the defence secretary, the foreign and cabinet secretaries along with the director IB. Thimayya was asked to explain the rationale for such a large force. He briefly summed up the threat that had emerged and the force level required to defend the border against the Chinese.[60]

During the consecutive meeting, Menon remarked that the force level recommended by him was "much too much" and he needed to "prune it down." Thimayya had no desire to give in and he explained that the raisings needed to be taken seriously as otherwise, the army when called to defend the borders, would be found lacking. And, he as COAS, did not certainly want it to be so. He further explained to Menon as to why he thought it was just the inescapable, the bare minimum. To this, Menon's stance changed from one of discussing the issues to admonition.

Unfortunately, after this, the file would be securely placed in the vaults of the MoD. About this time, Pakistani intransigence further increased. One had hoped that with the military coup and General Ayub Khan assuming complete powers, Indo-Pakistan relations would improve. That remained wishful thinking. Ayub was now openly hobnobbing with the USA and China, as a go-between for the two inimical powers in order to benefit from both, and plus – the plus being Kashmir.

In March-April, China had increased its border raids against Indian posts. While speaking at a mammoth ex-servicemen's rally in Mohindergarh (where he also opened a "Thimayya School"), Thimayya said, "If ever Pakistan tried to attack India it would result in its utter destruction." To this, a Pakistani paper highlighted: "General Thimayya in a destructive mood." [61] ■

NOTES

1. Quoted from *The Seven Military Classics of Ancient China* including *Art of War*.
2. *Thimayya of India*, p.305.
3. The change was promulgated with effect from 1 April 1955. In announcing this change, the prime minister said that "the process adopted was another step towards democratisation and total Indianisation." It warranted full reorganisation of the services and not merely dropping the title of C-in-C. Nehru also said, he would form a Defence Council, which never fructified. The philosophy of the government was to downgrade the services, keep them as disparate as feasible and so regulate their growth and finances that they survived in a state of "honourable poverty," as General Cariappa would quip.
4. **Air Vice Marshal Subroto Mukerjee, OBE:** Born 5 March1911. Trained at Cranwell RAF College and commissioned 1932. O.C. No. 1 sqn RIAF 1939-41. Staff College Quetta, 1941. OC RIAF Sqn Kohat, 1943-44. Dy AOA Air HQ India Command 1947. DCAS & Dy Air Cdr RIAF 1947-52. IDC, 1953. CAS-1 April 1954-1958 - November 1960.(Died November 1960.)
   Rear Admiral RD Katari: Born 8 October 1911. Trained at Dufferin. Commisssioned 1938. War service in Atlantic and Indian Ocean. In 1949-51, he was Commodore, as Chief of Personnel, IDC-1953. Dy CNS 1954-55. CNS April 1958.

General KS Thimayya: Born 31 March 1906. Was commissioned on 4 Februrary 1926. Chief, 8 May, 1957. (Was junior by one year to Lieutenant General Kalwant Singh, one of his army commanders.)
Colonel – KUMAON.

5. From *Reveille to Retreat;* also see *To Serve With Honour,* p.95
6. *USI Journal,* March-June 1957.
7. The Chinese would call them Chuva, Chunje, Shipki La, Puling Sumdo, Sangcha and Lapthal (not in the order mentioned). By 1956, the Chinese began to question whether these passes were situated on the common border.
8. The Defence Pacts. SEATO membership: Australia, France, New Zealand, Pakistan, the Philippines, Thailand, the UK and the US.
CENTO membership: Iran, Pakistan, Turkey and the UK with the US as an associated member.
SEATO was created in 1954 to primarily counter the Chinese expansion. Zhou En-lai told the SEATO members that China had no offensive intention and he offered to negotiate with the US on the status of Taiwan. India denounced it. In addition, the US had mutual defence pacts with Japan, South Korea and Taiwan.
9. This road classification in now class 36 with a daily capacity of 1,000 tonnes and its closure period is said to have been reduced to a bare 60 days. A larger network of laterals and feeders traverses up to the LAC all over Tibet, besides airfields and an oil pipe line, with a railway line in progress.
10. Author of *Spy on the Top of the World,* pp. 250-51. In the dedication, Wignall says, "General K S.Thimayya, DSO former COAS Indian Army, whose warning that the Chinese Communist military build-up in Tibet posed a threat to India's northern borders was ignored by Prime Minister Nehru."
Wignall says he had been assigned intelligence collection activity in areas of Taklakot by Lieutenant Colonel BN Mehta (1 Sikh) then in Military Intelligence, under instructions from Lieutenant General Thimayya, in 1955, while the latter was GOC-in-C Western Command. He brought considerable actionable intelligence but Nehru under the illusion of *Hindi-Chini Bhai-Bhai,* ignored the reports of Chinese atrocities in Tibet and as also the build-up.
11. Brief on Iyenger's and Karan Singh's patrol appears later in the text.
12. From private correspondence of Air Marshal PC Lal.
13. *Jawahar Lal Nehru's Speeches,* Vol III (March 1953-August 1957) in "Plan is the Country's Defence" and other speeches.
14. Ibid.
15. In any case, "diplomacy," as Theodore Roosevelt said a century ago, "is utterly useless unless there is a force behind it. In *Discovery of India,* Nehru himself emphasises the lessons of history by quoting the ancient Shukraniti. While one of India's poet laureates, Dinkar has said:
Shahansheelta, Kshma, daya to tabhi pujta jag hai
Bal ka darp chamakta uske piche jab-mag hai.

Transliterated it means:

Perseverance, forgiveness, kindness and such virtues or magnamity are respected only if mirrorised by power.

Even the Indian President (2002-) Dr APJH Abdul Kalam, India's leading scientist, a force behind India's 1998 Pokhran II, put it blunty: "In this world, fear has no place. Only strength respects strength."

16. It was this task force that was planned in 1957, which eventually became the autonomous Border Roads Organisation (BRO). A precious three years were lost.
17. Interview of Major General Munshi.
18. From Official records.
19. Official Documents.
20. *Behind the Scene*, p 33.
21. Ibid., pp. 50-51.
22. Courtesy Kumaon Regimental Centre.
23. It confirmed that J & K was an inalienable part of India.
24. Excerpted from *The Statesman*, 24 April 1957.
25. Official Records.
26. Official Records.
27. The two separate delegations – the first, besides General Thimayya, consisting of Major-General E. Habibullah, Brigadier Rajinder Singh, Air Commodore PC Lal and Air Commodore S N Goyal as its senior members, went to the USSR in response to a personal invitation of Marshal Zhukov. Commodore Chakravarti with Captain B N Lele and Captain S D Kale of the Indian Navy, who formed the second delegation, were officially invited by the Soviet government to attend Navy Day.
28. Carried by *Hindustan Times* of 30 July 1957.
29. From Official Documents. Some conjectural references on the subjects are available in Kevic and Maxwell's books.
30. The official document was based on an Intelligence Appreciation and MGO's projections.
31. Cariappa had an Army Order published in 1949 which enjoined that "recruitment to the Army will be open to all classes (and) no particular class of Indian nationals is to be denied the opportunity of serving in the Indian Army."
32. Based on a paper written officially by the adjutant general AHQ during this period. A decade later, Field Marshal Manekshaw would follow a similar but more flexible line on the recruitment policy, despite the growing influence of the Scheduled Caste/Tribes, under Jagjivan Ram as defence minister.
33. It may be recalledthat following the closure of the Suez Canal by Nasser, Egypt had become a victim of the Anglo-French aggression in November 1956 and the Israeli Army under Moshe Dayan had completed its lightning conquest of Sinai. Finally, however, these areas were restored to Egypt under the UN arrangements. A decade later, Sinai, the West Bank and Gaza Strip would be captured by the Israelis. The Sinai returned to Egypt after the 1973 *Yom Kippur War* but other areas continue to be a zone of conflict between the Palestinians

and the Israelis.
34. Narinder Kumar has several anecdotes to narrate. One of them relates to how he first got his first set of foreign skis. One day on a visit to Narinder's battalion, he found him getting a pair made by his carpenter and the contraption looked like anything but what it intended to be. Thimayya said nothing at the time but on return to his headquarters sent the Swiss pair of skis he himself had. Encouragement to the needy and keen, was his principle.
35 Courtesy: Archives, All India Radio, Delhi.
36. It was 0.52 per cent of India's G D P then. Such frightful disregard of the 36.272 million sq km of Indian territory made defence an object of pathos and even ridicule.. The Finance Ministry could use its scissors now freely. And the service chiefs could only air their views to the defence minister through the defence secretary. Regrettably, the whole mechanism of the Defence Council and other consultative bodies of the MoD had been overtaken by ad-hocism. The Opposition too could not be wholly faulted as both the prime minister and the defence minister assured the public and the Parliament that the country's borders were well guarded.
37. B N Mullik says the army considered the Aksai Chin Road as of little strategic importance, which is wrong as the records of the Ministry of Defence show otherwise. Publishing his book *My Years With Nehru: The Chinese Betrayal*, six years after Thimayya's death, he makes a case that "Thimayya knew the Chinese strength and capability (beyond the Indian Army's) ... Tried to play down the importance of the road and threw doubts on intelligence reports ...." pp. 201 and 205. Dissent and distrust, unfortunately between the services were haunting them and would continue.
38. The Indian "White Paper" mentions in some detail about the Chinese high-handedness with Indian patrols that would run into them in subsequent months. It excludes mention of these patrols, even Iyenger's, for which this officer of the Madras Engineering Group was awarded a special medal. (MEG Archives). Confirmation of the road alignment of the Aksai Chin was undertaken by high flying Canberras and also by a C-119 Fair Child Packet flown by AVM Pinto in September 1958.
39. From Official Records.
40. Mullik, in *My Years With Nehru: The Chinese Betrayal* says that Thimayya initially refused to 'rush forward posts' but later agreed. To Thimayya "forward posts" were a misnomer as deployment was inside own territory and the concept was not agreed to by him during his tenure. He would also repeatedly explain this fact to Menon, Nehru and others.
41. From the *USI Journal*, March-June 1958.
42. On this, the *Shankar's Weekly* of 8 December wrote: "Ah yes, first class leadership and second class technology for weapons turns the army second class. But has any second class army ever beaten a first class army? This mindset has to go."
43. Interview of Lieutenant Colonel PN Khanduri, who was GSO1, Cabinet Secretariat, Ministry of Defence during this period.
44. Some of the important men working directly under the Ministry of Defence were: Major General Pratap Narain – CGDP; Rear Admiral Daya Shankar – DG Ordnance Factories;

AVM Engineer /PC Lal – HAL Kanpur (for HF-24); Mr Baliga – BEL Bangalore, and so on.
45. "35 years in South Block" by A L Venkateshwaran, a serialised set of articles in *Sainik Samachar*.
46. *The Chinese Betrayal*, p. 269.
47. Interview of Major General Niranjan Prasad, who was commanding this force.
48. From Official Documents; he would reiterate this in every forum, discussions and presentation.
49. Excerpted from General Thimayya's talk at DSSC Wellington, 21 November 1958.
50. Interview of late Major General Munshi, who accompanied the general on his tour.
51. General Thimayya's views on Pakistan and China appear elsewhere but more specifically in *The Organiser* of July 1962. See Chapter 14.
52. On 5 December, 1958, Nehru announced in the Parliament the "selective age extension to some senior officers." The beneficiaries were General Thimayya, Air Marshal Mukerjee; NR Pillai, ICS; VKR Menon ICS and a few more. He also informed the Rajya Sabha of increases in the defence budget to "keep armed forces trim, vigilant."
53. From Official Documents.
54. The Chinese official media was highly critical of Marshal Tito at this time. They would even deprecate his friendship with Pandit Nehru in their White Paper of December 1962.
55. The 24-year-old 14th Dalai Lama, the Bodisattva Avalokiteshvara (the Buddha incarnate) escaped into India crossing Bum La on 31 March 1959.
56. General Thorat gives the outline plan in his *Reveille to Retreat* and says he carried its office copy to show to the prime minister after the Chinese attack in October 1962. The Thorat Plan of Defence of NEFA, as formulated after *Exercise Lal Quila*, according to DK Palit, was "vague." For, "the arbitary alignment of these (40-50 km back) Towang (Kameng Frontier Divison (FD)) – Ziro (Subansiri FD) – Along (Siang FD) – Tezu – Hayuliang (Lohit FD) – Jairampur could, by no stretch of the imagination, be viewed as a line of defence!" That the Thorat plan needed review and revision was quite clear.
57. On May 13 1959, when Kalwant retired after 34 years meritorious service, Thimayya said: "I personally feel I am losing a loyal and gallant soldier and a comrade-in-arms," (PN Thapar replaced Kalwant and JN Chaudhuri, on promotion, took over as GOC-in-C Southern Command.)
58. Unpublished official document, relating to History of 1962 India-China War. While 17th Division was raised from December 1959, the others would come up only from mid-1961.
59. These projections served as the basis for the quantum jump in force level after the Chinese debacle and adoption by the armed forces of the Defence 5-Year Plans. Also see Chapter 15.
60. From interviews of Brigadier PN Khanduri, Major General Munshi and Official Records.
61. *The Dawn*, 23 May 1959.

1. Captain Thimayya seen as a matinee idol.

2. Neena and the infant Mireille in Fort St George's, Chennai.

3. Married in the Kodav style. Capt. Thimayya in the centre. Neena, his bride, stands on his left.

4. A devastating scene of the Quetta earthquake, 1935.

5. Prime Minister Nehru during a visit to Tangdhar, June 1948.

6. The famous 'First Day Cover' issued by Cyprus Government in 1966.

7. Brig. Thimayya in wax, representing the Indian Army during the Japanese Surrender Ceremony at Singapore, August 1945. Courtesy National Museum, Singapore.

8. With the forward troops at Nastachhun, May 1948.

9. Thimayya visits troops in Leh, September 1948. Gen. Cariappa seen riding the second horse.

10. *TIME* took a full-size photograph of Timmy in his tent at the Hindnagar, DMZ. This photograph was especially presented to the author for this book.

11. At the zenith of the Thimayya resignation episode, the unconvincing defence of VK Krishna Menon (vis-a-vis Thimayya) by Nehru was depicted by the *Shankar's Weekly* as a Krishna suspended in thin air.

12. RK Laxman imagined Timmy's role in NNRC, Korea. He sent this old cartoon to the author.

13. Thimayya (third from left) with the Communist POWs in Korea.

14. Mrs and General Thimayya (as COAS) with their MA, Colonel and Mrs Munshi, 1957.

15. The Thimayya family in 1954. From L to R. Neena, Timmy and Mireille.

16. Thimayya (second from left) and V K Krishna Menon (right) at New York during his visit to the USA. Also seen are Lester Pearson and India's Ambassador to the USA.

17. Thimayya 'signing off' a 35-year service in uniform from Kumaon Regimental Centre, Ranikhet, April 1961. Courtesy Colonel Sandhanwalia.

18. Mrs Thimayya flanked by the Duke of Edinburgh and Nehru during the 1959 Republic Day 'Beating Retreat.' Courtesy *National Geographic*.

19. The grave of General Thimayya with a statuette on the right with a brief epitaph. Every morning, a 14-man guard of honour is mounted here by the ASC centre, Bangalore.

20. In Cyprus, in the company of Pauline, George and Bennades.

21. Thimayya as Commander UNFICYP, 1964-65.

22. Author holding Medhavi with Lalita (L) and Mireille (R). Bangalore, March 2003.

23. Dying in the cause of peace: A tearful last prayer from friend, Archbishop Makarios, President of Cyprus.

12
The Honourable Course

Thimayya was aware that the minister of defence had been "not too happy" with the earlier recommendations based on *Exercises Lal Qila* and *Sheel* but he attributed it to his perspective nuances as well as comprehension. After all, it was his job to make the prime minister, defence minister and president understand the strategic requirements of defence of the border and the country. None of them was a military man, nor exposed to the process of strategic thinking. He was perturbed at the "bickering" as he called it, that had ensued between him and Menon a month earlier. He sent the file back again to the minister – a lesson that he learnt from Field Marshal Bernard Montgomery. Like Monty, Thimayya believed that files, however inanimate, do activate some 'signature-shy' ministers!

Strategic Nuances

The overall deduction of the study in early 1959 saw clearly the "Chinese intention of crossing the Rubicon" and that "with the present state of development, the Chinese could launch a major incursion across any part of the border or create a situation where there would be the likelihood of a major operation taking place unless threatened by major retaliatory action by India."[1] Reiterating his earlier projections, he asked the government to:

(a) Approve the raising of approximately three divisions (along with naval and air force components as recommended by the COS Committee, earlier.)

(b) To equip all forces with modern weapons for which recommendations had already been sent.

(c) The progress of work on the strategic communications was anything but satisfactory. Once again, he recommended the development of these on a priority basis. It had become imperative, he said, to approve the Border

Map 9: Chinese Claims and Intrusions

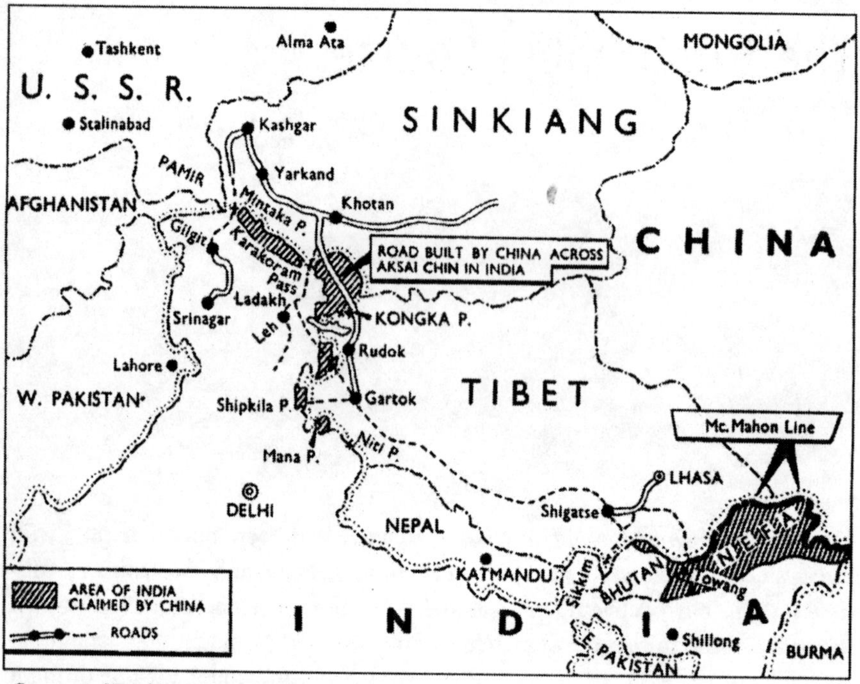

Courtesy: "Duel in Asian Deserts"

Roads Organisation (BRO) to act as an agency complementary to the other road building agencies, until the BRO could be solely responsible for strategic surface communications.

(d) The operational control of all agencies deployed or to be deployed on the border to be rationalised under one agency, preferably under the army, as and when it took over border responsibility.

Unfortunately, these vital recommendations would remain in the vaults of the MoD, until Nehru asked Thimayya to present another review in October end. The great hopes of the service chiefs for a golden period for the armed forces of India, with Menon as the helmsman, seemed to flounder. Although Menon's appointment had been warmly welcomed by the services – he was seen as an "energetic" and "politically viable" minister[2] – as time passed, the honeymoon seemed to be shortening, leading to distrust and resentment on both sides.[3] Thimayya was getting disenchanted, terribly disappointed that his "brilliant boss," was refusing to see reality.

Menon was the dictator whom the service chiefs chose to secretly nickname "God Almighty." Another problem with Menon, as observed by Katari, was his "inherently devious ways.[4] He would even go to the extent of tempting any officer pliant enough to be cultivated. In doing so, he often ran into the unexpected. Major General Manekshaw, for example, was asked by Menon what he

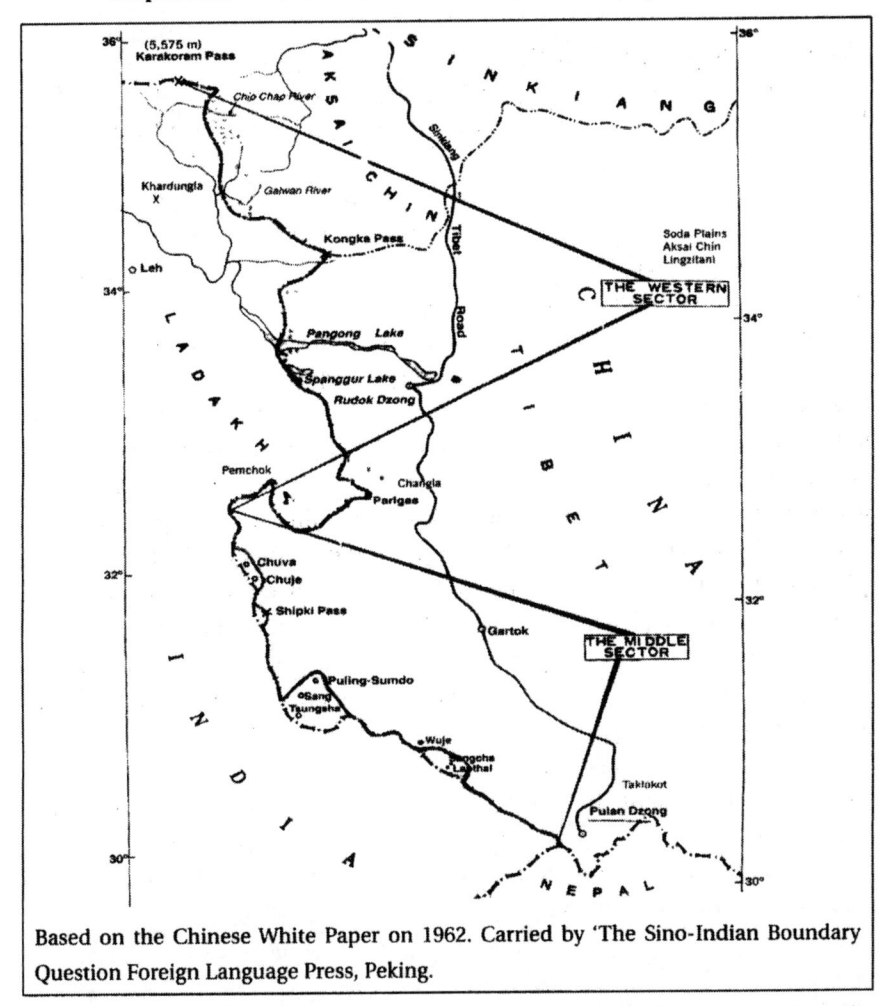

Map 10: The Western and Middle Sectors as Claimed by the Chinese

Based on the Chinese White Paper on 1962. Carried by 'The Sino-Indian Boundary Question Foreign Language Press, Peking.

thought of General Thimayya. Sam, blunt as ever, replied, " Sir, as a junior officer, we are not permitted to express an opinion on our superior officer. We respect our seniors and we have no two opinions on it." That was a good enough rebuff to see that a "rebellious" Sam was "fixed" at a suitable time!

Because Menon (contrary to his own tall claims) could understand neither technical nor tactical issues, he would call junior officers directly to explain cases to him although the same would already have been done by the chiefs themselves or their PSOs and directors. Worse still, he would issue orders to the chiefs through these officers. This did not appeal to the disciplined minds of the defence services. When the chiefs tried to explain the established ethos, protocol and operating procedures as norms for the services, he would not only get angry but also show contempt for their suggestions.

"I will not be bound by your sterile rules and procedures," he once told his chiefs angrily, "and I know how to manage the services. I will call any one, any time and for that I need no permission from you."[5]

His message was clear – he was the boss! It was civilian control and uniformed men should learn to obey orders implicitly – whatsoever the nature of the orders or instructions might be.

The prime cause of differences, besides Menon's abrasive personality, was one of perspectives. For, the chiefs, principally Thimayya, advocated that the strategy to be adopted by India against the two perceived enemies it faced had to be "dissuasive." Time and again, he would explain assiduously that it implied the "adoption of a strategy of adequate and appreciable counterpoise, causing damage to the aggressor, by striking deeper inside his territory and thus forcing him to recoil from his aggression." He would then explain through individual cases. Against China, he would emphasise that the strategy had to be one of a calibrated response – a mix of defensive-offensive postures that would be viable. But because Indian defence capability against China was limited, it had to be one of a mix of the military and diplomacy. It had to go along with a diplomatic flexibility of give and take. Concurrently, for the defensive capability to be effective, a build-up on the border, and raising and equipping of forces were imperative; so were improvement in logistics and communications. It called for an immediate evaluation of the threat posed, in both long and short periods of time.

Insofar as Pakistan was concerned, he advocated a total war, as and when it gave us cause to fight. But further build-up and creating of reserves were nonetheless necessary even in the case of Pakistan. Against Pakistan too, he advocated, diplomacy should form an essential part of our strategy to contain the Pakistani alliances of SEATO, CENTO and, indeed, China.

Menon's perspective was different. He harped on India-China friendship, while Pakistan to him was like a red rag to a bull. He saw no need for the growth of the army at the rate that Thimayya regarded as inescapable. He, however, accepted the need for modernisation, but only at his own pace of inducting indigenous equipment and arms. He was so obsessed with the public sector under the MoD, that the private sector dealing with defence production was ignored, starved to such an extent that they rebelled and cultivated the Opposition.

Menon's concept of indigenisation of defence industry and production, nonetheless, was a plausible one. But the policy he followed had mixed results due primarily to his own limited vision, obfuscation of priorities and obdurate belief in his own infallibility in everything, including tactics and strategy.

"If only tactics and strategy were so simple," reflected Thimayya, why would he and other masters, have wasted their life-time to learn, practise and relearn them. He began to wonder if Menon would ever develop the humility to learn from others or would continue to bully and bluster.

Then as if to exert his rights, as he had conveyed to them earlier, Menon began to call the chiefs for "consultations," at all hours of the day and even at odd hours of the night, at his home, at the office, at the airport and railway stations. In the office especially, they would have to wait in an ante-room while he scribbled through files, made long telephone calls, or dealt with other visitors, a number of whom would be sitting with him inside or waiting outside. This happened several times; so one day, while the mercury was at its height, and the chiefs waited in queue for a meeting, after a reasonable period of time had elapsed, they all decided to return to their offices, asking his secretary to recall them "when the minister could find time for them." This led to a further fouling of the working climate.

The Enigma of Kaul

In an effort to cultivate pliant officers, Menon picked on Kaul; he had in part, already successfully propped him up as GOC 4th Division at Ambala for his "intrepid energy" in pioneering the self-help type of army construction. *Project Amar* had been a resounding success, which had been followed by Harbakhsh and Manekshaw.[6]

In early April 1958, coinciding with the six-monthly Army Commanders Conference, the Army's Selection Board No 1, with General Thimayya as chairman, reviewed some 20 major generals to fill two vacancies of lieutenant generals. The board selected for promotion Major Generals P S Gyani and P P Kumaramanglam but also included Major General B M Kaul's name, as a formality. Ignoring the Board's recommendation Menon, replaced Gyani by Kaul. To add fuel to the fire, as a result of his manoeuvring, fully supported by Menon and Nehru, Kaul was appointed as QMG – ironically a principal staff officer to General Thimayya, in place of Lieutenant General Daulat Singh (who moved to command 11th Corps in Punjab). Although Kaul had not made the 'grade' as his superiors – Lieutenant Generals JN Chaudhuri (corps commander), Kalwant Singh (army commander) had confirmed his having reached his 'ceiling', he was still made a PSO!

Done secretly, this hush-hush affair nonetheless, could not remain confidential. Soon the Press and the Opposition were hot on the government's trail. With the announcement of the appointments and the skullduggery involved, it became clear to Thimayya that he had nurtured a very dangerous man all these years.

He spoke about it with Menon, pointing out the adverse repercussions of meddling with army promotions. Menon evaded the issue by saying that the decision was not his but that of the Defence Committee of the Cabinet, and, that he, as the army chief could be – and had been, in this case – overruled by the government. He further embarrassed him by inquiring why his (Kaul's) name, if not recommended, had been included in the list. The chief pointed out to him that the list also included names of others who had not been considered fit, for example, that of TB Handerson Brooks. Not to rake up the issue further, Thimayya decided to let things die down. But there were others who were watching.

Cariappa, keeping a tab on army discipline and morale, wrote to Pandit Nehru (the level at which he always chose to correspond) on 14 August. "This is about our army in which I have served for nearly 34 years. In recent months, I have been hearing from many sources, both civilian and services, of there being an undercurrent and dissatisfaction amongst many officers, over the policy of promotions and the place and prestige of the officers in the order of things today. I am told these feelings are very strong, particularly among some senior officers. It is only their sense of loyalty to you and their sense of discipline which have stopped them from bringing matters to a head. I am told 'politics' is getting into the army and the 'blue eyed-boys' of some higher authority are forming 'cliques', to plan their own future.... This is bringing in dual or changed loyalties." He urged the PM to "investigate the matter and rectify it, if found so,"

Nehru ignored the warning and admonished Cariappa for meddling in the affairs of the army.

The Opposition, already inflamed by the government's failures against the activities of the Chinese, led the attack in Parliament on this irregularity. Acharya Kripalani, the leader, demanded that a Parliamentary Enquiry Committee go into the "procedural twisting" by the government. But Nehru rose to reply to the queries in defence of Kaul's promotion. Ignoring the plea for an enquiry, he explained the circumstances in a splendidly articulated statement.

Thimayya realised that he had, in Kaul, a hornets' nest that he had allowed to grow in his own garden. Had he taken firm action against him for hobnobbing with politicians in getting *Project Amar* sanctioned, he could still have been cautioned on his moral dishonesty and indiscipline. He had erred in letting him go scot-free and, hence, it was his own *mea culpa*. So his (Kaul's) manoeuvring was now undermining his own position and lowering the morale of the army. Kaul's promotion through his political connections was a larger danger to the traditions of *camaraderie* and fair justice that the army was known for.

Storms: On the Horizon and at Home

In the meanwhile, in a deliberate attempt to pick a quarrel with India and locate gaps in the Indian defences along the border, the Chinese shifted their claim-line and military activities to NEFA. In June, they occupied Migyulten and pushed the Assam Rifles 10 km down south to Longju; their patrols also penetrated up to Walong but thereafter returned. And in the Bum La-Le areas, having crossed Khinzemane, they had travelled down to the Droksang Bridge. In Ladakh, they were firmly settled in the Khurnak Fort and on a feature that dominated Chushul. In their race against time to consolidate the unexpected gains in Aksai Chin, the PLA had also created a network of roads all over Tibet. These included roads Rowa-Rima, Gyantse-Phari, Parkha-Taklakot, Gartok-Tholingmath. Tsona Dzong and Lhuntze were also connected; so was the Chumbi Valley. There is a Chinese saying: "Roads are the key to military strategy," and they were effectively proving it in their strategic vision.

Thimayya met Krishna Menon immediately after the 28 July incident in which some policemen had been captured by the Chinese from Pangong Lake area and taken prisoner. He again impressed on the minister the need to expedite the raising of new units and formations, and reequipping, at least, those who would move up – eventually – against the Chinese. These requests were once again stone-walled.

On 7 August, the news of a fresh Chinese intrusion into Khinzemane, in NEFA, came in. It was on this day that Thimayya again met Menon, this time determined to convince the minister of the need to see the Chinese (and Pakistani) threats realistically, rather than ignore them.

He urged the minister to apprise the prime minister what the army felt about the defence of the Chinese border. He said, "The IB and police are there only for check posts and intelligence. That is how this patrol has been 'nabbed' by the Chinese. Nor do the Assam Rifles or J&K militia have the charter for it." He then reminded Menon that Generals Thorat and Kalwant had also appraised him about this need. (Both had met him in June as a matter of courtesy.) The point about additional troops, and equipment required for the purpose was repeated.

Thimayya saw Menon grow not only cold to anything he, or the other chiefs suggested, but actually hostile to them. While appeals for accretions were being ignored, their professional soundness was being questioned. What was bothering Menon? Thimayya wondered. Was it the case of the promotion of Kaul, or frank operational appraisals, or fear caused by the canard spread by the enemy of a coup by the army? Or had the government signed a secret agreement with the Chinese that had turned the leaders so overconfident. If so, why this exclusivity?

***

In his office, Thimayya called Bogey Sen, his CGS and asked him his opinion on how to handle Menon. Sen suggested an informal meeting with the other chiefs to find a way out.

Katari was in Burma and Mukerjee on a visit to Bombay and they returned by 10 August – a Saturday, a day for golf or sailing. Katari suggested sailing as even the caddies at the golf club could 'eavesdrop'! So while they sailed at the Okhla Sailing Club, the three having discussed the "grinding halt" they all had come to in their official functions, saw a ray of hope if they could persuade the prime minister to bring Menon back on track. For, they knew, he would change, if the prime minister prevailed; and the latter could be requested not to regard their meeting him as a "complaint" but one seeking "elderly help" to improve the overall working atmosphere. They, therefore, decided on a very honourable course of action: meet the prime minister at the Moghul Garden Party of 15 August and just tell him how "anxious they were to call on him." And if things did not improve, forgo their careers and resign.

Thimayya had been quite close to Nehru; so the mission to get the meeting arranged was left to him.

In the meanwhile, Nehru had been trying to pacify the people about events on the Chinese border, albeit not by telling the whole truth. A report read: "The situation on India's northern frontiers was discussed on August 13th in the Lok Sabha. The PM assured the House that everything would be done to safeguard the integrity of Indian territory. He further declared that....our frontiers are firm by treaty, firm by usage and right, and firm by geography." Addressing a meeting near Agra, Nehru again declared that the "Himalayas are the crown of India and constitute an essential element of India's culture, blood and veins." He laid stress on the many sacred places of pilgrimage in the Himalayas, revered by Indian people from time immemorial and mentioned in ancient Vedic scriptures.

All this, after all, was part of the political jugglery. And Thimayya understood this. Democracy, unlike closed societies (the military and Communists) is the most difficult form of government to manage – and Pandit Nehru was doing it well, as part of political expediency. But public announcements such as the frontiers are "firm by treaty" and so on, were merely a smokescreen and a bluff. Thimayya wanted to make the prime minister see the reality from the rhetorics, from which there was, unfortunately, no running away.

The garden party, despite the rain and humidity, served the purpose. Nehru said he would be delighted to meet him as he himself had been keen to meet him for some time and could he come tomorrow? Thimayya thanked the prime minister. The God-sent opportunity had appeared.

Admiral Katari and Air Marshal Mukerjee, the two other chiefs were, as a matter of protocol, at the party and they drove off to the army chief's residence for an at-home, where it was decided that they should remain available at their residences while Thimayya briefed Nehru on the problems they were facing with Menon. It was also decided that aspects of individual indignity they had suffered at Menon's hands should be played down, while the stagnation that had set in among the sevices and the demoralisation that was seeping in, called for some drastic change in Menon's attitude. In addition, the bad state of the services to face the enemies, lack of modernisation, inadequate funds for raising and equipping forces, and purchase of essential equipment from abroad were to be brought to his notice. And since Menon was out on a long trip to his home state Kerala, the meeting could not be taken as bypassing him in the chain of command. (In any case, Menon was continuously doing it with his subordinates!)

Meeting with Nehru and the Aftermath
In the meeting with Nehru, the following evening, Thimayya apologised for bothering him about defence matters when there was a full time minister and he was fully aware of the worsening situation on the border and of the imminence of hostilities.

He then drew Prime Minister Nehru's attention to the need to raise additional forces for the northern borders, equip them and develop communications at priority. He pointed out how averse the defence minister was to those inescapable requirements, that had, indeed, been based on professional deliberations and analyses. He highlighted the lacunae in the defence set-up and how it needed to be urgently refurbished.

He added, "I have personal knowledge of the Chinese military capabilities and with their vastly superior strength, improved communications, logistics, and so on, the threat they posed in 1956-57 has, at least, doubled." He continued: "The Chinese are angry over the Dalai Lama's entry into India and would do everything to let us down. Actions to further enlarge their area of occupation in Ladakh, and their ingression into UP, Sikkim and NEFA are probable. They are capable of playing 'Chinese Checkers' with us by virtue of their road communications. Under the circumstance, we need to locate troops on their most likely routes of ingress all over the 3,500 km of border. My worst fear is in Sikkim."

Nehru heard him uninterruptedly, sipping his whisky and smoking his cigarette. Thimayya then told him how Menon refused to see the service chiefs' points of view and how often he would 'tear his hair' when they persisted with their needs for improvement of their services, integration of resources, etc. for a real threat from China, and how treating them as school boys, they had been told to "look west" and "forget the north." He argued that politicians could understandably make political statements for general public morale, but as service chiefs, they could not "sweep the facts under the carpet."

He further said, "I have sent two sets of strategic analyses indicating threats and force requirements. They too have had no response. I wonder if it has reached you?"

Nehru said, he didn't remember having seen them.

Then Thimayya casually mentioned how Kaul's promotion had even embarrassed him (Nehru) and how such a thing needed to be avoided to keep the army's morale high. Though visibly annoyed, Nehru said, "Timmy, isn't that a thing worth ignoring.... But tell me, is it creating discontent among the ranks, as some papers say even now?"

Thimayya thought about it and said, "Now that you have explained things in Parliament, there is hardly any ill feeling except Gyani could be absorbed in a higher rank somewhere. But I would request that such things should be avoided."

Thimayya suggested that the prime minister should rather call Menon and make him see the gravity of the situation and if he deemed it fit, he and other chiefs could join him (Nehru) to review the border situation at a suitable place. Nehru insisted that Thimayya first talk to Menon in a day or two after he returned, telling him (Menon) that he had discussed the problems with him too. Thimayya demurred. "I doubt," said Thimayya, "if he would listen to me or any one of us. I fear he might misconstrue the whole thing."

Nehru said bypassing a minister may not be in order, though he would personally not treat the contents of the present discussion as bypassing him. And after Thimayya had spoken with Menon, he could meet him (Nehru) again. Thimayya could read the prime minister's mind and his desire. There could be no further argument over it. But Thimayya returned with an eerie feeling that his conversation had been secretly 'stored' or recorded.

As Thimayya returned, the prime minister called Mukerjee and Katari for a brief discussion with a view to ascertain their views.

Menon returned on the night of 19 August and dispensed with the regal reception at the airport. He met the prime minister the following morning and was badly upset. He then gave a diatribe on his chiefs and repeated his criticism of them – some of it in public. Still fuming. Menon told Nehru that he would ask Thimayya to "resign" and go, if he wanted.

"He is not indispensable. The others too could follow," he remarked caustically.

"None of us is indispensable," said Nehru, "but time is a vital factor. We need him but 'tame' him along with the other service chiefs." He advised Menon not to talk to Katari and Mukerjee as he already had talked to them. "Don't let them take up a collective stand," was the final word of counselling.

Having earlier met Mukerjee and Katari, Nehru then called Defence Secretary O Pulla Reddy. Personally, Reddy too had been a victim of Menon's impatience, arrogance and ridicule. (Menon often publicly called him a man who could neither 'pull' nor be 'ready' and such oddities!) But being a weak man, perhaps tolerant and afraid of Menon's vendetta, he decided not to be a 'bad boy.' He praised Menon for his brilliance and innovations, but admitted that the service chiefs were not happy as he did not "approve their projections." Then he added, "General Thimayya and Mr. Menon are strong personalities.... But General Thimayya is a gentleman, much respected and the armed forces have large expectations from him."

"Are there any temperamental differences between Menon and Thimayya?" asked Nehru, as a leading question.

"You have very appropriately summed it up, Sir," replied Reddy, with a gleam in his eyes.

Thimayya met Menon on the evening of 21 August. Dressed in a jacket and slacks, Thimayya walked in and wished the minister before sitting down. He gave him a summary of his meeting with the prime minister, the ensuing discussion on defence preparedness for the Chinese border, and, how things needed to be expedited. Menon asked Thimayya as to why he had met the prime minister without his permission.

"It was the prime minister who asked me to give him an update," said Thimayya.

Menon told Thimayya that he had no business to meet the prime minister without his specific approval. Thimayya reiterated that the prime minister desired to know about the preparedness, and the state of morale of the services, and he told him nothing that he had, over the period of 18 months or so, not discussed with the minister.

But Menon was furious and finally said: "No, General. It's downright disloyalty and impropriety."

To this, Thimayya said: "I make no allegations. You can call the other chiefs too. They will say the same that they and I have continuously said – that the services are being neglected and that their morale is lowering. These are the facts that we have told you earlier and the prime minister now. I am reiterating that by speaking candidly I and other chiefs are being loyal to you, the government and country. That's what loyalty means to me."

Thimayya saw no point in carrying on the conversation further with Menon. Deeply hurt at his remarks, he got up and said: " I have never been disloyal to anyone, least of all to you, my country and the government."

(Menon shouted at top of his voice). "You are disloyal to me and I have no place for disloyal generals around."

It was no longer possible to conceal the tension between Menon and the service chiefs. He left.

It was 9.30 p.m. when Thimayya reached home and told Nina to be ready to pack up and then murmured, "It's time to pack up honourably." He also talked to Mukerjee and Katari and told them he was seriously contemplating putting in his papers the next day or so. Both repeated their vow to 'follow the leader.'

"Sink or crash, we'll do it together," was the commitment.

"Unitedly, we will all," became the motto.

After Thimayya left, Menon met Nehru, who asked him not to rock the boat. He assured him that he would once again get the chiefs' willing cooperation, provided he showed patience.

Thimayya drafted his resignation letter the following morning and showed it to Mukerjee and Katari, both of whom confirmed their willingness to follow suit. "My conscience says, wait," Nina was saying.

Thimayya called Thorat, who advised the same. So was the suggestion of Bogey Sen, his CGS and Wadalia, his deputy chief. General Cariappa who was in

Delhi asked him to meet the prime minister again before he 'bunged in' his 'letter.'

While this was happening and Thimayya remained indecisive, he visited 50th Para (Indep) Brigade at Agra, a trip on which Nina joined him. Brigadier Niranjan Prasad, the brigade commander, was an old friend. He discussed nothing of the ongoing tension but did tell Niranjan that he was planning to leave prematurely! While returning from Agra, as the staff car drove back in a blinding monsoon downpour he could see that things had really been fouled up as Menon was equating his effort to improve the army as an "act of disloyalty;" Menon was not prepared to benefit from his professional advice and entreaties and was trying to politicise the army. In a situation such as this, where was the need for him to remain as the chief? He was getting more convinced in his mind that he should resign, perhaps sooner rather than later.

On his arrival on 24 August, Sen told him that the MoD was about to place NEFA under the army. This thought had taken root after the Chinese crossed Khinzemane in NEFA, on 7 August. The MEA and the IB had ever since been pressing the army to step in. A day later, the Chinese deepened their fangs with a bigger kill. The implication of the killing and capture of men of the Assam Rifles at Longju finally convinced Nehru that the border had to be eventually handled by the army.

So a meeting was held on the evening of 26 August under the chairmanship of Nehru, with Menon, Thimayya, the foreign secretary, the director IB and the finance minister attending. Nehru suggested that the army be made responsible for the entire 3,500-km-long border and all the existing resources under it. The army had also been asking for this and he (Nehru) was happy in doing so. But due to a suggestion from Menon and the director IB, however, only NEFA was to be handed over to the army, in the first instance. Thimayya saw this move as the age-old gaffe of passing the baby to the army when everyone else had raised their hands.

With NEFA being handed over to the army, Thimayya decided to move 4th Infantry Division located at Ambala to be deployed there. Orders were, therefore, issued. The GOC, Major General Amrik Singh, MC, was briefed at Delhi and told to reconnoitre the area, most of which was new. Thorat was to accept the division under his command.

Simultaneously, orders for re-raising of 17th (Black-Cat) Division and 114th Infantry Brigade were issued. "Things have begun to move," said Thimayya and tried to forget the ungracious words of Menon of 21 August. He thought the minister would acknowledge his blunder and would relent, if not proffer an open apology.

Unfortunately, there now came another occasion for a clash between the minister and General Thimayya – the Second Defence Production Conference (24-27 August). Menon opened it, with the prime minister in attendance, and gave out the 'marvellous progress' that had been achieved. The statistics seemed to justify the claim. Included in his well-prepared speech was the progress of the ordnance factories and the manufacture of armaments. He enumerated that the production in the ordnance factories had increased by 49.4 percent and BEL's production had multiplied 10.85 times. The production of Hindustan Aeronautics Limited on projects had also gone up steeply, particularly in the five months of 1959-60.

Thimayya, in his valedictory speech, which he had been invited to deliver, highlighted the more urgent operational needs, which he said, were being "ignored at the cost of services' efficiency for war." Analysing the operational-oriented needs, he went on to describe the future requirements of weapons and logistical support essential for fighting, which included 155mm guns, helicopters, good and wholesome rations for jawans, etc. The address was a testimony to his clear thinking besides giving a clarion call to the defence production agencies to accelerate production. He also suggested that by following a policy of debarring civil agencies from making useful contributions to defence, the services would suffer. He appealed for their inclusion in the venture, especially now that there was a need for a national effort. He was sad, he said, to learn that good progress on the AVRO 748 at Kanpur was being hampered by the trade unionists and local politicians with little or no sense of patriotism or love for the defence forces. He urged the government to look into it.

There was no irreverence in what he said – only urgency for a legitimate cause. There were no adverse comments on either the defence production or the man responsible for it, namely Menon. Yet, on 27 August, Menon, already keeping Thimayya on his 'hate list', called him to convey that even general suggestions by service chiefs to their minister did not go down well with him. The message was that defence production is "my preserve and any comments would draw fire." Thimayya would not relent either. He asserted, "AVRO is very fine but what about arms and equipment that we are deficient in and the additional units and formations we need to fight China and Pakistan?"

An angry Menon told Thimayya that the case for the raisings he had made, had "no justification vis-à-vis the threat? You are embroidering the Chinese threat. They have no design to attack India."

It was so ludicrous an exhibition of authority that Thimayya, already hurt at Menon's earlier remarks, was getting sick. Menon was treating him with scorn and contempt, like a bully.[a]

All through his service career, Thimayya had learnt to stand up to a bully, be he British or Indian – his superiors included. He had also never tolerated undignified treatment being meted out to anyone. He would rebel at indiscrimination being foisted on fellow Indians. And when honour or *izzat* was at stake, he had always been ready to relinquish his office and 'chuck' his commission

"I expect my officers and men to die doing their duty and do any other supreme sacrifice in its cause but never compromise on *izzat*. I follow the same principle for myself," he had repeatedly told everyone.

The damaging insinuation by Menon, accusing him of disloyalty to his superior, surpassed every irritant, irrational behaviour and even disrespect. A stage, therefore, had been reached when honour had to be redeemed through the only honourable mean available to a soldier. He decided to follow that honourable path: to offer to resign his commisision.

When Nehru called him on 28 August after the meeting of the Defence Production Board, Thimayya apprised him on how relations between him and Menon had continuously traversed towards an irreconcilable end. He told Nehru that under the circumstance it might be better to replace him as COAS by someone else "more amenable to Menon's perceptions and liking."

The prime minister sidetracked the issue and asked him if any progress towards restructuring of the armed forces had been achieved, to which Thimayya replied, "Nil."

Nehru looked visibly uncomfortable and Thimayya excused himself.

It was 30 August when Thimayya had decided to have tea with Katari (Mukerjee was already airborne for the UK) and told him in more or less coded language that he was firm in his resolve to leave and was planning to send a letter to the prime minister. Katari said, he would follow and inform Mukerjee too.

That night, Thimayya thought and re-thought about throwing away a career, the great honour the country had bestowed upon him and the trust his officers and men had reposed in him. It was one of the saddest nights of his life.

By 5 a.m. 31 August, his personal assistant, Subedar Major Prem Swarup Wal had reported to the ADC who was given a handwritten draft to type out. Gulu Nanda was ready with the fully typed letter by 6.30 a.m. Thimayya signed it. Marked "Confidential" and closed in double envelopes, Gulu Nanda, drove up to the prime minister's house, delivered it to Mathai, Nehru's personal assistant. "Please hand it over to the prime minister personally," he told Mathai. Mathai opened the letter, read it and passed it to Nehru. "Something urgent?", asked the prime minister. "Thimayya's letter of resignation," replied Mathai. Nehru read and re-read it:[10]

General K S Thimayya, DSO
COAS

31 August 1959

My dear Prime Minister,

You will remember, a few days ago I mentioned to you how impossible it was for me and the other two Chiefs of Staff to carry out our responsibilities under the present Defence Minister and that we sought your advice.

Since then, you have conveyed our feelings to the Minister of Defence who quite rightly feels that my talking to you directly is an act of disloyalty to him.

Under these circumstances, you will understand how impossible it is for me now to carry out my duties as Chief of the Army Staff under Mr. Krishna Menon. I, therefore, have no alternative but submit my resignation from my present appointment and (hope) that you will permit me to proceed on long leave pending retirement.

The interest of the Army and my loyalty to the country forces me to take the step after 33 years of service in the Indian Army both in peace and war.

Yours very truly
Sd xxx

Shri Jawaharlal Nehru
Prime Minister of India
Prime Minister's House

Menon was called to the prime minister's house within minutes. Mathai told him that he could come as he was. Arriving within an hour, Menon was shown the letter by Nehru and asked about the course they could follow. Menon said he would talk to Thimayya and ask him (Thimayya) not to resign. However, he did not. Then Nehru wanted to meet him at 2.30 p.m. after his briefing of the members of the Rajya Sabha on the Longju incident, calling it a case of "clear aggression by the Chinese."

On the afternoon of 31 August, when Thimayya met Nehru, after some pleasantries, Nehru, as Thimayya anticipated, returned to the main cause of his summons – the letter of resignation.

Putting his arm around Thimayya's shoulders, Nehru asked him why he hadn't met him, rather than sending in his resignation. "Please withdraw it straight away," ordered a visibly annoyed prime minister. "I will see you again at 7 p.m. with a letter withdrawing your resignation. In the meanwhile, I am keeping the letter with me." He then asked him to return at 7 p.m.[11]

In the meanwhile, Katari had informed Mukerjee, by now in London, that Thimayya had submitted his resignation and he was following suit. He expected Mukerjee to do so, although he made no such specific suggestion. He was expected to naturally follow them.

The period between 2.30 p.m. and 7 p.m. was used by Nehru to control the damage which the resignation of the chiefs would cause to the government, the services' morale, and the gains the enemy would make.

Nehru rang up Katari and told him that he had called Thimayya and he was withdrawing his resignation and he should not entertain any such proposal. (A similar message went to Mukerjee through the High Commission.) He told him that Thimayya would meet him again in the evening and he should meet him at 9.30 p.m.

So by the time Thimayya arrived at the Teen Murti residence of the prime minister at 7 p.m. through a carefully articulated manoeuvre, Nehru had distanced the other chiefs from Thimayya by "talking them out of it." Menon too was asked to keep a draft of his resignation handy. An emergency meeting of the Cabinet Committee of the Parliament was also called, to meet immediately after the Ayub-Nehru meeting at Palam, the following day.

And then he began to win over Timmy with his charm but Thimayya said that he had not changed his mind and instead urged the prime minister to accept his resignation. In his defence, he argued: "That's the only honourable course left to me and the other chiefs, When professional advice and recommendations are flouted at the drop of a hat, the chief loses his place and importance."

Nehru, however said: "We have sufficient problems. And at this moment of crisis, one should not do anything to encourage opponents or the enemy. Shouldn't it be so, Timmy?"[12]

Thimayya further explained that it was indeed a "moment of crisis" and it was his loyalty to him and his sense of patriotism to the country that had really moved him to sacrifice his job. But he repeated that Menon as defence minister had "made it impossible" for him and the other chiefs to work as head of the services, and unless Menon was moved out of defence, there could be little progress. But he understood that as this obviously could not be agreed to by the prime minister, he – and the other chiefs – should step aside, and, therefore, his submission of his resignation.

Nehru admitted that Menon, was a "difficult man," but he was simply "brilliant" and was doing service to defence which no one earlier had done. Thimayya agreed, but suggested that his methods of "man-management" were "outrageous" and even his brilliance was that of an "Oxford professor of philosophy" rather than of a man dealing with the country's defence forces which have to be prepared to fight enemies.

He reminded the prime minister that he was a soldier and he disliked politics. "I like straight talk. In politics, you say one thing and do another. Mr. Menon doesn't seem to appreciate that with soldiers he must talk straight."[13] He told him how Menon had begun to interfere with not only everyone's personal life, though trivial and ignorable, but still worse, there were cases of him dealing directly with subordinates as a calculated measure of undermining his and the other chiefs' position. Parallel groups of commands, he told Nehru, had been developed by Menon; in other words, politics had been introduced into an apolitical army.

And, finally, he truthfully said to his prime minister: "*With the present state of the army, I can hardly assure success. We are not prepared. All my efforts – as also of others – have failed for the past 24 to 30 months to make the armed forces a viable defence force.* So let someone else do the job.... I request my resignation be kindly accepted."

Nehru said that he appreciated that India had to be prepared for a war – whether a war came in the near future or not. India, he said, rhetorically, could not be weak or else no one would respect us. He said further that along with military preparedness, India, should pursue other means to "contain Chinese ambitions." Then he told him that now that the government had accepted the border in the east to be placed under the army, he could plan things in own expert way. "We'll take a decision on Ladakh responsibility soon," he said and looked at Thimayya.

Thimayya had been hoping that Nehru would also tell him that he had plans to shift Menon to some other portfolio. Instead, he said: "Menon is off to New York next week where he would remain, at least, for two to three months. I'll officiate. You can have my full attention then. And I promise, you all will have no problems. You can always walk up to me to get things moving. I'll also see that Menon creates no problems – temperamental or otherwise."

Thimayya wanted to leave nothing vital unexplained. It was also opportune, he thought, to speak about Menon's indigenisation plan. He said that he totally agreed with Mr. Menon's plans but if national security is the bulwark to all the planning, the services must be associated with the planning of not only defence factories but all factors of national importance. Then production should be based on the overall needs and operational considerations, based on strategic analysis for both the short and long terms. "Ad-hocism," he said, "is no substitute for all this. What we need is a national policy on it."

Nehru heard him out and said he agreed. Then he pleaded with Thimayya: "Timmy, I ask you to withdraw this resignation, I, as your elder and not necessarily your prime minister, am requesting you to do so. I promise to restore dignity to you and the other service chiefs' offices. We have to fight an enemy. For my sake, withdraw it."

The simple soldier, Thimayya was moved to see his prime minister, a man whom he admired and always trusted, making such a fervent appeal. He wondered if he could ignore his request any more. But a second thought overtook these emotions. He would think it over and take a firm decision only the next day. He told Nehru that he needed more time.

Warmly pumping his hand, Nehru saw Thimayya off. He drove back to his residence. At the gate, he saw a Press reporter, Narayan by name, trying to stop his car. As the car stopped momentarily, he asked: "Sir, has it been accepted?"

"Accepted what?" retorted Thimayya.

"Your resignation, " said Narayan.

Thimayya did not want to commit himself and asked the ADC to drive on.

Narayan rushed off to his *The Statesman* office and filed the report that Thimayya has resigned but one was not sure if it had been accepted.[14]

At home, after a light meal, he sat with Nina and narrated to her the contents of the discussion with Nehru. She asked him if the naval and air chiefs had sent their letters to the prime minister. He wasn't sure. Mrs Katari had said that the admiral had been called by the prime minister. So he expected a call. In the meanwhile, the Hindi service of the BBC quoted Mukerjee's statement to the reporters, saying that he was "surprised at the news."

"So he has developed cold feet," remarked Thimayya. "People do," he murmured.

Thimayya was now truly on the horns of a dilemma. The thought uppermost in Thimayya's mind was the genuine concern Nehru was showing for alleviating the distress of the chiefs and solving the urgent problems. Nina felt that under the circumstance he could consider withdrawing the letter before it became a bone of contention. "So far, things are between you, Menon and the PM. It may be for the better," she argued.

He dictated a brief letter to 'Gulu' Nanda and asked him to put it up by 7 a.m., on 1 September.

The previous evening, at 9.30 pm Katari had met Nehru who told him that they were "ganging up" against Menon and that "Thimayya had withdrawn his resignation" – both factually wrong. Katari, then decided to call off handing in his letter of resignation without even checking with Thimayya.[15]

Whether it was the charm of the prime minister or fear of retribution or the weakness of Katari – and Mukerjee – one will never know. But enormous damage was done to the chiefs' solidarity. He, however, recalled in his autobiography, "Menon, Menon," he (Nehru) exploded, "why have you got your knife into him? You people (services) do not realise what an intellectual giant he is."

"I do not know where I got the courage when I said, if he is, Sir, I have seen no evidence of it in the case under consideration."

(Katari's book in self-defence or abnegation could not be challenged by the others, as by 1982, when it was published, Mukerjee and Thimayya, and Nehru and Menon were all dead).

***

Soon, the whole of India was agog with the news and most of the capitals of the world too were buzzing with it. Thimayya was known as a great military hero; Nehru was the leading light of the Non-Aligned Movement: and Menon's marathon, witty and often exasperating battles in the UN General Assembly had made him an enigmatic character.

The conjecture that followed was that all was not well in the Ministry of Defence under Menon and the entire weight of sympathy swung to the cause of Thimayya, that led most to believe that a soldier of great repute was being made a scapegoat. There was a flutter in the market too, as prices of Tata Steel, Indian Iron, etc. plummeted.

The melodrama that would unfold on 2 September ranged from a tragi-comedy to the bizarre. It was comical in what Prime Minister Nehru would unfold in one of his cyclic letters to the chiefs ministers, on the one hand, and the psyche of India's leaders of the period vis-à-vis their perceptions of the defence forces, on the other.

The monsoon session of Parliament was in progress and the Nehru government was already under fire for having withheld the information on the construction by the Chinese of the Aksai Chin Road in Indian territory, and the incident leading to their other incursions from 1954. Mr Atal Behari Vajpayee from the Opposition benches had already compelled the government to publish a "White Paper" and to suggest "how effectively we can checkmate the Chinese military might massed in Tibet against our borders." [16]

Storm Over Army Chief's Resignation

Parliamentary storms, like natural ones, can sometimes burst suddenly and then blow over, leaving behind traces of ruin, according to their intensity. On Monday, 31 August, Parliament met in comparative calm, with no hint in the proceedings of either House that within 24 hours or so the MPs would be swept off their feet by developments, sudden and startling.

On the morning of 1 September, the capital awoke alarmed in the wake of the disturbing disclosures in the Press about Thimayya's resignation. In the Lok Sabha, eight members, the foremost among them being the veteran Acharya Kripalani, leader of the PSP, and Ganga Saran Sinha, member of the Rajya Sabha, felt that a particular newspaper report was bound to create "apprehension, demoralisation and to some extent confusion." V K Dhage (Democrat) found it no less "upsetting" and Bhupesh Gupta (Communist) also wanted the position to be cleared while cautioning the House against "sensation-mongering"!

From the chair came the final word that if there was truth in the Press report, the government should make a statement. The ensuing debate became prolonged and rancorous.

But Krishna Menon, not for want of courtesy to the House but for tactical reasons, would, like the Earl of Birkenhead, neither confirm nor contradict the report; he would rather leave it to the prime minister to deal with the situation. He had been briefed by Nehru to maintain a stoic calm.

In the Lok Sabha, the sailing was far less smooth, perhaps because of the very presence there of the defence minister over whom raged the entire controversy. And it became clear that the prime minister's absence at that hour (he had to be at Palam to receive the president of Pakistan) had two immediate results: first, the House was to endure some suspense; second, it could meanwhile concentrate on

Krishna Menon, according to the exigencies of the hour. While the House, prepared to await, however reluctantly, the prime minister's statement the next day, following the intervention of the minister for parliamentary affairs, had an exciting time making things uncomfortable for the minister for defence.

In a pointed attack, Acharya Kripalani blamed Menon for his seemingly strange silence over the Chinese aggression on the northern borders and for what were alleged to be "political considerations" that prevailed in the matter of army appointments or promotions. When there were some interruption from the Communist benches, Acharya Kripalani, with characteristic sarcasm, explained that his was no attack on the Communist Party! Among others, Ashoka Mehta (PSP) and Frank Anthony (Independent) tried to draw the defence minister out.

The prime minister was both frank and firm about it all when, the next morning he made his eagerly awaited statement, first in the Lok Sabha, and then in the Rajya Sabha. The reactions in the House seemed to vary from bench to bench, and even from member to member. *There was visible relief when it came to be known that, at the prime minister's instance, General Thimayya (who alone had resigned) had withdrawn his resignation.*

There was also considerable applause when the prime minister assured the House – and through it, the country – that *"under our practice, the civil authority is, and must remain supreme" (while it should, however, pay due heed to expert advice).* There was also applause when he referred to the army's "fine mettle" and "excellent morale."

But neither his vigorous defence of the policy in respect of promotions nor his handsome tribute to his colleague, the defence minister, was warmly acclaimed. Indeed, the latter provoked the vigilant N G Ranga, now no longer an occupant of the Congress benches, to ask the prime minister why he had not expressed equally enthusiastic appreciation of the COAS. Apart from saying that but for his appreciation of the general's record, he would not have persuaded him to withdraw his resignation, the prime minister referred to him as a "very gallant and experienced officer who had served his country well." But not happy over the interruptions from the PSP members, he also said, not happily either, that "General Thimayya was unwise in having resigned at all and he (the prime minister) could not really condone his action."

This observation seemed to jar on several ears.

The prime minister was also assertive otherwise. He felt so sure of the soundness of the policy at work in the matter of army promotions that he not only decried all talk of political considerations but threw out a general challenge to the "members to examine any file and substantiate the charge". He, however did not deny that there may well have been some "temperamental differences" between the general and his defence minister.

The exchanges that followed his statement revealed a partial desire in the House for a full discussion on the subject in camera, while the prime minister standing foursquare, said that he would not mind even an open debate, if necessary. That was, undoubtedly, a telling statement; yet one could see that the House did not feel reassured that everything about the Defence Ministry was all right. Some felt and, indeed, said, that General Thimayya's letter of resignation should be made public and others opined that much remained unsaid or undisclosed. *The prevailing impression was that while the prime minister had scored a personal triumph in tiding over a difficult situation, there was all the difference between a patched-up quarrel (however much owing to mere "temperamental" differences) and an amicable settlement.*

A side remark seemed to lighten the issue and to provide much-needed relief to ruffled tempers. It came from the unfailing Raja Mahendra Pratap, who described the state of relationship between Thimayya and Menon as "a cracked glass." He also made the interesting suggestion that Krishna Menon be shifted to the Foreign Office.

In the Rajya Sabha too, there was some discussion following the prime minister's statement during which the question of leakage of General Thimayya's resignation was raised by the Communist member, Bhupesh Gupta. "We should investigate how things leak out," admitted the prime minister, and devastatingly added: "But we should also know how things leak out to my friends sitting to my right." Thus, sometimes amidst interesting sallies, and more often amidst heated exchanges, the storm was over for the time being.[17]

***

During the Lok Sabha proceedings, The *Time* reporter George Power, who had called Menon a "crotchety, Mephistophelean," saw him sitting sprawled out on the second seat reserved for the prime minister. His eyes appeared to be withdrawn and his lips curled in a sardonic smile as he listened uncomfortably to Acharya Kripalani's attack on him. But when Nehru stood up to make his statement and as he admonished Thimayya for his resignation and concluded with a ringing tribute to Menon's "great energy and enthusiasm," Menon leaned back comfortably, his legs crossed, and his silver mane cushioned on a green upholstered bench. It was Menon's day all through – his triumph. He and his friend Nehru had seen the spanking, if not castigation of, a soldier in the arena.

***

It was Mireille who wept bitterly at the public condemnation of her father in the Parliament (where she sat alongside Indira Gandhi) by Pandit Nehru. When she recalled the scene to her father, tears welled up again. She understood nothing of politics, but surely had human sentiments, and spoke of these things to her father on the telephone at Secunderabad where he had gone for the forthcoming inauguration of the Joint Land Air Warfare School.

"Daddy you have been let down. Mummy was right in asking you not to withdraw your letter."

Thimayya said nothing. Later, on his return to Delhi, he showed her the office copy of his letter of resignation that contained the gist of what had transpired between him and Nehru, besides the appeals from the prime minister to withdraw his letter.

"You'll now on defend your father, I hope," he said.

"Always passionately, daddy," replied Mireille.

"If these are trivial, then I know of none other important issues," he told Nina, who was furious at the withdrawal and asked him to "re-resign" without a second thought, and expose the duo. He said he had accepted the advice and the assurances of his prime minister and had withdrawn his resignation. "For, in a democracy, a resignation is the only constitutional safeguard to a service chief against incompetent, unscrupulous or ambitious politicians," he murmured.

The supreme commander of the armed forces of India, Dr Rajendra Prasad was hurt and he "took umbrage at being kept in the dark about the crisis precipitated by the resignation of General Thimayya." This, he held, was a violation of his authority as supreme commander of the defence services. Krishna Menon, was reprimanded for the lapse and was made to apologise. Later, Dr Prasad also remonstrated with Nehru. "You are laying down bad precedents. A president who did not like you could have given you a lot of trouble."[18]

One of the major casualties, in the words of Rear Admiral Katari, was the "break-up of the friendly team of Chiefs of Staff."[19] This would be exploited by Menon.

Thimayya forgot most of the bitterness with the passage of time. He was, in fact, the first to drive down to Palam airport, when the dead body of Air Marshal Mukerjee was flown back from Tokyo on 10 November 1960. He was also the first to congratulate Air Marshal Aspy Engineer, the new CAS. Although the small men around who were jealous of Mukerjee's rise, meanly said that there was no "crane to pull the bone out of the air marshal's throat," he held only sympathy for a departed comrade.

Another fallout was "Menon's taming." Brigadier D K Palit observed that "Menon's obtrusive deportment as minister had been exaggeratedly portrayed as political interference with the army. But after the Thimayya episode, he had to grudgingly conform to the military bureaucratic protocol. In his dealings with the senior brass, he thereafter observed propriety – without grace." The last trait, in any case, was never a part of his psyche.[20]

The withdrawal of his resignation had its negative effects: Thimayya lost his hold over some of the officers who deified him and could not see him being humiliated; it gave Menon an opportunity to further strengthen himself with the aid of Kaul – the hatchet man – who became the *ghar ka bhedi Lanka dhaave* (roughly implying that inner conflict destroys great families and nations); it forfeited the giving of a jolt to Nehru, who not only seemed to link Thimayya's resignation with a hypothetically "questioning civilian supremacy" (and indirectly, a propensity for attempting a coup) but got a free run towards brinkmanship, leading to the debacle of 1962. Had Thimayya resigned, it was felt by the observers of the events of that period, the Indian government would have been forced to do some serious thinking about the Chinese threat and done a "course correction."

Thimayya would often remind his daughter, "When the chips are down, there is none one can fall back on. But my dear, God's justice is great; it grinds slowly but grind it does." It was the saddest period of Timmy's life.

The situation was now gradually coming to a point where the choice for Nehru was between Krishna Menon and India. As AD Goravala wrote in *The Indian Express* of 7 September, 1959: "*Whatever Nehru may say about 'trivial' differences and 'temperamental' incompatibilities, there can be little doubt that the real issue was the real defence of the country and the strong feeling in the Chief of Staff's mind that it was being seriously handicapped by Krishna Menon's occupying the position, as he does. Nehru's refusal to show to the Parliament the general's letter of resignation and the unwillingness he is expressing now to have even a debate on the subject, although he offered it during the heat of the discussion, are a clear indication that he is attempting to protect Krishna Menon. So too are his condemnatory remarks in Parliament about the general, all the more ill-judged and ungracious because only at his most pressing request can the general have consented to withdraw his resignation.*" He seemed to have got closer to the truth.

The editor-in-chief of *The Deccan Herald* of was also objective in his comments in the 7 September issue, "... *It is a great tragedy that Menon's departure has been delayed till he was able to reduce the armed forces to a state of near-demoralisation...* He played, in fact, for the creation at the highest level in the armed forces of 'officer cells' which would bear him personal loyalty. He sees the forces as an instrument of personal power. Many people passionately believe that Menon is a Communist. I doubt this. But the result is the same as if he was a Communist since he is widely regarded as one because of a consistent record of compromising activity ... The record is not one-sided. The Communist Party in Parliament has shown a consideration for Menon which is as open as it should have been embarrassing. *If knowing all this, Nehru still keeps Krishna Menon in office, the inference becomes almost unshakeable that his own mind is moving towards accepting the wishes of the Chinese Communists and the International Communism. Not all the people can be fooled all the time. Indeed, a large section of the people seem to have awakened to the fact that they have been fooled for quite a time. Mr Nehru may well find himself in extreme difficulty if he does not get rid of Mr Krishna Menon and oppose strongly Communist Chinese expansion."*

It must go to Thimayya's credit that as the senior service chief, he took upon himself to broach the issue with Nehru on behalf of the senior members of the suffering armed forces. Nor did his action spring from a sudden impulse. It had a deeper relationship to events and had, unfortunately, been sparked off by his meeting, at Nehru's behest, with Menon and, finally, by Menon's insatiable desire to treat him as a pariah. Nehru's role in igniting this dynamite rather than defusing it, also gains prominence. What were swept under the carpet were "various other matters" which had forced the government to accede to hold a parliamentary inquiry and toll the bell for Menon, on the one hand, and then forget about it, on the other.

The perspective that needed to be restored over the Thimayya resignation episode was urgent and Nehru did it by briefing the Opposition members, and the media; he even referred to it in his newsletter from the prime minister to the chief ministers:[21]

> There were tremendous floods in various parts of the country; there was the food situation which, without being really bad, yet gave us much trouble ; there was the big-scale rioting in Calcutta, stated to be over the food situation there; there was a few days' excitement over the reported resignation of our Army Chief of Staff, there were difficulties and internal conflicts in some states, and there were the rapid and disturbing developments on our borders with Tibet-China.

The resignation episode of General Thimayya had already become another historical landmark in Indian history. ■

NOTES

1. From Official Documents pertaining to the 1962 War.
2. *The USI Journal*, June 1957.
3. *India's China War*, p.190.
4. Katari and others were suffering, as he observed, "how difficult it was for a principled and straightforward Serviceman to function in complete harmony with the (Defence) Minister....... Thimayya being the head of the largest Service, was the worst sufferer..... Menon had a habit of dealing with subordinates as a matter of calculated preference (whose) irregular consultations inevitably developed undertones of intrigue..... there were already signs that a parallel lines of command inside was already developing in the army....." *A Sailor Remembers,*pp. 101-102.

5. Ibid.
6. By 1962, 4th Div would fail in its war in NEFA. The 5th when tested in a collective exercise was found untrained as its GOC, Major General D Prem Chand reported. 26th was on fixed defences and had chance to recover.
7. From *The Cariappa Papers*.
8. *The Times of India*, 30 May 1959.
9. *Soldiers and Politicians* see Chapter 6 (General Thimayya: A Victim of Personal Jealousy.)
10. Thimayya Papers.
11. General Thorat, a close friend of General Thimayya, remarked on it in *Reveille to Retreat* p.177: "When Timmy casually mentioned it to the prime minister, with whom he had excellent relations, he was told not to mind these idiosyncrasies of Mr Menon. Timmy did not pursue the matter further because he had great regard for the prime minister. Pandit Nehru had known him since 1947 when he was serving in the Boundary Force during the post-partition riots, and had much respect for his ability. He treated Timmy as a friend. But Menon undermined these sentiments by pernicious propaganda in which he was greatly helped by his able henchman. I refer to *Maj Gen B M Kaul who was destined to bring great disgrace to the Indian Army*." Thorat's version is only partially true.
12. It became a *Guru-Mantra* with Nehru, as he would use this sentence virtually in the Lok Sabha, in his addresses and letters. Nehru was repeating his sentence in the Lok Sabha specifically on 27 November 1959. "In a moment of crisis, one should not do anything to encourage the opponent or the enemy."
13. J P Narayan, a veteran respected social worker and politician, publicly stated that "he had no faith in Menon." In the public opinion poll, most of the papers had called Menon a "brilliant man" but faulted him on being "single track-minded," and "unsuitable to meet crises as defence minister." See also *Indian Nation* of 13 September 1959.
14. Interview of Mr Narayan in January 2000 before he retired as editor-in-chief of *Hindustan Times*.
15. *A Soldier Remembers*, p. 103.
16. Prime Minister, 1998-2004.
17. The entire proceedings were reproduced by all the leading dailies. The report is based on *The Times of India* of 4 September. Some excerpts of it have been juxtaposed from the parliamentary proceedings.
18. Durga Das, *India - from Curzon to Nehru*, p. 337 (as also quoted by IM Muthana in *General Thimayya*, p. 202).
19. n. 15, p. 105.
20. *War in High Himalayas*, p. 73.
21. *The Selected Works of Jawahar Lal Nehru*, Vol. 5, containing the letter of 1 October 1959.

13
A Distant Trumpet (1959-60)

The Visit to the Joint Land-Air Warfare School
Thimayya's popularity, despite the admonition by Nehru in the Parliament, continued to grow. In fact, it grew beyond description. One such example was his visit with Menon to Secunderabad a day after the inauguration of the School of Land-Air Warfare.

The School of Land-Air Warfare, Secunderabad, had been raised by the concerted efforts of Thimayya and other chiefs as a small example of integration of the services. Here it took shape when Menon inaugurated it on 3 September – and when the 'episode' was on everybody's lips. Thimayya had arrived here on 2 September, while Menon flew in on 3 September morning.

Opening this "first of its kind in Asia" institute, Menon took an opportunity to play up the issue of "friendly rivalry among the Chiefs of Staff." "Our Chiefs of Staff are not given to any sense of separatism but are bound by loyalty to the service of our land," said he. Then he smiled quizzically as he remarked, "Friendly rivalry, however, would be helpful to the development of forces."

Then Thimayya rose to speak and the whole gathering, including the VIPs, were on their feet, giving him a standing ovation. A tremendous ovation for a hero. So jubilant was the audience that a fly-past by a few Otters aircraft did not distract them, until the airborne troops began to "land from the sky." Menon's deep-rooted envy had already turned into malice; now it was pure and simple hatred, turning eventually into a mad vindictiveness, which he would show on his return from New York.

Return of Nehru's Trust
Nehru, a great leader, however, caught in his own web, tried to adopt more damage control measures. On 11 and 13 September, he told the MPs in the Parliament in

what was clearly a *mea-culpa*: "Unfortunately, far too much was being read into the Thimayya resignation. There are no basic policy differences but I myself have not been able to find 'missing links,' though earlier Menon and Thimayya were said to be 'thick pals'."[1] To clear himself, Menon, before he left for New York, told reporters that "there is no politics in the army, if there is politics, it is I...."[2]

Notwithstanding the rigmarole of the episode, a bigger and clearer admission came at the prime minister's monthly Press conference, when he said: "I do not consider General Thimayya's offer of resignation as a challenge to civil authority."[3]

Thimayya though was bitter at heart, no doubt, he refused to carry it on his sleeve or let it explode in any one's face. He was assiduously trying to contain the damage. Lieutenant General P N Kathpalia, an officer of the Kumaon Regiment, who was a gentleman cadet in the National Defence Academy when Thimayya was the commandant, remembers his visit to him in February 1960, a few months after the episode in Parliament. He recalls Thimayya saying:[4]

> My offer of resignation had several reasons, (the confidentiality of which I wish to maintain) but the basic cause was lack of growth of the army to do its role better, especially to meet the challenge from the Chinese. The prime minister promised me not once but twice on August 31st that improvements would take place – as, indeed, they are promising to show up. I have had meetings with him on various aspects of defence strategy and plans and I think there is gradual realisation of our requirements. Some of you may think that your chief has been publicly censured. I suppose that is true. That may have been for political reasons and beyond that I don't wish to say anything.

The resignation episode had to be erased from public memory, especially of the officers and men. By October beginning, as Nehru conveyed the correct impression, he wrote to the army commanders and commandants of the schools of instruction explaining the position. Belatedly there followed the deep and well-founded anguish of General Cariappa whose letter of 7 November made a deep impact on Nehru. For he wrote scathingly:[5]

> Thimayya put in his papers to leave the army for reasons, which he, after long and deep thought, must have thought, were strong enough to do what he did. It was a major decision in his life and could not have been taken just as a school boy 'joke.' Apparently, it was said in the Press, the other two Chiefs of Staff were likely to follow suit. However, you persuaded Thimayya to withdraw his resignation, which he, like a good soldier did, with his sense of unbounding loyalty to you and to our country. You then went to the Lok Sabha and told a packed house that Thimayya on your advice had withdrawn his resignation but you thought his reasons for sending in his resignation were very trifling, and, you could not congratulate him on what

he had done, and so on. You emphasised that civil is supreme, although this fact had never been even once raised by any one in the army and other Services. Panditji do you realise how humiliated Thimayya and the army are about your statement in the Lok Sabha?

Nehru replied post-haste to General Cariappa's letter on 19 November:[6]
I do not understand why you should consider what I said about Thimayya, taken as a whole, as unfair to him. You must remember that I was answering supplementary questions put to me after I had made the statement. I paid a handsome tribute to Thimayya. I certainly did say also that I did not congratulate him for his offering his resignation. I thought, then, and I still think, that it was not right for him to offer that resignation for the reasons he gave me and, and more particularly at that juncture when we were facing a rather difficult situation on the frontier. I told Thimayya so when I asked him to withdraw his resignation and he agreed to do so. He had mentioned some incidents to me which seemed to me rather trivial, even though they might have been irritating. It is to these incidents that I referred in the Lok Sabha and not to other causes that might have influenced him. It was, indeed, very far from my intention to 'humiliate', as you say, Thimayya. It would have been absurd for me to do so and yet ask him to continue in the high and responsible office that he holds. In fact, the whole trend of what I said in the Lok Sabha was different and was more of a compliment to him. When I am asked questions in the Lok Sabha, I cannot refuse to answer....

To tide over the problem created by the episode, Nehru diplomatically smoothened the rough edges of the matter. He pacified the aggrieved and deeply hurt army chief. Thimayya began to trust him again. Then he informed his chief ministers about the episode through his newsletters. He would pacify a deeply annoyed president. And finally, he told Menon to quit the 'battlefield' for two to three months by going into the UN, paradoxically, for preparing India's stand on the Chinese entry into the UN (besides taking a non-commital stand on the admission of Tibet's case in the UN, at the behest of the Dalai Lama. By these overtures to the Chinese in the world forum, Nehru was hoping to diplomatically win them over.)

In an overt display of full trust in Thimayya, Nehru visited Rawalpindi, Tehran and Kabul during the second half of September. With Menon in New York, the MoD virtually had Thimayya as the senior most, besides Majithia who officiated as defence minister. Thimayya and Majithia utilised this opportunity by visiting ordnance factories as also the Chinese border in NEFA.

"This is the time of productivity and consolidation," he told Majithia "and I hope we can get a few urgent cases through." Majithia helped. He began to pursue the old cases of Army Headquarters gathering dust over the past 30 months or so.

Menon had preceded Nehru on his 'official holiday' to New York via Bombay on 10 September, still bragging of the *Hindi-Chini Bhai-Bhai*, and garnering Communist support. However, by 6 September, Zhou En-lai had replied to Nehru's letter of 22 March, repeating his old allegations and causes for provocations. But the Chinese took specific care in not claiming either Sikkim or Bhutan – both of which had defence treaties with India. It was well-known in the case of the 3,000-sq-km Indian Protectorate of Sikkim, effective since the 1890 Anglo-Chinese conventions, futher confirmed through the 1950 Joint Treaty between the Maharaja of Sikkim and India that under the treaty relations, India was responsible for Sikkim's defence, external affairs and communications. In the design of India's defence, Sikkim had assumed a vastly significant posture, because a thrust by China through the Chumbi Valley in conjunction with East Pakistan through north Bengal could result in driving a wedge between the two halves of eastern India. The defence of Siliguri corridor and Sikkim had evidently become Thimayya's priority objectives.

The Chinese were also targeting the area of Darjeeling-Kalimpong, especially the latter, calling it a "centre of Tibetan revolt" in India. Nehru was determined and firm in handling China in this cartographic battle. On 26 September, he informed Zhou that "it was only after the 'recent unfortunate incidents' that we asked the army to take over responsibility of border protection (earlier being with the constabulary)." Discussing each sector, he suggested that the Indian troops withdraw west of the 1956 Chinese map line and the Chinese should do likewise to avoid clashes. It was a favourable solution for India but the Chinese would not oblige. The Chinese now made incursions across the Kongka Pass (21 October) and arrested 10 more Indian policemen.

Thimayya was very upset at this incident. Dave, a former officer of the IB, recalls that following this incident, Sir NR Pillai, the secretary general of the MEA had summoned a meeting, at which, among others, Thimayya was present. Sir Pillai called Ojha of the IB to explain the event. Instead, Thimayya volunteered to explain and summed up by saying, "This is what happens when the IB pokes its nose too far." Ojha was hurt and quoted the prime minister's direction in this regard.

"If that be so," said Thimayya, "I withdraw my words."

At this meeting, Thimayya also projected an urgent need to place the Ladakh-Tibet border under the army. It came about only after much haggling, explaining and even cajoling. For, by the autumn of 1959, the Chinese had spread west and south of the Aksai Chin Road and established new posts, disregarding the Indian protest. The Chinese also commenced construction of a road from Lanak La to Kongka La, the scene of some more activity. Besides road construction work was beginning from the north to Jilga–Sumdo–Samzumling and terminating at Kongka La; a southern extension was added via Shamul Lungpo. The network of these roads continued, with Chinese belligerence and Indian protests and feeble non-military responses.

A Chinese division with three regiments (brigades) had also been identified at Qizil Jilga, Lanak La, and Rudok, the divisional headquarters being located at Shahidulla. The Chinese divisions and border guards had strung in more than 50 company posts all along. They were determined to follow their claims to the territory in Ladakh with a full military presence, along with protests and counter-protests and a diplomatic offensive. From the Indian side, the entreaties from Thimayya were having some effect but compared to the Chinese it was merely marginal.

By 15 September, Thimayya was in Shillong to coordinate various issues involved in the defence of NEFA. Here he held a high level conference with civil and military officials. He warned that while there was no immediate danger of a flare up of any magnitude on the Sino-Indian border, the vast distances involved and difficult nature of terrain did not permit every inch of the frontier remaining inviolate. "Sporadic border incursions," he warned "could not, however, be ruled out." The meeting was attended by CP Sinha, governor of Assam, BP Chaliha, the chief minister, Colonel PN Luthra, commissioner NHTA, and General Thorat. The issues discussed included:[8]

(a) The Chinese influence in border areas of NEFA. While the Chinese had amassed some 25,000 troops and were constantly improving their communications, our side needed immediate improvement of communications and administration. NEFA's adviser was to help army's logistics.

(b) The Assam Rifles would remain deployed in their posts but act under the army's control, operationally.

(c) On the East Pakistan border, it was hoped that the situation would remain normal.

Evaluation of Threats and Suggested Strategy – Battle for Hearts and Minds!

There had been criticism from the president, governors and chief ministers that, thus far, the government machinery had not only proved unsatisfactory in keeping the Chinese out of the Indian border but also failed to keep them fully informed about developments on the border.

Nehru, very contrite and out of Menon's influence, thought of 'educating' the governors and others about the various aspects of development that had taken place and how the army intended to handle border defence. He asked General Thimayya to brief the august gathering. Nehru's letter of 7 October, fixed 28 October as the date of the presentation, which would also be attended, among others, by the president.

While opening the presentation to the governors, Nehru was generous. He said: "I have great admiration for General Thimayya's ability and experience. I am sure what he is going to present in his operational plans will benefit all of us. The Chinese menace has to be contained and I am sure it can be done militarily too. Over to him."

At the presentation, Thimayya began by highlighting the **deployment pattern of** the security forces on the Indo-Pakistan and India-China borders. He emphasised that the Indian Army, by its role and – hence, charter – was responsible for the defence of the border. "If the border is to be kept inviolable, I have been saying it for the past two to three years and reiterate it again," he said, "all other agencies now on the border – and those who would join – should be under the army for better coordination and operational control."

The **developments on the Chinese border**, the main issue, figured next. "An assessment of the Chinese offensive capability is, therefore, necessary at this stage," he stated. "I estimate the PLA have three armies of nine to ten divisions deployed both in Xinjiang and Tibet. The Chinese by 1959 have turned most of their highways capable of taking 40 ton tanks and a network of road arteries has spread from the main roads to the Indian borders, including the areas of the present incursions. While I see the entire force capable of switching axis, the most dangerous Chinese threat to India could be expected from the Chumbi Valley. It could develop across Sikkim into the Teesta plains." There he placed the Chinese ability to deploy two to three divisions.

Against Ladakh, his assessment of the Chinese strength was then of about one division and against NEFA, two to three divisions. These assessments, he pointed out, were subject to modifications based on intelligence updates. In NEFA, the main axes of ingress, he observed, were along Tawang-Bomdi La; and, Rima-Walong-Hayuliang. Self-contained battalion groups could always operate on numerous axes. This logically brought him to the pattern of defences the Indian Army should adopt.

"Because of its size and logistical problems," he remarked, "the army would be able to defend only vitally important communication centres, places and passes, but would gradually provide a larger tactical presence as the situation improved. But because the invading Chinese would inevitably lengthen their lines of communication, advantage could always be taken to disrupt it to own tactical benefit."

He was also candid that "in case of war, the government may have to accept loss of some territory initially but could rely on the army's ability to blunt major offensives in depth. And, eventually, defeat the enemy through a long-term strategy of cutting off the enemy's lines of communication, guerilla warfare combined with regular operations." He, nonetheless, made it amply clear that "although some measures had been taken, we will have to take immediate step to raise additional troops."

He recommended a **strategy of dissuasion,** namely, retaining a sufficiently adequate defence posture on the likely enemy axes of advance, and yet being able to strike into areas that would make the enemy recoil. Putting it plainly for the benefit of the audience, he said India needed to develop an offensive capability and those areas, he thought could well be Sikkim and Ladakh. He told them that eventually a force level of 15 to 25-30 divisions would be required to "squarely face" the Chinese.

However, it would have to be gradually raised. And the operational art required would necessitate the Indian Army supported by the IAF to fight a mobile warfare against the invading Chinese and render their operations untenable. That, he said, was for him and his commanders to decide.

Pakistan also figured in the presentation. In General Thimayya's views, Pakistan had not only adopted more aggressive overtures in J&K (and at the UN) but was constantly creating pockets of tension in Dera Baba Nanak by extending their control over the whole bridge, the Sulemanki head works and RS Pura in Jammu. These small pinpricks were indicative of larger designs. And as the Pakistani armed forces' potential had considerably increased, he, as army chief, was in no position to thin out the force level deployed against Pakistan for a probable employment on the Chinese border.

It was noteworthy that the prime minister continuously intervened to update the audience on the diplomatic efforts that India had made to contain both China and Pakistan. He repeatedly mentioned that he hoped "China would act more maturely in future." Even Thimayya did not apprehend anything big happening on the border for the time being, but as a soldier, he believed that "readiness for the worst is the best guarantee for peace."

Before Thimayya took his seat he concluded his **recommendations** and suggestions as:

(a) There must be **unity of command** while defending the country's borders and, hence, all areas of the borders which are still in the hands of the state police, Assam Rifles, militia and scouts, should be placed under the army. This will ensure better command of forces and control of resources. The present system, in his view, was highly unsatisfactory and needed to be remedied, as soon as possible.

(b) The minimum requirement of **additional troops in the next two years**, for the defence of the Chinese border, was three divisions plus. This would subsequently have to be doubled up in the following two to three years.

(c) He urged the prime minister to sanction the raisings as early as possible, as the training and equipping of troops take a long time. Similarly, with the limited capacities of training centres for men and academies for officers, more time will be required. Inevitably, while the corps headquarters at Srinagar could control additional troops for Ladakh, another corps headquarters was necessary for NEFA, NHTA, and so on.

The prime minister wanted to know the strategy to be followed with respect to Ladakh. Thimayya suggested that the Indian aim should be to PREVENT ANY FURTHER INGRESS INTO LAKAKH. He argued that the Indian Army – and the IAF – then needed two to three years to build up, to develop communications and infrastructures to be able to take on the PLA in a more deliberate manner. He further argued, "*We should firm in, strengthen the present line and look offensive only when we are capable of an offensive.*" Looking at the prime minister, he said, "*At present, diplomacy rather then military action may be the substitute to allow us to build up that capability.*"

At the end of the presentation, it was clear that all this time Menon had either kept the prime minister in what some of his critics called an "insulated glass case" or perhaps Nehru had left defence totally to Menon, ignoring even the calculus of the threats.[9]

Having agreed to the recommendations of Thimayya, the prime minister tasked the defence secretary to examine their implementation through various committees. The committees' reports reached Nehru in a fortnight but he wanted Menon to 'progress' them. As a result, only a fraction of them progressed. Nonetheless, with it came the approval for raising the Headquarters XXXIII Corps at Shillong, responsible for the areas of Sikkim, Bhutan, East Pakistan, northeastern states, including NEFA, and the Burma border. The corps was placed under Headquarters Eastern Command, Lucknow. Further, the results in part followed while Menon was still out: the Assam Rifles were placed under the army's operational control; the raising of 17th (Black Cat) Division began from 9 December; as was mentioned earlier, with Headquarters IAF Group at Shillong, the IAF too shot up to a 15 squadron force.

It was now that the Western Command would be allotted 114th Infantry Brigade for deployment at Leh and east of it, leading on from the Karakoram Pass to Chushul. Obviously, this force was highly inadequate and there would be need to raise a whole division for this task. That then set the foundation for the raising of the 3rd Himalayan Infantry Division.

Thimayya followed this presentation by writing two long letters, one summarising the presentation and the replies he gave to the queries raised by the governors and others. The second letter included his recommendations for phased raisings of army units, their equipping and deployment.

These letters also included the restructured and phased raisings as: three divisions by the end of 1959; three to four by 1961 and another three to four by 1962. This then laid the foundation of a 17 division army in the next two to three years. (The same plan would add another 10 to 12 divisions after 1962.)

Meanwhile, the 4th Infantry Division had moved in September to take up the responsibility of the border defences from "Sikkim to the Burma border." Despite problems of logistics and communications, 11th Brigade became responsible for the 225-km-long Sikkim border – basing its defences for northeast Sikkim while Assam Rifles got deployed in the north Sikkim plateau. The Maharaja of Sikkim, a friend of General Thimayya, helped. The 7th and 5th Brigades would look after 1,705 km of the NEFA border. The divisional headquarters was located at Tezpur. Naturally, much of the gap was to be filled by the Assam Rifles until new raisings replaced them. Thimayya asked for at least four battalions and more raisings for Sikkim so that 11th Brigade could join the division in NEFA, later.

By end September, Thimayya had ended his first inspection of the NEFA border and was said to be generally satisfied with the measures taken, although in his heart of hearts he was hardly happy to see the unsatisfactory arrangements existing on the ground. He had conferred with military officers as well as top civilian administrators. He found their morale excellent.[10]

***

Another challenge came not from the Chinese but the IB's Mullik wanting the army units to be deployed on the Chinese border. He thought it impractical. Thimayya suggested to the prime minister that any deployment in small penny-packets of sections (10 men) and platoons (30 men) of the army would not only make them easy prey to Chinese attacks but also cause demoralisation. The army's deployment, therefore, had to be in battalion and company defended localities, fully supported with artillery, air, logistics, communications, and so on. They had to be self-contained for fighting sustained battles, even under the contingency of being under siege. Nehru seem to appreciate the tactical logic and left the military matters with the army chief. It also cut short Mullik's adventurous shadow-boxing with the Chinese, who, he lamented, were creeping into the areas of Spangur Lakes, and so on. So there was to be deliberate army deployment in adequate strength, which would react to Chinese designs. In other words, no so-called 'forward policy' which Mullik was recommending.[11]

The welfare of the troops and ex-servicemen remained Thimayya's concern. Soldier boards were reorganised under a lieutenant general and cooperative societies of small industries and agricultural colonies were soon formed in large numbers. He had recommended doubling the pension under the old pay code, as was being done for civilians. He had also recommended 15 years service for every jawan, including a last year of technical training so that the men might get proper jobs in factories on retirement. He laid the foundation of the Army Welfare Housing Organisation and the Women's Welfare Organisation, called Army Rehabilitation Women's Association (ARWA), a forerunner to the Army Wives Welfare Association.

The 'episode' behind him, Thimayya was at his usual best. He was on the move, visiting the battalions and brigades on the borders, discussing their training and deployment. He asked them all to "train hard, dig hard and fight hard." He emphasised the need for training and extreme fitness in high-altitudes. From Leh-Chushul, he went to Bara Hoti, Badrinath and Mana, Nathu La and Jelep La to Giagong Plateau, Bum La to Tuting and, flew over Rima, opposite Tatu. At the 16,000 ft high plateau of Giagong, the Assam Rifles had a rickety jeep for him to travel in. He had a jolly good ride in it, crossing over to the Tibetan Shigatse plains. He made Brigadier Goraya drive him in a 15-hundred weight truck on the plains leading to Chaukan Pass on the Burma Border. "Put a flag on it, if you like but I'll be damned if I don't see the pass," he told Goraya.

With all the troops, it was *"Timmy Saab Ayo* (Timmy has come)."

With Nehru too, it was "Timmy." Nehru once said: "Timmy, you look after defence, let me handle politics and diplomacy."

Nehru had been asking him, if and when, the army could 'liberate' Goa. Thimayya firmly recommended against the diversion of resources for liberating Goa from the Portuguese. "We can always free it, even by well-trained police forces or through diplomatic efforts. I need troops for the border on the north and west," he told Nehru, who heard him out and agreed. But as soon as Menon returned from New York in late December 1959, he began to 'rock the boat,' again – against all diplomatic and strategic wisdom counselled by General Thimayya. That was evidently for self-glorification!

The Army Commanders Conference took place from 20 November for four days. General Thimayya reviewed the various defence commitments that had to be undertaken to protect India's frontiers, particularly the northern border. He referred to the engineering effort that was required to be put in to solve logistic problems, one of them being the construction of an elaborate network of roads in the difficult terrain of NEFA and other northern regions. He surveyed the activities of the army during the past six months. He gave an account of the aid given by the army during the floods in Jammu and Kashmir, West Bengal and Surat, as also the assistance extended by it to repair the Bhakra Dam, and in the building of a floating bridge for the forthcoming Kumbh Mela at Allahabad.

The reorganisation of the Military Engineering Service, he said, was well under way and he hoped that speed and economy would be achieved after the full implementation of the new scheme that integrated the military engineering construction of all the three services. A similar experiment was going on in the restructuring of the medical services and, hopefully, of intelligence. He also spoke of the successful execution of army housing projects, in the footsteps of *Project Amar*. A number of 'innovative ideas' had also been received from various army establishments. There was a proposal to grant monetary awards to those who had contributed original ideas.[12]

Limiting the Barrier Between the Thinking and the Fighting

Thimayya was a profound student of the art and science of war, who had totally imbibed the lessons of 'last wars' to fight and win 'future wars.' And, he recognised the need to persuade his officers and men to learn the hard way through education and training, so as to acquire the mental capability to adjust to the unpredictable future needs of war.

He encouraged all schools of instruction to invite experts and academicians to address students to increase the officers' knowledge and awareness in subjects other than purely military ones. While foreign exchange problems were keeping out even deserving officers from foreign tours and studies, he encouraged at least a small fraction to attend foreign courses and exchange programmes such as staff college, staff and command and technical courses.

Intellectual pursuits and search for excellence continued through "Gold Medal Essays," technical inventions and tactical innovations for which special incentives were offered. Similar grants were made to junior leaders and sportsmen.

One of the vital issues of intellectualism, of which he became a vocal exponent in the services, was the study of military history and technology and their influence on the future course of campaigns. He would tell the officers that unless the lessons of history were applied to our future campaigns, especially of the Korean and 1956 Sinai campaigns, we might miss their real significance. His emphasis on the study of amphibious warfare, especially of the Inchon Landing (Korea), Operation Lord (D-Day) with a view to apply lessons for carving out an amphibious doctrine for operations in the Indian Ocean and for the defence of Andaman & Nicobar and Lakshadweep Islands was well received.

As chairman, Chiefs of Staff Committee, he asked Admiral Katari to evolve an amphibious warfare doctrine for the defence of our groups of islands. The paper, when produced, was sent to the MoD, and disseminated to all schools of instructions. DSSC, Wellington, evolved an amphibious warfare exercise on it.

Along with these professional and intellectual pursuits, he was seized with another project: to improve the basic academic standards of the cadets at the academies so that a cadet was a graduate at the time of commissioning, with a BA or BSc degree. The project took roots during his tenure, but fructified only a decade later, due to bureaucratic procrastination and political apathy.[13]

A revision of syllabi that was instituted by him for all schools of instruction saw the rudiments of nuclear warfare taught to all officers attending courses at Wellington, Mhow, Pune (College of Military Engineers and Armed Forces Medical College). All these efforts were, as he often paraphrased the famous lines of Sir William Butler, "not to demarcate between the fighting man and the thinking man." "There has to be congruence between the two," he would stress.[14]

An Impetus to Logistics

We saw earlier that much to the chagrin of General Thimayya, Kaul was in the quarter master general's chair. Thimayya wanted Kaul to work effectively and improve the logistical capability of the army. He told him in May 1959 as to what he expected of him: the improvement of the logistical capability of the army both against China and Pakistan. 1st Armoured Division located in Jhansi-Babina needed to improve its response time of mobilisation. (He wanted it to be able to concentrate in a designated forward area in 72 to 96 hours rather than a week.) He wanted forward maintenance areas for troops operating in Nagaland-Manipur to be constructed at Dimapur, Misamari-Tezpur for NEFA, Siliguri-Bengdubi for Sikkim, Binaguri for Bhutan, Chandigarh-Leh-Chushul for Ladakh, Kalka for Himachal, and Dehra Dun-Rishikesh for the UP-Tibet border.

Thimayya knew Kaul would be hell bent to have the above accomplished. And by November, some progress had been achieved in terms of basic infrastructure. Kaul, typical of his character, would, however, tell Menon – and even Nehru – that he had "conceived and delivered the plans." "More babies, more mouths to feed, aye," was Menon's gaffe![15]

Kaul wanted to continue with his *Project Amar* and sought Thimayya's permission to initiate a project at Tezpur, where Headquarters 4th Division had begun to function. "Do it only if the command wants it and if troops can be spared," directed Thimayya. Kaul assured the command of financial resources. The command, hard pressed for funds, agreed. By April 1960, when Nehru was taken to inaugurate this *Project Amar-II* at Tezpur, a few barracks and a headquarters complex had come up. But people in the know were aware that Kaul was interfering with the operational tasks of the divisional engineer and the Signal regiments in NEFA.

All this could be tolerated but what irritated Thimayya about Kaul were his other activities: hobnobbing with politicians; doing tasks which were nothing but errands. He built up his public image (his known *forte*) by taking credit for the "Purr incident" of August, which was not liked by Thimayya. Then came Kaul's joining the trials of the Russian MI-4 helicopter in Ladakh and forcing its Russian pilot to land on a bad strip near Karakoram. It was brought to Thimayya's notice, who not being satisfied with his explanation, informed the minister for defence. A question was even raised in the Parliament.[16]

Kaul's insatiable thirst for publicity, professional advancement, power and fame had virtually begun to result in a parallel command being run at the Army Headquarters. An apolitical army being turned into a politicised one – all courtesy Menon and Kaul, supported by the prime minister. That, thought Thimayya, would only lead this fine army up a blind alley and perhaps to its annihilation. So he kept his ears to the ground on the goings on! But Kaul and Menon had become a cause of anxiety for Thimayya, with both having Nehru's ear.

Upon Menon's return from New York, Nehru told him how well Thimayya had worked in taking over the defence responsibility of the Chinese border and how the presentation to the governors, etc had had its impact. He said he had left some decisions on future raisings and import of weapons for him. He should take action for essential restructuring, and overall strategy. Nehru had hoped Menon would appreciate all he said about Thimayya to improve the so-called "temperamental incompatibility" between the two. He was sincere about it. Menon said, he was to get on with the job and return to him when required.

Already jealous about Thimayya's great rapport with the prime minister, Menon also had to face brickbats from the Parliament on his mishandling of the defence of the Chinese border. The bouquets, if any, were few.

The year, despite hard times and personal disappointments, was the year of triumph of Thimayya's honourable intention and life-long principle of faith in the honour and dignity of a general. It was the most difficult year of his 33 years of service of tribulation and a distant trumpet. ∎

NOTES

1. *Hindustan Times*, 12 September 1959.
2. *The Stateman*, 9 September 1959.
3. *The Times of India*, 12 September 1959.
4. Lieutenant General PN Kathpalia in an interview.
5. From Cariappa Papers, donated by the author to the National Archives, New Delhi.
6. From Cariappa Papers.
7. In an interview with Mr Dave.
8. Official documents, and *The Leader* (Allahabad), 17 September 1959.
9. That morning, Nehru was enlightened and his proclamation later (to General Thorat and others) that he never knew the army's threat perceptions may have only been a political cover-up.
10. As reported by *The Leader* (Allahabad), 17 September 1959.
11. In *The Chinese Betrayal*, Mullik refers to this meeting when after the Kongka incident, Thimayya had made Nehru agree to the IB being deployed on the border under the army. However, Nehru rescinded to Mullik's pleadings of keeping IB independent. The proposal had its merits and demerits.
12. As carried by *The Tribune*, 21 November 1959.
13. From Official Records (explained in preface).
14. Butler had said: "A nation that insists on drawing a broad line of demarcation between the fighting man and thinking man is liable to find its fighting done by fools and its thinking by cowards."
15. In an interview with Major Nanda.
16. Kaul also refers to these Quixotic acts in the chapter entitled "The Preparation", *The Untold Story*.

Additional Note

1. On the heel of Nehru's revelation on the Aksai Chin Road and other Chinese incursions till August 1959, the Opposition, led by J B Kripalani, and supported by A B Vajpayee, demanded that a "White Paper" be issued by the government. Made public on 7 September, it comprised the correspondence exchanged between New Delhi and Peking since the Sino-Indian Treaty of 28 April 1954 down to the latest Chinese incursion into Longju on 25

August. Running into some 120 printed pages, the "Paper" included 60 notes, memoranda, letters and statements. These related to border issues, Chinese allegations regarding the use of Kalimpong as a base for activity against Tibet and their (Chinese) infringement of the traditional rights and authority of Bhutan in regard to certain (Bhutanese) enclaves in Tibet. The salient facts are briefly mentioned below:

(a) The Paper showed a sequence of border claims and incursions into Indian territory by the Chinese in NEFA, Garhwal (Bara Hoti), Himachal (Shipki), and Ladakh. There had been a steady accretion of Chinese border claims ever since the signing of the Sino-Indian Treaty on Tibet, in April 1954.

(b) On 23 May 1959, the Indian foreign secretary told the Chinese ambassador in New Delhi that Peking had treated the Five Principles (*Panch Sheel*) not, indeed, as "matters of basic policy," but as "opportunism."

(c) In a note dated 25 July (1959), New Delhi expressed serious doubts as to whether the Chinese government really wished the Indian trade agents in the Tibet region to function, for not only were the facilities laid down in the 1954 agreement not provided for by them, but even the normal courtesies shown to foreign representatives and missions "are being denied to them."

(d) The position regarding Chinese maps and more specifically the McMahon Line was set out in an exchange of letters between Nehru and Zhou En-lai in 1958-59. The Indian prime minister's letter, dated 14 December (1958) made this point: "You will appreciate that nine years after the Chinese People's Republic came into power, the continued issue of these maps is embarrassing to us as to others. There can be no question of these large parts of India being anything but Indian and there is no dispute about them. I do not know what kind of surveys can affect these well-known and fixed boundaries." Again, reminding the Chinese prime minister in a subsequent letter dated 22 March (1959) that he (Zhou) had accepted the McMahon Line in 1954, Nehru made the point that it "was drawn after full discussion, was confirmed subsequently by a formal exchange of letters" and that there was nothing to indicate that the Tibetan authorities were in any way "dissatisfied with the agreed boundary." The Chinese countered by asserting (Zhou En-lai's letter dated June 23 1959) that the Sino-Indian boundary had never been formally delimited, that Peking did not raise border issues in 1954 since conditions were "not yet ripe for its settlement," that the McMahon Line was a product of the British policy of aggression against the Tibet region of China, that "juridically too it could not be considered legal" and, finally, that the Chinese maps were old which the People's government had not yet had the time to revise.

14
The Fateful Years (1960-1961)

During Menon's absence, Nehru was approachable, and Thimayya was hopeful that Nehru would continue to look after the defence portfolio, even after Menon's return. At least, the prime minister was not averse to listening to individual chiefs and would read through the Chiefs of Staff's papers. During this period, as the passes froze on the northern border, Thimayya found the time to visit ex-servicemen, and not only address their rallies but also look into their problems. He was also able to address youth rallies, where he urged them to join the army as patriotic citizens.

It was also the time for Thimayya to visit as many forward areas as possible and hold discussions, and attend to the problems of frontline troops. The visit that Thimayya undertook in an IAF Bell 47 G II helicopter in January 1960 to a far-flung post based at Limekin and later Tuting, gave him an insight into the problems of defending NEFA. Flight Lieutenant Johnson-Berry flew him there one afternoon. The company commander had been out for days together on a long range patrol, so typical of the Indian Army. Since its establishment, this remote, isolated post had not yet been visited even by the battalion commander. The sudden presence of the army chief almost overwhelmed the troops with joy. The post second-in-command, the subedar sahib, wanted to prepare lunch for the chief. Of course, due to shortage of time, only tea and *pakoras* could be served. During the *baat-cheet* or, chit-chat and quick *Sammelan*, Timmy Sahib asked how many of the men had been there for over two years. Half the hands went up. A few had been there for over three years. "That's too much of an exile for a man," he said to Johnson-Berry.

Timmy then told his ADC, "Nobody is to live behind God's back for more than a year; at the most two."

"Rotate the troops," he told everyone at Delhi. Five days later, he was with Major General Amrik Singh, visiting 4th Divisional Headquarters at Tezpur.

Earlier, on 25 February, he joined the Shah of Iran, the Turkish president and Prince Aly Khan at Lahore for the Pakistani Horse and Cattle Show. This was reciprocated by General Mohammed Musa, C-in-C Pakistan Army, who visited Delhi in March at Thimayya's invitation, for the Army's Annual Horse Show. He would watch polo where Thimayya played, have dinner at Hyderabad House and before flying off, have breakfast with Nehru. Among the invitees to dinner were General S M Shrinagesh, governor of Assam, N R Pillai, secretary general MEA, M J Desai, the Commonwealth secretary and Pakistan's high commissioner. Musa's visit was seen as a small glimmer of hope of *détente* with Pakistan.

But the Zhou En-lai-Nehru talks of April 1960 floundered. Menon attempted to sell the idea of "exchange of the Chumbi Valley, north of Sikkim, with the area of Aksai Chin occupied by China." But the proposal was shot down by the inner coterie of Nehru's advisers, consisting of Govind Ballabh Pant and Morarji, calling it "downright surrender and appeasement" and that it would inflame popular anger. Menon was not even asked to join the negotiators under S Swaran Singh. According to Mathai, Nehru had "lost faith" in him, due to his unpredictable behaviour. However, Menon would meet Zhou En-lai privately and try to sell the idea.

Zhou went back angry, accusing Nehru of "inconsistency" and fathering "Indian neocolonialism." It was evident to China-watchers, in fact, to everyone, that China would tenaciously hold onto every square metre of the Indian territory it had occupied, and it would attempt to grab and hold more, if it suited it tactically. India, no doubt, needed to do more than adopt a strategy of protest.

According to TN Kaul, during Zhou En-lai's April 1960 visit, an opportunity was lost owing to the Indian adviser's insistence on the Indian line being aligned to the Kuen-Lun range further east, rather than along Karakoram-Daulat Beg Oldi (DBO)-Lanak La (almost the McDonnel proposal of 1899). Kaul says it could have been accepted as a via media, but Nehru feared to face Parliament, which he considered a worse battlefield than one on the north or west.[1]

In March 1960, Thimayya, opening the Army Commanders Conference, reminded the minister that the plight of the soldiers and ex-servicemen had moved him, as "not sufficient" has been achieved to allow both serving soldiers and those out of service to lead a dignified existence.[2] He then pointed out several schemes he had forwarded, but which were still lying unapproved. He was also more specific on the threats, state of deployment, progress on logistics, and state of arms and equipment. Nehru attended the conference but made no comments. His presence nonetheless had its effect. Most of the schemes pending with the ministry were cleared in a fortnight.

As the Chinese belligerence grew further, the Border Roads Organisation (BRO) was grudgingly approved. It was not under the army's control but under a Board. On its opening day, Nehru said, "Necessary preparations have been made for the defence of Indian's northern border and in about a year or two, arrangements would be complete for developing communications to enable the Indian Defence Forces to move easily into difficult mountainous areas of the northern borders." Irrespective of a "Board" over which the MoD maintained financial control, roads and logistical capability became a priority concern for Thimayya. The border roads were to provide a priority road network in the border areas in consultation with the director of Military Operations.

The BRO formally took shape from April 1960 – too late to meet the needs of the emergency. All the same, work began on road New Misamari-Foot Hills-Rupa-Bomdi La-Se La. Similarly, construction of border roads in Ladakh and NHTA commenced. Subsequently, it proliferated into several task forces: Beacon (J& K); Vartak (NEFA); Swastik (Sikkim); Dantak (Bhutan); Deepak (HP); Sewak (Nagaland); Chetak (Uttaranchal); Pushpak (Mizoram); Yatrik (A& N Isles). It has continued to expand.

"You are the army's jugular vein, and, hence, the most vital but equally vulnerable part of our plans," Thimayya told the BRO.[3]

Thimayya had been working to establish an institution in India on the lines of the US War College and the British Imperial Defence College. The final touches to it were given by Lieutenant General K Bahadur Singh, the naval and air chiefs. Their efforts fructified only after two years of bureaucratic wrangling. Modelled on the Imperial Defence College, UK, it aimed at preparing the next generation of policy-makers from the defence forces and civil services for the higher direction of war through programmes of studies in national security and strategy.

"Along with the NDC," he told the prime minister, "there is a need to create a think-tank, in the form of an Institute for Strategic Studies." It would eventually take shape, but only after he had hung up his uniform.

While opening the National Defence College, New Delhi, on 27 April Nehru had said, "...India today has become positively and actively defence-conscious, more than at any time since independence." He added: "The defence apparatus has to be realistic and remain prepared for an emergency. The NDC has become a positive necessity to meet defence problems, as they are likely to be in future."[4]

Despite Menon's wishful thinking, the situation on the India-China border had begun to heat up, even in Ladakh. In February 1960, the Army Headquarters issued operational instructions (No 25) to Western Command, repeating its earlier instructions to deploy a brigade group for the defence of Ladakh, the Chinese capability then being assessed at about a division. The Command was tasked to "prevent any further Chinese ingress into Ladakh." Troops from Western Command had, therefore, moved to line Murgo-Tsogatsla-Phobrang-Chushul-Demchok with a view to prevent further incursion, although the Chinese were still on line Quizil Jilga-Dehra La-Samzungling (on the Galwan)-Kongka La-Khurnak Fort, roughly 35 km on the east. But the tactical requirement of deploying, at least, a brigade group, as recommended by Western Command and agreed to by Army Headquarters, needed to be expedited.[5]

As the Chinese increased their build-up, Western Command wanted a whole division for counter-infiltration and for the defence of Leh, which was to be deployed in two rings: the outer ring complex was to be on the DBO Complex, Chushul, Dungti and Phobrang area; and the inner ring complex based on Khardung La and Chang La passes, with adequate troops in Leh itself.[6]

The Pendulum of Forward Policy

As posts began to be established, the required logistics began to pose problems everywhere. The IAF and Air Kalinga were finding it difficult to cope with maintenance of the existing forward posts. Under the circumstance, Menon was 'activated.' He called an urgent meeting on 26 May. In the meeting, which was held at the behest of Thimayya, it was decided to maintain the existing posts by air and ascertain the feasibility of establishing additional air-maintained posts. However, despite the best efforts of the IAF (whose forward air bases were at Leh and Chushul), no additional posts could be established. So, no "forward policy" could really be implemented, even if, some newspapers called it so.

In the east, the IAF effort was reinforced by Biju Patnaik's Kalinga Airlines supplying the Assam Rifles, while the army was air-maintained by the IAF from bases at Guwahati and Jorhat. But even here the logistical support was minimum and unreliable. The basic problem here was of funds. Funds were not released for purchase or expansion, mostly due to Nehru's policy. "The opening of the purse strings," as Mullik observed, "came only after the Chinese aggression." And this was vindicated by Nehru by saying that earlier he saw "no reason" to do so, nor could he justify prioritising defence over development.[7]

With threatening developments on the frontier, the Opposition berated Menon for "defence unpreparedness" on the northern border. A B Vajpayee quoted Morarji Desai's conversation with General Thimayya (*Time*, 14 December 1959) and made a telling statement, which claimed that when in 1957, Thimayya had forwarded measures to safeguard the northern border, Menon had said that the "enemy was on the other (Pakistan) side and not on this (Chinese) side." Menon was castigated for not taking the Chinese threat seriously.[8]

A desperate inter-personal situation once again began to build up and tension heightened, as Menon set to poison Nehru against Thimayya, repeatedly telling him that Thimayya was a stumbling block to Nehru's "Forward Policy," and that he was not cooperating with him on enforcing this policy. There was, he told Nehru, tardy progress from Western Command to move troops forward and Thimayya was not doing enough to "push" them up.

Menon now began, what Thorat calls "a whispering campaign" against Thimayya.[8A] In this, aided by Kaul, he did not spare some other officers including Lieutenant Generals SPP Thorat, JN Chaudhuri, SD Verma, Umrao Singh and Major General SHFJ Manekshaw. The message Nehru was once again receiving from his minister was that General Thimayya was obstructing Menon's plan for "modernisation of the army," his indigenisation plans were being questioned by him, and that he, along with the branded coterie of a dozen others were "pro-British," "pro-American" – and, in another ludicrous canard, "anti-Congress."

The result was, as Thorat observed: "Kaul and Menon led this propaganda to the prime minister... A great man though he was, the gullible PM began to believe in this sort of persistent but subtle propaganda and slowly his mind became poisoned against these officers, including me and Timmy. Emboldened by the PM's changing attitude, Menon once again started to bypass him (Thimayya) and began to deal directly with his subordinate officers."[9] But that did not perturb Thimayya any more. "Time will tell how wrong," Thimayya would say, "the gentleman had been."

With Menon's support for the Forward Policy, Mullik would again create panic in Nehru's mind in June 1960. Mullik brought the news of the Chinese movement towards the Hot Springs and Demchok, besides NEFA and suggested that the army adopt a "Forward Posture," face to face.[10]

Thimayya was at pains to explain that he was no detractor of the suggested forward deployment (and not forward policy), but the ground reality did not help make it possible. He explained that, to be able to confront the Chinese whose forward posts were connected with roadheads based on 10 ton heavy vehicles plying, the Indian posts, with no roads, would take eight to ten days of foot or mule columns to maintain, unless assured air supply could be maintained for the posts. The air effort was, nonetheless, limited, due to both lack of resources and unpredictable weather. The IAF was finding it difficult to maintain even the existing posts. This logistical deficiency, he firmly told the prime minister, precluded any worthwhile army deployment beyond a few posts already ahead.

Nehru wanted Thimayya to explore the possibility of increasing this deployment and surveillance, to which, he assured the prime minister – and the defence minister – "until logistics were built up, patrols of larger strength would maintain contact with the Chinese." He ensured that maintaining a discreet distance, the Chinese forward build-up was under observation; and for the rear areas, the IAF Canberras were already active in reconnaissance.[11]

The talk of forward deployment and forward policy would resurface within months again. But then, again, it showed the discretion of the prime minister who, despite his minister's instigation, was still prepared to respect the professional wisdom of his army chief. Nehru's regard for Thimayya's professional competence and advice had not wavered, as Menon and others had assumed. It was, in fact, his steadfast and edifying approach to security that would triumph, eventually.

***

By 12 June, Thimayya was at the IMA, Dehra Dun. At the passing out parade his advice to the young officers was resounding:

Your conduct both as a soldier and gentleman, should be beyond reproach, and officers and men under you should always feel that they could obtain fair play at your hands. Everything you say or do – your behaviour in public, in the company of officers – and your turnout will be a reflection on the army as a whole. You should make every effort in helping build this country to its full stature. Your loyalty will be first to your men, to your army and your country and under no circumstance must you be involved in taking part in political life of the country.[12]

After coffee at the end of the parade, Mrs Sharda Nanavati, the wife of the commandant, Brigadier Nanavati, had barely opened the indoor exhibition when Menon entered the exhibition. And while Brigadier Nanavati conducted him around, Menon volunteered to distribute the prizes. It all happened in split seconds and then he was gone. It transpired that the minister had been holidaying at Mussoorie and while returning to Delhi, had decided to drive down to the IMA, almost uninvited. When Thimayya was told about it, he smiled and shrugged. "Ah yes," he said, "The minister is in love with me – in an utterly-butterly way." He did tell the commandant that he saw ominous forebodings on the northern border.

From the IMA he went to the Infantry School, Mhow, where, while addressing the officers, he said more forthrightly that he saw "war coming in not-too-distant-a future." He was frank again in telling them what he had disseminated to the group of Kumaoni officers about the "resignation episode." He was sanguine that his withdrawal of the letter to the prime minister was no aberration. "Both the letters had been addressed with a purpose which is being achieved," he concluded. He was seeing the army – and the other services – improving and there was method even in the madness.[13]

By 15 July, he was accompanying the prime minister on his visits to Srinagar and Leh, and getting him to appreciate the requirements of defence. The prime minister had an aerial view of the areas of Daulet Beg Oldi (DBO), the greater Karakoram, the lakes in eastern Ladakh, Demchok, before flying back via Manali. The Himalayas had always awed Nehru; in fact, he worshipped them, quoting their great glory. Becoming emotional, he told General Thimayya: "Timmy, we mustn't lose our Himalayas." For once, Thimayya hoped, the prime minister would even now see the real-time needs of defence and not forget them in the maze of politics in the capital.[14]

His inspection tours to Sikkim, Ladakh, and NEFA showed him that the Indian soldiers, indeed, have a great deal of capacity to adapt themselves to different climates, terrain, and altitudes, from arid deserts to snowy peaks. But considering that a large number of troops would now be deployed on the northern borders, where they would live in high altitudes and face the rigours of extreme cold and inclement weather, it became necessary to study both scientifically and medically, various aspects relating to problems pertaining to food, clothing, living, and mental attitudes. The Medical Directorate at the Army Headquarters examined the problems through studies, research and symposiums and were able to focus on the problems by early 1961; however, the progress here too had slackened off until September 1962 when war with the Chinese was a few weeks away.

During his visit to Sikkim and North Bengal, from 19 to 23 June, Thimayya saw the defences, met the troops, discussed plans with both Lieutenant General Umrao Singh (GOC, of the newly raised XXXIII Corps) and other commanders.[15]

The Chinese had a sizeable force in Shighatse-Khamba Dzong and the Chumbi Valley. His impressions of the Chinese build-up, indicated that they had certainly made heavy concentrations along some of "our border areas" but he was not unduly perturbed. What worried him was the further intention which motivated the build-up. Fully aware that the media served the purpose of disseminating the picture more accurately than other methods, he held a Press conference.[16]

While briefing reporters at the Himalayan Mountaineering Institute (HMI), Darjeeling, he said that the army was in overall control of the entire Himalayan border from Leh to NEFA, and "we are taking every step to build up our strength, to secure our frontiers against aggression and every effort is being made to develop communications in the Himalayan region and frontiers." He was aware that the PLA's arms and ammunition were of Russian origin, but some military hardware was now being manufactured in China. In their internal war against the Chinese in Tibet, the Tibetan guerillas seemed to be using all types of arms, from ancient muzzle-loaders to the most modern types, including those of Russian, Chinese, British and American makes. "Not everything is hunky-dory," he said, as he saw "the guerilla struggle petering out in a year or two, unless a strong external support went to their succour."

He then evaluated the overall advantages of the PLA and the Indian Army in this build-up. As far as the army build-up and communications in the border areas were concerned, he observed, the Chinese had the advantage of an early start in developing border communications and also the additional advantage of operating, in many places, in easier terrain. The Indian forward posts, on the other hand, had to encounter tremendous natural obstacles in some areas, particularly in the NEFA and Ladakh regions. However, communications were being developed in all these areas and he hoped India would soon have good and efficient communication lines to the forward posts.

On the likely future shape of developments on the Sino-Indian border, he felt that *unless negotiations between India and China broke down completely there was little likelihood of the present status quo in the border areas being disturbed. It was obvious that both sides were anxious to strengthen their border areas. A contributory factor to the build-up was the psychological element arising out of a fear complex that the other side was better equipped and better manned. It was, therefore, possible that the Chinese were securing their border in the normal way. Even if there had been a considerable build-up on the other side, he asserted that considerable logistical support was required, not merely for the daily maintenance of troops, but to develop a plan of attack, which cannot go unnoticed. He said a large build-up needs time.*[17]

He further added that there was, in winter, generally a withdrawal on both sides from forward areas and a return to these posts in summer. These also "contributed to exaggerated versions of troop concentrations and movements." However, as a precautionary measure to prevent incidents, which might lead to unfortunate skirmishes, "Indian troops manning forward areas had been given strict orders not to take any aggressive action" without permission from responsible officers. This would also help in maintaining the *status quo* in the border areas.

There arose differing perspectives about the PLA's capabilities. The IB had been propagating that the PLA was in a position to launch all three of its field armies in an invasion of India. Army HQ was not convinced until a 'logistical capability appreciation' was made that the courses opened to the PLA could be estimated. In 1960, there arose, according to Mr Dave, a former official of the IB, differences regarding the PLA's offensive capability: the army placing it as about three to four divisions as against nine to ten assessed by the IB. Eventually, in 1962, the PLA employed about four to five divisions – one each in Ladakh and Walong and about two plus in Tawang sector. The IB was, indeed, off the mark in its evaluation.

Till now, Thimayya had been able to contain Mullik's penchant for the so-called "Forward Policy." Translated into the ground reality, patrols were to stop two miles short of the Chinese-held line, except in places like Demchok (west), Khinzemane (east). From 1960 onwards, forward deployment had taken place but a border clash had been avoided.[18]

There was no war-mongering from the Indian side; the posts that had moved closer to the border were told to maintain surveillance up to the border – the McMahon Line in NEFA, the border in Sikkim, and the Chinese forward line held in Ladakh. Under the circumstances, there was no alternative but to build, wait and watch, and provide a graduated response as part of the strategy of dissuasion he had made the government accept.

Continuing Stand-Off with Menon Drags on: Proposal for CDS Ignored

The dichotomy of India's policy and the state of the Menon-Thimayya relationship is unveiled in a letter written by Lord Mountbatten. Just before the Chinese War (end 1960–beginning 1961, when Thimayya was still the COAS), Mountbatten had suggested to Nehru, to appoint Thimayya as Chief of Defence Staff (CDS).[19] For, having seen Thimayya and known his capability, Mountbatten knew that he alone could cut the proverbial Gordian knot of the Chinese, first by adopting adequate deterrence, and, second, by a successful counter-offensive strategy in the event of their aggression.

Though Lord Mountbatten did not specify the role the CDS could be assigned, in normal circumstances, it envisaged "to provide a single-point military advice to the government; to administer the integrated force; and to enhance efficiency and effectiveness of strategic planning and inter-services cooperation in war and peace." If adopted, the system of CDS would have accrued in adequate deterrence, in integrating the Ministry of Defence with the services and would have sharpened their cutting edge, through coordination of intelligence, integration of logistics and unified command.

Lord Mountbatten's letter of 27 September 1977 to Major General ML Chibber explains not only Nehru's dilemma vis-à-vis Menon but gives an insight into the strategic concepts of the period 1947-64, more objectively.

His letter said[20]:

> The main reason for not agreeing to an immediate appointment of a CDS was precisely that it would be a number of years before a naval or air force officer would be senior enough to be considered for the appointment. *I should perhaps add that the last time Nehru stayed with me here at Broadlands before the Chinese invasion on the North-East Frontier, I urged him to appoint General Thimayya to be the CDS right away as I could see trouble brewing up. He liked Thimayya immensely and Nehru was no longer opposed to the idea of a CDS provided it could be got through the Minister of Defence, at that time, our mutual friend, Krishna Menon. He said Krishna was so bitterly opposed to Thimayya – and indeed, all the really intelligent independent senior officers such as Muchoo Chaudhuri, that he could never get Krishna to agree.*[20]

It is paradoxical, to say the least, that as prime minister, Nehru could not prevail on his defence minister to accept Thimayya's retention and appointment as CDS; the prime minister evidently was firing his gun from Menon's shoulder. And even later, when the drum-beatings began from July 1962, Nehru could have intervened as he could not have failed to see the coming war with China. To meet the needs of national security, even Menon could have been persuaded to get Thimayya back in uniform, had Nehru cared to persuade him, or forced him.

But there is no evidence to suggest that the contents of Lord Mountbatten's letter ever reached the knowledge of General Thimayya.

***

At the six-monthly Army Commanders' Conference, which was opened by Menon, Thimayya reviewed the state of the new raisings, the equipment and arms. He said that although 4th Infantry Division had moved to Sikkim and NEFA, the state of logistics was preventing the deployment of a brigade at Tawang; he was, however, optimistic that the progress of Road Bomdi La-Dirang-Se La to Jang and Tawang would further facilitate this build-up by the summer of 1961. In Ladakh, however, troops would build up faster as the road was progressing well.

Among the other areas of progress was his decision to double the capacity of the

IMA from July 1960; to progress the Army Cadet College (ACC) Wing and increase the capacity of the NDA. These, he said, would not only help reduce the existing deficiency of 3,000 officers but meet the requirements of the new raisings which had commenced from December 1959. But he regretted the continuous disregard by the MoD of the strategic posture to be adopted against the Chinese. "It is refusing to take shape," he said matter-of-factly, "owing to lack of resources. All our projections for raisings and equipping have yet to be approved." He minced no words when he said that "in case of war with the Chinese, he could assure no good showing with the present state of affairs."

It raised Menon's hackles again, but ignoring Thimayya's plea, he chose to highlight the state-of-the-art in technology under his stewardship. He said the AVRO – 748 was operational, so were MI-4 and Aloutte helicopters; the Shaktimaans were on the assembly lines. He blamed the army for not accepting the Ishapore 7.62 rifles. He said the army was "finding too many faults with it." To this, Thimayya submitted that "several faults, indeed, were seen in the prototypes of the Ishapore rifles but he would accept them if field tests showed them improved."

A period of no communication, except strictly official formalities, followed. It was during the summer of 1960 that Menon asked Thimayya over and said that he would like him to overhaul his PSOs at Army HQ and have Kaul appointed as chief of General Staff in place of Bogey Sen. Menon argued that Kaul had been a brilliant QMG and was fully qualified to handle operational matters and evolve strategic plans. Thimayya told Menon that though he had his reservations about the proposal, he would place his recommendations on the file.

Thimayya examined the defence minister's point and then analysed the qualitative requirements for CGS and advised the minister against Kaul's appointment since he had no war experience and lacked a grasp of strategic manoeuvres.[21]

Inevitably, the note travelled up to Pandit Nehru, with Menon over-ruling Thimayya's recommendation. Nehru asked Menon to leave the matter in abeyance till Thimayya was on his way out. When Thimayya's remarks on this note were shown to Kaul, he felt aggrieved and began to pass remarks about his chief, which SK Sinha, then a major under Kaul (as QMG) saw clearly as disparaging. Reluctant to accept the truth with maturity and grace, Kaul is said to have connived with Menon in hatching up a grandiose theory of "politicians being informed" on the controversial issues (such as promotions and appointments, state of morale, by the staff officers of Army HQ, and how these showed Menon in a bad light in the international media, among the politicians and the foreign Press. These, it was alleged, had General Thimayya's "blessings!"

Menon is said to have discussed this with Mullik and asked for surveillance of Army HQ by a senior IB officer. Although Mullik says he rejected such a demand, several officers who served in Army HQ then confirm the presence of such a "spy ring" working under the IB.[22]

Thimayya knew about these machinations. His sixth sense warned him that it could well be the moment to wind up. But his sense of duty prevailed. He seemed to believe that the "northern storm," as he called the "yellow peril," would, sooner, rather than later, compel every one to unite against it. He would remark: "Then these 'God-dammit' small bickering and bellyaches would evaporate." He could never see the petty side of machinations. "Those are not insurmountable," he told Nina. "People would repent for their pusillanimous attitude and sins. God's ways are great. The army will survive."

With the prime minister, Thimayya's relations remained cordial and reverential. Nehru would always meet his army chief – and the other chiefs – with a friendly smile and a warm handshake. He would always want to listen to Thimayya. As the Chinese began to talk vituperatively of Nehru, he was still maintaining his dignity, Thimayya, however, knew that the Chinese were not merely thundering. Lightning and storm could be predicted with some certainty and he told Nehru so.

In May 1960, after his return from the Commonwealth Meet, Nehru asked Thimayya what he thought the Chinese would do after Zhou En-lai's failed mission. He was frank in telling him: "The Chinese are more bitter with the Americans than with us as they are helplessly watching Formosa (Taiwan) stay away because of American support; then they see American hands, more than Indian, in the Tibetan revolt. Inside China also there is growing opposition to the spread of godless Communism. There is a scarcity of resources in China while the population continues to grow. They have to show to the world that they are a mighty nation, the winner of the Korean War, fought against the Americans. They could prove it against India which, unfortunately, remains a weak competitor."[23]

Taking advantage of this meeting, Thimayya again urged the prime minister to support the plans for preparedness. There was little response, except that he had told Menon so. The defence minister evidently held full sway over his prime minister.

But it must go to Nehru's credit that he often doused the fire of hatred that was visible in Menon for Thimayya. Nehru would ask Menon to "pipe down" and say that though he (Menon) may consider Thimayya "a pain in the neck" because of professional differences, "Timmy is a good guy, a patriot and a good general." He would mildly tell Menon to show adaptability. But then his friendship and dependence on Menon would prevail, rather than firm directions.

On their part, the Chinese strategic aims were clear: to isolate India; and in a true Clausewitzian stratagem, employ force as a continuation of their strategy to legitimise territorial claims. They had made serious inroads into Nepal and were gathering information about the Indian Army, besides winning the whole-hearted support of King Mahendra. Their nexus with the hostile Nagas had been a painful realisation to India, and collusion between Pakistan and China had become an established reality.

***

A few days' sojourn cum official visit to the Haile Selassie Military Academy, Harar (Ethiopia), followed. The Haile Selassie 1 Military Academy was the first institution started by India since independence; besides providing the best officers as instructors, the Indian government took every interest in it. Here, the emperor honoured Thimayya with the "ORDER OF MENELIK – II." Its citation read:

Conquering Lion of the Tribe of Judah
Haile Selassie I
Elect of God, Emperor of Ethiopia

TO ALL THOSE WHO MAY SEE THIS TESTIMONY, GREETINGS.
WHEREAS, we are the Commander and Granter of the ORDER OF MENELIK II, an Order highly honoured in our Realm; and, WHEREAS, We had thought it fit and proper to have GENERAL THIMAYYA Honoured by conferring upon him the said order; NOW, THEREFORE, it is with unreserved great goodwill and happiness that, WE confer the GRAND CORDON of the ORDER OF MENELIK on GENERAL THIMAYYA. WE also ordain that GENERAL THIMAYYA is entitled to all the rights and privileges accorded to those recipients of this Great honour.
GIVEN in our Imperial Palace at Addis Ababa, on this Twenty-second day of Maskerem, 1953 (E.C.) and in the Thirtieth Year of Our Reign.

Signed
KETEMA YIFRU   **TSEHAFE TEZAZ AKLILU HAPTE-WOLD**
Minister of State   *Prime Minister and Minister of Pen*

In response, Thimayya said that the team of officers who left India in the middle of May 1956 had observed the progress of this academy, opened by his Imperial Majesty in October 1958. He praised not only the way the academy had been built up but the efforts of Brigadier N C Rawlley, MC and his officers in fostering a lasting relationship between the two governments and two peoples.[24]

Back at Delhi, 10 to 15 October kept him busy in the Army Commanders Conference. Here he asked Major General D Som Dutt, the director of Military Training to present concepts of operations of war in high altitudes vis-à-vis the Chinese known organisations, tactics and techniques. He also gave a broader concept of the "Himalayan Divisions" that the army would have to design and adopt for the northern border. Earlier, he had given some thought to modify the existing Infantry (Plains) Division which should be organised in battalion and brigade groups to be able to operate off the road axis and undertake special missions against the line of communications of the enemy; with support from both helicopters and own integral porter and animal transport.

The Land-Air Warfare School had also evolved a concept of joint operations in the mountains. He said he would want commands to hold joint exercises in Ladakh, NEFA and Sikkim, to test its feasibility. General Som Dutt had issued a comprehensive compendium on the Chinese organisation, equipment and tactics. Both 4th Division and Western Command were to test and adopt them before issuing out manuals for the training of troops. Similarly, the Jungle Warfare School, temporarily located at Dehra Dun, the High Altitude Warfare School, Gulmarg, and other schools of instruction were asked to test and put them into practice.

He was told by Director BRO, Brigadier K N Dubey that road Foot Hills-Rupa-Bomdi La was through for one ton trucks, and trace cutting over Se La was progressing. Similarly, road Leh-Chushul had progressed well. In NHTA, the road alignment east of Mokukchung to the Burma border was under survey; and the road Imphal-Ukhrul had been repaired. He wanted road Leh-Khardung La to be given priority. In this priority would figure the axes Gangtok-North Sikkim and extension of Bomdi La over the Se la. "You have a Himalayan task," he told the director BRO, "but our ability to fight will depend on your roads. In my view, it is not only the root of administration and logistics but the root of military strategy."

The raising of 17th Division in place of 4th which had been moved east, was progressing satisfactorily, although deficiency in equipment remained.

The Chinese, in the meanwhile, continued to improve their hold. In Ladakh, they had connected Qizil Jilga with Kongka La via Dehra Compase by a class 18 road. By now, they were leaning on a line, which they would call the "1960 Claim Line." In NEFA, their effort seemed to concentrate opposite the Kameng Frontier Division although having captured Longju and carried reconnaissance towards Kibithoo-Walong, their intentions could no longer remain undisguised. He asked Umrao Singh to further strengthen Assam Rifles there till regular troops could be moved up – perhaps from NHTA, if not from new raisings. There was also appreciable build-up in the Chumbi Valley, opposite Sikkim.

Upon his return from his tour abroad, he found the ghost of the Forward Policy haunting the HQ again. It was reemphasised by Menon even during the Army Commanders Conference. Thimayya questioned the very rationale of this posture as he said: "Because, the Chinese were playing their 'Checkers,' did we mean to be their pawn in the game?" He said, "We have taken adequate and deliberate measures, within our capability, for border defence. And although we'll continue to review our posture, we shouldn't play to the enemy's tune."

But then anything Thimayya said or wrote was taken by Menon as "defeatist," a phrase he seemed to have coined (or picked up from Kaul) to exhibit his displeasure. Unfortunately, Menon had, in his wisdom, now decided not to "share the common task," or even encourage "meeting of the two minds." His prejudice against Thimayya (and even Katari) had become so intense and unidirectional that communication with him was either through the CGS or the QMG. "The internal lines of communications," as even Khera observed, had been "clogged by Menon with dislike and suspicion.[25] It was an "allergy that Menon had developed for all outstanding officers with minds (and dignity) of their own, with impressive service records – a fact even Lord Mountbatten acknowledged."[26]

Menon was naïve to imagine that without strong armed forces there could be security; that without the willing cooperation of the team he was leading, goals could be achieved and final success ensured. The chiefs, on their part, wondered how a brilliant man could be so bereft of human feelings and humanity, especially when danger lurked around the corner. Thimayya was totally perplexed with Menon's attitude. One thing was certain, however: Thimayya would give opinions that were unbiased; he would not say something just to please an egoistic Menon, he would only give objective opinions.

Thimayya of India: A Headache!

The absence of Thimayya from his office, owing to his foreign tour, was also exploited by Menon to turn Nehru anti-Thimayya as well. One such opportunity was the book *Thimayya of India*... fortuitously in the market when Thimayya-Menon relations were at their nadir. In this ambience of distrust and suspicion, providentially, so it would seem – and to his unbounded delight – Menon was offered, what he thought was a cane to beat General Thimayya with. It was the publication by the Vanguard Press, USA, of *Thimayya of India: A Soldier's Life*. This 300-page book had been authored by Humphrey Evans, who had been following the general's life from Korea. That it was an unauthorised biography was clear from the beginning. But Menon wanted to make an "example" of it!

Thimayya learnt of the publication of the book some time in March (1960) when *Blitz*, the pro-Menonite paper wrote: "The Americans do not want General Thimayya (to live) in peace.... Evans had induced Thimayya to write a book on Korea, which was not approved for publication. *Thimayya of India*, it is hoped, will not put him into more troubles."[27]

Thimayya wrote to Evans post-haste on 11 March seeking clarification.

Evans was prompt to reply on 20 March, explaining the various aspects of the biography he had written vis-à-vis the autobiography General Thimayya had in mind.[28] He elucidated: "I obtained the information by the normal journalistic method of research and interview. I know that the larger news media in the US and UK have compiled similar biographical data on you; probably, the media in other countries have done the same. The quotations I have used are either from the occasional public statements you have made, from the stories you tell frequently within the circle of your social acquaintances, or from the several formal interviews I have had with you."[29] (He had edited the draft on Korea.) He conveyed the true picture of the MoD.

While Menon was rejoicing at seeing his army chief becoming the centre of yet another public controversy and was seeking his explanation and, thus, encouraging dissension within the house, the Chinese had built more than one division behind line Qizil Jilga-Dehra La-Samzungling-Kongka La-Khurnak Fort. Headquarters Western Command was wanting at least five more battalions added to 114 Infantry Brigade, located at Leh, for fortifying the forward defence line. So Thimayya was pressing the government to raise the whole of 3rd Division on the 114th Infantry Brigade group along with one armoured regiment, equipped with AMX – 13/30 tanks for the defence of Leh.

On 26 August 1960, while Thimayya was airborne for his foreign tour, Menon told the Parliament, "General Thimayya had supplied information for his biography to Humphrey Evans. But he had actually not collaborated with Evans, who unauthorisedly published his biography and the book had been published without his knowledge or consent. And he had remonstrated against the publication of material made available to him without his express approval." He also told the Parliament that the Ministry of Law was examining the legal aspects.

The Law Ministry examined the book for "lapses of security" or "violation of Army Rule 21 of 1954" (which provides that no person subject to this Act shall publish in any form or cause to be published any subject matter of a political question or a service subject without the sanction of the government.)

The file travelled back. In the meanwhile, public opinion also came through the reviews on the book. The reviews by Brigadier General SLA Marshal, critic Ralph Black, Justice GD Khosla, Frank Moraes (editor, *The Indian Express*) and several others, broadly came to the conclusion that the book said very little of a "soldier's life" which Thimayya was known for, although, it "succeeded in projecting the personality of a versatile humane and highly efficient soldier besides the intriguing background to evolution of independent India's Army." Most found the book fascinating but equally disappointing because, as Justice Khosla said in a review on AIR Jullundur, "*It does not fully bring out Thimayya's fearless courage, his unequalled quality of leadership, the confidence and (the) respect he inspires in his subordinates and the affection he is held in by everyone.*" Each reviewer-cum-critic claimed the book contained a one-sided story – and the "*hastily put together narrative of a brilliant career.*" They all hoped that the autobiography – or a good biography – would show Thimayya in a "full and objective" manner, so as to serve as part of the history of India.

Thimayya also produced every bit of correspondence and material and made his acts and intentions clear and the Parliamentarians ceased to fuss over the issue. It was agreed that the book did not jeopardise either security or service norms. Menon, who had hoped to make a case out of it, much to the chagrin of the Communist members, himself told the Lok Sabha, that "no action was envisaged against the general as Army Rule 21 had no relevance to the case."

The *Thimayya of India* ....episode had clearly further shown that Menon would exploit every situation that might emanate from any source regarding Thimayya and drag him into controversy and even public scrutiny, if not ridicule. General Thimayya was sick and tired of the politics of his bosses and subordinates like Kaul. He was, in fact, "a babe lost in the political woods, often rescued by the wrong search party," as the media humorously named his unenvious plight, generated by controversies created for him by others.

The thought of leaving the army prematurely again came to him. The break with Menon was complete since by now, frank and fair discussion between the minister and his chief was finally snapped by Menon's public fanfare on this trivial issue.

Crise de Conscience: The Agonising Period of Moral Uncertainty

It was because of this distressing ambience that Thimayya, baring his soul, wrote to General Cariappa, who had advised him to accept an extension of tenure, about which he had heard a possibility existed, and, that he should not "desert" the Indian Army at such a critical moment:

> Now regarding my staying beyond February 1961. It is not on. On my return from the UK, I have found a lot of intrigue between the army commanders (they being Thapar, Thorat and Chaudhuri) as who was to succeed me and I found junior officers wondering whom they should support...I am sure if you were in my place now you would not stay for a single day. *As soon as a chief ceases to be the only military adviser to the government, he must go. I cannot accept the position of one of the two advisers on the army side...* I am off to the Naga Hills on Monday to sort out the mess we seem to have got in there. I wonder if I will find the real reason.[30]

But he would be persuaded by the prime minister to complete his term. Despite such harassment he would not give up the cause of the army he had so loyally served and to which he owed unwavering commitment. In a talk on "Army as a Career" on AIR on 24 October, he painstakingly explained the organisation and function of each service and arm of the Indian Army..."We in the army are a happy family," he began. "We make great friendships, we look after each other's interests and we are the greatest community, and *I am proud that we are the greatest nation-building community that this country has. This in itself gives the satisfaction that no other life can give you. It is full of danger, full of toughness, and still a life full of glamour and romance.* Watch the faces of the people who march past on Republic Day Parade, their smart turnout, their precision marching to the strains of brass and pipes and durms, and you will realise how proud this country is of them. So, I tell you all, if you want to be a man, join the army."[31] (Emphasis added.)

The Spider's Web

While Thimayya was preparing to visit Nepal, the news of a coup (by him) kept demagoguely ranting around. This stupefying insinuation had amazed him even earlier when, on his return from Korea, Nehru called him and naively asked him if he planned a coup.

"Sorry, prime minister, I do not understand, who has told you so?"

He then counter-questioned Nehru who evaded further discussion. The matter died down. When he apprised General Rajendra Sinhji, the C-in-C about this piece of news, the benign elder had warned him to be careful, as his popularity, then at its apogee, could incite such allegations purely due to the envy of some people. "Understand the psyche of your leaders. They seem to be suspicious of us all," said the C-in-C.[32]

Prime Minister Nehru had earlier also informed the chief ministers that among the "troublesome issues" his government faced was Thimayya's resignation. The prime minister wrote: "...there were tremendous floods in various parts of the country (Gujarat, Orissa, West Bengal), there was the food situation, which, without being really bad, gave us much trouble, there was big scale rioting in Calcutta, stated to be over the food situation there; there was a few days' excitement over the reported resignation of our Army Chief of Staff; there were rapid and disturbing developments on our borders with Tibet-China."[33]

The genesis of all this was the fear psychosis that prevailed amongst the Indian leaders about the suspected propensity of the military in new democracies to grab power. A similar opinion was aired by General PP Kumaramangalam, DSO. Writing under the title of "Men of Straw" in *The Indian Express* of April 16, 1970, he remarked: ".... *An ambitious general can only take over if he can produce a valid excuse to the public. The general public likes stability, and are averse to coups and revolutions unless they are driven to it.*"[34]

And because Generals Ne Win (Burma) and Ayub Khan (Pakistan), already ruling their countries, were continuously attributing their military takeovers to the "politicians' failures", their "corruption and misgovernance," Menon was nurturing similar fears of Thimayya's likely military takeover in India. Howsoever imaginary, it was aimed at serving an ulterior motive: *to damage Thimayya's reputation and harass him, as part of a preemptive strategy. So, preemption was behind it.*

B K Nehru, a contemporary of Thimayya, also saw the 'muck' Menon had spread in the MoD and especially against Thimayya. He observed: "*Krishna Menon did not succeed in ousting the general – there was an outcry in the country – but what he did succeed in doing was to destroy the confidence of the prime minister in the Chief of the Army Staff and equally to destroy the morale of the army. After Thimayya's tenure, the army began to be politicised. What Krishna Menon wanted was a pliable head of the army so that there would be no two voices which the prime minister could hear. This he got in Timmy's successor, Pran Thapar, who raised no objection to favouritism being played within the army. It was this politicisation and the consequent inefficiency and loss of morale, which contributed greatly to the inglorious defeat at the hands of the Chinese of this once proud and till then, invincible force.*"[35] (Emphasis added.)

Nepal – A Monarchical Coup, Too

To rebut those obnoxious utterances and as a temporary reprieve, Thimayya asked for the ministry's approval for his scheduled visit to Nepal. Nina and Mireille joined him in what Thimayya felt, was a lifetime experience in Nepal. They flew to Kathmandu on 8 December. He inspected a ceremonial parade, then drove to Betrawati and trekked to the 14,000-ft-high Gosain Kund. An aerial trip to Jomsom and Mustang saw him return with "ruddy face and pure air in his lungs." He also wanted to see if the Tibetans reportedly still fleeing their homeland, and harbouring in Mustang, were really there. He had a fleeting glimpse of some of them – in fact, thousands of them.

At the Pokhra and Dharan Pension Paying Offices, he addressed thousands of ex-servicemen, widows and children of the Gorkha Regiments of the Indian Army. He told them, to their great delight, that their pensions had been enhanced and they would have better medical and travelling facilities.

King Mahendra was delighted not only to give him an "honoured audience," he hosted a dinner and accredited him as "Honorary General of the Royal Nepalese Army." General Subarna Shamsher Jung Bahadur Rana, the deputy prime minister in B P Koirala's Cabinet, an old friend from the Sandhurst days, volunteered to accompany the general on his *shikar* trip to Royal Chitwan National Park, Terai.

The External Affairs Ministry had been seized, not only of the Indo-Nepalese relations being at their nadir, but the need to do everything in reparation. Thimayya had been requested by the foreign secretary to assuage the Nepalese feelings and pave the way for improving the strained mutual relations. The Gorkhas of the Indian Army were Thimayya's consideration, but so was the need to arm the Royal Nepalese Army (RNA) for which Kathmandu had approached Washington, London, Moscow – and even Beijing – besides New Delhi. This was evidently to exhibit Kathmandu's annoyance with Delhi, as according to the treaties between India and Nepal, the supply of arms and ammunition was to be principally from India.

Thimayya won over both the king and B P Koirala to restore the old friendly relations. The arms and ammunition to equip the 17,000-strong RNA, costing Rs. 65 lakh would, of course, be supplied in 1962.[36] But the king conveyed through him a message to Nehru that he would expect India to support the "country under him."

In the meanwhile, there took place a serious development. On 17 December, while Thimayya was on his *machan* taking a shot at a young male tiger, the BBC news was covering the drama enacted by King Mahendra. He had dismissed the Cabinet; suspended the Constitution; and arrested the prime minister and others, for what the Singh Durbar reported as "vague but harmful differences of opinion between His Majesty and the Koirala Government." The official bulletin had alleged that Koirala was encouraging anti-national elements, *et al.*[37]

When Thimayya returned to Delhi, the Communist members were raising the question in the Parliament of his being honoured as "Honorary General of the RNA."

"Is it not distasteful to receive honour under such a circumstance?" they asked.

Nehru, however, rose to Thimayya's defence and told them, "General Thimayya has been honoured by many governments and people all over the world, including the Emperor Haile Selassie, and I am certain the honour the Nepalese Government and people have accorded him was deserving and was in the best tradition of our mutual relations. I hope he will continue to add more laurels to the country." [38]

Nehru was being extraordinarily generous; or perhaps his statement was serving a diplomatic cause.

On his return journey, Thimayya had driven back through the Gorkha Recruiting Depot Kunraghat, Gorakhpur, where some 30,000 pensioners awaited him. Gratuitously, their pensions had been increased, and there were plans for further raisings in the Gorkha regiments. They accorded him great honour at a civic reception.

Earlier, the Universities of Allahabad and Lucknow had invited him to chair their convocations and NCC day parades on 4 and 5 December. In both places, he highlighted the role of the youth in nation building. At the convocation at the Allahabad University, his humour was its best – referring to the convocation robe he wore, he said: "This academic black that I have been forced to wear is a camouflage. For, I have neither any qualifications to wear it nor is there any justification."

Journey's End

15 January 1961 was a day of both triumph and tragedy for Thimayya. In the morning, he took the salute at a spectacular annual Army Day Parade, where more than 3,000 men representing different arms and services took part. Commanded by Major General Bikram Singh, GOC Delhi and Rajasthan Area, it showed the army in fine fettle, but the fact that this was the last of the parades prior to his retirement gave it a touch of sadness, seen on every face.

In his address, he said: "I have had your loyalty and love which I can never repay." His eyes moistened, his throat became hoarse. And as the columns marched off playing a new tune, *Bharat Mata Ki Jai* (Glory to Mother India), he prayed to God to look after these boys. His solicitousness for the men was typical of all great military men – he believed that the jawans were the most important men. Never questioning their motives, and genuinely respecting them, he demonstrated what Emerson once wrote:

> *Trust men and they will be true to you;*
> *Treat them greatly and they'll show themselves great.*

Thimayya was coming to the journey's end. The last four years had been hectic and difficult. He realised how difficult the ambience had turned out to be. He had hoped to 'sprint' from the beginning – all those four years were to be spent in making an army he envisaged as "an army being capable of affording truly great support to the country." It turned out to be a gruelling and grinding time, especially after September 1959.

By February, Thimayya was on his farewell visits all over the three Commands and schools of instructions. The message he gave everywhere was the same: "Jawans have made our army one of the finest in the world. Challenges are many, be prepared to face them."

At the ACC Nowgong, he asked the young army cadets undergoing training for commissions as officers to "acquire qualities of leadership, impartiality, unbiased thinking and high sense of duty,"

To the IMA Dehra Dun, which held a special parade in honour of its old commandant, his message was: "You must become leaders of men, of high integrity and good character. Remain straightforward and dispense punishment with justice. And, politics is an anathema to you."

At Lucknow, where General Thorat would retire alongside Thimayya, he warned the Eastern Command: "You have great commitment on the frontiers of India which involves constant watch and alertness. You don't know when the drums can begin to roll." He told the gathering of senior officers later. "Prepare yourself for war."

He praised General Thorat for his "friendship, leadership and advice as one of his greatest assets, in carrying out my great responsibility."

By March 1961, Menon made sure that Thimayya was as good as retired. Thimayya's recommendation on his relief in April by Thorat was ignored by Menon whose selection was P N Thapar.[39] With S D Verma's resignation, Daulat Singh was earmarked to take over the Western Command. What was now pressed forward was "reactivation" of the appointment of CGS for Kaul – thus far held in abeyance. It meant keeping Sen on a temporary assignment before he could take over Eastern Command from Thorat in April. By 15 March, when Kaul moved into the powerful seat of CGS, another desire of Menon had been fulfilled. For Kaul, it was considered a springboard to larger "responsibility and glory." And, as if to shower blessings on General Thapar, the raising of two divisions and a brigade group (although already approved in principle) were affirmed by the Ministry of Defence.

Along with it, the operational directive was restated: "*To resist the Chinese to the full and evict any further incursion or aggression by the Chinese on our territory.*"

So, contrary to Thimayya's recommendations, Kaul had been shifted as CGS, around the same day that Thimayya was moving from Lucknow to Ranikhet, on the last leg of his farewell visit. It caused, naturally, an uproar in the Parliament, which Kaul says was "engineered by my contemporaries in the army." In Kaul's defence, Nehru added that Kaul was one of the "brightest and best officers" in the army.[40]

Fleeting Glimpses

For four years General Thimayya had calmly and resolutely borne the crushing load of responsibility. Despite working under enormous stress, he remained a "great chief," a man of principle, a patriot and an officer and a gentleman, whose fidelity was beyond doubt. For full four years, his prophecy of the Chinese intentions initially was met with derision and apathy. But he budged not an inch from his principal duty to prepare the armed forces to meet the "yellow peril" and advise the government on the military strategy to be followed. The plan of border defence he had adopted, if fully followed by his successor, would see India stand up to the invaders. An honourable man, who observed his principles to the letter and who fostered them as fully as possible.

Thimayya's operational achievements had been remarkable. He did not buckle under the pressure of Menon and Mullik to push an unprepared army forward. The buck stopped at his headquarters and did not trickle down. He ensured that Sikkim was adequately guarded; that 4th Division was not harried and moved up in the wilderness without proper logistical support. A new Corps Headquarters (XXXIII) had been raised, controlling the operations in the east. Troops were deployed in Ladakh. He persuaded the prime minister to unify the police, Assam Rifles, militia and Border Scouts under the operational control of the army when, from autumn 1959, the army was saddled with the responsibility of the defence of the Chinese border. "The move of the army," he told everyone, "will synchronise with our logistical and build up capability. No mad rush."

Then he managed to make Nehru see the prime need to raise new formations although due to Menon's obduracy, they would be activated only at the end of his tenure in 1961 – alas, two years had been allowed to whither away on the vine. A BRO was eventually extending road communications; an NDC had been raised; there were some semblance of integration – at least the base had been constructed. On the whole, Thimayya had galvanised the army and boosted its morale by giving better conditions of pay, pension, service and living and in the opinion of the knowledgeable and the media, "Officers and men were, once again, proud of their profession."[41] A great achievement, indeed.

"A Soldier's General," wrote another prestigious paper.[42] It reported: "General Thimayya has been fortunate in bringing much urgently-needed financial relief to the army, whose case often goes by default, because, unlike civilian government cadres, *servicemen have no means of publicly expressing their difficulties, and must perforce bear hardship in silence until someone strong enough is able and willing to champion their cause.* Previous army chiefs had originated some of the schemes which reached fulfillment in General Thimayya's time. But the fact that these were finally accepted and implemented during his regime not unnaturally rebounds to his credit in the eyes of the army."

"Thus, in many ways," wrote another paper "General Thimayya is legendary and like all strong men, a controversial figure."[43] And the image he had built was of being "bluff, tough and gay by temperament and popular among all ranks," one who "was worshipped by jawans, adored by younger officers and loved and respected by his colleagues, a typical soldier, outstanding in his own profesion, blunt and articulate of speech, who hated, if anything, politics but not necessarily, the politicians."[44]

The Thimayya legend had taken deeper roots. The media and the people who knew him – and those who had only heard of him – were agog with the story of this phenomenal man. All papers without exception were calling him:
- A Great Soldier – who is worshipped, adored, loved and respected.
- A Living Legend.
- A Soldier's Life: A Life that was Extraordinary and Dramatic.

***

Thimayya in his 'FINAL REPORT' to the government on 1 March, had greatly stressed on three vital aspects: one, raisings of accretions he had forwarded and which had been approved in principle by the prime minister since October 1959 could be delayed only at grave peril to the security of the northern borders; two, forward deployment of troops should be in conformity with the development of logistical infrastructure and build-up of communications; three, and lastly, all units and formations moving to the northern border must be fully equipped with clothing for the extreme cold and modern weapons and be fully acclimatised.

"While we raise and prepare troops," his last sentence read, "the Chinese should be kept in good humour rather than be provoked, or made to react prematurely. *A status quo suits us till the sinews of our defence have acquired sufficient strength. I feel the Chinese are under pressure both from the Americans and the Soviets and they may release their pressure toward us.*"[45]

A farewell dinner at the Hyderabad House saw the end of an era in Delhi. Before that, Mrs Thimayya, presented a fully mounted tiger head to the NDC.

Leaving Delhi for Lucknow, Patiala and Ranikhet, he was seen off by O Pulla Reddy, service chiefs and others. In keeping with the tradition of the services, he called on the prime minister in his office, and gave the last salute to his defence minister.

This then marked the fading away from public glare and the armed forces of General K S Thimayya, Padma Vibhushan, Distinguished Service Order – a gallant soldier, and international figure, a messiah of peace, the envy of his friends and the nemesis of India's enemies.

Personally, that night he scribbled in his diary:
I HAVE COME TO MY JOURNEY'S END.
AND I HOPE I GET ANOTHER CHANCE TO SERVE THE MOTHERLAND.
EVEN IF I DON'T, I PRAY TO GOD TO LET ME BE BORN AGAIN
AND AGAIN – AS A SOLDIER.

Although Thimayya was retiring from Delhi, it was at the Kumaon Regimental Centre, his real 'home,' that he wanted to change into 'civvies.'

The Statesman caught the spirit of Thimayya's last two days in Ranikhet before his leave pending retirement. It was a Kumaoni farewell:

"A week which will never be forgotten. A much loved and admired Army Chief,

General K S Thimyya, DSO, has gone," so wrote the paper, adding a touch of pathos.

> One heard it on all sides, from top-ranking officers and their wives, to the jawans, and old pensioners and in the bazaar. His unassuming courtliness and kindness has touched many strata of life...
>
> The week began with a large parade at Dulikhet under the overall command of General Thimayya, as colonel of the Regiment with the parade commanded by Lieutenant Colonel Teg Bahadur Kapur at which the 4th Battalion Kumaon Regiment were presented with new Colours by the president. They had just returned from a peace mission in Gaza with the UN. The 4th Battalion is the first battalion of the Infantry to have been honoured so...

8 April was not too far. The PTI of 10 April carried his parting message to the army he loved:

> I have now completed thirty-five years of army service and had the good fortune to reach the highest rank in the army, and for the last four years I have been your Chief of Staff. During this period, we have gone through difficult times and undergone various stresses and strains. Our problems have also increased, but with your fine traditions of discipline, loyalty and courage, we have coped with these problems adequately. Not only have you undertaken the defence of our own borders to the satisfaction of our people, but you have been, and still are, carrying out a number of international missions to the satisfaction of the world.
>
> I thank each of you for the unstinted loyalty and affection that you have shown me throughout this difficult period, and I have no doubt that you will go on doing so to my successor, General Thapar, and his successors. I wish you all God-speed and good luck for the future.

In a message to the All India Radio and *Sainik Samachar*, he romanticised his life in uniform as he scribbled:

> Finally, when I look back on my army career of 35 years, I think of my dashing subaltern days when I learnt to lead a hundred Ahirs from the Punjab, when I learnt to soldier and love and speak, eat and live with them. And then, as a captain and a major, I learnt to command the Jats and Kumaonis and to serve alongside Sikhs, Dogras, Rajputs, Gorkhas and Madrasis, and all the other classes that go to make up this fine army of ours. I feel I really know this country and its people. I think of all the fun I have had, of playing games with these men, playing polo, peg-sticking, shikar and think of all the places that I have visited both in peace and in war. Whether it was under the peaceful conditions of cantonment life, the glamour of the mess kit,

dances and polo, or whether it was in the humid jungles of Burma or the Himalayan snows of Kashmir with its sub-normal temperatures, service in the army has given me a fullness of life which cannot be gained in any other sphere of life.
Publish it or announce it, my friends. I have been the happiest man in all these years. By God, I hope to remain so all my living years. Good luck to you all.

It was splashed over all the papers the following day.

The next day Narayan of the *The Statesman* followed him in the cavalcade of cars returning to Delhi, before he boarded his saloon at Delhi Junction. As if on a mission of rediscovering a great life, he wrote:

> Thimayya has that touch of greatness which makes humble men feel he is at once their leader and their friend. This is not a qualification that can be acquired by academic study or distinguished patronage. It is an attribute bequeathed to few. That is why General Thimayya was known as the "Soldier's General." When "Timmy" (as he was affectionately known to the army) was to visit a unit, spit and polish were applied with extra care, not to impress a man who was too shrewd to be impressed by mere externals, but to honour him. For, wherever he went, he took with him a special soldierliness that was intolerant of inefficiency, a dignity of rank that sat easily on his boad shoulders, and the imponderable authority of experience, fearlessness and decision.
>
> But with these went the calm reasonableness with which he corrected errors, an amazing willingness to listen to explanations from subordinates, and above all the complete sincerity which he brought to bear on all things, completely devoid of the bluster and pomposity, which for lesser men are necessary props.

As part of the general's entourage another paper, also in quest of General Thimayya, would pick on an anecdote.

> Visiting a far-flung lonely outpost near Kibithoo in NEFA, accessible only by helicopter, on one occasion, he found a very young officer in command.
> "How long have you been here?"
> "Six months, Sir."
> "Jump into the helicopter. You are coming to a party with me tonight."
> "But Sir, my CO's orders...."
> "That's Okay. I'll explain to your CO. Hand over to your second-in-command and come along. That's an order."
> The next morning the dazed subaltern was back at his post writing a letter of thanks to his chief.

That was General Thimayya, the COAS. And if anybody felt that this was vainglorious trumpeting, all he had to do was to stop the next soldier and ask what he thought of General Thimayya. For, there was a saying in the army that you can often fool all the generals, but you can never fool the men. General Thimayya needed no trumpets. When he went away on retirement, the soldier lost a dear friend, and India a great soldier!

That is how the opinion poll of the media went. And, personally, he would say, he had been lucky all his life, the challenges and disappointments, notwithstanding. He rarely believed in sermons, but while addressing a spiritual gathering in the Rama-Krishna Mission at Delhi, he summed up his simple philosophy of life as two cardinal principles for happiness and contentment in life.

- Look down rather than look up. For there are better people below you, who perhaps could have been better than you, had luck been on their side, as on yours.
- Be generous. (He would quote a Buddhist verse that had touched his heart during those awful "September Days.") "And when others out of jealousy, treat me wrongly with abuse, slander, and scorn, May I take upon myself Defeat and offer to others, Victory."[46]

During his lifetime, and even now, if there was anyone in the country who practised Thy, Thine, Thou, in preference to I, Me, Mine, it was Timmy, the man, soldier and messiah of peace. ■

NOTES

1. *Diplomat's Diary 1947-1999*: excerpted in *Hindustan Times*, 6 February, 2000.
2. Official Documents. (Explained in preface.)
3. Official Documents. (Explained in preface.)
4. An extract from the speech delivered by Prime Minister Jawaharlal Nehru on 27 April 1960 while inaugurating the National Defence College (Courtesy NDC, New Delhi).
5. From the *Thimayya Papers*.
6. Official Documents.
7. From the *Cariappa Papers*.
8. Quoted in *Four Decades in Parliament (Defence & Security)* Vol I, pp. 202-203.
8a. From *Reveille to Retreat*, p. 177.
9. Ibid., pp. 177-178.
10. Mullik refers to it at pp. 546-548, generally supporting Menon and Nehru's policies adopted on the basis of his intelligence inputs. Kaul was behind the scene activist at this stage. But later, by April 1961 would be a co-sponsor. See *Untold Story*, p. 180, *War in High Himalayas*, p. 201.
11. Official Documents and conversations with Major DRL Nanda, and General Munshi. Such references were also made by Lieutenant General L P Sen DSO then CGS and who was colonel of the Regiment of 1st Gorkhas, the author's regiment.

12. Courtesy IMA Archives.
13. Reference to this was made in *The Infantry Journal* of June-September 1960.
14. From interview of Major DRL Nanda who accompanied the VIPs.
15. It was as the result of the 28 October (1959) presentation of plans by General Thimayya, that this headquarters was raised at Shillong on 10 May 1960; it was shifted to Siliguri in early 1963, its place having been taken over by HQ IV Corps.
16. All the newspapers carried detailed and comprehensive reports on this briefing. *The Times of India* report of 25 June becomes the basis of this section.
17. Interestingly, the news of the Indian Everest Expedition under Brigadier Gyan Singh came during this briefing. "An occasion to celebrate," he told the scribes. The Chinese were known to be competing with the Indian Everest Expedition about the same time, ascending from the Nepalese side. Supported by almost a battalion of climbers, the Chinese expedition assaulted the difficult and unbeaten gradient from Tibet. It failed to climb beyond 7,900 metres but it demonstrated the Chinese will to compete with India in every field.
18. The Army HQ had issued very specific orders not to provoke border clashes. Maintaining discreet surveillance through well defended firm bases was the policy, all through Thimayya's tenure.
19. Carried by *Indian Defence Review*, May-June 1992. There is no evidence, official or personal, to indicate whether Lord Mountbatten's suggestion to the prime minister on the appointment of Thimayya as CDS was disseminated to anyone else, including Menon. Also see n. 20 below.
20. Dr S Gopal in *Nehru A Biography*, p. 132, has more to offer on it: "Perhaps by now Menon had also placed in the prime minister's mind thoughts of the danger of a military *coup* – fear that is never absent in an under-developed country where the democratic tradition has no long history. The Indian Army had played no part in a national movement committed to non-violence; and one main reason for Nehru's defence, immediately after the war, of the Indian National Army had been his desire to bring the armed services into the mainstream of the national life of free India. The army, on its part, had not shown any interest in politics. But now Nehru seems to have begun to share Menon's distrust of the officer corps as a whole. This is the probable explanation for his rejection, over a year later, on Menon's advice, of *Mountbatten's suggestion that the post of Chairman of Chiefs of Staff be created and Thimayya appointed to it, for he was "one of the most outstanding generals that I have ever come across in any country."* Gopal also quotes his interview with Lord Mountbatten and the latter's letter of 9 December 1960 to Nehru.
21. From Official Records.
22. At p. 544, in *The Chinese Betrayal*, Mullik wrote: "At his best, Krishna Menon was a difficult person to work with. At his worst, he was devasting: What chance could then a serviceman – civilian or military – have against him?" Allusion to it appears at p. 557 of the *The Chinese Betrayal*. Generals Munshi and D Prem Chand, however, confirm it. For "disparaging comments," see pp 156-158, *A Soldier Recalls*. Sinha saw his QMG as a "politician among generals and general among politicians."

23. From personal documents of General Thimayya.

    How striking Thimayya's analysis had been is vindicated even by historical analysis by historians. Maurice Meisner wrote in *Mao's China and After, A History of the People's Republic*: "For over a century, China had been humiliated repeatedly by Western military forces, but now, for the first time, China held on its own against a consortium of Western military powers in a conventional war. This event perhaps more than any other, in China's modern history, served to stimulate intense patriotic feelings."
24. From the *Thimayya Papers*.
25. *Problems of India's Defence*, p. 205.
26. *Guilty Men of 1962*, p. 128.
27. *Blitz*, 5 March 1960. It called the book a "magnum dopus" and a "wet squib," highlighting Thimayya's propensity to resign, luck playing a major role than gallantry *et al*.
28. From The *Thimayya Papers*.
29. Ibid.
30. The incident related to Purr in the Naga Hills, where 301st Infantry Brigade under Brigadier Bireshswar Nath was in charge. Some time in mid-August (while Thimayya was abroad), the Naga secessionists had not only besieged the post but captured the crew of an IAF plane on a supply dropping mission that had force landed in a nearby field. Volunteering to handle the situation, Kaul (as QMG) claims to have lifted the siege and freed the crew. Later events and enquiries showed that Menon had assigned Kaul to ascertain facts for him to 'do down' the Eastern Command and General Thorat in the so-called "mishandling this issue." While Kaul glorified himself (see pp. 254, 255, *Untold Story*) the blame even for the failure of the earlier action was being passed on to the Eastern Command. Menon also went to visit it and said so. Then Thimayya, on his return from abroad, further investigated into the episode and told the ministry that there had been no "deliberate dereliction of duty by both the troops and commanders." The case was closed, though it served the purpose of Kaul's self-aggrandisement.
31. Courtesy AIR Delhi.
32. From Thimayya's private correspondence. But Nehru mentions it in his letter to the chief ministers. See previous reference in *The Selected Works of Nehru*, October 1958.
33. *The Selected Works of Nehru*, letter of 1 October 1959.
34. General Kumaramangalam's views emanated after listening to a taped lecture by General Thimayya, a copy of which had been handed over to him by Mrs Thimayya, while he was COAS. These tapes had been sent to Mrs Thimayya by Ms Pauline Phedonos from Cyprus, after the general's death.
35. *Nice Guys Finish Second*, pp. 378-374. *The Untold Story*, at p.264, Kaul also writes: "As soon as Thapar was chosen to succeed Thimayya, he came to my house and said he would like me to be his CGS. I felt deeply hounoured..." A travesty of the whole truth. Even if true, it showed how the traditions of the army had been destroyed so evidently that an army chief asks a politically-linked man to be his principal staff officer!
36. Documents in Historical Division, Ministry of Defence.

37. The events of December 1960 were replicated, in a way, on February 2005, when King Gyanendra imposed emergency, and dismissed the government in power. The seriousness of threat to the solidarity of Nepal as now, was not so in the 1960s.
38. Both *Hindustan Times* of 17 December 1960 and *Rising Nepal* of 18 December 1960 carried the news item.
39. That General Thapar owed his deep gratitude to Kaul for this appointment is nonetheless clear. All senior officers of that period affirm that Thapar's appointment as COAS was clearly seen by everyone as a "Menon-Kaul conspiracy." See *War in High Himalayas* by Palit, p. 73; *Fall of Towang* by Niranjan Prasad, p. 43.
40. Kripalani (to whom repeated references appear in the chapter and throughout the book) supported by the letter from General Cariappa had demanded that the prime minister institute a "Morale Committee" to ascertain the alleged lowering of morale of the Indian armed forces. Kripalani, rising on a point of correction, said that he had suggested a committee of inquiry composed of members of Parliament, or if that was not acceptable, another committee comprising eminent men, including some retired officers. To that, Nehru asked: "After all, he must have got his information on which he based charges against some individuals. If so, I should be glad if he tells me even privately who those people are. Then I can tell him about the facts." When Kripalani named Cariappa, Nehru fumed and remarked that the general was losing his senses. He said: "I have consulted the outgoing chief and he too does not agree to it." That seems to have given a shut-up call. *The Statesman*, 11 April 1961.
41. *The Times of India*, 20 March 1961.
42. *Hindustan Times*, 30 March 1961.
43. *The Indian Express*, 17 March 1961.
44. *The Statesman*, 18 March 1961.
45. Private papers.
46. One of the eight Buddhist verses on transforming the mind.

**Map 11: The Chinese Checker
(Link with Map 10 and observe discrepancies)**

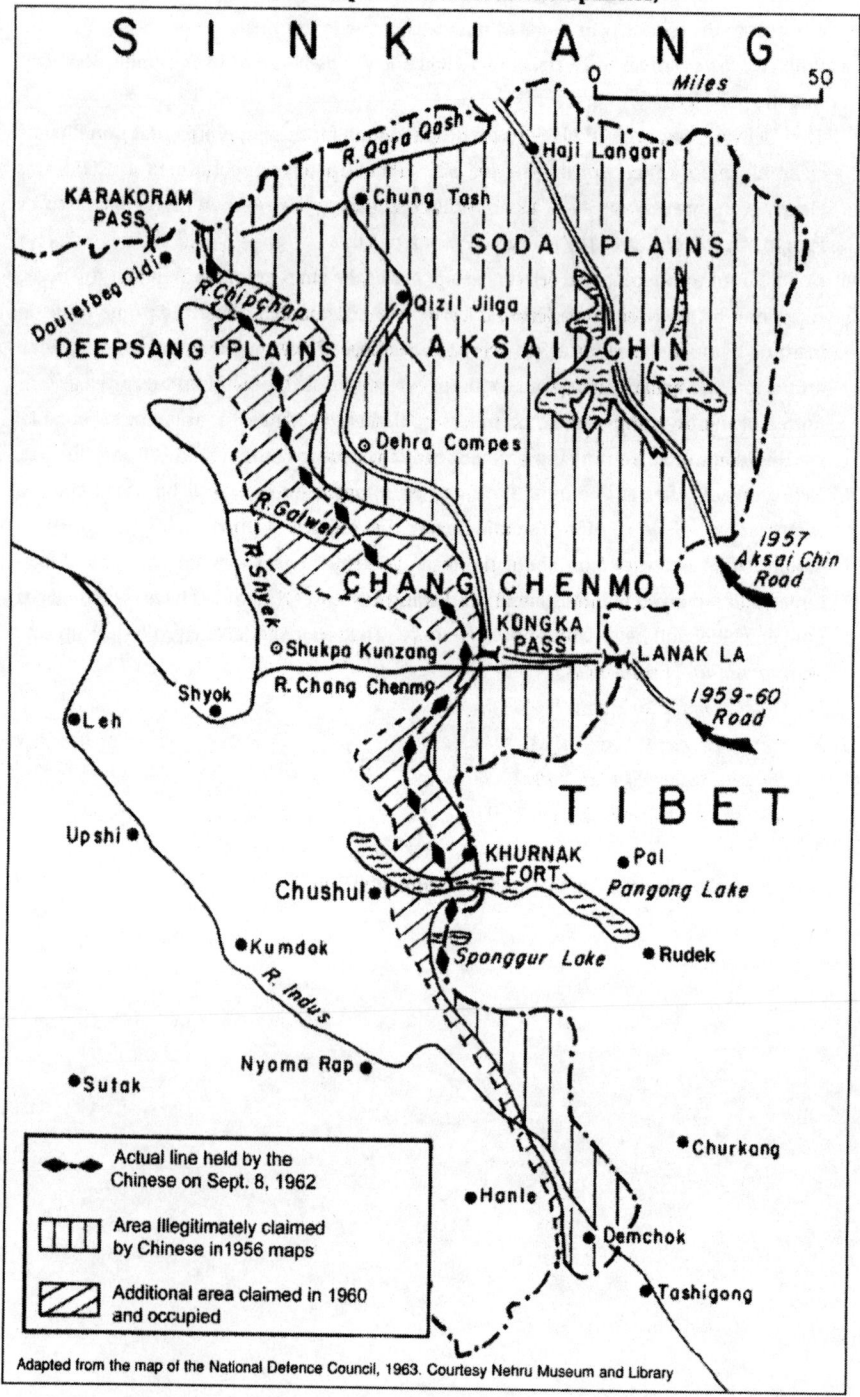

Adapted from the map of the National Defence Council, 1963. Courtesy Nehru Museum and Library

15
Refusing to Fade Away

Never a Dull Moment

At "Sunny Side," where Thimayya arrived by 15 April, the Kodava of Mercara poured in by the thousands. 'Dubbu' was back. "What do you intend doing now," many asked. "You are young and fit."

The job of vice president, United Planters Association of South India, (UPASI) awaited; they had asked him over to Coonoor (Niligiri Hills) as soon as possible, to see if the facilities they provided would need to be enhanced. And there was the annual general meeting of the world coffee planters to which UPASI invited his gracious presence on 20 April.

But his heart was set on doing something for the welfare of the soldiers out of uniform. Thimayya had been in communication with a dozen odd international organisations all over the world and wanted to learn from them so that he could incorporate some of their ideas and systems into what he and General Cariappa dreamt of: a national league for ex-servicemen.

General Thimayya had done much more for the cause of ex-servicemen than just lip-service. He had been constantly helping them, through visits, increments in pension, medical care, travelling allowances, and in improving the quality of their life and morale. He exhorted them to "work shoulder to shoulder with the rest of the countrymen, forgetting their past laurels of gallantry and romance."[1] "Realism and not idealism" was the motto he offered. A wave of enthusiasm spread wherever "Thimayya Sahib" appeared. It served as a tonic to the ex-servicemen as well as to those still serving. The results were not disheartening to see. Every state had begun to take the retired men into their service and business houses were responding to the call for employing ex-servicemen.

At the Ministry of Defence, Lieutenant General Sarda Nand Singh headed the

Resettlement Directorate. With his wide experience, he was expected to improve the conditions of these suffering people. But that was hardly sufficient. For, to be heard, the ex-servicemen needed to have their representative in the Parliament – either elected or nominated. All the efforts of Cariappa to move Pandit Nehru or the presidents were being ignored or conveniently sidetracked in the name of Constitutional proviso. In a personal letter of 26 June 1962, Nehru wrote to him:

> I am sorry I have been unable to recommend to the President the nomination of an ex-army officer to the Rajya Sabha. The number of those so nominated are very few; twelve in all, and a vacancy occurs every third year. It is a difficult choice, and we recommend scientists, educationists, artistes and others to the best of our knowledge.[2]

So soldiers had no place among the people at the helm of affairs.

Absymal Libels Borne Out of Malice

In April 1961, Menon was in the proverbial eye of the storm. Nehru was then touring the Afro-Asian countries and Deputy Prime Minister Morarji Desai officiated in his absence. There appeared, in all the national dailies, but more prominently in *Blitz* and *Organiser*, a pseudonymous letter addressed to Desai from what it claimed to be a set of "disgruntled, demoralised but well informed officers," which began to toll the euphemistic bell for Menon. It said:

> The treatment meted out to our Chief last year, the way he was chastised by no less than the PM Nehru, has left no doubt in our minds that our Prime Minister looks upon us as mere pawns in the political game... We have no doubt, it was done at the instigation of Menon...

The letter further said that Menon and Kaul had already done sufficient damage to the army's traditions of *camaraderie* and sense of sacrifice, and would compel General Thapar to follow wrong policies. Both Menon and Kaul were being identified "as enemies," intent upon "caving in the walls of cohesiveness of the army."

Morarji Desai, however, decided to defend Menon in the Parliament, dismissing the letter as being written with "political motivation." But once again the issues of the resignation, promotions, and the army's low morale would continue to haunt Menon. With the supersession and resignation of Lieutenant General Verma, it was alleged that appointments were being manipulated to suit the politically connected Kaul, and for his eventual elevation as COAS. This, as Kripalani pointed out in the Parliament, was lowering the morale of the officers, leading to "heart burning" and so on.[3]

As the papers and politicians continued their unabated tirade afresh, General

Thimayya, already under "Menon's surveillance" by his IB agents and the "Kaul Boys" was having all his movements, contacts and utterances – past and present – reported. Stories were built up, fabricated or tailored. A so-called compendium on this was prepared with a view to demolish his image of a "patriot," and an "officer and gentleman." It was also assumed that his pension could be stopped. Kaul was assigned to turn out his confidential document in this exercise in character assassination. Lieutenant General P N Thapar, COAS designate, signed the letter.

An official courier reached Mercara on 29 April, by which time Mrs Thimayya had begun to open her bags and was giving the house a shape. Thimayya had also met the planters in Ootacmond and he had been honoured not only by the people in the Nilgiris but by his school. He also found time to address the students and the teaching faculty of the DSSC, Wellington, on current strategic issues.

Thimayya returned from his tours by 4 May. He looked greatly relaxed and in a jovial mood. The weather was beautiful in the hill station and mild sunlight bathed the hills and the town. He wanted to relax and write a few letters. The letter brought by an officer courier was shown to Thimayya, who read it with anger and even some disdain. He reflected on the contents of the letter – evidently politically motivated libel and insinuations. He replied to Thapar hurriedly: "In view of the complete falseness of the allegations, please tell the prime minister that I am prepared to face anyone to disprove these fantastic allegations in an open court of law or an assemblage of a public enquiry or a tribunal."[4]

But Thimayya knew that the worst could happen. The government, under the directions of the prime minister, at whose behest, Thapar said, the letter had been written, could move the court, or order an enquiry. Harassment and bad publicity would still be there, although the truth would triumph in the end. He, therefore, consulted some eminent lawyers. The unavoidable reticence necessitated by the libel law had to be observed by Thimayya, in any case. He began to build up his defence.

General Thimayya was dismayed at Prime Minister Nehru being led astray by this coterie of detestable, vile people. But he hoped better sense would prevail. If not, he would fight it out.

Coincidently, about the same date in April 1961, General Verma, awaiting confirmation of his pension, instead, received a letter containing several allegations through a "special courier, a major." Verma worded a reply and gave it to the major but he was hurt that "things should have come to this pass. Vengeance was being wreaked by Menon and Kaul in this manner."[5]

Months passed and nothing happened. He thought that there were a few reasons for this: the failure of an enquiry which Kaul had instituted against Major General Manekshaw, commandant DSSC, proved all allegations "false and planted with malicious intent." General Daulat Singh, assisted by K G Handoo, IP, had exonerated "Sam" of all charges. The second could, perhaps, be the worsening situation on the Chinese and Pakistani borders that had been keeping this coterie fully engaged. The troop deployment as a result of a further push to the Forward Policy and the violent Chinese reactions to it was making everyone conscious of the precarious game they had embarked on. Diplomatically, China was accusing India of "refusing to hold negotiations" and complaining of the so-called "India's illegal occupation of territories in Ladakh and NEFA."

In order to avoid a "kangaroo court" being assembled against Thimayya, Nehru, on second thoughts, had sought the advice of the Law Ministry, Sardar Swaran Singh and Lal Bahadur Shastri. All of them thought that while the allegations were based on hearsay, the case might well take a political turn and, hence, was best ignored, till reopened by Thimayya or someone else. After some discussion, it was decided that in the course of a few months, Thapar could send a letter to Thimayya saying that the "allegations made against him on the basis of facts available to the government had not been proved and hence no further action was deemed to be taken." By September, when a similarly worded letter reached Thimayya, he was much relieved. His lawyer asked him to initiate a defamation case, challenging Thapar against calumny and abuse, but Thimayya wanted none of that. "I have had sufficient and I have no desire to put my neck into it again," was Thimayya's response.

Towards Brinkmanship

As Thimayya was leaving the service, the Chinese intelligence services had also become active in India, with PLA agents posing as Tibetan exiles (both in India and the Himalayan Kingdoms).[6] They had also begun to cultivate the locals in NEFA, West Bengal and Assam, through whom the PLA kept tabs on every military movement, the improvement in the state of communications and even the politico-military dissent, besides the state of the military morale under the new regime. They celebrated the news of the superannuation of Thimayya. They had known him from the NNRC days and envied his combat leadership. With his exit, they correctly assessed, there would be a void in the national military leadership.[7]

It was a pity that Nehru had ignored even Lord Mountbatten's sincere advice on retaining Thimayya as CDS. Even if his recommendation to make Thorat succeed him as COAS had been accepted, he would have perhaps stemmed the rot by following the "Thimayya policies." However, "civilian supremacy" over professional judgement, downgradation of their advice and recommendations, and playing down of Chinese belligerency seemed to colour the entire perspective. It had germinated distrust, a crisis of conscience and a loss of confidence never seen before. And the army would then be goaded into adopting a deployment, strategically unwise and tactically unsound.

As long as Thimayya was there, there had been the factor of "checks and balances," that stymied Quixotic adventures such as the Forward Policy. In fact, he felt that with inadequate fire and logistical support, each one of the forward posts would go the way of Dien Bien Phu (DBP) of the French. Thimayya would explain how the well guarded but isolated garrison of DBP was systematically destroyed by Giap's rag-tag band of guerillas in 1954. "We don't want DBPs to be offered to the Chinese," he would repeatedly say. The Forward Policy was, unfortunately, to be implemented with added enthusiasm. On his retirement, the baton had been passed onto Kaul and General Thapar.

Against the deliberate stonewalling of the "Forward Policy" by professionally responsible soldiers, Mullik began to cultivate Kaul in whom he found a keen enthusiast of the Forward Policy.[8] He would, in total irreverence, term Thimayya's nuances to this policy as "defeatist," while asking Thapar and Menon to support it. Consequently, and as a result of this goading, pressure and forcible obedience, the army was ordered to "quickly move up and forestall the Chinese from advancing further."

Accordingly, in the east in NEFA, 35 posts including 25 Assam Rifles posts came up, and, in Ladakh, some 36 posts were occupied by both the militia and the army. In this race of forward posts, the Chinese had set up some 47 posts in occupied Ladakh. India, by now, had to deal with not only a Pakistan Occupied Kashmir (POK) but Chinese Occupied Ladakh (COL).

The unimaginable damage that would accrue as a result of the Forward Policy made two fiery commanders with a great sense of honour i.e. Verma (XV Corps) and Umrao Singh (XXXIII Corps) put in their papers – Verma for repudiating Nehru's political claim that the "army was best prepared to face the Chinese" and resisting the Forward Policy, and Umrao, later, for protesting against denuding the nominated "Vital Ground" of Tawang by diverting 7th Mountain Brigade to the Nymka Chu, and into its "death trap."[9]

So, while Mullik had found in Kaul a great enthusiast of his Forward Policy, the latter would now outmanoeuvre Menon, as even Welles Hengen observed.[10] And the plot Mullik prepared was to surreptitiously sell the idea to Nehru and then make everyone accept it as a formalised doctrine of Forward Policy – the brilliant strategy of neutralising the Chinese menace.

Kaul, however, soon realised its political significance. He says that the very rationale of the Forward Policy of Nehru was principally for the "Parliament and Public," and, in passing, a strategy of "beating the Chinese at this game." For, Nehru believed firmly that neither China nor Pakistan was in a position to provoke a war with India as they had their own problems. Kaul further argues, "So far as defence was concerned, neither Nehru nor his ministers evolved a comprehensive defence policy, e.g. who were our political enemies, what was their relative strength, vis-à-vis ourselves, and what military and diplomatic moves and steps were necessary."[11]

Nehru was, indeed, under great tension due to his having held back from the public and Parliament the information about the Chinese violation of Indian territory from 1954 – and decidedly from 1957 – until he could no longer keep it under wraps. Then, having ignored Thimayya's professional advice on how to handle the Chinese military menace, he was influenced by novices to achieve a via-media, principally as

Kaul says, to assuage public feeling, which both Kaul and Mullik refer to in their books. General Thapar should have clarified the matter rather than leave it to Mullik and Kaul to interpret as they saw it with their limited tactical backgrounds. But perhaps Thapar himself had turned totally subservient or was incapable of offering a more pragmatic strategic alternative or perhaps, both.[12]

Although it appears that there was ad-hocism in evolving this strategy of Forward Policy rather than guidance by expert opinions, these posts created, out of this policy as the situation developed, were to act as a springboard to evicting the Chinese intrusions. On paper, it was still not too disparaging. But, on the ground, there was confusion and the field formations in both Ladakh and NEFA were finding it difficult to implement the Forward Policy, owing primarily to non-availability of force, lack of modernisation, lack of surface communications, and air maintenance and, generally, major logistical deficiencies.

The unpublished history of the 1962 War gives a further insight to the problem. It says, "In 1961, as the forward policy led to establishment of new posts in DBO and Changchenmo area, the load on the air force increased considerably. In September 1961, the air force intimated XV Corps, that it planned to withdraw Dakotas from Srinagar. Since Sultan Chuskee had no suitable dropping zone for packet aircraft, the air force pleaded inablity to further continue supplying the post... the post had to be held with reduced strength and supplied by land from Murgo."[13]

Adding to this, Brigadier Dalvi of the ill-fated 7th Brigade says: "To hide our military weakness and lack of preparedness which were seemingly inflexible postures, we mouthed brave words. We advertised grandiose schemes for building tanks and aircraft... we talked of self-sufficiency in defence production..."[14]

In the meanwhile, the defence budget for 1961 drew heat and bluster in the Parliament. Archarya Kripalani was determined to get the government into a corner and then thrash it. To the chagrin of Menon, he said that "the defence minister had made it easy for the Chinese to grab some 50,000 sq miles (80,000 sq km) of Indian territory without firing a shot." Menon evaded a response.

The 1962 general elections were around and Menon, fully supported by the prime minister, was to contest elections in northern Bombay against his nemesis, Kripalani. Something very spectacular had to be done to show Menon, the defence minister, as the real historic figure of the future and add another feather to his hat. A brilliant idea on how this could be achieved came from no less than Kaul, who suggested to both Menon and Thapar, that nothing could serve the purpose better than removing the last vestiges of the colonial stigma of Portuguese Goa from independent India's history. The idea appealed to Menon's wild imagination. Nehru was sounded and his approval obtained in principle, although he said it could be done only after his return from the USA in November 1961. Menon's election victory was assured with the Goa victory and the personal intervention of the prime minister, who publicly claimed that Menon had "brought about a complete reawakening in the army by giving it new life and spirit and equipping it with modern weapons." Kaul's prestige as a strategist was assured as also his place as a front-rank leader.[15]

The victory in Goa proved heady wine to Kaul, misleading to Menon and damaging to Pandit Nehru's image as a peace-loving, non-aligned Third World leader. Indo-US relations nosedived. Menon too began to be targeted as a war-monger.[16] And the Chinese had one more reason to diplomatically target India as a war-monger, howsoever uncalled for.

Thimayya was observing these developments. "One more such a victory," Thimayya said at a seminar at Ootacamond in December, "and we are doomed."

By now a series of operations to support the forward policy i.e. *Operations Onkar, Leghorn, Mahakal, Trishul*, and so on, had been launched. The maps in the Military Operations briefing room were being cluttered up.

View from Observer's Alley

Thimayya had been closely watching developments on India's borders. He had been interviewed on the developing situations, by various papers and journals. His views appeared regularly. In March 1962, the editor of *Seminar*, a prestigious journal, approached him for a 'piece.' "Adequate Insurance" appeared in its July issue – just in time to warn the government to follow a strategy of credible deterrence against China and Pakistan. It was in conformity with his strategic thinking, which had been the theme of his concept virtually from 1957. Its excerpts:

> The problem of the defence of India as posed by *Seminar* has to be discussed on the acceptance of the following premises: Pakistan and China are our immediate threats; we retain our foreign policy of keeping out of the Cold War and, consequently, out of military pacts; and the necessity of reducing our defence budget to the minimum to give us necessary 'insurance' to enable us to expand our national development plans."

Thimayya argued that adequate "insurance" could not be offered to our people by abolishing our present organisation of the armed forces, based, as it is, on modern concepts of war, equipped with modern expensive equipment, and replacing it by making use of our enormous non-mechanical manpower, served as far as possible with *indigenous equipment.*

In trying to reach the correct answer, he examined the potential of both Pakistan and China, the organisations of their respective armed forces and the topography of the area over which fighting could take place.[17]

There were psychological reasons from the Indian point of view, he argued. "There is a large section of the people which is convinced that *Pakistan intends to attack India, if not now, at some future date*. We must, therefore, take precautions and convince them of our readiness to defend ourselves against such an attack. We cannot defend ourselves by replacing our modern, well-equipped portion of the army on the Indo-Pakistan border with masses of militia equipped with light weapons as the type of country does not lend itself to guerilla tactics against a modern equipped army as that of Pakistan. In Kashmir, we are making use of our manpower and are only using the very minimum of heavy fighting equipment, most of which, in any case, is being made in India or likely to be made in the not too distant future."

He considered the two scenarios prevailing then. Whereas *in the case of Pakistan, he considered the possibility of a total war, he could not, even as a soldier, envisage India taking on China in an open conflict on its own*. China's present strength in manpower, equipment and aircraft exceeded India's resources a hundred-fold with the full support of the USSR, and India could never hope to match China in the foreseeable future. He thought it should be left to the politicians and diplomats to ensure our security.[18]

"Obviously," he said, "we cannot sit aside and do nothing about it: fortunately the terrain throughout the length of the India-China border favours us in the matter of defence. The country is a mass of mountains right up to the highest ridges of the Himalayas. The passes are practically impossible of crossing for over six months of the year except for men and animals, and that too with difficulty. China is, therefore, deprived of the use of its overwhelming superiority in heavy equipment of every kind, i.e., tanks, heavy-calibred artillery, etc. This is where we should make full use of our manpower and light equipment which, indeed, we are doing."

Because of the Indian logistical discrepancies, he enunciated the strategy that he had been recommending to the government since 1957. He said, "*If the Chinese do attack us with the intention of recovering territory which they believe to be theirs, we must meet them in those regions with commandos and highly equipped and fast-moving infantry. If the Chinese penetrate the Himalayas and are able to reach the plains and foothills, we must be in a position to take advantage of our superior fire power and manoeuvrability to defeat them and, at the same time, continue to harass their lines of communications by the use of commandos and guerillas.*"

He summarised India's requirements for the defence of the India-China border as follows:

(a) Large numbers of lightly equipped infantry to give early warning and to defend approaches into our territory; sufficient reserves which should be mobile to move across the country, if necessary.

(b) A strong organised force with heavy fighting equipment including tanks, armoured cars, artillery, etc., to defeat the enemy after he has penetrated the Himalayan main ranges.

"In my opinion, the present strength of the army and air forces of India, organised as well as modern armies," he wrote, "are even below the '*minimum insurance*' that we can give to our people. *That's why the requirement for at least three divisions to begin with.*" He emphasised that there can be no question of reducing the equipment required for a modern force; in fact, Indian Army equipment was below the minimum required and steps needed to be taken to remedy these deficiencies, either by purchase from abroad or accelerated indigenous production.

To what extent did the government learn from General Thimayya? Apparently, it learnt nothing, as events barely two months away, showed.[19]

While developments, as mentioned, were taking place, the Chinese had firmly established themselves on the 8 September 1962 Line and were claiming additional area as their '1960 Claim Line,' stretching themselves virtually from the Karakoram Pass-east of Daulat Beg Oldi-Dehra Compes, and heights dominating Chushul and Demchchok. Four to six battalions were deployed in Rudok-Tashigong, Spangur, Khurnak Fort-Dambu Guru, Kongka La-Hot Spring, and Quizil Jilga-Samzungling-Dehra La. The regimental group would soon build up to a division, supported by another in reserve in depth. It was then that the Western Command under Daulat Singh began to demand the induction of a whole division for the defence of Leh and areas forward of it.

On the Indian side, caution and even panic were also dawning. For, General Thapar had said in the 22 September (1962) meeting of the DCC that despite his professional assessment and advice, he was being asked to evict the Chinese, but he would do so only if a written order was issued to him. By insisting on a written order, he was hoping to dissuade the government from precipitating the crisis. The result unexpectedly, however, was one of binding him to an official order – a sort of *hara-kiri*. While Thapar and Sen (the Eastern Army commander) vacillated, it was only Umrao Singh who opposed, and he was forced to resign. It could not stem the rot.

Ironically, the war which was to break out in October 1962 was not on the Indian government's immediate agenda. Besides Nehru and Menon, Kaul was absent all through September. Even Brigadier Dalvi, commanding 7th Brigade, was granted leave and 114th Infantry Brigade was still in Leh. At Walong, the brigade commanders were being changed.[20]

While in England, Nehru had categorically told Lord Mountbatten that "the Chinese will not attack."[21] Was it an assurance by Zhou En-lai to him in April 1960 or the CIA-fed inputs, as Dave contends – nothing seems certain. Then on his return from the Commonwealth and Sri Lanka, Nehru decided to spring a surprise. He announced:

(a) The formation of the Special Task Force under Kaul on 4 October with the avowed aim of ousting the Chinese from their occupied territories of NEFA.

(b) A Press conference on 12 October where he said he had ordered the Indian Army to oust the invaders from NEFA.

If Mullik, Menon and Kaul had been the originators of the Forward Policy, it was Nehru's biggest *faux pas* that precipitated the entire border problem. Adding an igniter to an explosive situation, General Thapar, who knew what his army was capable – or incapable – of, saw the prime minister precipitating the issue to a point of no return. It was then that the drums of war grew louder. The die had been cast, and the Indian Army had been driven into a *cul de sac*, from which there was no withdrawal.

As it was, the publicity given to the formation of a task force under Lieutenant General BM Kaul as GOC IV Corps on 4 October, had raised the Chinese hackles regarding the impending Indian action. The Thag La incident of 8 September had given them an excuse to retaliate. They waited for an opportune moment. It came on 19 October when Washington gave a 24-hour ultimatum to Moscow to stay out of Cuba. The preoccupation of the two superpowers in a deadly stand-off that lasted 13 days, China knew, would minimise interference from them in the Sino-Indian dispute over an area whose geography the world hardly knew. They struck.

While the Chinese attack progressed, someone drew Thimayya's attention to his views contained in *Seminar* and asked whether he felt "vindicated" in his assessment. Thimayya told him that he had done so throughout his tenure, despite the displeasure of the leaders. " As a service chief it was my duty to support the government and air my professional views and add my professional advice without fear of displeasure or rancour. In so far as agreeing to my assessment was concerned, it was the government's discretion and prerogative – whatever they chose." To this, he added, "The general reluctance of the government to respond to urgent entreaties to make up deficiencies and the army's over-enthusiasm to abandon the rudiments of strategy and tactics did not augur well at all. One could see their brinkmanship leading to the path of disaster."[22]

On 23 October, General Thimayya was contacted by General Sen at Coonoor. He asked Thimayya, what, in his opinion, needed to be done to stop the Chinese, besides the locating of 62nd Brigade at Se La, and building up more troops at Bomdi La, and strengthening Walong.

"Use the air force against the Chinks inside own territory for the present," was the sincere advice of Sen's former chief. Sen was prompt to inform Thapar, who consulted Engineer, the IAF chief. "We are all for it," said the air marshal.

A meeting took place the next day to consider the employment of the IAF, now already providing transport and reconnaissance support. Earlier, the IAF on intelligence inputs and apparently under wrong paradigms of comparative performances of the PLA AF vis-à-vis IAF had rejected its employment in the offensive role.[23] All this apparently happened after Thimayya left. For, earlier, a full integration of the air with ground operations had been planned. But because Mullik (ostensibly on the CIA-fed input), began to predict larger strategic damage to Indian cities from the PLA AF, the offensive role was shelved in preference to logistical support operations against the invaders. However, both pessimism and external influence seem to have been the cause of the IAF taking the offensive missions off its operational plans.

As the IAF had discarded the offensive use of air, the Americans were stealthily trying to win over Prime Minister Nehru in this crisis. It was apparent that the US

Ambassador, John Galbraith succeeded in this stroke of American diplomacy to acquire the Indian willingness to be assisted by them. He began to advise Nehru immediately after Menon was forced to resign, virtually, from the last few days of October – and finally and officially on 1 November. It was also connected with the American willingness to supply arms, equipment and an 'air umbrella' to India. Such was the panic in Delhi that by 19 November, the draft of a request approved by Nehru to the US president to "release 12 squadrons of F-104s and two squadrons of B-57 bombers" was not even shown to Air Marshal Aspy Engineer! And the US Air Force, according to Galbraith, was to protect the Indian cities while the IAF would interdict the Chinese along their lines of communication in NEFA.[24]

Galbraith, according to his own memoirs (*An Ambassador's Diary*), read in conjunction with the memoirs of Sorensen and Schlessinger (1965), had "seen an opportunity to consolidate the American friendship with India." Acting with great sense and skill, he succeeded in working out air defence arrangements, and in case of a protracted war, India could expect American assistance.[25] The CIA had triumphed. And a bold and calculated use of the IAF in NEFA during the clear October-November months was discarded. In the event, it would have helped the ground troops to strengthen their resolve to fight defensive battles and make an orderly withdrawal, if a withdrawal was forced for tactical reasons.

There was more damage to the principles of NAM for which India stood. This turn of the tide, inevitably but unexpectedly, made Pandit Nehru forfeit his non-aligned policy. To add to it, Kaul as GOC IV Corps and commander Special Task Force, responsible for evicting the Chinese, was suggesting the induction of "foreign troops" and offensive air support to save his disintegrating 'corps.'[26]

Brinkmanship had become an unfortunate stratagem of the government. When brinkmanship proved the undoing of Menon and Kaul, General Thimayya was remembered. His strategy of "dissuasion" was recalled and his "military appreciations" and tentative plans browsed through; so was his wisdom of adequate insurance studied. Every right thinking Indian hoped that Nehru would have him recalled to service, though he would himself return reluctantly. Then politics again, Menon's unsavoury influence – once again – kept the prime minister indecisive. By 1 November, he would decide to call him not as chief, not as CDS, but as a member of the National Defence Council (NDC). In the end, as things went awry, Nehru admitted that General Thimayya had been right all along. ∎

NOTES

1. From the *Thimayya Papers*.
2. Nehru was leaning on Articles 80 (3) and 171 (5) of the Constitution which did not favour representation of ex-servicemen to the Parliament. But they were not debarred from making their way in through election.

3. In *To Serve With Honour*, Lieutenant General SD Verma says (at p. 124): "A lot of fuss was made about my resignation. Kripalani made a strong attack on Menon in the house and blamed him for ruining the fine structure of the Indian Army. He finished with the famous, 'I accuse, I accuse you' (J'*accuse*). It was Nehru who was a party to it."
4. An extract from personal file. *India's Quest for Security*, p.167 makes allusion to it. Kevic's version is based on his interview with the general. So does Maxwell's *India's China War*, p. 194.
5. Similar impressions are also contained in Minoo Masani's *Against the Tide* (now out of print).
6. Chinese documents and the 1962 Official Documents and the Thimayya Papers, NIMNL.
7. That the Chinese were generally aware of the Indian Army's state of morale under the new leadership, is evident from even Altaf Gauhar's *Ayub Khan – Pakistan's First Military Ruler*. He observes, at pp. 141-42, "The Chinese ambassador to Pakistan told Ayub that he had known General Thimayya ... He commented on the poor quality of the Indian Army's leadership, just before the war, which Ayub knew would be a limited one." The unhindered visits by the Chinese military delegations to military establishments, including firepower demonstration of May 1962 at Nalagarh (Ambala), showed the military capability and was being imaged and evaluated.
8. General Daulat Singh and other higher military brass always thought that generally Mullik was behind the gamble of "Forward Posture" and even dissuading the use of the IAF by inflating the PLA AF capability (p. 58, *Behind The Scene* and 1962 Official History). He was also using his 'secret services' and direct contacts with Nehru to the detriment of the army's image, and its correct deployment.
9. Official documents; G S Bhargava in the *Battle of NEFA*, quoted by Dalvi at p. 71, of *The Himalayan Blunder*.
10. *After Nehru, Who?* p. 72.
11. *The Untold Story*, pp. 330 and 321.
12. Mullik also refers to it at pp. 315-316 of *The Chinese Betrayal*; see *The Untold Story*, p. 330.
13. Official Document; Mullik refers to it at pp. 309-310.
14. *The Himalayan Blunder*, p. 99.
15. *Operation Vijay* never took off during Thimayya's tenure. But despite the imminence of the Chinese threat, Goa was cleared in December 1961. The troops who took part in it wore canvas shoes and carried World War II weapons.
16. During the Goa operation, for example, Kaul was in Belgaum and with advancing troops, according to Mullik, director IB, "to be present at the kill." That enthusiasm for being present at the kill, less than 10 months later, would take Kaul to his "Waterloo in NEFA."
17. Commenting on it, D R Mankekar wrote in the *Guilty Men of 1962*, "Such were also obviously the views of Thimayya officially, as Chief of the Army Staff, presented to the defence minister. But to Krishna Menon, his advice was redundant, as the government was convinced that the Chinese would never attack India! It did not, however, need a General (Thimayya) to state that patent truth. Even without Soviet support, China was infinitely stronger, militarily, than India. With the Sino-Pak collusion now a hard reality, in the next conflict with China or Pakistan, we would be up against a war on two fronts. It is as clear

as a pikestaff, therefore that our country has to be further reinforced through political and diplomatic channels."
18. This part has been quoted – and misquoted – by several writers to place Thimayya in a defensive and ineffectual posture against the Chinese. They fail to link the balance and supplementary strategy he offered now for public consumption and which, in fact, was the Dissuasive Strategy he had planned officially.
19. Coincidently, the IB, according to Mr Dave, had intimated to the government on 8 June 1962 that "China had decided to wage a war on India, unless it settled the border dispute, presumably at its own terms."
20. 1962 War Documents.
21. See earlier reference to CDS.
22. From personal correspondence.
23. *The Untold Story*, p. 441. Mullik, DIB responsible for strategic intelligence, had suggested that the PLA AF was vastly superior and should best be left unprovoked! He says so at pp. 350 and 387 of his book. But it was later learnt that most of the frontline fighters and bombers of the PLA AF were, in fact, grounded for lack of spares which the USSR refused to release.
24. In *Jawaharlal Nehru, A Biography* (Vol III), Dr S Gopal says (p. 233), "The position was rendered increasingly grave by a succession of military reverses. The strategy of dissuasion which Thimayya forwarded of lightly equipped and mobile infantry harassing the advancing Chinese had been abandoned." So is the overall opinion of the unpublished history of the 1962 War. Also see pp. 340-342, *War in the High Himalayas*.
25. Quoted by Gauhar, n. 7, p. 358, Also see John Galbraith's *An Ambassador's Diary*.
26. *The Untold Story*, p. 441.

ADDITIONAL NOTE

1. "The Chinese and Indian diplomacy," said Cheng Ruisheng, a former ambassador of China to India, "in 1962 was immature." Writing in the *International Studies*, an official journal of China Institute of International Studies of May 2004, Cheng said, "At different stages, the two countries had been emotional in dealing with their boundary question, which had finally led to the border conflict and consequently a major setback to bilateral relations." Cheng suggested that India make necessary adjustments to the MacMahon Line in the "Light of History and Reality."
Short of a breakthrough in Sino-Indian relations, the events of 2004-05 have paved positive ways to improving mutual relations. The acceptance by the Chinese of the fallacious stand point they had in 1955-62 and the realisation that they bore equal responsibility, if not the major one, for the war in 1962, is by itself indicative of the Chinese desire for reconciliation and settlement of the border dispute.

16
At the Altar of Peace: Commander UN Forces in Cyprus (July 1964-December 1965)

The Evening tells, how the day has been.

–Voltaire.

UN Secretary General U Thant had been looking for someone who would handle the sudden 'volcano' that erupted in Cyprus from early 1964. Names were suggested and shortlisted, and then he put his thumb on the name of General Thimayya. Since Thimayya was still in the Reserve List, the request reached Prime Minister Nehru, who agreed to spare him. But the President, Dr Radhakrishnan, had something bigger in mind for the general. He asked Nehru to utilise his services to refurbish the Indian armed forces, then under reorganisation, rather than fritter away this "national asset's talent."[1] Some discussion took place and finally by the end of April, it was agreed to loan the services of General Thimayya to the UN for an assignment in Cyprus. By the time the UN was informed, clearance obtained from Turkey and Greece and the approval of the Security Council received, it was June.

Thimayya's life had been going on at his own pace for the past two years or so: lectures, tours, ex-servicemen's welfare projects, speaking at the NDC, and so on. Nina was busy shifting to Bangalore; they were hoping Mireille would be settled soon. The Kumanonis had been in contact and he was hoping to join them during the Dussehra festival.

Then broke a tempest for him, as the UN secretary general telegraphed him, seeking his acceptance as force commander of the UN Force in Cyprus (UNFICYP) and the move forthwith. He was delighted at this opportunity to return to uniform and the international arena, and make a contribution to an organisation like the UN.

Amongst the many who congratulated him on this appointment was his old friend. Lord Mountbatten, then chief of Defence Staff, UK. His letter of 22 June reads:

> My dear Timmy,
> I am writing to tell you how delighted I am that you have accepted the nomination to relieve Gyani as commander of UNFICYP. This is a key appointment for the British as you can well imagine and I can assure you there is no general that the British Forces would sooner serve under than yourself. None is more delighted at this appointment than your old friend.[2]

Thimayya responded promptly on 27 June to Lord Mountbatten. He thanked him and added, "It will be my privilege to once again have British troops under my command. I have no doubt, I will get their unstinted support and cooperation and look forward to a pleasant, though I realise, difficult, assignment. I do hope we shall meet once again in the near future."

Before Thimayya left for Cyprus, Seyfullah Esin, the ambassador of Turkey to India briefed him at Delhi, giving, of course, his side of the story.

What was revealed was interesting – the tiny island was an example of 20th century conflict.

The four banners of Greece, Turkey, the UN and Cyprus, showed the divided loyalty of some six million Cypriots.[3] The Constitution, drawn up by Britain, Greece and Turkey, gave liberal rights to the Turkish Muslim minority, rousing thus the ire of the 82 per cent Christian Greeks. In that ambience of distrust and enmity, heavy fighting had broken out in 1963 that saw military intervention by Turkey and positioning by it of a brigade on the island. The Turks withdrew from the government in 1964 and set up a separate administration, which the Greeks never recognised. So, politically divided and redivided, its archaeology showed a violent past; the blending of cultures nevertheless more evident in places like Famagusta than Nicosia, for example.

Thus, although it was the Greeks who colonised the island from about 2400 BC, the Turks ruled from AD 1573 till 1878, when the British acquired control, retaining it till 1960. The major part of the freedom struggle was fought by the Greeks under Archbishop Makarios, one of the very few religious men who believed in both the Bible and the bayonet for the cause of national independence.

The disparate ethnic composition and mutual distrust led to conflict between the two communities, divided further by religion and politics. The UN stepped in and established its peace-keeping force, UNFICYP, from January 1964.

The map of the island shows its broad geography. The UNFICYP under Thimayya's command was wholly a European command.

By July 1964, when Lieutenant General Gyani and Major General Carver, his deputy left and Thimayya took over, the demonstrated usefulness of UNFICYP had

Map 12: A Divided Cyprus as Thimayya Saw it

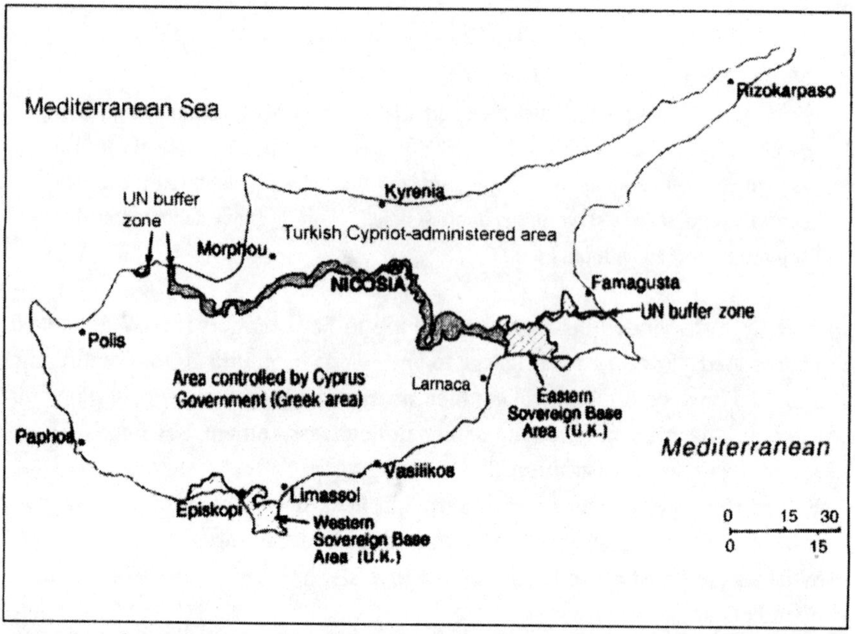

necessitated continuous extension to its mandate. However, despite hard work, restraint and good coordination, no real progress had been achieved in performing the triple tasks assigned to UNFICYP: to prevent a recurrence of fighting in Cyprus; to help, if possible, in maintenance of law and order; and, thus as a result of the first two tasks, help Cyprus return to normal conditions.

Analysing all these, Thimayya had come to the conclusion, right at the start, that the UN was there basically not to fight (unlike what happened in Katanga, Congo) but "one of my main tasks – and a new one to me and one of the essential differences of UN soldiering – is to prevent my men from shooting." For, in his considered opinion, the basis of which was his experience in the NNRC and his study of other peace-keeping operations, "Shooting nearly always leads to trouble."[4] He would, thus, lay the foundation of constructive peace by the UN in Cyprus which would serve as an example for other UN peace-keeping missions.

UNFICYP had built upto 20,000 combatants, police and civilians and had an organisation that existed on the ground. It could not, however, have been expected to normally take on either the Turkish or the Greece forces – both of which were, ironically, part of NATO, but also obsessed with individual interests, so characteristic of a world embittered by the Cold War. Although peace had been maintained, it was, however, as Harbotttle observed, "a precarious peace – more in the nature of an armed truce, constantly in danger of being broken."[5]

On 24 July 1964, when Thimayya took over as commander of the UNFICYP, *The Blue Beret*, a UN newsmagazine, carried his message:

I am very proud to have been appointed as commander of UNFICYP. I have been with you just a week and I am beginning to understand the very ticklish problem you are faced with here. I am beginning to understand also the difficulties, the stresses and strains under which all of you are operating particularly the men who have to deal with the day-to-day functions of this force. I convey my greetings to you all and look forward to my further association with you in the next few months in bringing our work to a successful conclusion. I hope you all enjoy reading the *Blue Beret*; it keeps you in touch with the happenings within this force and remember that it is by your own contributions that the *Blue Beret* can fulfill its obligations to you.

He was soon visiting the *Blue Beret* troops deployed on the "Green Line" that divided the Greek Cypriots and the Turkish Cypriots. During the tours, he invariably told them: "I want you all to be 'diplomat soldiers,' to be the 'envoy of your country and the secretary general's'. You must create a *niche* in gentlemanliness and neutrality."

General Thimayya, fully aware of the value of the Press in enhancing and projecting the image of the UN peace-keeping operations, and having especially learnt so in Korea, held his first briefing for the Press on Friday, 14 August. In his opening remarks, he spoke about the situation prevailing throughout the island, the recent ceasefire agreement, the problem in Nicosia and he praised the troops of UNFICYP.

"The whole question in Cyprus," he observed, "appears to be a matter of fear, where each community is afraid of the other." The minority community, he observed, had secluded itself within its village groups and was finding its day-to-day life rather difficult. However, the government of the island took the view that there was no need for this seclusion as the people have been permitted to live a normal life. The fear between the communities had brought about clashes, irrespective of the presence of the UN troops.

Highlighting his own mandate, General Thimayya said, "I have now been directed to supervise the ceasefire. I have assurances from both sides that there will be no firing." He admitted he was not happy with the position in Nicosia and other places where there seemed to exist a firm dividing line between the two sides. As a result, despite all efforts to stop the firing, the situation in Nicosia could not be controlled and General Thimayya said he was very keen to establish a "free zone."

Free and frank discussion with the media had a magical effect. If the process of winning the media over had been initially difficult in Nicosia during his predecessor's period, Thimayya found they were eager to support him from the beginning. They grew friendlier as they met him often and became his 'force multiplier'. To further improve the image of UNFICYP, *The Blue Beret* was organised as an effective media organ under the Office of Field Operations and External Support Activities (OFOESA). Thimayya directed it to be responsive to the media and see that truth, even in its manipulated form, was available to the correspondents.

Soon, however, he found himself in inflammable situations although true to his instinct he would anticipate them. He asked the Turkish and Cyprus governments to remove their forces lodged in the Kokkina and Mansoura areas as it could lead to serious trouble. He was assured it would not happen. But the clash still occurred. In August, within a fortnight of his taking over, fighting broke out at Tylliria (in the Kokkina Enclave) and the Turkish Air Force intervened, causing some casualties. The trigger-happy Greek National Guard under General Grivas caused more than two dozen casualties. Thimayya reinforced the UN units in the battle zone and ensured the safety of the inhabitants rather than getting involved in fighting or quelling the two disputants.

From the moment troops landed on the island, UNFICYP had been deployed and had been on the move. They had remained locked up over the "Green Line" and had no time to come to a common grid of functioning. It became imperative, therefore, to evolve a common doctrine for them to generate a prompt and adequate response to various conceivable contingencies. A study group under his Chief of Staff prepared the paper containing instructions for deployment, liaison, coordination, communications and actions to be taken against situations. These instructions serving more as guidelines rather than firm directions, were revamped and were issued to the units and sub-units. They would serve not only as an *aide-mémoire* but as a 'Bible' to the troops.

A few functional principles also began to be insisted upon by Thimayya. These included the tenures of units, removal of restrictions on movement of the UNFICYP in the island, reconnaissance procedures, and so on.

He asked the UN secretary general and his new civilian counterpart Carlos Bernades, the secretary general's representative, to see that the tenures of the contingents were extended to at least six months, if not a year, for effective and continuous employment. This was promptly agreed to. This then put the contingents in a better frame of mind and provided what U Thant himself acknowledged by the end of the year, "an effective move to prevent the danger of a larger conflagration and bigger disaster."

The mandate of the peace-keepers, Thimayya thought, needed larger functional expansion. It needed modification of the charter to cater for the extraordinarily difficult situations that affected almost every conceivable aspect of life in Cyprus. The first and foremost of these was to remove the restriction on the freedom of movement of the UN throughout Cyprus. Out of functional requirements again would follow the need to strengthen the UNFICYP's authority to control the activities of both warring groups from spreading violence, improve their potential to maintain peace, besides, indeed, to curb interference from both Turkey and Greece, the two vital external forces fighting their 'proxy war' in the island.

As all UNFICYP functions, of necessity, were carried out in contact and in consultation with the Government of Cyprus, the Turkish Cypriot authority, besides Greece and Turkey, Thimmaya began to hold regular meetings with all of them. He also encouraged his Chief of Staff and others to maintain constant liaison with their military and police, the Turkish brigade in Cyprus, the British force *et al.* He prioritised and assiduously worked for an agreement on the freedom of movement of the force throughout Cyprus. There was, inevitably, resistance to it as both the Greek and Turkish Cypriots saw in it their security being violated, but persistence and hard negotiations paid off handsomely. In fact, in addition, freedom of movement of the UN troops without searches (a condition which the UN did not have even in Congo) was agreed for the Limassol Docks, and a few other places. But this was not all. It had to be applied for the whole island.

The UN and the Cypriots, he felt, created frictions and conflict due to lack of procedures such as reconnaissance. A thorough review of the reconnaissance (recce) procedure of the UNFICYP as its standard operating procedure and battle procedures, therefore, became Thimayya's next operational priority. Although individual cases of infringement could not be prevented, the adoption of the procedures instituted by him saw major irritants minimised.

He also realised that he needed to train the UNFICYF to wholly meet the requirements of maintaining of absolute neutrality of the force and to see that his command worked as "soldiers of peace" rather than conventional soldiers. So training manuals and working procedures were written and disseminated. These, however, impinged in no way on the operational flexibility of the lower commanders. "Peacekeeping," his training manual emphasised, "needs common sense, patience, understanding of the people of this great, historic island. It is as important as intelligence, and military professionalism."[6] "Maintaining correct human relationships is necessary," he said, "to the fulfillment of our mission." He would emphasise it in all his tours, and the visits that he did almost daily.

One of the sad fallouts of the August flare-up was the effort of the Greek Cypriots to isolate and starve the Turkish Cypriots. It was then decided by Thimayya, supported by Bernades, to mount a comprehensive military economic assistance operation for sustaining the Turkish Cypriots. All the work related with provision of humanitarian relief began to be organised by the troops of the *Blue Berets*, which they did most enthusiastically, with Thimayya leading the first convoy – reminiscent of his days in the Boundary Force and the tank assault at Zoji La.

The force commander now also instituted a system of fixed posts, frequent patrols, on the spot intervention, and enlarging of the demarcation of the Ceasefire Line (the so-called "Green Line") aimed at reducing armed confrontation. Where confrontation did take place, his orders were to assist the civilians, evacuate the wounded, resolve the conflict, and alleviate the problem of the refugees.

"We are both the referee and the players in a game of football, we therefore, must act as impartial and honest, whose honesty and impartiality must be felt," he told his command.

Turkey, as mentioned, in order to provide succour to the Turkish Cypriots, had stationed a brigade group on the Nicosia-Kyrenia road. They had been stopping all traffic on the Nicosia road. It became Thimayya's priority task to force a redeployment of this brigade group from Nicosia-Kyrenia.

"We are here to provide basic security to the Turkish Cypriots. Reinforce me with your trust and faith to do my job, the brigade can leave," he pleaded. Of course, he could not get the Turkish brigade to abandon the island, but he succeeded in getting it redeployed and the road came under the exclusive control of the UNFICYP, who regulated the traffic for both communities.

Subsequently, when Turkey wanted to rotate its force by another brigade, they voluntarily agreed to have it done under the UNFICYP observation – a demonstration of great trust. For General Thimayya, these comprised an essential part of the "credibility and efficacy" of the UNFICYP, and his successes saw a natural aura of respect building up for him and his force. And when, by December 1964, fighting had virtually ended, the credit for this went to General Thimayya.

But Cyprus was an active volcano that could throw up lava and fire any time; and Thimayya knew this well.

Another recurring phenomenon of the conflict was the 'rat-like pot-holing' of posts and road-blocks that would spring up from nowhere. When confronted with these, both communities would blame the other for having started it. General Thimayya's battle was for withdrawal of troops from fortified posts, elimination of road-blocks which would sprout everywhere without warning, and lifting economic restrictions. President Makarios gladly accepted the normalisation programme in Larnaca, Limassol and Ktima but the Turkish Cypriots tried to sabotage the plan. He had to handle them very deftly.

He also suggested to the secretary general and both the governments to let the UNFICYP personnel inspect goods at the ports of Famagusta and Limassol. It was instantly agreed but it had to be later modified when in December 1964, a Greek shipment of arms was intercepted. He had to keep a tag on the 'pulse of the island,' and see that the uneasy peace remained, as any action or utterance, howsoever small and apparently insignificant, could cause the whole process to collapse. It was truly a house of cards that could collapse at the slightest disturbance. To ensure that the fragile peace process endured, he was forced to centralise both the policy and plans of his force. Personally, he had never liked centralisation but it became inescapable here.

By 24 October, Thimayya decided to let the world know the progress of peace-keeping on the island. "Peace-keeping is not synonymous with peace-making," General Thimayya told an audience at the United Nations Day luncheon in Nicosia. In his remarks, he recalled that UN Secretary General UThant, in his recent annual report to the General Assembly, had drawn attention to the danger that the "stalemated quarrels and peace-keeping operations may contain isolated explosive situations without, however, really affecting the basic cause of conflict."[7] He was of the opinion that a state of relative order and quiet must not reduce the sense of urgency of the search for a basic and peaceful solution of the underlying conflict. He said he was not happy with the concept of the UN adopting a static mentality and feeling satisfied in keeping the "fire from spreading out." The external interference has to end, if "the fire is to be fully put out, peace is to be strengthened, the so-called 'Green Line,' has to disappear and both the parties have to sign a non-proliferation treaty," he argued. Then he explained how his endeavours to unify the leaders – as a first step – were slowly and steadily yielding results in containing the spread of defence works, embrasures and pill-boxes.

"It's a long arduous road, I know and I need God's blessing and the blessing of the people of this lovely island," he concluded."[8]

That very afternoon, he would spread the gospel at another address to the people of Cyprus, on State Television, where he called the *UN "a mirror that reflects the world society in its present form. One may not be entirely pleased by what one may see; the answer is not to blame the mirror, much less to break it, but rather to improve the image it reflects..."*

General Thimayya was gradually winning over the entire international community, the islanders and every member of his force. However, his analyses showed that he had been able to achieve only a fraction of the goal of peace-keeping he had set for himself. There were dark spots, vulnerable points and areas that could take ugly shape. The distrust of both the communities, though somewhat mitigated, still persisted, and the fire of mistrust and hatred could ignite and manifest in any form. Winning of hearts and minds was, therefore, most vital. Secondly, the areas of Famagusta and Kokkina-Mansoura that could turn hot at any moment, had to be handled as a contingency.

As anticipated by him, the Famagusta bridgehead on the eastern coast became the scene of more intense activities. It arose as a result of what Harbottle called "the beehive-like activity on the part of both sides to enlarge and extend field defences." He wrote: "General Thimayya was at great pains to prevent this undesirable policy from escalating to such an extent so as to become a major obstacle to disengagement and demilitarisation... He imposed as much limitation as possible on defence construction. He was determined to prevent, so far as he was able, an extension of the defence system already constructed and, to a large measure, he was able to control particularly in the coastal areas where defences had begun to blossom."[9]

Thimayya even inspected the defence networks of both sides, in one of which he did what became the talk of the Island, if not the whole world. *The Cyprus Mail* of 30 January 1965 carried the story:

> Upon having been informed that the Turkish Cypriots had constructed a new set of defences, right under the nose of a UN picket, General Thimayya moved post haste to the site. It was pitch dark and he asked the unit to arrange a petromax and a ladder for him to climb up on a nearby tree to inspect the reported defences. Wearing his uni-

form and great coat, the general climbed up while a soldier held a petromax. What he saw infuriated him. He asked a few questions and said nothing at the moment. The following morning, the commanding officer of the erring unit was before him.

"You have failed in doing your duty," he said, "I am recommending your immediate return."

While the unit got its marching orders, a new unit reached the place and Thimayya himself saw a UN bulldozer level the unauthorised defences.

The story spread and both the UN troops and the Cypriots were on their toes.[10]

There was another story that spread but only within his HQ. It was Chhaju the 'stick orderly' who living in a foreign environment had learnt a few functional words of English – 'Yes Sir,' 'No Sir,' 'Yes Madam,' 'No Madam,' 'No, no Madam,' 'Good Sir,' 'Bad Madam,' and so on. So one day while delivering a file that General Thimayya sent across to James Wilson, now his COS, Chhaju sprang the greatest surprise for this last adjutant of the IMA at the time of the Partition in 1947.

"Madam, file," he told Wilson. Wilson looked up in disbelief.

"Chhaju, address me as Sir," Wilson said pleasantly.

"Yes, Madam," replied Chhaju, as he saluted and marched out.

Wilson brought this to the notice of General Thimayya at lunch, more as a joke.

"Ah, James," quipped Timmy, "Be careful about Chhaju's intentions."

Humour could never depart from Timmy.

***

The Famagusta situation could not, however, be controlled despite Thimayya persistently telling the Greeks and the Turks and President Makarios, almost in admonition and desperation: "The Turks say the Greeks are building new positions and we are doing nothing: Where is the need to build destructive fortifications?"[11]

Finally, Famagusta exploded on the first day of November 1965. On 5 November, when firing ceased, both sides had lost heavily and were licking their wounds. Once again, Thimayya toured the 'battlefield' of Famagusta, placed his UN troops between the warring Cypriots and brought in some sanity. As a result of these developments, a readjustment of the United Nations Force within the Nicosia Zone, to allow more functional operational control within the zone, took place on Wednesday, 9 December. The Canadian, Danish and Finnish contingents of the UNFICYP were involved in the redeployment.

Seizing on this initiative, Thimayya forced a programme of "defortification" of the area outside the walls of the Old City and dismantling of the Turkish positions on top of the wall, creating, thus, a DMZ manned by the UN troops.

Politically, the Cyprus government was moving a draft resolution in the UN General Assembly for "unfettered sovereignty and independence." Based on the

Cairo Non-Aligned Declaration of December 1964, it called upon all states to "respect the sovereignty, unity, independence and territorial integrity of Cyprus and to refrain from any threat or use of force or intervention directed against Cyprus and from any effort to impose unjust solutions unacceptable to the people of Cyprus." It further said that Cyprus, as an equal member of the United Nations, is entitled to, and should enjoy, unrestricted and unfettered sovereignty and independence, allowing its people to determine freely, and without any foreign intervention or interference, the political future of the country, on the basis of the principle of self-determination, in accordance with the Charter of the United Nations. It also recommended the elimination of the foreign bases in Cyprus and the withdrawal of foreign troops.

Undoubtedly, it was the vanguard of the UNFICYP under Thimayya that had helped the Government of Cyprus to undertake this diplomatic offensive in the UNO despite the opposition of the concerned parties. Makarios and his Turkish Cypriot counterpart's trust further increased in the "general from India."

Recording the impressions of his visit to Cyprus in December, GH Jansen, reported from Beirut: "*From both sides in Cyprus – Greek and Turk – I heard nothing but praise for General Thimayya's cool bravery and diplomatic sagacity. It was admitted on all hands that if Cyprus continued to remain at peace, it was largely because of the moral standing of the United Nations force and the charm of its commander's formidable personality.*"[12]

14 December was a memorable day for Thimayya. He had seen the DMZ coming up and had many words of praise for the Swedes at Famagusta. He then climbed the 'Rocas Bastion' again to have a grandstand view of the area and the blue, placid sea of the Famagusta Bay. While passing through the Palouriotissa suburb of Nicosia, he had talked to a young boy sitting on a stone.

"How are you, my dear friend," he said, as he gave him a piece of chocolate and shook his hand. The boy smiled and saluted him. He was happy that things looked upbeat before the coming Christmas and the New Year Eve celebration. Eighteen months had passed eventfully and he had reasons to be happy. He had begun to enjoy the job.

In his heart, he was still happier. The trust of both sides i.e. the Turkish and Greek governments, had grown more sanguine. The UNFICYP was not only controlling the feuding sides but helping the suffering civilians. Supplies were moving uninterrupted into the Turkish Cypriot area. The Turkish government was less trigger-happy and not escalating local situations by sending their air force or naval vessels. And he was overjoyed when the question of a ban on the movement of the Turkish Cypriots in Nicosia was left entirely in his hands by the Governments of Greece and Cyprus.

President Makarios was showing implicit faith in Thimayya's judgement and decisions. He provided UN security to him. Still greater was his satisfaction that the UN was constantly being looked upon by both contestants and even the superpowers as being able to handle the Cyprus problem by itself. Makarios opened his doors to Thimayya virtually all '24 hours'.

On the personal side of command, while Bernades, the UN mediator, was friendly and cooperative, the sector and sub-sector commanders (the British, Canadian, Danish, Irish, Finnish and Swedish) were ably led, motivated and "on the ball" as he often said.

The UN was lavish in offering facilities to Thimayya as commander UNFICYP. He had a large bungalow in Nicosia and a country home in Kyrenia on the sea. The Cypriots soon got to know him for the fine social animal he was and everyone wanted to befriend him.

When the opportunity occurred, he would not miss his humorous musings, calling them "crudos." Earlier in the week, while addressing the Swedish troupe "Flickery Files," that had come to entertain the UNFICYP, he told the pretty 16-year-old Eva Osterberg, "If you stay here long, I'll have a coup at Nicosia."

This great circle of friends of whom Pauline is most steadfast, has helped the author in innumerable ways – script, research papers from friends and HQ UNFICYP, photos, discs and special stamp. It speaks volumes for both Timmy and the wonderful people of Cyprus. The youth was always a focus of his attention, even in Cyprus. He would find time to address the university students regaling them with his war stories, India's wars with Pakistan and China and telling them how India had corrected the deficiencies and discrepancies and done well in 1965 – and would do better. His taped lectures continue to be preserved in the university and colleges he addressed. In doing so he was also imaging India as a progressive nation.

On the evening of 14 December, Phedonos had hosted a dinner in his honour, which was atteneded by the most important people of Nicosia. He was determined to relax and enjoy himself amidst his friends who would address him as Timmy.

Thimayya was a great *raconteur*. He was known to also spread his masculine charm with the fair sex as a class "from ages 16 to 76," as Fateh would recall. In social circles, they (the ladies) would sit around a table or fireplace and listen to his stories of war and peace, of men and women, as folk tales by admiring kids. Most wanted to listen to him and see his boyish smile and wanted to mother him.

At Phedonos' that night, there was a game of 'last wish' being played: people's last wish. People's wishes ranged from going to heaven or avoiding hell, or 'leaving no problem behind.' Then it was Timmy's turn. "I tell you the truth," said he, "I will ask God to let me die in this battlefield." Then he paused, "Or die in the arms of a beautiful woman." It was new to this great circle of friends; in India it was a pet joke. But here many beautiful women, including Pauline and Anne blushed. "Ah, the general, he is so sweet," they said. But they knew it was all for humour.

In doing so he became the darling of all those who believed in reducing the travails and anxieties of others through self-targetted humour. It was his philosophy of "contentment of comparative bliss" as Pauline would quote his serious sayings.

"General Timmy," she wrote, "told me how he used to grumble to his parents that he had no good shoes to wear. And then one day, his mother took him to a temple to see a man with no feet. From that day, Timmy wore whatever the parents offered. And he often mumbled, 'Ah, I had no shoes, and I grumbled, until I met a man without feet.'"

"Consider yourself lucky and laugh," he would say and often add, "Laughter is infectious and while it costs nothing, it gives a lot."

Thimayya was again the famed 'Pied Piper' in Cyprus, with the charismatic image of a man who could blend with Cypriot society, while remaining totally impartial and devoted to his impartial command.

Two of his close friends wrote of him to the author. Mrs Stella Souliotou, the former minister of justice and minister of health wrote:

> What I can tell you about General Thimayya is what has remained in my memory over the years as I did not keep a diary at the time on which I can draw. First of all let me tell you that Archbishop Makarios, president of Cyprus, had not only great regard for him but also great affection. He trusted him absolutely as commander of UNFICYP to do what was right and fair and he would always listen with great attention to any recommendations of the general with regard to the conduct of our own military forces which were only then being constituted as a body known as the National Guard. I also know that the archbishop took the general's advice on the situation in Cyprus generally. This esteem of the archbishop for Timmy was shared by all the ministers of Makarios' Council of Ministers, of which as you know I was a member, as minister of justice and concurrently minister of health. Timmy had access to President Makarios at any time of the day and night.
>
> Timmy was not only the serious and respected commander of the UNFICYP but was also a great favourite of Nicosia society. He became a regular guest in all our homes and he was always the soul of the party. As you probably know, he was full of life, becoming the centre of any social event, contributing with wit and intelligence to any serious or not so serious conversation.

Pauline Phedonos, an international artist, teacher and one with great reverence for the 'magic' in General Thimayya, wrote:

> My memories of the general are full of good thoughts and happy days. We spent many hours together both in Nicosia and Kyrenia. When his work for the day was over – it was never really over, of course. We would meet up either at home or night club or homes of friends for cocktail parties, dinner, etc. He never failed to remember the children's birthdays or Christmas.. His daughter Mirelle dressed up in her beautiful saris visited us. We went to nice spots, singing and dancing and laughing... there was no doubt he was a social animal. He had become an integral part of the Nicosia scene. Wherever he went people collected to meet him and in his turn, he

was most eager to meet them. In Limassol, where the carnival was held, he was feted and admired – always the toast of the party; always regal.

Among his other ardent admirers and friends were Michael Triantafilliades (ex-president of Supreme Court and now chancellor of Nicosia University), Spiros Kyprianou (foreign minister during Timmy's tenure and president of the House of Representatives), Tassos Papandopoullos (leader of the Democratic Party), and, of course, Makarios.

***

By 15 December, the body could no longer cope with the strain. Timmy had overworked and was suffering from a heavy cold. He was confined to bed for the next 10 days by the doctors. Despite this, he continued to deal with all matters affecting the force and was in regular contact with members of his staff.

One of the last documents written by him was a Christmas message to his command.

17 December was a calamitous day for General Thimayya. The news he received from Nina that morning proved most distressing: Krishna, his beloved sister, had lost her IAS husband on the way to Chakrata, near Dehra Dun.

At 4 a.m., the following morning, he walked into the toilet. While entering it, he stumbled and had a fall. He was rushed to the hospital. According to a UN signal, "A fall in his villa at 4 a.m. on December 18th, resulted in a heart attack and subsequent death."

Death had finally struck the formidable general in the early morning of 18 December.

More medical investigation of the causes of General Thimayya's death showed that it was the effects of high altitude which had killed him prematurely – all other causes aggravating the main cause. He had been travelling and living in high altitudes, from the time he took over the Sri Div in 1948 and then all through, whenever opportunity appeared. He had suffered its effects and was evacuated and rendered low medical category ('B' for six months) while he was commandant National Defence Academy, Dehra Dun. As army commander, too, he remained in the low medical category from August 1955 till March 1956.[13] The Indian government, on advice from the President, Dr Radhakrishnan, awarded Mrs Thimayya "Special Family Pension."

In New York, UN Secretary General U Thant, announced the death of General Thimayya to the United Nations General Assembly just as this UN body moved towards adoption of a resolution on the question of Cyprus on Saturday, 18 December.

The Assembly stood for a minute in silence and warm tributes were then paid by the heads of the delegations of Cyprus, Great Britain, Greece, Turkey and India.

In his statement, U Thant said: "His death comes as a great shock. His passing is a most serious loss to the United Nations peace effort in Cyprus, for General Thimayya has rendered distinguished and dedicated service to the United Nations and to Cyprus in his tour of duty in that island."

"He was highly regarded by all for his military ability, his wisdom, his integrity and above all his warm human qualities," said the secretary general, in a eulogy, "He was a splendid example of those soldiers of peace which the United Nations has uniquely inspired and employed." In paying further tribute to his memory and in expressing admiration of the services, he said that the *"general regarded his personal affairs and his failing health as of secondary importance compared to the serious tasks with which he was entrusted with by the United Nations. As a commander, he achieved a great deal for the UNFICYP under his command."* (Emphasis added.)

Dr Fazil Kuchuck, vice president of the republic, said that he was sure that he expressed the feelings of the entire Turkish Cypriot community in stating that the death of General Thimayya "has shocked us all very deeply, indeed. We had come to know him as a man of great integrity and wisdom, of justice and equanimity, enlivened by an excellent sense of humour with which he endeared himself to everyone he knew... The United Nations, and mankind at large have lost a very devoted servant of the cause of peace."

Among the others who paid warm tribute to Thimayya was Bernardes. He said, "General Thimayya was particularly conscious of the significance of UN peace-keeping operations and the role of those who serve in them. He was sure that apart from their importance in preventing the tensions and frictions in any particular area from extending into more serious conflagrations, they are simply indispensable for the new order."

Justice Triatafylliades praised "Thimayya's simplicity and quiet confidence, flavoured with kindness and good humour as the hallmarks of his personality." He argued that though he was buried in India, his memory should be inscribed in the hearts of all men of goodwill. He draw a Greek parallel to the worldwide crusade for peace by Thimayya: *Here lies the wrecked seafarer but sail on thou, for while we perish, the other ships sail over the sea.*

T Wainman-Wood, the Canadian high commissioner to India was eloquent when he wrote: "General Thimayya had a great record of service to the UN as many Canadians who served under him have been able to testify. His impressive leadership, calm and efficient ways in which he performed his duties, brought credit to the UN and himself."

Just 18 months and Thimayya's name was on everyone's lips: even in many hearts. An extraordinary human being with outstanding qualities of head and heart, much admired not only in India, but the world over. His early death robbed Cyprus of its adopted son, who, had he lived, would have put it on the road to reconciliation. Perhaps Cyprus was not so fortunate.

The tributes that were showered on him further constitute a brief but true biography of General Thimayya, certainly of his character and competence. Vignettes:

- The Commonwealth Secretary, Mr Bottomley, in a message sent to the British High Commission in Delhi, said, "General Thimayya will be greatly missed in Cyprus where his qualities of impartiality, patience and tact have been invaluable. I would be most grateful if you would arrange for my sincere condolences and those of Her Majesty's Government to be passed to the Government of India and to General Thimayya's family."
- The President, Dr Radhakrishnan expressed his deep distress over the death of General Thimayya. In a message of condolence to Mrs Thimayya, the president said, "I am deeply distressed to hear of the sudden passing away of your illustrious husband. He served with distinction our country and the international world in different capacities. Only the other day at Belgrade airport I met him. He seemed to be in quite good health. Please accept my deepest sympathy in your great bereavement."
- The Chief of the Army Staff, General JN Chaudhuri, said, "In General Thimayya's death we lose an Indian who was a fine soldier, a gay companion and a man who loved his country. He died doing a peace-keeping job for the world as a whole and he will be missed in many spheres."
- The Chief of Air Staff, Air Marshal Arjan Singh in a message to Mrs Thimayya, said, "The news of the sudden death of General Thimayya, has come to us as a great shock and we can well imagine what a tremendous blow it must be to you."
- The Chief of the Naval Staff, Vice Admiral BS Soman, in his message to Mrs Thimayya said, "General Thimayya was a towering personality of our times and his distinguished service for the army, the country and the UN had earned for him love, respect... discipline of a soldier... It is all these qualities as well as his organisational ability, which General Thimayya proved to possess in abundance, which made his task a success."
- On 20 December 1966, the President, Dr S.Radhakrishnan, received a message from Archbishop Makarios, which said, "I wish to express to you and to the government and the people of India the feelings of deep regret felt by everyone in Cyprus on the death of the Commander of UNFICPY, General Thimayya. *A distinguished son of India and a great soldier of peace, his memory will stay always with us and his invaluable services to the cause of peace in Cyprus will be remembered with the deepest gratitude by the people of Cyprus, the Government and myself.*" (Emphasis added.)

Earlier, on 18 December 1965 Makarios' official statement in the Parliament of Cyprus echoed both his personal sentiments and official gratitude, seldom conveyed to any other citizen of India in any capacity thus far. The statement read:

The death of the Commander of the United Nations Peace Keeping Force in Cyprus,

General Thimayya has grieved profoundly the Government and the people of Cyprus. His unexpected death constitutes a grave loss for the United Nations, for his own country and for Cyprus.

General Thimayya combined many virtues and capabilities and distinguished himself as a National Hero of India. Having taken over the command of the International Force in Cyprus, he offered very valuable services to the United Nations efforts to restore and maintain peace in the Island. The work of the Peace-Keeping Force relied to a great extent upon the strong personality of General Thimayya, a personality which radiated sincerity, kindness and goodwill.

The memory of General Thimayya will always be kept alive in Cyprus by a feeling of love and gratitude. General Thimayya fell at the altar of supreme duty, at the altar of the peace of Cyprus, as an apostle of the universal idea which the United Nations expresses.

His name has been linked with the history of Cyprus and his memory will always remain in Cyprus.

In a rare yet befitting overture, the Cyprus government issued a **First Day Cover** and a special commemorating stamp, and named a road, after him.

The Vision

To Cyprus he had left a parting gift: a thought on its future.

Its theme: "*Unified Cyprus Will Foster European Unity.*" The paper contended that Cyprus' unity, though inevitable in the long run, was being fractured by the hostility perpetrated by the two communities. Yet both these communities had every reason to recognise that their future lay in a unified republic. Then alone, the paper argued, would they be accepted into the European Common Market.[14] Included in the requirement were two more: reversion of the Turkish force, and, phasing out of the UNFICYP by an international police force. To ensure that NATO and Warsaw military pact did not interfere with Cyprus' security, he recommended the declaration of the "Mediterranean as a free zone."

The paper was with the secretary general just about the time when the UN body was paying its condolences. Today, Thimayya's vision has proved correct as Greek Cyprus is becoming a member of the European Union; and there can be no doubt that Turkish Cyprus would follow the example, as unified Cyprus.

That, then would vindicate the *coup d'oeuil*, of General Thimayya. *Coup d'oeuil*, the penetrating vision, it is said, is a gift of God. Thimayya had it in abundance. What could be better for a great soldier than to die for the cause of PEACE, still wearing his general's uniform with the UN beret. ∎

NOTES

1. According to Mirelle, Dr Radhakrishnan, said so when General Thimayya met him in Belgrade, a little before his death.
2. The British, by treaty, retained a small enclave in Cyprus. Upon induction of the UNFICYP into the island, it took upon itself to provide logistical support to it, for which it had positioned adequate logistical service units.
3. Alludes to an article in *The National Geographic* of February 1973 by Jonathan Blair entitled "Cyprus Under Four Flags".
4. From UN Papers, *Blue Beret*, 10 July, 1964.
5. In *The Impartial Soldier* by Brigadier Michael Harbottle, p. 52. He replaced Brigadier Yeo. Subsequently, Brigadier Wilson replaced Harbottle, just about a month before General Thimayya's death.
6. Based on the interviews of Lieutenant General D Prem Chand who took over the UNFCYP in 1969. Prem Chand is on record to say that standard operating procedures and instructions framed were in practice even then. "They are monumental," he said.
7. *The Cyprus Mail*, 25 October 1964.
8. *The Blue Beret*, 1 November 1964.
9. *The Impartial Soldier*, p. 58.
10. *The Cyprus Mail*.
11. *The Blue Beret*, 3 November 1965.
12. *The Times of India*, 15 December 1965.
13. Government of India, Ministry of Defence, letter dated 5 July 1968 reads: "I am directed to say that the President has decided that the cause of death viz. high altitude effects of late General KS Thimayya should be regarded as attributable to his military service."
14. A forerunner to the "European Union."

17
The Incomparable Thimayya: The Man of Magic – His Leadership Beyond National Boundaries

General

The great Nigerian novelist Chinua Achebe characterised society's need for three kinds of people. He called them "drummers" "warriors" and "storytellers." "Drummers," Achebe explained, are those who, developing a deep understanding of the past, carry out a realistic appraisal of the present and then drum up enduring causes for the future.

"Warriors" go forth to fight military, political and even social battles for great causes as many times as necessary. They demonstrate the enduring worth of the causes and consequences. The third category, "storytellers" recount the story of great events either verbally or in writing and leave the same for others to read and learn.

Thimayya falls in the second category – of "warriors" who fight battles in war and life because, in their esteemed opinion, war and peace, are bound in an inexplicable cycle.

His life moved with those cycles too. He was one who never ceased to think of war as a whole – someone like Freud, Sir Winston Churchill or Major General JFC Fuller, the analysts who agreed that the activities of human beings and wars are related to cycles of peace and war, both however springing, as Fuller said, from life force.

He saw more in its fundamental cause. "Wars cannot be wished away," he said, "there has always been fear of one another. And so long fear stalks individuals, groups and nations, there will be hatred, there will be violence and wars. As a soldier alone fights, he alone knows how he longs for peace. And if he survives the war about which he should never be squeamish, he must not hesitate to contribute to the cause of peace." This then became the philosophy of life of General Thimayya.[1]

In India, there is no more dramatic example of military leadership than the life of General Thimayya, both in peace and war, and peace-making-cum-peace-keeping.

His great abilities were recognised even by his harshest, and often unjust critic and detractor – Krishna Menon.

He was the quintessence of an ideal soldier – tall, tough, handsome, unflappable. His capacity for simplifying awful, irrating situations and his easy-going way endeared him to all fighting men. So did his wisecracks, uncanny sense of humour, vision, higher intellect and strategic grasp and width of knowledge admired by the intellectuals and the politicians.

Thimayya epitomised rare virtues of valour, chivalry and courage, the best, indeed, of the Kodav traits. A true patriot, who gave patriotism a different definition, through his acts more than words. In all his acts and exhortations to the youth, to the soldiers and to the public, his deep and palpably sincere love of the county would sway everyone.

His imperturbability, broad mental horizons, force of character, anticipation, level-headedness, common sense, and practical knowledge could get the best out of everyone to produce the most magnificent results from situations seemingly impossible to the others.

He had a great dream for India in which he would contribute in all its national security, defence, secularism, and democratic facets. It was to be principally a citizen army and a national army which would, true to its own tradition, be the finest army of the world. In a way, as a soldier, he was a freedom fighter in uniform.

The contribution of Thimayya to India's struggle for independence and its upkeep had been unique. In revolting against the British policy of denying the Indians their due share in higher command and leadership, he was one of the very few who gave a new form to Gandhiji's struggle for freedom. He simply refused to accept the British tradition of relegating the Indian officers to inferior positions.

"Why I can't have a quarter in Fort St. George's?" "Why not be posted as GSO2 (OPS) rather than GSO2 (SD)?" "Why not accept the Indian officers of the Indianised Units as equal and trustworthy?" "Why not I command my brigade?" "Why not split the Punjab Boundary Force (PBF) and let Indian and Pakistani officers handle the refugees?" And so on.

It was this rebellious attitude and occasionally offering to resign his commission that saw the Indianisation given an impetus. So, indeed, was his performance in the war which vindicated that, given an opportunity and treated as equals, Indians, could be better than the best British officers in any field. And he proved that good Indians, like him, could not be shackled under the British rules and regulations. And as opportunities came and luck held up, so tremendous was his image in the eyes of the British at the end of World War II that his superior, Major General G N Wood rated him as "outstanding," "an exceptionally good officer whose personality commands universal respect and liking by all ranks, British, Americans, Chinese, and Indians alike..." General Christison, his corps commander saw him as "the most outstanding Indian officer of the period." It was due to this image that– much to their chagrin –

he was entrusted to command a brigade during the war and as part of the Commonwealth Occupational Force in Japan.

Then sprang the challenges and the teething problems of the vivisected sub-continent: the Partition, the apocalypse of uprooting of the largest disapora of history. At its heel and almost concurrent with this, began the J & K War. Thimayya's role in both the PBF and the war was one of the highest leadership.

He would stretch his patriotic fervour beyond the uniformed gentry.

In the years preceding the Sino-Indian conflict, as the war clouds built up on the horizon, he began to marshal the youth of the country too, quoting Dr Samuel Johnson, "Every man thinks meanly of himself for not having been a soldier." He exhorted them.

"Our country is passing through a period of stress and strain, and we are in dire need of men and women of high quality and leadership. If you wish to serve your country and, at the same time, want an exciting life full of adventure, a life closely connected with human beings of the finest quality, I say join the armed forces." A service in the cause of nation, he would tell them, would also turn them as better citizens.

Youth, its motivation and direction, remained his life-long involvement.

There has been no other better example of a disciplined soldier who upheld the principle of equal justice for the Indian officers vis-à-vis the British while he himself observed absolute fidelity and allegiance to them. No one else had really provided the greater real time 'support' to the new independent nation as did Thimayya.

It does not in any way detract from the great yeoman services Thimayya rendered to the UNO in Korea and Cyprus as Chairman Neutral Nation's Repatriation Commission and Commander UN Force in Cyprus respectively. His objectivity, outstanding ability, devotion to duty, his integrity as a judge, wisdom and shrewdness of a statesman, the veritable Mahatma in uniform he had been acclaimed, the tact of a diplomat, the patience of a peace-maker and the discipline of a soldier, made him not only a distinguished soldier of both war and peace but also an historic person.

Right from the early days, Thimmya was able to lead by example. He would stand up for his principles and convictions while never dithering on his responsibility and obligations. He was heroic, heroically combative and could be romantic and dramatic too.

Imbued with the advantage of good upbringing and education and a tradition of an officer and gentleman, he had built up indomitable courage as an integral part of his character. Brave as a lion, he had the moral courage of Socrates and Rommel to drink his goblet of hemlock for the values he cherished and the principles he enshrined. He, however, had a visceral reaction to bullies. He could not tolerate it when a predator took unfair advantage.

In the mould of a true general, he was always ready to relinquish his office if it compromised his status or demanded subservience to political whims and neglect of his primary responsibility – the defence of the territorial integrity of the country and of those responsible for it. The disregard of his sincere and professional advice by his minister and inference to distrust, led him to sacrifice his authority and resign. It ignited a firestorm which refused to subside, eventually compelling Prime Minister Nehru to plead for his return. And he minced no words. "I'll leave," he would tell Nehru after he said that he hadn't congratulated him for offering to resign. Seen retrospectively and with the advantage of hindsight, his offer of resignation was both stately and dignified. He remained "Thimayya of India."

In Kodagu there is a saying: "Truth has three sides – the truth you say, the truth he says, and the truth itself." The truth was that Thimayya's patriotism and love for the country, his respect for the democratic system the country had adopted, his convictions that soldiers have only one duty – to defend the country, and contribute to the cause of peace – made him as an ideal CHIEF, the best the country could have ever asked for. Unfortunately, the discrepancies of the leaders of that period was too large and the neighbouring countries had, by being militarised, given some unfounded cause for anxiety. It was sad that in counting the trees, the entire forest was forgotten.

Thimayya's Personal Traits

Good, clean working habits had been acquired by him from childhood; these were refined in his school and service. As a sportsman, he had imbibed the best principles sports taught: play fair, play hardest, do not forsake team loyalty and leave the results to the referee, if not to God.

Independence of thoughts and actions were further ingrained in him as he left home when four years old. Out of these grew in him adaptability, a natural way with everyone, including the fair sex, and winning trust and friendship. His love of adventure and ability to take risks gave him physical courage. So blossomed his moral courage and ability to discriminate wrong from right and also to right the wrong.

Prejudice, jealousy and envy never touched Thimayya. "None of them," said General Mohd Azam Khan and Brigadier Khushwaqt-ul-Mulk of the Pakistani Army who had been with him through their regimental service before the Partition told the author, "could affect him – nor the bad Indo-Pak relations, nor the wars continuously being fought and the politicians fouling them." "He was respected in Pakistan as much as in India or elsewhere," they said in a tribute. Absence of malice, prejudice and vengeance plausibly arose in him from his basic conviction that "let defeat be attributed to me and success accredited to all others."

There were some traits that are essential to understand him as a man, a commander and a leader. Like a good Kodav, he was both bland and blunt, a straight-talking man of action. His background of schooling under missionaries, his education and service under the British right from the PWRIMC, Sandhurst days and commissioned service in various capacities, made him a happy blend of the East and the West. The British, he saw as both just and wavering but always as the ones "compromise against whom could be fatal." One had to stand up to them to acquire what was legitimate. On several occasions, he would go to the extent of offering to resign his commission. He believed that the British could be both just and uncompromising but because they had been empire builders, and possessed something of everything, good could be emulated from them. But he could never be subservient to them, highsoever high.

He could be **controversial** too, depending upon the decisions he took, the statements he made, the plans he followed, and the successes his genius achieved. It was part of his make-up. But it never rattled him. His priceless qualities of truth, honesty and resilience saw him encounter the situations which made lesser souls flee from the ring.

The **thoroughness and immaculate preparation** that he made for events, small and large, were legendary. Upon being given a task or being convinced of its need, he would labour and try hard to plan the events with operational precision and prepare for every conceivable contingency. His genius lay in conceiving a plan or a number of plans for every event with meticulous personal attention to details. It was so in preparing for Sandhurst, or making his Jats-Ahirs and Kumaonis play hockey against the champion Sikhs, or operational plans for war and his handling the 'non-repatriated' prisoners of the Korean War and finally keeping peace in Cyprus.

But because he believed in the principle that "every plan gets changed at the first contact with the enemy," flexibility became his second nature. He was always, not only anticipating but thinking: what next? "Think what would you do if you were on the other side," he would indefatigably quiz and harry his advisers and then having heard everyone, evolve a plan that would have basically his stamp of boldness. Creativity and innovation were equally strong with him. For himself, he would be sublime. "I have no inborn genius," he would say, "except hammering hard during the preparations." Whether it was the attack against the Japanese strongholds or the attack at Zoji La, or rescuing a damsel in distress in Iraq or saving millions from the 1947 apocalypse of the Partition, or the defence of the northern border, every act had Thimayya's stamp of study, planning and coordination.

To him there was no substitute of genius with hard work, meticulous planning and bold execution.

The *coup d'oeuil*, a penetrating vision is said to be a gift of God to a man. It was certainly so with him. "I can anticipate things well in advance, I can read a coming storm from nature and man. While God's role in it is not known to me, my professional knowledge and continuous search for it has been helping me see things with some degree of perfection. Consequently, I could, more often than not, see things through the fog – both of war and conflicts."

"So you see," he would quip, "one needs both God's gift and good training for what Napolean called *coup d'oeuil*. Then only, can one seize opportunities, the outcome of which becomes decisive." Out of this arose his ability to pick relevant facts from the general confusion of war and peace. So did his great ability to read the mind of his opponents.

Although Thimmya never claimed to be a historian, less still an intellectual, he had developed a historic imagination about every problem he faced. From the beginning, he had realised that history was responsible for the nuances in British behaviour in England and India, the traits they had developed and the way Indians needed to conduct themselves. Similarly, for the Kashmir, Korean or Cyprus problems. Assiduously studying them beforehand he would handle those problems dexterously. "Every man has a history, every tribe has it," he would say so and apply his knowledge to the Naga problem and the Chinese belligerency.

Complicated plans never appealed to him. "Simplicity is the heart and art of winning a battle," he said and would qualify it, "even in winning over a girl and in foxing the enemy. In both cases, do what they don't expect."

Lecturing once on common sense and principles of war, he argued : "Common sense, simply common sense, it comes instinctively to a properly trained soldier. And if he combines some rudiments which we have formalised as 'principles of war,' for example, in all his plans, he would know how to successfully react to various situations."

Risk-taking, like any bold risk-taker was a dominant trait of Thimayya. Indeed, boldness was in his blood and psyche. He had evolved his own method of evaluating the risk, based on the 'pros and the cons' of the risk. But when both weighed equal, he preferred action to inertia and *status quo*. "Act when in doubt," was his maxim, "and be prepared to face the consequence of a reverse even if a reverse is forced upon you." He did this by clearing the Japanese position under whose dominance he found his battalion stretched – shelled and demoralised, and possibly breaking down.

"The Japanese superman bogey," he told General Christison, his corps commander after capturing the dominating feature as his first action in the Arakans, "needed to be smashed. And my boys have done it." So would he say, "If the Germans had done *blitzkrieg* in Europe in better terrain, I needed to attempt it here (Zoji La)." Had he remained the COAS, and been given the freedom to put his own designs to practice while fighting the Chinese in 1962, the world would have seen another *blitz* and a better example to fight the invading enemy by employing to the maximum his strategy of dissuasion.

The risk boldly taken luckily invariably succeeded in his endeavours. Boldness, risk-taking propensity combined with luck saw great successes in his bigger battles of life, where he faced the impending adversities squarely. He truly epitomised what Field Marshal A P Wavell believed: "A bold general can be lucky but no general can be lucky unless he is bold."

Thimayya had remarkable **intuitive capacity** that helped him read the reaction and responses of others to a particular circumstance or developing circumstances.

Always invariably he could accurately gauge them. So anticipation of future developments always saw him better prepared to foresee situations that also became responsible for yet another great quality of his **imperturbability**, the *sangfroid*.

This great quality of remaining **cool in crises** permeated an ambience of confidence among his compatriots, superiors and subordinates. "Nothing could rattle him," was the observation of those who served with him in war, the Quetta earthquake, the problem of the PBF or later situations. Cool, calm and collected, he would radiate similar moods among those involved in the task.

Decisiveness was Thimayya's great trait. Most of his decisions were well argued, discussed, brain-stormed and even tested in mock-battles. At every opportunity, he would examine his 'plan from all angles, specially the opponents', and adopt it only on considering all factors that the circumstances favoured. His appreciations were thorough, the plans that he decided to adopt, simple and flexible. Rarely would he change his decision. A man of swift resolve who, having taken a comprehensive view of the situation, would pick and follow key result areas.

His **communication skill**, acquired through hard studies and reflections and preparations, were as legendary as those of the best military commanders. His correctness of diction, the rhythm in thought, rhetorical subtlety, made his addresses elegant and his writings direct, concise and ornate. Even his jabs and jests and countless puns, were well thought out. Thimayya was a born *raconteur* with great eloquence and a genius for keeping people spellbound. He would speak extemporaneously but never lose track of the 'issues in hand' or the points he wished to 'nail down.'

He spoke, without exception, what he thought what was necessary to speak, although always frugal and balanced with his words.

Quoting Winston Churchill, he would say, "Of all the talents bestowed upon men, none is so precious as the gift of oratory." One may be betrayed by friends, stripped of one's offices but whoever can command this power, remains still formidable." He would advise all to master this art. "You will be heard," he would add, "provided you speak well."

Both **wit and humour** remained his great strength, personally and for those who formed his audience. "The members of my Neutral Nations' Repatriation Commission, NNRC," he would say, "held the Democles sword over me." On another occasion, almost at the end of life, where addressing the Swedish troupe "Flickery's Flies," that entertained the UN troops in Cyprus, he told the pretty sixteen-year-old Eva Osterberg, "If you stay here long, I'll have a *coup* at Nicosia." He would be as charming with a 77-year-old lady! A man of singular joyness, after all.

Because he was always frank and fair, he expected people to reciprocate similarly. He would often err on that account. "His candidness and often humour," wrote a friend, Tara Ali Baig, "often was misunderstood and misconstrued. But that did not bother him in the least." No **maelstrom**, however sudden and powerful, could sweep him off his feet. In fact, he was loved for this grand fault of his. He could not be faulted even for his romantic and boyish platitudes, either.

Because he was free with the fair sex – he shared in a way his predilection for the fair sex with Nelson, Napoleon and Caesar – it could, on occasions, invite adverse comments from his contemporaries, especially the detractrs. There was in him no repression of sex, which often characterises the arch authoritarians and sexually deranged such as Hitler; or for that matter, VK Krishna Menon. Often ladies became the butt of his humour. There arose a scandal once when some parliamentarians, reading a report from a paper, said that Timmy had driven a lady over a 'restricted road.' It got over as he sent his explanation. But in one of the messes when an officer asked him about it, the reply he gave brought the roof down, "But to think my intention in driving her in the calm of the night was to show her the road is an insult to my manhood." These puns were to defuse tension and make others appreciate the value of laughter.

When in the wake of the Chinese continuous expansion in Ladakh and intrusion into NEFA, IB Director, Mullik began to press the army into the so-called "Forward Policy," he told him: "Military tasks are best left to me as I wouldn't like to take on your spying, snooping and sniffing networks. No, Mr Mullik."

His **frankness** was ever pervading. When one morning, Panditji sent for him in his office, he thought he must be wanting his views on the Chinese intrusion. Nehru surprised him, however, by saying that he should not be seen at public places late at night. Timmy asked him what specifically he had in mind, as he often did attend late night parties, when invited. Obviously, tutored by the intelligence, the PM had been told that Timmy had been dancing in the Ashoka Hotel till 3 a.m, that morning.

Thimayya thought for a minute and told Panditji: "I think our spy system is working well but it would be nice if our boys had reliable intelligence on our enemies too." He also humourously added, "Panditji, isn't it better to be enjoying late parties than planning a coup in the middle of the night!" Panditji laughed it off then but the thought lingered on, especially as events in neighbourhood had been frighteningly true! Both Burma and Pakistan were under military rulers.

Managing stress was his panacea to 'recharge' the system. His social 'beat ups,' forays into golf, polo, yachting and even dancing kept him fit and thinking.

He had seen a man like General Davies cave in under stress during the war. He had no desire to be a dead man before the war and ensured that rest, relaxation and recreation followed hard work and strenuous situations for himself and those under him. He would do that during the war or between the phases of a campaign – whether it was after the battle of *chhaungs* at Kangaw or operations of Sri Div. He would follow this panacea during the stressful days as chairman NNRC and as COAS.

A remarkable man, friendly and very correct, he was the life and soul of any organisation including the social ones. All his life Thimayya had developed a carefree attitude – both to life and death. But above all, he developed a philosophic attitude to criticism, both official and from the media. He accepted what he called the official 'raps' with *sangfroid*. Because, in terms of fame, he was virtually level with the best of leaders and newsworthy celebrities, he took pains to keep the needs of the media in mind. In most of the cases, the tensions generated even by his political superiors were transitory.

Lead by example, was his motto. It was always a character-based leadership combining and exuding honesty, courage and integrity. To him, image did not matter but character did.

"Character, besides luck," he would say, "is the bed-rock of soldiery." "Characterless people can never be true soldier and leaders," was his firm conviction. Out of his courage emerged the best in him which acted invariably to save a situation from defeat or destruction. His heroic roles in the Quetta earthquake; his deft handling of a few mutinies; his first and most audacious action to capture the Japanese positions, overlooking his defence and subsequent operation including the Kangaw; his employment of tanks at Zoji La and landing at Leh, his one-man mission into Pakistan to save the people of Sheikpura and so on, could serve many benchmarks of "Lead by Example."

His leadership was, therefore, synonymous with inspiring confidence borne out of results. In all these, he had proved to be a man of character, intelligence, with an inexhaustible reservoir of moral courage and resiliency.

A man with an impeccable military and civil background, Thimayya was a hero *par exellence*. "His personal qualities," wrote Brigadier J P Dalvi (in *The Himalayan Blunder*) "matched his military talents and experience. As a commander, he had magic touch with both officers and men." Dalvi recalls that in his long service, he never heard an ill-word spoken against him or heard of an unwise military decision attributed to him. " This," he assessed," is the highest tribute and praise that can be paid to an officer, a gallant gentleman and an outstanding soldier."

The secret behind this image was the great art he had mastered: Thimayya's unceasing **cultivating of human resources**, humanity through his uncommon warmth and human understanding. He saw that human frailty was as natural but also each individual was a reservoir of unfathomed source of energy and strength. "Treat every man well and you can tap all the best from him," were his golden words. He would often repeat Emerson's golden words too: "Trust men and they will be true to you; Treat them greatly, and they will show themselves great."

He could be both **humane and disciplinarian** in caring for his army. Of the two, he preferred humane treatment over punishment, care over pampering, warmth over authoritarianism. An open mind, quick to receive and disseminate new ideas, innovation, especially in tactics and technology, motivated his command. While he believed in pre-reconnoitring before committing the troops, leaving nothing to chance, he picked officers and men for their efficiency and determination for special tasks. Far from being a 'butcher' a 'yes man,' he repeatedly refused to commit his troops for voluntary sacrifices. "There will be forward deployment against the Chinese in keeping with tactical requirements and logistical build up. But I am afraid I cannot agree to this Quixotic Forward Policy," he told the government. To safeguard against such blundering march of folly, he offered to resign. He was not prepared to commit that cardinal sin of many generals who underestimate their enemies to later repent all their lives.

Personally, he was both loved and feared, envied and begrudged like an honest man of reputation. In fact, without exhorting support from his soldiers and officers, he got it; without inviting their appreciation, he gained it; and, without demanding their trust, he won it.

So endearing were his ways that even the common people could see greatness of a legend in the making in him. He was accepted as a living legend by most, including Serbjeet Singh or Captain (later Lieutenant General) E.Vas, General Shankar Roychowdhury, a one time Army Chief of Staff and now an Hon'ble member of Parliament, would deify him as "The INCOMPARABLE."[2]

Lieutenant General (then Brigadier) Harbakhsh recalled his exceptional opportunity of studying General Thimayya not only as a soldier on the battlefield in J & K, but also in peace-time as his principal staff officer, when he was Army Commander, Western Command. "I was able to see him both as a military leader as well as a man; in his official dealings, he would not let his personal interests or prejudices weigh with him. Yet whether in office or outside, he was always relaxed, joyous, friendly and freely exuding goodwill and bonhomie. People were fond of him as a man."

In the opinion of General K V Krishna Rao, General Thimayya was "India's best field commander who left an indelible imprint on the country."

"A proven soldier in the battlefield, his grasp of warfare was intuitive," remarked General Bhagat. "His handling of men," he said, "was characteristic of his personality – bold, imaginative, sympathetic and loyal. No general could have had a more loyal army, and no army a more loyal general."

Among the officers, VCOs (JCOs) and men of Thimayya's time, stories would be built up in a fashion that, say, entwined Rommel during his African Campaign. It was 'Ram Lal,' 'Ram Lal' with the Indian soldiers. There were long and short stories of Thimayya or 'Timmy Sahib.' To his men of the Hyderabad (Hybd) Regiment, his Gorkhas in Japan, his cadets of the NDA, his officers who served with him in various capacities, the civilians and everyone lucky to have been associated with him, his wit, humour, sincerity and concern for others were immense.

He had time for everything that human life and its challenges could offer. Colonel B B Moitra, an officer who had a long innings in the Defence Headquarters from the dawn of independence as a public relations officer has distinct memories of the "Thimayya couple." He says: "While General Thimayya was, indeed, the beacon, guide and philosopher of the armed forces, Mrs Thimayya spared no effort to help him look after the welfare and cultural needs of the army. She played a prominent role in improving welfare of families, and their children. General Thimayya also encouraged Housing Societies for serving and ex-servicemen, Army Officers' Dramatic Societies, adventure, sports and educational activities."

"There was no limit to General Thimayya and Mrs Thimayya's joint cooperation," he recalled. "You name anything and they were there, and they left their enduring imprints."

The way he encouraged a talented and determined creative young man, Serbjeet, an evacuee from Pakistan, struggling to pick up the threads of his life anew, is by itself the basic theme of Serbjeet's coffee table book *Zoji La: 1 November 1948.* "I have been posted to Srinagar," he told Serbjeet, "Now there is no problem to your making a war film on the Kashmir War."

And interestingly, he is perhaps the only one whose biography was written, like Nepoleon's, while he served. He is also one of the very few and distinguished people whose grave has been shifted. Unique honours both in life and death have been his share.

Major J Nazareth, having fallen foul of Major General Kaul, had been rescued by him. "The various confidential reports on me were not allowed to stand against my record and General Thimayya as Army Chief ordered them to be expunged; the only case where a junior officer was vindicated against two seniors and that too voluntarily," he wrote.

There were several such cases of 'vendetta,' which he would squash, or advise his PSOs to be more humane in dealing with erring youngsters whose cheques bounced, whose marriages floundered and who were wrongly booked. "Damn it 'P' (as he called, Kumaramangalam, the AG), don't be so harsh to ignore their contribution in war," he would simply rebuke. "Haven't we ourselves been naughty?" would be his last sentence on cases recommended to be 'cashiered,' 'dismissed' or 'monetarily penalised.' He would suggest that punishment be humanised. Many remained grateful to him. But that in no way meant showing laxity to the inefficient and the corrupt.

Thimayya's objective was to see that his officers and men served the country with their sacrifices but they themselves were not denied dignity and *izzat*. It was a recognised fact in the army that General Thimayya always set a high example of courage and steadfastness under most dangerous conditions in the battlefield and that was why he was so loved and respected by all ranks under his command. He was a born leader, he had continuously won the confidence of his subordinates through forthrightness, a practical and even-handed approach to both seniors and juniors. He was a hero to all.

Thimayya's greatest quality was that he never claimed for himself credit for success, but gave to his subordinates. Their failures, however, he attributed to his own planning failure or the hazards of war, unless there was downright lack of enthusiasm or cowardice. He was prepared to give a second chance and even a third as he did to Atal at Zoji La. He was after all practising his principle of 'accepting upon himself defeats and disappointments and while offering others, victory.' 'Passing the buck' was not to his liking, nor was the finding of the proverbial sacrificial goat.

And when thousands of ECOs of World War II and the J&K War were being asked to leave prematurely for not clearing their promotion examinations, he had them coached and passed – and confimed 'permanent.' "There is no better test for a soldier than doing his job well in war and they all have been good soldiers," he would say, asking military officers not to be bureaucrats! General Thimayya remained a custodian of the inherent honour of the army. But there could be no compromise on efficiency, devotion, loyalty and the overall performance of duty. Nor would he take kindly to people harming the cohesiveness and traditions of the army.

So, sharing credit, accepting his subordinates' mistakes as his own failings made him 'our Timmy Sahib'; yet while he was generous to others, he did not spare himself self-criticism.

"I failed," he would admit, "in rescuing the garrison from Skardu."

"It is impossible," his message conveyed, "to deceive the garrison any longer on false hopes of maintenance and relief." He asked permission for its "withdrawal or surrender." He would also admit that mistakes were made in Korea, and by resigning, had he not committed a blunder, and so on. But he would not hesitate to repeat Winston Churchill's famous line, "We must learn from misfortunes, (as) the means of future strength." Truthfulness was his habit and it was ingrained in him, not like that of the fabled Yudhistar of the *Mahabharat* but like the mythical Raja Harish Chandra. It gave him a raised moral high ground, higher than any one else's.

Thimayya's human relationship was, thus, the epitome of his great popularity and acceptance among the people. By nature generous and forgiving, it was inconceivable for him to think ill of anyone nor anyone inimical to him, although professional jealousy, if not that worm called envy, could never be ruled out. But Thimayya had no place for either prejudices or discrimination.

It was perhaps Colonel C L (Larry) Proudfoot who had served with Thimayya as a captain, public relations officer in Sri Div, who caught the true sprit of Timmy: "General Thimayya, the great 'Timmy,' was the one who did not 'lose the common touch,' as COAS. He was one of those special people who, even when he rose to be C-in-C, was the same simple person who made every soldier instinctively think of him as a friend, exuding kindness and consideration which in turn inspire, affection and confidence. It has been the treasured privilege of our family to have shared Timmy's friendship."

He recalled how in Mhow where he was posted as an instructor, Timmy as COAS, after a game of golf, would "take off his shoes and play with the kids on the carpet, as they clambered all over him."

In the club, Timmy would either be conducting the band or dancing till 5 a.m.

when after breakfast, he would thank the staff, tip them generously, before rushing to his room to change, and be inspecting the school under Brigadier Pat Dunn.

Sharing credit with others, being liberal in praise, restrained in condemnation and criticism were, indeed, his great attributes.

Tact, grace and *savoir-faire* were other outstanding traits of Thimayya. He used them not only as an art to bring back men from mutinies and revolts but to save situations moving to a collapse. A magical touch, he really had.

If tact gave him a magician's wand, his kindness, magnanimity and gratitude gave him the real Midas' golden touch. For he was most forgiving even to his enemies and detractors. He would attribute their failings to human frailty and say that they would some day realise the futility of their behaviour and acts.

He would even handle some of the new breed of Parliamentarians who, during their political life during the Raj, cursed the Indian Army as "real impediment" to their forcing the British leave India in the 1930s. Tabling various motions in the Parliament for not only reducing the army's strength but cutting down basic amenities like accommodation, rum ration, travel concessions, etc they would boast and say that they would tame this army. So when a team of these people were sent to Zoji La and Leh in the thick of operations in November 1948, no such questions were ever asked, thereafter. Thimayya saw that they spent a night at Matayan shivering, with their bone marrow frozen, sharing the frozen *chapathis* and wet tents with the soldiers. The same people would then 'fight' for better facilities to their 'dear soldiers.'

When that news reached Cariappa, he asked, "What did you do, Timmy?"

"Oh, the normal exposure, Sir."

Religion to Thimayya was a religion of mankind related to the basic human values, namely, sense of caring, sense of responsibility and sense of forgiveness. Without adopting the religiousity of his religion, he was a *Karamayogi* who, without allusion to the teachings of the scriptures, believed in total surrender to the dictates of Almighty God. He would say: "I never sat before the deity but I always have her in my heart." He would humanise his faith further by saying: "In my heart were also always the men who fought along with me, who lost their lives and limbs, yet never complained."

A practical dose of spiritualism had became part of his life. In fulfilling his mission of life, about which he had clear concepts, he realised that God may have had larger designs for him. " So long as I can do my duty, my conscience is clear," he would say. So nothing else mattered in fulfilling the duty God ordained and the light He (or She) gave him.

"I shall pass through this world only once," he would often recant and, "any good I can do, let me do now." That was what he would recall, those ascetic Irish brothers at his school at Coonoor had told him, although they treated others like robots. Those great words sunk deep in a young mind. So would the fable of Jesus Christ, asking the 'idealists' stoning an idolatrous woman, "Search your hearts and see how clean you yourself are."

Although in later life he became an ardent devotee of God, the Kodav deities and his ancestors, out of frustration, he would wonder about the ways "God's mankind moved." In one of his letters to his father after PBF, he questioned the so-called "ubiquitous benevolent design of the deity,' in a world full of pain, death, and disease. He had been witness to, he said, too much misery in Burma but equally in the PBF. He saw the trauma and agony in the hearts of the non-repats in Hindnagar, Korea. He had seen the emaciated skeletons of prisoners held by the Japanese. Cyprus was as bad as happenings on the LAC in J & K.

He was certain that all wars broke out not as a result of the folly of the men in uniform but those in civvies, who 'romanticise' war and who 'politicise' the armed forces. These people are too dangerous a species to be trusted with the vital business of war as are incompetent generals, admirals and marshals. And again, "Shouldn't the civilians be civilising the society rather than militarising it? I found most of these types showing cloven feet."

"A soldier,(therefore) has a greater responsibility to society," he believed, "than ever before in history and his duty is to learn to carry responsibility as well ... by being a citizen beyond narrow attachment of class and province and above the passions of political conflict." Personally, he would explain time and again that while being a soldier, he was not squeamish about war, like most famous soldiers, he could never love it either.

Benchmarks of Indomitability
National Security Concerns

Strategic vision and tactical excellence were the two formidable Thimayya traits. His tactical plans, although simple, were based on ingenuity, surprise and deception and bold execution. They always succeeded. So was his strategic concept of, say, "dissuasive strategy."

To him, strategy was balancing acts of war and peace, weighing up fully the probable enemy capability and ideological, political intentions, vis-à-vis own. "Read the indications that the enemy gives very carefully to figure out his intentions and if his intentions are hostile and yours are weak, he'll strike. But you strike him equally powerfully at a place of your choosing. Make him recoil. And further, strategy must combine diplomacy but diplomacy by itself is a poor man's wife, at whom every passerby looks."

His moral courage-courage to do a thing right, and stand for his convictions – was indeed, legendary. Take, for example, the case of NNRC. "By the nature of his assignment," as General Maxwell Taylor observed, "Thimayya was constantly in the contentious cross-fire between the communist and the UN representatives."[1] He saw him, "keep his temper and equanimity, displaying such sound judgement and impartiality in his decisions that they were rarely susceptible to challenge." That is what earned him great success and tribute to his skill as an intermediary between the hostile forces, in conflict in Korea for over three years. Nothing could move him from his principled straight path, not even his own government with sympathy for the Chinese Communists and the leftist proclivities of people like Menon.

As Chairman of NNRC, his statesmanship was recognised, besides India being honoured. And some people were comparing him with Mahatma Gandhi in uniform and the Nobel Laureate Ralph Bunche.

Take another example – the main threat developed from the Chinese from the mid-1950s, despite the blind faith being shown by the political leadership that it was cartographic aggression, and a bluff and did nothing to violate the mutual principles of *Panch Sheel* and *Hindi-Chini Bhai-Bhai*. However, the Chinese saw in it a situation to affirm their plan of expansion and illegal occupation of Indian territory.

Thimayya conveyed in unambiguous terms that "leaders responsible for strategic plans and execution cannot be surrounded by staff that blindly agree to everything they say. Instead, those who speak truth with courage are more loyal than these 'yes' men." That was his definition of loyalty.

Militarily, therefore, he had advocated a strategy of dissuasion – against both Pakistan and China. Against China, with its advantages of better preparations, large force level, and a more determined political leadership, he recommended to the government to contain it diplomatically. But he sought an accelerated military take-over of the border and adoption of a graduated defence plan, integration of all forces manning the border under one head and rationalisation of the command and control. It is a travesty of facts that his efforts in this regard are fallaciously equated with surrendering military initiatives in favour of the diplomatic. This factual error, copied enough times, to paraphrase historian APJ Taylor, tends to compromise the truth.

In asking the government to the follow this strategy he was *ipso-facto* weighing over-cautiousness against Quixotic over-reactions being propagated by the non-professionals. He was also fighting against the politicisation of the army. After he left, failure to follow his advice exacted a terrible cost through the brinkmanship of those at the helm of affairs. For, this then brazenly exposed the incompetence of Menon's generals and they had to be sacked. So was Menon publicity castigated. The fiasco was so great that Nehru never recovered. All this could, in fact, be predicted by very knowledgeable people. General Thorat, for example, told Eric Vas in 1961 that the military regime led by Thapar and Kaul would collapse like a "pack of card!" And by the time the Chinese opponents came up, their full-fledged offensive, Menon's was the story of corpse pretending to be the coroner.

There were frustrating periods when his minister refused to view the Chinese threat as a threat to national security and failed to see the need to prepare the armed forces for adequate deterrence. He demitted his office as an unhappy chief. But national security remained his great concern, as indeed, it should be so of every officer who reaches that status. In October 1962, while Chinese had invaded NEFA and

Ladakh, he told Nehru to replace Kaul by Sen or Harbakhsh, and use commandos and air if the Chinese advance was to be stemmed and stopped.

So he never gave up the crusade, not only to warn the government but to advise as late as June 1962, to follow the correct strategy and avoid the path of national disaster through brinkmanship. They paid no heed and suffered. His article, "Adequate Insurance" in *Seminar*, if perused in the spirit, would have helped.

Even when the Chinese invaded in October, he advised the PM to "employ air force in the offensive role rather than keep it on the tarmac" and hit the Chinese hard as they lengthened their lines of communications. The hesitancy and incompetence of those elevated to the levels of strategists and leaders, led to a humiliating defeat. But ignoring the paranoia of some people, he happily joined the National Defence Council where he helped evolve national strategy for security in the 1960s.

These future events showed Thimayya unsurpassed in strategic wisdom and professional sense; all those who libelled such insinuations as being "defeatist" and "stumbling block" to the 'Forward Policy' and so on, against him, obviously had ulterior motives. Or, they failed to comprehend the reality.

When everything went awry, he was painfully forthright as he told a group of scribes: *"The government should know, we have sustained a defeat without fighting a full war. We have lost our image without fighting and we have reduced our army to ridicule for no other reason but failing to listen to our pleadings and advice. The gross neglect and deficiencies of our defence forces have caused all these. I had told them that the Indian Army needed everything except courage but courage too had its limits."*

Playing calculated risks and sticking to phlegmatism, were, in fact ,Thimayya's bold traits. What he was advocating during his tenure was not only to be vindicated by the 1962 debate, but the underlying lesson of the humiliation was that India could no longer defer hard decisions. Mildly put, the "White Paper" of 1963-64, in vindication of his views, said, *"The massive unprovoked attack by China in 1962 brought into focus the grave threat to the security of the country... our ideas of overall stategy as well as the requirements of weapons and equipment had to be reoriented. The questions of acclimatisation of our troops to function efficiently demanded immediate attention."*[1]

This is what Thimayya has been pleading and fighting for.

So was he pleading for adequate defence expenditure, which would jump in 1963-64 to Rs 3,188 crore from the earlier Rs 300 crore and even of 1962's Rs 1686 crore. And it was now Thimayya's turn to tell the government, "Before the Chinese attack whenever we went to the Government to change and improve the defence forces, everyone asked why? Tomorrow it will be, please do it as you like but do it please."

Menon's relationship with the service chiefs threw up difficulties that were incredulous, to say the least. But he did not seriously think of resigning again. A letter that General Taylor wrote on his demise tacitly speaks of it. As chief of staff, he remarked, both he and Thimayya held "analogous positions."

"We were able to compare notes regarding the difficulties of chief of staff," he wrote mildly, "to chuckle over our common experiences in defending military budgets before civil authority. *I recall that both of us agreed that there must be better ways of earning a living than being chief of staff, but then, we confessed that neither of us was inclined to give up his job."*

More than Taylor's assertion, Thimayya's role in tackling the implausible was wrought with manifold difficulties: he had a megalomaniac minister to handle who thought the enemy was neither on the 'west' nor on the 'north' but his own chiefs – prominently, General Thimayya.

During his service itself, he had hoped that the storm would build up without more warnings and then hesitancy and distrust would be replaced by a national will to face the challenge. Realisation would then dawn and everything would be all right. He had been witness to the raising of larger storms of World War II and how complacency had resulted in reverses and humiliations.

It was Emil Ludwig, who, while commenting on Napoleon's place as a politician-cum-statesman had said, "It is the political genius that makes a military commander supreme." Even smaller souls had opinion on it. "The relationship of the service chiefs with the political authorities," so said a one time Defence Secretary, KVR Rao, " the standing capability and the reputation of the service chiefs, within and outside the service, all come into play and influence the outcome."[5] Similar views have been conveyed by General P S Bhagat, VC. The question remains, could Thimayya have handled Menon more prudently?

The relationship between General Thimayya and Mr Menon, to begin with, was said to have been excellent, until they clashed on several grounds: the perspective of threat and the need to enlarge and strengthen the armed forces; to delink Menon's long-term indigenisation programme from immediate requirements of arms and equipment to give some semblance of modernisation to an obsolescent force; to let the army take over its border management and rationalise the entire gamut of security under one head, principally under the army; to immediately develop the logistics and infrastructures for the northern border *et al*. Among the 'etcetra' also included pleading to maintain the tradition and ethos of the services by not injecting favouritism and politics. Menon, rejected one by one, his all pleadings and entreaties. It was only then that Thimayya and the other chiefs – driven to a corner – decided to offer their resignations. And, hence, a bad relationship.

Many critics of that time forget that the basic problem lay with Menon. Devoid of expertise and too full of egoism to accept advice, in the name of upholding the civil authority over the services, he fouled the entire working culture, destroyed trust and faith – the bedrocks of the military. In the bargain, what could have been the golden period of Indian defence was turned inglorious. The authoritarian and intolerant Menon carried such an awful 'chip on his shoulder' that rather than leading this excellent team to fight the Chinese, he tried to break it and particularly Thimayya, by initially hinting at, and poisoning Nehru and diffusing stories of a 'probable' *coup d'etat* by him. Several authentic sources have been quoted in support of this grandiose canard, but more specifically, D R Mankekar also refers to it at pp. 128-130 of his work, *Guilty Men of 1962*. More potently, this fear psychosis is evident from the letter Nehru wrote to Bertrand Russell after the Chinese invasion, alluding to the "danger of military mentality spreading" in India. It clearly showed how the ghost of coup haunted the government of the day, ignoring the national security imperatives.

"There was wild imaginative speculation," wrote Harbakhsh to the author, "of a political future for General Timmy. (But) his loyalty for his leaders and India gave no room for thoughts of such ambitions in his mind." Fortunately, Thimayya's reputation remained intact, although he suffered the anguish in his heart. The biggest sufferer, however, was the country and its armed forces, albeit, upon realisation of this 'Himalayan blunder,' things improved. Nevertheless, what could have been the great unifying moments had been turned into divisive ones. It was a difficult battle to convince the unconvincing politicians but during his own time, he maintained some sanity through his advice.

A Visionary

Thimayya, as often said, believed in a 'thing called luck.' "I don't know what fate had destined for me but luck has been with me even in the worst days," he repeatedly said. It was with this great optimism but not fatalism, that he had developed a positive personality, magnanimity, sociability and a crusade like mission to every task that came his way. Out of this also arose his visions of a new India, a new reorganised army, a new breed of youth and politicians, his actions in war and peace.

After the war in J&K, like a good soldier, he longed to see peace between Pakistan and India as the two 'separated brothers.' So were his views on the futility of the superpowers bid to have an NNRC to solve their 'irreconcilable' problems.

But the NNRC proved that while neither side could be judged right or wrong on the non-repat issue, the "issue itself need not and should not have arisen." He had, in the words of Henry Evans, graduated to a professional status to appreciate the complexity of the ideological conflicts. It was obvious that the general was deeply convinced of the value of neutrality which has great value for the soldiers and politicians alike, more so the latter who bring about these "senseless wars." He went one step further: "If a world holocaust is to be avoided, each side must begin with the determination to maintain the integrity of its own values. If that were done, much of the bloodshed in and out of the battlefield could surely be avoided."

He heard a lot of criticism of the UN peace-keeping and peace-making operations from even those who contributed little or nothing to its upkeep but who were benefitted the most. His advice to them all – those who had turned UN as their own preserve or catalytic agent for policies – was most forthright. "The UN," he said in October 1965, "is a mirror that reflects the world society in its present form and

The Thimayya Gate at RIMC Dehra Dun

shape. If one is not entirely pleased by one what sees, the answer is not to blame the mirror, much less to break it, but rather improve the image it reflects."

To the superpowers, his advice was to go beyond the 'barricades' of the Berlin Wall, the 38th Parallel or their self-destroying strategy of Mutually Assured Destruction (MAD). Had Thimayya been alive, he would seen the end of the Cold War, dramatic reunification of the two Germanys besides sincere efforts at the reunification of the Koreas.

In Cyprus, to whose "history and memory he has been linked," he was offering leadership beyond the 'Green Line' by pursuing the concept of a 'unified Cyprus essential for European unity.' His premature death snatched away a great opportunity of an early settlement of the Cyprus problem. Nonetheless, Cyprus split on ethnic lines since 1974 when Turkish forces invaded the Island in response to a Greek-inspired coup, now seems to be seriously planning a settlement. Initiated in the January 2002, the UN special envoy Alvaro De Soto , managed to get the two rival leaders, Cyprus President Glafcos Clerides and Turkish Cypriot leader Rauf Denktash, to begin negotiations. It is quite possible that a reunification would be achieved as Cyprus joins the European Union by 2004-2005.

For the Indian Army, which was one of the dearest things for him, his vision had been sufficiently highlighted as Sri Div commander. Way back in 1959, his vision was one of a self-reliant, modern force that was to be built up to act as deterrence and counter-poise to the twin threats that had begun to seriously challenge India. Even then he had visualised :

It would be ideal for us to have a number of specialist or tailor-made divisions/formations, but we cannot have them as this is an expensive way of running our Army, and, therefore, we must organise ourselves on a general purpose organisation, which at the same time is flexible for adoption for every type of fighting. The Army, therefore, has to be trained for all types of warfare and they must be trained to use every type of weapon. In the deserts, we want fast moving units trained to function in small contact teams with hard-hitting weapons but not too heavy. In the cultivated regions, we need a normal organisation with plenty of armour and river crossing facilities, with medium and heavy artillery. In the mountains, tough infantry with lots of automatic fire, mortars and mountain guns. In the jungles, small compact parties with plenty of automatics and good means of logistical support.

His genius had undoubtedly been at work in Kashmir in several ways but there was something more important that he wrote: "We have been experimenting with several manoeuvres, tactics and techniques, besides strategy in J & K; some succeeded, some failed, although overall with the resources and the political constraints, we have the satisfaction of doing well. We could have done better, had we followed our operations with better resources," and he continued:

The obvious lessons of these are two: one, we as senior officers now responsible for strategy, must change further by exposing ourselves to the best of the strategic thoughts being studied the world over and not be content with what we have ourselves learnt. Two, we must candidly evaluate our performance, and learn lessons so as to dovetail them for our future plans against our enemy.

In a footnote-cum-post script, he added: "It will be naïve to ignore the fact that a new border is being exposed to us in Tibet. No border, in a military sense, could be considered peaceful if troops across follow a different ideology."

His was a constant battle with his political leaders. In several discussions, presentations, and letters (which the author was fortunate to have read in the MoD) he asked the government not to ignore the enemy threats. But even in mid-1962, he was warning the government to consider: "In case of total war with either Pakistan or China, or both, the most we can do is to have the whole nation trained to operate against the enemy in the border to prevent them from establishing a permanent foothold within the country, and to harass and demoralise them."

For the Indian Army too, he had a vision and that is why he had reason not to abandon this post for what has already been suitably highlighted and for more: *the eventual build up of the army from seven to 17 divisions – that in just three to four years, added another eight.* So he left it as a 'will'.

Summation

This essay is an endeavour to fathom and discover the greatness of Thimayya, as a man and as a leader. Among all the rare traits of Thimayya, what gave him the most sterling qualities of leadership were:
- His character and integrity.
- His courage and optimism.
- His wit and humour.
- His loyalty and patriotism and the trust he inspired.
- His visions and dreams.
- And, above all, his unceasing cultivation of human resources.

At the end, one is tempted to ask: Why does Thimayya still stand out as the most eminent general of the Indian Army?

The answer lies in the excellence of his leadership, his integrity, his loyalty, his influence on the people and above all, his courage – all unsurpassable. It would perhaps not be exaggeration to add that General Thimayya was loved by his army and the people of Cyprus more than anyone else.

As a human being, he was the noblest of the Kodavs and the Indians. And the life he led was extraordinary, romantic and even dramatic. Like all visionaries and men of action, he could be both a realist and a dreamer.

He achieved success in his life. For, he lived well a principled life. He had successfully fought through his wars. He had laughed the most and had made others join him in it. He had loved much and was loved equally. He had gained the respect of his soldiers, civilians the world over and his name, actions and reputation were known internationally. He had become the darling of all those who believed in humanity and human goodness, and in that he had won the respect of all intelligent men and women, and of little children and youth. And through his indomitable courage, wit and rationality, he had shown by his sense of duty and self-sacrifice that even peace exacted a price – the price of his own life.

He had filled a *niche*, the place among memorable persons and by his contributions to peace and war, had left this world a better place than he had found it. Such was the man Thimayya.

A Thimayya was, indeed, born in Kodagu, but a "Thimayya of India" and of history was born in the jungles and *chhaungs* of the battlefields of Burma, as in Zoji La and Leh. But more decisively, in Hindnagar of Korea, and later in Cyprus. These were all to be beyond the excitement of the moment. Although it may be unfair to say that he was a leader made and not a born one, he was a great leader, who in the words of Rudyard Kipling, would "meet with triumph and disaster and treat those imposters the same."

Thimayya was a military phenomenon that, like a Leonide, occurs only at rare intervals, over the Indian skies and its history. A man of bravery, with the courage and daring of Shivaji, the brains of Vivekananda, more tenacious and of cool and balance like Rana Pratap, and the diplomatic sagacity of Maharaja Ranjit Singh. His tactical excellence could easily compare with that of Erwin Rommel and strategic visions with Robert E. Lee. Above all, he was an apostle of peace, as much as an eminent soldier. India's history has been immensely enriched by General K S Thimayya.

***

His life epitomises:
To die a soldier's death, live and be remembered as a 'peacenick.' ∎

NOTES

1. Even Freud thought that all human history could be seen as a tug of war between EROS and THANATUS – between the urges to laugh and preserve and to destroy – a replicate of the Hindu divinities of Brahma (the creator), Vishnu (the perpetrator) and Mahesh (the destroyer).
2. In his autobiography, *Officially At Peace: Reflections on the Army & Its Role in Troubled Times*, at p. 148, Gen Roychowdhury wrote: "When our senior military commanders had warned him (Nehru) of the storm gathering over the North-East after the Chinese repossessed Tibet in 1950, the advice of experienced professionals like Generals Cariappa, Thimayya, Thorat, and others to develop requisite operational capabilities for defence of the Himalyan regions was peremptorily brushed aside by Nehru."
3. Private Correspondence (part of it quoted later)
4. The Government "White Paper" of 1961: "The morale and efficiency of the Armed Forces remained high."
5. In the USI lecture "Some Facts of Decision Making" (*USI Journal*, 1970).

Appendix
What the only Child Thought of Her Father?
At author's persuasion Mrs Mireille Chengappa wrote a piece:

My Father
It is not easy for parents to bring up an only child. Thanks to my mother, she kept me in check. I was made to tidy up and dust my own room, and polish my shoes.

Of course, in my father's eyes, I could do no wrong.

The atmosphere in our home was most informal and we were a close-knit family. When the parents were not dining or lunching out, we had our meals together and talked about the day's events or any amusing episode. Everyone had his say at the table.

Since people were in and out of the house most of the times, I felt comfortable with adults as well as friends of my own age (and) there was never a dull moment. I met the most interesting personalities from all over the world and accompanied my parents on their trips.

My father never discussed his work with us and kept his thoughts to himself – nor did we ask. However, no matter how late I would return from a party, he would wait up for me in his office room pretending to work on his files. My mother would be fast asleep. We would then talk far into the night with cups of coffee and sandwiches, and Zarir, his German shepherd, lying at his feet – she was so possessive of him. Those conversations are still clear in my mind – they covered my friends, events, my outings and people in general.

If he felt I needed advice, he would give it to me or kept quiet.

He enjoyed life to the full and expected me to do so. In spite of a very busy schedule, he never lost track of me. He had a great sense of humour.

In Pune, when I was learning how to ride his scooter (once) I went straight into one of the guards at the gate and I fell off. He was watching from the balcony of the house and exclaimed, "Oh my poor scooter," ignoring obviously the injury I might have caused to the guard or to myself..

I am thankful to both my parents for imbibing in me certain principles and values which are so important these days.

***

She would recall her last holidays with him in Cyprus in her letter of 14 April 2002:

I can see that you are devoting a lot of time and doing a tremendous amount of research on my father's book...

Yes, I spent six months in Cyprus with my father, and what a beautiful place! Very historical and teeming with life. I met people from all over the world; knowing my love for dancing and being an extrovert, my father took me out to the best restaurants with wonderful bands and I made friends easily.

I believe in living life to the full. Then on my own, I did a cruise to the Greek Islands, the Dalmatian coast, Italy and Haifa and, of course, Greece. Unfortunately, I didn't make it to Israel. Later, I made another trip to Lebanon, visited Beirut and also Damascus, the latter being an elegant city with lovely architecture.

Yes, my father doted on me but never once did I take either of my parents for granted. They did so much for me and brought me up with high principles and certain values. I am grateful to them.

I was selected for the New York fair but they would not pay for my fare so I said, "No, thank you"! My parents were taken aback. It wasn't the end of the world for me. I saw New York 20 years later and spent about a week there with Kittu.

(I had asked her if the general told her about Menon). She wrote : "My father never aired his opinion about people, politicians or otherwise. Like him, I also believe that God takes care of people who harm one. Eventually, they pay for it. Now you know why I have so much faith in the Almighty. Heaven and Hell is on this earth.

***

As I discussed with Mireille more, I found her a genial person, always looking at the positive side of life. " My father told me," she said, "never look back. Look at the present and the future. The past has its lessons but sometimes it is retrograde." She shrugged her shoulders and said, "Personally, I feel people who look backward are not progressive and are always regretting what they were and what they are. Kittu and I keep ourselves busy and are happy with the life that we are leading."

But she would equally – and most fondly – remember her father for his great observation on the changing world. " I believe there are no strangers in the world- which is getting smaller everyday. We all will have to be involved in everything."

This, she said, he wrote from Hindnagar, Korea in 1953 and even from Nicosia twelve years later.

General Thimayya would have cherished Mireille's letter; as he would Faiz's four lines written in an eulogy on his magnificent efforts at saving the suffering humanity after the Partition. ■

Thimayya at a Glance

Born on the last day of March 1906 in Mercara, Coorg (now Kodagu), Thimayya was educated at Coonoor, Bangalore, Dehra Dun and England and commissioned as a KCIO on 4 February 1926.

The Indian Army List of August 1947 (Special Edition) recorded the biographical data of Thimayya as: "AI-944. Unattached List... DSO Acting Major – to February 26, 1941, Temporary Major February 27-February 26, 1941, and April 1, 1942. Acting Lieutenant Colonel – May 19, 1944-August 18, 1944. Temporary Lieutenant Colonel – May 19, 1944-August 18, 1944. Lieutenant Colonel October 1, 1945. Acting Brigadier October 1, 1945. By April 1948, he was shown as Major General and Commandant JAK Force."

The Army List of December 1955, showed only two officers senior to him: General SM Shrinagesh, the COAS, and Lieutenant General Sant Singh, the GOC-in-C Eastern Command. Below him was once his senior officer, Lieutenant General Kalwant Singh, though commissioned one year before him, in January 1925. His course-mates were Major Generals Tara Singh Bal, and PN Thapar, both of February 4 1926 seniority. By 1955, there were only 59 KCIOs left in the Indian Army.

Thimayya served with 2nd Highland Light Infantry at Bangalore. He also served with 4th/19th Hybd in various appointments from 1 January 1927 till 24 March, 1936. He had played a commendable role in the Quetta earthquake. Then he became Adjutant 5th Battalion UTC, Madras, till August 1941. Reverted back to 4th/19th Hybd, being mobilised for service overseas in Singapore. His battalion changed to 8th/19th Hybd and after attending the Staff College Course at Quetta, was posted as GSO2 (Operations) 25th Indian Infantry Division in India and the Arakans, on 20 September, 1943 and in less than nine months, took over the command of his battalion in the same area, on 19 May 1944. Promoted as commander 36th Indian Infantry Brigade on

25 March 1945. Subsequently moved to 268th Brigade as part of the Occupation Force in Japan.

Recalled in December 1946 from Japan to become the Service Member, Armed Forces Nationalisation Committee, where he worked another five months till 15 May 1947. He later became a member of the Reconstitution Committee, too, while he commanded 5th and 11th Brigades of the 4th Division.

The banquets and historic speeches of independence by Jinnah and Nehru notwithstanding, the crisis of transmigration engulfed the whole of north India, on the one hand, and incapacitated the PBF under Major General Pete Rees, GOC 4th Division, on the other. As a consequence, Thimayya was promoted to eventually replace Rees. Thimayya played a commendable role in controlling the situation, which, but for his skilful handling, threatened to turn into a civil war.

He took over the Sri Div in the Kashmir Valley and directed the critical phase of the 1948 J&K War from 4 May till March 1950. After being briefly hospitalised due to high altitude sickness, he was moved to NDA, Dehra Dun, whose commandant he was from March 1950 till August 1951, whence he became QMG wherein he undertook several internal reforms.

As threats developed, Thimayya was one of the very few army commanders who moved from one command to another, to handle the situations as they emerged – Chhad Bet, Naga insurgency, Chinese, *et al.* In the meanwhile, he was moved to Korea to handle the non-repat POWs, one of the most difficult legacies of the Korean War. As COAS from 1957-61, he had to fight continually with an uncooperative ministry to prepare for battle with the twin enemies on the border. As a result, the four-year tenure he had as COAS was somewhat frustrating. It must, nonetheless, be said that had he been under a different defence minister, the "1962 Debacle" would most probably have been averted. And, had he not passed away prematurely in Cyprus, the problem there would have, in all probability, been solved.

Honours and awards came naturally to Thimayya, although he never hankered after them. A DSO of World War II with Mentioned-in-Dispatches, he was honoured with the award of the Padma Vibhushan for his grand role in Korea. Nepal made him an Honorary General of the Royal Nepalese Army and the Emperor of Ethiopia awarded him Order of Menelik II. The biggest honour, however, he always felt, was the love of his officers and men, and the trust of the country as its first soldier.

General Thimayya was a keen sportsman. He played polo, did skiing and sailing as a chief, besides playing golf and tennis.

He was a smoker and one who enjoyed a few 'chhota pegs' on party days. Very social, he was always the centre of any function. An eloquent speaker, who spoke with effect and charm – and often extempore. His writings were precise and easily understood, besides being ornate.

A great soldier, a great peace-maker and still a great man whose place is well established in the history of India, the UNO and the world.

As Thimayya was proceeding to Cyprus, the Kothari book of 'Who's Who' wrote of him on 25 February 1964:

THIMAYYA, Padma Vibhushan, Distinguished Service Order, GENERAL K.S; b. Mercara Coorg, 31st March 1906; d.Mireille Asha Lata; Educ: Commissioned Military College (Academy) Sandhurst, retired Chief of Indian Army Staff May 1961; Chairman, Neutral Nations' Repatriation Commission, Korea, 1953; Vice-President, All India Council of Sports; Vice-President, Royal Institute for Strategic Studies; President, Indian Ex-Services League; Deputy President, United Planters' Association of Southern Indian.
Address: Glenview, Coonoor, Nilgiris, South India.

The general died at Nicosia on 18 December 1965, owing to heart failure; his death was attributed to the cumulative effects of service in the high altitudes of India's northern borders. Mrs Nina Thimayya was the sole executrix of his will.

The Indian nation has also honoured him in several small ways such as naming roads, schools, etc after him. His grave has been relocated in the ASC Centre, Bangalore, where a statue also stands. The rightful place for it is at Rajghat, New Delhi.

The Government of Cyprus has, however done him the most singular honour by issuing a special stamp and naming a boulevard after him. Even today, his name remains on the lips of most Cypriots, as, indeed, it is in every soldier's heart and in the minds of those who value humanity, world peace and believe in leaving a better world behind.

Thimayya, to sum up, was:
- First in war.
- First in peace.
- First in the hearts of people.
- First on whom two books were written while he served.
- The first in India whose grave has been shifted.
- And, above all, he could be equally happy amidst the fragrance of people and high places or with the smell of blood, sweat and tears. ∎

Glossary

(Other than those expanded in text or internationally recognised)

bn	billion
CFL/LOC/LAC	CeasefireLine/Line of Control/Line of Actual Control.
CIA	Central Intelligence Agency (US)
COAS/CNS/CAS	Chief of Army Staff/Chief of Naval Staff/Chief of Air Staff
DSO	Distinguished Service Order
ECO	Emergency Commissioned Officer
HQ	Headquarters such as Air HQ, Army HQ, Naval HQ
INA	Indian National Army (of WW II, created by Japanese)
IS/ID	Internal Security/Internal Defence
ICO/KCIO	Indian Commissioned Officer/King's Commissioned Officer
MC	Military Cross
MVC	Mahavir Chakra
M(m)	Million or metre
NDA	National Defence Academy
NEFA	North-East Frontier Agency (now Arunachal Pradesh)
NWFP	North-West Frontier Province (now in Pakistan)
Offr...	Officer. During the British period, there were King Commissioned Indian Officer (KCIO), Indian Commissioned Officer (ICO), Viceroy Commissioned Officer (VCO), etc.
PLA/PLA AF	People's Liberation Army/PLA Air Force.
Point (Pt)	indicates the above mean sea level height marked on map
PsOW (POWs)	Prisoners of War
PVC	Param Vir Chakra
QMG	Quarter Master General
VC	Victoria Cross

(Note: Appointments special to the services have been expanded in the text, to the extent possible)

Bibliography

It is stated at the outset that the oft-repeated reference to Official Documents and Personal Documents in the text, allude, in many cases, to still "classified" and "confidential" documents maintained at various service headquarters. These were allowed to be browsed through by the author with a strict "oath of confidentiality." Specific details of such documents such as references to files, letters, memorandums have, therefore, been omitted, all through the text and in End Notes.

1. Primary Sources

(a) Documents relating St George's School, Coonoor; Bishop Cotton School, Bangalore; PWRIMC (now RIMC), Dehra Dun; National Defence Academy, Dehra Dun & Khadakvasla and Indian Military Acedemy, Dehra Dun; Staff College, Quetta, Naitonal Defence College, New Delhi College of Combat (War College), Mhow (earlier Infantry School).

(b) Histories of 2nd HLI: 4th/18th and 8th/18th Hyderabad (now 4th Kumaon), 26th Infantry Division, 4th Infantry Division; 19th (Sri) Division and histories of components of these formations.

(c) Study of the syllabi and general curriculam of RMA Sandhurst, for the period 1924-26 by the author, although the final report by RMA was not made available, despite several efforts.

(d) Family papers of the Thimayyas.

(e) Thimayya's papers in NIMML, New Delhi, and relevant papers in the National Achives (NA).

(f) The Cariappa and INA Papers in NA.

(g) Papers on the Quetta earthquake, 1935, including those maintained by 4th Kumaon and Kumaon Regimental Centre.

(h) Army HQs documents on Arakan Campaign, J&K War, 1962 India-China War (including unpublished official history on website).

(i) Papers on the INA and mutiny in 4th/18th Hybd.

(j) Papers on the Commonwealth Forces, especially of the "Brindiv", Japan.

(k) Papers relating to Chhad Bet, Naga Uprising in History Division, MOD, RK Puram.

(l) Reports and documents on Nationalisation Committee, Reconstitution, Punjab Boundary Force.

(m) Parliamentary and Selected Works of Nehru, Patel, Vajpayee, Kripalani and those relating to the "Thimayya Resignation" episode.
(n) Original unpublished papers of Lt Col Parab (Leh), Brig Thapa (Skardu), Maj Gen S. Shah, VrC (Sri Div), Thimayya Papers (Korea), Maj Gen Niranjan Prasad papers (Forward Policy in NEFA).
(o) UN papers on Korea, Kashmir, J&K and Cyprus.
(p) Original papers of "Exercises Lal Qila and Sheel," etc for defence against the Chinese.
(q) Original letters of Thimayya, Nehru, Ayub Khan, Cariappa.
(r) White Papers of GOI and China on Sino-Indian border dispute.
(s) Gazette, citations and reports of Thimayya.

2. **Interviews of individuals as mentioned in the text.**

3. **Magazines and Periodicals**
- *USI Magazine* April-July 1957; July 1997.
- *TIME*, 19 October 1953; 1-6 Sep 1959; 14 Dec 1959.
- *Sainik Samachar* for the period 1957-62.
- *The Blue Beret* (1964 - 65)
- *The National Geographic* of Feb 1973.
- *Foreign Affairs*, USA, Fall, 1953.
- *The Economist*, November 15, 1953.
- *USI Journals*.

4. **Newspapers/ Periodicals**
- *Morning Post* (Peshawar), June 1 to 5 1935.
- *Stars & Stripes* (US Forces), Sep-Dec 1953.
- *Asahi* (Japan), Sep 9 1953.
- *The Bombay Chronicle*, Apr 23 1957.
- *The New York Herald Tribune*, Oct 8 1953.
- *Christian Science Monitor* Mar 8 1953.
- *The Statesman,* Jan 15 1957, Mar 24 1957, Sep 1, 10, 24 1959.)
- *The Dawn*, May 23 1959.
- *The Tribune,* Feb 17 1957.
- *Hindustan Times,* Mar 10 1957, July 30 1957, April 1961, Dec 15 1965.
- *The Times of India,* Mar 11 1957, May 30 1959, Dec 15 1965.
- *The Indian Express,* Mar 13 1957, Sep 7 1959, Apr 16 1970.
- *The Deccan Herald,* Sept 7 1959.
- *Blitz,* Mar-Sep 1959, Mar 5 1960.
- *Organiser,* Throughout 1957-1959-Jul 1962.
- *The Cyprus Mail,* Jan 30 1965.
- *The Pakistan Times,* Aug 14 1979.

5. Books

Akbar, MJ	: *Nehru, the Making of India,* New Delhi, Viking, 1988
Anand, Mulk Raj	: *VK Krishna Menon's Marathon Speech on Kashmir at the UN Security Council,* 1992
Arif, Gen KM	: *Khaki Shadow (Pakistan 1947-1997),* Oxford University Press, Karachi, 2001
Azad, Maulana	: *India Wins Freedom,* Orient Longmans, 1959
Baig, Tara Ali	: *Portrait of An Era,* Roli Books Pvt Ltd
Vajpayee A B	: *Four Decades in Parliament* (Defence & Security) Vol 1, GOI Publication
Barnett, Corelli	: *The Collapse of British Power,* London, Eyre, Methuen, 1972
Bhagat, PS, VC	: *The Shield and the Sword,* New Delhi, Vikas (2nd Edn), 1974
Bhargava, GS	: *The Battle of NEFA,* New Delhi, Allied, 1964
Bidwood, Lord	: *Two Nations & Kashmir,* London, Robert Hale, 1956
Bloeria, Sudhir S.	: *The Battle of Zoji La, 1948,* New Delhi, Har Anand, 1997
Brecher, Michael	: *Nehru: A Political Biography,* Oxford, 1959
Cohen, Lt Col, Maurice	: *Thunder Over Kashmir,* Orient Longmans, 1955
Collins & Dominique	: *Mountbatten and Independent India,* Vol. 1, March 22- August 15, 1947, New Delhi, Vikas, 1982
Connel, John	: *Auchinleck: A Biography of Field Marshal Sir Claude Auchinleck,* Cassell, 1959
Dalvi, Brig JP	: *The Himalayan Blunder: The Curtain-Raiser to the Sino-Indian War of 1962,* Thacker, 1969
Daniel, Clifton	: *Chronicle of the 20th Century Chronicle Publication,* (Ed), New York. Chronicle, 1987
Das, Maj Gen CN	: *House of Glory – The Famous Battles of the Indian Army 1801-1971,* New Delhi, Vision Books, 1987
Das, Durga	: *India From Curzon to Nehru and After,* Collins, 1969
Dasgupta C.	: *War & Diplomacy in Kashmir 1947- 48,* Delhi, Sage

6. Publications, 2002.

Dixit, JN	: *India - Pakistan War & Peace,* India Today Books, 2002
Dixon, Norman	: *On Psychology of Military Incompetence,* London Jonathan Cape, 1976
Evans, Humphrey	: *Thimayya of India : A Soldier's Life,* New York, Harcourt Brace, 1960
Fischer, David	: *The Proudest Day*
Galbraith, John Kenneth	: *An Ambassador's journal – A Personal Account of the Kennedy Years,* New American Library Hamish Hamilton,1969. Massachusetts,1989

Gauhar, Altaf	: *Ayub Khan, Pakistan's First Military Ruler*, Karachi University Press, 1996
George, TJS	: *Krishna Menon*, Bombay, 1963
Gopal, Dr S	: *Jawaharlal Nehru: A Biography*, Jawaharlal Nehru Memorial Fund, 1984
Hangen, Welles	: *After Nehru, Who?*, London, Rupert Hart-Davis 1963
Harbottle, Brig. M	: *An Impartial Soldier*
Hoffman, Steven A	: *India & China Crisis*, 1990
Katari, Adml, RD	: *A Sailor Remembers*, New Delhi, Vikas, India, 1982
Kaul, BK	: *Reminiscences: Discreet & Indiscreet*, New Delhi, Lancer, 1982
Kaul, BM	: *The Untold Story*, 1967, Delhi, Allied Publishers, 1962
Kaul, TN	: *A Diplomat's Diary (1947-1999): China–India–USA, The TantalisingTriangle*, New Delhi, Macmillan India, 2000
Kavic, J Lorne	: *India's Quest for Security – Defense Policies 1947-65*, USA University of California Press, 1967
Kennedy, Paul	: *The Rise & Fall of Great Powers – Economic Change & Military Conflicts from 1500 to 2000*, Random House, New York, 1987.
Khan, FM Ayub	: *Friends & Not Masters – A Political Biography*, Oxford, 1967
Khan, Lt Gen Gul Hassan	: *Memoirs*, Oxford Press,1993
Khanduri, Brig PN & Chandra B	: *Soldiers & Politicians*, New Delhi, Om Publications, 2001
Khanduri, Brig PN	: *Field Marshal KM Cariappa – His Life & Times*, New Delhi, Lancer, 1995.
Chandra B	: *Generals & Strategists – From Kautilya to Manekshaw*, New Delhi, Gyan Sagar Publications, 2000
Khan, Maj Gen Akbar	: *Raiders in Kashmir 1947-48 (The Story of Kashmir War)*, Army Publishers, Delhi, Pak Publishers, Karachi, 1970
Kundu, Apurba	: *Militarisation In India – The Army & Civil Society In Consensus*, New Delhi, Viva Books, 1998
Lal, Air Chief Marshal	: *My Years With the IAF*, New Delhi, Lancer, 1986 (Ed: Ela Lal)
Lapping, Brian	: *End of Empire*, London, Grenada, 1985.
Mankekar, DR	: *Guilty Men of 1962*, Bombay, The Tulsi Shah Enterprises,1968.
	: *Leaves From A War Reporter's Diary – 1977*, New Delhi, Vikas 1977
Masani, Minoo	: *Against the Tide* (Out of Print)

Mathai, MO	: *Reminiscences of the Nehru Age*, New Delhi, Vikas, 1978
Maxwell, Neville	: *India China War*, Natraj Publishers, Dehra Dun, 1970
Meisner, Maurice	: *Mao's China & After - A History of the People' Republic*
Menon VP	: *The Transfer of Power*, Bombay, Orient Longmans, 1957
Moon, Penderal	: *Divide and Quit*, London, Chatto & Windus, 1961
Mullik, BN	: *My Years With Nehru - 1948-1964 Chinese Betrayal*, Delhi, Allied Publishers, 1972
Murphy, Ray	: *The Last Viceroy - The Life & Times of Rear Admiral The Earl Lord Mountbatten of Burma*, London, Jarolds, 1948
Musa, Gen Muhammad	: *Jawan to General*
Muthanna, IM	: *General Thimayya*, Bangalore, Orient Power Press, 1972
Narain, Maj Gen Pratap	: *Indian Arms Bazar*, New Delhi Shipra, 1994
Narayan, Col BK	: *Gen JN Chaudhuri: An Autobiography* (As told to Col Narayan), New Delhi, Vikas, 1978
Nayar, Kuldip	: *India, the Critical Years*, New Delhi, Vikas, India, 1975
Nehru, BK	: *Nice Guys Finish Second*, Delhi Viking, 1997
Owen, Frank	: *War in Burma*
Palit, Maj Gen DK, VrC	: *War in High Himalayas*, London, Lancer, 1991 *Maj Gen AA Rudra: His Services in Three Armies & Two World Wars*, Reliance Publishers House, India 1997
Ponnappa, Lt Col KC	: *The Study of Origin of Coorgs*, Bangalore, New Delhi, 1997
Prasad SN & Dharam Pal	: *Operations in J&K 1947-48* (GOI), MOD,1987
Prasad, Maj Gen Niranjan	: *The Fall of Towang 1962*, New Delhi, Palit & Palit, 1981
Praval, Maj KC	: *The Indian Army After Independence*, New Delhi, Lancer, 1987
	: *The Red Eagles – A History of Fourth Division of India*, New Delhi, Vision Books, 1982
Proudfoot, Lt Col CL	: *We Lead – The 7th Light Cavalry 1784-1990*, New Delhi, Lancer, 1990
Rao, Gen KV Krishna	: *In the Service of the Nation – Reminiscences*, New Delhi Viking, 2001
Raph D Sawyer(Translator)	: *The Seven Military Classics of Ancient China*, Colarado, Westview Press, 1993
Rikhye, Ravi	: *The War That Never Was: The Story of India's Strategic Failures*, Delhi Chanakya Publication,1988
Rommel FM Erwin	: *Infantry Attacks*, London Green Hill Books, 1990 (Ed: Alfred Rommel)
Roychowdhury Gen S	: *Officially at Peace - Reflections on the Army & Its Role in Troubled Times*, New Delhi, Viking, 2002

Russel, Bertrand	: *The Autobiography of Bertrand Russel (1944-67)* Vol II, London George Allen.
Sehgal, Lt Col JR	: *The Unfought War of 1962: The NEFA Debacle* Bombay, Allied, 1979
Sen, Lt Gen LP	: *Slender was the Thread*, New Delhi, Allied, 1979
Shaukat, Sardar	: *The Nation That Lost Its Soul*, Karachi, Jang Publications
Singh, Dr Karan	: *Heir Apparent*, Bombay, Oxford Press, 1982
Singh, Jaswant	: *Defending India*, Bangalore, Macmillan, 1999
Singh, Maj Gen Joginder	: *Behind the Scene – An Analysis of India's Military Operations 1947-71*, New Delhi, Lancer, 1971
Sinha Lt Gen SK	: *A Soldier Recalls*, New Delhi, Lancer, 1992
Sinha, Dr SN	: *China Strikes* (Foreward By Gen Thimayya, New Delhi, Rama Krishna, 1964
Slim, FM William	: *Defeat Into Victory*, London, Landsborough, 1958.
Tsuiji, Col Massauoby	: *Singapore, the Japanese Version*, London, Constable, 1960
Tewari, Maj Gen KK	: *A Soldier's Voyage to Self Discovery*, Pondicherry, All India Press, 1959
Thimayya, Gen KS	: *General Thimayya's Korean Diary: Experiments in Neutrality*, Delhi, Vikas Books, 1981
Thorat, Lt Gen SPP	: *Reveille to Retreat*, New Delhi, Allied, 1968
Tucker Lt Gen F	: *While Memory Serves*, London, Cassell, 1950
Yew, Lee Kwan	: *The Singapore Story: Memoirs of Lee Kwan Yew*, Singapore, Times Edition, 1998
Vas. Lt Gen EA	: *Fools & Infantrymen: One View of History 1923-1993*, Meerut, Kautilya Publications, 1995
Venkateshwaram, AL	: *35 Years in South Block* (Serialised in Sainik Samachar 1981-82)
Verma, Lt Gen SD	: *To Serve With Honour* : Kasauli, 1998
Vira D	: Memories of Civil Servant, Vikas, 1975
Wignall Sydney	: *Spy: On Top of the World*, Delhi, Penguin, 2002
Wilson Lt Gen Sir James	: *Unusual Undertaking: A Military Memoir*, Leo - Cooper, UK, 2002
Zeigler, Philip	: *Mountbatten*, London, Collins

Index

Abdullah, Sheikh, 150, 211
Abu Naser, 90
Achebe, Chinua, 342
ad-hocism, 259
Afghanistan, 42, 206
Afrika Korps, 70
Agnew, Captain, 46
Agra, 65, 66, 68-69
Ahimsa, 37
Ahirs, Ahir Company, 31, 35, 52, 60, 63-64, 73n', 76, 81, 86, 94, 304
Air Kalinga, 285
Air Observation Post (OP), 103
Ajaib Singh, *Brigadier*, 159
Ajit Singh, Captain, 130
Akbar Khan, 119
Aksai Chin Road: Chinese intrusion in the Indian territory, 206, 208-11, 218, 222, 236, 241n', 249, 260, 271, 283
Akyab, 81, 85, 89, 90
Alexander of Macedonia, 11, 19
Algiers: American invasion, 70
All India Council of Sports, 219
All Indian Brigade, 83
Allaha, 40
Allen, George V, 228
Allied Occupation Force, 97-99
Alvares, *Captain* CG, 204
Aly Khan, Prince of Iran, 283
American Military Government (AMG), 97
Americans, 66-67, 70, 97; and the Korean War, 169, 180
Amrik Singh, *Major General*, 204, 254, 282
Amrit Kaur, Raj Kumari, 219

An Pass, 88-89
Andaman-Nicobar Islands: Japanese advances, 70
Anglo-American Treaty, **1922**, 32
Anglo-Saxon occupational forces, 97
Angub, *Brigadier* TH, 77, 80
Anne, 3
Anthony, Frank, 262
Aracuzos, Andreas, 6
Arakan Hills, 86
Arakans, 72, 88-89, 93, 366
Argyll Highlanders, 64
Arjan Singh, *Air Marshal*, 338
Armageddon, 217
Armed Forces Academy, 150
Armed Forces Nationalisation Committee, 99, 149, 367
Armed Forces Reconstitution Committee (AFRC), 103, 104-5, 367
Armistice Agreement, **1953**, 163
Army Cadet College (ACC), Nowgong, 225, 291, 301
Army Commanders Conference, **1957**, 211-12, 218; **1958**, 219, 224, 247, 277, 293; **1960**, 283
Army Headquarters Mountaineering Association, 219
Army in Indian Reserve of Officers (AIRO), 14
Army Rehabilitation Women's Association (ARWA), 276
Army Supply Corps Centre, 7
Army Welfare Housing Organisation, 276
Army Wives Welfare Association, 276
Arnold, SC, 76, 77
Aryans, 11

Asarappa, *Major General* RE, 204
Assam, 314
Assam Regiment, 192
Assam Rifles, 192, 196, 236-37, 248, 249, 254, 272, 275, 276, 285, 294, 302
Atal, *Brigadier* HL, 122, 134, 139, 353
Atma Singh, *Major General*, 118
Attfield, *Lieutenant Colonel* Charles, 66-67, 69
Attlee, Clement Richard, 104
Auchinleck, *Field Marshal* Claude, 97, 105, 108, 118, 141n'', 151
Austerlitz, 81
Australians, 98
Auxilliary Force, 19
Avadi Heavy Vehicles Factory, 224
Ayub Khan, *General* M., 30n', 106-7, 110, 114, 207, 218, 229-30, 232, 238, 258, 298
Ayyangar, *Sir* N. Gopalaswamy, 102
Azad Kashmir, 127, 148
Azad, Maulana Abul Kalam, 107

Backward Policy, 42
Badhwar, *Lieutenant Colonel* MR, 164
Baghdad, Iraq, 32
Bagso, 129
Bahadur Singh, *Lieutenant General* K, 164, 204, 284
Bahadur Singh, *Subedar*, 46, 58, 78
Bahri, *Captain* KS, 184
Bahri, *Captain* SK, 164
Baig, Tara Ali, 54
Bajpayee, Girija Shankar, 150, 156
Baker, Noel, 119
Bakshi Ghulam Mohammed, 128, 211
Bal, *Major General* Tara Singh, 30n', 150, 366
Baldev Singh Committee Report, 223
Baldev Singh, Sardar, 109, 102, 113, 114, 153, 158, 204
Baldwin, *Wing Commander*, 182
Baltal, 137

Baluch16th/10th, 83, 92
Baluchs, 86
Balwant Singh, 46
Bandung Conference, 205
Banerji, *Major General* PC, 204
Bara Hoti, 205, 218, 276
Baralacha La, 126
Barltrop, *Brigadier*, 151
Basra Club, 33
Basra, Iraq, 32
Batala, Muslims killed, 109
Batkundi, 138
Batra, TS, 30n'
Bay of Bengal, 88
beliefs ad practices, 13
Berberoglu, AM, 6
Berlin Wall, 360
Bernades, Carlos, 3, 4, 5, 328-29, 337
Bhagat, *General* PS, 155, 351, 358
Bhatia, SP, 164
Bhilai Steel Plant, Bhilai, 213
Bhonsale, *Captain*, 45
Bhutan, 206, 226, 236, 275; Chinese claim, 271
bickering, 243
Bihar Regiment, 68
Bikram Singh, *Major General*, 300
Bird Nalla, 77-79
Birdwood, *Lord*, 123
Bishop Cotton School, Bangalore, 17-19, 82
Black, HD, 181
Black, Ralph, 296
Black Sea, 70
Blitzkrieg at Zoji La (Pass), 133-38, 347
Boer war, 24, 26
boldness, 134
Bollu (sister-in-law), 67
Bopanna, *Captain*, 52
border issue in defence, 221
border management, 358
Border Road Organisation (BRO), 225, 227, 283-84, 302

Border Scouts, 302
Border Security Force (BSF), 199
Bose, Netaji Subhash Chandra, 4
Boswell, James, 26
Bottomley, 338
Brahmagiri Hills, 13
Brahmins, 13
Brar, *Brigadier* DS, 30n[1]
Brar, *Captain* Harbishan Singh, 32
Brass Tacks Operation, 165-69
brigade group system, 217
brinkmanship, 314-17, 356-57
Bristo, *Brigadier* RCB, 110
British: and non-British, discrimination, 24-25; Commonwealth, 97; Crown, 154; Imperial Defence College, 284; Indian Division (Brindiv), 97, 99; influence, 14; intelligence failure, 65; policy of aggression against Tibet, 281n[1]; policy of globalisation of Indian goods, 34; sense of superiority, 33-34
Brook, Charles, 51
Brooks, TB Handerson, 248
Brown, *Captain*, 68
Brown, Major AD, 64
Browning, *Captain Sir* Robert, 23
Bruce, *Major General* GS, 100n[5]
Brucker, Welbur, 228
Bucher, *General Sir* Roy, 125, 132, 142n28
Bulganin, *Marshal*, 213
Bull, *Captain*, 34, 36, 48
Bunche, Ralph, 356
Bunker, Ellsworth, 228
bureaucracy, 225, 232, 248, 284, 353
Burgess, *Captain* CW, 76, 78
Burgess, *Sergeant* John, 19
Burma, 60, 87, 206, 355; British forces, withdrawal, 70; Campaign, 88; military rule, 229
Burns, *General*, 217-18
Butler, *Sir* William, 278
Buxton, *Major*, 76, 77, 78

Cabinet Committee for Partition, 104
Candeth, *Brigade Commander*, 139
Canteen Services Department, 158
Cargill, *Vice Marshal* Stephen, 204
Cariappa, *Field Marshal* KM (brother-in-law), 12, 13, 27, 28, 53, 56n15, 68-69, 115, 118-19, 126, 130, 132, 134, 140, 142n28, 150, 154, 155, 157, 158, 190, 203, 209, 216, 229, 248, 254, 269-70, 297, 311-12, 354
Carter, *Sir* Norman, 48, 49
Carver, *Major General*, 325
caste and class composition, concept of,
caste system, 14, 216
Caucasus: Russian offensive, 11, 70
Cauveri river, 13, 14
Cauvery Purana, 11
Ceasefire Line (CFL) *see* Green Line
Central Reserve Police, 191
Central Treaty Organisation (CENTO), 206, 246
Century Club, 26
Chakravarty, BN, 164, 182
Chakravarty, *Commodore* A, 214, 240n[27]
Chaliha, BP, 272
Chandravarma, 11-12
Changchenmo: Chinese intrusion, 316
Changi POW camp, 67
Chapathi Operation, 126, 129, 131
Chapman, *Air Marshal* Ivelaw, 154
Chatru, *Naik* MM, 130
Chaturvedi, *Commodore*, 207
Chaudhuri, BS, 30n[1]
Choudri, *Commander* H. Mohammed Siddiqui, 102, 103
Chaudhuri, *Major General* JN, 25, 30n[1], 173, 176, 207, 247, 285, 290, 296, 338
Chaukan Pass, 277
Chengappa, *Major* KM (son-in-law), 2, 7
Chengappa, Mireille (daughter), 1-2, 4-5, 7, 8, 53, 57, 58, 81, 87, 263-64, 299
Chhad Bet, 189-91, 367; Pakistani intrusion, 190

Chhaungs war, 88-96, 349, 362
Chiang Kai-shek, 66
Chibber, *Major General* ML, 290
Chief Controller of Research and Development, 223
Chief of Defence Staff (CDS), 289-90
Chiefs of Staff (COS) Committee, 203, 233, 243, 268
Chien Ye, *Marshal*, 207
Chiling, Pakistani offensive, 127
Chillas, 117
Chimni, *Major General* SBS, 109, 157, 159
China, 218, 225-27; border, deployment pattern, 273, 284; Chinese People's Voluntary Force (CPVF), 162, 166; communism, 265-66; military capability, 251; neo-colonialism, 205; India relations, 199, 206-7, 246; People's Liberation Army (PLA), 147, 162, 206, 207, 210, 213, 215, 227, 236, 249, 273, 288-89, 314-18; repatriation, 172; support to North Korea, 162; intrusions/threat to India, 203, 206-11, 213, 215, 221-23, 225-27, 234, 243, 246, 248, 254, 257, 261, 265, 271-78, 283-86, 288, 293, 298, 301-2, 313-14, 347, 356-57, 359, 361; and the Tibet issue, 189-90, 205-6, 222, 235-38, 249, 261, 271; war 1962, 289, 316, 344, 361
Chindits, 90
Chinese Occupied Ladakh (COL), 315
Chipman, Warwick F, 153
Chitralis, Jammu & Kashmir: Pakistani offensive, 131
Chopra, MS, 159
Choudri, *see* Chaudhuri
Christian Greeks, 325
Christianity, 16
Christison, *Lieutenant General* Sir AR Philip, 72, 83, 88-89
Chu Teh, 207
Chumbi Valley, Jammu & Kashmir: Chinese intrusion, 236, 237, 271, 273, 283, 288

Churchill, *Sir* Winston, 19, 24, 26, 65, 103, 342, 353
Chushul, 319; Chinese skirmishes, 235, 248; Indian army deployment, 275, 285
Chuskee, Sultan, 316
civil war, 109
Clark, *General* Mark, 165-66, 172-3, 178
Clerides, Glafcos, 5, 360
Clive, Robert (1725-74), 52
Cobb, *Sir* Henry, 14
Cochrane, Sir Charles, 23
code of conduct, 43
coercion, 171
cohesiveness, 66, 353
Cold War, 9, 164, 172, 178, 183, 206-7, 213, 217, 326
colonial arrogance, 20
colonial wars, 23
Colour Party, 38
Colsey, *Major*, 46
Combined Operations Pilotage Parties (COPP), 88-89, 91
Commando brigade, 3rd, 88, 90, 94
Commonwealth Army Chiefs of Staff, 217
communal violence, 110
communication skill, 348
Communist Party, 262, 265
Communists, 163, 166, 168-69, 174, 176-77, 179-80, 194, 216, 271
competition, 44
competitiveness, 44
Congress, 83, 262
conscience, 297
Constitution of India, 149, 198, 212
contractor system, 157-8
conversions, 33
Coonoor, 28
Coorg, Coorgs, 12, 13, 22
corruption, 298
counter-insurgency operations, 193
coup d'oeuil, 346

Cowan, *General* DT, 97-98
creativity and innovation, 346
Cromwell, Oliver (1599-1658), 8
Cubbon, *Sir* Marc, 26
culture, 14
Custodian Force India (CFI), 163-64, 165-66, 167-9, 172-74, 177-78, 180-82, 184
Cyprus problem, 1, 2, 3, 4, 6, 324-40, 344, 346, 348, 355, 360, 362, 367-68; *see also* United Nations
Czechs, 173, 174

D' Company, 60, 91, 92
d'Isle, *Colonel*, 67
Daenikkar, Dr. Armin, 164, 166
Dalai Lama, 235, 251, 270
Dalip Singh, 38, 41
Dalvi, *Brigadier* JP, 316, 319, 350
Daly Cadet College, Indore, 27, 55n7
Darjeeling-Kalimpong, Chinese intervention, 271
Dasgupta, *Captain* KC, 76
Dash Capture of Poland Operation, 85-88
Daulal Beg Oldi (DBO), 283, 285, 287, 316, 319
Daulat Singh, *Major General*, 32, 34, 39, 99, 204, 228, 229, 247, 301, 313
Dave, AK, 164, 172, 271, 289
Davies, *General* HL, 71-73, 77, 85, 349
Daya Shankar, Rear Admiral, 241n"
Dean, Arthur H, 177
decisiveness, 348, 362
Defence: Estimates, 207; expenditure, 1963-64, 357; self-reliance, 221
Defence Committee of the Cabinet, 233, 247
Defence Ministry (MoD), Government of India, 202, 204, 208, 216, 222, 225, 228, 232-33, 237, 244, 246, 254, 263, 270, 278, 284, 290-91, 295, 298, 301, 361; hierarchy, 203
Defence Production Board, 223, 256
Defence Production Conference, **1959**, 254-55
Defence Services Staff College (DSSC),

Wellington, Nilgiri Hills, 231, 278, 313
Delhi Golf Club, 219
Delovie, *Lt Gen* M, 148
Demchchok: Chinese intrusion, 286-87, 319
Demilitarized Zone (DMZ), 9, 163-64, 165, 166, 167-169, 333
demobilisation, 102, 105, 108
democracy, 250
demoralisation, 250
Denktash, Rauf, 360
Derian-Mercara Committee, 229
Desai, MJ, 283
Desai, Morarji, 212, 283, 285, 312
Dhage, VK, 261
Dhargalkar, *Major General* KP, 204
Dharma Vira, 219
Di Chu Valley, Ladakh: Chinese intrusion, 225, 226
dichotomy, 289
Dien Bien Phu (DBP), 206, 314-15
Digra, Ladakh, Chinese intrusion, 225, 226
discipline, 98-99
discrimination and prejudices, 17, 24-25,33-35, 45, 53, 57-58, 65, 112
dissuasion strategy, 273
divide and rule policy of British, 44, 59
Divisional Ski School, 138-39
Dobbie, *Lieutenant General Sir* William, 70
Dogra Regiment, 164
Dogras, 124, 129, 178-79, 304
dominion, 149
Dommel-Muzaffarabad, Indian Army operations, 119, 122
Dras, 136; occupied by Pakistani forces, 127
Drill Square, 23, 24
Droksand Bridge, 248
Dubey, *Brigadier* KN, 180, 294
Dulles, John Foster, 177, 182
Dunn, *Brigadier* Pat, 354
Duns, 92
Durham Light Infantry, 20

Dutt, *Captain* Ranjan, 125
Dzerzinski Artillery Academy, 214

Earl of Birkenhead, 261
East India Company, 12, 52
Eastern Command, 69, 191, 204, 227, 233, 235, 236, 275, 301
economic stratification, 17
Egypt, 32, 217-18; Army Chief of Staff, 217
eight Indianised units, 20, 25, 40
Eisenhower, Dwight, 182, 218
El Alamein, 70
Elle, *Sir* Hugh, 64
Elmhirst, Air Marshal TW, 125, 132
Elphic, Peter, 64
Emergency Commissions, 83
Engineer, *Air Marshal* Aspy, 264
Engineer, *Air Vice Marshal* MM, 182, 224
Esin, Seyfullah, 325
ethnographic differences, 67
euphemism, 35
European races, 65
European Union (EU), 340, 360
Evans, Henry, 360
Evans, Humphery; *Thimayya of India: A Soldier's Life*, 295
Exercise *Lal Quila*, 227, 235, 243
Exercise *Sheel*, 227, 236, 243
ex-servicemen, 282, 311
extra-regimental employment (ERE), 52

Fabian, 26
Faisal, Heshemite, King of Iraq, 32, 35
Faiz, Ahmad Faiz, 9, 113
Famagusta, 330-31
Faqir Singh, *Brigadier*, 130
Faqirs of Ippi, 43
Far East, 70
Fateh Singh, *Captain*, 2, 3, 4, 5, 6, 334
favouritism, 298, 358
Fazal Ali, 198

feudal chiefs, 32
Field Companies, 135-36
Fitzsimons, *Major General*, 59, 61, 63-64, 70
flexibility, 139, 210, 246, 346
Foot Hill-Rupa Bomdi La road, 294
foreign policy, 217
Form of Affirmation, 149-50
Formosa (Taiwan), 292
Fort Sandeman, 45-47
Forward Policy, 42, 285-89, 314-16, 351, 357
Fowler, *Major* AL, 90, 94
Fowler, *Major* Bobby, 76, 78
France: fall of, 96
frankness, 349
freedom struggle, 67
Freeman, J., 51
Freud, Sigmund, 342
Frontier Division Administrative Service, 196
Frunze Military Academy, 214
Fuller, *Major General* JFC, 342

Gable, Clark, 48
Gajewski, Stanislaw, 164
Ganapathi, Barrister Kaubiranda (brother-in-law), 15
Ganapathi, Gangoo (Thimayya, sister), 15
Ganapathy, *Colonel* CM, 14
Gandhi, M.K., 27, 37, 39, 47, 67, 83, 111, 114, 195, 343, 344, 356; assassination, 115
Ganga Singh, *Captain*, 133
Gangtok, Sikkim, 236-37, 294
Garwal Rifles, 164
General Officer Commanding (GOC), 71-73, 77, 94, 110-1, 119, 128, 138; 4th Division, 105-15
Geneva Convention, **1949**, 163, 165, 170
Gentleman Cadets (GCs), 23, 25, 154-5
George, Remmy, 3, 4
Germans, 70; and Russian Peace Treaty, 54
Ghazi Khan, 42
Ghenzis Khan, 128

Ghose, SK, 30n¹
Ghosh, BB, 175, 187n11
Gibbs, *Lieutenant Colonel* FW, 75
Gibraltar: acquisition of, 41
Gibson, Jack, 152
Gilani, *Colonel* MS, 120
Gilgit, Jammu & Kashmir: Pakistani offensive, 125, 127, 131
Gilgit Scouts, 117, 119
Gill, *Lieutenant Colonel* Inder, 218
Gill, Niranjan Singh, 30n¹, 39, 46, 60, 64, 73
globalisation, 34
Gokak, Vinayak Krishna, 8
Gollan, HR, 153
Goraya, *Brigadier*, 277
Batallion, 72, 83
Gorkha Regiment, Gurkhas, 43-4, 78, 97-98, 104,124, 127-29, 134, 126, 137, 149, 155, 206, 299-300; 2nd/5th battalion, 98-9; 8th battalion, 42
Gorman, *Major*, 20-21
Goyal, *Air Commdore* SN, 240n27
Gracey, *General* DD, 118-19, 125, 141n9
graded staff and window of opportunity, 71-73
Graham, *Dr*, 155
Grantzer, *Mrs*, 64
Graves, *Sir* Robert, 28
Gray, DC, 76
Great War, *see* World War II
Greek National Guard, 328
Greeks, 325, 332
Green Berets, 90
Green Hill, 76-77
Green Line, 4, 148, 189, 326, 329, 331
Grevas, SG, 6
Grewal, *Major*, 172
Grivas, *General*, 328
GSO 2 (staff operations), 71-72, 75
Gudalcanal: Japanese advances, 70
guerilla warfare, 237, 273
Gumri, 136

Gun Carriage Factory, Jabalpur, 224
Gupta, Bhupesh, 261, 263
Gurais (Gurez), Jammu & Kashmir: Indian Army action, 125, 127
Guraya, *Brigadier* Ajit Singh, 190
Gurbakhash Singh, *Brigadier* 164, 166
Gurdaspur: Muslims killed, 109
Gurkha, *see* Gorkha
Gyani, *Major General* PS, 204, 247, 252, 325

Habibullah, *Major General* E. 25, 34, 213, 240n27
Haile Selassie 1 Military Academy, 293
Haji Langar, 296
Haksar, PN, 164
Hall, *Major*, 46
Hamilton-Britton, *Colonel*, 33, 36
Hammrskjold, Dag, 229
Handoo, KG, 313
Handwara-Kupwara, Operation Summer Offensive, 122
Haralu, *Dr*, 192-93, 220
Harbakhsh, *Brigadier*, 122-23, 139, 351, 356, 359
Harbottle, 331
Hardy, *Brigadier* Campbell R., 90, 91, 94
Hari Chand, *Major*, 126, 128
Harjinder Singh, AVM, 224
Hasan, *General* Mohamed Rashad, 217
Haughton, *Lieutenant Colonel* JL, 20, 21
Hazare, *Lieutenant Colonel* P, 164
High Altitude Warfare School (HAWS), Gulmarg, 294
Highland Light Infantry (HLI), 25, 26, 28-29, 38, 47, 366
Hikitt, *Lieutenant Colonel*, 28
Hillary, Edmund, 194
Himalayan Infantry Division, 275
Himalayan Mountaineering Institute (HMI), Darjeeling, 219, 288
Himalayas, 287

Himmatsinhji, 209
Hindnagar, 163, 165, 174, 184, 362
Hindu regiments, 108
Hindus, Hinduism, 13, 36, 59, 105, 109
Hindustan Aeronautics Ltd (HAL), 224, 255
Hitler, Adolf, 54, 65, 96, 349
Hodgson, *Lt*, 35
Hong Kong, 59
Horsford, *Major* HN, 76, 90
Huddleston, *Major General* H.J., 51, 52
human relationships, 329
human resources, 350
Humanyun, 40
Huns, 11
Hussain, *Lieutenant* SM, 58
Hutton, *Brigadier* RA, 85, 92
Hydari, *Sir* Akbar, 195
Hyder Ali, 12, 16
Hyderabad, Nizam, 55n^1
Hyderabad Regiment, 149; 4th/19th battalion, 29, 31-32, 34, 36, 38, 40, 43-44, 46-47, 50-51, 52, 54, 59-63, 65-66, 76, 96, 98, 366; 8th/19th battalion, 66-69, 75, 76, 78, 83, 89-90, 202, 366

Ibrahim, Mohamed, 217
idealism, 311
Idris, KM, 30n^1
Iliff, *Colonel* AD, 149
imperialism, 154
imperturbility, 343, 348
Imphal, 85
Independent (Undivided) Armed Forces of India, 103
Indian Air Force (IAF), 191, 196, 204, 207, 221, 274, 275, 285, 286
Indian Armed Forces, 55n^1
Indian Arms and Amendment Act, 14
Indian Army, pre-partition, 117
Indian Brigade, 74th, 93
Indian Commissioned Officers (ICOs), 33,
36, 41, 46
Indian Grenadiers Regimental Centre, Nasirabad, 149
Indian Journalists Association, London, 217
Indian Military Academy (IMA), Dehra Dun, 20, 22, 23, 27, 55n^3, 56n^{12}, 151-53, 156, 213, 286-87, 291, 301,332
Indian National Army (INA), 14, 35, 65, 67, 71, 83, 95, 117, 166
Indian Ocean, 278
Indian Tank Brigade, 50th, 72
Indianisation, 34, 36, 38, 103, 343
indigenisation, 223, 224, 246, 259, 286, 358
Indo-Tibetan Border Police (ITBP), 237
Indo-US relations, 317
Indus valley, 127
industrialisation, 221; civil and defence, 223-24
Infantry Brigades: 11th, 105; 112nd, 190; 114th, 254, 296; 123rd, 106; 190th, 164; 268th, 97
Infantry Division, 4th, 275, 290, 366
Infantry School, Fort Benning, 229
Infantry School, Mhow, 287-88
insurgency, 195
integration of services, 232-34, 268, 356
Intelligence Bureau (IB), 189, 209, 215, 222, 233, 238, 249, 254, 271, 276, 289, 291, 313
Internal Defence (ID), 36-41
international communism, 265
Iraq: British Battalions, 30-36
Islam, 33
Ismail, Nawab Mohammad, 103
Ismay, *Lord*, 113
Iyappa, *Major General* AC, 204
Iyengar, *Lieutenant*, 222

J& K Infantry, 120, 129, 131
J&K Mountain Battery 11th Field Regiment, 138
Jackson, *Major*, 23

Jacob, *General Sir* Claude, 21
Jagjit Singh, Captain, 219-20
Jagjivan Ram, 240n^{32}
Jagmal, *Naik*, 94
JAK Corps, 148
JAK Force, 119
Jallianwala Bagh massacre, 26, 40
Jam Sahib of Junagadh, 111
Jammu and Kashmir (J&K), 105, 106; militia, 249; Pakistani offensive and Indian Army action, 117-25, 351, 361; plebiscite, 148; State Force, 117, 130; tribals' invasion, 117; War, **1947-48**, 110, 212, 344, 352-53, 360, 367
Jan, *Lt Col* Khalid, 110
Janardan, Major KV, 164
Jansen, GH, 333
Japan, Japanese, 85-86; American Military Government (AMG), 97; Commonwealth Occupational Force, 344, 367; defeat at Kohima and Imphal, 80; war against British, 59, 64-65, 70, 79-80, 86, 88, 91-94; surrender, 96, 97
Jasbir Singh, *Captain*, 164
Jat Regiment, 164
Jats, Jat Company, 31, 35, 52, 60, 63-64, 73n^{1}, 76, 79, 81, 86, 92, 304
Jetley, *Lieutenant Colonel* TR, 164
Jhansi-Babina, 278
Jihad, 110
Jinnah, Mohammad Ali, 37, 105-7, 111, 113, 117-19, 149, 366
job satisfaction, 65
Joginder, 211
Johnson, Dr. Samuel, 26, 50
Johnson-Berry, *Flight Lieutenant*, 282
Johore, Malaysia: reconnaissance, 60
Joint Chief of Staff, 203
Joint Defence Council (JDC), 105, 109, 111
Joint Land Air Warfare School, Secunderabad, 264, 268
Joint Service Wing (JSW), 151-53, 155

Jung, Nawab Ali Yavar, 217
Jungle Warfare School, Dehradun, 294

Kaladan Valley, 72, 93
Kalan, *Lieutenant Colonel* Sarup, 164
Kalapanzin Valley, 72
Kale, *Captain* SD, 240n^{2}
Kalimpong, 236-37
Kalkat, Major General OS, 141n^{50}
Kalwant Singh, *Major General*, 30n^{1}, 115, 118, 189, 204, 218, 227, 228, 230, 235, 236, 247, 249, 366
Kameng Frontier Division, 294
Kamikaze assault, 92-93
Kangaw, the war in Chhaungs, 88-96, 349, 350
Kannauj, 40
Kapur, BC, 195-96
Kapur, *Brigadier* BD, 228, 229
Kapur, *Lt Col* Teg Bahadur, 304
Karakoram Highway (KKH), 206
Karakoram Pass, 133, 283, 287; Indian Army operation, 147, 275, 319
Karam Singh, 222
Karan Singh, Dr., 139
Kargil, 138; Pakistani offensive and Indian Army action, 120-22, 127, 129, 131, 132
Karlill, *Admiral*, 225
Karnataka and Tamil Nadu, contention, 11
Karnatic Regiment, 33
Kashmir issue, 155, 207, 213, 318; *see also* Jammu & Kashmir
Kashmir, Maharaja, 115, 118
Katari, *Rear Admiral* RD, 204, 225, 244, 249-50, 252-53, 256, 257, 260, 278
Kathpalia, *Lieutenant General* PN, 269
Katju, KN, 191, 202, 213
Katoch, *Brigadier*, 122
Kaul, *Brigadier Lieutenant General* BM, 102, 103, 164, 166, 167, 230-31, 247-48, 251, 265, 278-79, 285, 286, 291, 297, 301, 308n^{37}, 309n^{41}, 312, 313, 315-17, 319, 352, 356

Kaul, TN, 283
Kelly, *Major* FJO, 76, 78, 90
Khampas, 218
Khan, *General* Mohd Azam, 345
Khan, M.A., 46
Khan, Mohammad Ismail, 102, 103
Khan, NJ, 30n1
Khanduri, *Major* PN, 164
Khanna, *Colonel* M.M., 156
Khanolkar, *Major General* U.R., 34
Khera, 294
Khinzemane, Chinese intrusion, 248-49, 254
Khosla, *Justice* GD, 296
Khrushchev, Nikita S, 213
Khullar, *Major General* Niranjan, 138
Khurnak Fort, 248; Indian Army operation, 147
Khushwaqt-ul-Mulk, *Brigadier*, 345
Kim Il-Sung *Marshal*, 162, 174, 182
Kim Yon Mo, *Lt*, 175
King's Colours, 153-54
King's Commissioned Indian Officers (KCIOs), 20, 22, 32, 33, 35, 37, 40, 46, 51, 203, 366
Kipling, Rudyard, 42
Kirpal Singh, *Brigadier*, 130-1
Kishan Ganga, Operation Summer Offensive, 122, 125
Kitchener, *General*, 20
Kittermaster, 20
Klaung, Malaysia: reconnaissance, 60
knowledge and awareness, 278
Kochar, *Major General* RK, 60, 192-93, 196, 197
Kodagu Hills, 11
Kodagu, *see* Coorg
Kodavs, 2, 11, 12, 13, 33; women, 13-14
Kohima, 85
Koirala, BP, 226, 299
Kongka La via Dehra Compase, 294
Kongka Pass, Chinese intrusion, 271
Korea, 298, 344; division, 162, 206; prisoners of war (POW), 166, 167-74, 176-77, 180-82, 183; War, 161, 164, 182, 190, 292, 346, 367

Kothari, Dr. DS, 228
Kripalani, Acharya JB, 221, 248, 261-63, 280n', 312, 316
Krishna (sister), 4, 15
Kuala Lumpur, Malaysia: reconnaissance, 60
Kubinka Air Force Station, 214
Kuchuck, Fazil, 6, 337 (Spell Check)
Kuldip Singh, 78, 90
Kumaon Regiment, 149, 269, 304
Kumaonis, Kumaoni Company, 31, 35, 52, 73n1, 76, 79, 81, 86, 93, 95, 124, 211, 346
Kumaramangalam, *Major General* PP, 235, 247, 298
Kumbh Mela, 38, 277
Kundan Singh, *Captain/Lt General*, 155
Kunzru, Pandit H.N., 102, 103
Kuomintang (KMT), 66
Kutch-Sindh boundary dispute, 190
Kuttappa, KK, 7, 8
Kyprianou, Spiros, 336

Ladakh, 205; Chinese intrusion, 209, 251, 273, 279, 284, 287, 288-89, 294, 314-16, 349; Indian Army deployment, 222, 302; Pakistani offensive and Indian Army action, 117, 127; Tibetans, exodus, 189
Ladakh Scouts, 216
Lahiri, *Gentleman Cadet* MK, 153
Lakshadweep Islands, 278
Lal, *Lt Col* NK, 149
Lal, PC, *Air Commodore*, 207, 240n[27]
Lamayaru; Pakistani offensive and Indian Army action, 125, 127, 129
Lamba, B.S., 46
Land-Air Warfare School, 293
language, 21, 29
Lapthal, Ladakh: Chinese presence, 225, 226
Latif, *General* Mohamed H A, 217
lawlessness, 110
Lawton, *General*, 171, 172
leadership quality, 45, 98-99, 150, 156, 202,

344, 350, 362
Lebanon: under France, 32
Lee Sang Cho, *Lt General*, 166-67
Lee, Robert E., 363
Leech, *Major*, 46
Leghorn Operation, 317
Leh, 285, 287, 288, 296; crisis/Pakistani offensive and Indian Army action, 120, 121, 125, 127-29, 138
Leh-Khardung La, 294
Lele, BN, 240n²⁷
Lemnitzer, *General* Layman L, 228
Lentaigne, *Major General* WD, 190
level-headedness, 343
Lewis, *Colonel*, 43-45, 46
Liaquat Ali Khan, 105, 107, 109, 110, 189
Liberators, 92
Libya, 32
Light Cavalry, 7th, 97
Lila Ram, *Havildar*, 219
Limassol Docks, 329, 330
Line of Actual Control, 148
Line of communication (L of C), 85, 120, 125, 131, 273
Lockhart, *General Sir* Rob MM, 105, 111, 112, 114, 141n9
logistics, 278-80, 303
Lohit Frontier Division, 225
Longju, 254
Lord Operation, 278
Lorried Brigade, 43rd, 128
loyalty, 99
Lushai hills, 194
Luthra, *Colonel* PN, 192, 272

Maan, *Lieutenant* Dilkhush, 58
MacArthur, *General* Douglas, 97
Macdequigley, *Major* FW, 76
Macek, *General*, 214
Machaia, Codanda Jappu, 15
Machoi, 137

Madikeri (Mercara), 13
Madras Engineering Group, 241n38
Madras Pioneers, 45
Madras Sappers, 136
Mahadeo Singh, *Brigadier*, 151
Mahakal Operation, 317
Mahar Machin Gun Battalion, 110
Mahendra Pratap, Raja, 263
Mahendra, King of Nepal, 292, 299
Majid, *Captain* MI, 73n'
Majid, Mohammad Istifaq, 32, 46
Majithia, Surjit Singh, 201, 202, 270
Makarios, Archbishop, 3, 5, 325, 330, 332, 333, 335-36, 338-39
Malakand Field Force, 26
Malaya: British invasion, 59-60, 65;—forces, withdrawal, 70
Malviya, Madan Mohan, 37
man-management, 98-99, 156
Manali–Leh route, 128
Manekshaw, *Field Marshal*, SHFJ, (Sam) 125, 240n32, 245, 247, 285, 313
Manipur, 279; Naga hostility, 197
Mankekar, DR, 89, 95, 359
Manyera, Niazi, 6
Marathas 3rd/5th infantry battalion, 32
Marlowe, Chritsopher, 54
marriage and challenge of the Quetta earthquake, 46-51, 54
Marshal, *Brigadier General* SLA, 296
Martin, *Rear Admiral* BCD, 88
Mason, Philip, 34
Master General Ordnance (MGO), 215
Matadin, Subedar, 94
Matayan, 136, 138, 354
Mathai, 256-57
Matterson, *Lt General* J.S., 46
Maungdaw, 85
Mawai, Malaysia: reconnaissance, 60
Mayu Peninsula, 72, 85-87
McCauley, Lord, 67

McLeod, *Major*, 73
McMahon Line, 205, 207, 209, 226-27, 235, 280n[1], 289
McNamara, *Brigadier* PR, 104
McNeil, RSM, 24
Measure, Philip, 40
media, reaction to Thimayya's resignation, 265; role, 175-6, 304-6
Meghalaya, 12
Mehar Chand, *Justice*, 105
Mehar Singh, *Wing Commander*, 102, 103, 125-26
Mehdi, BR, 195
Mehta, Ashoka, 262
Mehta, *Lieutenant* IN, 219
Mehta, KL, 195
Melrose, 93
Menon, V.K. Krishna, 163, 177, 202, 205, 207, 210-11, 212, 215, 216, 219, 221, 223-25, 229, 231, 234, 235, 237-38, 243-47, 249-66, 268-71, 275, 277, 279, 280, 282-86, 287, 289-98, 301-2, 307n[22], 308n[30], 312-13, 315-17, 319, 343, 349, 356-58
Menon, V.P., 118
Mesopotamia: colonised by British, 32
Messervy, *General Sir* Frank, 105, 116n[20], 141n[20]
Middle East, 32, 70
Migyulten: Chinese intrusion, 248
Miles, *Vice Admiral* Geoffrey, 102
Milford, 91
Military Commanders Conference, 277; 1960, 283
Military Demarcation Line, 162
Military Engineering Service, 277
Military Evacuation Organisations, 109
Military Intelligence (MI), 189, 233
Military Wing, 151-53, 155
Milkha Singh, Jemadar, 219
Mills, *Major General* AM, 149
Milner, *Lord*, 38
Mirza, *Major General* Iskandar, 113, 207

misgovernance, 298
Miyazaki, *General*, 89, 93
modernisation of Army, 216, 223, 285, 317, 358; lack of, 250
Mohenjodaro, 11
Moitra, *Colonel* BB, 351
Mongols, 129
Montgomery, *Field Marshal* Bernard, 109, 243
Moraes, Frank, 296
moral ascendancy, 202
moral failure, 132
moral uncertainty, 297
morale, 59, 66, 81, 127, 208, 253, 314
Mounbatten, 325
Mountain Brigade, 7th, 315
Mountbatten, *Lord*, 96, 104, 107-8, 110-1, 113-15, 117-18, 151, 190, 289, 291, 295, 319
Muftizade, Bejmal, 6
Mughals, 129
Mukerjee, *Air Marshal* Subroto, 204, 211, 249-50, 252-53, 256-57, 260, 264; died, 264
Mullik, BN, 209, 210, 222, 226, 227, 241n[37], 276, 285, 286, 289, 291, 302, 315-16, 319, 349
Munir, Justice Mohammad, 105
Munshi, *Major* YM, 164, 204
Musa, *General* Mohammad, 102, 108-9, 283
Muslim League, 108, 113
Muslims, 59, 105, 108-11
Mutiny of 1857, 12, 44, 67
mutually assured destruction (MAD), 217, 360
Myochaung, 89

Naga Hills and Tuensang, amalgamation demand, 195
Naga Hills-Tuensang Frontier Agency (NHTA), 192-94, 197-99, 272, 274, 284, 294, 297
Naga National Council (NNC), 191, 195, 199
Naga problem, Nagas, 191-99, 207, 218, 220, 227, 292, 367

Naga, federal government, 191
Nagaland, 279
Nagar, Ganpat Ram, 39, 46
Naidu, Sarojini, 37
Nanavati, *Brigadier*, 287
Nanavati, Sharda, 287
Nanda, Gulu, 256, 260
Nanda, *Major* D.R.L., 56n[7], 204
Napoleon, Bonaparte, 54, 81, 86, 138, 212, 346, 352, 358
Narain Singh, *Lieutenant Colonel*, 138
Narain, *Major General* Pratap, 60, 241n44
Narinder Kumar, *Captain*, 219
Nasser, Gamel Abdel, 218
Nastachhun: Operation Summer Offensive, 122-23
National Cadet Corps (NCC), 152, 213, 225, 229-30
National Defence Academy (NDA), Dehradun, 46, 55n[3], 55n[8], 140, 147, 150, 151-57, 164, 213, 269, 291, 336, 351, 367
National Defence College, Delhi, 284
National Defence Council (NDC), 324, 357, 302-303
national security concerns, 355-59
National War Academy, 151
Nazareth, *Major* J, 352
Nazir Ahmed, *Major General*, 106, 110, 148
Nazis, 54
Ne Win, *General*, 298
Nehru, Betty, 39
Nehru, BK, 298
Nehru, Jawahar Lal, 9, 37, 107-10, 113-15, 117-19, 153, 164, 176, 141n[3,20], 158, 159, 177-78, 182, 185, 190-92, 194, 196-97, 199, 204, 205, 207-11, 213-15, 218, 220-21, 223-24, 226, 229, 231, 234-35, 237, 244, 247-48, 251-61, 263-66, 268-72, 276, 277, 279, 282-87, 289-92, 295, 298-302, 312-17, 319, 324, 345, 356, 358, 366
Nehru, Moti Lal, 37, 39, 53
Nene, *Major* WS, 129

neo-colonialism, 283
Nepal, 206, 292, 297; India relations, 206; monarchical coup, 299-300
Neutral Nations' Repatriation Commission (NNRC), 1, 9, 95, 161, 163-86, 189, 201, 206, 210, 326, 344, 348, 355-56, 360
Nicolls, *Colonel*, 39
Nicosia, 327, 330, 334
Nicosia-Kyrenia road, 329-30
Nicosia University, 336
Nicosia Zone, 332
Nilgiri Hills, 28
Nimu: Pakistani offensive, 127
Nine Point Agreement, 195
Nizam of Hyderabad, 111
Non-Aligned Declaration, Cairo, 1964, 333
non-aligned policy, 208, 260
non-combatant unenrolled (NCU), 73
Non-Cooperation Movement, 83
North Africa, 70
North Atlantic Treaty Organisation (NATO), 217, 326, 340
North Bengal, 288
North East Frontier Area (NEFA), 196, 199, 205, 216, 218, 270, 272, 277, 279, 282, 286, 287, 288, 289, 290, 294; under Army, 254; Chinese intrusion, 226, 227, 235-37, 248-49, 251, 273-77, 314, 316, 319, 349, 356
North Korea: prisoners, 166; repatriation, 172
North Korean People's Army (NKPA), 162, 166 Northern Command, 162, 167-69, 172-4, 178, 179, 183, 210
Northcote, *General*, 97
North-West Frontier Province (NWFP), 40-46, 117; military operations, 54
Norton, *General*, 53
Nubra: Pakistani offensive, 127
Nye, *Sir* Archibald, 153, 154
Office of Field Operations and External Support Activities (OFOESA), 327
Oil Agreement, 1925, 32

Onkar Operation, 317
Onkareshwara temple, Coorg, 13
opportunism, 281n'
ordnance factories, 223-24
Osterberg, Eva, 348
Owen, Frank, 100n'

Paed, HD, 76
Paintal, *Brigadier* RS, 164, 166
Pakistan, Pakistanis, 207, 211; Army, 109, 118, 125, 127, 131; coup, 229; fundamentalism, 110; and India relation, 105, 199; military rule, 229; non-Muslim refugees, 108-9, 110; –killed 132-33; intrusion/threat to India, 115, 203, 206-7, 211, 221, 227, 234, 237, 246, 273-74, 278, 313, 317-18, 356, 361; –in Chhad Bet, 190-91; refugee issue, 230
Pakistan occupied Kashmir (PoK), 125, 148, 206, 315
Palit, *Brigadier* DK, 264
Pandu, Jammu & Kashmir: Indian Army operation, 147
Panikkar, KM, 205
Pant, Pandit Gobind Ballabh, 193, 283
Papandopoullos, Tassos, 336
Para Field Regiment, 138
Parab, *Colonel* HS, 128-29, 138, 139
Parachute Brigade, 77th, 138
Parachute Training School, Agra, 226
Parliamentary Enquiry Committee, 248
Parry, Vice Admiral, 154
Partition Committee, 103
Partition Council, 105
Partition of India, 104, 105, 106-14, 157, 190, 195, 332, 345
Patel, H.M., 153
Patel, Vallabhbhai, 55n', 107, 108, 124
Pathans, 110, 137-8
Patiala State Forces, 166
Patnaik, Biju, 285
patriotism, 234, 258, 362

Peace Accord, 1975, 199
peace clause, 97
Peace Mission, 1964, 199
Peace Pagoda, 167
peace process, 199
Pead, *Major*, 90
Peakes, GR, 228
Penn, *Lieutenant Colonel* P., 46, 51
Pentagon, 228
Percival, *General*, 70, 96
Persian Gulf, 32-33
Perth, 89, 92-94
Pettengell, *Lieutenant General*, 153
Phedonos, Pauline, 3, 334-35
Phizo, AZ, 191, 192, 194-95, 207, 220
Pillai, Raghwan, 187n"
Pillai, *Sir* NR, 271, 283
Pindras, 136
Pinner, 91, 92, 93
Pinto, AVM, 241n"
Pioneer platoon, 91
Pirpanjal, 117, 134
Plumer, Fazil, 6
Pokos, 6
Poland: Nazis' invasion, 54
Poles, 173, 174
Political Conference, 165, 183
political thinking, 36-41, 53
politics, 39, 248, 250, 258, 277, 286, 298, 301-2, 312, 315, 318, 345, 358, 360
Polk, *Lieutenant General*, 69
Poonch, Jammu & Kashmir: Pakistani offensive and Indian Army action, 118, 120, 122
Praja Socialist Party (PSP), 261, 262
Prasad, *Brigadier* Niranjan, 254
Prasad, Rajendra see Rajendra Prasad
prejudice, 107
Prem Chand, *Brigadier* D, 204
Prince of Wales Royal Indian Military College (PWRIMC), Dehradun, 19-22, 23, 345
Prithi Chand, *Major*, 127, 128

Probhat Singh, *Captain*, 130
Project Amar, 230-31, 247, 248, 277, 279
Project Amar II, 279
Proudfoot, *Colonel* CL, 353
Punjab 2nd/2nd, 83
Punjab 7/16, 93
Punjab Boundary Force (PBF), 164, 343-44, 355, 367; and General Officer Commanding (GOC) 4th Division, 105-15
Purr incident, 279

Qizil Jilga, 294
Qizil Jilga-Dehra La-Samzungling-Kongka La-Khurnak Fort, 296
Quarter Master General (QMG), 228, 247, 291, 294
Quetta Cantonment, 47, 48, 52
Quetta earthquake, 48-51, 63, 69, 91
Quigley, *Major*, 90, 92

racist patriotism, 38
Radcliffe Award, 106
Radcliffe, *Lord Sir* Cyril, 105
Radhakrishnan, *Dr* S, 324, 336, 338
RAF, 32, 49, 88
Raghu Ramiah, Kotha, 202
Rai, *Lt* Colonel Ranjit, 34
Rajagopalachari, C.R., 54, 57
Rajendra Prasad, *Dr*, 264
Raji (Reconciliation) Operation, 192
Rajinder Singh, *Brigadier*, 240n27
Rajinder, *Lieutenant Colonel* (Sparrow), 135-36
Rajindra Sinhji, *General*, 161, 185, 298 (chk spl)
Rajputana Rifles, 124, 164
Rajputs, 31, 35, 53, 137-38, 304
Raleigh, Walter, 39
Ram Lal, 351
Ram Singh, 81-82, 86, 148-49
Rampal, Gentleman Cadet KD, 154
Ramree Island operation, 89, 94

Rana, *General* Subarna Shamsher Jung Bahadur, 299
Randhir Singh, 24
Ranga, NG, 262
Rangaswamy, K, 175
Ranjit Singh, Maharaja, 363
Rao, *General* K.V. Krishna, 110, 351
Rao, KVR, 358
Rao, NV, 164
Rau, B.N., 156
Rauf, *Dr* MA, 165
Rawlinson, *General*, 20
Rawlley, *Brigadier* NC, 293
reconnaissance, 59-60, 90-1, 134, 125, 135, 222-23, 328
recruitment policy of the government, 216-17
Red Cross, 164
Reddy, O Pulla, 203, 225, 252, 303
Rees, *Major General* T.W. (Pete), 105, 107, 109, 110-11, 114, 367
regimental sergeant majors (RSMs), 22-24
religion, 354
reservations policy, 216
Revolutionary Communist Party of India (RCPI), 194
Rezang La, Chinese skirmishes, 235
Rhee, *Dr* Syngman, 162, 163, 166, 175, 177, 178, 184
RIASC Battalion, 58, 138
Rickets, *Major*, 46
righteousness, 97
Rinchin, Colonel, 128
risk-taking, 347-48
Roberts, *General* Andrew, 20, 116n25
Robertson, *Lieutenant General* Sir Brian, 97
Rommel, Erwin, 5, 70, 81, 344, 363
Roning, Chester A, 228
Roosevelt, Theodore, 239n15
Ross, *Captain Sir* Ronald, 78, 90
Royal Artillery, 149
Royal Indian Air Force (RIAF), 102-3, 125-26,

128, 131, 149
Royal Indian Artillery Engineers, 103
Royal Indian Navy (RIN), 102-3
Royal Marathas, 45, 97
Royal Marine Commando Brigade, 3rd, 89-90, 94
Royal Military Academy (RMA), Sandhurst, 15, 19, 21, 22-25, 39, 151, 152, 155, 345
Royal Nepalese Army (RNA), 299, 367
Royal Scottish Borderers, 23
Royal Sikhs, 20, 149
Roychowdhury, Shankar, 351
Rudra, *Captain* AA, 45
Rukmani Devi, 53
Russell, Bertrand, 359
Russell, *General* Dudley, 112
Russell, *Sir* Henry, 55n1
Russians, 70, 213
Ruthven, *Sir* Hore, 19

Sachdeva, *Brigadier* BL, 194
Sagar, *Lieutenant General* Moti, 7
Salabat Khan, Nawab of Hyderabad, 55n'
Sampuran Bachan Singh, *Lieutenant Colonel*, 102,130-1
Sandeman, *Sir* Robert, 42
Sangcha Nalla, Ladakh: Chinese presence, 225-26
Sant Ram, *Subedar*, 61-62
Sant Singh, *Lieutenant General*, 24, 30n', 192-94, 366
Sarabjeet Singh, 110, 136
Sardanand Singh, *Lieutenant General*, 159, 311
sati, 41-42
Satyagraha, 67
schooling and growth, 16-19
Scots, association with, 25-29
Scott, JGC, 20, 21
Scottish-British rivalry, 25
Seagrabes, *Lieutenant Colonel Sir* Robert, 27
secularism, 16, 343

Selassei, H, 300
self-criticism, 353
self-rule, 54, 57
Semas, 196
Sen, *Lieutenant Colonel* LP, 46, 83, 86, 93, 102, 120, 122, 124, 139, 204, 215, 249, 254, 291, 319
Serbjeet Singh, 136, 351, 352
Services Nationalization Committee, 102-3
Services Sports Control Board, 218
Shah of Iran, 283
Shah, *Major General* Surendra, 141n^{1}
Shahzada, *Colonel*, 131
Shaksgam Valley, 206
Sham Nath, 184
Sharma, *Major General* AN, 73, 149
Sharma, Som Nath, 74n^{12}, 78, 90, 149
Shastri, Lal Bahadur, 314
Shatt-al-Arab, Iraq, 32
Shaw, George Bernard, 5, 26
Sheikpura: communal violence, 110
Sher Shah Suri, 40
Shergill, Brigade Commander, 139
Shighatse-Khamba Dzong, 288
Shiva, 12, 13
Shrinagesh, *Lieutenant General* S.M., 45, 46, 55n^{12}, 60, 64, 73n', 119, 134, 140, 150, 159,191, 192, 194, 196, 202, 224, 233, 283, 366
Shyok Valley, 127
Siddhartha, King of Matsyadesha, 11
Sikh(s), 44, 105, 106, 129, 133, 136, 148; 47th battalion, 42; Regiment, 108; religious war against Muslims, 110
Sikkim, 206, 226, 273, 275-76, 279, 288-90, 283, 302; Chinese ingression, 271, 287, 251; Maharaja of, 275;–and India, treaty, 271
Sikorsky Helicopter Factory, Connecticut, USA, 228
Simovic, *Colonel* Ladislav, 164
Sinai, Egypt, 278
Singapore, British move, 59-60, 65; Japanese prisoners of war, 166; mutiny by Indian

soldiers, 61
Sinha, CP, 272
Sinha, Ganga Saran, 261
Sinha, *Lieutenant* NK, 86, 90
Sinha, *Major* SK, 291
Sino-India relations, see China, India relations
Sino-Indian Treaty on Tibet, 1954, 281n1
Skardu, Jammu and Kashmir: Pakistan's intrusion and Indian Army action, 117, 119-21, 125; under siege, 129-33, 148
Skeen, Sir Andrew, 27
Ski and Winter Warfare School, Gulmarg, 226
Ski Club of India, 139
slavery, 24
Slim, *General* William, 71-72, 80, 86, 93, 94, 96
Smolett, *Major Sir* Telfer, 27, 29
Sobbarayan, Dr P, 219
social disorder, war and, 97
social interaction, 33
social status, 38
Soin, LS, 30n1
Som Dutt, *Major General* D, 293-94
Somaiah, Cheppudira (father-in-law), 14
Soman, *Vice Admiral* BS, 338
Soto, Alvaro De, 360
Souliotou, Stella, 5, 335
South Korean Army, 162
Southeast Asia Treaty Organisation (SEATO), 206, 246
Southern Command, 189-90, 204
sovereignty, 212
Spangur, Ladakh: Chinese presence, 225, 226
Sparrow, see Rajinder, *Lieutenant Colonel*
spiritualism, 147
Sri Div, 120, 128, 131-32, 137, 150, 226, 336, 349, 353, 360, 367
Srinagar, Jammu & Kashmir: Pakistani offensive and Indian Army action, 118-19
Sri Lanka, 206
St George College, Coonoor, Nilgiri Hills, 16
Staff College, Quetta, 190; and staff appointment, 69-71
Stalingrad, 70
standard divisional system, 217
status quo, 157, 347
Steering Committee, 104
Stewart, *Major General* W. Ross, 44
Strategic developments in neighbouring countries and Indian response, 205-8
strategic nuances, 243-47
strategic wisdom, 357
Strauss, 231
Streenivasan, *Lieutenant Colonel*, 164, 175
Strenstrom, *Major General* Jan, 164, 166
stress management, 349-50
Stuart, *Lieutenant Colonel* D, 57, 64, 134
Sturgess, Lieutenant Colonel, 23, 25
Sudan, 151
Sukh Dev Singh, *Brigadier*, 192
Sukhjit Singh, *Captain*, 172
Summer Offensive Operation, 119, 120-26, 130, 131
Supply of Services (SOS), 66
Suri, *Dr* Balwant Singh, 163
Surya Operation, 123
Sutherland Highlanders, 64
Swaran Singh, Sardar, 283, 314
Swede, 179
symbolism, 153
Syria: under France, 32

Tagore, Rabindranath, 26-27
Taiwan, 206
Tambis, 136, 138
Tangdhar: Indian Army operation, 147
Tara Singh, Master, 106, 108, 110-11
Tawang-Bomdi La sector, 236, 237, 273, 315
Taylor, APJ, 356
Taylor, *General* Maxwell, 228, 234, 355, 357-58
Teja Singh, *Justice*, 105
temperamental, incompatibility, 279
Temple, *Major General* B, 104

Templer, *Field Marshal Sir* Gerald, 217
Tenzing Norgay, 194
Terms of Reference, 165, 168, 183; dichotomy of, 169-71
Tezpur, 275, 279, 282
Thadiyanda Mol, 12
Thagaraju, *Major*, 138
Thailand: coup, 229
Thakur Singh, 172
Thanarat, *General* Sarit, 229
Thapa, *Gentleman Cadet* Puran Bahadur, 153
Thapa, *Major* Sherjung, 120, 129-32
Thapar, *Lieutenant General* PN, 30n1, 204, 218, 296-98, 301, 312, 313-16, 319, 356, 366
Tharu: Pakistani offensive, 127-28
Thimayya Memorial Committee, 7
Thimayya of India: A Soldier's Life, by Humphery Evans, 295, 296
Thimayya, Bopayya (cousin), 22
Thimayya, Cheppudira Sitamma (mother), 14, 15-16
Thimayya, *Colonel* Ponnappa (brother), 14, 15, 17-18, 19, 65, 67, 95
Thimayya, Kodendra Kuthayya (father), 14-15
Thimayya, *General* Kodendra Subbayya: as Chief of Army Staff (COAS), vii, 192, 194, 201, 204, 208, 210, 215, 232, 238, 256-57, 262, 305, 312-14, 347-49, 353, 367; awards and honours, 149, 185-86, 303, 367-68; born, 15, 366; as chairman of Chiefs of Staff Committee, 278; communication skill, 348; competitiveness, 44; death, 1-5, 336; opposed discrimination, 38-39; early life, 16-19; family, 14-16; humanitarian aspect, 113; humour, 157, 159, 226, 348-49, 362; hunting, 15, 152, 154; at Hyderabad 4th/19th infantry battalion 29, 31-32, 34, 36, 38, 40, 43-44, 46-47, 50-51, 52, 54, 59-63, 65-66, 76, 96, 98, 366; intelligence/intellectual pursuits, 152, 278; job satisfaction, 65; leadership quality, 45, 98-99, 150, 156, 202, 344, 350, 362; meeting with Nehru, and the aftermath, 251-61; Naga problem, psychological approach, 195-99; as commandant National Defence Academy (NDA), 151-57, 164; as Chairman of Neutral Nations' Repatriation Commission (NNRC), 9, 161, 163-86, 189, 201, 326, 344, 355-56, 360; operation Summer Offensive, 119, 120-26; personal traits, personality, 156, 343, 345-55; political thinking, 36-41; Prince of Wales Royal Indian Military College (PWRIMC), Dehradun, 19-22, 23, 345; as commander Punjab Boundary Force (PBF), 105-15, 164; as quarter master general (QMG), 147, 157-59, 367; quality of life and principles, 202; Quetta earthquake, 46-51; reputation image, 35-36, 147-50; resignation, 259-66, 269-70, 287, 298; at Royal Military Academy (RMA), Sandhurst, 15, 19, 21, 22-25, 39, 151, 152, 345; honorary general of Royal Nepalese Army (RNA), 299, 367; visit to Russia, 214-14, 231; schooling and growth, 16-19; with Scots, 25-29, 60-63; evaluation by senior commanders, 33, 36, 44, 46; sportsmanship, 152-53, 318-20; as General Officer Commanding (GOC), Sri Div, 120, 128, 131-32, 137, 150, 226, 349, 353, 360, 367; as Head of Chiefs of Staff Committee, 232-33; visit to United Kingdom, Egypt, 217-18, 231; as Commander of United Nations forces in Cyprus, 324-40; winning over Nagas, 191-99; visit to Canada and United States, 227-30, 231; a visionary, 359-62
Thimayya, Mireille *see* Chengappa, Mireille
Thimayya, Nina (wife), 2, 4, 7, 27, 48-51, 53-54, 57, 63, 65, 67, 68, 69, 70, 72, 81-82, 87, 140, 151, 152, 201, 299, 303, 336, 338, 351-52, 368
Thimayya, Somayya (brother), 14, 15, 68, 124
thinking and fighting, limiting the barrier, 277-78
Thomas, *Dr*, 7

Thomas, *Lt* Mathew, 155
Thorat, *Major General* SSP, 30n[1], 83, 156, 159, 163, 164, 165, 172-73, 177, 179, 204, 218, 227, 235, 236, 249, 253, 254, 272, 285, 296, 301, 314, 356
thoroughness and immaculate preparation, 346
threat perceptions and projections, 215-16; and suggested strategy, 272-77
Tibet, Tibet issue: Chinese intrusion/ intervention, 205-6, 222, 235-36, 249, 261, 271, 273, 288, 298; Khampas, 218
Tibettans, 189-90
Tikka Khan, *Major General*, 191
Tilak Raj, *Second Lt*, 206
Tilawana, SS, 58
Ting Kuo Yu, *General*, 166-67
Tipu Sultan, 12
Tithwal, Operation Summer Offensive, 122-24
Tito, *Marshal* Josip Broz, 234, 242n[54]
Tiwana, Brigadier Munir, 110
Tolstoy, Count Leo, 38
Toman, *Lt Gen* YS, 154
Tottenham, *Major General* Loftus, 100n[5], 119-20, 125
Townsend, *Colonel*, 98
Trans-Jordan, under British, 32
transparency, 231-32
trekking, 15
Triantafilliades, Michael, 336-37
tribal marksmanship, 43
Tri-Service Academy, 151
Trishul Operation, 219, 317
Triveni river, 38
Tunisia, 128; American invasion, 70
Turkey, Turkish, 32; Air Force, 328; Cypriots, 326, 328-31, 333; Muslim minority, 325; Ottoman Empire, collapse, 32
Turks, 332
Twain, Mark, 66-67
two-nation theory, 103
Tyagi, Mahavir, 165

U Nu, 192, 197
U Thant, 3, 324, 328, 330, 336
Udal, 40
Ujjal Singh, *Lieutenant Colonel*, 164, 175
Umrao Singh, *Lt General*, 285, 288, 294, 315
Unattached List Indian Army (ULIA), 25, 26, 27
United Nations (UN), United Nations Organisation (UNO), 125, 156, 205-6, 213, 222, 260, 270, 324, 333, 344, 355, 367; Emergency Force in Cyprus (UNFICYP), 1, 2, 3, 4, 6, 324-40; Emergency Force (UNEF) in Gaza, 6, 217; General Assembly (UNGA), 330, 336; role Korea, 162-63, 165, 167-74, 176-79, 181, 184; Observer Group for India and Pakistan, 148-49; peace-keeping and peace-making operations, 360; Security Council (UNSC), 155, 161
United Planters Association of South India (UPASI), 311
United States of America: Central Intelligence Agency (CIA), 206, 228, 229 Civil War, 39; and Japan Trade Treaty (1919), 59; PX system, 158
University Training Corps (UTC), Madras (Chennai), (1937-1939), 51-55, 57, 366
unpredictability, 166
Upadhyaya, SP, 226
Uri, Jammu & Kashmir: Pakistani offensive and Indian Army action, 118, 120, 122, 124
Usman, *Brigadier*, 118
Uttar Pradesh: Chinese ingression, 251

Vajpayee, Atal Behari, 261, 280n1, 285
values, 344
Vanguard Press, United States of America, 295
Vas, *Lieutenant General* Eric, 107, 114, 351, 356
Veer Shiva Raja, 13
Vellodi, MK, 203
Venus Operation, 119
Verma, Major General SD, 204, 285, 301, 312, 315

Versailles Treaty, 32, 65, 96
Viceroy Commissioned Officer (VCOs), 36, 44, 51, 75-77, 351
Victoria Cross battalion, 97
Vidarbha, King of, 12
Vidhyachal, 12
Vietnam War, 206
Vijaynagar Empire, 12
violence, 342
Virajrajendra, king of Coorg, 12
Virendra Singh, *Lieutenant Colonel*, 97
Visveswaraya, Mokshagundam, 26
Vivekanand, 8
Vohra, N.N., 155
Voroshilvo Higher Military Academy, 214

Wadalia, *Major General* M.S., 45, 55n12, 156, 204, 254
Wade, *Major General* DAL, 102
Wainman-Wood, T, 337
Wal, *Subedar Major* Prem Swarup, 256
Walker, E. Ronald, 181
Walong, 289
Walter Reed Army Hospital, 228, 229
War Course, 7th, 69
War Memorial Academy, 151
War Office, London, 59
Warsaw Pact, 217, 340
Wavell, *Field Marshal Lord* AP, 138, 347
welfare system, 157-8
West Bengal: Chinese intelligence activities, 314
Western Bloc, 163
Western Command, 163, 189, 204, 222, 227, 233, 235, 275, 284-85, 296, 301
Western Ghats, 11-12
Western systems, 228
Wheeler, *Brigadier General* K, 66
Wheeler, *Brigadier* Tyrrwhit, 105

Wignell, Sydney, 206
Wilkinson, *General* JH, 156
Wilson, *Brigadier* AJ, 4, 6
Wilson, James, 332
Wilson-Effendon, *Lieutenant Colonel* EL, 60, 64
Wingate, *Major General* Orde, 90
women, the war victims, 97-98
Won Chu, *Sergeant*, 172
Wood, *General* Sammy, 85
Wood, *Major General* GN, $100n^5$, 343
World War I, 132
World War II, 9, 23, 25, 31, 32, 35, 39, $55n^1$, 56n12, 57, 76, 96, 132, 135, 147, 151, 212, 213, 230, 343, 353, 358, 367

Xinjiang-Tibet Road, 206

Yadav, *Lieutenant* YK, 219
Yadunath Singh, 39, 46, $55n^9$
Yamashita, *General*, 96
York and Lancaster 8th (Y&L), 83, 85
Young, *Colonel*, 90, 91

Zaban-e-Hindwi, 41
Zahir, *Captain*, 60-64, 73
Zanskar: Pakistani offensive, 127
Zatar, *Colonel* MV, 7
Zechal-Dor, 122
Zhob Independent Brigade, 42
Zhob river, 42
Zhou En-Lai, 182, 205, 206-7, 235, 271, 280n1, 283, 292, 319
Zhukov, *Marshal* GK, 213-14
Zhukovski Air Academy, 214
Zoji La, Jammu & Kashmir, 110, 346, 350, 353; Blitzkrieg, 133-38, 347; Pakistani offensive and Indian Army action, 117, 120, 125-27, 147